(R)Evolution

(R)Evolution
Organizations and the Dynamics of the Environment

Rob Dekkers
Delft University of Technology
Delft, The Netherlands

 Springer

Library of Congress Cataloging-in-Publication Data

A C.I.P. Catalogue record for this book is available
from the Library of Congress.

ISBN-10: 0-387-26125-7   e-ISBN-10: 0-387-26159-1
ISBN-13: 978-0387-26125-6   e-ISBN-13: 978-0387-26159-1

Printed on acid-free paper.

Printed in the United States of America.

9 8 7 6 5 4 3 2 1   SPIN 11357780

springeronline.com

SUMMARY

Adaptation as a process requires the generation of variation by companies, and the subsequent selection of mutations by the environment when drawing an analogy with evolutionary biology. The research aims at revealing both processes and structures that contribute to the generation of variation by companies, and that make it possible to anticipate on the selectional forces of competition and the product-market combinations. Companies differ from organisms to the extent that they can create a larger impact on the environment, they have the capability of foresight, and they possess relatively open boundaries. Additionally, mutations are induced and implemented in the organisation rather than creating offspring, the mechanism for organisms to adapt. To provide a structure for adaptation, not equalling one-time interventions but continuous change, the research has proposed a Framework for Dynamic Adaptation, encompassing:

- the Model for the Dynamic Adaptation Capability, containing both the externally oriented Dynamic Capability and the Internal Innovation Capability. Although both thrive on the interaction with the environment, the main purpose of the Dynamic Capability is to deal with environmental change and the impact of internally induced variation on the environment. The Internal Innovation Capability describes mostly the generation of variation;
- the Innovation Impact Point Model, which describes the impact of innovations on decision-making within companies. This model has been included in the Model for the Dynamic Adaptation Capability;
- the Collaboration Model. This model shows the interaction between companies for horizontal and vertical integration.

INTERACTION WITH THE ENVIRONMENT

Companies do depend on the actions of other companies in their industrial branches as well as the preferences by the customer base. Outcomes of these competitive pressures entail always chance. Nevertheless, the capability of foresight and monitoring of the environment, assist industrial companies to anticipate. The interaction with suppliers generates further possibilities to adapt to changes in the competitive pressures and changes in the product-market combinations.

The capability of foresight calls for a more dynamic approach than the static strategy schools at the moment present in management science. Thereto, the research has proposed a model for dynamic strategy, and, separately, a scenario planning based on game theories. The model of the dynamic strategy tells simply that companies should not focus on a singular strategy with a predetermined outcome; realising that strategy becomes virtually impossible because of chance events happening in the course of time, and maintaining that singular strategy carries the danger of pursuing it at all cost. In addition, a scenario planning based on game theory will help companies to anticipate better on the future; current scenario methodologies lack a coherent background or fall back to predicting one single future. Although the research has not developed yet this scenario planning, Adaptive Dynamics, a recent development within evolutionary biology, has been identified as theoretical base.

The second method to deal with competitive pressures is the monitoring of the environment, for the emergence of dominant designs and for decision-making on concepts of innovation. Eras of ferment results in periods of selection whereby preceding the emergence of a dominant design, elements of this design become visible. Monitoring the environment by industrial companies will result in early detection of these elements, and the possibility to integrate them into a product architecture that fits with the emerging dominant design. That monitoring connects to the internal processes and structures of dealing with innovation and breakthrough processes for which the Innovation Impact Point Model has been developed. In this model, innovations are assessed on their merits to contribute

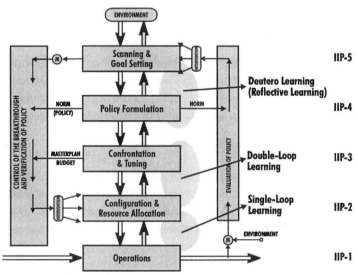

Model for the Innovation Impact Point. The breakthrough model shows the learning modes and the identified Innovation Impact Points (IIP). The higher the Impact Point, the more changes and innovations from lower levels affect organisational decision-making. Architectural, and often radical, changes and innovations come about through accumulation of minor changes and innovations.

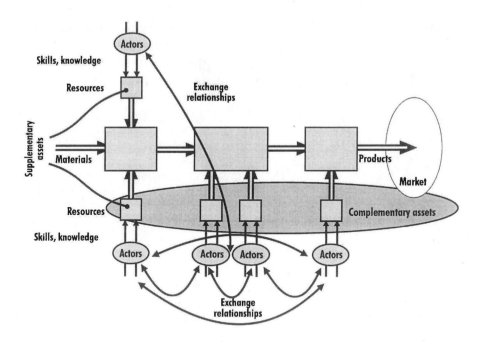

Collaboration Model. Exchange relationships occur through vertical and horizontal integration. Vertical collaboration indicates the capability of actors to manage the supply chain. Horizontal collaboration contributes to the dynamic capabiltiy of the network by reallocating resources or creating substitution.

to the concepts of innovation: incremental, modular, architectural, and radical innovation.

Thirdly, the research proposes a model to enhance collaboration with suppliers, the Collaboration Model. This model embeds both the steady-state process of managing the supply chain and the breakthrough processes; labeled as horizontal and vertical substitution. Additionally, it breaks ground to combine process models with actor models. The model as such has not fully been developed to include control, etc., but it does link to the capability of foresight and monitoring of the environment. Technology leverage by suppliers is seen as essential to sustain competitiveness at the long run, hence the effects might be captured by using the Innovation Impact Point Model and the Model for the Dynamic Adaptation Capability. The principle of self-organisation derived from evolutionary biology finds its place here but has not yet been converted to practical approaches.

Hence, the organisation responds to the environment by constantly putting variations to the test of selectional forces. By intended mutations, organisations shape their own future, an active rather than a passive role. The interaction with the environment requires a shift in management paradigm from the supposed effectiveness of one-time interventions (i.e. linear thinking) to managing the opportunities from the interaction with the environment (emergent thinking), supported by the generation of mutations (markets, products, performance).

GENERATION OF VARIATION

For the generation of variation, in processes and structures, industrial companies might revert to the theories of technology management, innovation, process innovation, Business Process Re-engineering, Learning Organisation, and Knowledge Management. The review of these theories on their merits for the development of organisations showed that some of these concepts have similarities resulting in the proposition of the Innovation Impact Point Model. Especially, the conscious deployment of possibilities for architectural innovation within this model might increase the competitiveness of firms.

Yet, the biological concepts of adaptive walks and developmental pathways have received little attention in management science. The dominant model of the punctuated equilibrium serves as retrospective explanation of phenomena, it does not possess predictive characteristics to indicate periods of turmoil and consolidation for industry. Rather, the accumulation of gradual changes might, in terms of the Innovation Impact Point Model, evoke the assessment of internal developments at higher Impact Points. If an accumulation occurs that fits with

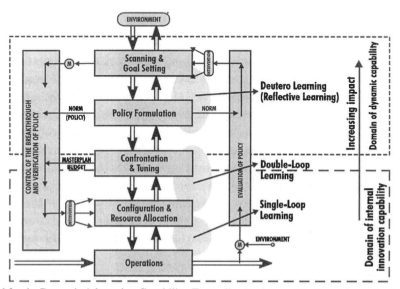

Model for the Dynamic Adaptation Capability. Expanding on the model of the Innovation Impact Points, this particular model distinguishes the Internal Innovation Capability and the Dynamic Capability with its external orientation.

adaptive zones (emerging product-market combinations or shifts in existing markets), then the mutation rate might temporarily accelerate, thereby giving the impression of a period of turmoil. At the base of beneficial mutations, speciation and bifurcation, always lies mutations inclusive deleterious ones and the existence of adaptive zones.

However, the study into the development of the Dutch economy during the Golden Age and the end of the 20th century indicates the relative slow change of an economy's capabilities (indicating that organisations might change slower than we want). Accumulation of changes, sometimes resulting in macromutations, compares to the mechanisms of micromutations and the phyletic gradualism. Macromutations come about from organisations themselves and might change the environment, calling for impact analysis through foresight (based on game theoretical principles).

The research has confirmed that industrial companies seem to move at the principles of gradualism, gradual change more than radical change. Revolutionary change hardly beholds, it draws heavily on the resources of companies. Other management scientists have proven that companies might be better off not implementing radical change or that companies slowly turn back to the old ways of working and old structures. Six case studies showed that topics for structural change, the domain of the methodology of the Delft School Approach, concern increasing local fitness, i.e. optimisaton, rather than considering evolvability, therewith confirming of the principles of gradual change. Therefore, the concepts of the Innovation Impact Point Model and the related Model for the Dynamic Adaptation Capability provide processes and structures for companies dealing with such. Models based on evolutionary biology seem to have validity for the domain of organisations, particularly their development.

RESEARCH METHODOLOGY AND OUTCOMES

The quest into the adaptation by companies has taken this research along evolutionary biological models to look for models for adaptation and to convert them to the domain of organisations. The exploration of the evolutionary models resulted in the development of a new reference model and the formulation of hypotheses. The reference model denotes organisations as allopietic systems with fuzzy boundaries and the capability of foresight; the development is based on five issues: (a) the distinction between genotype and phenotype, (b) the undertaking of adaptive walks, (c) the existence of developmental pathways, (d) the criteria sustained fitness and evolvability, and (e) the principle of self-organisation. This basic model generates additional insight in current theories for organisational development and organisational ecology. The reference model has served throughout the investigation as both predictive model for generating an integral approach to adaptation, and as explanatory model for reviewing existing theories in management science. The reference model assisted in expanding the hypotheses of the research in more defined ones for testing in the six case studies and the review of approaches in management science (technology management, innovation, process innovation, Business Process Re-engineering, Learning Organisation, and Knowledge Management). The belonging evolutionary mechanisms define the developments that companies experience, except for the principle of self-organisation. It seems that the principle of self-organisation has great impact on the development of industrial companies, it requires more research to expand it in workable models. The review of main hypotheses leads to the conclusion that continuous change prevails above one-time interventions as effective approach, and that environmental interactions at the contemporary boundary of an organisation drive evolution (companies have the capability to shift boundaries in contrast to organisms).

Since the research also questioned the validity of the so-called Delft School Approach, its methodology has been briefly reviewed. The methodology accounts for strategic intents, sometimes in contrast to other approaches of process innovation and Business Process Re-engineering. The implementation of its solutions requires the development of additional theories for adaptive walks and

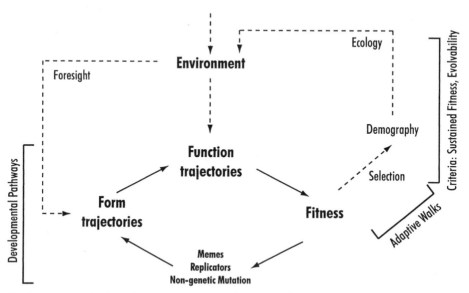

Evolutionary mechanisms for organisations as reference model. Memes and replicators serves as input for genetic formation, which exists besides non-genetic formation. Developmental pathways determine the form and function trajectories. These pathways also relate to organisations being a class of allopietic systems. The selectional processes select beneficial phenotypes on fitness following adaptive walks based on the criteria of sustained fitness and evolvability. Organisations have the capability of foresights in contrast to organisms.

developmental pathways to increase the effectiveness of its deployment. The research also proposes to adapt the theoretical model for a process (from Systems Theory), and to adapt the breakthrough model to suit the more dynamic views.

The research, the examination of biological literature, the review of existing management literature, the case studies has yielded models that did not exist before:

- the reference model derived from evolutionary biology to the domain of organisations, the view on organisations as allopietic systems with fuzzy boundaries;
- the Framework for Dynamic Adaptation, consisting of the Model for the Dynamic Adaptation Capability along with the Innovation Impact Point Model, the Collaboration Model, a proposal for dynamic strategies, and a proposal for scenario planning based on game theories;

and some additional proposals for:

- the assessment of factual innovations against the concepts of innovation and their impact;
- the implications of architectural innovation;
- the modelling of the Learning Organisation;
- the modelling of Knowledge Management.

The research has not ended. It should continue with expanding the models of the Framework for Dynamic Adaptation, developmental pathways, adaptive walks. Furthermore, the research base should be extended to include change management, culture, and leadership. Finally, the number of case studies has to be increased. This will open the possibility to conduct a study like the one of the aviation industry to more detailed mechanisms and models of adaptation.

PRACTICAL IMPLICATIONS

The principle of homeostasis, implicitly present in most theories of management science and therewith aiming towards describing a steady-state, views the environment as certain. The driving principles of evolution have shown that continuous interaction between the generation of mutations and the selection process in the environment enables the development of organisations. Especially, the mathematical models of Adaptive Dynamics demonstrate this interaction to the extent that organisms (and therefore also organisations) might influence their environment as a continuous process. Hardly, any equilibrium exists. Through successive minor modifications, potential major shifts are being prepared, creating potential opportunities for sustained fitness, optimisation within the current product-market combination, and evolvability, aiming at bifurcation and dispersal for emerging opportunities. The changes take place because of the continuous interaction between the generation of variation and the selectional processes.

This requires that industrial thinking should convert from the ideas and behaviour based on the effectiveness of one-time interventions to managing continuous change. So far, one-time interventions have dominated management science, and practice based on the classical view on leadership as invested power. The research has shown that changes takes place at all levels within the organisation and the environment. Hence, static thinking has only its place in relatively calm environments, which we perceive as existing less and less. The dynamics of the environment call on different ways of managing industrial organisations, according to this particular research directed to continuous change happening in and around the organisation.

CONTENTS

FOREWORD

It is always a great satisfaction for a research director and doctoral supervisor when one of his students' dissertations ends up as a book. This is the recognition of the quality of the research achievement by the student. But it is also an honor since such a publication demonstrates that the supervision has been done satisfactorily. It has to be pointed out that, in their professional life, academic researchers have very few occasions to be proud of a public recognition of their contribution.

Rob Dekkers has been one of my most committed doctoral students during the last five years and he has constantly demonstrated his interest as well as his competencies for academic research in the field of technology and innovation management (TIM). In his dissertation, Rob aimed at investigating the possible changes needed for industrial organisations to adapt to their evolving environment. This issue is clearly a very "hot" topic, which is dealt with by numerous researchers worldwide but mostly through partial and disciplinary shaped approaches.

Obviously increasingly faster scientific discoveries and technological innovations are crucial factors in business environment changes. Unfortunately, there is no more challenging research question than trying to contribute to fill – even very modestly – the gap of our knowledge on science, technology and corporate strategy. By chance, theoreticians did not get to a unique model or a stabilised body of knowledge and understanding, partly because this is by nature a multi-disciplinary exercise, potentially implying personal faith and belief.

It has to be pointed out that most recent reflections are targeting the relationships between science, technology, and the society in general (STS). In social sciences, the topic is very popular with sociologists, philosophers, macro-economists, and government scientists. But it is also an occasion for heavy contests amongst politicians and policy makers. Unfortunately, since corporate strategy is a micro-economic and largely managerial issue, there is only a limited amount of scientific research on the issue in economics and management sciences.

Two basic assumptions might be emphasised since the majority of scholars shares them:
- Knowledge, ideas, and artifacts produced or derived from science and technology are complex social constructs that are continually influenced by and influence society, including strategies developed by the business community;

- Science and technology are key sources of progress and wealth for human communities but might also have negative impacts as well.

There are indeed several rationales preaching for a reflection on the link between science and technology and corporate strategy. Recent innovations did generate new diseases, such as the mad cow disease and the Gulf War syndrome. Other products are causing environmental degradation, like air and water pollution, and global warming. Other artifacts are producing new criminal attitudes, for example mass terrorism and cyber crime. Forthcoming inventions might provoke ethical issues, e.g. genetic engineering. Above all, technology increases the wealth gap between North and South, i.e. between rich and poor populations and countries.

Nobody would contest that technology, partly derived from science, is today omnipresent and omnipotent and has already and will again revolutionise human being's ways of living, thinking, communicating, manufacturing, working, travelling, etc. In industrialised societies, it is hard to find any aspect of life that has not been touched by technologies rooted into the science developed in the last fifty years.

Moreover, applications of science will still be growing during the 21st century thanks to the already significant increase in research-development expenditures worldwide. Most observers agree that science and technology clearly have an *intrinsic power*, but they are still essentially and irredeemably *human and social activ*ities.

It should be pointed out that advance in philosophy of science, sociology of innovation, economics of technological change, technology management, in the general knowledge on science and technology is allowing a better understanding as well as forecasting of such impacts on societies, organisations (e.g. companies), and individuals. In the scientific community, there are intense debates on appropriate technologies, equal opportunities, sustainable development, planet survival, ethics in science and technology, science and democracy, science and corporate governance, etc.

The issue of science, technology, and society is so important that most advanced countries, such as Canada, the United States of America, France, Germany, Italy, Japan, and the United Kingdom, or regional authorities, e.g. the OECD and the European Union, have set up specific bodies for science and technology assessment, in charge of foresight and evaluation exercises as well as scenario building.

There are two opposite visions of the process of technology diffusion through innovation:

- The **traditional vision,** which is opposing two separate "worlds", science and technology, on one side, economic activities, on the other hand. Therefore, science is a black box in which entrepreneurs are selecting ideas for innovation. Such a vision might well work for innovations that are necessarily based on significant discoveries and advances in basic sciences such as pharmaceutical and chemistry. But even for such industries, the market acceptance is crucial and based on extensive testing procedures, including sociological and marketing knowledge. This theoretical dichotomy between the world of science and the world of business is largely explaining the weaknesses of literature on the issue of the relationship with corporate strategy.
- The **modernist vision,** which is considering science and technology and business as co-determined. Innovation is a social process with actions and reactions of many different stakeholders. The success of any innovation is the result of a consensus, i.e. of a true compatibility and coherence between market value, i.e. commercial "vendibility" as well as industrial feasibility and profitability, scientific and technological feasibility and political, cultural and social acceptability. Plenty of examples of successes and failures sustain this model. The failure of the supersonic civil transportation (Concorde) is mainly due to contradictions and oppositions by different groups and lobbies even when its scientific and technological feasibility was proven. The systemic approach is indeed much more complex to be implemented in action at corporate level since it requires a comprehensive approach and a permanent dialogue internally between all functions (marketing, R&D, finance, etc.) as well as externally, with suppliers, customers, government agencies, political and environmental lobbies, etc. This systemic approach of innovation has become more popular in academic literature in economics and management sciences in recent years but is still relatively neglected in business school curricula and corporate practices.

Business strategy is about creating wealth through manufacturing and selling profitably goods and services. Three main weapons are allowing profitability: decreasing costs; expanding volumes and market shares; creating new products and services. Therefore, science and technology are part of business strategy when they can offer new business opportunities through incremental and disruptive or radical innovations.

Nevertheless, there are several gaps between science, technology, and corporate rationale:

- The very first one, and probably the most important, is about the inherent contradiction between new knowledge integrated in innovative activities and routines, which are underlying business operations and without which there will be no profitability and business sustainability;

- The second one is about the possible contradiction between the social responsibility of firms with their employees, their customers, and the society, and their search for profitability;
- The third one is about the opposition between the activism and pessimism of the scientific community and the positivism as well as optimism of the business community as far as innovation is concerned.

Another crucial difficulty is concerning the "contextualisation" of science and technology at corporate level since they have always been and they still are two different social systems with different objectives, values, and even languages; additionally, the business community has no particular rationale or incentive to support science and technology *per se*. Up to very recently, management science has speaking in general excluded any reflection on science and technology since it would require a pluri disciplinary approach involving, beside traditional **management sciences and economics**, at least the following disciplines:

- **Sociology,** which looks at human behaviours as social artifacts and deals with issues related to the communication of information and knowledge within groups;
- **History,** which aims at explaining how scientific progress is made and to what extent history of science and technology might explain business behaviours and corporate culture;
- **Philosophy,** which shows that the key concepts informing science and technology at any given time are not *true* in any absolute sense and could therefore be challenged by stakeholders;
- **Anthropology,** which points to the *culture* of the tribe of scientists and technologists, who share a body of beliefs which is not readily apparent to outsiders;
- And but more for methodological purposes, **biology and genetics**.

It is worth pinpointing that such disciplines are not normal practice for entrepreneurs and businessmen and are not even included in business schools curricula.

Obviously, such a research agenda is endless and should be permanently updated. The research effort to be implemented is huge and will require building up a network of excellence within Europe, getting together scientists, social scientists, industrialists, as well as policy makers in order to investigate these issues. Multi-disciplinary implies the ability to use and transcend more than one disciplinary framework in order to examine issues and "contextualise" science and technology within the corpus of social sciences and in particular in management science. On the more practical side of management, i.e. developing implementation tools and methods, building up best practices, and experimenting with them in the business community, there is also a lot of action research to be done.

Rob's main area of contribution to these very difficult issues and challenging debates is embedded in his ambitious attempt to borrow from evolutionary biology and genetic not only metaphors but also concepts and models to be adapted to the management of business organizations. He provides us with a comprehensive vision of adaptation and variation in the business community integrating various intellectual inputs which are based on the evolutionary vision of economic behaviour integrating innovation and technological change as key variables of corporate strategy when such changes are vitaly needed.

Embracing and merging most major contemporary developments in the theories of change into a comprehensive integrated approach, Rob's book is also forming a text book which will be very useful for post-graduate students, in particular those entering doctoral studies and specialising into the management of technological change.

Rob's book is then more than a single brick on the wall of scientific knowledge. It is refreshing and expanding from the existing body of literature and it will lead to further research and insights.

Professor Jean-Jacques CHANARON

Research Director for the French National Center for Scientific Research
Senior Scientific Advisor for the Grenoble School of Management
2004 IAMOT Award for Research Excellence in Technology and Innovation Management

Grenoble, 26 March 2005.

PREFACE

This book is no more than an endeavour to use ideas from evolutionary biology for managers and management science. Some famous people have preceded my steps in this matter, among them Ludwig von Bertalanffy, Stafford Beer, and Kenneth Boulding; although known for their contribution to systems theories, they linked to biological models, somehow. Their thoughts have found their way in this book, and even though one might question the validity of their ideas for the contemporary competitiveness of organisations, they have looked at organisations as something incomprehensible, and yet, something to be understood.

Many others have tried to understand organisations, no more than a construct of the human mind, as a thing that we humans can manage. But the thing is not merely matter, it is made by and out of people. The many changes in organisations, many drastic in our managerial culture of doing, often affect people working in it more than considered. Managing a thing makes it easier to implement changes, drastic or not, that turn out later in ways not expected or not wanted even. Our culture of moving on gives us insufficient time to reflect what organisations are really about. People are at the heart of the enterprises. Avoiding drastic interventions, witnessed in many cases and with the only victims being the employees, became the start of the book, and then quickly turned into why do we not consider organisations as living entities, having a different perspective, a more natural approach to organisations.

The journey to writing this book has passed through the world of evolutionary biology. Great dedication to understanding the natural phenomena drives these scientists to expand theories and to find better or new ones. Most strikingly, their interdisciplinary approaches have made it possible to advance natural science, connecting different levels of aggregation, different fields of specialisation, different phenomena. Although I have barely touched on the available works, theories, and findings, it makes one envy their collaboration and their debate, not equalled in management science. May be that is the biggest lesson to learn for a management scientist, collaboration and debate, even questioning one's own propositions, will advance insight, not preached but done.

Rob Dekkers.

Rotterdam, March 2005.

Acknowledgements

Writing this book has become an evolution in itself. I want to express my gratitude to all the people without whom my own evolution would have reached a standstill.

Nil and Mert endured five long years of absence, other priorities. Yet, they did so patiently and encouraged me, giving leeway more than I did expect, and showing tremendous interest in the topic. Working at home proved the most academic environment, raising questions to why, what and how, carefully considering obtained insights. During early stages, weaknesses in the approach came about, even though you were not always aware of the true impact of words said. Thank you to donate your valuable time, Jean-Jacques Chanaron, all the time with much enthusiasm and encouraging remarks, until the end. Jeroen van den Bergh took the time to comment and to work on the evolutionary approaches, and Ferry de Goey, did not only support the work done but also looked at the historical correctness of the work. Klaas Smit who never doubted the outcome of the research at some critical stages. Also, I want to extend my thanks to Sean Lorre who supported the completion of this book and gave time where it was needed. Each of them guided me in all the chaos in the right direction with their patience, expertise, and wisdom. Last but not least, their encouragement never failed me to go on.

These acknowledgements might be far from complete, for which I extend both my apologies and my gratitude to these ones not mentioned. The long time it took, I have shared with many thoughts.

Rob Dekkers.

PROLOGUE

During the Golden Age, guilds in Amsterdam objected against the introduction of windmills to replace labour while the shipbuilding industry expanded. The area Zaanstreek, not far from Amsterdam, took over the supply of timber to wharves, which did never to return to the cities again (de Vries, 1995, pp. 350-358).

Companies do regularly alter their strategy, change their structures, and introduce new products. This causes the environment in which companies operate to differ and requires actions by other companies to react or anticipate. A lot of approaches have been developed in management science to understand these dynamics, either describing these changes or prescribing ways to deal with them. Similarly, many academics have looked into the matter of how companies do react to changes in their environment. This gives reason to explore these approaches before developing hypotheses and the research methodology into the underlying laws and mechanisms of adaptation (taken in the biological sense, i.e. the process by which entities acquire structures and functions enabling them to cope successfully with conditions of the environment). The extent and scope of these existing approaches implies that most likely this particular study does not cover all theories and it will not pretend to unlock all available literature.

The question arises whether those approaches suffice or that we have to review the patterns that underlie these dynamics and adaptation. Many of these approaches reside in case studies and the search for contingencies; this research's quest focuses on a more fundamental approach to generate more appropriate insights into adaptation by companies. Given the interaction between the environment and organisations, the next question to answer will be how internal processes and structures support these interactions or, alternatively, which internal processes and structures are necessary for these interactions.

The prologue, consisting of the first four chapters of this book, will expand on this brief problem definition for the research. Gradually it will move from exploring the environmental contexts in which companies operate to firms seen as individual entities and their adaptation. Chapter 1 relates the dynamics to the Delft School Approach, the methodology for analysing and designing organisational processes and structures as practised at Delft University of Technology. The chapter shortly describes the research objectives and the fields of application for the models for the interaction between organisations and the environment, to set the stage for the chapters to follow. Chapter 2 will continue by investigating patterns of the development of the Dutch economy during the Golden Age and the end of the 20th century. This is followed by an analysis of the airline industry. These two studies will indicate that establishing change is not easy and that change is necessary to adapt to the environment. The search into existing approaches in management science is the topic of Chapter 3. The main streams of thought will be explored and this will raise a number of issues for later chapters to deal with. Finally, Chapter 4 will review the research objectives, formulate hypotheses, and propose a research methodology, also based on the findings in Chapter 2 and 3.

1   INTRODUCTION

One wonders, what drives companies to restructure their organisations repeatedly. Almost everyday, industrial companies' press releases announce cut-downs, alliances, restructuring of organisations as a reaction to changing conditions. The initiatives mostly aim at reducing operational costs and developing new products through enlarging the scale, e.g. Boeing, Mercedes-Chrysler, Compaq, Fortis-Generale Bank during recent years. The continuous stream of announcements[1] makes us believe that organisations do adapt themselves to the environment (see Appendix A for the case of Boeing). Yet, a closer examination of these cases would reveal that one might categorise not all of them as adaptations rather than efforts to regain competitiveness on the short term. This might indicate that companies do react more than that they anticipate, a notion already brought forward by Brandligt (1992, p. 44, 55) in a literature survey about management during stasis; this survey aimed at revealing how companies might counteract during decreasing sales or market share. Management capabilities to deal with stagnation and perturbation prove essential in dealing with external changes.

Right away, the question comes to mind, why do managers of these companies not anticipate on developments within the market or why do they doubt the vitality of their companies' capabilities? Companies can be seen as a blend of processes, structures, human behaviour, culture and leadership in this respect. Do the dynamics of the environment pose insoluble puzzles to the management of companies? Do managers of companies miss the signals of weakness and how should they act? Should they actively read the developments occurring in the environment and create new capabilities for companies? How can they influence the capabilities of an organisation to prepare for the future? Which influence do external and internal factors have on the development of a company? All these questions raised relate to the emergence of change as driver for management, calling on leadership and vision, and change as a process.

What has become obvious is that during the past decades the speed of change has accelerated to a level not known before[2], calling for different perspectives on the development of companies. Management has moved away from the simple efficiency paradigm and related control processes, introduced in the 18th century

---

[1] *These announcements might also originate in the need to increase shareholders' value or from the necessity to sustain their (financial) support. Or ...? (Micklethwait & Wooldridge, 1996).*

[2] *The research will focus on the dynamics of the environment and not on the absolute levels of change. One might wonder if this notion is merely the result of perceptions.*

by Adam Smith (1776) and by Frederick the Great of Prussia (Morgan, 1997, pp. 15-16), to the notion of embedding companies in the environment and to the need for management to act as creator of conditions for change. Still, companies do exist that mainly rely on the efficiency and control paradigm, McDonalds being a famous example. Many industries do experience the need to anticipate and react to changes in the competitive positions and technological developments, e.g. as happening in the consumer electronics and software industries. Simultaneously, the performance requirements put forward by clients and the constraints imposed by the environment have increased. The environmental changes result in the need for approaches that guarantee continuity and sustainability. Embedding companies in the environment, creating conditions for change, improving working methods turn out to be important issues for management of industrial companies in this world of accelerated change.

1.1　CHALLENGES FOR INDUSTRIAL MANAGEMENT

Adapting organisations to the ever-changing environment and meeting performance requirements has grown into a continuous process and major concern for management; adapting should account for external developments and internal factors which influence the continuity of the company as an entity. The turbulence of continuous change does not only affect management, it also affects the people working within and for the organisation, certainly during severe interventions. Employees will look for stability and certainty about jobs, a home group to work with, the creation of their own expertise. The human factor is considered the most valuable asset and most important pivot for change. We need to create organisations and processes for and around people (e.g. Fischer & Hafen, 1997, pp. 44-45), even during the era of information technology with its huge influence on the way of working and during times of recession when companies tend to cut down on the labour force (but not always accounting for viability and longevity). Or otherwise, we will take a mechanistic view on employees, a consequence of a mechanistic view on organisations (Morgan, 1997, pp. 26-27); this statement has been recently emphasised by Mintzberg (2004). In return, this view will lead to indifferences by the work force (Maier, 2004), creating a vicious circle. Adapting to the changing circumstances becomes paramount difficult, since these organisations tend to "segmentalism" (Kanter, 1983, pp. 28-31); the compartmentalisation created by mechanistic divisions between hierarchical levels, functions, roles, and people tends to create barriers and stumbling blocks (Morgan, 1997, p. 28). The high degree of specialisation in different functional areas makes it more difficult to respond to changing circumstances. The question rises which processes and organisational structures support and enhance the so-called dynamic capabilities[3]; such capabilities reduce the need for radical change thus avoiding late and deep interventions with severe effects on the organisation and on the people (a notion also brought forward by Bruggeman [1996, p. 24]).

Therefore, industrial organisations should address the issues concerning change and they should develop a strategy that incorporates the external changes, the possibilities offered by globalisation, reach and richness, adoption of technology, partnerships, etc., and the internal developments within the organisation, or better to say the mobilisation of available resources and skills. Then organisations will innovate and change at higher speeds through both reacting or anticipating to external changes and managing internal developments. Innovation refers in this context to new product development creating value for customers and change stands for modification of the organisation. If industrial organisations want to increase their competitive base, they should incorporate innovation, technology management, and change in their strategic intents. Both product development and process innovation create give rise to new opportunities and allow companies to meet performance requirements. How do companies manage both different focal points and how do these points connect?

1.2   PROBLEM DOMAIN

Theories of change do not generate answers which structures apply for continuous change and about the link between these focal points. They consist of very generic concepts for the change process (e.g. Beer et al., 1990; Berger, 1994; Schein, 1993); change management is considered a necessity during one-time interventions and it has a top-down focus (Section 13.3 will briefly expand on this matter). Change management comes often along with cultural change which managers perceive as difficult to implement (see Section 13.4). At the same time, it requires modifications of the organisational structure along with the implementation. Practitioners of change, for example general managers of companies, have a need for understanding the processes of adapting to the market and they regularly ask for models to support these processes. That includes concepts for structures or even statements about optimal structures for meeting the challenges imposed by continuous change.

1.2.1   Delft School Approach

For example, the methodology for designing organisational structures practised by the Section Production Technology and Organisation, from the Delft University of Technology, attempts to design organisational structures that meet environmental demands and criteria derived from a company's strategy. The

---

3   *The dynamic capability constitutes the knowledge and skills to respond to changes in the environment of an entity. Chapter 3 will elaborate on the term dynamic capability.*

methodology is also known as the Delft School Approach[4]. According to ten Haaf et al. (2002, p. vi), the approach has three characteristics:
- *As being directed towards processes and the relevant accompanying functions.*
- *As dealing with the application of systems theory and its modelling approach.*
- *As being interdisciplinary.*

It limits itself to equifinality[5] through the exploitation of the steady-state model, for the modelling of recurrent processes, the related organelle structure, and the breakthrough model, for processes of change. Appendix B elaborates on the methodology and its models; within the framework of the research, the most important aspects of the methodology constitute the design approach, closely linked to the socio-technical design of organisations, and the application of a systems theory described by in 't Veld (1998 [8th edition]) during the 1970's.

The link with the socio-technical movement in the 1960's becomes apparent through the link with the work of Emery & Trist (1972). First of all, Emery & Trist as well as in 't Veld deploy systems theories as base for both describing and improving the organisational structure. Secondly, Emery & Trist (1972, p. 293) use the terminology: differentiation and grouping to point to what in 't Veld (1998, pp. 283-292) calls the architecture of the organelle structure (grouping of resources into units, departments). De Sitter et al. (1994) have expanded on the design of the socio-technical design at the level of the work place whereas in 't Veld has mainly used it for the design of the organelle structure. Nevertheless, both points of view consider organisations as open systems, to put it as Emery (1972, p. 9): ... *the early recognition by Ashby and Somerhof that if living systems are to be treated as open systems we must be able to characterise their environments.* He considers organisations as living systems.

The socio-technical movement emerged simultaneously with the rise of system theories. Some attempted to arrive at a General Systems Theory, like von Bertalanffy (1973). Others attempted to develop systems theories aimed at applications to the domain of organisations[6], like:
- Cybernetic approaches by Beer (1959, 1985);

---

[4]   *Recently, ten Haaf et al. (2002) have put this approach in writing based on lecture notes issued earlier, e.g. Bikker (1993). The approach has existed for about 30 years and has been practised mainly in The Netherlands, resulting in about 450 case studies. Since 2004, this approach has been transferred to the Section Technology, Strategy and Entrepreneurship at Delft University of Technology.*

[5]   *Equifinality refers to achieving a set objectives through a dynamic balance during changing circumstances (Baker, 1973, p. 9; in 't Veld, 1998, p. 44).*

[6]   *Ironically, the emergence of systems theories during the 1960's and the 1970's came about by the longing to create an universal language for science to bridge the diversity of disciplines*

- Soft Systems Methodology by Checkland (e.g. Checkland, 1981; Checkland & Scholes, 1993).

These two theories have not yet developed into a consistent approach for analysing and designing organisational structures; nevertheless, they have had a profound influence on the application of cybernetics and systems theories in the domain of organisations. The theory of in 't Veld, from now on marked as Systems Theory, has expanded on the systems theories by developing two main models: the steady-state model and the breakthrough model. The steady-state model (in 't Veld, 1998, pp. 236-241) resulted from control models applicable for both technological and organisational studies. In addition, the model for breakthrough processes demonstrates the related steps (a) to identify new needs and changed requirements and (b) to use these for the design of a new structure of the steady-state process (in 't Veld, 1998, pp. 330-331). The models generate answers to how to structure and organise and to a lesser extent what (Dekkers, 2000a).

The methodology of the Delft School Approach deploys Systems Theory to model organisations from a cybernetic point of view, the third system level of Boulding (1956). The design of organisations firstly pays attention to appropriate control structures, then correlate these during the next design steps to the organelle structure, and finally to the hierarchy (Appendix C contains an example of the application of the methodology). Since organisations represent the eight' system level, the Systems Theory might need elaboration by the adoption of theories of complex systems, networks and biological models; for that level the validity of the design approach might be questioned. The design approach has the characteristics of one-time interventions which companies might have to avoid because of their severe effects on the organisation. The review of other theories, like those of complex systems, networks, and biological models, might facilitate the search for the structures of organisations, needed for adapting to changes in the environment and continuous change.

Especially, the process of continuous change and adaptation poses additional challenges for industrial organisations. Production and Operations Management constitute the traditional domain of the Delft School Approach; its design approach has been applied to a variety of industrial problems. Although generic in its concepts, the application of the methodology has focused on the organisational problems of commercial industrial companies. Similarities that might be drawn for other areas within companies, such as financial management, or to other branches of business, e.g. service-oriented organisations, are considered beyond

(von Bertalanffy, 1973; Boulding, 1956) and by the interests into adaptation of systems to the environment (e.g. Terryberry, 1973, pp. 194-195). It seems that the research into adaptation by systems, as expansion of the General Systems Theory, slowed down because of biologists going their own way and the rise of the socio-technical design approach for organisations.

the scope of this particular research of the study. Within the manufacturing domain, changes are strongly driven by the skills and knowledge of human resources present in operational routines and the deployment of available assets, concurrently representing the capability to change. Operational structures embed the required skills, knowledge and technology within the resources and assets, thus decreasing the flexibility. Therefore, management of these industrial companies takes a strong interest in the issues surrounding adaptation to the continuously changing environment. The changes result in additional challenges for linking manufacturing to product development and engineering, managing the value chain, and exerting an effective manufacturing strategy.

1.2.2   Research Objectives

This research presented in this book aims at developing a methodology for analysing and designing process structures and organisational structures to fit continuous change and adaptation for industrial companies. Very limited research by others has taken place in the area of adaptation, creating the need for exploring the scarce literature and developing a new theoretical base. The literature survey has yielded limited available literature on this matter, e.g. time-pacing (Eisenhardt & Brown, 1998). The movement of Continuous Improvement claims continuous change (Bessant, 1997; Bessant et al., 2001) but hardly linked it adequately to adaptation; thereto, Chapter 11 will discuss Continuous Improvement as part of Business Process Re-engineering and Chapter 12 as part of the Learning Organisation and Knowledge Management. The basic research that has been undertaken has resulted in practical methodology, by using theories from other areas of research, such as theories of complexity, models of evolutionary biology, and mathematical optimisation, complemented with new models.

The methodology from the research into adaptation has been applied to Strategic Capacity Management, i.e. the development and deployment of resources, technologies in the manufacturing domain. To allow the application of the methodology, a framework has been developed for Strategic Capacity Management as a view on operational management of industrial companies (Dekkers, 2003). The subject of Strategic Capacity Management gets little or no attention in literature besides the continuing emphasis on organisational designs. After exploring the literature and developing a framework for the manufacturing strategy, also based on case studies, the link is made to the methodology for adaptation resulting in specific guidelines for production and operations management.

The research aims at developing practical approaches as well. Companies seek for inspiration, conceptions and methods to meet the industrial challenges for continuous change and adaptation. During case studies the research has covered the validation and the verification of the framework for dynamic adaptation. To verify the hypotheses, approaches, and methodologies, and to ground the methodologies, participation has been sought by industry during the development of the framework. The research has created models for adaptation but not yet a robust method; since this study is a first of its kind, further research needs to elaborate the frameworks and models, and to convert these conceptual methods for implementation in industry.

1.3   OUTLINE OF RESEARCH

Before detailing the research methodology in Chapter 4 of the prologue, Chapter 2 will focus on current industrial challenges for change and Chapter 3 will evaluate current approaches in management science to deal with continuous change and adaptation. Additionally, Chapter 3 will present information about studies in literature into industrial practices and challenges, like social-economical developments and longevity of organisations. Five streams of current approaches found in management literature, and their evaluation on merits for adaptation, are found in this chapter, too. Chapter 4 will outline the research methodology and connect it to the remaining parts of this book (see Table 1.1).

Part I will continue by exploring the field of evolutionary biology to find models for adaptation. Based on the comparison between systems levels of Boulding, the quest for models for continuous change and adaptation leads us to the models found in evolutionary biology and palaeontology, looking for the interaction between entity and environment. Recent advances in this field have

Table 1.1:   Overview of the different parts of the book, indicating main topics and outcomes.

	Topics	Outcomes
Prologue	Surveys of Dutch economy and aviation industry. Existing approaches to the dynamics of the environment.	More gradual change might be expected. Main hypotheses.
Part I	Comparison between organisms and organisations. Evolutionary biological models.	Reference model for development of organisations. Refined hypotheses for testing.
Part II	Review of existing management approaches. Testing hypotheses on 6 cases of Delft School Approach.	Limited effectiveness of one-time interventions. More gradual change of companies than anticipated.
Part III	Integration of findings into models for adaptation. 3 additional case studies for application of models.	Models for the Framework for Dynamic Adaptation (processes and structures).
Epilogue	Review of conclusion and findings. Recommendations for companies and research.	Proposals for modifications of Applied Systems Theory, breakthrough model, life-cycle of organisations.

been included in the investigation, like the science of complexity, the search for the origins of order by Kauffman (1993, 1995), and the application of game theories. Part I presents a new theoretical reference model for assessing the development of organisations and for reviewing literature on adaptation.

The search goes on in Part II, looking for models, findings, propositions, methods on this matter within the state-of-the-art of management science. This part will explore technology management, innovation, learning processes, Business Process Re-engineering, and briefly change management and culture. The findings of Part II lead to additional insights to the reference model. Six case studies, linked to the Delft School Approach, are used for testing hypotheses.

Part III creates the Framework for Dynamic Adaptation and models for continuous change. The evolutionary reference model and the findings from management science are transformed into the models for adaptation; additional exploration of literature grounds these models in theory and practice. The models are used to expand the models for Strategic Capacity Management. Earlier research into Strategic Capacity Management had already yielded some of the models (Dekkers, 1999, 2003), yet uncompleted. This part will conclude with three cases, to which the models of the Framework for Dynamic Adaptation have been applied.

The epilogue reviews the conclusions of the research and it proposes recommendations for implementation and further research. It examines the validity of the Systems Theory, the Delft School Approach, and looks at the strand of research into evolutionary approaches for industrial organisations.

1.4 SUMMARY

Industrial organisations need to adapt to the changes in the environment; at the same time, they need to manage their own (internal) development. How do companies adapt to changes in the environment? Which capabilities will avoid late and severe interventions affecting the people in the organisation? The research aims at revealing answers or possible routes to these questions.

The methodology known as the Delft School Approach aims at designing organisational structures based on principles of Systems Theory, and it deploys a design and engineering approach in line with one-time interventions (the redesign of the organisational structure). Although practised for a long while, does the methodology still hold in contemporary views on the organisation? How should we modify this approach to meet the challenges of adaptation and continuous change? The research aims at proposing improvements in the methodology that fit with the need for adaptation. The scope of the research limits itself to industrial organisations and to the processes and structures underlying adaptation.

2   STAGNATION AND EVOLUTION IN INDUSTRY

Does industrial change follow distinctive patterns and how does the patterns link to capabilities present in organisations? The research into adaptation will have to explore the existence of distinctive patterns as a possible roadmap to industrial change. The design approach assumes that one-time interventions, i.e. the design and implementation of new organisational structures, will suffice for adaptation requirements dictated by the changes in the environments. As a consequence of one-time interventions or the design methodology as present in the Delft School Approach, a sequence of reorganisations should follow in more dynamic environments to keep up with the changing circumstances. The organisation is changing continuously, at the integral level and the level of functional or business units. The changes taking place concern beside the new organisational structure also the path to the new blue print of an organisation. Mark Hillen[7] (Dekkers, 1996) says when asked about these frequent changes of structures:

> *The new blueprint follows market developments and the anticipation on these developments by setting a strategy. Because of the ever-increasing speed of changes in the environment, the blueprint is itself a moving target not being realised.*

Not adapting to the environments seems hardly an option. This is very well recognised by management of industrial companies paving the way for a continuous stream of reorganisations, restructuring, etc.

Does this continuous stream of change really hold under more dynamic circumstances? To answer this question, this chapter explores the development of the Dutch economy during the Golden Age (16-17th century) and its recent revival (at the end of the 20th century) in Section 2.1. This part of the research has been conducted by Saris (2003), supported by the Erasmus University Rotterdam and others, within the scope of the research into adaptation. The regional development of the Netherlands tells about local optimisation by an organisation, in this case the economic development of a state by comparing two particular periods of prosperity. Section 2.2 looks at the aviation industry, a relatively young industry, which came to rise during the 20th century, and at the airplane industry. A literature survey by Smeets (2003) as part of this research served as a base for the investigation of the aviation industry. The aviation industry (embedded in its nature) has been a true global industry from the very beginning

---

[7]   *Partner of Accenture, The Netherlands (beforehand known as Andersen Consulting).*

and the investigation will point to strategies followed by companies in that specific industry. Finally, Section 2.3 presents some findings of other researchers about the so-called one-time interventions and their effectiveness for sustainability of industrial organisations. This chapter addresses the levels of economies, industries, and individual companies to look for patterns of adaptation; the findings will make it possible to evaluate existing approaches and which theory the research should explore for understanding adaptation.

2.1   SOCIAL-ECONOMICAL DEVELOPMENT OF THE NETHERLANDS

All of us have observed in history the many examples of rising and declining regional and world powers, for example the Egyptians, the Chinese, the Inca's, the Spanish, and the English. All these highly developed societies served as a model for a modern and innovative society in their times, but they all fell at some moment into decline (Olson, 1981, pp. 1-2). It is impossible that a country sustains its dominating influence forever, nations come and nations go, as history points out. The law of the *restraining lead* also indicates that a specific nation cannot succeed in dominating the world development; one example is the economic dominance of the Republic of Seven United Provinces during the Golden Age (1580-1680). During this period Dutch innovations, Dutch entrepreneurship, and Dutch industrial products outflanked its competitors. This period of dominance did not last, new powers came to rise and threatened the small Republic. Eventually the Golden Age ended and a period of decline followed that lasted after the Napoleonic era (Jansma, 1991, pp. 191-244).

At the end of the 19th century, the Dutch society entered the phase of industrialisation that was continued after World War II when the economy flourished again (Griffiths, 1980, pp. 1-11). After a global crisis during the 1970's and the first half of the 1980's, the *poldermodel* was introduced to regenerate the poor Dutch economy (van Rossem, 1999, p. 5). This concept of a deliberation economy between employers and employees in combination with a guided wage policy solved many of the problems of the economic crisis of the 1970's and 1980's. The new period of forceful economic growth has recently ended in a global ICT crisis since 2000, when many of the newly founded ICT businesses went bankrupt. The economy of the Netherlands fell back on its competencies. What are those competencies and do these capabilities differ from those of the Republic during the Golden Age?

---

[8]   *For a full list of references used in the survey, I refer to the study by Saris (2003).*

2.1.1 The Republic during the Golden Age

During the Golden Age the Republic was the most important power in Europe[8], but like an Englishman once stated: *the Dutch economy was like a bird suited with goodly borrowed plumes; but if every fowl should take his feather, the bird would rest near naked.* Four exogenous developments set the environment in which the Republic did evolve towards an economic power. The four exogenous developments were the climate change, the shift in economic power from the Mediterranean area to the northwest of Europe, the shift in religion that caused competition between religions, and the population growth in Europe. Additionally, four endogenous factors stimulated economic development: (a) the population growth in the Republic causing a bigger domestic market and the import of know-how and capital, (b) the high degree of urbanisation, (c) the high degree of regional specialisation, and (d) the high autonomy of cities compared with the weak role of the central government. During the Golden Age, the Republic had to deal with protectionist measurements of other countries, especially those supplying natural resources, like timber and grain.

In this changing environment and with the endowments present in the Republic, economic activities were strengthened. The important economic activities in the Republic were dispersed over the primary sector (the part of the economy concerned with agriculture, fishery and the extraction of natural resources), the secondary sector (that part of the economy concerned with the manufacturing of goods), and the tertiary sector (that part of the economy concerned with provision of commercial services)[9]. Although the primary, secondary, and tertiary sector were closely linked to each other, the agriculture and the industry developed both partially independent from trade, the main activity of the tertiary sector; both agriculture and industry were capable to respond to new market opportunities by specialisation and commercialisation. For instance, the industry benefited from several technological innovations, like windmills for mechanised power. Besides being an agricommercial economy, the Republic was also an industrial nation!

At that time, the primary sector was by far the largest and most important sector, employing approximately 80-90 % of the professional population. The agricultural area in the sector was specialised due to the changing environment, in which the demand conditions caused an increasing need for basic products. Because grain could be transported in large amounts from the Baltic countries, the Dutch agricultural sector could concentrate on the production of cattle, meat, dairy products, horticultural and industrial crops. The fishery, especially the herring fishery, could benefit from the climate change that moved fish populations

---

[9] *Following the definitions by the SBI of the CBS (2003).*

Figure 2.1: Drawing of flute (Landström, 1972, p. 155). The flute represents the innovations in the shipbuilding industry, especially the crew size (about 10 rather than the usual 30 for a ship of 100 tonnes), the reduced armament, and the payload due to its characteristic design. The design of the flute was partially a reaction on Danish toll rules, tells Landström.

to the surrounding waters of the Republic. The primary sector grew in importance as base for trade relationships with neighbouring countries.

These changes in the primary sector initiated industrial activities, such as a high quality shipbuilding industry (see Figure 2.1). Generally spoken, the amount of natural resources relates to the size of a country. The small Republic lacked large amounts of natural resources, except the energy source peat. The lack of resources encouraged inevitably the establishment of traffic industries (bulk industries like the sugar refining industries, the salt works and the saw mills) in the urban regions. Additionally, the availability of peat allowed the setup of several energy-intensive industries (breweries, distilleries, textile bleaching and clay-processing industries). Besides the industries mentioned here, the Republic also had some important, traditional textiles centres for linen and wool.

The developments in the primary and secondary sector could not go without the expansion of the tertiary sector. The shift in economic power from the Mediterranean area to the northwest of Europe was important for the role of the Republic as *Gateway to Europe*. The Republic succeeded in creating a distribution network of domestic and colonial goods spanning the globe (dominated by the Vereenigde Oostindische Compagnie, also referred to as the state within the state). At the end of the Golden Age, the financial sector had developed, because the rich merchants withdrew their money out of the Dutch economy and invested in other countries (e.g. England).

One characteristic of the economic activities of the Republic was that the industries were mainly located in the urban regions, where the infrastructure of canals supported the connection between the primary, secondary sector and the market. In these urban regions, sufficient capital, know-how and a tradition to build up industry was available. Eventually, it was the textile industry, first in Europe and later in the Republic, that was transferred from the high wage urban regions to the low wage rural regions; this way the guilds of the cities were bypassed with the putting-out industry[10] in rural regions. This putting-out industry, in which independent home-workers were employed by entrepreneurs, was the starting point of the development of factories and of the rise of the proletariat, both the exponents of industrialisation. The guilds were useless then and were abolished by the central government.

The second characteristic is the strong interaction between the three economic sectors. The developments in the primary sector influenced heavily the course of events in the other two sectors. The development of energy-intensive bulk industries, the manufacturing industries, and the traffic industries traces back to the developments in the primary sector. Especially, these traffic industries were the goodly borrowed plumes the Englishman spoke of. The vulnerability of the Dutch economy with its small domestic market, its lack of sufficient raw materials and natural resources made it easy for the protectionist measurements of its rivals to appear; that meant competition with which the inflexible Dutch economic activities could not cope. As a result of this inflexibility, it became clear that several industries, like the shipbuilding industry, were not innovative anymore, and according to Porter (1991), more dynamic rivals will eventually sooner or later overtake that inflexible nation: *the bird would rest near naked.*

2.1.2 The Dutch Economy after World War II

The Industrial Revolution was an important turning-point in the economic history of the world. It triggered a new way of dealing with organisations and technology. Besides, the newly industrialised countries were also supposed to be modern, a society in which full-time industrial occupation was more significant than the employment in the primary sector. Despite its industrial history, the Netherlands were among the late industrialisers and experienced accelerated economic growth based on the secondary sector at the end of the 19th century (see Figure 2.2 for

---

10 *The putting-out industry, also known as the domestic system or Cottage Industry, was a popular system of textile production. It existed as early as the 15th century but gained more prominence during later centuries. Independent labourers would work from home, manufacturing individual articles from raw materials; these articles were either bought by merchants for which these labourers would work exclusively on pre-set prices or brought to a central place of business for assembly and sales. The putting-out industry preceded the large-scale manufacturing industry. The region Twente in the Netherlands serves as an example for this development: first, the textile industry based on craftmanship settled there away from the urban areas, then the putting-out industry emerged, followed by large-scale manufacturing industry.*

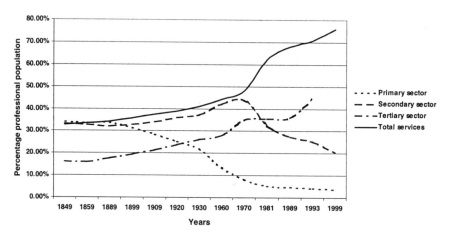

Figure 2.2: Composition of the Dutch professional population 1849-1999 (Saris, 2003, p. 41). The depicted data in the figure are based on data from the CBS (1994, 2001), Griffiths (1979), Wennekes (1993). The figure shows the shift caused by the 2nd Industrial Revolution and the 3rd Industrial Revolution.

employment data in the economic sectors). To pinpoint this age of industrialisation, van Zanden (1997, pp. 15-20) uses the term long century that started with the first Industrial Revolution[11]. Generally, it is accepted that the large-scale application of the steam engine marks the beginning of this first step in industrialisation. The cradle of these developments was England where this new economy started in the 1750's and it became the model for industrialisation. In comparison to European countries, like France (1829), Germany (1850) and Denmark (1870), it becomes clear that the Netherlands were late in their uptake of strong economic growth. This fact would be of huge importance for the Dutch economy during the 20th century.

Not until after World War II, in which a total destruction of capital and infrastructure had taken place, the Netherlands experienced a remarkable economic recovery. This economic recovery was especially based on the expansion of the secondary sector, by continuing the industrialisation process that had already started in the 1890's. This period of economic prosperity that

---

[11] *Generally, historians divide the Industrial Revolution in three phases, all marked with some elemental innovations. The First Industrial Revolution covers the large-scale applications of steam power and railways which triggered the textile industries. The Second Industrial Revolution is characterised by the large-scale applications of the internal combustion engine and the electromotor fueling the development of chemical process industry and the electronics industry. The Third Industrial Revolution concerns the large-scale applications of micro-electronics and ICT, setting the stage for advances in telecommunication and data-communication.*

lasted until the oil crisis of 1973, was based on the second Industrial Revolution; the Netherlands experienced its growth spurt on industrialisation and could profit from the knowledge available at that moment. To enter this stage, the Dutch had to deal with some unfavourable conditions (no optimal demand conditions in a too small domestic market, large public debt due to the Napoleonic era, available capital invested in foreign countries, high taxation, perennial shortage of some natural resources, non-optimal infrastructure and power supply, prevailing entrepreneurial attitude focusing on short-term gains). The industrialisation that started in the 19th century went together with the foundation of some companies that turned later into large corporations. The emergence of labour unions as part of the social-economic system and the system of social security arose as a reaction to the bad labour conditions and exploitation in manufacturing industries. These industries found their base in the putting-out industry of the 17th century. The rise of the Dutch economy during the second half of the 20th century was the logical consequence of the preceding era.

Mostly dependent on the world economy, the Netherlands gained from some favourable exogenous trends: (a) the liberalisation of trade, (b) the globalisation, (c) the shift from a seller's to a buyer's market, (d) technological progress, and (e) the founding of the European Community. At the same time, some endogenous developments, e.g. the role of the government in the social-economic policy with the guided wage policy, the geographic position as Gateway to Europe, the independency of the colonial trade and the demographic structure that build a society with political consensus and compromise, led to further prosperity. The Dutch economy was turned from an agricommercial into a multilateral industrial-commercial economy with a strong connection to a high productive and mechanised agricultural sector.

The main industrial activities of the 20th century were exponents of the Second Industrial Revolution, like the (petro-)chemical industry, other process industries and electronics. Besides these industrial activities, the food and luxury goods industries performed well, because of the existence of a competitive agricultural sector. As always the transportation and trade constitute a large part of the Gross Domestic Product.

Generally, after World War II, the tertiary sector, that includes the financial services and other commercial services, attracted an increasing part of the professional population. This conversion process was accelerated during the crisis of the 1970's and 1980's because of the large reorganisation processes in the bureaucratic industrial systems that had emerged (caused by the prevailing efficiency paradigm); only the process industries and manufacturing industries with a high energy-intensity and capital-intensity survived the crisis. Some of the traditional industrial activities, like the textiles and shipbuilding industries, came under heavy foreign competition. These processes of reorganising and of evaluation of the industrial activities took place during the crisis years. During the postwar period the role of the government in the social-economic policy did increase.

The excessive growth of the 1950's and the 1960's was attributed to the consensus policy of moderating wages; the reaction on the crisis of the 1970's and early 1980's was the re-establishment of that policy with the poldermodel. A period of growth during the 1990's followed, but still some branches of industry did not withstand this period of turmoil, like airplane manufacturing (Fokker). The year 2000 marked an end to the excessive growth of the ICT sector, causing a new period of recession and instability.

2.1.3   Competencies of the Dutch Economy

The comparison of major economic activities during the two periods in Table 2.1 is remarkable. The primary sector of the Netherlands in the present day seems to be founded on the basis already laid in the Golden Age. The strong sectors in the present day, horticulture and cattle-breeding, were also of huge importance during the Golden Age. During this period already some technologies were implemented to improve the quality of the products and also much arable land was converted into grass land; the land reclamation projects can be placed in this perspective. All these indicators pointed to expanding the amount of grass land to increase the number of cattle. If we look at the competitive agricultural

Table 2.1:   Comparison between major economic activities during the Golden Age and the end of the 20th century (derived from Saris, 2003, pp. 59-60). The columns of each period list the major activities in each sector with the most pronounced products.

Economic Sector	Golden Age	Postwar Period 20th century
Primary	Industrial crops (except grain), horticultural sector (e.g. vegetables, flower bulbs, trees), cattle-breeding (e.g. meat and dairy products), fishery (e.g. herring and whale), extraction of natural resources (peat)	Horticultural crops (e.g. flower bulbs, trees, cut flowers, vegetables), cattle-breeding (e.g. pig-breeding, poultry farming, cows), extraction of natural resources (e.g. petroleum, natural gas, salt)
Secondary	Traffic industries (e.g. saw mills, sugar refining industry, salt-works), energy-intensive industries (e.g. breweries, distilleries, linen bleaching, potteries), traditional industries (e.g. textile industry, shipbuilding industry)	Process industries (refineries, chemicals), energy-intensive industries (e.g. basic metals), food and luxury goods industries, knowledge-based manufacturing industries
Tertiary	Distribution network spanning globe, transportation sector, financial sector	Transit trade of goods, transportation sector, financial sector

sectors at this moment, it seems that they are embedded in an infrastructure of knowledge and innovation.

The secondary sector at the end of the 20th century basically consisted out of the same activities as during the Golden Age. The traffic industries of that period are comparable with the present process industries. The geographic position of the Netherlands and its shortage of some natural resources were the main causes for founding these activities near trade hubs. The existence of energy-intensive industries depends on the closeness to the extraction of natural resources. During the Golden Age the energy source was peat, which was available in large amounts for the energy-intensive industries; during the postwar period the energy-sources were petroleum and natural gas, the Netherlands happened to have large natural gas reserves. The special case of the food and luxury goods industry is closely related to a strong and highly productive agricultural sector, just like in the Republic during the Golden Age. The manufacturing industries remained the most vulnerable part of the Dutch economy. The innovative manufacturing industries of the Republic were the textile industry and the shipbuilding industry; these two industries were lost due to heavy competition of low wage countries. At the end of the 20th century, only the knowledge-based manufacturing industries could survive, like the electronics industry, but these were still subject to the higher wage level in the Netherlands. The agricultural and industrial goods could profit from the excellent geographic position of the Netherlands as Gateway to Europe.

The main difference in the tertiary sector is the share of the financial sector. During the Golden Age, this sector was also responsible for the decline of the Republic, because the Dutch economy lacked capital to invest in new innovations (investments were placed abroad). At present the financial sector has large shares in many industrial and commercial services and provides these sectors with capital to improve its competitive position.

2.1.4 Dynamics of the Dutch Economy

The competencies of the Dutch economy follow from the comparison between the economic activities of the Republic during the Golden Age and the Netherlands at the end of the 20th century. These competencies are:

- process industries;
- food and luxury goods industries;
- energy-intensive industries;
- knowledge-based manufacturing industries.

These four industrial activities are based on a strong and highly productive agricultural sector, an excellent geographic position of the Netherlands as Gateway to Europe, a global spanning network with the historically based trade capabilities, a strong financial sector for the provision of capital, the lack of some natural resources, and the availability of sufficient cheap energy. Much of the success of the Netherlands in the Golden Age was a result of her technological innovations which complemented her commercial achievements (Mokyr, 1994, p. 564), a true Schumpeterian thought. Again technological advances related to the competencies did drive economic development at the end of the 20th century.

Despite that these technological advances have changed the appearance of society, the driving economic activities of the Dutch economy have remained practically the same. The economic development seems to root in competencies, innovation, and knowledge surrounding these main activities. Many others nations all around the world have shared the same phenomena and fate (Goldstone, 2002, p. 378). Companies operate in that environment and, if what Porter (1991) states is true, the chances of success and progression seems to be related to the industrial environment. This does not say that an individual company with a different line of business has no chance of emerging. A famous example is Philips that profited from both the commercialisation of an invention and the presence of a latent workforce in the area of Eindhoven. On the other side, look at Nedap, a company that focused on advanced electronic systems for identification, but sought first applications in the agricultural industry. Albeit, economic systems exist because of the indivudual entities, e.g. companies, the elements depend very much on the evolution of the economy with its industries as a total.

2.2   GROWTH OF THE AVIATION INDUSTRY

The evolution of the aviation industry shows the connection between economic growth and the development of an industry; and the progress of individual companies in an industrial context. The aviation industry has gained a vast position as part of economic activities and as an industry itself during the past century. Its close relationship to the world economy have made it also sensitive to the social-economic developments, reason for the literature study by Smeets (2003)[12]. Additionally, the airlines depend on the management of their resources to serve customers (by having an adequate fleet of airplanes), hence linking weakly to Strategic Capacity Management. Smeets explores the trends in the industry to compare these with actual reactions by individual companies.

2.2.1   Short History of Aviation

The history of aviation is described following the model of Baum & McGahan (2004), which recognises four phases in the life-cycle of an industry: fragmentation, shake-out, maturity, and decline. During the first phase, the

---

[12] *For a full list of references used in the survey, I refer to the study by Smeets (2003).*

Figure 2.3: Major innovations of the airplane industry. From left to right: Wright brothers' first flight, DC-3, Boeing 747, and Airbus 380. These aeroplanes characterises the four phases of the life-cycle of the aviation industry: the Wright aeroplane the phase of fragmentation, the DC-3 laid the base for the designs of the era of shake-out, and the Boeing 747 and Airbus 380 the period of maturity.

entrepreneur is seen as the prime mover in the genesis of the new industry because he has to turn the invention into an innovation. This phase has as characteristic the existence of many small firms (e.g. the number of car producers in the USA during the early stages of the automotive industry [Geroski & Mazzucato, 2001]). The success relates to the institutional context and the social context during the development. The shake-out period follows in which a dominant model emerges; this model allows the possibility of efficiency and a strong growth of the industry. The next phase, the phase of maturity, occurs when technological advances associated with the shake-out begin to yield only incremental operational and product improvements, thus changing the basis of competition to favour industry leaders emphasising the efficiency enabled by the dominant model. This leads to growing importance of inter-firm collaboration and competition. The life-cycle ends with the phase of decline and saturation of the market occurs. The inertia of large firms impedes the growth as wars of attrition and bureaucracy leads to customer dissatisfaction and poor profits.

The historic flight of the Wright brothers in 1903 marks the beginning of the aviation industry and therewith the period of fragmentation (1903-1945). The real applications started at the end of World War I, until that time pioneers like Fokker struggled to turn aviation into a profitable industry. The major part of airplane manufacturers, building airplanes for the war, was put out of order right after the war, only the pioneer companies largely survived. After 1918, the industry started especially in Europe, with its poor railway system. The industry was dominated by European firms like Junkers, Fokker, Farman, and Handley Page. Yet, the European air services operated at high costs and aviation enthusiasts soon discovered that the industry could not run without subsidies. At the other side of the Atlantic Ocean, the American counterparts did not become state-owned companies and remained in private hands. The industry continued to be unprofitable until the year 1938. From that moment on, the emphasis moved to speed, economy, profitability, and cost reduction. The introduction of the DC-3 offered the possibility for low ticket prices and speed. Further technological innovations followed, such as the DC-4, Boeing Stratoliner, and Lockheed Constellation. At the outbreak of the war, the USA had a vigorous airline industry in contrast to Europe. The war gave also strong support to other developments like the airports, five hundred were built in the USA at an expense of 383 million dollar. At the end of the war, the leading airplane builders Douglas, Lockheed, and Boeing dominated the world's airline fleets while American airlines had the reputation for best operating practices.

After the war, the air traffic jumped at an annual growth rate of about 15% and a trend towards ultra low fares started, the era of shake-out (1945-1978). It was this growth that would give the industry its regulations. Because the European airlines did not operate on competitive levels with the American ones, the American authorities did not open the market. In 1944, the Chicago Convention placed a firm regime on the airline industry containing a web of rules and regulations, fare-fixing pacts, and bilateral agreements. Both the European countries and the USA benefited from the market options by using the rights between European capitals and American main hubs for bilateral agreements, and by not allowing each other to service domestic destinations.

The British started a new wave of airplane design by bringing the Comet into commercial service equipped with a turbojet engine; the new jet designs did put pressure on airports since the airplanes needed longer runways. Further innovations in jet engine design led to the turbofan jet engine which also solved the problems with the runways. At the same time, Boeing laid the foundation for its hegemony as airplane builder due to a large order of Pan Am in 1957 for 20 707's and 25 DC-8's[13]. At that stage, the number of passengers was still growing rapidly and the airports and traffic control could not follow the demand. The

Boeing 747 marked the introduction of airplanes with an increased airlift capacity. The development of competitive airplanes by Lockheed and McDonnell-Douglas brought these companies to bankruptcy. The recession in 1970's reduced passengers' traffic and eventually the airplane manufacturers had to reduce their workforce (Boeing from 83.700 at its peak to 30.000 in 1970). Later on, after some major setbacks, Boeing thrived on the orders it received for the 747. In 1966, the initiative was made to found the Airbus industry. After a troublesome start, the oil crisis gave the Airbus airplanes a new advantage: their design had a better fuel economy. Airbus started to catch up with Boeing. Airbus had only been capable of doing this by the subsidies it received from the governments but also Boeing was no stranger to federal aid and had received huge amounts for defence contracts.

The maturity phase started with the Airline Deregulation Act in 1978. After the deregulation new airlines entered high volume point-to-point markets with costs 30-40% lower than that of the traditional carriers, largely driven by low cost non-union-labour and the wide availability of inexpensive second-hand airplane. The reaction by the old carriers was cutting prices on all their routes destroying almost all new entrants by 1986. A new round of air wars was sparked off, resulting in the increasing of carriers' fleet by leasing airplanes. The marginalisation of almost all smaller independent carriers by the larger carriers ensured that competition was effectively eliminated. By 1998, 20 years into the US airline deregulation, its industry had consolidated into two distinct market segments: the hub-and-spoke market dominated by the established and powerful carriers, and the peripheral market serviced by point-to-point carriers, exemplified by Southwest Airlines. In contrast to the situation in the USA, the dominance of European carriers at each hub was defended through market entry barriers imposed by the regulatory authorities. When this defensive protection was removed, European flag carriers responded by consolidating their position of dominance on the national market. Subsequently, more cross-border acquisitions took place. Gradual liberalisation made collaboration develop between major flag carriers and paved the way for participation in alliances at a global scale. The deregulated European airline industry therefore turned out to be very similar to that in the USA, dominated by three large carriers: British Airways, Air France, Lufthansa. The current move seems towards global consortia or alliances, each comprising lead airlines from all three major regions of the world.

Most recently, wars and diseases on a global scale have struck the aviation industry. The attack on the World Trade Centre in 2001 has dropped passengers' demand, in combination with USA's response to evoke war against Afghanistan

---

13   DC-8's were built by Douglas Aircraft Company, which merged to become McDonnel-Douglas, and in 1997 merged with Boeing.

and Iraq. This changed setting together with the SARS epidemic caused the aviation industry to suffer from large losses and the consolidation of that industry does not seem to end yet.

2.2.2   Market Analysis Aviation Industry

Within the scope of this research, Smeets (2003) has studied time series against two models to assess the developments in the aviation industry. The first model is that of Miles & Snow (1978), they distinguish four strategic types: Prospectors, Defenders, Analysers, and Reactors. Prospectors are the creators of changes in their industry. They make use of non-permanent groups, low degrees of structural formalisation, short horizontal feedback loops, and complex, expensive forms of coordination. This gives the opportunities to innovate and to move into more profitable markets. Their strategy contrasts to Defenders, who use functional organisational structures, extensive divisions of labour, high degrees of formalisation, long-looped vertical information structures, and uncomplicated, inexpensive forms of coordination. The Defender depends on the continued viability of a single narrow market domain. Analysers operate in two types of product-market domains, one relatively stable, the other dynamic. Hereto, they have a simple and a more complex form of coordination. The formalisation is both high and low for which they use a matrix structure in the organisation. In their turbulent areas, top managers watch their competitors closely for new ideas and then they rapidly adopt the most promising concepts. The Reactors lack a consistent strategy-structure relationship, they seldom make adjustments of any sort until forced by environmental pressures. Those companies are mostly not capable to adjust effectively to the environment. The second model arrives from Farjoun (2002) and it relates four factors: Organisation, Environment, Strategy, and Performance (see Figure 2.4). Farjoun shift from a mechanistic view to a more organic one, in which strategy becomes the planned or actual coordination of the firm's major goals and actions. His proposal for the reciprocal causality between the organisation and the environment gives new insights to strategic management processes which come forward in the notion of dynamic fit.

Appendix D contains a full description of the analysis by using these two models. Data have been used from the Bureau of Transportation Statistics to describe the total airline industry (covering data from 1970-1991). Additional data have been examined from the International Air Transport Association, Annuals Reports issued by the Faculty of Economical Sciences from Erasmus University Rotterdam, data from Dienel & Lyth (1998), Morrison (1995). The data concern both American airlines (7 from which 3 did not survive the turmoil)

---

[14]   *During 2004, two of the European airlines did merge: Air France and KLM.*

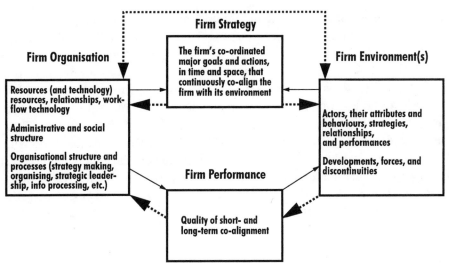

Figure 2.4: Organisation-Environment-Strategy-Performance model (Farjoun, 2002, p. 573). The firm's organisation is viewed as an open system that interacts with related elements in the environment through resource exchange, communication, other relationships, and boundary activities. The environment includes political, economic, social, institutional, informational, technological and demographic aspects, conditions, and developments. The firm's strategy co-aligns with the environment by building on and by modifying the firm's internal attributes. The performance can be represented by growth, profitability, survival, and other indicators.

and European airlines (4)[14]. The next paragraphs will list the major findings from this analysis.

The reaction to *changes in demand* were mostly well adopted by the airlines by changing their Available Tons per Kilometre (ATK), an indicator for available capacity, and Revenue Ton Kilometre (RTK), an indicator for income and capacity utilisation. For example, Braniff had increased its Available Tons per Kilometre on a high pace before 1979 and was not able to adjust its capacity in the critical period between 1980 and 1981. Air France was not able to adjust its price level after the crisis in 1973 due to institutional limits. From the analysis we can derive that the performances in 1973 were lower than those during the crisis of 1979. The reaction to *market changes in sort* could not be visualised but changes in the service strategy were an indication for this phenomenon. However, a higher service level led not to visible changes in the performance, since the number of employees per Revenue Passengers Kilometres was decreasing during the whole period. The reaction to *market changes in routes* could not be visualised. In 1987, the extension of the network of Delta Air Lines led to better performances. Furthermore, the Available Tons per Kilometre changed up and down after 1978; a good network most likely led to higher chances of survival. After 1978, the hub-and-spoke systems became more important for survival and airlines with margins in their cost structure and with extensive networks had clearly a competitive advantage.

In 1978, the introduction of the Deregulation Act causes a few interesting phenomena. The Prospector strategy leads to higher performances before 1978. Not influenced by competition, a high cost structure is more profitable in this period. After 1978, the Analyser or Reactor strategy performs better; for TWA the Defender strategy yields better performance. The Analyser strategy with the use of different markets can be an interesting strategy in the aviation industry. It deploys a combination of keeping costs as low as possible with an exploration of the market for new opportunities. The uncertainties should be covered with different scenarios which enable a company to react as fast as possible during turmoil.

2.2.3   Developments in the Airplane Industry

The strategy of airlines and the airplane industry are uniquely linked together. If the Analyser or Reactor strategy in the aviation industry seems to outperform the other two in competitive environments, does it have effects on the airplane industry? Because of their unique entanglement, the strategies of the airplane industry should follow each other, but which one follows? Obviously, not all launched concepts of airplanes are commercially successful; think about the French-British Concorde which came to operation on a limited scale and the concept of Boeing's Sonic Cruiser that never came beyond the design stages. Therefore, a brief exploration will follow of three manufacturers from the 1960's onwards: McDonnell-Douglas, Airbus, and Britten-Norman; this exploration serves no other purpose than to look into the effect of improvement in airplane design on the operations by airlines.

In the late 1960's, the DC9-15 of Douglas Airplane Company was a version offering more fuel and capacity in comparison to the initial DC9-10, a popular commercial airplane. This model was introduced on the base of customers' needs for a short-range variant of the four-engine DC-8. The DC9-10 was the first in the twinjet family accommodating up to 90 passengers. In the 1960's, McDonnell-Douglas (in the meanwhile Douglas Aircraft Company had merged with McDonnell Company) was the first to launch a model paving the way for a family concept. The next descendant, the Series 20, flew in 1968 and was designed to operate from very short runways thanks to its high-lift wing and ability to produce more thrust. The Series 30 that followed had a stretched fuselage for up to 115 passengers. The Series 40 has a further increased seat capacity, up to 125 passengers. The last series to be introduced were the MD-80's series, basically representing an upgrade of the DC9. Each one of that series has a longer fuselage, stronger engines. The MD-87 and MD-88 represent the last modifications with new cockpits, aerodynamic modifications, and stretched fuselages. The DC-9/MD-80 series shows that enlarged seat capacity and broader range of use were achieved by successive modifications to meet customer demands. The DC-10 a tri-engine jet, initially a wide-body to compete with Boeing's 747, follows similar patterns of improvement: increasing capacity and fuel economy while upgrading the technologies of the airplane. It appears that McDonnell-Douglas did mostly keep up with developments by upgrading its existing products and scarcely by introducing new airplanes.

The other two companies, Airbus and Britten-Norman, have followed similar strategies for their products. Airbus produces a range of similar airplanes as a family concept, the A318/A319/A320/A321 and a range of less related airplanes, the A330, A340, and now the A380. All these airplanes have been successively developed and use components from each other although designed for different markets and capacities. At the same time, each airplane design has improved features to meet the changing customer demands. Britten-Norman is a small manufacturer of under-16-seat propeller driven airplanes and produces the B-N Islander, Trislander, and Defender-4000. The B-N Islander is the best-selling airplane produced in Western-Europe. The Trislander with its three engines was a response to offer more thrust for a stretched version of the Islander. The Defender-4000, a derivative of the Islander, differs in terms of extended fuselage, internal fuel capacity, improved cabin layout, and enhanced vision from the cockpit. Again, like McDonnell-Douglas, these companies have maintained their competitive position by continuously offering upgrades of existing products and components.

Although the strategies of the airplane and aviation industry are entangled, it looks that step-wise improvement prevails during the maturity era. New versions are launched as versions of previous designs or offers as separate airplanes having a large commonality. Each of these versions offer either improved performance on seat capacity, fuel economy, range or enlarged capabilities, such as shorter runways. Disconnecting the strategy of the aviation industry from the airplane industry proves difficult; it is hard to tell whether these developments in airplanes are technological-driven or customer-driven. Major innovative designs have hardly made it to the market, the Concorde one of the few and may be the Airbus A380 the last one. It seems that incremental changes in product design prevail above radical innovations.

2.2.4 Dynamics of the Aviation and Airplane Industry

The analysis with the typology from Miles & Snow shows the deployment of different strategies in the aviation industry. Similar results appear during a study by Forte et al. (2000) using the Miles & Snow typology for the hospital industry of Florida; the most useful strategies are the Analyser and Prospector. A paper by Sabherwal (2001) on the interaction between information systems and the organisation also indicates the importance of the Analyser strategy. One should note that the Miles & Snow typology operates at the border of entity and environment. Sabherwal uses it to analyse the internal, functional strategy of ITC for which the typology was not developed. Hence, his findings that relate the typology to the "market domain" seem inappropriate. Additionally, Miller & Chen (1994) have noted that organisational changes appear frequently as incremental rather than radical. Despite the turbulence and uncertainties, these studies point all to the significance of moderate dispersal and incremental organisational change for companies.

The incremental changes make the differences in performance between companies very small. Most of the airlines did balance the development of available capacity and utilisation; they also adapted to changing market requirements by adopting the hub-and-spoke system for destinations besides the point-to-point connections. The hub-and-spoke system required increased capacity of airplanes and the point-to-point connections called on airplanes with both long flight ranges and increased capacity. Mostly, these were achieved by incremental steps in design of existing airplanes, and sometimes by the introduction of new airplane designs which did build on experience gained with previous models. Some radical steps in design proved successful at the long-run, like the Boeing 747, some designs were less successful. A study by Achilladelis & Antonakis (2001) into innovation in the pharmaceutical industry shows similar findings, incremental innovations play a larger role in the total than radical innovations. The findings also indicate that dispersal into different product-market domains might be necessary (looking at the aviation industry), as a consequence of the Analyser strategy. Also, the findings indicate that relatively incremental changes result in a better fit. To know more about effectiveness of strategies, incremental and radical design changes, the processes of adaptation of companies should be investigated in more detail. The research will come back on the themes of the strategies, dispersal, incremental change, and the specific studies during later chapters.

2.3   INDICATIONS ABOUT INDUSTRIAL CHANGE

Industrial dynamics have a large influence on the sustainability of individual firms. The investigation by Mickelwaith & Wooldridge (1996) shows that contemporary approaches in management science hardly contribute to competitiveness and firms' health on the long run, and that dynamics have a profound effect on firms' performance without necessarily that management can exert effective control. Within this perspective, Meyerson (2002) sketches the following data, similar to the more qualitative findings of Mickletwaith & Wooldridge:

- A full 70% of the largest firms in 1955 no longer exist (bankruptcy or dissolved).
- As many as 10% of the 1980 Fortune 500 have disappeared.
- Only three of the top ten companies in the world in 1972 remain in the top ten today.
- The average life expectancy of a large industrial company is 40 years.
- Employment and security are no longer mainstays of the economy. Companies have downsized and cut employment ranks significantly.
- Investors and Wall Street are demanding that companies take action by rewarding cost cutting and downsizing.

The statements show at least part of the dynamics that companies experience. It also tells us that companies should actively seek a fit to the environment. Jack Welch, the former CEO of General Electric, said once that when change imposed from outside the company is faster than the ability of the company to change internally, it is doomed. It still leaves us with the question how industrial companies should adapt to the dynamics of the environment.

At the same time, the effects of one-time interventions seem limited. Take Business Process Re-engineering as an example of one-time interventions, Hammer & Champy (1993) estimate that only 30% of these did succeed while they advocate the merits of the approach. The study by Jarrar & Aspinwall (1999) shows that only 25% of Re-engineering efforts reached acceptable performance improvements. Sabherwal (2001, p. 193, 195) also points to the limitations of redesign of organisations, alignment between strategy and structure is hardly achieved, and a redesign is inhibited by cultural and structural inertia. Gordon et al. (2001, p. 933) state that convergent patterns of adaptation see more common than episodes of revolutionary organisational transformation after studying longitudinal data of 75 software firms and 45 furniture firms in the period 1987-1993. In addition, they note that rapidly changing environmental conditions are more likely to result in an organisational transformation to realign organisational activities and internal processes with competitive circumstances. In their study only 16.2% of the firms exerted an organisational transformation. Zajac et al. (2000) show in their longitudinal study of 4000 loans and savings institutions that companies should follow environmental forces to maintain a strategic fit based on their organisational resources. Hence, the chances for optimisation by one-time interventions seem limited. Gordon et al. (2001) find that a change of CEO will more likely trigger an organisational transformation, in accordance with other studies on this mater. The present powers attributed to managers and the strong influence of shareholders calls for the interventions; they disregard the actual chances of succeeding and the draw it has on the resources of companies, leaving them unfit to face future challenges.

If it is not, what then? This pleas to explore the possibilities of adaptation to the environment. How do adaptation processes take place? It is not so much a matter of what but how, typical for engineering and physical sciences, the quest which processes and structures in companies do support the continuous adaptation.

2.4 SUMMARY

The Dutch economy hardly seems capable of moving away from its origins rooted in history. Although the world today does not look like anything like the one in the 16-17th century, the major activities still relate to the agricultural sector and industry, energy-intensive industries, trade, transportation, and the financial sector. Since companies operate on both a global and regional scale, it seems likely that their growth and development mostly resides in the present capabilities. National economies rely on their strong points, historically bound, maybe companies do too.

The development of the aviation industry shows that specific reactions suit the dynamics of the environment. A profound difference exists between the period of regulation and the period of liberalisation. During the era of maturity, two main strategies dominate: the Analyser strategy (active in both a stable market and dynamic markets) and the Reactor strategy (follower of strategies by other companies). Only one company exerted the strategy of the Defender, most likely due to its focus on a niche market. Hence, generalist companies have two options: either to disperse into new, dynamic markets from a stable base or to observe others and copy. The brief study of the airplane industry linked to aviation industry tells that incremental changes might contribute to a greater extent to viability than presumed in many cases, calling for an investigation into this matter.

Large one-time interventions do not equal adaptation by companies to the dynamics of the environment. By exerting those, management of industrial companies does not necessarily increase the fitness of the organisation. The interventions have limited effects and draw heavily on the resources of the company involved, maybe even to the extent of losing its health. How companies should respond to environmental changes is still at the heart of the research. It seems that continuous change differs quite from the concept of reorganising.

3 EVOLUTION AS MODEL FOR BUSINESS GROWTH

The theme of continuous change and adaptation has not only been identified during this study. Others, like the founders of systems theories, have already searched, but did they find approaches that really reflect how industry evolves? The facts from the previous chapter indicate that drifting away from existing capabilities seems hard (shown by the case of the Netherlands in Section 2.1) and changes in industrial settings come along with turmoil (the case of the aviation and airplane industry in Section 2.2). Additionally, the effectiveness of one-time interventions seems very limited. Did management science recognise these difficulties and present viable theories for continuous change?

This question of continuous change did underlie the earlier attempts to generate generic concepts of systems theories and the socio-technical stream for structuring organisations. As the Delft School Approach links both the development of the systems theories and the socio-technical approach, this paragraph will account briefly for these attempts to create more viable organisations. Von Bertalanffy (1973, p. 46) mentions the main characteristic of adaptive behaviour by open systems: *by trial and error reaching a state where it no longer comes into conflict with critical values of the environment*. This thought, aiming for a specific state, returns in later literature about system theories, e.g. Kast & Rozenzweig (1974, p. 110) and Brown (1973, pp. 236-240). The Socio-Technical School, being considered successful at that time, has taken up this approach and centred it at its heart. Miller & Rice (1970, pp. 9, 34-35) use system models based on conversion processes to maintain the balance with the environment. In the Netherlands, the socio-technical design school has found its propagator in de Sitter (1994), and additionally it has been connected to Systems Theory (in 't Veld, 1998) by the Delft School Approach[15]. In the emerging theories about systems thinking during the 1960's, adaptation is reduced to a matter of searching for a homeostatic balance through trial and error (Scott, 1973, pp. 111-112) or social-technical design creating involvement of employees (Katz & Georgopoulus, 1973, pp. 130-131). At the beginning of the 1990's a fierce discussion put question marks to the adaptation capability of socio-technical design. An article by Adler & Cole (1993), on the subject of the Lean Production[16]

---

[15] *Both de Sitter and in 't Veld have already published their approaches during the 1970's as lecture notes and books.*

[16] *Lean Production, arriving from Japanese production methods, has served as a model for the automotive industry in the 1990's and later other industries for effective and efficient production by using traditional production lines (Womack et al., 1990).*

versus the human-centred model, and the reaction on it by Berggren (1994) provides insight in the difficulties implementing socio-technical design for adaptation to the changing environment. It seems that adaptation became an issue for biologists, one of the origins of system theories, and it has not got sufficient attention from those dealing with social-technical design (they seemed concerned with the Quality of Working Life and less with the dynamics of the environment).

Searching for models and theories of continuous change that address somehow adaptation, a limited number of principal approaches to evolutionary development of organisations exist within management science. They can be divided in social-economical perspectives (Mokyr, 1990, 1992, 1994), organisational ecology (Hannan & Freeman, 1989), approaches to the evolution of life-cycles of companies (Lievegoed, 1972; de Geus, 1999; Greiner, 1998), developmental pathways (Prahalad & Hamel, 1990; Teece et al., 1997; Brown & Eisenhardt, 1997; Eisenhardt & Brown, 1998), and flexibility issues (Volberda, 1998; Warnecke, 1993). Other attempts than those in this chapter might exist, yet these were neither convincing about the mechanisms of adaptation nor insightful to the interaction between organisation and environment. The following sections will review each group of existing approaches and link them to the evolution of companies.

3.1 SOCIAL-ECONOMICAL PERSPECTIVES

The social-economical perspective pays attention to the role of technology in society and its effects on economies. Section 2.1 has already looked at the development of the Netherlands during the Golden Age and the second half of the 20th century, concluding a remarkable similarity in economic activities driving the nation's economy during both periods. The interaction between the economic activities, the levels of competition and the rate of innovations contributed to a healthy economy in both periods. It indicated as well that the competencies did not change although the world of yesterday does not look like the one four centuries before. The Netherlands has had its ups and downs, but how did those relate to the role of technology in society in general?

Technological systems, like all cultural systems, must have some built-in stability, says Mokyr (1992, p. 327, 329), indicating the self-induced resistance to change in a society as a relatively closed system[17]. The term technological system refers to the skills, capabilities, and resources at hand within an economy that tend to self-organise and to evolve finding its own applications. But looking

---

[17] *Von Bertalanffy (1973, p. 40) did already point out that stability in closed systems is relative. Starting conditions will determine the final state of the system.*

at technology as a purely self-organising system is an oversimplification. Technological developments might encounter forces that resist change, and get trapped in current settings within a society. Labour has been a factor in resisting change[18]. In the early days of the Industrial Revolution, artisans and domestic workers feared that machines would reduce the demand for labour and cause technological unemployement; later many historians and economists have shown that technological change creates more jobs than it destroyed. Resistance came about from the environment of a technology in a society, especially; it mostly takes place through non-market mechanisms. Firstly, the success of a potential innovation depends on the intensity of the opposition's motivation. Secondly, the degree to which the benefits and losses were concentrated among the winners and losers determined the extent to which political organisation is possible on either side. Finally, the attitude of the authorities is crucial precisely because resistance takes place outside the market domain. All together, the resistance to technological progress resides in social and political effects in a relatively closed society, such as the former East European countries, hence competitiveness and technological progress to reach for innovation do not link in such a case. Does competitiveness and technological progress link only in purely open societies?

This question requires looking at the interaction between countries. Which forces undergo societies from other countries and their achievements? The diversity of single economies, as demonstrated by Europe, lends itself to technological creativity (Mokyr, 1994, p. 562). Diversity is neither a sufficient nor a necessary condition for technological creativity, political fragmentation is neither also. The Chinese developments show so, some Western technologies relate to (or depend on) early Chinese inventions, reached in a time of relative prosperity (Chanaron & Dekkers, 2004). Cardwell's law states that most societies that have been technologically creative have been so for relatively short periods (Mokyr, 1994, p. 563, 573). Such a law might hold when economic systems are viewed as equilibrium systems in which bodies of movement gradually lose their momentum and come to a standstill. Thereto, Mokyr explores the effects of innovations and acceptance on the dispersal within a local economy, as a single unit, and a global economy, consisting of more related units. Rather than following Cardwell's law, it appears that in the case of Europe continuous technological progress has been reached through pluralism and competition.

In addition, Mokyr (1990) reflects on the nature of macroinventions and microinventions as drivers for technological change. The reflection finds its base

---

[18] *During the Golden Age, guilds in Amsterdam objected against the introduction of windmills to replace labour while the shipbuilding industry expanded. The area Zaanstreek, not far from Amsterdam, took over the supply of timber to wharves, never to return to the cities again (de Vries, 1995, pp. 350-358).*

in an analogy with evolutionary biological phenomena which has also drawn attention from economists (e.g. Chanaron, 1990, p. 529, 532). The changes in biological systems appear at different levels of impact, and therefore in competitive systems have four different classes according to Mokyr (1990, p. 351):

- phenotypical changes without genotypical causes (phenotype: visible features, genotype: pool of genes). Much of the observed variation resides in reversible changes of the phenotype to changes in the environment, such as shedding of the fur or population sizes adapting to food resources (behaviour of lemmings). The equivalents of these in business management are changes in packaging of products and the dynamics of seasonal patterns;
- changes in gene frequency. Given some genetic variation, the genes with higher fitness might dominate populations, an analogy to the diffusion process of new technologies;
- mutation, a change in the genotype. Most mutations are rather small and can hardly be regarded as the beginning of new species, just as most inventions are individually insignificant cumulative improvements on existing technologies;
- speciation, a minority of mutations might result in the generation of new species. For that matter, macroinventions constitute technological breakthroughs as discontinuous leaps.

Mokyr demonstrates the strong interactions between microinventions and macroinventions through the example of telegraphy. Successive microinventions might lead to accumulation into a macromutation; after the introduction of a macroinvention, microinventions contribute to further optimisation and dispersal of the new technology. Landes (2003, pp. 80-108) shows a similar pattern for the Industrial Revolution in the United Kingdom during the 18th and 19th century. Hence, technologies do hardly all of a sudden appear, they come about through national settings and through successive steps in the development of technologies (Wezel & Lomi, 2003).

3.2 ORGANISATIONAL ECOLOGY

Another strand of research in the social-economical domain that draws on analogies with biology is called organisational ecology. This type of research investigates the factors that influence changes in the population, which leads to the perspective on populations of organisations and not on the individual companies themselves (the analysis of the aviation industry, Section 2.2, is also part of this strand of research). These theories view organisations as relatively inert to environmental changes (Bruggeman, 1996, pp. 21-22). This implies that most of the time organisations are not capable of substantially changing their structure in a way that results in successful and timely adaptation to new environmental conditions. This assumption is in line with the Darwinian perspective, and in the view of organisational ecology the selection process creates the diversity of forms[19] and not the adaptive behaviour of an individual organisation.

A crucial question in organisational ecology is which internal factors of a population and which environmental ones determine both the entry of new organisations and the survival, change, and failure of existing ones in product-market domains (Hjalager, 2000, p. 272). Configurations of core features of the organisations are made to determine if certain forms and companies with the corresponding form belong to the same population. Hjalager states that the organisational ecology has often been accused of ignoring firms' strategies and unique compositions of individual enterprises. However, this strand of research assumes that firms' choices on a population level determine the occurrence of crucial life events. Bruggeman (1996, p. 24) explains rational adaptation in organisational ecology as changes in the structure of individual companies in the case of substantial reorganisation and with that changes in the core features and form of the company. Organisational ecology consists of a few sub-theories (see Table 3.1), focusing on different aspects of the interaction between environment and population.

Surely, the environment in which companies operate determines for a large part the prospects for the development of an organisation as an entity. For example, work forces might resist technological changes, reason to include employees in the (technological) development of a company when competition provides a base for technological progress; this depends also on the organisational culture whether such a style of leadership might hold (see Hofstede's assessment of cultures [1994]). The case of the Dutch society (Section 2.1) shows that competitiveness and innovation (as technological development) have a strong link, therefore both a prerequisite for development and growth. Although the thoughts of the social-economical perspectives casts some doubts on the further integration of the European Community, it means for companies that pluralistic approaches offer opportunities for development (pluralistic refers to the markets, products and technologies). Yet, Hannan & Freeman (1977, p. 933) state that the evolution of industries as aggregate of individual companies follows different dynamics than those of individual companies. According to them, events at the higher level cannot be reduced to events at the individual level. Following the

---

[19] *Hannan & Freeman (1977, p. 935) state that forms are seen originally as the characterisation of the key elements of the blueprint as seen within a decision-making framework. Forms have two purposes: to inform about the state of the external environment, and to activate responses to information.*

Table 3.1: Overview of approaches in organisational ecology (Hjalager, 2000, p. 273). The original table has been complemented with major findings reported in her paper and the results of studies by Arthur (1989), Mokyr (1992, 1994).

Approach	Variables	Major findings
Demographic processes	*Age.* Studies of the probability of survival/failure as a function of organisational age. Liability of newness, e.g. newness as a cause for succes or failure.	Most studies agree that size and age correlate positively with the probability of survival (Baum, 1996; Singh & Lumsden, 1990). Hjalager's own study confirms this relationship.
	Size. Studies of the probability if survival/failures as a function of organisational size, e.g. the importance of advantages and disadvantages of scale.	
Ecological processes	*Niches.* The inclination of specialisation or diversification and their impacts on survival and exit from and entries into the population.	Turbulent environments will favour generalists (Freeman & Hannan, 1983; Hannan & Freeman, 1989). Success of large generalists creates gaps in product portfolio, attracing specialised entrants that co-exist for periods of time (Freeman & Hannan, 1983).
	Population dynamics. States the effects of new entries as a function of previous patterns of entries and exits.	Regulations and deregulations change the competitive environment, albeit not always in predictable ways (Barnett, 1990; Silverman et al., 1997). Impact depends whether new technologies enhance or dissolve existing frameworks or competencies (Tushman & Anderson, 1986; Baum, 1996).
	Density. The total number of enterprises in the population is investigated for its effects on entries, exits and survivals.	
	Dependency. Studies that focus on complementary or competitive cross dependencies between two or more populations in a community.	Positive correlation between institutionalisation and survival (Ingrid & Baum, 1997; Baum & Oliver, 1992; Miner, Amburgey & Stearn, 1990).
Environmental processes	*Institutional processes.* The impacts on organisational survival, change, entries and exits of political regulations or turmoil, change in associative arrangements, etc., are investigated.	Resistance to technological progress greater in a relatively closed society. Pluralism and competition favour techological progress. (Mokyr, 1992, 1994)
	Technological processes. The theme is the adaptive actions of enterprises connected to major technological changes.	Increasing returns create technological lock-in, not per sé the most appropriate technology (Arthur, 1989).
Managerial processes	*Managerial processes.* Impacts of mergers, joint ventures, etc. on survival rates.	

major findings of organisational ecology as listed in Table 3.1, age and size of an organisation matter for increased chances of survival and additionally a strong link exists between competitiveness and innovation (or technological progress). How do companies reach this age and size so critical for their longevity? Which processes and structures should exist to adapt to the environment?

3.3 EVOLUTION OF ORGANISATIONS

The evolution of the individual company has already received attention in management literature. Focusing on phases of growth[20] and features of individual organisations to sustain ageing, this section explores three core concepts of life-cycles for companies: the growth model by Greiner (1998), the life-cycle model of Lievegoed (1972), and the investigation in longevity by de Geus (1999).

A reprint from an article by Greiner (1998) describes five phases of growth that a company goes through: *creativity, direction, delegation, coordination, and collaboration* (see Figure 3.1). Each phase begins with a period of evolution, with steady growth and stability, and ends with a revolutionary period of substantial organisational turmoil and unrest in which organisations exhibit a change of management practices. Each evolutionary phase is characterised by the dominant management style used to achieve growth; each revolutionary period is characterised by the dominant management problem that must be solved in order to enhance organisational performance and maintain continuity. We should remark that both axes in Figure 3.1 represent the two main dimensions for survival according to organisational ecology: age and size.

It is important to note that each phase in the development of a company emerges from the previous one and acts as a cause for the next phase. For each phase, managers are limited in what they can do for growth to occur. A company cannot return to previous practices; it must adopt new practices in order to move forward (Greiner, 1998, p. 56; Lievegoed, 1972). Greiner describes the five phases as follows:

- *Phase 1: Creativity.* In the earliest stages of the organisational life-cycle, the emphasis is on creating both a product and a market. The company is largely void of formal policies and structures, and often led by a technical or entrepreneurial leader. But as the organisation grows, production runs require more knowledge about the efficiency of manufacturing. Increased numbers of employees cannot be managed through informal communication alone. At this point, a crisis of leadership emerges, because of the lack of managers

---

[20] *Ferry de Goey (Erasmus University Rotterdam) remarks that more than 90% of the companies remain small, hence these notions apply especially to middle-sized and larger companies.*

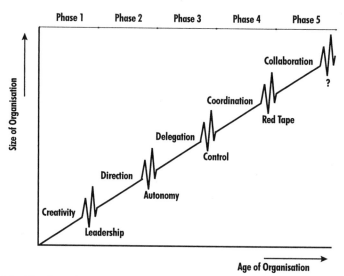

Figure 3.1: The five phases of evolution according to Greiner (1998). This classic approach distinguishes phases of growth interchanged by periods of turmoil moving into a next stage of development of a company.

that have the necessary knowledge and skills to introduce new business techniques. A new type of control structure is required.

- *Phase 2: Direction.* Those companies that survive the crisis of the first phase usually embark on a period of sustained growth, introducing a functional organisational structure. In most cases, departments arise, like marketing and logistics, where teams of lower-level managers are treated more like specialists than as decision-making managers. Although the new directive techniques channel the organisational resources more efficiently into growth, lack of autonomy on the lower levels becomes more and more problematic. Lower-level managers have to possess more direct knowledge, for example about markets and machinery, than their leaders at the top do. This introduces the second crisis, the crisis of autonomy.

- *Phase 3: Delegation.* The next period of growth evolves from the successful application of a decentralised organisational structure. The organisation will be divided into different units and the control paradigm becomes management by exception based on periodic reports from the field. This can only be done if operations and functions are narrowly described. A serious problem eventually emerges as top-level management feel that they are losing control over a highly diversified field. The organisation falls into a crisis of control as top management seeks to regain control over the company as a whole.

Those companies that move ahead find a solution in the use of new coordination techniques.

- *Phase 4: Coordination.* The evolutionary era of the coordination phase is characterised by the use of formal systems for achieving greater coordination and by top management taking responsibility for the initiation and administration of these systems. These new coordination systems will allocate the organisation's limited resources more efficiently. The systems prompt field managers to look beyond the needs of their local units and will therefore make the company more externally oriented. Although these managers still have a great deal of decision-making responsibility, they learn to justify their actions more carefully to a watchdog audience at headquarters. Eventually, the company will become too large and complex to be managed by formal programs and rigid systems. Procedures take precedence over problem solving; a red-tape crisis is introduced.
- *Phase 5: Collaboration.* The last observable phase emphasises spontaneity in management action through teams and the skilful confrontation of interpersonal differences. Social control and self-discipline replace formal control. The collaboration phase builds around a more flexible and behavioural approach to management.

The question of what will be the next phase in response to the collaboration phase is difficult to answer. Greiner (1998) imagines that the next phase will centre on the psychological saturation of employees who grow emotionally and physically exhausted from the intensity of teamwork and the heavy pressure for innovative solutions. Although companies might experience periods of evolution interchanged by revolutionary periods of substantial organisational turmoil and change, each phase builds on capabilities acquired in the past and on decisions taken rather than projections of the future on the present.

The view on life-cycles of organisations has also been elaborated by Lievegoed (1972, pp. 54-85, 98-99). He distinguishes three phases in the life-cycle of companies:

- *Pioneering phase.* The strength of a company in the pioneering phase is its potential and its powerful identity, concentrated in the founder or those who continue this style. Objectives and goals are visible at all levels within the company, everybody knows what to do and how to contribute to these objectives, even though the policy and strategy have not been formalised. The planning on long term lacks but the organisation displays an enormous flexibility. The organisation is based on historical growth and tailored to the personal skills of the employees. Renewal and innovation happen through motivated personnel that directly applies their own ideas. Managerial control processes are focused on direct contact with clients. The pioneer's models has its limitations in the health of the pioneer, the complexity of technology, and the market in which it operates.

- *Differentiation phase.* This phase finds its base in an hierarchical structure aiming at the expansion of the technical system, both for advancing production technologies and improving the organisation. Specialists have entered the company and the expansion leads to increasing the layers of command. (Sub-)optimisation of departments starts to take over and the attention of management shifts to control of the internal processes and structures, even into the direction of a mechanistic view on the labour force of the company. The rationalisation of the internal processes reflects also on the position of the client. The market becomes anonymous and the organisation moves away from the personal approach during the pioneering phase. Inside and outside of the organisation the resistance builds up and companies find themselves more and more in conflicting situations.
- *Integration phase.* This phase calls for connecting all processes, departments and employees to a meaningful whole. Lievegoed states that this transformation should start at the top management level; eventually it should lead to a management style of guidance rather than directing. The internal organisation should allow participation of employees. It requires rethinking of all primary and control processes to suit the needs of clients and to appeal to the capabilities of employees. Decentralisation becomes a key-concept in this line of thought and the clients regain their position as focus of the internal processes.

The life-cycle of product does show similar patterns as the growth of companies and we know that an intervention is needed when we want to extend the product life-cycle to sustain growth and avoid decline (Brandligt, 1992; Whetten, 1980).

The same question, renewal of companies, is at the heart of the studies performed by Shell, tells de Geus (1999). The shift from forecasting to scenario-analysis for strategic planning and the implementation of business concepts has driven this study by a practitioner rather than an academic. This concept of the *Living Organisation* has four main principles:

- The capability of foresight by an organisation to anticipate on the future through the development of scenarios strongly determines the possible reactions to the shifts taking place in the environment. De Geus makes it clear that such an activity should not reside within the Financial or Accounting Department; rather it requires participation by all actual decision-makers to prepare for and envision the future.
- Through learning, organisations develop an image of the effects of their actions and set the course for future actions. Thus, a continuous process of decision-making, studying effects of actions and evaluations enfolds which

provokes learning cycles by which an organisation might increase its effectiveness.

- The organisation has an identity it wants to uphold and maintain, the so-called Persona. Continuous managerial attention focuses at the behaviour and attitude of people in the organisation.
- A solid financial policy not only governed by the circumstances of the day. A study by Laitinen (2000) confirms this thought. His comparative study shows that in the medium term, investment in product development and marketing and in the acquisition proves the most successful strategy while a strategy heavily based on negotiating finance contracts and restructuring was the most unsuccessful.

The concept of the Living Organisation has been strongly influenced by sociological themes of identity and learning. The idea: the organisation as a living thing, arrives from the works of Maturana & Varela (1980) on autopoiesis for organisms (see Section 7.4); organisations differ from organisms in the capability of foresight, a theme that will return in the chapters to follow. Essentially, the importance of evolutionary biology returns again to describe adaptation, hence the further research within the scope of this research should pay attention to importance of these theories for adaptation processes and structures.

3.4 Developmental Pathways for Organisations

Prahalad & Hamel (1990) have introduced the concept of core competencies[21], to explain how companies interact with their environment, followed by many other authors expanding this notion. They subtly expand the view of technology from a broadly described feature, whose importance is determined by its support of the corporate mission, to a specific source of corporate uniqueness. Competencies represent in their view the collective learning of the organisation, especially how to coordinate diverse production skills and integrate multiple streams of technology. It seems true for the Netherlands as a nation building today on capabilities present in the past. This notion resembles to the paradigm of growth rooting in the past whereby organisations follow certain patterns of growth and experience transformations from one phase to another.

Elaborating on this concept, the concept of operational routines from Nelson & Winter (1982), Teece et al. (1997, p. 515, 523) denote that dynamic capabilities

---

[21] *The term core competency creates confusion. According to the The New Oxford Dictionary of English (1998) capability means the power or ability to do something while competency means the ability to do something successfully or efficiently. Hence core competency as concept is already included in competency. Therefore, it is more appropriate to use the word competency instead of core competency.*

comprise two aspects that were not present yet in other perspectives on strategy. The term *dynamic* refers to the ability to renew competencies so as to achieve congruence with the changing business environment. They call it the possibility to generate innovative responses when the time-to-market is critical, the rate of technological change is rapid, and the nature of future competition and markets difficult to determine. The term *capabilities* emphasises the adaptation, the integration and reconfiguration of internal and external skills, resources, and functional competencies to match the requirements of a changing environment. The organisational processes shaped by the firm's asset positions and moulded by its evolutionary and co-evolutionary path, demonstrate the essence of the firm's dynamic capabilities and its competitive advantage. Both managerial processes and organisational processes shape the competitive advantage through the developmental pathways the company has followed. Teece et al. denote that the importance of path dependencies where conditions of increasing returns exist. The competencies create competitive advantage if they are founded on a collection of routines, skills, and complementary assets that are difficult to imitate. Replication, transferring or redeploying competencies from one setting to another, is one strategy to expand capabilities but in practice true replication is difficult. Another way is imitation, simply replication performed by a competitor. This

Table 3.2: Types of flexibility, managerial requirements and outcomes (Volberda, 1998, p. 200). Note that absorptive capacity refers to the ability of management to recognise the value of new, external information, to assimilate, and to apply it to commcercial ends and that it constitutes part of the dynamic capability (Volberda, 1998, p. 110). The concepts of single-loop, double-loop and deutero-learning will appear in Section 12.1.

Type of flexibility	Flexibility repertoire	Managerial requirements	Outcome
Steady-state flexibility	Specialised routines	Static control Limited expertise Low absorptive capacity Fixed managerial mindsets (no experimentation) Single-loop learning	Increasing efficiency of response
Operational, structural and strategic flexbility	Dynamic capabilities	Dynamic control Broad and deep knowledge-base Medium absorptive capacity Broad managerial mindsets (experimentation) Double-loop learning	Increasing variety and speed of response
Metaflexibility	Metacapabilities	High absorptive capacity Deutero-learning	Facilitating unlearning and relearning Developing industry foresight

strategy has a low likelihood of succeeding as competencies and capabilities strongly rely on organisational settings and routines. Although, the conceptual understanding of dynamic capabilities carries a strong base for competitive advantages, the authors do not demonstrate its impact on the management and control of firms, the domain of the research.

Eisenhardt & Brown (1998) expand on the views of dynamic capabilities through adding time-pacing. They propose that companies that operate in dynamic environments should regularly renew themselves, in particular the organisational structure or the product range. The higher the dynamics, the more transitions occur in organisations to keep up with the changing markets. Their basic thought is that companies should acquire the skills to manage the rhythm of change by changing at regular intervals and the execution of transitions through perfecting these.

The view on competencies strongly relies on the recognition of the strongholds of firms, their competitive advantage and future development. Competencies indicate where companies come from and to what they evolve. For competitors, these competencies seem hard to imitate, even transferring to other domains of product-markets seems limited, and they retain the competitive advantage of a firm to its environment. It also tells that companies likely will not easily evolve towards a new direction but evolve from their present capabilities.

3.5   FLEXIBILITY AND CHANGEABILITY

Volberda (2000, p. 21) states the shift from static to more dynamic competitive environments highlights the already existing tension between the capabilities for exploitation and for exploration (a notion highlighted also by Fowler et al. [2000])[22]. The current, changing market environments require flexibility after the call for efficiency during the 1950's and 1960's and the call for quality during the 1970's and 1980's (Volberda, 1998, pp. 12-13). The elaboration on flexibility results in three types of flexibility to anticipate on the dynamics of the environment (see Table 3.2). To assess and improve a firm's flexibility, Volberda (1998, p. 226) has developed a method called Flexibility Assessment and Redesign, supported by questionnaires. For the design of the organisation he deploys input-and-output analysis and characterisations that resemble a combination of the organelle structure and hierarchy from the Delft School Approach. The analysis should indicate whether firms should improve their approach to the environment and by what improvements.

---

22   *Pierre Ch. Malotaux, prof.em. Delft University of Technology, has always reffered to the "Nu-Straks-klem" indicating the dilemma (klem) for management to solve operational problems (Nu) and to prepare for the future (Straks).*

For the arrangement of the organisation, Volberda (1998, pp. 268-275; 2000, pp. 24-27) introduces four concepts. The Network Corporation, in which companies outsource a major part of their activities, addresses the tension between change and preservation by the capabilities of others to further develop specific competencies. Although widely embraced, these networks might converge to tight control or fall apart due to continuous lowering synergy of its members, each going their own way. The Dual Corporation solves the tension between change and preservation by splitting the modes for exploration and exploitation in different parts of the company (the Analyser Strategy from Miles & Snow [1978] is such a strategy), by separation on level, function or location, e.g. creating different business units. Volberda states that the redesign of General Electric by Jack Welch represents an advanced version of this type of corporation, having a hierarchical divisional structure. The Oscillating Corporation moves between spatial modes of exploitation and exploration. In a given space of time, such a company searches for new opportunities, consolidates in the next phase and moves again to explore new possibilities. The Balanced Corporation encourages entrepreneurial behaviour and innovation with its structural context. Volberda does not state explicitly which corporate form suits which contingencies, he rather warns that bureaucratisation does inhibit the challenges posed by the more and more dynamic environments companies encounter.

Especially, the issues of networks and collaboration between companies have got attention from scientists to address the needs of the dynamic environments. The foremost characteristic of industrial companies and networks constitutes the capability to capture market opportunities and adapt to the changes of the environment. Within these two issues the collaboration with other companies has a significant impact on the capabilities of a network. Thereto, the dynamic capability equals the changeability, in the view of scientists. Milberg & Dürrschmidt (2002) denote the changeability as the sum of flexibility, the capability to operate in a wider space on certain dimensions of business management, and responsiveness, the ability to handle emerging changes of the environment. Changeability indicates thus the total changes the environment imposes on an organisation or network (Wiendahl & Lutz, 2002). Sometimes, the sacrifices to obtain flexibility in a given production system exceed the benefits from it. This looks very much like the distinction Volberda makes in different types of flexibility.

To anticipate on the changing dynamics of the environment, Warnecke (1993, p. 137) proposes the Fractal Factory, an integrating approach not only based on technology and organisations but also on accounting for the human factor. Self-organisation constitutes the driving principle of this network-like approach; fractals within this concept are either part of the organisation itself or independent agents when he denotes fractals as an independently acting corporate entity whose goals and performance can be precisely described. Fractals are self-similar, practice self-organisation and self-optimisation, generate a system of goals to fit within corporate goals, perform self-assessment, evaluate; these fractals are networked via an efficient information and communication system. One might wonder how this differs from an organisational structure based on semi-autonomous groups. The real difference is found in the performance evaluation and goal setting processes that characterise the Fractal Factory, two conditions for the simultaneous forces of exploitation and exploration from Volberda.

3.6 Brief Review of Existing Evolutionary Approaches

Within the scope of the research, the question remains how companies should adapt to the changing environment. The five principal approaches that describe the evolutionary development of companies (social-economical perspective, organisational ecology, evolution of organisations, developmental pathways, flexibility and changeability) hardly address the questions raised during Chapter 1: how do companies adapt to changing circumstances, and which internal processes and structures are needed to adapt? While the social-economical perspective and organisational ecology are grounded in research, the approaches of the developmental pathways look more like concepts. The theories of the evolution of organisations and the concepts of flexibility appear to be more of an empirical nature. Therefore, the five principal approaches differ quite on validity and applicability.

The found literature about the principal approaches has very diverse applications to continuous change; each of them addresses quite different facets that might matter to answer the question of adaptation and linking these will become another problem. According to Kuhn (1988), fundamental new insight and vital progress in science will only come along with a shift in the underlying paradigms - anything else can only yield incremental improvement. Hence, the research has to continue and to find ways to describe continuous change and adaptation.

Especially, when looking at the Delft School Approach, a further investigation is needed. This approach aims at designing organisational structures and follows a deductive process, given criteria result in the internal structure of the organisation. One of the major research questions moves at this level. Do companies have to follow a deductive pathway or an inductive pathway? The deductive pathway reasons from external development to countermeasures internally, while the inductive pathway leads to the influence of an organisation on its environment. Yet, none of the approaches accounts directly for such. The further search for internal processes and structures that support or enable continuous change, should lead to verification of the Delft School Approach to dynamic environments.

Describing the interaction with the environment, some of the studies deploy models of evolutionary biology, like Mokyr does, and others use similar techniques as biologists do to investigate the evolution of organisations, like organisational ecology. The interaction between entity and environment moves at the heart of evolutionary biology. Since not all of the presented approaches explicitly refer to evolutionary biology, including this domain might yield a better background for understanding the interaction between organisation and environment. This extends beyond the efforts of organisational ecology which deploy techniques aimed at discovering factors of influence looking at a total population; most of these techniques find their base in data analysis, like the investigation in the aviation industry during Chapter 2. The particular research at hand aims at reviewing internal processes and structures, therefore searching for other factors in addition to those of organisational ecology.

3.7   SUMMARY

Industrial companies operate within the context of societies defining technological progress and social attitudes towards innovation. Nations' competitiveness depends on it, as shown by the self-sufficiency in Dutch society after the Golden Age. Europe's pluralism and competition drove technological progress at this continent.

Does this hold for companies, too? Technological innovation becomes an important issue residing in competencies of a company. Developmental pathways determine the development of organisations, some management scientists advocate time-pacing to enforce regularly adaptation which does not tell which processes and structures behold for continuous change.

The application of evolutionary biology in the domain of organisations, especially, development and growth, opens possible new perspectives for understanding the continuous change of individual companies. Organisational ecology, also exploring evolutionary patterns, seems mainly concerned with capturing the underlying patterns for industries. The individual organisation needs more attention. This search aims to extend the concept of continuous change beyond the topics of flexibility and changeability, which direct themselves to better design parameters for a given company at a specific moment in time.

4 Research Objectives and Methodology

Management science has reacted to challenges, induced by changes of the environment, by producing new theories or new versions of older theories, at the risk of confusion by practitioners; likewise for adaptation. Fischer & Hafen (1997) present an overview of these trends, merely Taylorism, mechanisation, automatisation during the second Industrial Revolution to the current range of managerial concepts, e.g. Agile Manufacturing, Virtual Company, Business Process Re-engineering, Process Management, TQM. They question whether these theories or practices address adequately the nature of change. The practice of these theories, mostly top-down enforced onto the organisation, should increase the fitness of the organisation to anticipate on changes of the environment. The world of management has been overfed by theories that might have been adequate to some enterprises to deal with the contemporary challenges facing industry but not to others (Micklethwait & Wooldridge, 1996). All these theories have in common that their foundations stem from a variety of presuppositions pertaining to different factors that might directly influence the rate of success of an organization at one place and time. Direct transferences of these approaches to adaptation and continuous change will fail as they lack problem-oriented interdisciplinary inferences. The previous chapter did briefly show that bottom-up practices have encountered limitations as well: the socio-technical design has been discussed intensely, e.g. the discussion on the NUMMI plant vs. the Uddevalla plant (Adler & Cole, 1993; Berggren, 1994). Lewin & Volberda (1999, p. 520) remark that writers have speculated about new organisational forms, such as the virtual corporation, hollow company, cellular organisation, dynamic network form, etc. and done so by retrospective accounts of single cases. They indicate that further development remains necessary to transform these single case studies into organisational theory. Adaptation requires the development of organisational theory based on scientific foundations rather than the expansion of contingencies and the draw of generalisations that hardly befit companies.

The exploratory chapters did already generate interesting notions about how companies might deal with the dynamics of the environment. First of all, evolutionary models constitute a strong base for describing adaptation by industrial nations, industries, and industrial companies (industry continues to be the prime area of interest, even though the findings might be applicable in other economic areas). These models root in theories of evolutionary biology, raising immediately the question how evolutionary biological models and models for adaptation by industrial companies relate. Secondly, the analogies with biological models introduced learning capabilities as characterisation for living organisms and for organisations; organisations possess the capability of foresight. Thirdly, technological progress and innovation link strongly to competitiveness, as noticed during the studies in the development of the Netherlands and the aviation industry. Additionally, the principles of Business Process Re-engineering look like one-time interventions, which most likely have limited effects and they drain the resources of the company. Hence, all these topics should find their place within the scope of the research.

This chapter reveals how the research will contribute to the domain of theories and approaches for dynamically changing environments and how it will cover the issues raised; additionally, the research methodology will be elaborated. Section 4.1 will introduce the research objectives, linking it to the methodology for designing organisational structures of the Delft School Approach. Section 4.2 will expand on the research domain and the choice for Strategic Capacity Management as domain of application; the relation to the specific research will be briefly discussed. Section 4.3 will outline the research methodology and expand on the actual execution of the research.

4.1 RESEARCH OBJECTIVES AND PROPOSITION

The research is rooted in the tradition of the Delft School Approach in two ways. First, one will find the origin of this approach in the design of processes and structures of organisations (see Section 11.2 for a more detailed explanation, Appendix C describes a case), especially the control processes and organelle structures with a strong link to the socio-technical design school. The approach has proven that successful redesigns of organisations are possible in combination with the tools provided by Systems Theory (from the 450 case studies to date a substantial part has been implemented). Secondly, looking at the application of the Systems Theory, it appears that the methodology limits itself to equifinality through the exploitation of the steady-state model, for describing recurrent processes.

4.1.1 Equifinality

Von Bertalanffy (1968, p. 40) writes about equifinality, when introducing the concept as part of the General Systems Theory:

> In any closed system, the final state is unequivocally determined by the initial conditions... If either the initial conditions or the process is altered, the final state will also be changed. This is not so in open systems. Here, the final state may be reached from different initial conditions and in different ways. This is what is called equifinality, and it has a significant meaning for the phenomena of biological regulation... It can be shown, however, that open systems, insofar as

they attain a steady state, must show equifinality, ...

Equifinality directly connects to homeostasis (von Bertalanffy, 1968, p. 46):

> *... equifinality, the tendency towards a characteristic final state from different initial states and in different ways, based on dynamic interactions in an open system attaining a steady state; the second, feedback, the homeostatic maintenance of a characteristic state or the seeking of a goal, based upon circular causal chains and mechanisms monitoring back information on deviations from the state to be maintained or the goal to be reached.*

Later scientists developing the General Systems Theory confirmed this thought (Kast & Rozenzweig, 1970, p. 467; Hagen, 1973, p. 79). Furthermore, Hagen (1973, pp. 79-80) denotes that in case of homeostasis one variable could return to its old value only if another one changed permanently in magnitude. This overlooked phenomenon, homeostasis implies an alteration in another value, called heterostasis, acts as a signal of weakness for the effect of one-time interventions; these interventions must draw on the resources at the disposal of an organisation. All authors within the domain of systems theories do connect the maintenance of a homeostatic state to boundary control, as part of the transformation processes, taking place in organisations; indicating the inclusion of the exploration of the interaction between entity (organisation) and environment.

In addition, there should be processes for innovative decisions (organisations as adaptive systems), which move the organisation along its life-cycle in response to external and internal stimuli (Kast & Rozenzweig, 1970, p. 467). The model for breakthrough processes, as part of Systems Theory (see Appendix B), demonstrates the related steps to identify new needs and changed requirements and translate these into a new structure of the steady-state process. Although, the equifinality assumes that different internal structures might produce the same or similar results and performance levels of systems and processes, the growth of organisations might require the evaluation of internal structures for future fits. Neither the models of the systems theory nor the design approach have been assessed at this point.

4.1.2   Search for Reference Model and Proposition of Main Hypotheses

Such an assessment needs a reference model; where do we find such theoretical concepts for a review of Systems Theory and the design approach? Systems Theory aims at modelling organisations from a cybernetic point of view, the third system level of Boulding (1956), as also mentioned by Lievegoed (1972, p. 47). Since, organisations represent the eight' system level, the adoption of theories from biological models and the strongly related science of complexity provide additional insight for the reference model and the belonging structures of organisations (Section 5.2.1 will elaborate on this matter). This assumption might apply best to the dynamics of the market and the response by organisations. Thus, insight gained by this comparison, between organisations and organisms, might create new guidelines for adapting organisations to the contemporary developments of the market and environment.

Additionally, this research aims at developing a methodology for analysing and designing process structures and organisational structures to fit continuous change. Very limited research has taken place in this area creating the need for exploring the scarce literature and developing a new theoretical framework. This basic research should result in practical methodology by using theories from other areas of research into this field, such as science of complexity, models of growth, and mathematical optimisation. Although organisations have a position at the eight' level of Boulding, theories exceeding that third level should generate complementary views on fitting organisations to the uncertainty of the dynamics of the environment. Hence, the main proposition of the research will centre on the following statement:

> *Despite the uncertainty of the dynamics of the environment, processes and structures within organisations do exist to increase the chances of successful adaptation to the changes taking place in the environment. Hence, if companies do not employ such processes and structures, they are forced to exert severe interventions heavily drawing on resources within and in reach of the company, decreasing the chances of survival.*

Although the statement might seem obvious, the current quest of many academics and sincere practitioners into this area should lead to comprehend the (related) phenomena. The research should reveal the underlying mechanisms that should increase the chances of a fit in the dynamically changing landscape of the competitive environment of industrial companies.

Therefore, a wide scope of models from evolutionary biology focusing on speciation and landscape fitness will be addressed to find possible ways to answer the main proposition of the research, centring on the two following hypotheses:

Hypothesis A
The principle of boundary control based on homeostasis limits the evolution of organisations in response to the dynamics of the environment.

Hypothesis B
Adaptation to the environment constitutes of continuous processes within the organisations rather than one-time interventions.

Both hypotheses rely on the belief that, despite the uncertainty of the dynamics of the environment, processes and structures within organisations do exist to increase the chances of successful adaptation to the changes taking place in the environment. The first hypothesis indicates whether we have to revise the main principle that seems to dominate management science. Homeostasis, balancing the internal structure and the environment, might not fit as model for change when talking about dynamically changing environments in which less time remains to implement gradual changes. If the structures for increasing the Complexity Handling Capability (Boswijk, 1992, p. 101), the ability of an organisation to deal with the imposed complexity by its environment, exist, homeostasis does not drive adaptation. As mentioned before, if companies do not employ such processes and structures, they are forced to exert severe interventions heavily drawing on resources within and in reach of the company, decreasing the chances of survival. This call for the second hypothesis which partially justifies the exploitation of homeostasis, gradual change might rely on maintaining homeostasis. Might such a contradiction of opposing forces, like yin and yang, drive the successful adaptation of companies to the ever-changing environment and serve as a model for internal processes and structures?

4.1.3   Research Methodology

Some methodological notes will be made before continuing with the contents of the research. According to Popper (1999, p. 10), the two hypotheses should be falsifiable. This is not yet the case, the further investigation of theory and practice should reveal whether a refinement becomes possible such that testing will allow the assessment of these theories (Popper, 1966, pp. 52-55). The refinement can become possible after reviewing literature on evolutionary biology; the knowledge about evolution of organisms and mechanisms for adaptation in biology has grown tremendously during the past 10-20 years, giving ground for a profound look at theories in this field. For testing of hypotheses, it is necessary that the class of opportunities to falsify the theories should not be empty on beforehand. The generic character of theories allows no verification, but they could be open to falsification (Nola & Sankey, 2000, p. 18). Looking at the two hypotheses, it seems that both have been stated in general terms. Hence, a refinement becomes necessary for which models might be found by exploring evolutionary biology.

The second point of Popper's philosophy towards scientific discovery, induction logic, warns for drawing generalisations where possibly inappropriate (Popper, 1966, pp. 98-99); a thought rooted in the research of Selz (1913, p. 97). Hence, the research will take this into account whenever applying analogies from evolutionary biology to the domain of organisations (Chapter 5 will expand on this matter), Kuhn's thoughts allow to take interest in these theories as the choice between theories is subjective (Nola & Sankey, 2000, p. 28; Leavitt, 2001, p. 6). The four-stage model of scientific discovery (Popper, 1999, p. 14) should also lead to caution with respect to hasty conclusions; the four stages consist of: (a) the old problem, (b) the formation of tentative theories, (c) the attempts at elimination, (d) the new problems. Before arriving at this chapter, one cycle has already taken place (current theories do insufficiently tell how to adapt and have little predictive value), leading up to the need for a further study into evolutionary biological models.

As a result, the research should lead to revealing the underlying mechanisms that should increase the chances of a fit in the dynamic changing landscape of the competitive environment of industrial companies. Within evolutionary biology, both the theories of the phyletic gradualism and the punctuated equilibrium[23] have sought to find an answer how species adapt to the changes in the environment. They assume totally different mechanisms for the adaptation to the environment; the phyletic gradualism pronounces the growth from within the organism (Encyclopaedia Brittannica, 1986) and through natural selection whereas the punctuated equilibrium places more emphasis on natural changes affecting the existence of species. The phyletic gradualism roots strongly in biology and the punctuated equilibrium is favoured by palaeontologists (Teed, 2001; Prothero, 1992), even one might suspect they deploy different time-scales and they either look at a system or explore the impact of changes in its environment. In addition, the research presented here will also explore the mechanisms of evolutionary biology, palaeontology, and their implications for fitness landscapes in more detail. It will also pinpoint how industrial companies can be deploying the strategies of this kind. Although these theories are treated as such in the context of evolutionary biology, the underlying paradigms should answer the quest for adaptation strategies for companies to the dynamics of the environment.

4.2   RESEARCH DOMAIN

Pfeifer et al. (1994) refer to this matter when mentioning: *In view of the variety and complexity of changing boundary conditions, the question presents itself as to what methods can be best employed to sustain the competitiveness of a company.* Achieving and sustaining competitiveness means paying attention to all aspects and processes within the company, according to their view. This implies that we should address all aspects of a company to develop a coherent theory. A

---

[23] *Hans Metz (Leiden University) points out that it would be better to speak of theory of punctuated equilibria because periods of equilibrium are interchanged by periods of turmoil.*

choice has already been made to limit the study to processes and structures, a further limitation is necessary to increase the feasibility and grounding of the theories to be developed.

For the field of application and verification of the theory, the research will address Strategic Capacity Management for manufacturing. The choice for such has two main reasons:

- The Delft School Approach[24] has mainly focused on industrial companies, particularly the manufacturing area. Therefore, to develop and to detail the theories of the research, a broad spectrum of research, industrial findings and experience is at hand.

- Especially, for Manufacturing Management the process of continuous change poses additional challenges. Changes are strongly driven by the skills and knowledge of resources and the deployment of available assets, concurrently representing the capability to change. Operations and Manufacturing might embed the skills, knowledge and technology within the assets decreasing the flexibility. Thereto Manufacturing Management takes a strong interest in the dynamic capability for adaptation to the dynamically changing environment. The continuous changes confront Manufacturing Management with additional challenges for the link to product development and engineering, for managing the value chain, and for exerting an effective manufacturing strategy.

With the focus on Strategic Capacity Management and to allow the application of the methodology, first a framework has been developed for Strategic Capacity Management as a view on operational management of industrial companies. Methods have been developed within an overall framework to support decision-making on a strategic basis, consisting of (a) process mapping, (b) an evaluation framework, (c) a master plan for sourcing decisions, technology acquisition and process development, and (d) resource management, including managing the value chain and organisational structures (see Chapter 15).

During case studies fragments of these methods have been implemented, particularly the strategic processes, the management of outsourcing, and the selection of organelle structures. These case studies result from initiatives by industrial companies for postgraduate dissertations, thus connecting theory and practice. On the cases, reverse engineering has been applied to link actual analysis of problems within industry and their solutions to theories. The interplay between

---

[24] *Since 2004, the Delft School Approach has been transferred from the Section Production Technology and Organisation (Faculty Design, Construction and Production) to the Section Technology, Strategy and Entrepreneurship (Faculty Technology, Policy and Management), Delft University of Technology.*

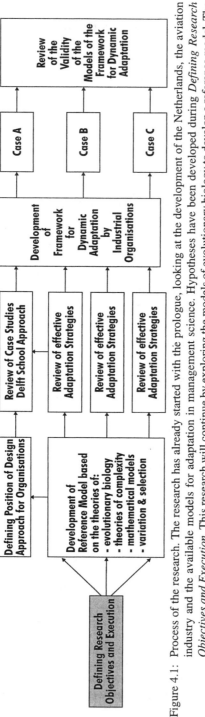

Figure 4.1: Process of the research. The research has already started with the prologue, looking at the development of the Netherlands, the aviation industry and the available models for adaptation in management science. Hypotheses have been developed during *Defining Research Objectives and Execution*. This research will continue by exploring the models of evolutionary biology to develop a reference model. The reference model will serve as a basis for looking at theories of management science and the design approach for organisations of the Delft School Approach (six cases will be examined). At the end, the a Framework for Dynamic Adaptation will be developed which will be applied to Strategic Capacity Management and will be verified by conducting three case studies (A, B, C).

academic literature and empirical fieldwork results in grounded theory (Glaser & Strauss, 1967).

The research aims at developing practical approaches as well. To verify the approaches and methodologies, and to ground the methodologies active participation has been sought by industry in the manufacturing domain. By conducting and reviewing the three final case studies, the research will also verify the Framework for Dynamic Adaptation.

4.3   RESEARCH METHODOLOGY

Before, conducting these three final case studies, the research will review existing theories in the fields of evolutionary biology and management science, implying that the research will follow an additional heuristic route (see Figure 4.1). Biological models have been very well documented, reviewed, verified in the field's literary sources. This should generate sufficient material for a reference model. Management science lags behind on the scientific approaches of evolutionary biology but covers a wide array of literature as well, describing (onset to) theories, findings, etc.[25] For example, van den Bergh & Gowdy (2003, p. 67) write that micro- and macro-evolution in biology has been more discussed than the similar controversy in economics, fuelled by the more advanced specialisation, interaction, and integration of subdisciplines in biological sciences. The reference model helps to review all the pieces and parts present in the literature of management science.

4.3.1   Research Process

Firstly, the research will include an extended survey into the models for adaptation to the changes taking place in the environment. These evolutionary models go beyond the current findings as applied in organisational ecology, as propagated by Hannan & Freeman (1997). Organisational ecology covers partially the same base as this research, though researchers use few references from biological science to develop and to review models. Based on the biological evolutionary theories, findings from literature in management science will be reviewed. This part of the literature survey will also pinpoint the relevant factors in adaptation. These results will be combined with the evaluation of six case studies, undertaken by students for their postgraduate dissertations, and it will also highlight the performance of the current design approach of the Delft School Approach. The literature survey in combination with the case review will generate the findings necessary for developing a Framework for Dynamic Adaptation.

---

25 *Lewin & Volberda (1999, p. 523) date the interest into evolutionary science by management scientists back to 1978.*

As mentioned before, the search into evolutionary models will take us to the world of biological models, theories of complexity, mathematical models for the reference model. The second step in the research, the review of existing management literature, will cover the fields and disciplines[26] of:

- technology management;
- innovation management;
- redesign of processes and organisations;
- Knowledge Management;
- Continuous Improvement.

These two steps will lead to indications for adaptation as found in literature. The review of these theories and their findings will lead up to the development of a Framework for Dynamic Adaptation, the third step, which will be connected to Strategic Capacity Management in the fourth step. This will describe the underlying mechanisms shaped into processes and structures to ensure a fit with the dynamics of changing environment. That will also enable to define the dynamic capability of the manufacturing domain and the implications for its management. Finally, the research will describe the connection between theory and the final case studies revealing the practical relevance of the developed theory. Verification of the methodology and validation of the hypotheses will prove very difficult because the development of organisations might cover many years of existence and even then we should derive the link to the specific area's of the methodology to the phenomena of the company embedded in its own complexity and that of the environment. Within the duration of this research, such a lasting study in the development of companies has not been possible. The field of application that has been chosen (Strategic Capacity Management) will ease the submission of evidence for the validity of the theory and will create more definite statements on the practical utilisation of the underlying mechanisms.

4.3.2 Methodological Notes

The setup of the research process points to a mixed methodology, it is neither completely qualitative nor quantitative in nature. The past decades have seen a rise of mixed model research approaches, according to Tashakkori & Teddlie (1998, p. 4). These approaches overcome partially some of the problems associated with either type, such as Hempel's paradox for empirical research (Leavitt, 2001, p. 228). The research process complies with the general research cycle (Tashakkori & Teddlie, 1998, p. 25): inductive reasoning is used to create

---

[26] *Originally, the research scope included also change management and culture. For two reasons, the research has been limited to the listed topics: (1) change management and culture do not directly connect to processes and structures and (2) time prevented an adequate expansion into these areas.*

a reference model by the generalisation of evolutionary biological theories to the domain of management science, and hypothesis derived from this conversion are tested, or rather attempted to be falsified, following Popper's thoughts, by the review of management approaches in Part II and the six case studies of the Delft School Approach. Only the review of the six case studies of the Delft School Approach can be qualified as being quantitative.

A deliberate choice has been made to base the review of management approaches in Part II on archival research. The choice has been driven by the availability of literature that relates somehow to this specific research. Findings on archival research needs to be assessed on validity and reliability (Tashakkori & Teddlie, 1998, p. 109); this has been done by eliminating published research papers that did not comply with this requirement, e.g. single case studies, dubious methods of recording the research, unspecific findings. The dependency on other researchers, with their own way of looking at data collection and their findings, poses some problems to draw conclusive statements (Leavitt, 2001, pp. 199-200). However, it allows to get information from many sources in support of the hypotheses (or for the falsification). The archival research makes it possible to investigate a wide range of literature rather than limiting the scope of the study. To make the comparison possible between the rather disparate areas in management science, the reference model serves as denominator; it allows to compare findings on a normative model. The review of existing literature in the different areas of management science also meets the principle of triangulation (Tashakkori & Teddlie, 1998, p. 41), especially data triangulation, therewith reducing bias from researchers in a specific field and increasing consistency.

The position of the six case studies of Delft School Approach deserves some attention. They are based on individual dissertations at postgraduate level for an organisational redesign following the methodology of the Delft School Approach. Each of these case studies can be viewed as an experiment in which a proposal has been made for an organisational redesign. Since the design approach for organisations proves to be one of the theories for adaptation to the environment, an investigation will be done into the efficacy of the methodology. The efficacy of the proposal for the design of the organisational structure is determined by the adoption by a company and the effectiveness of the solution. To assess how the approach fits the requirements of successful and continuous change, the dissertations will be reviewed following the methodology outlined by Boyer & Pagell (2000). Case studies, if necessary complemented with interview with multiple respondents, will provide detailed information on the deployment of the methodology in practice. Looking back at dissertations that were finished earlier will provide information of how strategies of companies and organisational redesigns hold over time.

4.3.3   Adaptation Strategies to the Dynamics of the Environment

Current literature does provide little or no guidance for developing an approach to continuous change and adaptation, although frequently mentioned in studies on survival in dynamic environments as a relevant issue for companies. Based on an examination of existing theories and applications the methodology for adaptation will be constructed to solve the tantalising question how companies might adapt to the changes taking place within the environment. We should bear in mind that, like Morgan (1997) remarks in his book, no matter the theory on organisations, it might create more limitations than truth. The development of the methodology will not create a new comprehensive view on organisations but shed light on the additional measures and contingencies necessary to create continuous change and avoid one-time interventions with their severe effects on organisations.

From different theories, sometimes in other fields, constructs will be drawn to create processes, structures, and organisational designs for continuous change. The fields of organisations and management might include strategic management, value chain management, innovation, change management, Knowledge Management, etc. Other disciplines that provided additional insight into the development of organisations will cover ecology of biological systems, mathematical optimisation methods, science of complexity. All of these theories will provide a piece of the puzzle for the methodology.

4.4   SUMMARY

To advance insight in the adaptation by organisations to the dynamics of the environment, this research will rely on insight of evolutionary biology. The reference model as an outcome of this investigation of evolutionary models will guide us to look at some fields of management science, such as: the Learning Organisation and Business Process Re-engineering. The research follows a mixed model research approach based on heuristic approaches (by developing a reference model based on evolutionary (biological) theories), archival research (for assessing theories and methods in management science), six case studies of the Delft School Approach for testing hypotheses, and three final case studies to verify the application of the generated models. The research should lead to a methodology and contingencies for continuous change as guidelines for processes and structures that support adaptation and continuous change.

PART I: EVOLUTIONARY MODELS FOR ORGANISATIONS

The picture shows the heavily discussed Archaeopteryx *(Nedin, 2002), based on fossils found. It finds itself at the crossroads of evolutionary biologists and Creationists. The latter have not generated biological models of evolution as Section 9.3 will briefly touch on. The views on evolutionary biology in Part I of the research might raise questions to which models do hold. The purpose is to look at biological models to explain the evolution of organisations and not to discover truth about the origins of life.*

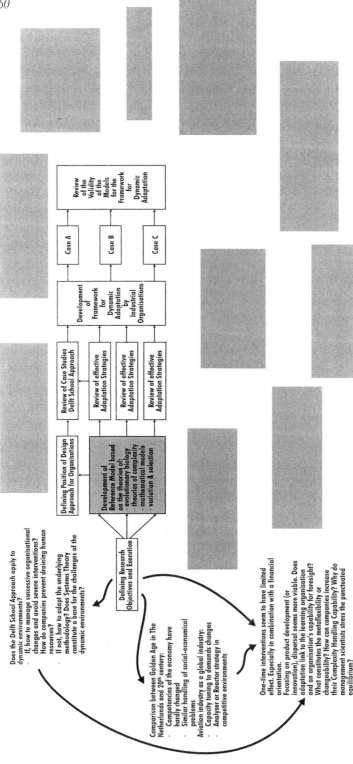

Figure I.1: Overview of the research, based on the prologue. At the centre of this figure we do find the research methodology presented in Chapter 4. So far, the findings indicate that one-time interventions might have limited effects, reason to question the effectiveness of the Delft School Approach. Current theories in management science do answer this question and the processes of adaptation insufficiently, creating the need to explore models of evolutionary biology directed towards mechanisms of adaptation during Part I.

Might companies experience a similar pattern of development as states? It seems that nations move hardly away from their existent competencies (if the case of the Netherlands is representative); a similar notion is brought forward by others for companies (e.g. the theory of competencies from Prahalad & Hamel [1990]). Reacting to the dynamics of the environment within a given industry follows pattern as described by organisational ecology and a preferred strategy of the Analyser or of the Reactor type (Miles & Snow typology), with its inherent exploration of new product market combinations, will yield better chances for survival (provided that the aviation industry has characteristics that allow comparison between industrial branches). Also, one-time interventions to close the gap with the environment seem to strain the resources of the organisation and do not achieve envisioned effects. A strategy dictated by financial motives does not improve a firm's health. What then?

The recurrent theme of the development of organisations centres on evolutionary models from biology. Management scientists frequently refer to these, particularly to the theory of the punctuated equilibrium. Although mentioned, it seems that authors use only a fraction of the available literature of biology that might link to the development of companies. It raises the question which theories and models from biology relate to the adaptation by industrial companies and which ones to choose for the creation of a reference model (to assess management theories).

The purpose of the study captured in this part of the research is to compile theories and approaches from evolutionary biology, to create a complete picture of evolutionary mechanisms, and to describe the interaction between organisms and their environment. To explore evolutionary mechanisms, the development of industrial organisations compares to the development of individual organisms. At the same time, companies are part of industrial branches and market forces, so when reviewing the theories of evolutionary biology attention will be paid to the development of species and taxa. The study provides an overview of different concepts of evolutionary biology that might apply to organisations. In hindsight, it cannot compete with overall views on biological models and evolution as by Jablonski (2000), though some of the references in this research reflect state-of-the-art in evolutionary biology not referred to by him.

Before reviewing theories and findings of evolutionary biology, Chapter 5 will look at the comparison between organisms and organisations. Such a comparison should clarify to which extent the models have validity for organisations, a theme that will return at the end of this part, too. This chapter also pays attention to the modelling of the dynamics of the environment.

Chapter 6 will elaborate on the literature survey to explore which evolutionary theories exist, which will create eventually insight into the viability of industrial companies. From the different disciplines focusing on the evolution of species themselves the theories have been drawn that describe genetic variation in relation to the environment. This chapter will cover most existing theories on speciation although we will not be able to address all matters, since Jablonski (2000) makes it clear that advances in theoretical and practical frameworks still have to be made. These advances should substantiate theories and gaps that exist, which gives ground for at least many years of research in this field. Based on his writing, a selection has been made from the existing theories based on the interaction between species and environment as well as the limited understanding of the researcher of the field of evolutionary biology. It appeared during the study that researchers in the biological field are not always able to pinpoint which theories hold under which circumstances, limiting the validity of the outcomes of this study for the domain of biology itself.

Chapter 7 will discuss the theoretical base of the interaction between species and environment, especially concentrating on speciation, following the classical Darwinian process of the origin of variation, subject of the previous chapter, and the sorting of variation (Jablonski, 2000; van den Bergh, 2003, p. 3). Although (natural) selection acts mostly as mechanism for the survival of the most adapted, different views exist on how we should look at the environment. Four different views have been found on this matter, ranging from natural selection to autopoiesis.

Chapter 8 will integrate the models found in this search, by introducing the hypotheses derived from the evolutionary biological models for the purpose of studying the evolution of industrial organisations. The evolution of species and the role of the environment will be dealt with separately. Additionally, this chapter introduces the reference model for Part II. Finally, the chapter reviews the existing models on the evolution of organisations, presented in Chapter 3.

Finally, Chapter 9 concludes this report by summarising the approaches of biology and pays attention to various views on evolution including ones that criticise the modern theories of evolutionary biology.

5 INTERACTION BETWEEN ORGANISATION AND ENVIRONMENT AS EVOLUTIONARY PROCESS

Originally, the systems theories for organisations, with their focus on the interaction between a company and its environment, were derived from biological perspectives on entities. These systems theories lie at the heart of this research. Do these theories hold in dynamic environments, and, more in particular, do they retain their validity in an environment that we perceive as changing at rates not known before? A lot of management literature tells us about changes taking place, but do they tell us how to cope with change in a generic way? The research will question whether the systems theories appraise the true nature of the dynamic environment, thereto the study might challenge their foremost principles based on homeostasis; the study will link also the understanding of current theories in management science to homeostasis.

For the rise of systems theories, von Bertalanffy's drive to establish a discipline to enhance communication between fields of research, created ground for cross-fertilisation, and initiated the so-called General Systems Theory (von Bertalanffy, 1973), as universal language between sciences. In the spirit of his thoughts, the interaction between the many different fields holds the promise of new perspectives. The communication and exchange between practitioners allows the emergence of new concepts through cross-fertilisation (Boulding, 1956, p. 201), like the ancient cities of Cordoba, Spain, and Baghdad, Iraq, represent two historical sites at crossroads of cultures that boosted advances in science in their times of prosperity. From literature it is known that Faust (Goethe, 1832) became the last single person to encompass all knowledge existing that time. He embraced this thought of mastery at the expense of his soul. Since then sciences have developed in many different directions and displayed unawareness of each other's progress and understanding in the nature of phenomena. Particularly now, advances in theory should be drafted not only from the specific field of research but should also give way to the spirit of cross-fertilisation[27].

Do other fields than management science provide sufficient understanding of the adaptation by organisations to the dynamics of the environment? Within the framework of the research, recent progress in biological evolutionary theories might generate impulses towards a better understanding of the interaction between environment and organisation; the search might drift away from the original

---

[27] *Recently, the Rector Magnificus of the Delft University of Technology (Fokkema, 2003, p. 56) has underlined the importance of cross-fertilisation to advance technology and to support the development of a sustainable society. He refers to the advances made by biologists tying together the expertise of mathematics, computer science, physics, chemistry, biology.*

views of systems theories, rooted as well in biology, to new perspectives. Many more times, management science has deployed theories from biology. So far, most of these did focus on phyletic gradualism and the punctuated equilibrium (topics of Chapter 6) and then especially based on generalisations of evolutionary biology (van den Bergh & Dekkers, forthcoming). The studies of evolutionary biology concern themselves with the development of organisms over time and their interaction with the environment.

This chapter will compare organisms and organisations to justify the conversion of biological models to the domain of organisations. Section 5.1 will address the concepts of homeostasis, found in both evolutionary biology and management science. The systems hierarchy of Boulding will serve as base for the comparison in Section 5.2. The adaptation acts at the boundary of organisation and environment. Thereto, Section 5.3 will explore the features of the dynamics of the environment. Taking into account, the differences and similarities between organisms and organisations, the following chapters will treat the evolutionary models in more detail.

5.1 HOMEOSTASIS AND CHANGE

For the study into the interaction between organisations and their environments, the concepts of evolutionary biology offer insight into the dynamics that companies do experience. As Morgan (1997, p. 34) states when introducing the metaphor of organisations as organisms:

> ... *organisation theory has become a kind of biology in which the distinctions and relations among molecules, cells, complex organisms, species, and ecology are paralleled in those between individuals, groups, organisations, populations (species) of organisations, and their social ecology. In pursuing this line of inquiry, organisation theorists have generated many new ideas for understanding how organisations function and the factors that influence their well-being.*

The distinction of different aggregation strata within biology parallels those within industry and organisations. One of the main topics towards the understanding of organisations as systems is the concept of homeostasis (Morgan, p. 40), which describes how entities maintain the balance with the environment, given the internal structure. The methodology of redesigning organisations through the use of Systems Theory deploys the concept of homeostasis as base for process structures, control structures, and organelle structures (all three part of the total organisational structure that includes also the hierarchy). In the domain of dynamics of the environment and the interaction with organisations, the concept of maintaining a steady-state does not provide sufficient insight in underlying mechanisms.

The research into the dynamic adaptation of organisations focuses on the existence of processes and structures that industrial companies need to deal with external changes and the dynamics of the environment, thereby abolishing the thoughts about achieving any kind of long-lasting balance. The research aims at addressing which alternative paradigm might be used to solve the following problem statement (in addition to the main proposition in Section 4.1), and how such a paradigm should be evaluated:

> *Industrial organisations are innovating and changing at higher speeds than before. This leads to the situation where the implementation of changes falls behind the speed of internal developments driven by innovation as well as emerging market needs and performance requirements. The deployment of technology plays an important role in the adaptation. Does Systems Theory provide answers for these situations of continuous change since the underlying paradigm relies largely on equifinality and a controllable flux of changes?*

The concept of homeostasis does not provide an alternative paradigm for dealing with continuous change and adaptation at the level of the organisation. Factually, Boulding (1956, p. 201) has already pointed out that important differences exist between equilibrium theories, the focus of many authors according to him, and growth theories, to which little attention was paid at that time. Maybe this study will do justice to his words. Seeking for homeostasis would imply that any change in the environment either should be absorbed by the current capabilities of the organisations or should lead to defining a new homeostasis. Absorption of environmental changes means reacting to direct small deviations like changes in demand and their effect on production capacity. Such a deviation does not mean that an organisation should design a new internal organisation structure to meet the new demands given that these changes remain within the limits of the current capability of an organisation to fulfil its function within the environment.

When the environment truly changes, it requires the design of a new organisational structure. This has occurred during the past years when consumers have been requesting for a greater variety of products and innovation, thus calling for organisational concepts that incorporate more flexibility. When the rate of change of the environment increases, the view driven by homeostasis will cause interventions in the structure to succeed each other in ever-increasing speed, causing instability and drafting a heavy toll on the resources of companies. All together, a homeostasis-based approach might provide a too narrow base for dealing with the dynamics of the environment and the internal processes and structures companies need for such.

Additionally, the problem statement refers to equifinality. This concept more or less assumes that different internal structures might yield similar performance or capabilities (in fact, a technological approach to designs and structures). Hence, management science has a choice to provide any concept for companies as long as it fits performance characteristics. If organisations have to adapt to the environment, does the assumption that internal structures do not matter hold as long as they meet performance requirements?

Adapting organisations to the dynamics of the environment requires more than one-time interventions seeking for equilibrium. Industrial companies will have to increase their Complexity Handling Capability, the ability to cope with the changes in their environment and the complexity imposed by the environment (Boswijk, 1992, p. 101). Adaptive landscapes in which firms operate play an important role in the complexity enforced on organisations. To strengthen their Complexity Handling Capability, organisational entities might reduce their internal complexity through redefining their organisational structures and their product structure (products seen as output to the environment and fulfilling the function of an organisation as a system, according to the Systems Theory). The effect of these internal measurements seems limited; an organisation might win more by learning to increase its base of capabilities for dealing with the imposed complexity of the landscape in which it operates.

The development of capabilities by organisations to fit the environment holds parallels to the development of species in biology and palaeontology for which two main opposing models seemed to exist for a while: punctuated equilibrium and phyletic[28] gradualism. Punctuated equilibrium theory supposes that periods of relative peacefulness within a landscape are interrupted by periods of fermentation giving rise to new variants and species. Key innovations in species change the trait space and a fortiori the fitness landscape whereby the trait space determines the development. The theory of phyletic gradualism assumes the development of characteristics in species related to the fitness landscape that are initially hard to detect but will lead at the end to the evolution of species and possibly new species. Within this classical view, the ecology determines the selection processes, e.g. the bifurcation processes and Evolutionary Stable Strategies. Whatever might be true for biology and palaeontology, these two models appear as a possibility to review the theories of organisational change. The models of evolutionary biology focus on the adaptations of organisms to the environment, the internal structures to support these adaptations and the resulting new behaviour or "outputs"; both models provide also additional insight into the rise and decline of companies. This gives ground to explore the evolutionary models and adaptive landscapes in more detail which should lead to more pronounced paradigms on the interaction between organisations and their environment.

---

[28] *Phylogeny refers to the evolutionary development of groups of organisms.*

Mokyr (1990, p. 350) recognises this when stating that the evolutionary models of biology have drawn the attention of economists during recent years; van den Bergh & Gowdy (2003, pp. 67-68) recognise this, too. A lot of research has been done in the field of organisational ecology resulting in the findings as displayed earlier in Table 3.1. This research moves at the level of industries and industrial branches, not the adaptation by individual companies, the area of interest. Riechert & Hammerstein (1983, p. 377) make a similar remark but for the reverse case: optimisation models for economics have enhanced biologists' insight into the mechanisms explaining phenomena of evolutionary processes: natural selection, operating on biological variance, and optimal fine-tuned responses to environmental variables. Riechert & Hammerstein look at the application of game theories in the field of biology; we might conclude that economists and management scientists have embraced the core thoughts of evolutionary approaches.

Most of all, in the domain of management sciences the theory of the punctuated equilibrium has led to a number of publications especially oriented at describing technological advancements and innovations (e.g. Sabherwal, 2001; Tushman & Anderson, 1997); the theory has been applied less to the development of companies on the long-term. Especially, the concept of turmoil seems to attract academics in management science. No matter the debates in the (biological and palaeontological) development of species which also discuss the validity and interaction between the two main streams of thought, the theories tell something about the mechanisms, processes, and contingencies of evolution. The discussions have led to further expansion of the application (fields) of each of the theories, the differences, the resemblances, the models of evolution at different levels, and a profound insight into detailed processes of evolution.

5.2   COMPARING ORGANISATIONS AND ORGANISMS

Before applying the theories derived from biological models, the parallels between species and companies needs clarifying. The taxonomy of biology distinguishes specimen, species, genera, families, and higher groups as different levels of aggregation (Encyclopaedia Brittannica, 1986, p. 1003). Individual specimens might be characterised as mutants when they possess characteristics different from the parent species. Selection takes place within species, characteristics change over time, while genera and families have a historical relation with regard to predecessors. Likewise, for the purpose of the research, we might discriminate between companies, industrial branches, and industries. In this perspective an individual company compares with a specimen (entity) and an industrial branch with a family (set of entities), leaving out the stages of species and genera (partial sets of entities); higher groups find their analogy in industries. Species and genera would compare with companies aiming at niches or specific product-market combinations allowing to bridge the gap between a general industry branch and a specific company. Mutants will appear then at the level of individual companies. For example, a company might develop a new product-market combination, acting as a mutant, which will attract other or new companies to do likewise creating competition and a bigger cluster of companies as offspring. A company and a specimen differ in the sense that spin-offs of companies might become new, individual companies whereas a single adaptation of a specimen, here used as those structures and functions specialised for a particular role, cannot become a single entity. It would require a more profound study to assess the biological distinctions on their merits to these economic classifications; the results of such have no bearing on this particular study at hand.

5.2.1   Levels of Systems Hierarchy

At this point, the comparison between the development of companies and species encounters the remark by Boulding (1956) that lower levels of his systems hierarchy are a prerequisite for higher levels but do not per se suffice for describing systems of a higher order (note the parallel with emergent properties and behaviour). Even though, might we consider organisations as systems? Boulding (1956, pp. 202-205) points out that we do when outlining his hierarchy of systems, distinguishing nine levels[29]:

- level of *static structures* or *frameworks*. This level describes static systems, not accounting for processes that might influence any parameter of the elements. He claims that without the geography and the anatomy of the universe no accurate or functional dynamic theory becomes possible;
- level of *simple dynamic systems* with predetermined, necessary motions, such as clock works. At this level static processes occur, according to Boulding. He notes that most physical and chemical reactions and most social systems do in fact exhibit a tendency to equilibrium; or otherwise, he remarks, the world would have exploded or imploded long ago (a question that still puzzles modern astronomers);
- level of *control mechanisms* or *cybernetic systems*. The processes that determine the moves of the system to maintain any given equilibrium, within its limits. The homeostatic system is an example of a cybernetic system and such systems exist throughout the empirical world of the biologist and the social scientist, according to Boulding;
- level of *open systems* or *self-maintaining structures*. This level is characterised by open systems, able to survive in the environment and respond to changes

---

[29] *The descriptions used here are also based on von Bertalanffy (1973, pp. 27-29).*

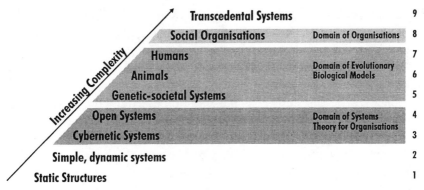

Figure 5.1: The nine levels of Boulding (1956). The domain of organisations moves at the eight'
level, which indicates the importance of meaning, value systems, and symbolisation
(levels also indicated by numbers). The domain of systems theory and some other
approaches in management science (e.g. information technology) find themselves at
the third and fourth level. Models from evolutionary biology might bridge the gap
between some of the approaches in management science and the actual organisational
domain.

in it. At this level life begins to differentiate from non-life. The property of
self-maintenance of structure becomes of paramount importance for systems
of this complexity or higher complexities;

- level of *genetic-societal systems* (it refers to simple biological systems).
  Grouping of cells occurs which leads to organelles for specialised functions
  and the interaction with the environment. Also, a sharp difference occurs
  between the genotype (i.e. the genome present in organisms) and the
  phenotype (the visible traits of organisms), associated with the phenomena
  of equifinality or *blue-printed* growth;
- level of *animals*, characterised by increased mobility, teleological behaviour,
  and self-awareness. The development of receptors allows processing of
  information, though the relation between the receipt of information and the
  building up of an image remains complex. The difficulties in the prediction
  of the behaviour of these systems arise largely because of the mental processes
  that might also determine the responses to stimuli;
- level of *humans*. The systems develop self-awareness and consciousness
  connected to the phenomena of language and symbols;
- level of *social organisations*. These systems exist longer than the elements
  themselves; both do not provide guarantees for survival of the system. At
  this level we must concern ourselves with the content and meaning of
  messages, the nature and dimension of value systems, the transcriptions of
  images into a historical record, the subtle symbolisation of art, music, poetry,
  and the complex gamut of human emotion;

- level of *transcendental systems*. These philosophical systems are the ultimate, the absolute, and the inescapable unknowable, and they must also exhibit systematic structure and relationship.

Boulding (1956, pp. 205-207) doubts even if advances in management sciences might exceed the fourth level. The conversion of evolutionary models of biology to the domain of organisations has the ambition to extend the current state of management sciences at the fourth level but these will never lead to descriptions at the eight' level, driven by the need for simplification to model organisational systems. Specifically, Boulding (1956, p. 206) writes:

> *Beyond the fourth level it may be doubted whether we have as yet even the rudiments of theoretical systems. The intricate machinery of growth by which the genetic complex organises the matter around it is almost a complete mystery. Up to now, whatever the future may hold, only God can make a tree. In the face of the living systems we are almost helpless; we can occasionally cooperate with systems which we do not understand; we cannot even begin to reproduce them.*

Figure 5.1 depicts the hierarchy of systems. Organisations rank at the eight' level of this classification; the Delft School Approach provides models for structures at the third and fourth level. Models simplify the reality to serve a specific domain of research. Hence, we, as researchers, will never be able to develop profound, comprehensive models that reflect reality; rather we have to make choices how to represent the problem domain in understandable pictures (Checkland, 1981, pp. 162-183). The evolutionary biological models move at the fifth, sixth and seventh level. The structure of organisations might differ from the structures of lower levels; then our prime area of interest becomes which theories and models govern the behaviour when deploying an analogy between organisations and organisms. Therefore, evolutionary biological models will create more profound insight in the evolution of organisations, that way describing the reality for organisations with a higher validity than the existing approaches. Nevertheless, the models based on a more profound insight of evolutionary processes will also show deficiencies with regard to the development of organisations.

From the evolutionary perspective, Colby (2002) considers the differentiation between the fifth, sixth and seventh level a mistake, no distinction exists between "lower" organisms, such as bacteria, and "higher" animals, e.g. mankind. All these three levels move at a lower level of complexity than organisations. At the same time, they exceed the models of the third and fourth level, like the Systems Theory and the methods of the Delft School Approach. For the purpose of this research, having a distinction in three levels or one for biological entities, does not affect conclusions or analogies.

According to the definition of a system (Appendix B, Section B.1), it does not make a difference whether we are talking about biological systems or organisational systems. The research focuses on systems of the eight' level of Boulding; biological systems are found at the fourth to the seventh level. This means that ideas and contingencies developed during this research might not be true entirely for systems of the social level. It is the implication of the research that principles found at a lower level might also hold true at higher levels to a certain extent. Gould (1980, p. 121) makes a similar remark when stating that *emergent* features not explicitly present in the operations at lower levels of evolution, may control events at higher levels. However, the Systems Theory aims at modelling organisations from a cybernetic point of view, the third system level of Boulding (1956). Since organisations represent the eight' system level, the adoption of theories from complex systems, networks, and biological models will provide additional insight into the structures of organisations.

When reviewing the evolutionary concepts of biology and palaeontology for the application in the domain of organisations, we should definitely consider the differences between macroevolution and microevolution (Jablonski, 2000). An explanation of this distinction between these types of evolution will follow in Section 6.4. The field of evolutionary biology and palaeontology considers genetic and molecular pathways as well as clades (sets of taxa, an equivalent for higher groups), covering a large range of phenomena related to evolution at different levels. The study into models for adaptation by organisations emphasises the interaction between organisations and environment, a more limited scope than that of evolutionary models. The difference between the clades and molecules is great but at the same time strong interrelationships exist, which explains why the descriptions of evolutionary biology in the chapters to come move at different aggregation strata. For a clearer treatment of these concepts and their effects, Figure 5.2 shows the comparison between biological aggregation strata and organisational strata at relevant levels; this comparison will serve as a guideline during the discussion of models.

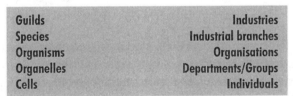

Figure 5.2: Levels of aggregation for evolutionary biology and management science. Note that within the level of below organisms and organisations a split occurs in organelles and cells (organisms) and departments and groups (organisations). This split finds its origin in the complexity of each which does not allow a single notion of lower levels. Organisational ecology moves at the level of guilds and species in biology.

5.2.2 Analogy between Organisms and Organisations

Morgan (1996, pp. 4-8) states that different views on organisations lead to a variety of concepts and assumptions surrounding the organisations. One of the views he introduces, concerns the metaphor of the organism, the view of biology. At this stage, one should note that his metaphor of the organism strongly focuses on the development of system theories, and attention is given to the ecology and evolution of species. The origin of systems theories dates back to von Bertalanffy (1973) whose attempts to create an interdisciplinary science resulted in the rise of General Systems Theory and many other systems theories. According to Morgan (1996, p. 41), the concept of homeostasis, the interaction with the environment in a boundary, refers to the ability for self-regulation and therefore to the capability of maintaining a steady-state. The methodology of the Delft School Approach for organisations thrives on this concept. At the heart of the methodology lies the thought that one can derive requirements from the environment to assess and to improve the control processes and organisational design. Morgan even highlights an example of a systems approach to demonstrate its integrative character. The resemblance between the development of organisations and the evolution of species relies on Darwinism[30], in particular the theory of the phyletic gradualism, with its main characteristics of variation, selection, retention, and modification (Morgan, 1996, p. 61).

The metaphor of the organisations as organisms has six major strengths (Morgan, 1996, pp. 67-68):

1. It provides an understanding of the relations between organisations and their environments. Both organisms and organisations operate in environments that consist of the population itself, other species or (industrial) branches, resources, etc.
2. It focuses on needs, consequently through the primary goals and processes, that must be satisfied. The fulfilment of needs and primary goals by an organisation might improve through systematic attention by management.
3. It assumes that organisations do have a range of options, in parallel to the thought of the existence of different "species" of organisms. Mutants, either organisms or organisations, interact with selectional processes that eliminate the less fit variants.
4. It stresses the virtue of organic forms of organisations in the process of innovation. In contrast to the thoughts of the contingency approach and the design approach, it focuses on the (natural) development of organisations.
5. It contributes to the theory of organisational development, especially through the contingency approach. Although the metaphor contrasts with the

---

[30] *Darwinism refers to evolutionary process connected to the thoughts of Charles Darwin (1859), esp. the role of natural selection.*

contingency approach in terms of one-time interventions, variance in organisations come about through step-wise mutations; therefore the metaphor might complement the contingency approach.

6. It makes important contributions through the focus on "ecology" and interorganisational relations. Organisms and organisation will be viewed as parts of the total environment in which they operate.

As well as having strengths, the metaphor also shows major limitations driven by the principal differences between organisations and organisms (Morgan, 1996, pp. 69-71):

a. The view on organisations is far too concrete. Organisational environments are made through the actions of individuals, groups, and organisations who populate them, according to him; it should be noted that these actions by all kind of actors have different impacts on the organisation.

b. It assumes "functional" unity. He might mean that this view relies on the belief that employees, groups, departments share the same vision on the external goals for internal cooperation.

c. The danger that it becomes an ideology. The study aims at investigating the interaction between entity and environment through the analogy between the evolution of organisms and the evolution of organisations. Yet, the study should account for the differences, avoiding the dogmatic trap.

These setbacks force the careful application of the theories from evolutionary biology to the field and discipline of organisations.

Morgan (1996) explicitly refers to metaphors. When using metaphors, an author attempts to draw a picture of organisations through a comparison to explain and to clarify structures or phenomena, mostly to someone who does not know yet. This is not the case for this research. The aim of this study heavily relies on analogies, the possibility of explaining similar behaviour of systems unlike but yet sufficient resembling each other in some particular aspects. This resemblance should lead to transfer of thoughts and insight. An analogy, and not a metaphor, creates the insight to transfer evolutionary biological models to the domain of organisations.

5.2.3 Opportunities for the Comparison

Can evolutionary biological models truly help to understand the evolution of organisations, fuelling our knowledge about firms? This takes us back to the question what to compare. If we believe Boulding (1956), the comparison will show limits but at the same time might shed light on organisational phenomena not yet captured by management sciences; equally, Morgan (1996) puts forward the metaphor of organisations as organisms to arrive at valuable insight into organisations.

Some authors have taken the understanding of biological phenomena as starting point to describe the development of organisations, for example the developmental pathways. Maynard Smith et al. (1985, pp. 265-266) describe an approach to developmental constraints and their impact on the evolution of species as part of the pathways they follow. They present the origin of these constraints and they make a distinction between developmental constraints and selective constraints. A similar thought has been brought forward by Teece et al. (1997, p. 523) when introducing the concept of developmental pathways for organisations, in which path dependency exists (see Section 3.3). Hence, we might conclude that the processes of evolution for organisms and the processes organisations will have parallels if we are looking for mechanisms governing change.

At the level of organisations, it might be necessary to consider organisations comprised of different agents or entities. Boulding (1956, p. 205) tells that these agents (or entities) do not necessarily have to equal humans, depending on the situation under review. Organisations consist of individual entities that display their own behaviour and at the same time collective behaviour. This study focuses on the interaction between organisation and environment, happening at the level of the organisations as a whole; the interaction might materialise through contacts of individual persons. During the comparison by deploying analogies, the unit of analysis might differ, from entities or units within an organisation, to single organisations to sets of organisations, creating a complete picture of relevant interactions.

5.2.4   Limitations of the Comparison

The description and analysis of the evolutionary models should lead to the point where a profound understanding of the relationship between organisms and environments is reached enabling the application of the analogy (especially focusing on the dynamics of the environment). Yet, organisations and organisms do differ: we observe organisms as physical entities whereas organisations constitute a construct of the human mind, even when we create physical realities in which they operate (e.g. office buildings). This directs the analogy towards specific situations in which the comparison might hold.

In fact, as remarked before, most of the (evolutionary) models within management science take the principle of homeostasis as a starting point. The principle of homeostasis for organisations assumes that organisations can maintain balance with the environment for a period of time, approves implicitly one-time interventions as adjustments of homeostatic structures. One-time interventions and solutions to fix contemporary problems for companies dominate management science. The world of management has been overfed by theories that might have been adequate to some enterprises to deal with the contemporary challenges facing industry but not to others (Fischer & Hafen, 1997; Micklethwait & Wooldridge, 1996). These theories have in common that their foundations stem from a variety of presuppositions pertaining to different factors that might directly influence the rate of success of an organization at one place and time. Direct transferences of these approaches to issues with a broader scope regularly fail as they lack problem-oriented interdisciplinary inferences (Dekkers et al., 2004). Moreover, a static view on the interaction with environment will lead to theories that assume one-time organisational design as starting-point will suffice. This has the danger of ignoring the need for continuous interventions in truly dynamic environments.

As reaction to changes in the environment, organisations have the option to redefine their resource base and their structure. At the level of organisms, new specimens appear as mutations of the original species, sometimes in the course of several generations, but they will never convert themselves into new specimens during their own lifetime. Hence, adaptations in organisations might occur at higher speeds than in biological evolution. These adaptations would take a number of mutations, and therefore generations in organisms, before manifesting itself in a changed phenotype (the manifestation of an organism to the environment). Additionally, in biology the genotype-phenotype distinction is very clear, in economics no such distinction exists (van den Bergh & Dekkers, forthcoming). No singular equivalent in economics exists to the most basic unit of selection in biology, i.e. the gene. Related to this is the fact that 'ontogeny' – development of an organism – and 'phylogeny' – 'family tree' or evolutionary history of a group of organisms – have no counterparts in economics; only recently McCarthy (2005) has advocated attention for phylogenetic phenomena for organisations, although others like Wollin (1999, pp. 360-362) have described rudimentary principles of industrial branching. Both these differences relate to the fact that biological evolution is genetic evolution, whereas social-economic evolution is a combination of genetic and non-genetic evolution, where the latter is dominant because of different timescales. Nevertheless, some authors have tried to impose the genotype-phenotype analogy to economics (Boulding, 1981; Faber & Proops, 1990). The evolution of organisations is greatly determined by the capability and the pathways of artificial mutations.

5.2.5 Research Methodology

Therefore, a wide scope of models from evolutionary biology focusing on speciation and fitness landscapes will be addressed to find possible ways to answer the main proposition of the research, centring on the two hypotheses (Section 4.1). This search will explore the meaning of evolutionary biology, including the theories of phyletic gradualism and the punctuated equilibrium, to find adaptation strategies[31] for organisations; the phyletic gradualism relies on gradual mutations taking place leading to adaptation, while the punctuated equilibrium focuses on accelerated speciation. In addition, the research presented here will also explore in more detail the mechanisms of evolutionary biology, palaeontology, and their implications for fitness landscapes. It will also pinpoint how industrial companies deploy strategies of this kind. Although these theories are treated as such in the context of evolutionary biology, the underlying paradigms should answer the quest for adaptation strategies for companies to the dynamics of the environment.

5.3   DYNAMICS OF THE ENVIRONMENT

But what do the dynamics of the environment constitute? We all know that dynamics refer to changes, but how should we define these changes? These dynamics directly connect to the state of the environment. At a defined point of time, one might describe the environment of a company through the external relationships that the company has with entities in that environment (in 't Veld, 1998, pp. 26-27). Entities in its environment might comprise: clients, suppliers, government, institutions, banks, shareholders, trade unions. The relationships might be described in terms of aspects, a group of specific relationships with underlying features and parameters; the values of relevant parameters at a certain point in time describe the state of the system. An example of such is the stock value. At a specific moment in time, the set of relationships from the company with the environment is called the external structure, which possesses a specific state. The dynamics of the environment indicates when the state of the external relationships changes or the external structure is redefined.

The practical implication of the terminology derived from Systems Theory lies in the fact that either existing relationships with the environment change or companies face a changed (or new) set of external relationships. In the first case, the demand for a product expressed in volume of sales might change, or clients might shift their priorities, for example, the stronger emphasis on lead-time during the 1980's and 1990's. Short-term variations in relationships have been extensively researched. For example, the variations in demands and the logistic performance in known parameters have evoked new concepts for logistic control. In the second case that companies face a changed (or new) set of external

---

[31] *In the biological sense, adaptation has two meanings, according to the Encyclopaedia Brittannica (1986, p. 985): "Adaptation is the biological process by which advantage is conferred on those organisms that have structures and functions enabling them to cope successfully with the conditions of the environment. .... The word adaptation is also used to denote those structures and functions specialised for a particular role." Within this study adaptation refers to the first meaning.*

relationships, a firm may change its client base due to globalisation or it might change its suppliers. Although quite different in nature, this research will treat both these dynamics and consider them primarily as changes in external relationships.

5.3.1 Changes of Aspects, Features and Parameters

For static environments, the creation of the organisational systems, with their elements and their relationships, seen as an one-time activity, allows companies to create a structure focused on internal optimisation and a known environment. No changes in the environment take effect during the period of observation resulting in stability for the internal organisation. Currently, we as humans perceive these environments not to exist any more. For organisations, and increasingly for technical systems, the responses to changes in external relationships (events), which determine the potential behaviour under varying conditions and fast changes, have become a more critical capability.

How do companies react to the dynamics of the markets? How does a computer network react to loads of requests for web-sites? The external dynamics might lead to changes in the values of relationships or changes in the set of external relationships leading to internal changes, even affecting the internal structure of the system. When we restructure companies, we do so by adapting the external structure and the internal structure, hence companies in dynamic environments tend to behave as dynamic systems.

When the internal structure or external structure changes, the system will display new behaviour in its environment. Through changes in the relationships or even changes in elements within the system, the interaction with the environment will alter. The changes affect the aspects with their underlying features and parameters of the relationships. Hence, keeping an eye on the dynamics of the environment by a company requires paying attention to shifts in aspects, features, and parameters acting at different levels of aggregation. These events will lead to reactions by companies and consequently to adaptations to the environment.

5.3.2 Emergent Behaviour of Environments

The notion that in dynamic systems processes happen when events lead to activities to act on the entity, which eventually leads to changes in the external relationships or internal relationships of the system, has implications for the adaptation strategies of industrial companies. A so-called activity indicates an event induced by another event and activities generally consume time. That means that it takes a while before the changes in relationships take effect, and particularly for industrial companies this implies that they will achieve a new state after a while. Therefore, the state of a system depends also on previous events, the so-called *memory*. Instantly, this raises the question for the research, what role does the memory play in the adaptations to the environment for boundary control and does previous events affect continuous change?

For dynamic systems, we focus on processes rather than on the elements as such. Although organisations are driven by their (potential) capabilities present in the resources they utilise, the research should uncover which reaction the dynamics of the environment provokes within companies and which structures suit these processes. This search exceeds the concept of competencies introduced by Prahalad & Hamel (1990). The research should look at the processes for displaying behaviour that the environment requires, especially the capabilities and competencies of organisations to adapt to the environment.

Returning to the hypotheses, changes in relationships are preceded by other events in the boundary of the company, and these events might relate to events outside its boundary, outside its own external structure. When competition puts pressure on clients by offering competitive prices or new products, this pressure requires a reaction by a company. Consequently companies should extend their horizon beyond the direct external relationships to monitor environmental trends even though one might not be able to predict every outcome of variations happening in the universe; in Systems Theory, the concept of universe points to elements and relationships, known or not yet known, external to the system, beyond the system's boundaries. For practical reasons, the research will use environment to describe all the elements and relationships that affect directly or indirectly an industrial company, thereby deviating from the earlier definition of Systems Theory. In his literature survey about scenario planning, Brouwer (2002,

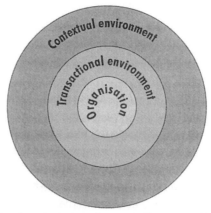

Figure 5.3: Transactional and contextual environment (Brouwer, 2002, p. 11). A company has direct relationships with entities in this environment. Other entities that influence the transactional environment are found in the contextual environment.

p. 11) makes a distinction between the transactional environment and the contextual environment of a company (see Figure 5.3); this distinction is based on van der Heijden (1996, p. 155). The transactional environment stands for those entities and elements that a company directly has relationships with, e.g. clients and suppliers. The contextual environment includes also the elements and entities that influence the transactional environment, for example demography as related to the composition of clients of a company (the universe would contain all elements that have no bearing on an organisation). This extended environment causes reactions by companies, which display particular behaviour given the state of the environment; in general, we should note that the memory of an organisation limits recurrent and predictable behaviour.

Especially, when we describe complex systems, the whole may have properties that refer to the whole only and are meaningless in terms of the parts which make up the whole (Checkland & Scholes, 1993, pp. 18-19). These we call emergent properties of the whole system. When we strive for reducing systems by distinguishing elements, the emergent properties might be lost, as indicated in the remarks by Pfeifer et al. (1994) to consider companies on all their aspects. Organisations often achieve performances that exceed the sum of the individual capabilities (often referred to as synergy). Jablonski (2000, p. 34) defines a feature as emergent at a given level if its evolutionary consequences do not depend on how the feature is generated at lower levels. These performances elevate the organisation from being a collection of elements to a level of self-reference. For organisations as well as technical systems, this points to an integration step when discussing the properties of a system. When looking at the whole system, we might attribute different properties than when reviewing the elements themselves.

The concept of emergence applies equally well to systems as to the environment. Especially, the dynamics of the environment might lead to the combined behaviour of elements that exceeds individual behaviour. For example, a group of clients might move to a more sophisticated product line while an individual client still puts a high priority on pricing. In this case, concentration on individual needs by developing competitive priced products would eventually lead to loss of market share by the company. Monitoring environmental developments, on different aggregation strata and different time scales, becomes a capability for adapting to the dynamics of the environment.

5.4 SUMMARY

The theories and models from biological science will improve the current insight into the evolution of industrial organisations and their adaptation to the dynamics of the environment; even though that the comparison between organisms and organisations does not entirely hold true. However, the parallels between these different entities will create a more profound understanding of the interaction between organisations and their environment. So far, management science has mostly focused on the interpretation of the punctuated equilibrium and its consequences, thereby ignoring alternative explanations and underlying mechanisms governing adaptation.

Two themes do return, linked to the hypotheses at the heart of the research. The first one concentrates on homeostasis, which has been a leading theme in the dominating theories on the interaction between companies and their environment. The external structure, connecting the internal structure to the environment, interacts on different levels of aggregation strata, from aspects to parameters. The research extends beyond the effects on defined parameters, such as seasonal sales patterns. Rather it might focus on the total interaction acting on companies as systems and point to the events in the boundary, which evoke actions by the internal structure. The second theme targets at discovering whether adaptations are the result of continuous processes. Within evolutionary biology two main models exist: the phyletic gradualism and the punctuated equilibrium. The theories of phyletic gradualism point to more gradual changes taking place; the theory of the punctuated equilibrium assumes abrupt changes interlaced with relatively quite periods of consolidation. Management literature so far has emphasised one-time interventions more than the continuous processes, maybe risking severe interventions and neglecting the dynamics of the environment.

6   EVOLUTIONARY MODELS FOR GENETIC VARIATION

Today we attribute the origin of evolutionary theory to Darwin who shocked the scientists of his days with the publication of *On the Origin of Species by Natural Selection* in 1859. Up until that time biologists spend their time on classifying species on the base of comparative taxonomy, whereby species were perceived as fixed, unchanging species (Kauffman, 1993, p. 4), resulting in the systematic approach of the Linnaean taxonomy. Kant considered organisms as fundamentally self-reproducing and therefore self-organising wholes. In early stages, this (liberal) line of thought appears also in management sciences dating back to the 18th century (Mokyr, 1992, p. 326):

> *Adam Smith's greatest insight into the economy has been that it is a self-organising system, one not created by human design but by uncoordinated human action.*

According to Kauffman (1993, p. 5) four conceptual strands lead from the Rational Morphologists, propagators of the comparative taxonomy, to contemporary biology; Darwin's theory being the first (the other three are Mendel's discovery of the basic laws of transmission genetics, Weismann's concept of the continuous germ plasm[32] from which each organism grows, and the advent of population genetics in the effort to account for Darwinian evolution by selection acting on single genes). The evolutionary view was mostly translated into Darwin's principle of natural selection. The environment acts as a selector of viable variants, survival of the fittest, a theoretical base still found in contemporary competitive models in biology and management science.

This chapter will explore the role of variants within the Darwinian theory (Section 6.1) while Chapter 7 will focus on the role of natural selection, the second factor of this theory. As Colby (1996) states: *Evolution requires genetic variation.* Section 6.2 explores the punctuated equilibrium, introduced by Gould & Eldredge (1972), a model for evolutionary growth and speciation with additional explanations to the Darwinian theory. Contemporary theories have included and linked the concepts of macromutations to the Darwinian theories (Section 6.3). Additionally, modern views on evolution have recognised the potential of macromutations to connect phyletic gradualism and punctuated equilibrium, therewith reconciling macroevolution and microevolution (Section

---

[32] *Weismann recognised the existence of diploidy, cells having two copies of each chromosome (usually one from the mother and one from the father), and genetic recombination (Hanes, 2005).*

6.4). Bell (2002) strongly recommends that modern theories should include both views from palaeobiology and population biology.

While evolutionary biology has moved on, management sciences have had a strong fixation on viewing organisations as mechanisms, as constructions of hierarchical control and cybernetic principles (Morgan, pp. 11-31). It makes one wonder whether management science has progressed really in past years to explain the evolution or revolution of organisations. Some researchers in management sciences have taken interest in the theory of the punctuated equilibrium (e.g. Brown & Eisenhardt, 1997; Mokyr, 1990, 1992; Tushman et al., 1986), a way of offering insight into sudden changes in the industrial landscape or the turmoil that individual companies experience.

The analogy of the evolutionary punctuated equilibrium to the development of organisations has stronger implications than most of the times assumed by management scientists. It stretches beyond the notion of disruptions interchanged by longer periods of stability since the mechanisms underlying the phenomenon of the punctuated equilibrium reside in the ability of mutations and species to appear in *new* environments. Only through mutations and speciation species adapt to their environment. The discussion about the phenomenon and the mechanisms of the punctuated equilibrium has not yet settled between evolutionary biologists and palaeontologists, and certainly induced a lot of research into the mechanisms of biological evolution (see Jablonski, 2000).

The chapter attempts to present thoughts about the evolutionary biological theories, most relevant to the evolution of organisations, before applying these theories to the domain of organisations in Section 6.5. Such a conversion seems justified because adaptations in species emerge in their constituent individuals (Maynard Smith et al., 1985, p. 266), and organisations represent individual entities. That section will also reflect on the original problem definition of the research on the hypotheses proposed in Section 4.1.

6.1 INCREMENTAL VARIATION AS BASE FOR GRADUAL CHANGE

According to our understanding of evolution, the development of species has followed the idea developed by Darwin, known as phyletic gradualism (Prothero, 1992). In this view, species display a continuum of gradual changes in anatomical characteristics over time, through which new species arise from the slow and steady transformation of entire populations (Eldredge & Gould, 1972, p. 84). Darwinian Theory tells that a certain amount of diversity in life forms might develop once there are various types of living organisms already in existence within a closed system (Johnson, 1993). The underlying premise is that the variational basis of the evolution occurs as very small changes that are difficult to detect, and initially appears to have little significance for natural selection

(Southgate & Negus, 2001). The other part of the Darwinian Theory lies in competition between species and subspecies given an appropriate niche for their operation and survival. It should be noted that this particular version of Darwinism cannot cope with the saltational development of not yet existing species.

The complexity of living materials and the significance of evolutionary adaptation as a fundamental feature of life are visible in the vast differences among the principal groups of living organisms (Savage, 1969, pp. 12-13). Phylogenic studies, rooted in evolutionary and biochemical studies, reveal that all kind of organisms - about 2 million different living species and the millions of extinct types - are descended from a common early form of life. The diversity of living organisms has been produced through adaptation to the world's many environments.

Before Darwin developed his theory of natural selection for the process of adaptation, Lamarck introduced the concept of evolution in 1801 based on two premises (Savage, 1969, p. 17):

• the structures of specimen appear because of an inner want of the organism;
• these structures are acquired in response to need and then inherited by later generations.

Lamarck published a further development of his theory about evolution in 1809 (Colby, 1996). The hypothesis of Lamarck reads that progressive changes in species have been produced by the attempts of animals to increase the development of their own organs, and thus modify their structure and habits. This thought has been repeatedly refuted by all writers on the subject of varieties and species. The Darwinian theories render such an hypothesis quite unnecessary, by showing that similar results must be produced by the action of ordinary principles. A well-quoted example states that the giraffe[33] did not acquire its long neck by desiring to reach the foliage of the more lofty shrubs. And not by constantly stretching its neck for the purpose, but because of any varieties which occurred among its phenotypes with a longer neck than usual. At once, that secured a fresh range of pasture over the same ground as their shorter-necked companions. On the first scarcity of food the longer-necked giraffes were thereby enabled to outlive them (Rance, 2002), which has caused a shift in the phenotypes present in the population. Hence, the environment induces gradual directional change from randomly generated variation.

That gradual change of genotypes or phenotypes might eventually lead to the diversity of species was perceived during the 19th century through the investigations of both Darwin and Mendel. Based on two observations, Darwin reached two conclusions to explain the diversity of life and life forms (Savage,

---

[33] *Rance (2002) notes that factually Darwin never wrote about the length of a neck's giraffe.*

1969, p. 21). The two observations especially made at the Galapagos Islands were:

- All organisms exhibit variety in their phenotypes. This stochastic view meant a break with the Linnaean, deterministic way of describing species so far.
- All organisms reproduce many more offspring than survive.

These two observations led Darwin to the conclusions that:

- The environment selects those individuals best fitted to survive, while individual variants fail to reproduce (so-called natural selection).
- The characteristics thus favoured by selection are passed on to the next generation.

During the 1920's Darwin's views were amalgamated with the results of J. Gregor Mendel's research into the principles of evolutionary genetics. It took a long time before Mendel's ideas were accepted (Colby, 1996; Lönnig, 2001). Mendel studied discrete traits, the appearance of the coat on peas that are either wrinkled or smooth, and it turned out that he could influence this property by purposeful interbreeding of the different types. The observations during these studies led him to generate two laws (Dorak, 2002):

- Mendel's first law (law of segregation). The two alleles (or genes) received, one from each parent, are segregated in gamete formation, so that each gamete (two of which combine to form a individual offspring) receives one or the other with equal probability.
- Mendel's second law (law of recombination). The two characters determined by two unlinked genes are recombined at random during gamete formation, so that they segregate independently of each other, each according to the first law.

The original theories of Darwin expanded with the principles of Mendel have evolved into *Neo-Darwinism* centring on two major premises (Gould, 1980, p. 119):

- point mutations[34] are the ultimate source of variability. Evolutionary change is a process of gradual allelic substitution within a population: gradualism, continuity of evolutionary change by the gradual transformation of populations;

---

[34] *Mutations are permanent, transmissible changes to the genetic materials. Generally, these can be caused by copying genetic errors during cell division, by external causes, or by sexual reproduction at cell level. Point mutations are a type of mutations that cause the replacement of a single base pair with another pair. Point mutations are usually caused by chemicals, malfunction of DNA replication, and exchange a single nucleotide, an organic molecule, for another.*

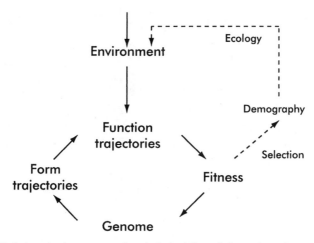

Figure 6.1: Variations in the genome, the whole heriditary information of an organism encoded in the DNA, might lead to variations in form. These variations might lead to better performance of individuals in certain environments and to new functions. Selection acts on the fitness of individuals that establishes a characteristic demography at the level of species, which partially determines the environment in which individuals operate; the other part of the environment consists of the physical habitat.

- genetic variation is raw material only. Natural selection directs the evolutionary change of species, new species. Finally, the selection process leads to adaptation of organisms to their environment.

The evolutionary mechanism consists out of two intertwined cycles as depicted in Figure 6.1. The first cycle generates variability through mutations of the genome, which might lead to different forms of individuals in populations; ultimately these forms result in adapted phenotypes, on which the forces of natural selection act, the second cycle (subject of Chapter 7).

Max (2001) describes a famous example of gradual changes occurring as a result of selection. This concerns the darkening of the peppered moth population, which took place when the soot-darkened trees resulting from heavy industry made light-coloured moths easier targets for hungry birds. According to Colby (1996), Kettlewell found that dark moths constituted less than 2% of the population before 1848. The frequency of the dark morph increased in the years following. By 1898, 95% of the moths in Manchester and other highly industrialised areas were of the dark type. Their frequency was less in rural areas. The moth population changed from mostly light coloured moths to mostly dark coloured moths. A single gene primarily determined the moths' colour. The change in frequency of dark coloured moths represented a change in the gene pool brought about by natural selection. Figure 6.2 shows the gradual changes that took place in the evolution of the extinct titanotheres. The two examples

Figure 6.2: Gradualism in the evolution of the extinct titanotheres, sharing a common ancestry with the horse. During the Eocene, the ancestors of many modern animals appeared. Through gradual changes, the animal evolved to a height of 2.5 metres at the shoulders and acquired the two pairs of large horns at the front of the skull.

Titanotheres had bony protuberances extending from their noses. The sequence of fossil skulls from these animals shows that evolutionary changes in the size of these "horns" were not random; instead, changes were biased in the direction of increasing horn size. And in fact, several different titanothere lineages experienced the same sort of change in horn size. The titanotheres reconstructions shown here range from about 55 mya (A) to 35 mya (D), according to H.F. Osborn (University of California Museum of Paleontology, 2004).

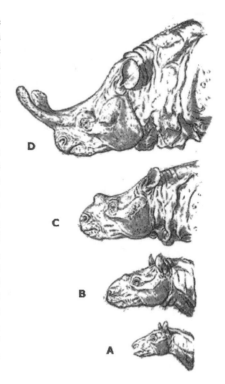

show that through gradual changes influenced by natural selection species will eventually evolve to possess different traits.

If equilibrium with the environment is maintained, evolution is impossible (Savage, 1969, p. 42). When the equilibrium shifts, caused by any factor or any combination of factors, evolution occurs. The equilibrium may be upset if conditions change, either within the population through origin of additional variations or through environmental changes (the effects of the environment will be elaborated in Chapter 7). Biologists recognise mostly three primary forces for evolution (Savage, 1969, pp. 50-51):

• Mutations. A change in gene frequency might appear through either one of evolving subspecies or "spontaneous" change. Mutations might involve gradual steps or macromutations, size of step large (Section 6.3 will come back on this specific matter).

• Natural selection. Environmental factors may operate to favour the reproduction of certain alleles or gene combinations over others present in the population. The impact of the total environment on the reproduction of gene combinations is the force of natural selection. The effects of natural selection alter as the environment changes, so that slightly different conditions

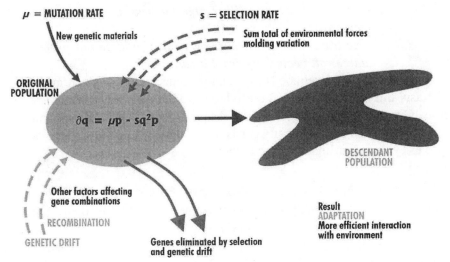

μ = MUTATION RATE

New genetic materials

s = SELECTION RATE

Sum total of environmental forces
molding variation

ORIGINAL
POPULATION

$\partial q = \mu p - sq^2 p$

DESCENDANT
POPULATION

Other factors affecting
gene combinations

RECOMBINATION

GENETIC DRIFT

Genes eliminated by selection
and genetic drift

Result
ADAPTATION
More efficient interaction
with environment

Figure 6.3: Symbolic representation of the elementary evolutionary processes, adapted from Savage (1969, p. 85), resulting in an adapted population. Evolution of populations consists of the interaction between mutation, recombination, selection, and genetic drift to produce adaptations. The area of the original population symbolises variation in gene combinations generated by mutation, recombination and genetic drift; the area and shape of the descendant population represent the new range of variation in gene combinations produced by gene elimination and genetic drift. The symbols in the formula stand for: μ: mutation rate, p: gene frequency first allele, q: gene frequency second allele, s: selection rate.

for each generation favour slightly different gene combinations. Natural selection moulds the genetic variation present in a population, but it cannot directly produce new genes or gene combinations.

- Genetic drift. In small populations, completely random fluctuations in the reproduction of alleles or gene combinations occur, even under constant environmental conditions. These fluctuations constitute genetic drift, which makes its impact felt as random effects upon the genetic variation present in the population. Ultimately, this random walk can produce phenotypes that may have a selective advantage or may be deleterious (Prothero, 1992).

These three forces determine the adaptation, the speciation, and the changes in the diversity of life through microevolution, where adaptation is the process in which species might evolve into ones better adapted to the environment (see Figure 6.3).

Eldredge & Gould (1972, p. 89), when introducing the punctuated equilibrium, identify the following tenets for the concept of phyletic gradualism:

(1)   *New species arise by the transformation of an ancestral population into its modified descendants.*

(2)   *The transformation is even and slow.*

(3)   The transformation involves large numbers, usually the entire ancestral population.

(4)   The transformation occurs over all or a large part of the ancestral species' geographic range.

For these reasons, the likelihood of speciation seems low although during periods of stasis this mechanism of the phyletic gradualism might hold. The low probability of effective change linked to the phyletic gradualism makes it difficult to explain why so much diversity exists in life, and how all the present and past species evolved into and from each other.

6.2   DISRUPTION AS BASE FOR THE PUNCTUATED EQUILIBRIUM

Rather than through gradual change, the punctuated equilibrium theory assumes that change occurs through periods of turmoil, eventually, caused by changes in the environment. During these periods of turmoil, there will be a burst of new species creation (Price & Evans, 2001), filling spaces in the fitness landscape that did not exist before by mutants as offspring of existing species. Or the sudden changes might result in the extinction of species, the most well-known example being the demise of the dinosaurs. During periods of net stasis, species display small reversible changes accompanied by environmental changes. This stasis is interrupted by abrupt extinction and speciation events (Teed, 2001).

Elsberry (1996) indicates that the essential features that make up the concept of punctuated equilibrium consist of:

- Palaeontology should be informed by neontology (branch of zoology dealing with living forms).
- Daughter species usually develop in a geographically limited region.
- Daughter species usually develop in a stratigraphically limited time-period, which is small relative to the total residence time of a species.
- Sampling of the fossil record will reveal a pattern of most species in stasis, with abrupt appearance of newly derived species being a consequence of ecological succession and dispersion.
- Adaptive change in lineages occurs mostly during periods of speciation.

Theobald (2002) notes that it appears, from the quotations of Eldredge & Gould's original paper on the punctuated equilibrium, that the concept arose as a logical consequence from the allopatric speciation model. Allopatric speciation refers to the development of sustainable variants in isolated habitats; because the gene pool in those isolated populations may not entirely resemble the gene pool of the original population, and therefore possesses a different linkage disequilibrium[35]. The tie to macromutations and saltational leaps appears later (see Section 6.3).

---

[35] *The linkage disequilibrium is a measure of association between alleles of two different*

According to Theobald (2002), Eldredge & Gould (1972) arrive at three conclusions in their original paper:

- Most species experience stasis for most of their existence.
- Adaptive change usually corresponds with speciation.
- Natural selection at the species level has important macroevolutionary implications (species selection).

Theobald (2002) states that the evidence is still mixed as to whether adaptive change usually accompanies speciation. Furthermore, Eldredge & Gould (1972, pp. 114-115) remark that phyletic gradualism has a strong link to viewing species - and individuals - as amazingly well-buffered, i.e. able to resist change and to maintain stability in the face of disturbing influences. Speciation becomes a rare and difficult event that punctuates a system in a homeostatic equilibrium.

6.2.1 Creation of New Species

Essential to understanding the punctuated equilibrium is the comprehension of the processes which create new species, the so-called punctuated speciation introduced by Richard Goldschmidt (Gould, 1980, p. 124), a feature still heavily debated today. It inspired Eldredge & Gould (1972) to introduce the punctuated equilibrium theory, describing speciation, and thereby deviating from the conventional theories related to Darwinism. Within the view of the punctuated equilibrium theory, a period of intense selection wipes out most of the newly appearing mutants, they do not possess viable phenotypes or they have maladaptive phenotypes. The selection leads eventually to phenotypes that will not any more breed with the parent species and reduce genetic variance, resulting in a long period of stasis. Genetic variance and intense natural selection during that period of turmoil comprises the key to the process of speciation.

The major mechanism underlying the punctuated equilibrium theory is peripatric speciation (Elsberry, 1996); peripatric speciation states that a population of an ancestral species in a geographically peripheral part of the ancestral range is modified over time until even when the ancestral and daughter populations come into contact, there is reproductive isolation. Elsberry explains also that punctuated equilibria postulates that speciation events comprise most of adaptive

---

genes. [allele: alternate version of a gene] If two alleles were found together in organisms more often than would be expected, the alleles are in linkage disequilibrium. If there two loci in an organism (A and B) and two alleles at each of these loci (A_1, A_2, B_1, and B_2) linkage disequilibrium (D) is calculated as $D = f(A_1B_1) * f(A_2B_2) - f(A_1B_2) * f(A_2B_1)$ (where $f(X)$ is the frequency of X in the population). [Loci (plural of locus): location of a gene on a chromosome] D varies between -1/4 and 1/4; the greater the deviation from zero, the greater the linkage. The sign is simply a consequence of how the alleles are numbered. Linkage disequilibrium can be the result of physical proximity of the genes. Or, it can be maintained by natural selection if some combinations of alleles work better as a team. (Colby, 1996)

evolutionary change, as a consequence of the inhibitory effects of gene flow, genetic homeostasis, and large population sizes that are otherwise operative. These factors no longer restrict the newly speciated daughter populations because of reproductive isolation. Relaxed competition allows larger mutational steps. The presence of punctuated equilibria explains the abrupt appearance of new species in the fossil record during relative short periods. The splitting of lineages in the mode of allopatric speciation followed by ecological dispersion and succession would result in geologically abrupt appearance of the daughter species everywhere except the limited geographic area where the speciation took place. The cases of introduced species in modern times, e.g. the starling in North America, demonstrate the extreme rapidity in which a species may spread across large geographic extents. Furthermore, the punctuated equilibrium theory explains the relative stasis of species. A species may produce a few daughter species during its existence. Large interbreeding populations are unlikely to change much due to genetic homeostasis and gene flow from far-flung parts of the range. Finally, the punctuated equilibrium theory asserts *species selection* as the way in which major trends proceed. Closely related species are often likely to overlap in niche spaces when relaxed competition appears between related species. Ecological processes may cause the displacement and possible extinction of certain species due to competition with other species. If adaptive change in large populations is largely inhibited, then each species represents a hypothesis that is tested in competition.

6.2.2 Causes for Turmoil

At the base of the punctuated equilibrium theory there should be a period of turmoil that may be caused by three major reasons:

- Macromutations. These mutations occur as a phenotype deviation from the original species, and may give rise to new species or subspecies with characteristics not known before as long as these are adaptive. Macromutations require a separate treatment (Section 6.3).
- Extinction of species. Recently, evolutionary biologist have added (mass) extinction of species to the causes for the punctuated equilibrium (Jablonski, 2000, p. 40).
- Change of environment (topic of Section 7.3).

The extinction of species gives ground for further discussion in this subsection.

Colby (1996), Dorak (2002), and Maynard Smith (1989) describe extinction as the ultimate fate of all species. Causes of extinction vary: the competitive exclusion by a closely related species, a disappearing habitat, the emerging unbeatable defence of an exploited species, and the appearance of new diseases. Maynard Smith (1989, p. 245) explains that the introduction of foreign species causes habitat destruction, a phenomenon demonstrated by the many examples of human intervention in nature. Colby (1996) mentions that most believe that if the environment stays fairly constant a well-adapted species could continue to survive indefinitely.

In contrast to the ordinary extinction, Colby (1996) remarks that mass extinctions shape the overall pattern of macroevolution. The history of life on this earth includes many episodes in which many groups were wiped off the face of the planet. The Permian extinction, about 250 millions years ago, was the largest extinction in history, with an estimated 96% of all species meeting their end (Dorak, 2002). Periods of adaptive radiation[36] follow after mass extinctions where new species evolve to fill the empty niches left behind. After the rapid development of many new species, lots or most of them die out as quickly as they appeared. The surviving species are almost perfectly adapted to the new environment. From that moment on, the rise and fall of new species will progress very slowly, compared to the initial outburst of species. Colby (1996) says that surviving a mass extinction largely depends on luck; thus mass extinctions give ample space for the role of contingencies in contradiction to macroevolution.

6.3   EMERGENCE OF MACROMUTATIONS

This section will explain the phenomena of macromutations; it will bridge the punctuated equilibrium theory, periods of turmoil interchanged by long periods of stasis, and the gradual change characteristic for the theory of the phyletic gradualism. The text will follow the outline of variation as extensively described by Jablonski (2000, pp. 16-26). Within evolutionary models, genetics are considered the base for variation, even if the inadvertent changes in the genetic make-up are rare (Seaborg, 1999, p. 2). Jablonski distinguishes four ways for arriving at macromutations: changes in genetic control pathways, heterochrony, heterotopy, and epigenetics. These macromutations, visible at the level of phenotypical change, supposedly influence the change of populations, mostly because of their effects on evolution, each of them linking to chromosomal changes and genetic networks.

---

[36] *Adaptive radiation describes the rapid speciation of a single or a few species to fill many ecological niches. This is an evolutionary process driven by mutation and natural selection. Adaptive radiation often occurs when a species is introduced to a new ecosystem, or when a species can survive in an environment that was unreachable before. For example, the Darwin's finches on the Galapagos Islands developed from a single species of finches that reached the islands. The dynamics of adaptive radiation is such that, within a relatively short time, many species derive from a single or a few ancestor species. From this large number of genetic combinations, only a few can survive on long term.*

In certain population structures, particularly in very small and circumscribed groups with high degrees of inbreeding, major chromosomal changes can rise to fixation in less than a handful of generations (Gould, 1980, p. 123). Speciation may be more a matter of gene regulation and rearrangement than of changes in structure that adapt local populations in minor ways to fluctuating environments. Max (2001) describes extensively the experiments of biologist Richard Dawkins with a computer model and his own experiments showing that changes occur through a number of mutational steps, and that active selection by the environment directs the changes. An unusual forced reorganisation of the epistatic supergenes might occur within the system's limits of variability[37]. This cycle of disorganisation and reorganisation can be viewed as the core of the speciation process.

6.3.1 Genetic Control Pathways and Networks

One way that genes express themselves in mutations is through the network of genes present in a specimen. Hox genes have been found to regulate the pattern of the body axis and appendages across the entire breadth of animal diversity, to specify positional information, and thereby to regulate the transcription of a large number of downstream genes. An example of such a Hox gene is the one that controls the number of toes at our feet; sometimes human beings will have six toes rather than five, a consequence of a "mismatch" in the regulation of the body pattern by the Hox genes involved. Hence, it becomes clear that genes of large effect do play a role in the origin of adaptations and the divergence of species (Jablonski, 2000, p. 18). Even then, mutations take place along limited paths, the successive steps in the development of mutants, to succeed in bringing about beneficial genotypes.

Genetic paths, i.e. series of mutations, determine the possible routes of change for organisms, as Colby (1996) denotes that complex traits must evolve through viable intermediates; the evolution of species happens through mutations, each of which should reach higher degree of fitness for sustained viability of the species. These paths might also be affected by the existence of developmental and selective constraints (Maynard Smith et al., 1985; Maynard Smith, 1989, pp. 241-242). Developmental constraints are those constraints arising from the non-feasibility of certain forms (see Figure 6.1: these are form trajectories that do not result in function trajectories with improved fitness). Jablonski (2000, p. 28) defines developmental constraints as the resistance of the phenotype to selection in certain directions, owing to the configuration of developmental

---

[37] *This mechanism works only for simple organisms, according to Hans Metz (University Leiden).*

networks and pathways. Selective constraints result from the step-by-step transformation (of the gene pool). The difference between developmental and selective constraints can be explained by the interactions between the organism and the environment. We might speak about developmental constraints when an evolutionary stasis exists while little or no stabilising selection is exerted (a feature difficult to notice in fossil record). Developmental constraints exert their influence when no features are available for selection. Selective constraints come about through the capabilities present in an individual, general developments, and mimicry. A second way of discovering selective constraints is by the presence of stabilising selection on heritable variation and by fluctuating directional selection in appropriate succession of environments. Maynard Smith et al. (1985, p. 283) remark that

> *it is worth inquiring whether mechanisms fostering genetic responsiveness to environmental challenge have evolved because of the speed with which they enable lineages to adapt to changing environments.*

Worden (1995) developed a model for linking the evolution of species to speed limits present in the phenotype of organisms. He arrives at the conclusion that it is reasonable to assume that:

- if some feature fluctuates caused by the environment and has been fluctuating for a very long time, it can be expected that species have developed evolutionary mechanisms to change the feature rapidly. The rate of evolution of the phenotypical response comes close to speed limits induced by formulas and calculations proposed by him. Two possibilities appear for the phenotypical response: either the developmental system allows many mutations in a relevant direction or large amounts of variation are present;
- for some completely new environmental challenge, which a species has never faced before, the expected rate of evolutionary response will be very slow (far below limitations in speed) until the first effective response by chance. This first effective response will have the opportunity to spread within the population (adaptive radiation).

He refers to the example of body size, which species often need to evolve in order to move into new habitats, cope with climatic changes, and so on. One should expect the genetic mechanisms that control body size to be capable of rapid evolutionary response - changing body size as fast as the limits allow; the response to selectional forces depends on the variation present in the gene pool and the mutation speed. Experience with breeding domestic animals shows that body size can be rapidly controlled by selection.

Furthermore, Worden (1995) mentions that small or large populations[38] might respond equally well. In this spirit, he recognizes that three factors might favour small populations:

- Small populations, living in a particular habitat, are more likely to come under some special localised selection pressure (which leads to rapid evolutionary response) than large ones.
- Random genetic changes, when they occur, can become fixed in a small population more rapidly than in a large one (less variation present).
- Speciation, which may precede a period of rapid evolutionary change, may be more likely in small isolated populations.

Concluding, network of genes provide pathways (and also constraints) to the development of mutants. Each of these pathways beholds speed limits that are also affected by population size; smaller population sizes evoke some responses at higher speeds than those that happen in larger populations.

6.3.2 Heterochrony and Heterotopy

Heterochrony, a source of macromutations, defined as a change in rate or timing during the development of individual organisms, has received much attention as a potential avenue to dramatic morphological evolution (Jablonski, 2000, pp. 18-20). Heterochrony has often profound effects upon adult phenotypes through small changes in developmental rate (Gould, 1980, p. 127), and can lead to significant alterations in form. Sometimes it is called a change in a change, indicating that heterochrony is a deviation from the expected kind of change during the development of an individual organism. Heterochrony does not represent an evolutionary mechanism, rather it points to the generation of variant phenotypes.

Jablonski (2000, pp. 18-20) makes a distinction between global or systemic heterochrony and local or specific heterochrony. Global heterochrony is the development of organisms in which the entire phenotype is shifted relative to ancestral ontogeny (the development or course of development of an individual organism). Deviations in the development of offspring generate differences in genetic population structures and phenotypes. Such changes might occur easiest during saltational changes, such as metamorphosis (Jablonski gives the example of salamanders that mature in the aquatic larval state). The phenomenon is most visible in species that undergo substantial phenotypical changes during ontogeny. Specific heterochrony, changes in rate or timing of development of particular structures within an organism, can break allometric relationships and generate

---

[38] *In small populations there might be also little chance for random genetic changes to mutate through recombination. Some populations, too small, might not even have the opportunity to drift away from the original set of traits.*

new and coordinated morphologies, again by drawing on established developmental interactions but this time within a localised region or developmental field. The scope for evolution is far wider than implied by global heterochrony alone. It focuses on restricted areas of the body or cell line in contrast to global heterochrony that affects a total organism.

Heterotopy represents an evolutionary change in the site at which a particular development occurs, in other words: the alteration in the location of a developmental event (in Figure 6.1 these correspond to the form trajectories). For example, a wing of a fruitfly appears attached to a different part of the body. Spatial changes in development may prove to have greater evolutionary impact than temporal ones, i.e. heterochrony, and hold the promise of a gradual change. Heterochrony depends strongly on the shift of an entire phenotype. Selection determines the feasibility of macromutations.

6.3.3   Epigenetics

Jablonski (2000, pp. 20-21) and Seaborg (1999, pp. 3-4) state that local cell and tissue interactions that help to integrate the developing parts of an organism into a functional whole, constitute a fourth source for macromutations; the other three sources are genetic networks, heterochrony, and heterotopy. By drawing on a set of preprogrammed responses to local signals, such interactions allow the developing embryo to accommodate evolutionary changes in particular morphological elements without a host of independent but mutually beneficial mutations. The epigenetic interactions that help generate complex forms do have limits to the changes they can accommodate, as attested by many "failed" embryological manipulations or the gene regulation experiments. The important questions for macromutations revolve around where those limits lie for particular clades or particular kinds of changes, and how evenly the potential directions of permissible change are distributed in morphospace.

In addition to this view on epigenetics, Riedl (1977, pp. 352-362) reasons that insight derived from morphology give way to the notion that feedback loops exist linking different strata of complexity. The interest in these feedback loops within organisms, linked to their development, arose from homologues, similar structures in different organisms. A closer look at these similarities, which might even exist under totally different circumstances, evokes the thought of universal patterns of organisation of organisms, and offers a possible explanation for developmental pathways for species. The feedback loops acts as master switches at different strata of complexity in an organism. When such a master switch changes through genetic variation, followed by a number of gene transformations at lower levels, the species might produce viable variants with different traits, a new phenotype, open for selection by the environment. According to Riedl, this process is propelled by tremendous selection pressure which is itself a feedback cycle between accessible niches in the environment as well as conditions within the organisation of the organism. The consequence is a structural response of adaptive traits. He particularly notes that an amplification of successful adaptation occurs at the expense of flexibility. One more consequence of such directed revolution is the high probability that, if a species is to survive, the accessibility of adaptive niches is narrowly circumscribed.

In his paper, Seaborg (1999) draws the attention to two key points for epigenetics: (1) organisms are feedback systems whose genes and phenotypical traits interact with each other and with natural selection, profoundly affecting rates and direction of evolution (much like the descriptions of Riedl), and (2) changes in the phenotype, genotype, and gene frequencies can greatly change natural selection, in both intensity and direction. Regulatory genes serve as master switches to control other genes for development. Switching of the regulatory genes results in coordinated macromutations (adaptive, successful mutations of large phenotypical effect), because organisms are hierarchical, integrated genetic systems. The integration of an organism itself assures that only a very small percentage of mutations will be adaptive and even a smaller percentage will be adaptive, and with a large phenotypical effect. Especially, Seaborg (1999, p. 6) points to key innovations (a macromutation, a gradual accumulation of many small mutations, genetic recombination, or a combination of these) to occur. These new, critical adaptations might allow access to resources previously unavailable to the lineage. Sequential evolution, caused by positive feedback, might lead to maximising probability if the direction of the mutations appears beneficial to selection by the environment. Also, Seaborg (1999, pp. 2-3) points to the fact that such directional change does not exist without changes in the environment, i.e. directional selection determines the fitness of phenotypes. For example, Jablonski (2000, p. 26) mentions that regulatory molecules that suppress phenotypical variation can be disabled not only by mutation but also by environmental extremes, like high temperatures.

6.4 Evolutionary Processes at Different Levels

There is a discontinuity in cause and explanation between adaptation in local populations and speciation; they represent two distinct, though, interacting levels of evolution. Johnson (1993) quotes Mayr that macroevolution is nothing but an extrapolation and magnification of the events that take place within populations and species. Gould (1980, p. 128) positions macroevolution as a different model for substitution, and therefore it is not an extrapolation of gradual allelic substitution as a model for all evolutionary change. Its mechanisms distinguish macroevolution from speciation and variation within local populations. According

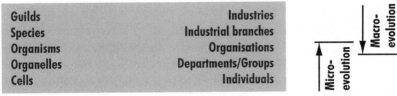

Guilds	Industries
Species	Industrial branches
Organisms	Organisations
Organelles	Departments/Groups
Cells	Individuals

Figure 6.4: Distinction between microevolution and macroevolution. Microevolution describes the evolutionary processes for entities; the domain of macroevolution stretches from populations to branching, speciation, etc. The research looks at microevolution while accounting for the mechanisms of macroevolution.

to him, the concept of speciation separates microevolution from macroevolution. When applying the evolutionary concepts of biology and palaeontology to the development of organisms and species, we should definitely consider the differences between macroevolution and microevolution (Jablonski, 2000, p. 26). Figure 6.4 shows the general distinction between microevolution and macroevolution.

6.4.1 Positioning of Microevolution and Macroevolution

Gould (1980) discusses three levels at which evolution takes place, not necessarily with the same modes of change. As he notes himself, evolution is grounded in development at the molecular level where tiny variance may strongly affect forms of life, and at the level of (developmental) genes and morphology, where individual development can exert strong effects on species. Gould distinguishes these three levels:

- variation within populations. These variations and their selection are the subject of the theories of the Modern Synthesis (Neo-Darwinism);
- speciation;
- patterns of macroevolution.

Speciation, the basis for macroevolution, is a process of branching. At all these levels, evolution takes place through (Gould, 1980, p. 129):

- punctuational change at all levels (sudden changes since homeostatic systems change by abrupt shifting to new equilibria);
- essential non-adaptation, even in major parts of the phenotype (change in an integrated organism often has effects that reverberate throughout the system);
- channelling of direction by constraints of history and developmental architecture.

Henceforth, Moran (1993) indicates that the Modern Synthesis Theory has advanced from early Darwinism in three important respects (especially because Darwin did not focus on the background of variation):

- It recognises several mechanisms of evolution in addition to natural selection. One of these, random genetic drift, may be as important as natural selection.
- It recognises that characteristics are inherited as discrete entities called genes. Variation within a population is due to the presence of multiple alleles of a gene.
- It postulates that speciation is (usually) due to the gradual accumulation of small genetic changes. This is equivalent to saying that macroevolution is simply a lot of microevolution.

At the level of species, evolutionary biologists prefer to speak about species selection rather than natural selection. The criterion for species selection is that the performance that determines survival is one that could be measured only on the species as a whole and not on an individual (although the performance, the rate of evolution, depends on a characteristic of individuals, namely sexual reproduction) (Maynard Smith, 1989, p. 248).

6.4.2   Choosing between Phyletic Gradualism and Punctuated Equilibrium

Initially after the launch of Eldredge & Gould's paper (1972), the debates among palaeontologists and neontologists seemed fierce whether the theories of phyletic gradualism and punctuated equilibrium hold true. After the emergence of Neo-Darwinism during the 1940's, most researchers attributed the differences between paleaobiology and population biology to incomplete fossil records (e.g. Bell, 2000, p. 1457). A more complete record would reveal species transition through mechanisms observed in extant populations. The postulate of Eldredge & Gould changed all that: other approaches to evolution might contribute to understanding evolutionary change. Bell (2000, pp. 1458-1459) indicates that the model of the punctuated equilibrium is fundamentally Neo-Darwinistic; palaeobiology is the primary source of the knowledge about biological diversity as well as evolutionary tempo and mode, but its potential to elucidate evolutionary mechanisms is limited. Population biology is limited by lack of temporal scope but it offers the most tractable systems to study evolutionary mechanisms. Both Prothero (1992) and Teed (2001) point to the weak evidence for the theories of the phyletic gradualism and the punctuated equilibrium, and they stress their different origins; sometimes others (like Elsberry [1996]) point to the evidence both schools have collected to substantiate their reasoning.

Reading the overview by Jablonski (2000), one sees however that both views have made tremendous progress, and at the same time many questions remained unanswered. However, the theory of the punctuated equilibrium seems deeply rooted in the study of fossil records which differs from biological studies into the behaviour of species; an explanation might be found in the very different time-scales of the approaches (also remarked by Bell [2000, p. 1457]). The model of the punctuated equilibrium offers perspectives for the long-term development of industrial companies: periods of intense selection (competition on products, performance, resource allocation) interchanged by longer periods of developmental homeostasis. This view combines both theories as complementary to each other, having their own field of application or rather specific periods have specific selection mechanisms. In this respect, it should be noted that Maynard Smith (1989, p. 241) remarks that whether the pattern of evolution is punctuational or gradual, they are both compatible with genetic theory. In other words, different mechanisms might be active at different levels of evolution, different aggregation strata so to say, they all root in the variation brought about by mutations of organisms. Prothero (1992) and Teed (2001) do offer similar conclusions on the evolution of species. In addition, Jablonski (2000, pp. 37-38) remarks that evidence supports both the model of phyletic gradualism, especially newer insight, and the model of punctuated equilibrium. Elsberry (1996) states that the theories of punctuated equilibrium and phyletic gradualism are not mutually exclusive.

Additionally, Prothero (1992) points out that the development of simple organisms relies more on the models of punctuated equilibrium while organisms that are more complex show patterns of developmental stasis, as noted before. Simple organisms tend to live in enormous populations that span entire oceanic water masses, so they do not form many small, isolated populations (Prothero, 1992), a condition more in favour of the application of the theory of punctuated equilibrium. Isolated populations of more complex organisms allow also mutations to become allopatric, creating their own space of living (e.g. geographically separated). According to Southgate & Negus (2001), Gould stresses that the evolution of higher organisms is not a matter of inevitable progress to greater sophistication, but rather that higher systems are more subject to environmental change. During this process of adaptation to the environment organisms try out new properties without prematurely losing the benefit of the old ones. Teed (2001) highlights that allopatric species might even substitute the parent species when invading the original territory and thus becoming competitive. Would this mean that the size of organisations acts as factor the active evolutionary processes, i.e. the processes related to the punctuated equilibrium or the processes of the phyletic gradualism?

As Lemmon (2002) concludes, phyletic gradualism is evident; although it does not predominate, gradualism seems to be important in at least some taxa. The evolution of life has proceeded by evolutionary processes, described by models of punctuated equilibrium and phyletic gradualism, but current data suggests that the abrupt speciation likely plays a more significant role.

6.5 CONVERSION OF VARIATION TO THE DOMAIN OF ORGANISATIONS

This chapter has mostly described the origin of variations for the evolution of species. The evolutionary processes happen at different levels from individual organisms to species (microevolution and macroevolution), giving way to diversification at different levels. The same might be true for organisations. According to Section 5.2, parallels and differences exist between organisms and organisations. Firstly, following the theory of Boulding, models from lower levels of the systems hierarchy might induce insight in the behaviour of higher levels but not predict behaviour entirely. Secondly, an organisation consists of (groups) of entities that might show evolutionary patterns like at the level of microevolution. This might happen at the level of the total organisation, evoking the need sometimes to consider organisations as a whole and sometimes to consider organisations as a constellation of groups. Thirdly, the fact that an organisation is a construct of human thought and behaviour constitutes a major difference. Finally, organisations might display evolutionary patterns like species. Similarly to the development of species and taxa, the evolutionary development of organisations acts at the level of individual entities to groups, i.e. microevolution, and it contributes to macroevolution (described by organisational ecology for the domain of organisations). Although limitations do exist, we can transfer the theories from biological evolution to the domain of organisations.

6.5.1 Evolutionary Mechanisms for Organisations

So far, one of the major differences between organisms and organisations did not receive any attention: the base of the variation is found in the gene pool of species, something that is not present in organisations as such. A way to explore such would be the analogy of genes to knowledge, habits, and rules; a route that does not seem directly connected to the research at hand. All variation in organisms finds its origin in the mutations of the gene pool. The variation is expressed through the phenotype on which the environment exerts selection. It also became clear that the gene pool contains levels of complexity, regulatory genes, and feedback loops. Mutations of organisms appear through gametic formation in which the genotype of each organism participates, through developmental deviations (Hox genes, heterochrony, heterotopy), and through environmental stress (enabling or disabling regulatory genes, selection).

What should this research consider instead of the gene pool that expresses itself in the phenotype? How do we observe organisations? Not only this study touches on the basic unit of selection, the gene, and the genome, the genetic material present in a cell or organism. Some suggestions have been made to what to consider the equivalent of the genes and the genome on which the evolutionary mechanisms build. One possible view concentrates on the division

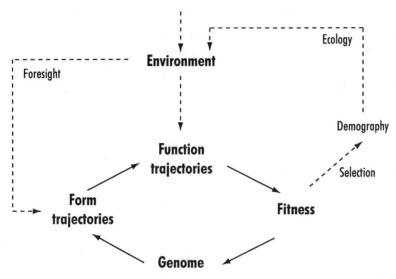

Figure 6.5: Evolutionary mechanism for organisations. The two intertwined cycles consist of the same steps as for organisms. The evolutionary mechanism for organisations has two major differences in comparison to the mechanisms for organisms: (a) the equivalent of a genome does not exist, it seems most appropriate to describe the organisational genome by skills, capabilities, memes, technology, and (b) the concept of Lamarckian evolution depicted by the foresight loop.

of an organisation in departments, groups, individuals, etc. Morgan (1996, p. 34, 43) did propose such when introducing the image of an organisation as an organism. Another view would be to look at organisations as a collection of resources with skills and knowledge present, expressing itself in the form of capabilities (capabilities express themselves in function trajectories), like Nakane (1986). Dawkins[39] (1989, p. 192) has proposed memes, as unit for imitation and recombination. Memes constitute elements of a culture or system of behaviour that may be considered to be passed from one individual to another by non-genetic means, especially imitation. Dawkins extends this concept to a wide variety of topics like ideas, artefacts, including people, products, books, behaviours, routines, knowledge, science, religion, art, rituals, institutions, and politics. In organisational studies memes enjoy a high degree of popularity. Kauffman et al. (2000) take technology as starting point for recombination. That way they connect the development of technology as genetic evolution to evolutionary biological models, esp. fitness landscapes. The well-known study of Nelson & Winter (1982) use organisational routines unit for selection. Knudsen (2002, p. 459) remarks that Nelson & Winter use the term routine in the sense of

---

[39] *The first edition of this book was published in 1969 and did already contain the proposal for the distinction of memes as unit for evolution.*

both replicators (routines as the genes of the organisation) and interactors (routines as recurrent patterns of behaviour among interacting social agents). These different explanations suit different purposes for different analysis of business.

Following the thoughts of this research, it matters less what to take as the equivalent of genes. The generation of variation becomes more important and whether that generation of variation has effects on the form and function trajectories; either brought about through genetic mutations or non-genetic mutations. Only then selection will elect the fitter variants for evolutionary steps. For example, the capabilities of a firm will change over time through non-genetic formation. But also memes and technology could be seen as components of genetic formation that creates mutations. Within the evolutionary mechanism for organisations the variation should result in form and function trajectories for selection by the environment (see Figure 6.5).

6.5.2 Variation in Organisations

Organisations exhibit also phenotypes, the visible traits of an organism, to the environment; these visible traits result from function trajectories. Whereas in biology the genotype-phenotype distinction is very clear, in economics no such distinction exists. There is no singular equivalent in economics to the most basic unit of selection, i.e. the gene. Biological evolution is genetic evolution, whereas social-economic evolution is a combination of genetic and non-genetic evolution, where the latter is dominant because of different timescales. Nevertheless, some authors have tried to impose the genotype-phenotype analogy to economics (Boulding, 1981; Faber & Proops, 1990). Selection will act on the phenotypes and those with characteristics favoured by the environment will evolve.

In contrast to organisms, organisations do not have to rely solely on the stochastic selection operating on variants. Through the adequate development of feasible traits and the appropriate design of organisations, industrial companies might create mutants with higher chances of success than possible in evolutionary biology. Lamarckian or goal-oriented evolution occurs on various levels in economic systems: individuals, groups, and sectors. This is due to social and individual learning and search. In biological systems and most animal species this type of learning is largely absent, and mutations are largely random and certainly not the result of purposeful search processes. Therefore, the distinction between selection as social learning (selection, diffusion) and individual learning (limited) is clear-cut in biology. In contrast, in economics and management science such a distinction is blurred, as technologies developed and lessons learned in one sector can be easily transferred to other sectors. Essential for economic-cultural evolution is the fact that information can be purposefully accumulated and that changes (mutations) can be purposefully stimulated (see Figure 6.5: the inclusion of the foresight loop). At the same time, if the models of evolutionary biology hold true in some respects for organisational evolution, it becomes impossible to eliminate chance. The testing of hypotheses, when each mutation is seen as a hypothesis, happens in the market domain in which a specific company operates or in which it wants to enter. The testing of viability happens through the visible traits of the company.

When performing the Future Manufacturing Survey, Nakane (1986) took these capabilities, or should we call them traits now, as starting point for selection. In addition, the postulate of the Delft School Approach for the analysis and design of organisations relies heavily on the distinction between the control structure, the organelle structure, and the hierarchy. The hierarchy with its division in departments, groups, and individuals constitutes the centre of change management and leadership (leadership was excluded from this research when defining the scope of the research); change management aims primarily at changing organisational behaviour through influencing attitudes and decisions by individuals and groups, therewith affecting the organisational culture. The focus on resources and capabilities links more directly to the concept of the processes and structures needed for adaptation, the quest of this specific research. To obtain a complete record, the evaluation of change management should be part of the research (Chapter 13 will briefly touch on this matter); the focus on resources and capabilities offers more perspectives for transferring the models of evolutionary biology to the domain of industrial organisations as the next subsection and the next chapters will demonstrate.

Anyhow, within industrial populations, companies serving a specific product-market combination, a wide variety of organisational forms exists, one not necessarily excluding others and all having different fitness. Wollin (1999, pp. 360-362) builds on Simon's seminal work (1962) on the architecture of complexity, for social systems theory. Within this view, the organisation of deep structure consists of a nested hierarchy where elements or subsystems at less fundamental level are subsets, and therefore dependent on elements or subsets at more fundamental levels in the same branch. This description looks like the ones of Riedl and Seaborg when they tried to explain the phenomenon of feedback loops (Subsection 6.3.3). Wollin uses the nested hierarchy to explain the impact of the punctuated equilibrium and incremental change; he ignores the fundamental principles of the theories of punctuated equilibrium and phyletic gradualism as phenomenon of speciation. The nested hierarchy looks more like the mechanisms of macromutations without the rich background the biological models offer; hence the writings of Wollin do not influence the research into adaptation.

McCarthy (2005) proposes to use a classification for describing organisational diversity, in his words: ... *the cladistic focus on shared patterns of common ancestry is an evolutionary logic compatible with the variation, selection, and retention explanations for how and why new organisational taxa emerge.* He mentions that some, like Miles & Snow (1978), have already attempted to arrive at a classification; Miles & Snow link the organisational form, he notes (configuration) to the conditions and demands of the environment. McCarthy (2005) shows that a more comprehensive approach towards classification is needed, akin the practices in biology. For the study at hand, a classification does not mean that the underlying mechanisms of diversity and variation are understood. Despite the fact that it might be worthwhile to pay more attention to classification, this investigation will continue without go into more detail about this topic.

6.5.3   Mechanisms for Variation

It becomes clear from the evolutionary biological models that equilibria hardly exist. Continuous emergence of mutants cause disturbance of an equilibrium and might cause genetic drift. Hence, for companies continuous change and adaptation is not any more a question but a necessity. These continuous processes are driven by the coexistence of evolutionary development, e.g. captured in the concepts of the phyletic gradualism, the punctuated equilibrium, and the macromutations. The models are strongly related to each other: the punctuated equilibrium does not exist without the gradual changes during the longer periods of stasis. Likewise, in both the theories of the phyletic gradualism and the punctuated equilibrium, macromutations cause evolutionary change. Whenever the conversion of the concepts takes place, attention should be paid to the level at which the evolution takes place (microevolution and macroevolution). Although primarily aiming at the development of individual companies, the study should also look at changes happening in product-market combinations and in branches (a study was presented in Chapter 2; much more the focus of the next chapter). This subsection will consecutively transfer the thoughts about phyletic gradualism and punctuated equilibrium to the evolution of organisations.

How do we translate the models from gradualism to human constructs like an organisation? Gradualism tells that the accumulation of variations in the genotype might result in favourable traits to the environment. In other words, the variation should lead to visible characteristics to the environment (especially driven by large numbers and many successive steps). In case of an organisation, its environment consists of suppliers, resources (qualitative and quantitative), clients, boundary shapers (government, regulators, etc.). All these entities might perceive changes in the behaviour and characterisation of a company that will provoke selection. On top of the changes in traits, companies might change their borders with the environment through:

- changing the borders with suppliers (integrating suppliers in their system or by outsourcing);
- changing the borders with clients;
- combination with or decomposition into other units (of the same firm or another firm);
- integrating technologies and skills from resources or abandoning these for differentiation.

If gradualism applies, companies would go through these changes by gradual steps, on each outcome the forces of selection will act. Dorak (2002) mentions that evolution means not necessarily progress because it is about adaptation to the surroundings over a period of time. However, no progress can take place without evolution. Each of these steps and the final adaptation reside in the capability of an organisation to generate variations, especially those which result in diversification of visible traits to the environment.

According to the biological models, not changes in the environment affect industrial companies in the first place but variations from within organisations (e.g. organisational structures or organisational formats). The principles of the punctuated equilibrium theory tell that longer periods of stasis, ruled by developmental homeostasis and adaptation, alternate intense periods of competition and elimination. During those periods of resilience organisations face a relatively stable environment, a period in which hybridisation (translated as mergers, acquisitions, alliances aiming at synergy), stands higher chances for allometry given the presence of abundant resources, even though the success of hybridisation is extremely low. This would point especially to periods of (stable) growth in the presence of sufficient resources. The survey on biological models showed that not the selection of viable adaptation but the elimination of weak or inviable mutants dominates the survival during turmoil. Even then industrial organisations need to create mutants by changing their behaviour, internal processes, and structures. The theory of punctuated equilibrium recognises four influences on speciation:

- allopatric speciation and the founder effect;
- macromutations;
- extinctions;
- environmental changes.

These four influences might cause periods of turmoil in which speciation occurs (see Chapter 7) and in which mutants of organisations have a chance to become a beneficial allele for an organisation.

Macromutations, as source for mutations besides the gradual changes of Darwinian theories, come about through four patterns of creating diversity. First, the developmental genes might guide organisms into variations; especially those genes with large effects do so. These variations express themselves in the morphology of the organism. Secondly, the mechanism of heterochrony also finds its way in diversity in the structure of organisms. Thirdly, heterotopy does the same (note that heterochrony and heterotopy also depend on the presence of developmental genes). Finally, epigenetics change the structure as well but then at the level of the integration of developing parts into a whole. For organisations, this concept of macromutations means that changing structures over the life-cycle, and that changing structures through regulatory controls might increase their fitness to the landscape in which they operate. The effects of macromutations, whether brought about by developmental genes, heterochrony, heterotopy or epigenetics, look very much like one-time interventions. These macromutations have large effect but appear mostly deleterious; do one-time interventions share the same fate? In addition, certain developmental pathways should be followed because of developmental constraints and selective constraints. The evolution of companies during the life-cycle and in their structures occurs along the lines of specific pathways.

Before concluding this subsection, three more points require attention. Firstly, small populations favour quick changes of the gene pool, which means that companies operating in product-market combinations with a limited number of competitors should prepare for dynamic environments. Small populations appear sometimes through the exploitation of new or niche markets or the splitting of the market domain. Secondly, according to the thoughts of Worden, a first effective response to the changing environment will evoke a quick shift of populations. During periods of changing environments, the likelihood that a first response strikes, increases. This accounts for organisations then too, the longer competitors hold their horses though the environment calls for change, the more dramatic the response after a first strike will unfold. Such cases might lead to previously beneficial phenotypes of organisations to become all of a sudden deleterious. Thirdly, the evolutionary biological models indicate that organisms of higher complexity are more sensitive to the models of the punctuated equilibrium than simple organisms. That would imply that larger organisational structures, as a monolithic company or as a networked structure of companies, would be more sensitive to the phenomena of the theory of punctuated equilibrium. According to the system hierarchy of Boulding, organisations move at a level of higher complexity. Even then, industrial organisations display a total range of complexity along the dimensions of size, processes, specialisation, resources, etc. In addition to the mechanisms of evolution, three factors influence the adaptation of industrial organisations: the size of the product-market combination, the speed after the first effective response, and the internal complexity of an organisation.

6.5.4 Evolution of Industrial Organisations

Evolution takes place at many levels in the hierarchy of specimen, species, taxa, etc. This applies to organisations, too. Organisations operate in a industrial branch, belong to conglomerates, etc. Our concern is mostly the interaction between an individual organisation and its environment. Analogous to biological evolution, the development of an individual organisation is tied to the development of its own species. Although the research focuses on the adaptation of individual firms, the development of higher levels should be included. For example, Lewin et al. (1999) have started research in the co-evolution of new organisational forms; it appears though that they have chosen a different path than historians like Mokyr (Section 3.1). At the end of their paper, they state also that the development of the organisational forms resides in individual organisations (Lewin et al., 1999, pp. 546-547). The development of an individual firm relates to the shifts taking place in its customers base, the competitive environment, the technological developments, etc.

Preliminarily, the outcomes of research so far might force the conclusion that organisations are never at equilibrium with their environment. To ensure evolution, continuous adaptation must take place. Even so, we might state that variation is a prerequisite for adapting to the environment rather than that the environment proclaims changes companies should adapt to. Then the research should strongly focus on how these mutations evolve continuously. If organisms could directly compare to organisations both hypotheses stated in Section 4.1 would be answered already, adaptation is a matter of continuous evolution and a homeostatic equilibrium proves to be an illusion. Nevertheless, the question remains whether theories in management science acknowledge the principles of evolution, and whether current practices in industrial organisations exhibit bottlenecks for companies to implement effective and dynamic adaptation.

To conclude this chapter, the literature research into evolutionary biological models leads to a few preliminary conclusions and remarks:

- First of all, the creation of variance at the level of phenotypes, as evolutionary force, depends on the recognition of genes and alleles. Although a comparison might be made with individuals and groups, as Morgan (1997) proposes for the metaphors, at first sight it does not generate additional models for adaptation by industrial companies. Some authors have proposed memes, capabilities as substitute for genes and alleles; some have taken technology as starting point for analysis of evolutionary processes. However, the principle of recombination by genes does not directly find its kin in organisations.
- The appearance of macromutations beholds more promises to analogies for industrial companies. The recognition of developmental pathways, Hox genes, regulatory genes, and feedback loops resembles the internal complexity

of the development of organisations. Adaptation might have effect when accounting for these type of mechanisms.

- Furthermore, periods of intense selection and longer periods of developmental homeostasis interchange. For small and simple organisations the mechanisms of phyletic gradualism dominate; gradual changes of the phenotypes, traits, occur and selection by the environment determines the overall evolution. For larger, more complex organisations, the models of the punctuated equilibrium and the mechanisms for generating macromutations exert stronger effects. This indicates that larger organisations might be confronted with quicker changes, more turmoil, and more disruptions.

- Finally, the major differences between organisms and organisations, the less fixed boundaries and the capability of foresight, allow managers and designers to intervene in developmental pathways; this is referred to as Lamarckian evolution. This applies to the levels or strata at which the change should focus and the possibility to redefine the boundary.

6.6   SUMMARY

This survey of the evolutionary models for (genetic) variation has also resulted in three remarkable notions, which the further research might have to answer. First of all, the mechanisms related to the punctuated equilibrium might apply more to bigger and complex organisations rather than relatively small and simple organisations, indicating the need for internal complexity reduction for bigger companies. Secondly, the changes from one homeostasis to another one through a period of turmoil might occur quickly once adaptive zones or vacant niches exist or an accumulation of changes topples internal integrative mechanisms to other point of stability. Thirdly, industrial companies in overlapping habitats, markets, and resources, should emphasise differences. If not, these companies should isolate themselves in different areas for survival, the mechanism of allopatric speciation, to allow growth into a stable environment before exposing themselves to the competition with parent species, the original cluster of companies to which they belonged. Depending on their size, companies might enhance growth and sustainability through applying the principles of the punctuated equilibrium, emphasising differences between companies in similar competitive environments and creating energy for change.

7 LANDSCAPE FITNESS AND ADAPTATION

The environment of a specimen consists of other individuals of its population, other species, and resources (one might also add the circumstances). The interaction with that environment determines the course of the development and adaptation of species. Evolutionary theories include this interaction as driving force for selection, a notion Darwin (1859) formalised. Section 7.1 will describe the concept of natural selection and adaptation. This paradigm arrives from the Darwinian theory on the origin of species, but is still found in other emerging theories, and has not been abandoned, yet. For example, a cybernetic view on punctuated evolutionary change reveals three mechanisms by which adaptive mutations occur (Seaborg, 1999, p. 20):

1. Macromutations. Organisms represent holistically interrelated systems, each trait interconnected to several other traits. A change in one character of an organism can change the fitness and evolutionary change of other characters. Any major alteration will tend to be deleterious since most feedback loops will be negative, resisting change; even though such a major alteration might be a successful adaptation in both its internal mechanisms and its external relationships. The hierarchical nature of genetic and developmental systems of organisms, present in regulatory genes, might give way for coordinated changes in the whole organism that are adaptive and of large effect (as described in Section 6.3).

2. Directional selection driven primarily by the external environment. In this case, strong selection favours one of the extreme phenotypes (Dorak, 2002) while thereby reducing the variation that exists in a population. Stressful conditions from the environment might be very effective in shifting the mean of a trait by directional selection (Hoffmann & Hercus, 2002, p. 217).

3. Directional selection driven primarily by statistical phenomena occurring in a population (and the belonging phenotypes and genotypes) and the interactions of these with natural selection.

The latter two indicate the importance and central role of natural selection in the process of adaptation, whereby natural selection constitutes part of the environment. As Maynard Smith (1989, p. 242) tells: "evolution takes place even if the environment does not change". On the other hand, events like the complete disappearance of a landscape, like an island sinking in the sea, can hardly be counteracted by speciation. However, the mechanisms of selection and its effect on speciation operate in many different ways. Recent insight in mathematical models offers the possibilities to expand these theories to the domain of the theory of the punctuated equilibrium and the domain of macromutations. Especially, Jablonski (2000, p. 35) indicates that more complex social structures might have higher speciation rates than those with breeding systems that are more open. An indication that organisations may experience relatively strong influences of the models of the punctuated equilibrium and the emergence of macromutations.

After the exploration of the more classical approaches of natural selection in Section 7.1, the next section will pay attention to landscape fitness which principles have been applied to the domain of organisations. Evolutionary biology has included the mathematics of the landscape fitness into the metaphor of the polyhedron. Section 7.3 focuses on recent insight into selection mechanisms that take dynamics of the environment into account when species move along the axis of development and evolution. In addition to these environmental influences, Section 7.4 will briefly discuss the theory of autopoiesis as launched by Maturana & Varela (1980). Section 7.5 deals with the transfer of the theories of selection and landscape fitness to the domain of organisations.

7.1 NATURAL SELECTION

Environmental factors may operate to favour the reproduction of certain alleles or gene combinations over others present in the population. The impact of the total environment on the reproduction of gene combinations is the force of natural selection, a feature of the Darwinism, which has so far directed the research into evolutionary biology. The effects of natural selection vary as the environment changes, so that slightly different environmental conditions for each generation favour slightly different gene combinations. Natural selection moulds the genetic variation present in a population, but it cannot itself produce new genes or gene combinations. In reality, people often confuse natural selection with evolution. Selection merely favours beneficial genetic changes when they occur by chance (Dorak, 2002), reason to explore the mechanisms of natural selection in more detail.

7.1.1 Decreasing Variation

Natural selection does not have any foresight. It makes organisms adapt to their current environment whether the environment changes or whether it remains in a stable state. Structures or behaviours do not evolve for future utility, as in the doctrine of Lamarckian evolution. Organisms adapts to their environment at each stage of their evolution through successive steps as the distribution of a gene pool shifts to a new position in the landscape. New traits may be selected for when the environment changes. Large changes in populations are the result of cumulative natural selection, no population changes overnight (except in the case of environmental catastrophes). Changes in the population are introduced by mutations; the small minority of these changes that result in a greater reproductive output of their bearers are amplified in frequency by selection.

Natural selection as mechanism for evolution of species maintains or depletes genetic variation depending on how it acts. Most commonly, the action of natural selection removes unfit variants as they arise via mutation. Natural selection is the only mechanism of adaptive evolution: it is defined as differential reproductive success of pre-existing classes of genetic variants in the gene pool (Colby, 1996). When selection acts to weed out deleterious alleles, or causes an allele to sweep to fixation, it depletes genetic variation. When heterozygotes are more fit than either of the homozygotes, selection causes genetic variation to be maintained. This is called balancing selection. Balancing selection is rare in natural populations since most species find themselves at disequilibrium with the environment: either "the population evolves or the environment changes" or "both the population evolves and the environment changes".

One way of disequilibrium roots in the interaction between closely related organisms. Helping closely related organisms can appear altruistic: but this is also selfish behaviour in terms of evolution and fitness. Reproductive success (fitness) has two components: direct fitness and indirect fitness. Direct fitness is a measure of how many alleles, on average, a genotype contributes to the subsequent generation's gene pool by reproducing and determining its fitness to the environment. Indirect fitness is a measure of how many alleles identical to its own it helps to enter the gene pool. Direct fitness plus indirect fitness is inclusive fitness. Natural selection favours traits or behaviour that increase a genotype's inclusive fitness. Closely related organisms share many of the same alleles. In diploid species[40], siblings share on average at least 50% of their alleles. This percentage is higher if the parents are closely related. Although helping closely related organisms proves beneficial, it generally contributes to maintaining a status quo of the mean of a gene pool (Hoffmann & Hercus, 2002, pp. 218-219). Therefore, this mechanism, the interaction between closely related organisms, does not necessarily increase fitness.

7.1.2   Allopatric Speciation

Mayr has introduced the concept of allopatric speciation in 1954 (Prothero, 1992), expanding the Darwinian theories to explain the diversity of life. According to him, small subpopulations which are genetically isolated from the main population are more likely to change, because an evolutionary novelty has a much better chance of dominating a small population than a large one. In small populations

---

[40]   *See introduction of Chapter 6.*

variants will evolve that in later stages might penetrate the parent species' landscape. In case of invasion, the new species might die out quickly, or it might drive its ancestor to extinction, or both might persist side-by-side, typically by exploring slightly different ecological niches. Recent insight in the development of mankind shows that human invaders from Asia following a route from Africa to Asia into Europe drove the Neanderthal population to extinction about 50.000 years ago. This theory of allopatric speciation promoted the importance of small founding populations and relatively rapid rates of change. Nevertheless, the theory of allopatric speciation remains rooted in the belief that changes in gene frequencies will accumulate over time, and that selection pushes separated populations in different adaptive directions if they live in slightly different habitats.

Allopatric populations occupy different geographic or ecological ranges separated by spatial barriers (Savage, 1969, p. 92). This leads to isolated reproduction, a consequence of sufficient isolation (Gould, 1980, p. 122). In allopatric speciation, evolution may take place in two spatially isolated populations descended from a common ancestor (see Figure 7.1). Differences in the interaction of variation, selection, and drift will operate in these fragments in exactly the same process of microevolution. Through sequential mutations, lack of gene flow, continued different selection, the subspecies continue to diverge until they can no longer interbreed with the sister species (Teed, 2001). Also, in small populations, genes which are rare in the parent population can drift to high frequency. If the population remains separated for a long enough time, and if the

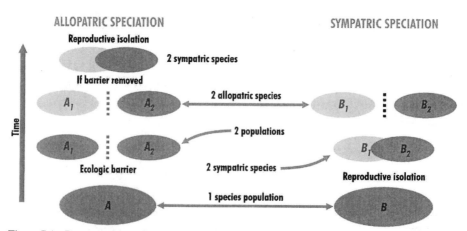

Figure 7.1: Representation of allopatric and sympatric speciation (Savage, 1969, p. 110). Through the emergence of an ecological barrier, species might involve into allopatric species, even to the extent that the removal of the original barrier maintains the reproductive isolation. Sympatric species evolve in the same habitat, but will lead to allopatric species at the end.

interacting forces of evolution - particularly selection - operate to produce divergence, allopatric species result.

As a special case of allopatric speciation, we find peripatric speciation, a term introduced by Mayr (1942). The term refers to the situation where a small colony derived from a more widespread "parent" population diverges and acquires reproductive isolation. Sympatric speciation, the production of a daughter species within the geographic range of the parent species, after Dobzhansky's (1966) ostracysm: "sympatric speciation is like the measles; everyone gets it and we all get over it" (Bush, 1998), is currently making a comeback in the both the theoretical and experimental literature as a definite and maybe even common possibility.

7.1.3 Sympatric Speciation

Species are called sympatric when they share a portion of ecological ranges (Savage, 1969, p. 92). Sympatric speciation may produce similar results as allopatric speciation (see Figure 7.1). If reproductive isolation between segments of the same population were to rise instantaneously and directly, two reproductive isolated populations would result. If one or both populations moved out of the original habitat, the species would become allopatric. If the two populations remained in the same area, sympatric species would be recognized. Once reproductive isolation is established, each population follows its own course. Elsberry (1996) states that allopatric speciation prevails above sympatric speciation. According to him, sympatric speciation is a rare event, if existent primarily seen in insect and parasite lineages. Savage (1969, p. 113) remarks that the mechanisms for sympatric speciation are relatively clear. Either the genotype or gene distribution is unsuitable for interbreeding or the interbreeding ceases to act. At the same time, the actual reasons why isolating mechanisms become established in a specific population, remains unsolved; Section 7.3 will elaborate on a possible mechanism to act on speciation.

According to both the allopatric and the sympatric models, speciation is simply a matter of time, an accumulation of continuously-accrued change, not the result of unlikely mutation (like the rare occurrence of macromutations). According to Teed (2001), Rice & Hostert have found that divergent selection dominates above loss of gene flow between two separated populations. After sympatric speciation, one of the two populations might move out of the original habitat, that way establishing an allopatric population (Savage, 1969, p. 111). The other way around, an allopatric population might move into the habitat of the parent population causing sympatric species to exist; this seems unlikely since genetic drift will create quickly divergence between the two populations through their own course of mutations.

7.1.4 Frequency-dependent and Density-dependent Selection

The distribution of mutations and their individual fitness determine the long term evolutionary path, as new mutations invade and drift towards fixation at a rate determined by their fitness. The linkage disequilibrium (see Section 6.2) is a sample of frequency-dependent selection where the fitness is not fixed but variable, and the values they take on vary as functions of the frequencies of the diploid genotypes they characterise (Gromko, 1976, p. 438), under certain conditions. Another point is that fitness needs not be constant, in fact, they rarely are, but may be density- and frequency-dependent; a special, but important, case is the situation where fitness values vary to favour rare types, and become approximately equal as an intermediate frequency is approached. The terms have been introduced to allow the comparison of more realistic but less tractable models for evolutionary change, where fitness is allowed to vary with ecological circumstances, with the earlier simpler models in which fitness was assumed to have constant values.

Additionally to frequency-dependent selection, density-dependent selection exists. Wallace (1975, p. 466) gives as an example of this type of selection: the death of individuals who fail to establish private territories (had fewer individuals existed, all individuals could have had territories). Density-dependent selection relates strongly to the availability of resources for species to continue to survive,

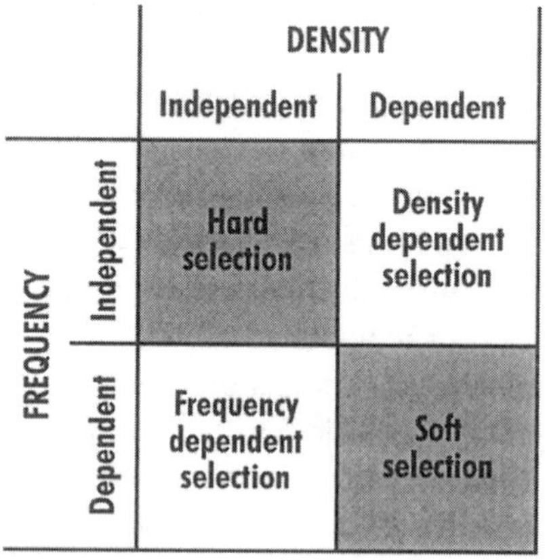

		DENSITY	
		Independent	Dependent
FREQUENCY	Independent	Hard selection	Density dependent selection
	Dependent	Frequency dependent selection	Soft selection

Figure 7.2: Illustration of the four types of selection: hard, soft, density-dependent, and frequency-dependent (Wallace, 1975, p. 470). Frequency-dependent selection occurs when the fitness of a genotype depends on its frequency; it is possible for the fitness of a genotype to increase (positively frequency-dependent) or decrease (negatively frequency-dependent) as the genotype frequency in the population increases. Density-dependent selection occurs when the fitness of types in a population depend upon the size of the population. For example, overcrowding may decrease average fitness, and underpopulation may increase it. If that is the case, we could expect the population size to oscillate about an equilibrium value. Hard and soft selection indicate the absence or presence of both types of selection.

and plays an important role in mathematical modelling of evolutionary processes. In contrast to frequency-dependent selection, in the case of density-dependent selection the fitness as such from an organism relates to competing for resources, and not the occurrence of other organisms within the population with similar phenotypes.

Wallace (1975) has introduced the soft and hard selection thereby combining frequency-dependent selection and density-dependent selection (see Figure 7.2). Hard selection points to independence of frequency and density, one can compare this concept with the appearance of deleterious mutations (in Wallace's words: lethal genes). Soft selection acts both through frequency-dependent selection and density-dependent selection. This combination receives comments from Gromko (1976, p. 440) since it has been demonstrated explicitly that although fitness values appear not to be dependent on frequency in uncrowded cultures they become so in crowded ones. A prerequisite for such is the existence of heterogeneous cultures. In addition, it becomes clear that the population size relates to factors as territories, while available resources determine strongly the directional selection.

7.1.5 Stressful Environmental Conditions

When evolving, species might encounter adaptive limits, and simultaneously environmental stress will strengthen the speed of evolution, according to Hoffmann & Hercus (2002). In their paper, they explore the effect of stressful conditions from the environment on rapid evolution. They conclude that periodically stressful conditions may influence evolutionary rates by generating and maintaining variability, and by overcoming adaptation limits caused by gene flow; these phenomena help to explain diversification patterns in the fossil record.

Adaptive limits might have five causes (Hoffmann & Hercus, 2002, pp. 218-220). First of all, species might possess insufficient genetic variability for adaptive changes to occur; a high level of potential variability is necessary to create a linkage disequilibrium or the appearance of extreme phenotypes. Secondly, the genetic variability present in a population may not be used. Especially, major genes or control genes display more resistance to evolutionary change than minor genes. Additionally, gene flow might also prevent adaptive divergence (also mentioned by Bell [2000, p. 1458], based on findings by Futuyuma). Gene flow causes homogenisation of the gene pool, making it more difficult for adaptations to appear under marginal conditions and restraining a population to common conditions. Fourthly, so-called trade-off depresses evolutionary change. Genes favoured under marginal conditions are often associated with low fitness under favourable conditions, and vice versa. Finally, the selection of deleterious mutations is more efficient in environments that are commonly encountered by organisms than in those that are rarely encountered.

Stressful environmental conditions might induce rapid evolutionary change. The paper by Hoffmann & Hercus (2002, pp. 219-222) mentions three causes through which environmental stress expresses itself in evolutionary change. Originally, they mention four factors for rapid evolutionary change but the factor of increased mutation and recombination is also mentioned later as part of the factor of phenotypic variation, and therefore both are considered one factor in this research. The first cause is increased phenotypic variation, as mentioned in Sections 6.1 and 6.3. A few extreme phenotypes produced by localised stress are likely to be diluted by gene flow in populations unless the phenotypes have large phenotypic effects on the fitness of organisms. This suggests a much more dynamic interaction between the environment and genetic systems than has previously been appreciated. Secondly, restricted gene flow can have a positive effect on adaptation (similar to the founder effect). Lastly, the cause of persistent genetic variation generates adaptation.

The size of populations has a dual role, restricting and enhancing evolutionary change (Hoffmann & Hercus, 2002, pp. 222-223). If isolated populations become smaller, then genetic variation can become lost. The only exception is when epistatic interaction occurs, which can result in a release of genetic variability following a population bottleneck. A small population size will also lead to inbreeding depression, which occurs when there is an increase in the relative frequency of genotypes with homozygotes for recessive deleterious alleles. Decreased population size might also allow the base of genetic variation to decrease allowing a shift of the mean of a trait by directional selection enforced by environmental stress.

7.2   LANDSCAPE FITNESS

According to Colby (1996), natural selection may not lead a population to a state in which it possesses the optimal set of traits. In any population, a certain combination of possible alleles exists that would produce the optimal set of traits (the global optimum); but there are also other sets of alleles present that would yield a population almost as adapted (local optima). Transition from a local optimum to another optimum may be hindered or forbidden because the population would have to pass through less adaptive states to make the transition.

7.2.1   Wright's Adaptive Landscape

Natural selection only works by bringing populations to the nearest optimal point. This theory is referred to as Sewall Wright's adaptive landscape (Wright, 1982), even though others have shown that, mathematically, his landscapes do not exist as envisioned. The fitness of species develops by moving from one to another selective peak (see Figure 7.3). As Wright wonders, which force will act against the pressure of selection moving species from one peak to another one? According to him (Wright, 1982, pp. 8-9), an effective shifting balance process involves three phases: first, extensive local differentiation, with wide stochastic variability in each locality; second, occasional crossing of a saddle leading to a higher selective peak under mass selection; and third, excess proliferation of, and dispersion from, those local populations in which a peak-shift has occurred, leading to occupation of the superior peak as a whole. Not only species adapt to the landscape, the surface of selective values changes with changes in environmental conditions. With changing conditions, the location of the species follows the movement of the peak if the change does not lead to extinction. Old adaptations are lost as new ones are acquired.

Referring to the development of species, Worden (1995) encourages the application of genetic algorithms for mimicking natural selection as attaining fitness peaks. He remarks that the development of species through the deployment of genetic algorithms is subject to the speed limits he proposes (see Subsection 6.3.1). The adaptations to the environment, homeostatic development, inhibit moving the development of a species to the next successful set of adaptation, like a ball rolling across hilly terrain. Then species are always trying to reach the adaptive peaks of the landscape, and are continually modified in response to the shifting of the peaks. Gould (1980, p. 129) refers to the metaphor of Galton's polyhedron borrowed by St. George Mivart to describe the evolution of organisms and the state of equilibria. Prothero (1992) proposes to use the metaphor of the polyhedron, which can roll rapidly over from face to face, but resists change

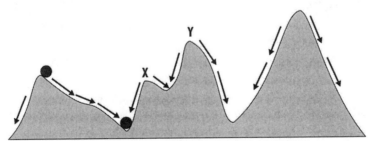

Figure 7.3: Representation of Wright's adaptive landscape (adapted from Heylighen, 1999). Species move from one peak to another (represented by the circle, being at a fitness peak, a stable position, and a saddle, representing a stable point with low fitness). During the move they might experience reduced fitness before reaching the more adaptive saddle. The ball will move most likely from the saddle to the nearst, highest fitness peak (on the left) or reach point X because each adaptive step yields higher fitness than moving left. Point X and point Y indicate stable positions of high fitness. A species at point X will have to move through a saddle with lower fitness before reaching the higher fitness peak Y.

when it is sitting on one of its stable faces. Change only occurs when the threshold necessary to tip it over has been exceeded, and then the polyhedron will resist further change until that threshold is once again reached. Between stable states (the faces), the transitions occur very rapidly. The practical implication for companies is that a lot of energy and momentum is required to initiate a change process but once the company approaches a possible stable state in relation to the environment, the intended change will unfold very fast.

7.2.2   Random Fitness Landscapes

Kauffman (1993, 1995) has extended the concept of the fitness landscapes to explain the diversity of life and the common origins of life. His two publications cover mostly the same grounds, and provide different texts for the same phenomena during the evolution of life on earth. The theory of his fitness landscapes directly connects to the impact of natural selection. The framework of adaptation on rugged fitness landscapes (Kauffman, 1993, pp. 36-67) applies to adaptive evolution in sequence spaces, spaces in which the successive steps depend on the preceding steps (the underlying mechanism for mutations to appear in a population), indicating the exsitence of developmental pathways.

To explain his thoughts about the fitness landscape, this subsection captures the text for explaining the N-model before moving on to the NK-model in the next subsection. Fitness resembles height, a measure for expressing the fitness of a genotype, equal to thoughts of Wright's adaptive landscape. Fitter genotypes are higher than less fit genotypes. Consider a genotype with only four genes, each having two alleles: *1* and *0* (i.e. a Boolean representation of the state of each gene), resulting in 16 possible genotypes, each an unique combination of the different states of the four genes. Each vertex corresponds to one of the 16 possibilities (see Figure 7.4). Each vertex differs only by one mutation from the neighbouring ones, representing the step of a single mutation, thereby stating that each mutation as such is independent from the state of the other genes. Each genotype is arbitrarily assigned to a fitness value ranked from worst (i.e. *1*) to best (i.e. *16*), representing a peak in the fitness landscape (in Figure 7.4 this is indicated by the fitness value instead of the height within the fitness landscape). An adaptive walk might begin at any vertex and move to vertices that have higher fitness values. An adaptive walk ends at a local optimum, not necessarily the highest optimum, a vertex that has a higher fitness value than all its one-mutant neighbours. In the figure it shows that there are three local optima at which adaptive walks may end.

Kauffman (1993, p. 39) refers to Gillespie (1984), who has shown that an the process of an adapting population corresponds to the undertaking an adaptive walk. If the population begins at the less fit allele, a single mutant will eventually

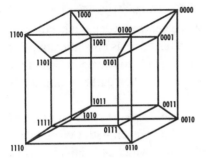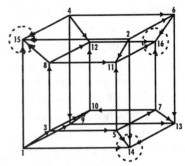

Figure 7.4: The N-model as proposed by Kauffman (1993, p. 38). 16 possible peptides of length 4 aminos are arranged as vertices on a four-dimensional Boolean hypercube. Each peptide connects to its four one-mutant neighbours, accessible by changing a single amino acid from 1 to 0 or from 0 to 1. The hypercube on the left represents this four-dimensional peptide space. In the hypercube on the right-hand side, each peptide has been assigned, at random, a rank-order fitness, ranging from the worst, 1, to the best, 16. Directions of such moves between adjacent positions are shown by arrows from the less fit to the more fit. Peptides fitter than all one-mutant neighbours are local optima (three in this case).

encounter the fitter allele. Either that mutant dies out before leaving offspring, or a few of the fitter mutants are produced. Once the number of fitter mutants produced is sufficient to reduce the chance of fluctuation leading to their death, the fitter type rapidly takes over the entire population. Thus the entire population moves to the fitter genotype. Gillespie has shown that the entire adaptive process can be treated as a continuous-time, discrete-state Markov process.

As Kauffman (1995, pp. 166-167) states, evolution requires landscapes that are not random. In fact, on random landscapes, finding, the global peak by searching uphill, is totally useless; we have to search the entire space of possibilities. From any initial point on a landscape, adaptive walks reach local peaks after some number of steps. Additionally, no matter, where an adaptive walks starts, if the population is allowed to walk only uphill, it can reach only an infinitesimal fraction of the local peaks. But in reality, the fitness landscapes that underlie the mutation steps of gradualism are correlated, and often local peaks do have similar heights.

7.2.3 Rugged Fitness Landscapes

As noted in Section 6.3 (developmental pathways, regulatory genes, and epigenetics), each gene does not exists on its own, it correlates to other genes; hence, the notion of the random landscape has limited meaning for the evolution of life forms. Some of the genes do have correlations to others, e.g. the hierarchy of genes, or sets of genes exist all contributing to particular appendages, organelles, or epistatic control genes exist. As Kauffman (1995, p. 170) notes himself: the fitness contribution of one allele of one gene may depend in complex ways on the alleles of other genes. This is often referred to as epistatic coupling or epistatic interactions. Rugged landscapes are those landscapes in which the fitness of one gene depends on that part and upon K other parts among the N present in the landscape (Kauffman, 1993, p 40).

The NK-model offers further insight in the mechanisms of evolution and selection. Again consider an organism with N gene loci, each with two alleles, *1* and *0*. Let K stand for the average number of other loci which epistatically affect the fitness contribution of each locus. The fitness contribution of the allele at the ith locus depends on itself (whether it is *1* or *0*) and on the other alleles, *1* or *0*, at K other loci, hence upon $K+1$ alleles. The number of combinations of these alleles is just 2^{K+1}. Kauffman selects at random to each of the 2^{K+1} combinations a different fitness contribution from a uniform distribution between *0.0* and *1.0* (see Figure 7.5). The fitness of one entire genotype can be calculated as the average of all of the loci:

$$W = 1/N. \sum w_i \qquad\qquad (Eq.\ 3.1)$$

It becomes clear again that more than one local optimum exists.

Despite the importance of fitness landscapes for evolutionary processes, Kauffman (1995, p. 161) states that biologists hardly know what such fitness landscapes look like or how successful a search process is as a function of landscape structure. The landscapes may vary from smooth, single-peaked to

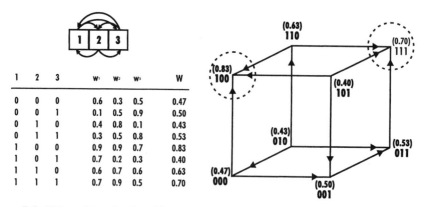

Figure 7.5: NK-model as developed by Kauffman (1993, p. 42). In the upper left corner it shows the assignment of $K=2$ epistatic inputs to each site. The assignment of the fitness values to each of the three genes 1, 2 and 3. These fitness values then assign fitness to each of the $2^3=8$ possible genotypes as the mean value of the fitness contributions of the three genes, as given in Equation 3.1. The figure depicts the fitness landscape on the three-dimensional Boolean cube corresponding to the fitness values of the eight genotypes. More than one local optimum exists.

rugged, multi-peaked landscapes. During evolution species search these landscapes using mutation, recombination, and selection, a process for which the NK model provides insight into particular phenomena accompanying the adaptive walk. From the study of Kauffman into evolutionary biological phenomena by deploying the NK model, a number of conclusions can be drawn:

- On smooth surfaces and rugged surfaces of the fitness landscape, the search process might fail to find the high peaks (Kauffman, 1995, p. 161).
- When on smooth surfaces the high peaks are found by a population, mutations might cause the complexity error catastrophe (Kauffman, 1993, p. 96; 1995, pp. 161, 183-184). Normally, when a species or population reaches a peak in the landscape, smooth or rugged, it remains stable at the peak. Through higher mutation rates, the population might increase by number and diversity (the interpretation of Kauffman's statement about complexity), causing a greater area of spread. This spread might extend so far from the peak itself that part of the population starts the search for new peaks. Kauffman labels this phenomena the complexity error catastrophe therewith indicating that the mutation rate exceeds the equilibrium force of remaining at the peak.
- On random landscapes, finding the global peak by searching uphill is useless, the entire space of possibilities needs to be searched (Kauffman, 1995, p. 168). At the same time, wherever the adaptive walk starts, only a fraction of the local peaks will be reached.
- When the population climbs higher to a local or global peak, it becomes exponential harder to find the direction uphill (Kauffman, 1995, pp. 178, 193-194). As complexity increases, interpreted as number and diversity, blind long jumps become a more wasteful strategy, even on the best of landscapes (Kauffman, 1993, p. 74).
- Fitness can increase more rapidly near peaks when mutation and selection are joined by recombination (Kauffman, 1995, p. 182). This covers both local and large-scale features of the fitness landscape.
- Complex artifacts or real organisms never find the global optimum of the fixed or adapting landscape (Kauffman, 1993, pp. 77-78).
- A breakdown of populations in patches enhances adaptability of species and populations, especially in changing landscapes (Kauffman, 1995, p. 263).
- Mass extinction opens the possibilities for finding new fitness peaks (Kauffman, 1993, p. 78).

As Kauffman (1993, p. 118) remarks, adaptive evolution is a search process - driven by mutation, recombination, and selection - on fixed or deforming fitness landscapes. Nevertheless, the dynamics of the environment are driven in his view by the shape and form of the landscape. The deformation of the landscape is explained qualitatively; hence the shifting dynamics of the landscape are less present in the models and mathematical approaches underpinning this theory. The search in these (semi-)static fitness landscapes is directed to finding fitness peaks, and to which mutation types (one-step, multi-step or long jumps) fit best to the shape of landscape.

7.2.4   Self-organisation and Selection

In addition to the models of the fitness landscape, Kauffman connects the concept of self-organisation as one of the driving forces for evolution (as a partial explanation for the origins of order and the existence of life) to the search processes. The concept of self-organisation of systems arose from early studies by Prigogine (1980). Kauffman (1993, pp. 567-568) connects the NK-model to the concept of self-organisation.

Self-organisation has drawn the attention of researchers in many fields of science (e.g. Mikulecky, 1995). The interests of all directs to the explanation of emergent behaviour, and the establishment of patterns that cannot be explained only by the actions of agents or reduced to the agents' behaviour (Stacey, 1996, p. 63). The explanations for the emergence of behaviour and patterns vary.

Let us look closer at Complex Adaptive Systems; they consist of components (or agents) that interact with each other according to sets of rules that require them to examine and to respond to each other's behaviour. Their responses aim to improve the behaviour of individual agents, but at the end it influences the behaviour of the system they comprise (Stacey, 1996, p. 10). An explanation of the behaviour of these systems states that simple rules might lead to complex behaviour. The famous and often quoted example concerns the flocking behaviour of birds (Stacey, 1996, p. 73). A simulation of Boids, an artificial creature, in a computer program shows the complex behavioural pattern of flocks that emerges when a Boid adjust its behaviour by only looking at its neighbour's position and speed. With no more than these rules, Boids learn to flock, fly around obstacles and regroup. Although this experiment points to simple rules for complex patterns, it does not explain the adaptation of organisms to their environment, the quest of the research.

A second explanation for complex behaviour arrives through the insight of Lorenz attractors (Kauffman, 1993, pp. 178-179; Morgan, 1996, p. 264; Stacey, 1996, pp. 58-60). When the control parameters in a deterministic non-linear feedback network are tuned up (e.g. when information or energy flows are increased), the behaviour of the network follows a potential bifurcating path in which it continues to display regular, stable patterns but they become increasingly complicated. A critical level of the control parameter moves the system in a state between stability and instability. All authors report sensitivity of these patterns to initial conditions, tiny deviations in initial conditions might result in vast differences in the subsequent behaviour of the system. An attractor does not per se mean bifurcation. Attractors only indicate points of stability with high or low dimensionality that form states to which the behaviour of a system evolves. Low dimensionality of attractors is mostly related to more orderly behaviour (Kauffman, 1993, p. 179).

The theories of Prigogine & Nicolis (1977) expand this matter by introducing dissipative structures, whereby away from the point of homeostasis a temporary and complex order is maintained. Only a part of the exchange with the environment, such as the energy flow, sustains the order, most of it dissipates to the environment. At the end, a new state arises in which the internal complexity has been increased, and new structures and behaviour do emerge. The theories of self-organisation most focus on state transitions and their meaning for the explanation of emergent behaviour and the rise of new structures.

Four particular states arise when the NK-model is analysed for the principles of self-organisation (referring to more extended models than in Figure 7.5) (Kauffman, 1993 pp. 191-203). Firstly, at $K=1$, the orderly regime appears, in which independent subsystems function as largely isolated islands with minimal interaction. At $K=2$, the network is at the edge of chaos, the ordered regime rules at maximum capacity but chaos is around the corner. At values ranging from $K=2$ to $K=5$ the transition to chaos appears although indications are that this transition happens already before $K=3$. From $K>5$, the network displays chaotic behaviour. All these four possibilities of K indicate that the behaviour of networks strongly varies according to the connectivity.

Kauffman (1993, p. 198; 1995, p. 91) claims that a position in the ordered regime near the state of chaos affords the best mixture of stability and flexibility. Such a state optimises the performance of the complexity of connected tasks and optimises evolvability of complex systems. Although, Kauffman's models merely generate fitness landscapes, they imply the similarity between structures within forms of life. Optimisation is bound by the developmental pathways embedded in the fitness landscape and the principles of self-organisation. Hence, the resemblance in existing life forms is no matter of chance but a result from previous mutations and developments.

7.3   GAME THEORIES AND ADAPTATIONS TO THE ENVIRONMENT

The paper of Seaborg (1999, pp. 5-7) sets the stage for expanding the view on the landscape. He introduces sequential evolution as main source for the appearance of (macro)mutations that occupy spaces in the landscape which particular species did not occupy before. His reasoning find its base in the presence of feedback loops in organisms that operate on negative feedback. When negative feedback is maintained, the species and organisms are experiencing stasis, while positive feedback might create enough momentum for species to enter a zone of punctuated evolution. The mechanism of sequential evolution consists of the following steps (like the evolutionary mechanisms of Figure 6.1):

- A macromutation of a gradual accumulation of gradual changes occurs which allows a species to enter a new adaptive zone, setting the stage for adaptive radiation. These adaptations may have large phenotypic effects, may be rapid and abrupt.
- This adaptation spreads throughout the population because of the superior fitness it confers on its bearers.
- This results in an adaptive advantage among those members of the population who have a behaviour that best allows the use of the new morphology. Directional selection for this new behaviour and its intensification follows.
- The behaviour selected for increases in frequency in the population.
- This may result in the exploitation of a new habitat. This step does not always occur and it is not a necessary condition for the process.
- The new adaptation results in directional selection for the morphology to become more extreme.
- The morphology becomes more extreme among individuals in the population.
- A period of post-adaptive adjustments follows in which the genetic background adjusts to the new adaptive mutation.
- The directional selection fuelled by the positive feedback between morphology and behaviour continues with the resulting intensification of both until equilibrium is reached such that the benefits of increasing them equal the efforts.
- The above changes may result in the species entering a new adaptive zone where it is free from interspecific competition. If this is the case, the result could be adaptive radiation, with concomitant speciation. If not, this step does not occur.

The idea of sequential evolution connects to the Evolutionary Stable Strategies, topic of the next subsection, although these theories have not met yet in literature on evolutionary biology. As Dorak (2002) mentions unstable environments drive and induce evolution. These instabilities might present vacant niches to species that can be occupied: (a) the species may enter relatively uninhibited territory; (b) it may survive a catastrophe that has eliminated other species in related niches; (c) it may achieve a breakthrough in the slow process of improvement that opens up previously nonexistent niches (Wright, 1982, p. 16).

7.3.1 Evolutionary Stable Strategies

In addition to the application of genetic algorithms, which assume a static landscape, game theories have been deployed for explaining and predicting evolutionary phenomena in more dynamic situations. Von Neumann & Morgenstern (1944) developed originally game theories for the economic, social, and organisational field. These game theories envisaged the mathematics to deal with situations of uncertainty, and the development of contingencies during time. Maynard Smith & Price (1973) transferred these thought to the domain of biology (for an explanation of basics in game theory, see Appendix E). In the evolutionary game, players inherit their strategies (Brown & Vincent, 1987, p. 143). This is unlike the classical game theory, where players choose their strategies. Hence, the focus is on pay-offs associated with a strategy rather than pay-offs to an individual. This strategy orientation is more appropriate because strategies, rather than individuals, persist through time. Within this research field, the term Evolutionary Stable Strategy plays a central role. Maynard Smith & Price (1973, p. 15) conceptualised an Evolutionary Stable Strategy as a strategy such that, if most members of a population adopt it, there is no mutant strategy that would give higher reproduction fitness. Many have searched for strategies to define this strategy or to find algorithms for this optimal strategy. In course of time, this concept and the simulation by matrix games has elevated from simple 2-person matrix games to continuous, complex games (Brown & Vincent, 1987, pp. 140-141).

From a simple 2-person matrix game Maynard Smith & Price (1973, pp. 17-18) draw already conclusions with regard to the stability of the population in relation to their strategy. In this case, they examine the behaviour of male animals during the contest preceding mating. These simulations lead to the conclusion that an evolutionary stable population is either genetically polymorphic or that its consists of individuals whose behaviour differs from contest to contest. Therefore, no pure stable strategy exists, and no behaviourally uniform population remains stable. This means that as long as variation exists, selection acts on the variances present in a population, residing in its individuals, and always instability gives ground for the emergence of distinct phenotypes (Maynard Smith & Price, 1973, p. 15):

> *Group selection, traditionally seen as a consequence of natural selection, cannot account for the complex anatomical and behavioural adaptations found in so many species but there must be individual selection for these.*

The matrix game theory has been applied to continuous games for populations (Hines, 1980, p. 602) in which it shows that although the mean strategy of a complex population must be an Evolutionary Stable Strategy, a complex population means mostly a polymorphic population. But it does not imply necessarily that the evolution of the population changes the mean (it might change the distribution). Also, the consideration how strategies are distributed among entities in the population strongly affects outcomes. Hines (1980, p. 608) concludes that an Evolutionary Stable Strategy does not equal to a competitive strategy that protects the population from changing in composition. The expected population strategy can possess characteristics of stability. The population composition is affected by increased diversity in strategy resulting from the selective advantage enjoyed in periods of non-equilibrium by users of strategies close or equal to the Evolutionary Stable Strategy. Smaller population sizes are sensitive to disturbances caused by invaders with sufficiently different strategies. Brown & Vincent (1987, pp. 150-152) build further on this framework, and confirm the findings of Hines that mixed strategies matrix games are only neutrally stable.

Zeeman (1980) considers polymorphic populations in which each individual plays a pure strategy. The payoff is related to reproductive success. Brown & Vincent (1987, pp. 152-153) reformulate the mathematical models to conclude that in polymorphic populations and continuous games factually not only frequency-dependent selection exists but also density-dependent selection. In that case the mutant strategies that can invade also relate to the population size. Therefore, changes in population size are not merely ecological processes but they constitute evolutionary change.

7.3.2 Adaptive Dynamics

The models of the Evolutionary Stable Strategies have evolved to models that do not take fitness as a constant but as a variable. The application of these so-called Adaptive Dynamics yields additional insight into the evolution and co-evolution of species and populations (Geritz et al., 1997, Meszéna et al., 2001), see Appendix E. Geritz et al. (1997, p. 2025) claim that a Pairwise Invasibility Plot allows convenient display of how mutants spread in a given population. It indicates the effect of a mutant with strategy y in an equilibrium population with x strategists. The different evolutionary scenarios for populations depend on four properties of stability that can be depicted in Pairwise Invasibility Plots:

a) Evolutionary stability. A singular strategy is evolutionary stable if no initially rare mutant can invade (Meszéna et al., 2001, p. 202, Geritz et al., 1997, p. 2025). Other strategies than the optimal singular strategy have less changes for survival on the long run.

b) Convergence stability. A singular strategy is convergence stable if a population of nearby phenotypes can be invaded by mutants that are even closer to x^* (the singular stable strategy present in a population). The singular strategy moves towards an asymptotically stable fixed point of the canonical adaptive dynamics, through a sequence of small steps that constitute a stochastic evolutionary path (Meszéna et al., 2001, pp. 201-202).

c) Invading potential. A singular strategy can spread in other populations when it itself is initially rare. A singular strategy that is evolutionary stable and convergence stable may nevertheless be incapable of invading other populations if initially rare itself (Geritz, 1997, p. 2025). Meszéna et al. (2001, p. 202) remark that this differs from convergence stability. Such a singular strategy can be reached only asymptotically through a series of ever-decreasing evolutionary steps.

d) Dimorphism stability (Geritz, 1997, pp. 2025-2026). Two strategies x and y can mutually invade, and give rise to a dimorphic population. This process of divergence of strategies is evolutionary branching and the singular strategy in the Pairwise Invasibility Plot is a branching point. The dimensionality of the environment sets an upper limit to the number of different types that can coexist, and hence to the maximum diversity that can be reached by branching of the evolutionary tree. The picture of evolution that arises is that of a random walk in a state space of a dimension given by the number of the different strategies present. The direction of the steps is given by the local fitness gradient. At each branching event the dimension of the state space increases.

These four different kinds of stability indicate different modes for a singular strategy. To determine the position of a singular strategy and to evaluate the evolutionary potential, assessment of all these four different kinds of stability should take place. Evolutionary change occurs when the requirements for the four properties of evolutionary stability are not met.

The application of these models exceeds the thoughts of the NK-models as proposed by Kauffman (1993, pp. 41-43). In the NK-model, the type with the highest fitness peak will in the long run out-compete all others since the separate fitness peaks possess unequal heights (Geritz et al., 1997, p. 2027). Although Kauffman explains coexistence and branching, he deploys additional qualitative descriptions to arrive at conclusions towards the diversity of life. During his discussion of the adaptive walks two main criteria appeared: sustained fitness and evolvability, which have a connection to the four properties of stability of Adaptive Dynamics. The first two stability requirements, evolutionary stability and convergence stability, have strong parallels with sustained fitness. Evolvability resembles invading potential and dimorphism stability. The models of Adaptive Dynamics effectively explain the underlying mechanisms of evolution but hardly connect to the genotype as is the case with the NK-model of Kauffman.

For the research, the mechanisms linked to Adaptive Dynamics do not only explain evolutionary processes, they also allow predictions about the evolutionary direction. This theory has yielded explanatory models for the punctuated equilibrium, through the criteria for the invading potential and the dimorphism stability; once these criteria are not met speciation will occur. However, the stability requirements or rather the instability requirements indicate the pathways of evolutionary development. At moments of instability, described by the four properties of Adaptive Dynamics and the aggregate of Kauffman focusing on two criteria, organisms either evolve or speciate. Whether species experience periods of turmoil depends on the mutation rates of populations, and speed of branching that might occur.

Several strategies exist in a population. The question remains: do these strategies retain a species naar an optimum or does the population evolve? To ascertain stability, deviations among strategies should be maintained and selection should favour a singular strategy (i.e. evolutionary stability). The models of Adaptive Dynamics explain bifurcation processes within populations, and describe the basic processes of the punctuated equilibrium.

7.3.3 Environment in Models of the Punctuated Equilibrium

But how exactly the environment interacts during the extinction and rise of species, those who adhere to the punctuated equilibrium hold different views (the knowledge of game theories puts these thoughts in a different perspective). Prothero (1992) claims that species demonstrate stability in spite of well-documented environmental change, even though when these changes might have dramatic effects on the existence of a species. Rather than adapt to the new environments, species migrate back and forth in response to them, preserving their own characteristics. His own research shows that with high probability species remained unchanged through an interval or became extinct with new species replacing them; in any case none showed the panselectionist prediction of gradually evolving to track their changing environment. Teed (2001) remarks

> ... that during the course of a species existence it will be forced to adapt to a new or changed habitat every few thousands years undoing the centuries of adaptation to the old environment. Simply migrating south to find an environment similar to the old one is unlikely to work in most cases...

Both views indicate that species adapt to changes in their environment or remain stable with the risk of extinction. For companies that results in the notion: change or maybe die. Adapting to the environment becomes an essential prerequisite for survival in changing environments.

The environment plays also a crucial role in the chances of survival of hybrids. Essential to the theory of the punctuated equilibrium as posted by Eldredge & Gould, is that mutations particularly occur in small populations (Mokyr, 1990, p. 354). Teed (2001) stresses that selection might happen in relaxed environments during the initial periods in which mutants survive and reproduce, especially, through hybrid offspring. These hybrid offspring and backcrosses are genetically and phenotypically variable, and may have the opportunity to speciate, certainly in abundant periods. Transferring these thoughts to companies, should they merge, form alliances, etc. in periods of abundance rather then out of need in famine periods? If so, the acquisitions, mergers, and alliances aiming at creating synergy, properties not yet existing in each of the parent organisation, should occur in times of abundance.

Species in overlapping habitats should emphasise differences (Teed, 2001). Through exaggeration distinction becomes possible and the opportunity arises for further development of a species. If speciation results in blurry species these must isolate themselves to survive.

Last but not least, the selection of species is not a source of innovation but the elimination of new mutations and gene combinations (Gould, 1980). Three mechanisms for punctuated change exist for driving evolutionary change (Seaborg, pp. 20-21):

- macromutations;
- directional selection driven by the external environment;
- directional selection driven primarily by the organisms. This type fits very well the concept of dynamic landscapes.

Disruptive selection leading, in one or two opposing directions, will ultimately result in species selection making it a main cause for the punctuated equilibrium. This disruptive selection thrives on sequential evolution through (positive) evolutionary feedback. In terms of the environment, it relies on the presence of a dynamic landscape.

Maynard Smith (1989, p. 249) refers to Mayr who demonstrated that stability becomes less likely as the number of species, and the number of interaction per species, increases, based on Lotka-Volterra dynamics (i.e. a common model for describing interrelations between species, for example the relation between the size of predator in relation to the dynamics of the prey population) with randomly chosen parameters. Complexity of interaction itself is not sufficient to describe stability.

Game theories have found their way in explaining evolutionary process, yet literature have linked them weakly to explain the phenomenon of the punctuated equilibrium, a strand of research which needs further exploration. As seen in the previous subsection, game theories detail the mechanisms of adaptive radiation.

7.3.4   Extinction driving Speciation

Lemmon (2002) draws attention to the fact that adaptive radiation tends to follow mass extinction. Jablonski (2000, p. 27) mentions the importance of habitat tracking for stabilising selection. Casagrandi & Gatto (2002) show through the deployment of Markov models for metapopulations that extinction of species links to habitat destruction and environmental catastrophes. Metapopulations consider local populations described by Markov chains (a mathematical model for describing successive events) connected by dispersal, which resembles the idea of allopatric speciation without the effects of genetic drift. In these models a patch hosts an integer number of individuals (see Figure 7.6). Environmental catastrophes increase the risk of extinction for both frequent dispersers and infrequent dispersers, while the random loss of patches has a much larger influence on frequent dispersers (the rate of dispersal exceeds the rate of demographic increase). The influence of catastrophes can be counterbalanced by active dispersal. Local erosion of habitat fragments has a larger influence on infrequent than on frequent dispersers.

According to Casagrandi & Gatto (2002, pp. 135-136), the effects of random habitat loss are more complex than by previous models, such as Lande's one for establishing threshold values. At very low dispersal rates, demographic stochasticity brings the population to extinction. At higher, but still low dispersal rates, the rescue effect due to immigration allows to counterbalance local extinction. At higher dispersal rates, the negative effect of dispersing organisms ending up in unsuitable habitat starts showing up: the risk is now higher for organisms that disperse too much. At low dispersal rates, habitat erosion is more

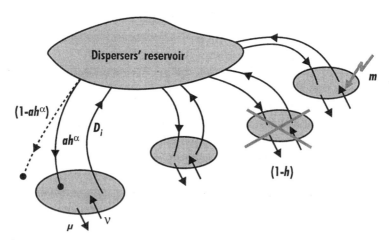

Figure 7.6: Diagram of the metapopulation model by Casagrandi & Gatto (2002, p. 129). The model consists of an infinite network of equal patches subject to disturbance. D_i is the rate of dispersal from the patches. A fraction $(1-h)$ of the patches is permanently destroyed because of habitat loss while some local populations can be wiped out by environmental disasters (which occur at rate m). The propagule rain from a common reservoir of dispersers can rescue from extinction any local population via colonisation, whose success depends on the colonising probability a, the fraction h of undestroyed patches, and the ability to search for suitable patches.

harmful than random loss of entire patches, at high dispersal rates it is the converse. Frequent dispersers are hit more by random loss of entire patches than by habitat erosion. Species that are able to recognize suitable patches have better chances of surviving when the proportion of destroyed habitat is large.

Casagrandi & Gatto (2002, p. 137) have tested their models for environmental catastrophes. They conclude that habitat loss drives frequently dispersing species to extinction (can be counterbalanced by non-random search for suitable patches). Frequent and infrequent dispersers are equally endangered by environmental catastrophes.

7.4   AUTOPOIESIS

Does the influence of the environment dominate? To answer that question, Morgan (1997, pp. 253-258, 413-414) points to another theory offered by Maturana & Varela (1980) to explain evolutionary processes: autopoiesis, the ability to self-create or self-renew through a closed system of relations. In this view, living systems engage in circular patterns of interaction whereby change in one element of the system is coupled with changes elsewhere, setting up continuous patterns of interaction that are always self-referential. A system enters only interactions that are specified by its organisation. A system's interaction with its *environment* is a reflection and part of its own organisation. An autopoietic system interacts with its environment in a way that facilitates its own self-production; its environment is really a part of itself.

During the study of living systems, Maturana & Varela (1980) have observed when looking at biological entities, in particular one-cell organisms, fundamental notions on biological systems:

- individual systems are characterised by their autonomy. Even when they are part of organisms or populations and when they undergo environmental influences, the individual entities remain internally closed and self-defined entities;
- living systems consist of components with different properties. These components, and their interaction with adjacent elements, determine the total behaviour of living systems;
- all explanations and descriptions of these living systems are generated by observers external to the system. Such an observer will denote the entities and the environment in which they exist. Components within the entity do not possess this capability of observation and will only react to behaviour of other components existent within the entity;
- Only an observer can describe the objectives and functions of components present in the entity; the living system itself is incapable of to make these

observations. Only the interactions of component with adjacent internal components can be observed.

The development of autopoiesis is a reaction to the cybernetic movements within the General Systems Theory and aims at explaining the unique features of biological systems and entities. Three principles dominate the thoughts of autopoiesis.

7.4.1 Principles of Autopoiesis

At the heart of the theory of autopoiesis lays the possibility for self-reproduction. This concept of self-reproduction is also found in the attempts of Kauffman to explain the origin of life when he deploys the concept of autocatalytic sets (Kauffman, 1993, pp. 298-341). The concept rests on the combinatorial consequences of polymer chemistry. As the maximum length in a system increases, the number of reactions by which polymers can interconvert rises faster than the number of polymers present. Then, a sufficiently complex set of polymers has very many potential reactions leading to the synthesis of any of these polymers. As a consequence, for many possible distributions of catalytic capacity for those reactions among the same set of polymers, autocatalytic sets will emerge, such as peptides stepping up to DNA. The hypothesis that life is a collective emergent property of complex polymer systems seems likely to give an answer to the critical question why free-living systems exhibit a minimal complexity. The self-reproduction principle of autopoiesis tells that the structure[41] of all components and processes together produce the same components and processes to ensure the continuity of the living system (Maturena & Varela, 1980). This principle creates an autonomous, self-producing entity.

Autopoietic systems are structurally closed which does not imply that no interaction takes place with the environment. For example, living entities feed themselves through input (food) taken from the environment. These inputs do not account for changes as such in the living entity, and generally support the continuity of the system. However, within the definitions of autopoiesis, perturbations lead to disruptions within the system. The environment has little grip on the reactions by the system and the consequences for the structure and composition, and vice versa. The connection to the environment is called the structural coupling. Structural coupling between living systems eases the realisation of autopoiesis. If the homeostasis created by the organisational closure of the systems can no longer be maintained, the disintegration of systems occurs

---

[41] Maturena & Varela (1980) denote structure as organisation (van der Vaart, 2002, p. 6). For the sake of this research the wording has been changed to avoid confusion and maintain similar meaning throughout the entire text of this book.

which leads van der Vaart (2002, p. 5) to the statement: *Autopoiesis is all or nothing!*

Autopoietic systems (see Figure 7.7) are defined as a composed unit with a network of components that

- completes through interactions repeatedly the production process of components by which the very self-production sustains;
- realises a unit for self-production in a space in which the system exists by creating and specifying boundaries in which only components are allowed that participate in the realisation of the production process.

7.4.2   Interaction with Environment

The structural determinism of autopoietic systems and the related principle of structurally closed entities constitute the most important principles for evolutionary processes. Structural determinism tells that all changes are embedded within the organisation and structure of the entity. Each change of a composed unit is a change of the structure moulded by the properties of the components of the structure. A true change will occur as a reaction to the internal dynamics of the system or the interaction with the environment, and even then the internal relations of components shape the change rather than the environment dictates the internal adaptations.

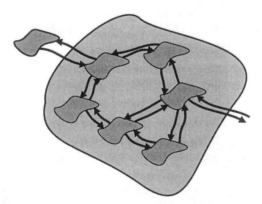

Figure 7.7: Representation of an autopoietic system. The type of system has relations with its environment, as an open system, with which it interacts as a steady-state. The system is structurally closed and perturbations that would require modifications of the internal structure do not directly affect the components, structure and composition. The modification of the system is driven by its internal structure as a reaction to perturbations.

This view does not tell that these systems are isolated. They interact through a circular pattern of interaction which has no end or beginning since it is a closed loop of interaction. The theory of autopoiesis accepts that systems can be recognised as having environments but insists that relations with any environment are internally determined. The boundary of the system consists of components generated by the interactions of internal components of the system with the environment. The boundary is maintained by relations and interaction with adjacent components in the boundary. Without these components, the autopoietic system does not sustain self-referential processes for retaining its autonomy and steady-state.

The structural coupling governs by which interactions a component of living system is influenced. When interactions initiate changes in the structure and composition, the structure is called plastic. Through repeated interaction and initiations, selection of subsequent structures happens by the environment. The selection is driven by the environment and by the plasticity of the structure by its own components and internal interactions. The environment does not determine the internal adaptations! Therefore, autopoietic systems are interactively open and structurally closed (van der Vaart, 2002, p. 11).

One of the foremost reasons for the research into autopoiesis stems from the quest for the nature of perception and cognition. Perception and cognition derive from the nerve system realised by the autopoiesis of the organism. To exist, continuously interactions should be repeated since the structural coupling exists; in this sense cognition represents gathering knowledge about all effective interaction for sustainability. Learning as a process of cognition originates in the properties of self-reference of the system. When learning exceeds the level of direct interaction and moves towards orientation in the common domain of two

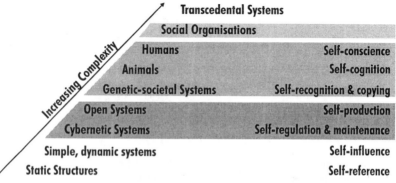

Figure 7.8: Connection of the theory of autopoiesis to the systems hierarchy of Boulding according to Mingers (1995). The interaction with the environment changes because of the model of reference to the environment, which induces internal processes at the higher levels of the systems hierarchy.

autopoietic systems, communication is established. When descriptions lead to being observer of its own behaviour, self-conscience arises. The composition of a system related to an external point of reference defines the identity of an autopoietic system (van der Vaart, 2002, pp. 7, 24-25). The identity is strongly related to the composition of the entity, changes in the composition lead to a changed identity; through self-reference autopoietic systems seek to maintain their identity unless perturbations provoke adaptations. These notions leads Mingers (1995) to connect the theory of autopoiesis to the systems hierarchy of Boulding (see Figure 7.8).

7.5 SELECTION AND LANDSCAPE FITNESS FOR THE DOMAIN OF ORGANISATIONS

Before converting the evolutionary models to organisations, this section offers a synopsis of the main models of the interaction between environment and species. Without doubt, the driving force of evolution is selection. The insight of the mechanisms of selection have evolved from Darwinian insight, natural selection and accumulation of gradual changes, to complex mathematical models describing the interaction between genotype and selection through fitness tests, e.g. the adaptive walks of Kauffman and Adaptive Dynamics. Species show evolution by successive changes and selection acts on it (genetic drift). The capability of species to disperse and invade offers the opportunity that they expand their base for existence, and that they develop variations that fit specific environments (allopatric speciation). Moderate dispersal into new habitats if exerted intentionally ensures the continuation of species even if the environments appear to be instable. Splitting of lineages might occur in accordance with the models of Adaptive Dynamics. These models root in the theories of the Evolutionary Stable Strategies and introduce four properties of stability that determine the evolution of species based on the fitness functions; the resulting simulation of bifurcation processes explains the phenomena of allopatric speciation and sympatric speciation. Extinction as the ultimate fate of variants and species also clears the way for new species to develop. All together four different models of evolution might occur in any population: genetic drift, speciation (allopatric, sympatric), dispersal, and extinction.

The interaction of species and the environment is mainly described by three main mathematical models, i.e. the NK-model, Adaptive Dynamics, and dispersal models. The NK-model assumes that fitness landscapes remain constant in a certain extent in contrast to the models of Adaptive Dynamics that take the dynamics of evolution into account. Dispersal and invading potential play an important role in the interaction. The capability to evolve is also found in the criterion for evolvability, and determines mostly the pathways organisms will follow during evolution. Sustained fitness finds it way in the capability of organisms and species to optimise their local fitness and sustainability. The two subcriteria are: local evolutionary stability and convergence stability. Species find themselves in local evolutionary stability if no other mutant can maintain itself within this population on the long term. Convergence stability indicates whether a species reaches an optimum after a number of steps. The assessment of the two main criteria, sustained fitness and evolvability, provides insight into the direction the development of species takes. When will optimisation take the lead? When will new bifurcation resulting in new subspecies occur? This raises the question whether it becomes possible to use these criteria in the domain of organisations.

7.5.1 Evolutionary Mechanisms and Selection for Organisations

The evolutionary mechanisms do connect to the evolution of organisations in two ways (see Figure 7.9). The first constitutes the alternation of mutation and selection, called the harmonica model by van den Bergh (2003). Some authors refer to the cycle of variation, retention, and selection (as propagated by Campbell [1969]). Organisational ecology (Section 3.2) has also aimed at revealing the evolutionary mechanisms of mutation and selection. However, they seem to focus

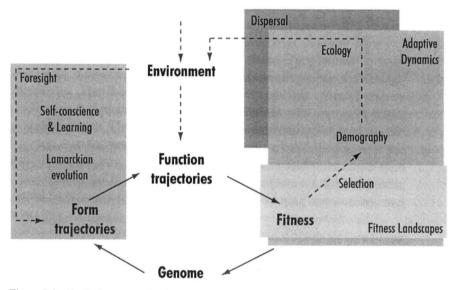

Figure 7.9: Evolutionary mechanisms related to main topics of selection. On the left the figure shows the reach of Lamarckian evolution. The topics on the right are strongly interrelated. The fitness landscapes as described by Kauffman offer limited insight into the evolutionary mechanisms: they are static. Adaptive Dynamics offers an explanation for dynamic changes but addresses only partially the dynamics of dispersal. Further progress will depend on the integration of all theories into a whole approach.

on parts of the two cycles present in Figure 7.9. The second one is through learning. Connecting it to the capabilities of autopoietic systems, de Geus points to learning as characteristic for organisations (similar to learning by organisms). Learning becomes possible through self-cognition as typical for the higher levels of the systems hierarchy of Boulding. Although, the evolutionary mechanisms differ in detail due to specific characteristics of organisations, the same selectional process applies to organisations.

The search for fitness determines the developmental pathways and the adaptive walks for both organisms and organisations. Due to the properties of autopoietic systems, despite the absence of a direct connection to self-reproduction, organisations will mutate determined by the internal structure and components of the organisation. Also the search for fitness determines the paths of development, the connectivity K in the NK-model of Kauffman.

The main differences between organisations and organisms remain the capability for foresight and the self-induced capability for mutations. Mutations are induced by the internal structure more than the enforced perturbations of the environment, which cause imbalance and threaten the homeostatic equilibrium, the maintenance of the steady-state. The paradox is that organisations can purposely mutate, Lamarckian evolution, while chance operates, and at the same time, mutations are limited by the internal structure.

7.5.2 Evolution of Organisations and Selection

Do companies during their development follow know evolutionary paths as we know now from evolutionary biology? What is clear that companies undergo the forces of selection, expressed in phylogeny, ontogeny, and developmental pathways. Industrial companies as a cluster (population) in a product-market combination experience the same processes of mutation and selection. Also, at the level of the individual company these processes act. In fact, the evolutionary processes resemble those of organisms but show a greater diversity since product-market combinations either know a very few competitors (sometimes large companies) or many dispersed, different companies for fragmented markets. Companies demonstrate a large diversity in life-cycle and life-time. Despite these differences, it seems impossible that companies emerge out of nothing. In their own evolution they build on existent capabilities and features, and even newly founded companies expand on the base of already existing skills and knowledge.

In analogy to the theories of evolutionary biology, the four properties of stability for the interaction with the environment exist to describe the evolution of companies (derived from the models of Adaptive Dynamics). To describe the interaction with the environment assessment of these properties should take place using the developments in the environment, the evaluation of fitness, and the developmental pathways of capabilities. Evolutionary stability indicates a period of stasis for the organisation. During such a period of time, optimisation of traits becomes the foremost principle for managing the development of companies. Dispersal might also lead to further stability, expanding the base of product-market combinations. The adequate deployment of principles of dispersal might even reduce the sensitivity of a company or companies to instable environments. Bifurcation might appear as a result of dispersal (founder effect) or within a particular habitat.

The dynamics of the environment indicate that the relative importance of selection criteria changes: either converge to another strategy or invade or bifurcate. The NK-model and the theories about Evolutionary Stable Strategies provide insight into how these processes affect organisations seen as organisms. Therefore, these models will assist the quest into the processes and structures for adaptation to develop mechanisms and criteria for evolution; given that the understanding of organisational development through the analogy with evolutionary biology generates more profound insight. Romme & van Witteloostuijn (1997, p. 65, 69) doubt that corresponding mathematical models of complexity, chaos (and related self-organisation) have found their way in organisational models, basing their observations on the work of Gleick (1988), Prigogine (1980), and Stacey (1993). Nieuwstad (1997) has shown the importance of the behaviour of Complex Adaptive Systems for the understanding of organisational dynamics; at the same time, the exact application to the organisational domain has a limited meaning, and remains global of nature. The application seems limited to econometry. However, the recent addition of the game theories and the true implications of mathematical models tell more about how organisations evolve in a dynamic fitness landscape.

Such evolution in a fitness landscape gives rise to describe the interaction of the development of organisations. From the evolutionary biological theories six notions emerge for the interaction between organisation and environment:

- Again, the phenotype is input to the selection process, no matter the difficulty of defining it in an organisational context. As shown in Chapter 2, traits that are relevant to the environment will be selected by the environment, thereto stressing the importance of variety. The interaction models show that individual development of traits is subject to selection, and that individual development of traits not necessarily means that such a mutation fixes.
- Organisms do not have any foresight; organisations might deploy the capability to shape their own structures and processes therewith anticipating on the future (the notion of Lamarckian evolution).
- The strategy of optimisation holds only true when organisations find themselves near fitness peaks. During optimisation the effect of next steps

decreases quickly as well as the possibilities for optimisation (hill climbing reduces the effect of the next step by half and the number of possible steps too). Under certain conditions the complexity error catastrophe might occur moving part of a population into the search for a nearby fitness peak.

- The strategy of evolvability has most effects when organisations reach behind the critical Hamming distance. New fitness peaks are only found if an organisation manages to reach the neighbourhood of another fitness peak. The higher the correlation between traits, the bigger the distance to travel, which increases the chances of not finding new peaks.
- During the transition from order to chaos, the chances for both sustained fitness and evolvability rank highest. However, this transition phase requires the existence of a dissipative structure implying intense interaction with the environment.
- The mathematical models based on the NK-model from Kauffman and on game theories, especially Adaptive Dynamics, reflect the evolution of organisations and the interaction with the environment.

We might conclude that the evolutionary biological models yield understanding of the development of organisations in relation to their environment. It becomes possible to understand which processes and structures support adaptation to the dynamics of the environment.

7.5.3   Autopoiesis and Organisations

Will this insight about the interaction between entity and environment lead to an universal understanding of the way organisations relate to their environment, and in how far will organisations be able to manage this relationship? According to Morgan (1997, pp. 256-258) the theory of autopoiesis has strong implications for the understanding of organisations. First, a creative interpretation of this theory envisions that organisms are always trying to achieve a form of self-referential closure in relation to their environments, enacting their environments as extensions of their own identity. Secondly, problems that organisations experience in the interaction with the environment are intimately connected to the kind of identity they are trying to maintain. Thirdly, explanations of the evolution, change, and development of organisations must give primary attention to the factors that shape the patterns embracing both organisation and environment in the broadest sense. The figures and pictures that an organisation produces on market trends, competitive position, sales forecasts, raw material availability, and so forth are in fact projections of the organisations's own sense of identity, interests, and concerns. They reflect its understanding of itself. It is through this process of self-reference that organisational members can intervene their own functioning, and thus participate in creating and maintaining their own identity.

Because the concept of self-production does not reside as such in organisations, the principle of autopoiesis applies partially to the domain of organisations. In this respect, one would denote organisations as allopietic systems. Van der Vaart (2002, p. 26) remarks that the other two principles of autopoiesis dominate the view on organisations: autonomy and structurally closed. He adds that Biggiero (2001) comments that the boundaries of organisations are more fuzzy than those of biological entities. Other approaches to transfer the theory of autopoiesis to the domain of organisations lack clarity (Morgan, 1997; Luhmann, 1986). Maturana (1981) and Varela (1981) have always objected against the application of their theory to social systems. However, it seems when organisations are considered as allopietic systems (i.e. systems without self-reproduction, avoiding the definition of the organisational genome), the principles of autonomy and self-reference apply; these principles have meaning to the understanding of the interaction between organisation and environment.

Autopoiesis means also that *fitness-as-is* and *fitness-as-seen* differ, even to the effect that similar organisations enacting with the same environment might have different views on that very same environment (self-reference). This notion particularly requires considering that organisations might be adapted to the environment by self-induced signals rather than that the environment directly affects the internal structure. This will show that organisations possess strong inhibitions within their structure to adapt to their environment. Only sufficient self-reflection will induce adaptations meaningful to the dynamics of the environment.

Self-reflection invokes learning processes within organisations through the interaction between entity and environment, as de Geus (1999, pp. 111-115) explains. Hence, foresight is at reach and connected to the capability for self-reflection empowered by senses that interpret the environment. From another point of view, foresight is necessary as well. It has been demonstrated that recombination acts as a powerful tool for evolutionary processes for organisms, largely depending on stochastics for finding fitness peaks. We can hardly imagine that recombination acts as a driver for evolution of organisations, what might replace this process of recombination? Subsection 6.5.1. has highlighted that genetic mutation (of memes or replicators) and non-genetic mutation equal the process of the generation of variation through recombination. Foresight constitutes a complementary mechanism for organisations as a capability to reach out for fitness peaks in the landscape wherein organisations do operate; that the selection of beneficial mutations will not only depend on chance might as a side-effect increasse the speed of change in comparison to biological evolution. Organisations might deploy foresight by the learning processes present within the structure, and as replacement for self-production and recombination.

The theory of autopoiesis adds three notions to the ones mentioned in Subsection 7.5.2 about the interaction between an organisation and the environment:

- Through being structurally closed, organisations evolve from their current processes, structures, and compositions to new processes, structures, and compositions. The changes occur from within as a reaction to changes in the environment or perturbations. The composition and structure define these changes, the environment acts as catalyst to induce internal reactions.
- The principle of self-reference means that organisations will look from within at the environment. Acting and learning reside in the capability of organisations for observing the environment, and their capability to define changes in their composition and structure. Self-reflection seen as the capability to take on the role of observer to one's own behaviour stimulates the organisation to discover relationships within itself and to the environment (also mentioned by Romme & van Witteloostuijn [1997, p. 67]). Such self-reflection might support the creation of adaptations when the environment changes.
- Boundaries in organisations are to be considered fuzzier than those of organisms. Living organisms define and maintain a boundary separating it from other autopoietic systems and the environment. At the boundary they exert homeostasis. Organisations have boundaries, too, as a consequence of choices made by the organisation. The organisation might decide to shift these boundaries; nevertheless organisations tend to maintain their boundaries as well, including striving for homeostatic integrity.

7.6   SUMMARY

The role of selection has a profound effect on the existence of species and the diversity of life. Advancement in the past decade has made it possible to describe evolution better, mostly supported by mathematical models; these mathematical models should be viewed as complementary rather than synthesised theories. The models focus on the role of selection. Although species might display a higher variety over time while maintaining a mean, mutants exist by the grace of the environment. The environment might even favour these variants rather than the mean of a population. The descriptions of traditional evolutionary biology relied strongly on the models of allopatric speciation and sympatric speciation. Evolutionary biology has moved from these qualitative explanatory models to quantitative mathematical models to create insight in phenomena underlying the evolution of life forms. Especially, the insight generated by the NK-model and the concept of Adaptive Dynamics contribute to understanding the evolution of species into new mutants and the branching of species. Dispersal contributes to the processes of evolution by its possibilities for finding new habitats when existing ones disappear or deteriorate.

In particular, the requirements of sustained fitness and evolvability require the attention for the research into adaptations by industrial organisations to the dynamics of the environment. The assessment of these criteria leads to the direction of adaptive walks. If all four subcriteria (evolutionary stability, convergence stability, invading potential, dimorphism stability), derived from Evolutionary Stable Strategies, indicate instability then the future of an organisation becomes very unclear; the landscape has turned into an extreme random fitness landscape where every step to adapt may not even produce better fitness. However, the actual values of the four subcriteria might also point to evolution. The evolution might be dispersal into new habitats and finding new resources, bifurcation which increases the dimension of the landscape and gradual change towards a new point of optimisation. It is even possible that the criteria tell that an organisation finds itself at a local point of stability, an evolutionary trap. Although clear in their meaning, further works needs to be done to expand these models to the domain of organisations and such efforts should result in the development of a Framework for Dynamic Adaptation.

The principles of allopietic systems indicate that self-reference dominates the adaptations by organisations to the dynamics of the environment. In fact, autonomy and the organisational closure of organisations might inhibit effective adaptations unless the system possesses adequate capabilities for self-reflection.

8 REFERENCE MODEL AND HYPOTHESES FOR THE EVOLUTION OF ORGANISATIONS

If the study aims to elevate the models and theories describing the evolution of organisations through biological models, then the first thing that comes to mind is the comparison of the morphology of a specimen in biology and an individual organisation. The previous chapters have already shown that a comparison might be difficult for internal structures (with the danger that it will end up being more a metaphor than an analogy). At the level of species, the comparison might hold better: species or subspecies compare to industrial branches or product-market combinations. The opportunity for organisations to implement self-defined mutations over periods of time creates the possibility that the variants that organisms create through offspring are present in the individual life-cycle of organisations. Ontology for organisations, by detecting (tiny) differences in the individual development among different organisations, will encounter difficulties because of the small sample sizes in some branches and the often unique character of organisations. Hence, organisations compare to both specimen and to (sub)species in their evolutionary processes although their structures differ and a similar process to recombination does not exist.

By shifting the emphasis on laws that govern the development of organisations and their evolutionary processes, the need arises to integrate the view of the origin of variations as expressed in Chapter 6 and the effects of natural selection as portrayed in Chapter 7 in an comprehensive model. For the purpose of exploring the theories and mechanisms of evolutionary biology, these two subjects have been treated separately. Even then, it becomes clear that the process of mutations and the mechanisms of selection interact wholly with each other, and that no feasible theory exists without considering both (van den Bergh, 2003). Some biologists made attempts to expand the evolutionary theories to the domain of organisations. For example, Kauffman (1995, pp. 203-206) pays explicitly attention to the meaning of sustained fitness, and clarifies the background of learning curves by expanding on the criterion of sustained fitness, as adaptive walks near a local optimum. So far, management science, if looking at models derived from evolutionary biology, has focused on the models of the punctuated equilibrium. Although, the high level of complexity of organisations might justify the attention for this model - periods of turmoil interchanged with longer legs of relative stasis - the previous chapters made it clear that evolutionary models span a wide range of (often detailed) mechanisms. The details of the evolutionary processes of variation and selection in the previous chapters offer sufficient perspectives for the conversion to the domain of evolutionary development of organisations. The study so far has generated comprehensive theories about the evolution of organisms, and that way possibly of organisations.

The evolutionary principles from Chapter 6 and Chapter 7 might help to refine the hypotheses that Chapter 4 proposed on the limitations of the boundary control through homeostasis and on the continuous processes of change. Section 8.1 will describe the integration of the theories into a reference model for adaptation by industrial organisations. This reference model roots in the evolutionary biological models, and will be used for the evaluation of existing theories in management science further on in this investigation. Section 8.2 will assess the original hypotheses and expand them for the review based on the reference model from evolutionary biology. The newly proposed, refined hypotheses will serve as a base to discuss the existing models for evolution of organisations (see Chapter 3) in Section 8.3.

8.1 Internal Processes and Structures Interacting with the Environment

According to the view of evolutionary biology, the creation of a new species, a new class of industrial companies, comes about primarily through variation, the creation of mutants. These mutants are seen as offspring of the parent companies, and might replace the parent species or live in a separate landscape, either way enhancing the competitive environment through a variety of phenotypes. The key to speciation lies in the elimination of inviable or maladaptive phenotypes, mutants of companies that are less successful; speciation is seen here as successful adaptation, the survival of companies with phenotypes that fit with the competitive environment.

Hence, if companies create variations to ensure adaptation, they might do so by generating internal changes to cope with the dynamics of the environment; these changes comprise differentiation in product-market combinations, performance, interaction with the market domain, etc. The internally generated changes could cover a wide range of options as long as they lead to differences between industrial companies in product-market combinations through which the elimination process will start.

8.1.1 Requisite for a Reference Model

Romme & van Witteloostuijn (1997, pp. 63-64) state that classical organisational models assume that you might achieve a balance between the internal structure and the interaction with the environment of an organisation (as a system). Once the balance has been established through the implementation of a strategy, the internal structure and the external requirements have to match to each other. These models assume that one might control and predict the behaviour of an organisation, a similar assumption as found in cybernetic modelling (e.g. Kramer

& de Smit, pp. 109-115; in 't Veld, 1998, p. 64). We might denote such as a deterministic view on organisations, which hardly accounts for the subsequent elimination processes exerted by the environment. This view denies the continuous motion of the environment as well. One should remark that this view creates the possibilities to specify the requirements for the design of organisational systems on the short-term. In this case, the build-in flexibility, to ensure adaptation, should correspond with developments foreseen on the long-term.

Grant (1996) proposes that industrial companies should base their (long-term) strategy on organisational capabilities rather than product-market strategies, for coping with unstable market conditions caused by innovation; the strategy should incorporate the effects of increasing intensity and diversity of competition. Selecting product-market combinations becomes a tactical issue rather than a strategy, and requires a higher state of awareness of the organisation and higher speed of adapting to the changed market conditions (Dekkers, 1996). Fowler et al. (2000) propose a similar approach when they find that companies should focus on:

- building market-driven, technological, and integration competencies, and not only a stream of product improvements;
- decoupling these competencies from current products in order to create and exploit new opportunities.

This shifts away from the traditional competitive strategy to a more comprehensive approach for competing in dynamic environments.

8.1.2   Representation of Organisations as Evolutionary Entities

It becomes clear that the generation of variation interacts with the dynamics of the environment seen from an evolutionary biological perspective. These two components are inseparable. Whether selection acts on either mutants or on order caused by mutations, variation as such is the input for selection. However, some of the theories tell the organisms also influence their own environment (state space dimensions in Adaptive Dynamics and shifts in fitness landscapes depending on mutations by the entities of the population) or they only perceive the environment as a result from their internal mechanisms, processes, and structures (organisations as allopietic systems). The reference model that will be developed will not discuss the value of each of these views but rather integrate them into items for selectional processes.

The reference model also thrives on two views on industrial organisations: (a) the organisation as a whole consisting of processes that deliver output to its environment, and (b) the organisation consisting of smaller units (the metaphor of Morgan). The first view will compare the development of organisations at the level of a whole with the evolution of organisms; it is difficult to compare processes of organisation with processes of organisms. The evolutionary biological models that have been reviewed do not account for such a comparison. As a metaphor of explanation it might serve, may be the appetite of organisations exceeds the appetite of organisms. The second view allows to compare the internal details of organisations and organisms: looking at both the behaviour of groups, individuals and the role of skills and knowledge as genes (i.e. replicators or memes for genetic mutation and mechanisms for non-genetic mutation). That offers the opportunity to include change management and culture. Although primarily aiming for processes and structures that support adaptation to the environment, the research can not separate the issues of culture and change management from how organisations could adapt to the dynamics of the environment. The internal structures of organisations and organisms do differ much; would we use this second view to compare, it would become a metaphor to explain rather than an analogy to predict. Hence, the research will continue to look at organisations as a whole adapting to the environment.

To describe the interaction between organisation and environment, the study had to revert to evolutionary biological theories assuming an analogy between organisations and organisms. The comparison between organisation and organisms in their development strongly roots in the systems hierarchy of Boulding; higher levels in this hierarchy have characteristics that resembles those of lower levels, nevertheless a study should account for the differences. Mutants appear at the level of individual companies.

For the purpose of the research into adaptations of organisations to the dynamics of the environment, the differences between organisms and organisations for evolutionary processes are summarised:

- organisations do not have the possibility for self-reproduction in contrast to living entities. Recombination might occur through the concepts of memes and replicators; such recombination as a genetic formation exists in addition to non-genetic mutation in organisations. Reproducing through recombination has very positive effects on finding fitness peaks in the adaptive landscapes as demonstrated through the NK-model developed by Kauffman (Section 7.2.3). Organisms have genes that allow recombination to occur by alleles. The direct deployment of the thoughts of genes to the domain of organisations carries the danger that the study will end up as a metaphor rather than an analogy;
- organisations have the capability for foresight already latently present at the level of animals and present at the level of human beings. Through senses, organisms acquire information about the effects of actions, and have the capability to learn by self-reference embedded in the structure of the entity (so-called Lamarckian evolution). However, the evolution of organisms

depends on the creation of mutations and selection of these by the environment. At the level of organisations, it becomes possible to influence the behaviour of other organisms, and to include foresight in the evolutionary process;

- organisations have fuzzy boundaries. Organisms as autopoietic systems not only reproduce, they also retain a boundary to the environment, they consist of components that compose a total functional entity, and they are structurally closed. Through these boundaries, the environment can only induce changes that are already present in the composition and structure of the entity. Organisations have boundaries too but have the capability to shift these[42]. Additionally, some components of an organisation cross the boundaries back and forth, e.g. employees.

Although these differences exist, an analogy becomes possible when sufficient similarities constitute a base for transferring the models of evolutionary biology to the domain of organisations. This particular study has found these similarities:

- selection acts on mutations. Biological evolution generates a variety of phenotypes, and the environment selects phenotypes for survival. Such a process exists also for organisations where the selection process finds itself in the competition for the customer base, the acquisition of resources, e.g. suppliers, and the acknowledgement of existence by society;
- organisations and organisms are structurally closed with relations between components and boundaries to the environment. The relationships between the components determine how the entity absorbs perturbations by the environment. Changes in the structure of organisations reside in the current structure and capabilities and depend less on principles of equifinality; that means that the design of organisations should account for the ontogenic development of the current organisational structures and capabilities;
- organisations have the possibility of self-reference and learning, also found at the 5th, 6th and 7th level of Boulding. The autopoietic principle of self-reference appears for both organisms and organisations; the latent changes are present in the structure of the entity, and the environment may induce these changes. Learning becomes possible because both organisations and organisms will deploy a set of sensors to acquire information about their behaviour although self-reference limits the possibilities to detect all changes and perturbations in the environment;
- developmental pathways seem to exist for both organisations and organisms. Organisms can increase their fitness by undertaking an adaptive walk in a

---

[42] *Primarily, the research focuses on internal processes and structures for adaptation. Because of this scope, the development of companies through shifting the boundaries (e.g. mergers, acquisitions, outsourcing) has been ignored.*

fitness landscape where selection acts on the phenotypes. Organisations can also create mutations by an adaptive walk.

Organisations can be best described as allopietic systems with fuzzy boundaries, having the unique capability of foresight and maybe following similar laws of development as organisms (see Figure 8.1).

The study has revealed a large number of conceptual models for the origin and diversity of life as well as biological models for adaptations to the environment. What became apparent during the study is that organisations need to create variety in their phenotype, visible traits to the environment, to expose these mutations to selection by the environment. These mutations might fix within a population, a product-market combination, or they might be deleterious. Linkage disequilibrium might favour these mutations to appear and fix. In addition, (extreme) mutations can appear and coexist even if the mean of a group of companies does not shift. Such a phenomenon will result in the complexity error catastrophe in large populations when the high mutation rate increases, causing bifurcation processes to create diversity.

Especially, the effect of macromutations deserves attention for the domain of evolution of organisations:

- Firstly, the emergence of these macromutations follows developmental pathways due to the existence of related networks of regulatory genes.

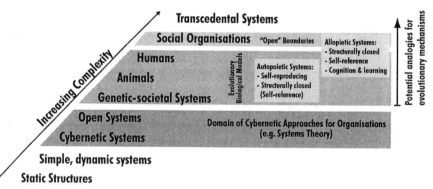

Figure 8.1: The nine levels of the systems hierarchy by Boulding. The domain of organisations moves at the eight' level indicating the importance of meaning, value systems and symbolisation. The domain of Systems Theory and some other approaches in management science (e.g. information technology) find themselves at the third and fourth level. Models from evolutionary biology might bridge the gap between some of the approaches in management science and the actual organisational domain. However, differences exist between organisms and organisations mostly denoted by the difference between autopoietic systems and allopietic systems. Additionally, the boundaries of an organisation are relatively open; companies might shift the boundaries and employees are part of other social organisations and contexts.

Following this thought of evolutionary biology, genes relate to each other and at certain moments genes controlling other genes might topple and quickly provoke changes taking part in a large part of an organism; this cascade of changes might prevail above the gradual change of individual pool sets of genes. Such toppling might also result from the accumulation of many changes in genes at lower levels. Genes do not exist in organisations as an analogy, but control networks and aggregates do. The developmental pathways specify the possible routes that organisations might have to follow since each step should ideally result in higher fitness.

- Secondly, heterochrony and heterotopy, as specific forms of macromutations, indicate the possible effects of viable deviations during development on the timing and the positioning of organelles, and the structure of organisms. Organisations might profit from such an approach because the relocation of components and organelles together with the change of structure can create new capabilities.

- Thirdly, the mechanism of epigenetics tells that integrating mechanisms, like control or regulatory structures, serve as a powerful source for adaptations to the dynamics of the environment. An integrating mechanism ties all the loose components together and shapes it into a meaningful whole.

It should be noted that macromutations in evolutionary biology have a rare chance of becoming beneficial due to the (internal) complexity of interactions; might this also be true for organisations? The quick accumulation of incremental changes seems a more likely mechanism to succeed. Nevertheless, developmental pathways shape the first adaptation and successive mutational steps to reach new fitness peaks. It appears that developmental pathways seem to rule all possible changes and the search for increased fitness strongly determines the route and development of organisations.

In the development of species, evolutionary biology makes a distinction between macroevolution and microevolution. During the past decades, it has become clear that the phenomena at the level of species are not necessarily the same as those at the level of individuals and populations. This indicates that the adaptation processes at the level of industries might not look like those on the level of organisations, a warning for drawing hasty conclusions at different levels of aggregation. Because of the existence of the linkage disequilibrium quite different organisations might coexist in product-market combinations, while the general development of a niche follows the evolutionary processes. This might mean that a deleterious mutation of an individual organisation holds an initial potential for survival. On the long run, selection mechanisms mostly remove these mutations; some mutations develop into viable phenotypes. Bifurcation might occur when specific mutations have fitness characteristics that suit a more specialised niche for existence.

8.1.3 Reference Model for Evolutionary Development

It becomes time to connect the developmental models from evolutionary biology to models to a reference model for organisational development. Although the analogies might have its restrictions, it also might lead to remarkable visions about the interaction between environment and organisation. The evolutionary cycles of variation and selection for organisations have been depicted in Figure 8.2. (Non-)genetic mutation leads to form and function trajectories as the generation of variation, following developmental pathways embedded in the structure of the organisational entity. These mutations are selected by the environment based on adaptive walks and the criteria of sustained fitness and evolvability. The reference model for adaptation by organisations to the dynamics of the environment encompasses the following items:

i)   the distinction between phenotype and genotype. At the level of the interaction between entity and environment, the phenotype contains the visible traits, on which selection by the environment operates. The visible traits of an

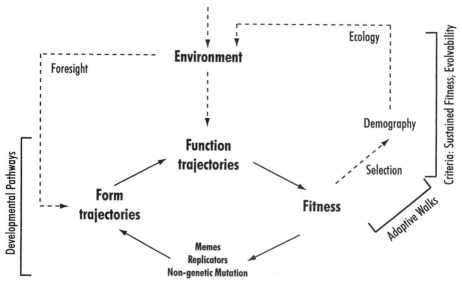

Figure 8.2: Evolutionary mechanisms for organisations as reference model. Memes and replicators serves as input for genetic formation, which exists besides non-genetic formation. Developmental pathways determine the form and function trajectories. These pathways also relate to organisations being a class of allopietic systems. The selectional processes select beneficial phenotypes on fitness following adaptive walks based on the criteria of sustained fitness and evolvability. Organisations have the capability of foresight in contrast to organisms.

organisation, sometimes referred to as capabilities, find themselves at the boundary of the organisation and its environment. Variation leads to mutants, and the environment selects these entities that display the combination of traits that it favours. This concept holds also for organisations since a certain capability, take value for money for products of a certain company (the trait), requires skills, resources, etc. that are not necessarily visible to the outside world. Maintenance of the phenotype in a company requires then also the development of the underlying subset of the elements of the genotype. The principle of allopietic systems dictates that the observed relationships to the environment strongly root in the definition of these through the identity of the organisation itself (structure, boundaries, and organisational inhibitions). These relationships can only change when the company internally changes its capability for dealing with the environment;

ii) the undertaking of adaptive walks and the constraints imposed by developmental pathways. Through linked step-by-step mutations, organisms search for optimisation of their fitness to the landscape. The combined effects of mutation, selection, and recombination allow effective searches. Organisations might exert adaptive walks to increase their fitness as selection acts on individuals rather then on species or any other combination of entities. These adaptive walks take the form of one-step mutants, more-step mutants or long jumps. One-step mutants prove less effective than more-step mutants (two to five steps per mutation) for reaching local fitness peaks which means that gradual but not extreme changes in companies fit the search for continuous optimisation. Long jumps, forced macromutations, might prove very effective on rugged fitness landscapes, where many fitness peaks exist, though they become a weak strategy as the complexity (diversity and numbers) increases. These macromutations have only effect when such a jump reaches across the critical Hamming distance (Kauffman, 1993, p. 199). The Hamming distance represents the number of positions in which the two states are different given a number of elements. The rate of finding successively fitter mutations by long jumps decreases rapidly on very rugged landscapes and on smooth fitness landscapes. Recombination as mechanism for optimisation poses problems to organisations although valuable for organisms. Should companies produce offspring through recombination that has a higher fitness than the original parents? Or does this phenomenon point to the effects of mergers between companies? If the latter appears to be true, these parent companies should merge to find a higher fitness peak in between their local fitness peaks.

iii) the assessment of the capability of sustained fitness. Two main criteria determine the extent of sustained fitness: local evolutionary stability, as indicator of the stability of a singular strategy, and convergence stability, as indicator of evolving of organisations to a stable strategy. The convergence stability resembles the statements of Kauffman on decreasing effects of adaptive walks. When reaching a local optimum, the effect of each step reduces by half and the efforts increase by a factor two. The theory of Adaptive Dynamics indicates that each next step has less effect (asymptotic functions). In an evolutionary stable point or at an Evolutionary Stable Strategy, organisations get trapped at this optimum, moving in each direction will decrease fitness. Local trapping at the level of populations of organisations might by avoided by increased complexity, numbers, and diversity (the complexity error catastrophe).

iv) the evolvability of organisations. This capability depends on the assessment of two criteria: the invading potential, as a capability to disperse and to penetrate into new habitats, and the protected dimorphism instability, as the possibility for splitting lineages. Dispersal rates play an important role in combination with the mutation rate. Dispersal, seen as invading other habitats, decreases the sensitivity of organisations against environmental catastrophes. Especially, moving into carefully selected habitats with higher fitness proves an effective strategy. The dispersal depends on mutation rates amounting to sufficient levels to sustain the invading potential or otherwise diluting will appear, reducing the chances of survival. Once a singular strategy finds itself near two attractors, dimorphisms, splitting of the lineage will appear. Bifurcation opens the possibility for the founder effect and further evolution but also requires the capability to deal with increasing complexity since the dimensions of strategies increase. These moves away from an original singular strategy depend on the existence of adaptive zones (they link the concept of macromutations to bifurcation processes).

v) the emergence of self-organisation. Phase transitions during which organisations intensively absorb and dissipate through relationships with the environment, provide the possibility of emergent behaviour and emergent structures to adapt to changes within that environment. Such trajectories, moving to an attractor, a point of the state space, closely relate to bifurcation processes. Low-dimensionality of the attractor allows a more orderly regime. Furthermore, low connectivity in networked systems provides the possibility for seeking a state in which a system moves between the orderly regime and chaos. At such a state transition, adaptation that meet the criteria of sustained fitness and evolvability provide most opportunities.

The five items relate to different parts of the evolutionary mechanism for organisations in Figure 8.2. Biological models define the distinction between genotype-phenotype quite clearly, in economics and management science no such distinction exists. This differences relates to the fact that biological evolution constitutes genetic evolution, whereas social-economic evolution is a combination of genetic and non-genetic evolution, where the latter is dominant because of different time scales. Some authors have tried to impose the genotype-phenotype analogy to economics (Boulding, 1981; Faber & Proops, 1990). In the reference model both genetic evolution and non-genetic evolution are addressed. Secondly, the developmental pathways and the adaptive walks indicate evolutionary routes organisations will have to follow to generate fitter mutants. The concept of developmental pathways has got recognition in the fields of evolutionary economics and management science, but it requires a link between form and function trajectories to fitness landscape; that link lacks in evolutionary economics and management science. Thirdly, the items of the criteria sustained fitness and evolvability tell how entities evolve in a fitness landscape (following both the NK-model of Kauffman and the models of Adaptive Dynamics). Fitter mutants, after going through form and function trajectories, will only fix if they meet those criteria based on their phenotype. Finally, the principle of self-organisation suggests a principle of how organisations evolve internally in addition to the structurally closed allopietic systems. All together, the reference model comprises of two cycles, variation and selection, with additional, detailed information about the steps described by the five items.

From the above processes it becomes clear that both the theory of the phyletic gradualism and the theory of the punctuated equilibrium (more at the level of macroevolution) describe processes for evolution. When looking in more detail at the mechanisms, some remarks should be made to the underlying concepts of macromutations and fitness landscapes:

- The recognition of the importance of heterochrony for evolutionary biology does not directly translate to models for organisations. Heterochrony would indicate differences in developments between organisations; at the moment, management science has very limited (and coarse) models for the development of organisations, the life-cycle approaches from Section 3.3. Also the sample size and differences between companies in a product-market combination will make it difficult to draw conclusions based on heterochrony.
- The concept of heterotopy resembles one-time interventions (i.e. form trajectories). If the similarity with evolutionary biology holds, such interventions have little chance for survival.
- The existence of developmental pathways, epigenetics, and regulatory genes carries more resemblance to possible processes of adaptation in organisations. Like organisms, organisations constitute of components with links between them (defined by epigenetics and regulatory genes, which equals the control mechanisms of organisations). The developmental pathways come about

through the structural closedness of organisations and the pathways for searching fitness peaks at fitness landscapes.

- The landscape describe the fitness of different positions of the phenotype. As Kauffman (1993, pp. 77-78) states: *landscapes cannot be fixed in general, if only because the physical environment changes.* In landscapes that change heavily and rapidly in time, there exists uncorrelated fitness forcing the organisation to assess evolvability. In slower changing landscapes, local search prevails (sustained fitness).

- Organisations operate in dynamic fitness landscapes as indicated by the models of Adaptive Dynamics. The fitness landscape deforms according to the mutations generated by the population itself. Especially, this should be viewed from the capability of foresight; most likely, organisations adapt by higher mutation rate with more purpose the organisms. Since this investigation focuses on the evolution of single entities, the concept of co-evolution has been excluded from the scope but definitely will yield additional insight into this phenomenon.

Yes, the models of evolutionary biology have meaning for the adaptation by organisations as described by the reference model (organisations as special allopietic systems, evolutionary mechanisms for organisations, five items). However, the scope of the evolutionary models indicates the necessity of a better link to the real development of organisations and other fields in management science.

Some management scientists, like Lewin et al. (1999, pp. 536-538) and Volberda (1998; 2000), strongly advocate the distinction between the process of exploitation and exploration to describe the evolution of individual companies and industrial branches. This differs from the introduced reference model for several reasons. First of all, the reference model contains criteria rather than internal processes of adaptation such as exploitation and exploration, and the model sets constraints for the outcomes of these. The criteria act at the same time, each single step is neither exploration nor exploitation but a step that should simultaneously increase sustained fitness and evolvability. Secondly, evolvability and exploration are not exactly congruent with the search processes of the reference model. Evolvability describes particularly the invading potential, very similar to the potential results of exploration, and dimorphisms as base for splitting lineages. Within population ecology and hence organisational evolution, also bifurcation drives evolutionary processes. This should be considered. Thirdly, sustained fitness resembles exploitation but its distinction between evolutionary stability and convergence stability increases the descriptive capability of models for evolutionary processes. Exploitation might simply be the input and output of a company, a far more limited description in view of evolutionary models. Hence, organisational ecology might profit from the reference model to better understanding of the development of organisations.

8.2   HYPOTHESES LINKED TO THE EVOLUTIONARY BIOLOGICAL MODELS

Taking the reference model as starting point, this section will introduce the expansion of the hypotheses launched in Chapter 4. Originally, this research has proposed two main hypotheses for review:

Hypothesis A
The principle of boundary control based on homeostasis limits the evolution of organisations in response to the dynamics of the environment.

Hypothesis B
Adaptation to the environment constitutes of continuous processes within the organisations rather than one-time interventions.

Both hypotheses state the responses of an organisation to the dynamics of the environment, through maintaining the boundaries (except mergers, acquisitions, etc., which are outside the scope of this particular research), homeostasis, and through one-time interventions. The biological evolutionary models have revealed that internal processes exist for variation as well as external processes for selection. The interaction between the internal processes and external processes results in the diversity of life and evolution of species. Although species exists of many individual specimens, the research looks at organisations as single entities in their industrial environment.

The reference model incorporates the adaptation strategies for companies. The adaptation strategies evolve from the reference model: mutations (whether or not resulting from recombination of memes, replicators or coming about through intended mutations), state transition, adaptive walks, long jumps; the reference model also presents criteria for development: sustained fitness, evolvability. Additionally, it has mentioned the phenomenon of the complexity error catastrophe. With the detailed mechanisms of the reference model it becomes possible to review existing approaches for continuous change and adaptation (Chapter 3), existing approaches in management science, and case studies of the Delft School Approach.

With reference to the research approach, these strategies, criteria, and the phenomena will be tested during the stage of elimination as presented in the four-stage model of Popper (1999, p. 14). The first two stages of his model consist of formulating the old problem and the formation of tentative theories. We have already concluded that current approaches do insufficiently address the adaptation to the dynamics of the environment and continuous change. The search for tentative theories has lead to the reference model comprising detailed mechanisms for the evolution of organisations. The third stage of the Popper's model concerns the stage of elimination by testing the tentative theory, i.e. the reference model in this case; this stage of elimination is found in Section 8.3 and Part II of this book. The original hypotheses serve as a base for testing the reference model.

8.2.1   Review of Original Hypotheses

Let us look at the first hypothesis; it strongly relies on the application of the orderly regime of networks, e.g. the models of Kauffman, and the effects of gradualism. The orderly regime of networks indicates the existence of functionally separated subsystems that act almost independently and display stability to perturbation. This stability or homeostasis remains the bottleneck for adaptation to the dynamics of the environment. Albeit, if industrial organisations want to adapt to the environment, they should not exert control to the highest limit and not isolate the organisation as a subsystem. Rather, the organisation should increase interaction with the environment at the edge of chaos within the orderly regime. Gradual changes have less effect the more dynamic the environment, also indicating that operating within an orderly regime creates boundaries for the evolvability of organisations. Higher step mutations, not necessarily long jumps, create better possibilities for adaptation.

The second hypothesis has been proven already if evolutionary biological models are entirely true for organisations. Adaptive walks are continuous searches for beneficial mutations. Organisms display no stability, they evolve even if selection remains stable, but in the case of dynamics of the environment adaptive walks become a necessity. The search should lead to adaptive zones in which negative feedback flips to positive feedback and new adaptive zones or local peaks become attainable.

Both hypotheses seem already addressed by the inclusion of evolutionary biological models into the reference model. Still, we need to review the proposed theory included in the reference model; that will only be possible if the hypotheses are refined and made suitable for testing.

8.2.2   Limiting Growth through Maintaining Homeostasis

The first main hypothesis states that the principle of boundary control based on homeostasis limits the evolution of organisations in response to the dynamics of the environment, implying the inhibitions of change the organisations exposes itself to. This situation is characterised by gradual boundary changes, relatively small changes within the organisation, and relatively closedness of an entity. Most of the biological models mention the appearance of mutations as a sequence of steps with decreasing effects towards a new state of the entities, either representing genetic drift or bifurcation. The first hypothesis therefore strongly roots in the principles of homeostasis, maintaining balance with the environment, and consequently, gradual steps towards a new local optimum. Almost the opposite, the dissipative structures of self-organisation require an intense interaction with the environment. During such a period of transition and a state between order and chaos, even the boundary of the system might diffuse, certainly considering the increased exchange between system and environment. These quite different models about the system boundary lead to a bifurcation of the first hypothesis:

Hypothesis A.1 Mutations
The organisation maintains its homeostasis through the introduction of small changes to its phenotype, outer traits, to adapt to the dynamics of the environment.

Hypothesis A.2 State Transition
In dynamic environments, organisations should increase their exchange with the environment and create a dissipative structure through which new behaviour and structures arise. The interchange with the environment should expand the relationships beyond those defined by structure, composition, and identity (allopietic systems).

Both hypotheses can be observed, a necessity for the stage of elimination. In the first case, the generation of variation takes place without consideration of the environment or without interaction with the environment. The organisation evolves more or less independently from the environment. Selectional forces act as feedback to the system by the acceptance of the variation. The second hypothesis relies on the interaction with the environment through dissipative structures, and the environment determines in that sense the outcomes of the evolution. Interaction might consist out of requests for renewal as well as knowledge and skills introduced by additional resources the company interacts with. Hence, both refined hypotheses exclude each other.

8.2.3   Processes of Adaptation

The second main hypothesis aims at explaining the mechanisms of adaptations or adaptive walks. The biological evolutionary models comprise the idea of undertaking adaptive walks, whether the environment is stable or dynamic, towards finding new optima for organisations. Then one-time interventions look like the long jumps of Kauffman. For these long jumps, he has stated that they only become effective when such a long jump reaches beyond the critical Hamming distance, getting beyond the nearby local peak and finding other fitness peaks in the landscape, and when it appears on rugged fitness landscapes. Hence, two main streams of adaptations occur: adaptive walks which represent continuous adaptation, and long jumps that resemble the ideas of one-time interventions. This results in two hypotheses for further review:

Hypothesis B.1.A Adaptive Walks

An organisation undertakes continuous adaptive walks to increase its fitness in the landscape it operates thereby taking the characteristics of the landscape into account. These adaptive walks follow developmental pathways by which the fitness increases.

Hypothesis B.1.B Long Jumps

An organisation exerts one-time interventions to adapt to the environment taking into account the Hamming distance, exceeding the differences necessary for reaching a nearby adaptive peak in the landscape.

The first hypothesis of these two can be reviewed by looking at how companies account for the requirements dictated by the landscape (shape and correlation). Each mutation should yield a higher fitness to the environment. The consequence of the second hypothesis is that when the developmental pathways require long jumps or when companies exert long jumps, these mutations should really make a difference in the phenotype of the company. Earlier during this research doubts have been casted to the effectiveness of this strategy. These two hypotheses direct themselves at determining the development of fitness in landscapes.

Additionally, the research into the adaptation has revealed two main criteria that determine how organisations evolve if the biological evolutionary models do hold in the domain of management. Sustained fitness indicates the capability and possibilities for optimisation. Evolvability should indicate whether an organisation has the possibility for invading other product-market combinations or that it should bifurcate, split itself in lineages. The combination of both criteria tells about the presence of adaptive zones for organisations. Both criteria have been taken apart to assess against management practices and the theories in management science:

Hypothesis B.2.A Sustained Fitness

The organisation maintains its homeostasis through the introduction of small changes to its phenotype, outer traits, to find a local optimum. Through gradual steps it becomes gradually harder to reach the local fitness peak.

Hypothesis B.2.B Evolvability

A company moves into new adaptive zones either by deploying an appropriate strategy: dispersal, invading, or bifurcation.

These two mechanisms represent two different ways of looking at adaptation by companies (taking into account that organisations possess the capability for foresight). The choice is between local optimisation and the search for product-market combinations. Theoretically, companies might pursue both since these criteria both determine the development of individual firms.

Furthermore, when organisations get trapped at a local fitness peak, the market segment might display the characteristics of the complexity error catastrophe. If the rate of mutations increases together with (relatively) large numbers of competitors, some companies find optima at the edge. They slide down the fitness peaks and might find nearby optima. These optima might not necessarily have a higher fitness value than the original fitness peak, but be of sufficient value for the organisations to maintain themselves.

Hypothesis B.2.C Complexity Error Catastrophe
An increasing number of competitors, mutations, diversity in the product-market combination(s) force a company to reposition itself by choosing either to increase sustained fitness or to search for a nearby local fitness peak.

All seven hypotheses constitute a refinement of the original hypotheses from Chapter 4. However, the research should test them and look at how organisations evolve over time. The elements of the hypotheses have not yet been used in literature to determine the development of organisations, also in more dynamic environments.

8.2.4   Testing of Refined Hypotheses
Following the thoughts of Feyerabend on methodological pluralism (Leavitt, 2001, p. 6; Nola & Sankey, 2000, p. 12), the testing of the refined hypotheses will happen through the review of existing literature in management science (as archival research) and the six case studies of the Delft School Approach. The explorative character of this study does not allow at this stage to formulate hypotheses that encompass both cause and effect, as the Popperian view prescribes. Rather, the hypotheses focus on the presence of mechanisms for the evolution of organisations. The review of existing literature has only accounted for those that relate the (internal) mechanisms to the adaptation by companies; this explains partially the limited number of research papers that contributed to findings of this particular study. Furthermore, only studies that have performed quantitative analysis, in-depth case studies or testing grounded theory have been considered. Each review of existing literature within a specific field in management science is preceded by a general description of that specific field.

The six case studies are considered as individual experiments through which the outcomes can be compared with the refined hypotheses.

Since the literature in management science and the six case studies do differ, the reference model has acted as common ground for content analysis (Tashakkori & Teddlie, 1998, p. 54). To make this content analysis possible, the link between the reference model and the refined hypotheses has been made through defining features related to the each of the hypotheses (see Appendix F). Each publication in literature in management science has been assessed on its validity and reliability before considering its outcomes in relation to the features. After relating findings to the features, it becomes possible whether a specific publication supports or refutes the refined hypotheses. The features will also be used for assessing the six case studies of the Delft School Approach.

8.3   Review of the Existing Models for Evolution of Organisations

Some archival research has already been introduced during Chapter 3, the existing approaches towards adaptation and continuous change; the reference model will serve as a basis to discuss these in this section. These existing approaches did direct themselves at explaining the evolution of organisations. The studies into the development of the Netherlands and the aviation industry (Chapter 2) will be used as examples to relate the approaches to the reference model where appropriate.

8.3.1   Social-economical Perspective

The social-economical perspective carries many of the characteristics of the evolutionary biological models. Especially, Mokyr (1990) has emphasised the use of evolutionary models to explain technology development in a historical context; he seems to technology (macro- or microinventions) as "genes" for the evolutionary process. As Mokyr noted, minor and major inventions are strongly related, a notion that has resemblances with innovation processes in companies. The relationship between minor and major inventions in the development of technology looks like the developmental pathways for organisms. In retrospect, they contain too few details to account for an accurate picture of how organisations adapt to the environment and which mechanisms prevail.

The social-economical perspective demonstrates the utmost importance of dispersal for adaptation, and the need for advancing the internal (technological) capabilities of economies. Also, it indicates that the internal capabilities have a strong influence on the future development of economies, and that looks like the thoughts about developmental pathways. The findings of Mokyr, presented in Section 3.1, indicate that inertia are found in organisationally closed structures (when examining the development of nations). Hence, internal forces hamper the adaptation processes; such is the case for the Netherlands at the end of Golden Age. May be the end of the 20th century and the beginning of the 21st century will present this nation the same fate. An individual nation might temporarily fall behind on overall developments, yet the greater the gap, the more it induces revolution overthrowing reactionary institutions, e.g. Japan after 1853 (Mokyr, 1994, p. 569). Such development of nations at different, varying speeds, as present in Europe, has strong parallels to the need for dispersal. Dispersal represents the development of product-market combinations.

8.3.2 Organisational Ecology

The research into organisational ecology has underlined that developmental pathways, especially those that point to age and size, increase the chances of survival for an organisation. Organisational ecology has underlined that age and size matter, hence managing transitions from one stage to another in the life-cycle of organisations becomes important. Barnett (1997) analyses breweries in the USA and telephone companies in Pennsylvania, reaching the conclusion that small companies might become more competitive than the larger ones. Size matters but quite differently than expected, selectional forces on small organisations drive them to enhance competitiveness while institutionalisation offers large companies a way out. This phenomenon is not directly part of this research because most of the time age and size are reached through acquisitions, mergers, etc. with their own specific problems.

Organisational ecology recognises the role of niche players as well, comparable to the existence of linkage disequilibrium. The reaction by industrial companies on changes in demand are followed pretty well (seasonal patterns), like in the aviation industry. The aviation industry pointed to the importance of the Analyser (and Reactor) strategy. Technological lock-in appears as phenomenon, linked to finding a local fitness peak and the speed of step-wise mutations.

Key point in organisational ecology is the organisational form which looks like the concept of the phenotype. Still the concept of forms as such seems a mix of visible features and strategies. McKendrick & Carroll (2001, pp. 661-664) note the lack of definition of organisational forms; they build on the work of Pólos et al. to define organisational forms as external identity codes, meaning that the perceptions and opinions from outside matter. Such a definition bears a resemblance to the phenotype. To define organisational forms, organisational ecology could profit from the theories from evolutionary biology. Hannan & Freeman (1977, p. 935) introduce the concept of organisational form by defining it as the blueprint for organisational action (transforming inputs into outputs):

- the formal structure of the organisation in the narrow sense: tables of organisation, written rules of operation, etc.;
- the patterns of activity within the organisation: what actually gets done by whom;
- the normative order: the ways of organising that are defined as right and proper by both members and relevant sectors of the environment.

Some other authors, like Forte et al. (2000, pp. 754-756), take organisational forms as equal to the classification of Miles & Snow: Prospectors, Defenders, Analysers, and Reactors (as used to study the aviation industry). Lewin & Volberda (1999) strongly advocate the research into new organisational forms, however, without defining or describing such. Yet, they remark that new organisational forms results from mutations from the old stock of forms in a population in industry induced by new entrants or radical technological innovations (Lewin & Volberda, 1999, p. 529).

8.3.3 Evolution of Organisations

The evolution of organisation carries strong resemblances to the evolutionary biological models. The transitions between phases in Greiner's model look like the transition states between chaos and order (including the concept of dissipative structures). Zuijderhoudt et al. (2002) have described the phase transitions in greater detail using the theories of chaos and complexity. Lievegoed's model finds its base in the phase transitions and optimisation models of sustained fitness. Although usable, the exact mechanisms of adaptation have not yet become clear. The adaptation thoughts seem to follow mostly those of ontogenic development of individuals, and they do hardly address evolvability. De Geus's concept partially acts as a metaphor, and partially resides in the principles of autopoiesis and learning (de Geus, 1999, pp. 111-115). Especially, the concept of self-reference, linked to autopoiesis has hardly emerged in the existing management approaches as theme for the dynamic capability. Additionally, the need for foresight has not yet been addressed; de Geus is the only one talking about this issue. The concepts for the evolution of organisations hardly address the internal processes and structures necessary to adapt to the dynamics of the environment.

The study of Laitinen (2000) into the effectiveness of five different adaptation strategies shows the importance of the need to invest on the acquisition of customers, new product development, and marketing (he examined financial-economical data from 750 companies). The adaptation strategies, he reviewed, are: efficiency improvement, marketing improvement, short-term assets and expenses cutting, debt restructuring strategy, and fixed assets realisation and share emitting strategies. On the long-run, the efficiency improvement strategy and the marketing improvement strategy seem to be the most successful, very much like the findings in the aviation industry. Hence, dispersal by product development and the development of product-market combinations determine the survival of an industrial organisation (evolvability) as well as efficiency improvement (sustained fitness).

A study by Sabherwal et al. (2001) into three cases uses the punctuated equilibrium model to study the alignment between (i) business strategies and information strategies, and (ii) business structures and information system structures. One of their findings states that alignment or misalignment does not correlate to evolutionary change, following the punctuated equilibrium model (Sabherwal et al., 2001, p. 195). In addition, structural and cultural inertia exist within an organisation resisting the implementation of a redesign (this looks like the prediction by the models of autopoiesis). They do not touch on the evolutionary model of punctuated equilibrium to assess mutations as driving force, therefore the conclusions on the applicability seem limited. Hannan & Freeman (1977, p. 931) mention the existence of structural inertia in organisations; our interest has especially (a) the mentioning of investments in plants, equipment and specialised personnel and (b) the normative agreements on standard procedures and the allocation of tasks and authority.

8.3.4 Developmental Pathways for Organisations

The approach of dynamic capabilities and competencies roots in the thought of developmental pathways (and adaptive walks). Competencies indicate the strongholds of a current market position of a firm but hardly point to the adaptive zones. Prahalad & Hamel (1990, p. 82) show that companies build products and business areas based on competencies present in an organisation. Business development resides in competencies present in the firm's organisation, requiring thinking in competencies rather than in products; this proved also true for the development of the Netherlands. The identification of competencies has shown great difficulty because of the retrospective view of the theory, according to Walsh & Linton (2001, p. 167); they propose a method to assess the competencies of individual firms and industries. Such a thought does not resemble developmental pathways; it only takes the current situation into account. The principle of self-reference justifies that developments reside in the current capabilities, however the method does not describe how to develop a company. In fact, Teece et al. (1997, p. 523) mention the increasing fitness, expressed as increasing returns, and as adaptive zones into which markets might evolve. However, the theories do not generate an answer to which processes and structures should exist to support the dynamic capabilities and the evolution of competencies.

A few studies consider part of the developmental pathways. Ruef (1997, p. 850) has found that adaptivity decreases with the degree of generalism when investigating the Californian hospital industry. Such a finding indicates the importance of specialisation for adaptation. In addition, Forte et al. (2000, p. 770), examining the hospital industry in Florida, found that Reactors and Defenders (enacting changes appropriate to the emerging environmental conditions) failed to make a complete and coherent transformation to a new organisational form, and were not expected to achieve higher performance. Again, these findings tell the importance of searching for new markets and opportunities, the profiles of Prospectors and Analysers in Miles & Snow typology.

According to Nelson & Winter (1982), operational routines are embedded in knowledge and skills as successive stages of learning take place. These operational routines develop into practices from which the organisation evolves. Hence it becomes harder to move away from these routines, even though the environment calls for change. The organisational routines might point to a possible application of recombination. Such a strand requires the consideration of other processes and mechanisms from a different point of view, such as exploring linkage disequilibrium (this has been omitted from the research by Nelson & Winter). Although the organisational routines might be seen as the memes for the evolutionary mechanism, it requires the consideration of the total evolutionary cycles from the reference model.

8.3.5 Flexibility and Changeability

In any case, two different criteria prevail in evolutionary processes, sustained fitness and evolvability. According to Volberda, his array of different organisation types (Network Corporation, Dual Corporation, Oscillating Corporation, Balanced Corporation) offers managers the choice to face the dynamic challenges of the environment. The Balanced Corporation might shift its emphasis to exploitation or exploration following internal forces in a company. The reference model indicates that successive mutations follow the selectional forces, incorporating both sustained fitness and evolvability. Sorenson (2000, p. 588) shows that in more volatile environments product variety yields competitive advantages, more than culling on product lines (when looking at the computer work station industry). The advantages of monitoring market preferences assist companies to recognise shifts in-time, and to anticipate on uncertainties in accurate predictions of demand. When many competitive rivals exist, focusing on certain product lines becomes more productive. Both thoughts are embedded in those of developmental pathways.

Fowler et al. (2000) relate competitive advantage to a competency-centred approach rather than a product-centred approach. In more dynamic environments, the development of technological competencies, market-driven competencies and integration competencies, should contribute to more appropriate reactions to environmental shifts. This notion has many characteristics from the theories of competencies and the dynamic capability. However, the authors do not address the necessary organisational processes and structures to create these competencies.

Popular reviews of evolutionary change take the punctuated equilibrium as departing point. Industrial changes have their forebodes in earlier developments, according to the evolutionary models, which might trigger revolutionary changes through (accelerated) mutations (separating causes and effects). This view occurs in Romanelli & Tushman (1994, p. 1159) when they state that the model of punctuated equilibrium is a principal means by which organisations fundamentally alter their systems, strategies, and structures. Their research into the minicomputer industry in the USA shows that (1) a large majority of organisational transformations were accomplished via rapid and discontinuous change over most or all domains of organisational activity, (2) small changes in strategies, structures and power distributions did not accumulate to produce fundamental transformations, and (3) major environmental changes and chief executive officer succession influenced transformations. This study typically has not investigated the role of minor and major inventions by looking at the contents of a technology development.

8.3.6 Evolutionary Models for Processes and Structures

Based on the discussions in the previous subsections, Table 8.1 links the contemporary approaches to the reference model, and it displays the intentions of each of these approaches to the components of the reference model. The social-historic view adds the importance of dispersal. The research at hand focuses on which mechanisms, processes, and structures underlie the adaptation of organisations to the dynamics of the environment. The current main approaches to the evolution of organisations do not answer this quest. Additionally, it is not possible to review the hypotheses at this stage, and to elaborate the models of adaptation such that they result in clear guidelines for companies.

The overview in Table 8.1 also illustrates the dispersal of the topics covered by the contemporary management approaches. They hardly do connect to each other, while some of them present conceptual approaches. Current literature mainly emphasises the concepts of dynamic capabilities and developmental pathways, without following truly the concepts of these evolutionary approaches. So far, it seems that especially the social-economic perspective has taken an interest in evolutionary models derived from biology. This conversion still resides in simplified models of evolution, thereby reducing its potential for adequate descriptive and predictive models. If this research develops models for internal processes and structures, it should look into both descriptive and predictive models for continuous change and adaptation, other than in the contemporary approaches found in Chapter 3. It becomes necessary to evaluate and to include, if appropriate, theories of management science.

The next stage of the research focuses on theories and approaches in management science that closely relate to processes and structures for adaptation. The theories are found in the fields of technology management, innovation, process innovation, Business Process Re-engineering, Learning Organisation, Knowledge Management, change management, and culture to answer how industrial companies can adapt to the dynamics of the environment. Table 8.2 lists the most pronounced questions for this further search, based on the link between these fields and the reference model. The questions arose from connecting the intents of the reference model to the topics of these theories, such as technology

Table 8.1: The main contemporary approaches related to the items of the reference model. The columns show that so far each of the approaches offers partial explanations of evolutionary change. Each of these approaches resides in different aspects and theories. Metaflexibility refers to the capability to anticipate on future developments (Volberda, 1998, pp. 200-201).

Management Approach	Phenotype/ Genotype	Adaptive Walks	Developmental pathways	Sustained Fitness	Evolvability	Self-organisation
Social-economical History			Major/minor inventions. Structural inertia in societies.		Pluralism and competition between nations. Dispersal.	
Organisational Ecology	Organisational form (although not defined).		Age and size. Technological lock-in.	Turbulent environments: generalists. Large generalists induce specialised entrants.		
Life-cycle of organisations		Periods of turmoil. Capability of foresight.				During change of phases.
Dynamic Capabilities		Time-pacing.	Core competencies. Organisational routines.			
Flexibility/ Changeability		Exploration and exploitation.		Steady-state flexibility. (Dynamic capabilities) (Metacapabilities)	(Dynamic capabilities) (Metacapabilities) (Changeability)	

Table 8.2: Relation between the fields of investigation and the items of the reference model. These questions will direct the research in Part II.

	Phenotype/Genotype	Adaptive Walks	Developmental pathways	Sustained Fitness	Evolvability	Self-organisation
Technology Management Product Innovation	How do technological advances and product innovation contribute to competitiveness?	Which paths do lead to increased fitness of an organisation? Does technological lock-in decrease or increase fitness? How does technology and product innovation link to foresight? How do periods of turmoil affect industrial companies? Does time-pacing offer a solution for dynamics environment?	Can one distinguish between major and minor inventions? Do minor inventions accumulate into major breakthroughs? Which inertia exist? Does technological lock-in set out developmental pathways? Do technology and innovation relate to core competencies?	How do technological advances contribute to sustained fitness? And product innovations? Should organisations specialise or generalise (depending on environment)?	How do technological advances contribute to evolvability? And product innovations? Do the pluralism and competition mean anything in this respect?	Which intense interactions enhance state transitions? Role of suppliers and customer base?
Process Innovation Business Process Re-engineering	How does Process Innovation contribute to the phenotype? How about Business Process Re-engineering?	Does the capability of foresight relate to Process Innovation and Business Process Re-engineering? Do these concepts improve fitness?	Does the implementation of Process Innovation and Business Process Re-engineering account for developmental pathways? Do they affect organisational routines? Do they consider core competencies?	Do Process Innovation and Business Process Re-engineering enhance sustained fitness? Do they link to generalisation or specialisation?	How does Process Innovation contribute to evolvability? And Business Process Re-engineering?	Which intense interactions enhance state transitions? Role of suppliers and customer base?
Delft School Approach	Does it differ from Business Process Re-engineering?	idem	idem	idem	idem	idem
Learning Organisation Knowledge Management Continuous Improvement	How do these concepts relate to the phenotype? Do they focus on genotypes or phenotypes?	Do these concepts relate to adaptive walks to increase fitness? How do they link to the capability of foresight? Relation to time-pacing?	Do these concepts relate to core competencies? And to organisational routines?	Do these concepts increase sustained fitness? Do they link to generalisation and specialisation?	How do these concepts contribute to evolvability?	Which intense interactions enhance state transitions? Role of suppliers and customer base?
Change Management Culture	Do these really affect the organisational form or genotype?	Which link exists between change management and adaptive walks? Idem culture.	Do change management and cultural change affect organisational routines? And core competencies?	Do these concepts increase sustained fitness? Do they link to generalisation and specialisation?	How do these concepts contribute to evolvability?	Which intense interactions enhance state transitions?

management. Partially, the search has already paved the way for answers; the focus on processes and structures forces us to explore the management concepts in more detail. Table 8.2 shows that many questions need to be answered before developing a Framework for Dynamic Adaptation.

8.4   SUMMARY

Although organisations and organisms have different structures, the theories and models of evolutionary biology might find their way to management science as underlying mechanisms governing the (evolutionary) change and the interaction with the environment. The principle of self-reproduction has no direct counterpart in organisations, but organisations can transform themselves through teleological mutations. So far, the research into the adaptation by organisations has resulted in a reference model for evaluation, based on organisations as a special class of allopietic systems and evolutionary mechanisms similar to those of organisms, described by five items:

- the distinction between phenotype and genotype, the difference between the visible traits and the underlying gene pool;
- the adaptive walks and developmental pathways;
- the criterion of sustained fitness;
- the criterion of evolvability;
- the concept of self-organisation.

Each of these items affects the outcome of evolutionary processes by organisations, and how organisations adapt to the dynamics of the environment. Within these issues, defining the landscape fitness remains an unsolved matter. Given certain landscapes, it becomes possible to investigate the reference model (organisations as allopietic systems, evolutionary mechanisms, five items) to evaluate the performance of companies, and to review existing management approaches.

The existing approaches in management science do not clarify detailed mechanisms and processes that are necessary for adaptation. They stress the importance of dynamic capabilities, developmental pathways, and sometimes dispersal. It becomes necessary to extend this study to other theories in management sciences to gain more detailed insight in the processes and structures necessary for adaptation. Especially, since it becomes clear that not the environment determines which processes and structures fit best but the internal capabilities to create those. The environment merely selects.

9 CONCLUDING EVOLUTIONARY BIOLOGY

To conclude the evolutionary biological models, this chapter will elaborate briefly on the different opinions surrounding evolutionary biology, therewith partially questioning the findings so far. Looking at evolutionary biology, it seems a lot of complementary research takes place though not all biologists agree with each other. Section 9.1 will shortly expand on this matter. The evolutionary theories have been criticised, and it makes no sense for completeness if we do not pay attention to some criticisms on the modern theories of evolutionary biology. Especially, the views on the origins of variation and the origins of order have been attacked by the Creationists, rooted in the thoughts of pure Christianity. These critical views of Creationists root deeply in religious beliefs, and therefore have a strong impact on secular views; for the area of research, it will not result in clearer or different views on evolution of organisations. The nature of the criticisms might justify another study which should account for different beliefs. Hence, it will result in different outcomes for the adaptation of organisations to the dynamics of the environment, and it might even require a different approach to this study. Section 9.2 will only briefly address this matter for the sake of completion. At the end, Section 9.3 reviews the thoughts and the meaning of the evolutionary biological models for this particular research. Section 9.4 addresses the initiatives that might result from the meaning of evolutionary biology for management science, and its sets out possible pathways for enhancing research in this area.

9.1 STREAMS OF THOUGHT

Until the 1970's the actual research into evolutionary biology has been dominated by Neo-Darwinism. For example, Johnson (1993) quotes Mayr that macroevolution, evolution at the level of species, is nothing but an extrapolation and magnification of the events that take place within populations and species, i.e. the concept of microevolution. The paper by Gould & Eldredge (1972) sets out another course for evolution of species although it came about from palaeontology where some phenomena of the extinction and the emergence of species needed different views to arrive at a valid theory. During the years after their publication, many have disputed their thoughts led by eminent scientists like Mayr (1976). At the end of the 20th century, these streams have come together and the coexistence of the models of phyletic gradualism and punctuated equilibrium has become a fact. Rather, the models seem complementary and one might even doubt that the originators, Darwin for the theory of phyletic gradualism and Gould & Eldredge for theory of punctuated equilibrium, excluded the existence of other explanations. The search for alternative mechanisms of evolution has led to the attention for macromutations. Jablonski (2000) tells us that the exact mechanisms have not yet been discovered while pointing out the utmost importance of enhancing our insight into the appearance of macromutations. Recent developments in evolutionary biological models show the impact of heterochrony and heterotopy. Yet, it remains to be seen if these new insight will expand the views on both the origins of life and the bio-diversity of life.

Since the acknowledgement of Darwin's *On the Origin of Species by Natural Selection*, the role of natural selection has not really been disputed. The modelling of the interaction became the work of population scientists, during the second half of the 20th century aided by theoretical evolutionary biology, combining mathematics, optimisation theories, simulation tools, etc. Some scientists note that during the shift to include other disciplines, the art of morphology has somewhat disappeared to the background, and that this shift disconnects recent developments in theoretical biology from phenomena in nature. The theoretical models have a great power to explain the diversity of life at both the level of microevolution and macroevolution. However, a comprehensive theory for evolution of species has not yet emerged, and therefore Jablonski (2000) rightfully concludes that at the verge of the new century much more work has to be done.

Wilkins (1998) discusses the various oppositions to Darwinism, and creates therewith an overview of the theories related to Darwinism and the varieties of anti-Darwinism. By no means, the account is complete but it provides an astonishing list of all kind of views that come along with evolutionary biology. Wilkins makes a distinction in eleven separate theses of Darwinism:

1. *Transmutationism.* Species change form to become other species (Section 6.1).
2. *Common descent.* Similar species have common ancestors.
3. *Struggle for existence.* More offspring is born than can survive (Section 6.1 and 7.1).
4. *Natural selection.* The relative better adapted organisms have more offspring (Section 7.1).
5. *Sexual selection.* The more attractive organisms of sexual species mate more (and have more offspring), causing unfit traits to spread.
6. *Biogeographic distribution.* Species occur close by related species, explaining the distributions of various genera (Section 7.1).
7. *Heredity.* Alleles are transferred by recombination from one generation to the next (Section 6.1).

8. *Random mutation.* The notion that changes in genes are not directed towards *better* alternatives; in other words, that mutations are blind to the needs imposed by the ecology in which organisms find themselves (Section 6.1).

9. *Genetic drift/neutralism.* Some changes in genes are due to chance or the so-called *sampling error* of small populations of organisms (Section 6.1 and 7.1). Molecular neutralism tells that the very structure of genes changes in purely random ways.

10 *Functionalism.* Features of organisms are neither due to or are constrained by the shapes (morphology) of their lineage, but are due to their functional or adaptive benefits (Section 6.3).

11. *Gradualism.* Changes do not occur all at once; there are intermediate steps from an earlier stage to the next (Section 6.1).

During the past 150 years, Darwinism has been challenged on several accounts and by several streams of thought (Wilkins, 1998). From each of these challenging theories, this overview lists the proponents, including modern ones:

- *Special Creationism*: the view that species are created *specially* in each case (subject of Section 9.3, last biologist to be a Special Creationist: Louis Aggasis). This stream especially challenges concepts 1, 2, 6, and usually 8 of Darwinism.

- *Orthogenesis*: evolution proceeds in direct lines to goals, also sometimes called teleological evolution or progressionism (Lamarck, Nägeli, Eimer, Osborn, Severtsov, Teilhard de Chardin). The proponents question especially the theories 8 and 9 of Darwinism.

- *Neo-Lamarckism (a.k.a. Instructionism)*: the environment instructs the genome and changes occur to anticipate the needs of an organism (Darwin [1859]), Haeckel, E.D. Cope, S. Butler, Kropotkin, G.B.S. Shaw, Kammerer, Koestler, E. Steele, Goldschmidt). This theory disputes in particular the concepts of 7, 8, and 9.

- *Process Structuralism*: laws of change that determine some or all of the features of organisms (Goethe, Geoffrey, d'Arcy Thompson, Goodwin, Salthe, Gould [1980], Løvtrup, Kauffman [1993, 1995]). The advocates of this view object to points 3, 5, and 10 of Darwinism (Section 6.2, 6.2, 6.3).

- *Saltationism*: changes between forms occur all-at-once or not at all (Galton, T.H. Huxley, de Vries, T.H. Morgan, Johannsen, Goldschmidt). They oppose 10 and sometimes 11 (Section 6.2).

- *Monism*: all evolutionary and biological phenomena can be brought under a single set of consistent theories of mechanisms (Dawkins [Max, 2001], Maynard Smith [1982]).

None of the opponents has ever disputed the role of natural selection, making it look like that Darwin's proposition still holds. Wilkins (1998) concludes that defying Darwinian views comes easy but hard empirical work needs to be done before disestablishing any of the theories. He mentions that Maynard Smith did convince Kauffman that his thoughts were Darwinian after all. For our study, it seems that the compilation of evolutionary biology has touched on most of the theories whether Darwinian or not and explored those that tell most about the interaction between entity and environment.

9.2   VIEW OF THE CREATIONISTS

The views on the origins of variation and the origins of order have been fiercely disputed by the Creationists, people who take the creation account in the Book of Genesis to be true in a very literal sense (Johnson, 1993). That means that those take as a starting point that:

- the earth was created in a single week of six days no more than 10.000 years ago;
- the major features of the geological diversity were produced by Noah's flood;
- no more major innovations emerged in the forms of life since the beginning.

Not all within the Christian belief oppose the theories of evolution that have sprouted since Darwin drew the focus to natural selection. According to Johnson (1993), most Christian scientists share the view that Darwinism can be interpreted as consistent with Christian belief. He concludes that Darwinism is not empirical at all but rather an implication of a philosophical doctrine called scientific naturalism, which is based on the a priori assumption that God was absent from the realm of nature. Olson (2003), as propagator of Creationism, refutes such and declares theistic evolution incompatible with Christianity.

According to Max (1999), the Creationists focus on three favourite arguments to discuss the phenomena of randomness linked to evolutionary models and design as created by God. First, Creationists proclaim that mutations are harmful. If you take a well-running complex biological machine and subject it to random alterations, you could scarcely expect to have made any improvements and almost certainly will have harmed the organism. To explain adaptive changes in populations, the Creationists argue, for example, that the variant genes for dark and light colour were present in the original population, designed by a creator to allow moths to live in varying environments (an alternative explanation for the example of the peppered moth in Section 6.1). The shift towards darker coloration resulted from shifts in the frequencies of existing designed genes without requiring new random mutations. Selection in this view acts conservatively to weed out individuals with mutations and to prevent the spread of mutations into a population. Secondly, Creationists tell that random mutations cannot increase the information content of a system. Since the information content of the human genome is vastly larger than that of bacteria, if mutation cannot play a role in this increase then the foundation of evolution by mutation and natural selection would seem to be in question. Thirdly, the role of random mutation in biological origins is a stochastic process supposedly proving the impossibility of an evolutionary origin of proteins. The Creationists ask: What is the probability that the correct sequence of amino acids of a specific protein could have been selected by chance? According to them, this chance seems so negligibly small that they compare it with the likelihood that a tornado blowing through a junkyard could assemble a 747 airliner. These three arguments (harmfulness of mutations, information content, stochastic process) make Creationist believe that insight from the evolutionary biological models is unlikely to explain the diversity of life.

Some of the counter arguments have been presented in this research. Firstly, beneficial mutations occur even though they are rare (Max, 1999). A beneficial mutation can confer a survival or reproductive advantage to the individuals that carry it, thereby leading, over several generations, to the spread of this mutation throughout a population (Chapter 6). Furthermore, a large part of the increase in information of human genomes compared with those of *lower* organisms apparently results from gene duplication processes followed by independent evolution and differentiation of duplicated copies into multiple genes with distinct functions (Max, 1999), as described by the theories of macromutations (Section 6.3), the models of Kauffman (Section 7.2), and the various adaptive theories (Section 7.3). Finally, Max (1999) presents the statistical impossibility to be possible by expanding on an experiment by Dawkins using a computer simulation; this looks very much like how Kauffman (1995) explains the origins of order. The counter arguments against Creationism originate from the theoretical models of evolution from which many have been reviewed in this report.

Arshad (1996) draws our attention to the peculiar fact that the idea of natural selection and the evidence for evolution has been subject of study for Muslim scientists, even one thousand years before Darwin published his findings. He states:

> The Muslim scientists ibn Kathir, ibn Khauldun, ibn Arabi, ibn Sina, among other scientists, such as the Ikhwan school of thought, arrived at the same conclusions as Darwin with a convincing amount of evidence. Every Muslim school and mosque used to teach evolution up until a few hundred years ago. Some Westerners, including Darwin's contemporary, Sir William Draper, called it the Mohammedan Theory of Evolution. Draper admitted that the Muslim version was more advanced than Darwin's, because in the Muslim version, the evolution starts out with minerals.

Now remember, that Kauffman proved that the origin of life might originate in autocatalytic sets; catalytic reactions might be stimulated by minerals, a known fact from chemistry. Therefore, the study of life strongly relates to the total interpretation of the world and its relationships to other topics than evolutionary biology and management science. Arshad (1996) links the view of the Creationists to the concept that Babylonians had, God changes all the laws of nature in order to accomplish something, very much unlike the interwoven thoughts of Jews and Muslims on this point. Also he points to the fact that Creationists disprove evolution mostly by negative arguments: the present theory is false, therefore creation is true.

The interpretations show that even religious beliefs might have ambiguous views on the evolutionary processes. The view that the diversity of life originates in designs by a Creator might also lead to similar views on the processes and structures of organisations to adapt to the dynamics of the environment. Neo-Darwinism will lead to restricted perspectives on the evolution of organisations. The Talk.Origins Archive (www.talkorigins.org) demonstrates this notion by paying attention to both the contemporary ideas of evolutionary biology as well as the controversies that surround any of these theories, including those of secular beliefs. Looking at the study at hand, the study has compiled all kind of different insight and theories to a set of related concepts that might help to explain the evolution of organisations and their adaptation processes. It has not looked at the roots of these theories and their philosophical impact on beliefs. These might affect topics like leadership (Wood, 1992, p. 196). It will require another study to reveal the meaning of beliefs on the way organisations deal with their environment.

9.3   ADAPTATION OF INDUSTRIAL ORGANISATIONS TO THE DYNAMICS OF THE ENVIRONMENT

Only during the past decades, the interest by management scientists into biological models for the evolution of organisations has got more attention. This stream of thought has not yet reached sufficient levels of maturity in comparison to the methods and the advances in the domain of evolutionary biology. Wobben (2001, p. 89) notes that many applications of the theories on chaos and complexity focus on metaphors rather than on analogies. He adds that one of the reasons for such is the lack of interest by managers, scientists, and consultants for describing and understanding reality rather than the pursuit of explaining and predicting reality by causality and deductive-nomological models. Romme & van Witteloostuijn (1997, pp. 69-70) suggest that the theoretical base in the descriptions for organisations lacks in most theories. As a result, the insight of management science has an superficial character, and therefore offer hardly new points of view though potentially they should. Even then, most of the management studies root in *morphological* studies of organisations to highlight differences; in the domain of biology, scientists are aware of their limitations. Both theoretical work and practical studies should enlighten the theories on the evolution of organisations.

The diversity of the theories on evolutionary biology and their relations justify a comprehensive reference model for the evolution of organisations, accounting for the differences between organisations and organisms. The investigation has shown that the interaction between organisation and environment constitutes a continuous process. One-time interventions, comparable to the long jumps of Kauffman's NK-model, hardly seem effective, and even then organisations need to undergo the forces of further development and optimisation to reach nearby fitness peaks in the adaptive landscape. The connection of the reference model to strands of management theories and managerial practice should lead to more profound insight in the evolutionary processes within organisations; these theories and managerial practice will be presented in Chapters 11-13.

Recently, the literature on management science has seen a vast rise on the numbers of publications on the flexibility of organisations. Although such approaches rightfully take the dynamics of the environment into account, they abolish the thought of continuous adaptation. To cope with the dynamics of the environment, the concept of changeability has been introduced as a more comprehensive concept than flexibility (e.g. Milberg & Dürrschmidt, 2002). Changeability comprises flexibility and change of the organisational structure. Yet, this theme has hardly been explored as Volberda (2000, p. 28) notes.

The study of the biological theories demonstrates that the current approaches of management science hardly suffice. The continuous interaction between organisation and environment requires continuous processes and structures to shape the interaction and evolve organisations to fitness for the future. Although the reference model sets out leads to unveil the mechanisms in organisations underlying adaptation, it does not tell how to shape the processes and structures needed, the original quest of the study. The model highlights a number of issues that surround adaptation instead of pointing to a singular theory to describe all.

9.4   Further Research into the Evolution of Organisations

The vast, extended amount of literature on evolutionary biology made it impossible to study all possible evolutionary mechanisms; for example, altruism and co-evolution might offer additional perspectives, and the theories of the science of complexity have been limited mostly to the models of Kauffman. Therefore the results so far might suffer from inconsistencies or gaps that have not been accounted for, and might have restricted value for the field of management science. The current compilation of literature on evolutionary biology developed into a view on how the interaction between organism and environment takes place. The transfer of this knowledge to the domain of organisations, a higher level of complexity within the systems hierarchy of Boulding, yielded a reference model for the interaction between organisations and their environment.

At the same time, it becomes clear that a lot work still has to be done. The statements of Wobben (2001) and Romme & van Witteloostuijn (1997) indicate that only elaboration of existing models in management science will yield newer, different insight exceeding the abstract statements about the evolution of organisations so far; these statements should converge to contemporary models for addressing the imbalance organisations experience between the dynamics of the environment and internally generated adaptations. In this regard, the elaboration of the next chapters will bring this understanding closer to implementation in industry and managerial practice.

Hence, the next stage will consider the organisation as a living entity for which the research cumulates issues from current theories of management science, which are relevant to the reference model. The selected theories that describe the interaction between organisation and environment comprise the fields of:

- technology and innovation management;
- Business Process Re-engineering;
- Learning Organisation, Knowledge Management and Continuous Improvement;
- change management and culture (briefly discussed in Chapter 13).

The theories of these fields attracted much attention during the past decade, and direct themselves primarily to the interaction between the environment and the structures and processes of individual organisations. The assessment of these fields, by looking at literature, in combination with a review of practices in companies, both from available literature and cases in practice, should lead to a Framework for Dynamic Adaptation by industrial organisations.

PART II: REVIEW OF MANAGEMENT APPROACHES

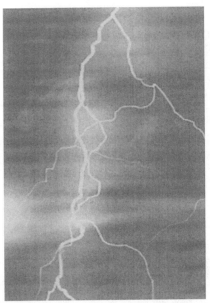

Management science has moved away from the simple efficiency paradigm and related control processes, introduced in the 18ᵗʰ century by Adam Smith (1776) and by Frederick the Great of Prussia (Morgan, 1997, pp. 15-16), into the many branches of specialisation that exist today. Evolutionary processes require a more integral view.

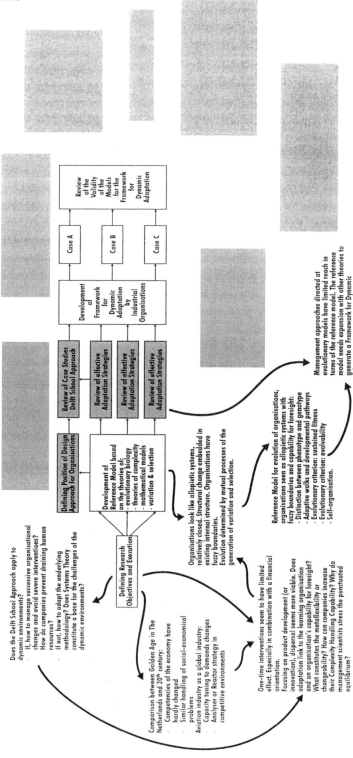

Figure II.1: Overview of the research, based on the findings during the prologue and Part I. The evolutionary biological models indicate the mechanisms of evolution for organisations. Although organisations do differ from organisms, partially the same theories and mechanisms do apply to explain the development and adaptation of organisations. This has resulted in the development of a reference model for the evolution of organisations. Part II will focus on connecting the reference model to existing theories in management science in the domain of technology and innovation management, Business Process Re-engineering, Learning Organisation, Knowledge Management, Continuous Improvement.

That adaptation plays a large role in the evolution of organisations has become clear during the first stages of this research. The analogy of the development of organisations with the evolutionary biological models created insight into the detailed mechanisms that underpin adaptations. Such adaptations should be highly listed on the agenda of management teams, reason to focus research on the processes and structures that industrial companies need to deal with external changes and the dynamics of the environment. The prevailing notion that companies achieve equilibrium with their environment rarely seems to hold, both are in motion, driven by quite different phenomena. Companies mutate which creates disequilibria, even in seemingly stable markets, as the evolutionary theories tell. The environment constantly changes, caused by mutations of other companies, shifting landscapes, and further increasing complexity of the state space of landscapes. The evolutionary models from biology give ground to extensively reviewing the existing approaches in management science.

The journey continues from the evolutionary biological models to the domain of contemporary approaches in management science to seek for answers into the quest of adaptation strategies for industrial companies in dynamic environments. So far, we have collected different models from evolutionary biological models and transferred them to the domain of organisations. This resulted in the creation of a reference model, introduced in Subsection 8.1.2, based on organisations as allopietic systems whose development is described by evolutionary mechanisms with five items: the difference between genotype and phenotype, the undertaking of adaptive walks, the optimisation by searching for sustained fitness, the evolvability of organisations to disperse, bifurcate, etc., and the self-organisation in combination with dissipative structures. The next phase of the research focuses on the value of technology management, innovation management, process innovation, Business Process Re-engineering, Learning Organisation, Knowledge Management, Continuous Improvement, change management, and culture for the adaptation strategies of companies. The reference model points to the mechanisms and theories that describe evolutionary development of organisations. Many of the contemporary approaches in management science reside in empirical studies of organisations as entities and industries. The comparison of the reference model with theories, propositions, and findings in management literature on evolutionary approaches or adaptation sets out the pathway to expand those with additional findings to generate a Framework for Dynamic Adaptation.

Hence, the next stage of the research will consider the organisation as a living entity for which the survey of contemporary approaches in management science cumulates issues for a framework (see Table 8.2). The reference model supports the assessment of current theories in the themes:
- technology and innovation management, two closely related topics of management science (Chapter 10). Viewing the organisation as a living entity,

the concepts of innovation and technology management capture directly the model of the input and output of an allopietic system. The implementation of technology and innovation has lead to remarkable notions for increasing competitiveness. Both the theories and practice of technology and innovation will be tested against the issues of the framework and the hypotheses;

- Business Process Re-engineering (Chapter 11). The primary aim of Re-engineering has always been directed at creating a different structure for an organisation to control and manage its primary process. Furthermore, the chapter will explore the contingencies and circumstances needed for expansion of the theories. This chapter will also link to theories and contingencies to the Delft School Approach, testing the viability of the methodology, and assessing the value of the theories found so far in practice. This allows to ground the theory in practice through investigating case studies in detail;
- Learning Organisation, Knowledge Management, and Continuous Improvement (Chapter 12). Self-reference and cognition lead to the capability of learning whereby Knowledge Management and Continuous Improvement resemble more defined principles of learning processes in organisations;
- change management and culture (Chapter 13). These topics aim at changing the behaviour of an organisation mainly looking at the composition (and sometimes the structure). Originally, the issues of change management and culture were not part of the research. Since the search for adaptive walks looks at the behaviour of organisations, the effective changes in the organisation deserve some attention, too. However, this is not the core of the research which looks at processes and structures as such for adaptation.

The assessment of these areas in combination with a review of practices in companies should lead to a Framework for Dynamic Adaptation by industrial organisations.

From the insight so far, it has become clear that the adaptation to the environment happens through the creation of mutations, through forms and functions, in performance towards the environment, whether it concerns meeting performance requirements, offering new products or utilising resources. These mutations might go through a period of elimination before those that survive enter an era of stability in which gradual changes take place. The turmoil is caused by all the variants, mutants appearing at that time, which created the need for testing the adaptation of each to the changing environment. Hence, industrial companies should create mutations of themselves as a continuous process that way reducing the chances for creating and maintaining homeostatic balance. This model of punctuated equilibrium has received much attention from management scientists in the field of technology management and innovation, two closely related topics.

The justification for innovation as driving factor for current business practices of change stems from Schumpeter who was wondering why we were better off than our parents. He arrives at a powerful insight: the prime driver of economic progress is technological innovation. Most economics of his day concentrated on achieving the state of perfect competition. Schumpeter pointed out, however, that people were better off in the 1940's than they had been at the turn of the 19th century because of technological advances, and because industries had approached the perfect state of competition. Eisenhardt & Tabrizi (1995, p. 84) mention that many authors proved that product development and innovation is a dominant path by which they adapt to the environment. This chapter will explore how the necessary mutations come about for industrial companies by looking at technology and innovation.

The approaches towards technology and innovation rank under the aggregate of descriptions of phenomena related to discontinuity, including technological discontinuity, product innovation, and process innovation. When speaking about innovation in this chapter, it refers the renewal of products and markets for a given company. This includes developing new products such as the new laptop computer without its own operating system for use at Internet or the application of existing products in new markets. Renewal takes also place when a company redefines its position, its activities, and its policy as a total. When this is the case, the renewal is called breakthrough to distinguish it from innovation directed at product-market combinations. Innovation as defined above might be part of the total breakthrough for a company. Technology is a reflection of the skills and knowledge base of a company (Section 10.1) and will eventually generate new products and processes. Product innovation refers to the renewal of products in the market place (Section 10.2). Process innovation directs itself to improving the performance of the primary process, i.e. order processing and delivering products to the market (subject of Chapter 11). Although process innovation is discussed later, it is not quite possible to treat product innovation and process innovation separately, for which Chapter 11 will expand on the relationship between product and process innovation.

Many relate technological advances and innovation to the models of punctuated equilibrium. With the dynamic changes within the environment, does the premise of the punctuated equilibrium hold? How should a structural approach to technology management and innovation the competitiveness of an industrial organisation? These questions will be explored during Section 10.3 by exploring the existing literature on approaches to support adequately technology management and innovation in industrial companies. Section 10.4 will examine the findings so far and subject them to the reference model for the evolutionary development of organisations.

10.1 TECHNOLOGICAL DISCONTINUITY

How does technology relate to the development of organisations and their products? Since the 1980's technology is recognised as an important element of business definition and competitive strategy in academic literature. Abell (1980) identified technology as one of three principal dimensions of business definition, noting *technology adds a dynamic character to the task of business definition, as one technology may more or less rapidly displace another over time.* Porter (1983) observes that *technology is among the most prominent factors that determine the rules of competition.* Friar & Horwitch (1985, pp. 145-147) explain the growing prominence of technology as the result of historical forces: the disenchantment with strategic planning, the success of high-technology firms in emerging industries, the surge of Japanese competition, a recognition of the competitive significance of manufacturing, and the emergence of an academic interest in technology management. Nowadays, we contribute to high-tech firms elevated levels of competitiveness.

But what precisely constitutes the role of technology in a firm's strategy? Before expanding on the role of technology in business management, what does technology stand for? According to the *Oxford Dictionary* technology means the application of scientific knowledge into practical purposes, it notes especially in industry. When we look at the original Greek words where it is derived from: τεκηνε (art, craft) and λογια (subject of study or interest), we see two components. First of all, the reference to craft implies the application of skills and knowledge into practice. The second component indicates that technology looks for general rules for the application of those skills and knowledge. Hence,

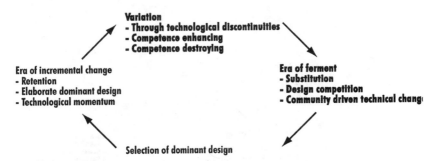

Figure 10.1: Technology cycle. Periods of turmoil, eras of ferment and selection of dominant design, are interchanged by periods of homeostatic stability, eras of incremental change and variation. This cycle corresponds to the selectional processes of the evolutionary mechanisms.

technology relates to the available skills and knowledge within the reach of an organisation, identified as key factors for achieving sustainability.

10.1.1 Technology Cycle

Gomory & Schmitt (1989), Morone (1993), Deschamps & Nayak (1995), Burgelman et al. (1995), and Tushman & Anderson (1997) investigated technology as a part of business management. They remark that the next state of the environment arrives through long periods of incremental change and continuous improvement, broken by radical, revolutionary change that in turn leads to further incremental change, interrupted by a subsequent revolutionary event, and so on. These revolutions are triggered by discontinuous environmental shifts, one of which is the introduction of new technologies. Considering this cyclical model, they developed a technology cycle containing four phases: technological discontinuities (variation), eras of ferment, dominant designs, and eras of incremental change (like the theory of punctuated equilibrium). The phases of technological discontinuities and dominant designs mark the transitions between eras of ferment and eras of incremental change, as illustrated in Figure 10.1. Technology exceeds the individual capabilities of firms for diffusion: acceptance of technologies relates strongly to the overall introduction and application by more firms, yet individual companies strongly contribute to the overall technology base of an industry.

Additionally, Mokyr (1990, pp. 352-354) believes that macroinventions, he means in fact technologies, mostly require a number of microinventions, micro-advances, before taking effect. Only few major technological advances revolutionised a whole technical mode in one bold stroke, as he states. Generally, technologies need complementary micro-advances to reach sufficient levels of perfection. For example, the invention by Lewis and Paul in 1740 of the roller

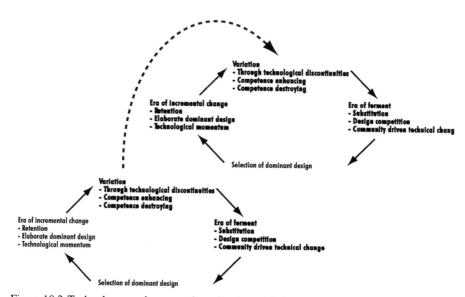

Figure 10.2: Technology cycles over time. During periods of variation, significant different technologies might appear that result in new consequent technology cycles. The era of variation does not only yield further technological advances within the scope of an existing technology, it also might end in new technologies that enter their own technology cycles. The development of technologies resides in the performance and development of earlier technologies. The eras of variation and ferment represent periods of turmoil like in the evolutionary model of the punctuated equilibrium. A period of stability follows that expands on the selected dominant design.

replacing human fingers as a yarn twisting device *had to wait until it was complemented a quarter-century later by Arkwright's relatively marginal but crucial insight to use two (instead of one) rollers.* In contrast to micro-advances that result from dedicated research and development, macroinventions depend on chance discoveries, luck, and inspiration.

Technological advance is driven by the combination of chance events (variation), direct social and political action of organisations in selecting between rival technical regimes (artificial selection), as well as by incremental, competence enhancing, puzzle solving actions of many organisations through learning-by-doing (retention)[43]. This retention stage provides a context for the subsequent technological discontinuity. This subsequent technological discontinuity then triggers the next wave of technical variation, selection, and retention (see Figure

---

[43] *Subsection 7.5.1 remarks that the model of variation, retention, and selection has limited reach for describing the total evolutionary mechanism (for both organisms and organisations).*

10.2). The next subsections will examine each phase of the technology cycle, stressing the roles of social, political, and organisational actors in the course of technological evolution. Elaborating the four stages in the technology cycle brightens the insight how technology might contribute to the adaptation strategies of a company, by creating new competencies and by developing new, marketable products. However, it becomes clear that the continuous development of new technologies and the elaboration of dominant designs cause the instability within the population of industries; very similar to the development of species.

10.1.2 Technological Discontinuity

Technological discontinuities represent those rare advances of a relevant technological frontier by an order-of-magnitude, which involve fundamentally different product or process designs; but they might not yet have a commercial impact (Sepers, 1998, p. 35). *Product discontinuities* constitute of fundamentally different product forms, which command a decisive cost, performance or quality advantage over prior product forms (e.g. jet engines, diesel locomotives, and quartz oscillation). *Process discontinuities* are fundamentally different ways of making a product, which are reflected in order-of-magnitude improvements in the cost of quality of the product or new levels of performance. Process discontinuities might affect the product design by opening up new possibilities for parts, components, etc. Both discontinuities reflect on the performance of products, the output of companies, towards the market; only when these discontinuities convert into commercial success, they will be considered innovations.

Not all technological discontinuities are alike. Technological discontinuities might be characterised as competence destroying or competence enhancing. Competence destroying discontinuities are based on fundamentally different technological knowledge or concepts and, as such, obsolete expertise required to master existing technology. For example, the mechanical watchmaking capabilities were rendered irrelevant by quartz movements. Competence enhancing discontinuities, on the other hand, build on existing know-how. In watch technology, for example, automatic mechanical movements represented a fundamentally different way of providing energy to the spring, but built on prior mechanical competencies. Competence enhancing innovations introduce a new technical order while building on, not obsolescing, the existing technical regime.

10.1.3 Eras of Ferment

Technological discontinuities open eras of ferment, as radical technical advances increase variation in a product class. Technological discontinuities usher in an era of experimentation as organisations struggle to absorb (or destroy) the innovative technology. Two distinct processes characterise this era of ferment: competition between old and new technological regimes, and competition within new technical regimes. Given a certain product class, this period of substantial product class variation and, in turn uncertainty is closed by the emergence of a dominant design.

Competition between old and new technologies is fierce; older technological orders seldom vanish quietly. The response of the existing community of practitioners often is to increase the innovativeness and efficiency of the existing technical regime. For example, piston jets and mechanical watches both experienced sharp performance advances in response to technological threats. Given the innovative response of practitioners rooted in the existing technical order, technical discontinuities do not always dominate (e.g. bubble memory, Wankel engines).

Concurrent with competition between technical orders is the process of design competition within a technological order. Several, often incompatible versions of the discontinuity appear both because the technology is not well understood, and because each pioneering firm has an incentive to differentiate its variant from rivals. Substitute technologies will dominate existing technologies only if they add an important functional parameter and do as well on existing parameters; or if they dominate existing parameters, contributing to the company's business growth. However, during eras of ferment, neither dimensions of merit nor subsequent technical performance are yet clear.

10.1.4 Dominant Designs

For variation and selection to cumulate in an evolutionary process, there must be a retention mechanism; a successful variation must be preserved and propagated. A dominant design is the second watershed event in a technology cycle, demarcating the end of the era of ferment. A dominant design is a single architecture that establishes dominance in a product class. Once a dominant design emerges, a future technological progress (until the next discontinuity) consists of incremental improvements elaborating the standard: technological uncertainty decreases. Technical clarity and convergence on a set of technical parameters permit firms to design standardised and interchangeable parts, and to optimise organisational processes for volume and efficiency. Practitioner communities develop industry wide procedures, traditions, and problem-solving modes that permit focused, incremental technical puzzle solving. Dominant designs permit more stable and reliable relations with suppliers, vendors, and customers. From customers' perspectives, dominant designs reduce product class confusion and promise dramatic decreases in product cost. Finally, if the product is part of a larger system, industry standards permit system compatibility and integration.

The crucial point is that with the exception of the simplest products, the emergence of dominant designs is not a function of economic or technological determinism; they do not appear because there is one best way to implement a product or process. Rival designs are often technologically superior on one or more key performance dimensions. For example, the IBM PC was not the fastest personal computer, Matsushita's VHS format did not offer the sharpest videocassette reproduction, and Westinghouse's AC power systems were not the most efficient. Indeed, dominant designs may not be particularly innovative; they often incorporate features pioneered elsewhere. If dominant designs do not arise from inexorable technical or economic logic, how do they evolve? Because a single technological order rarely dominates alternative technologies across critical dimensions of merit, community level sociopolitical processes adjudicate among feasible technical and economic options. A process of compromise and accommodation between suppliers, vendors, customers, and governments shapes the closing on critical dimensions of merit. Dominant designs then emerge not from technical logic, but from a negotiated logic enlivened by actors with interests in competing technical regimes.

10.1.5 Eras of Incremental Change

After dominant designs emerge, technical progress is driven by numerous incremental innovations. These innovations elaborate and extend the dominant design. During periods of incremental change, informal know-how trading occurs between competitors. Practice traditions are socially constructed and, unlike scientific progress, cross-disciplinary boundaries. Where dominant designs are established by the visible hand of a few powerful organisations competing for dominance, in the era of incremental change, technological progress is driven by the invisible hand of a multitude of organisations competing within sharp technical, social, and normative constraints.

Eras of incremental change persist until they are ended by subsequent technological discontinuities. Technological discontinuities directly challenge technical premises that underlie the prior period of incremental change. However, these technological threats are met with resistance by technological momentum within competing organisations, especially because any discontinuity is originally associated with substantial uncertainty, ambiguity, and implementation costs.

10.2 PRODUCT INNOVATION AS KEY POINT FOR ADAPTING

As discussed, chance events combined with selection between technical regimes, as well as by incremental, competence enhancing, puzzle solving actions drive technological advance. How do these technological advances contribute to the adaptation strategies by industrial companies? Within the management literature, a strong connection exists between innovation and technology: the variation, the selection, and the incremental change eras are powered by innovation. But what constitutes innovation and how does it work?

The innovation process according to Herbig (1994) consists not merely of discrete occurrences but of a flow of events. Figure 10.3 illustrates the development of an innovation, which begins with the fundamental science (the discovery of new principles, theories, etc.), and ends with the diffusion of the innovation throughout the market. With this framework, Herbig focuses on the heart of the innovation process: the stages of discovery, feasibility (invention), and commercial production. Examples of the discovery of the principle or theory (fundamental research) include Maxwell's equations regarding electromagnetism and Einstein's famous equation denoting the relationship between energy and matter. Discovery is an event that is most often credited to a single individual, and is often done in isolation. But discovery is only the first step. At times, a period of many years is required before the practical application of a discovery may be turned into a real product (as can be readily seen from da Vinci's drawings of helicopters). Though the discovery is important, it is the application of that discovery rather than the discovery itself, which becomes critical to the development of a company.

The invention step is the first working prototype that resulted from the discovery (technical invention or applied research). Many inventions do not immediately enter the stream of commercial or industrial application. In fact, many never get beyond the stage of conception, while others are abandoned during the period of development. How marvellous a technological invention may be, it does not constitute innovation if it creates no growth or profit in the market economy. Given a certain field of application, thus a 'survival of the

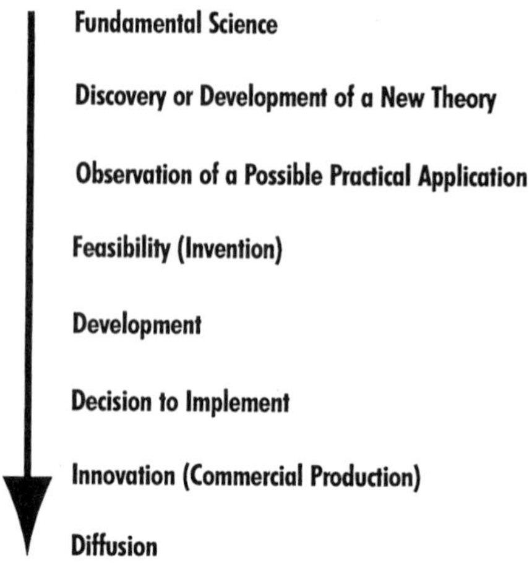

Figure 10.3: Innovation process from discovery to commercialisation. Only when innovations reach the market stage, we speak about innovations. Such innovation should also find their way to customers (diffusion). Please note that the position of innovation suggests a different definition than in the text. It seems that Herbig wants to indicate by this

Fundamental Science

Discovery or Development of a New Theory

Observation of a Possible Practical Application

Feasibility (Invention)

Development

Decision to Implement

Innovation (Commercial Production)

Diffusion

fittest' occurs as a direct result of the marketplace; multiple inventions lead to competition, resulting in lesser numbers of innovations, until one standard emerges as the innovation diffuses. This standard is often named dominant design.

According to Herbig (1994), the innovation is the first commercial demonstration of the invention. Innovation is the conversion of that invention into a used application. If there is no market (or use) for the product, there cannot be innovation. Unlike invention, innovation is related to potential uses and potential markets, and related to the development of a company:

Innovation = Invention + Exploitation.

Burgelman et al. (1995) approach innovation in a similar way. They state that innovations are the outcome of the innovation process, leading to new, marketable products and services or new production and delivery systems. They say that the criteria for success of technological innovations are commercial rather than technical: a successful innovation is one that returns the original investment in its development plus some additional returns.

10.2.1 Incremental and Radical Innovations

As pointed out in the previous section, the technology cycle is characterised by different eras. These phases represent different approaches, and with that different types of innovation. Abernathy & Clark (1985), Iansiti & Clark (1994), Tabrizi & Eisenhardt (1995), Burgelman et al. (1995), Sanderson & Uzumeri (1995), and Tushman & Anderson (1997) write that in competitive, technology-intensive global markets, competitive advantage can be built only through a combination of different types of innovation – not only through the creation of product substitutes, but also through architectural innovation, continuous, incremental innovation, and radical innovation. It is the ability to produce streams of different kinds of innovation that drives sustained competitive advantage:

- *Incremental innovations* involve the adaptation, refinement, and enhancement of existing products and services, e.g. the next generation of a microprocessor. Incremental innovation often reinforces the dominance of established firms. Although it does not draw from dramatically new science, it often calls for considerable skills and ingenuity, and might have significant economic consequences.
- *Radical innovations*, in contrast, are based on a different set of engineering and scientific principles. Radical innovations involve entirely new product categories, service categories, production and delivery systems (e.g. wireless communications). It often opens up whole new markets and potential applications.

Radical and incremental innovations have such different competitive consequences because they require quite different organisational capabilities. Organisational capabilities are difficult to create and costly to adjust. Where incremental innovation reinforces the capabilities of established organisations, radical innovation does force them to ask a new set of questions, to draw on new technical and commercial skills, and to employ new problem-solving approaches.

10.2.2 Architectural Innovations

The same authors however agree that the distinction between radical and incremental innovations has produced important insight, but is fundamentally incomplete. There is growing evidence that there are numerous technical innovations that involve apparently modest changes to the existing technology but that have quite dramatic competitive consequences. Existing models that rely on the simple distinction between radical and incremental innovation provide little insight into the reasons why such apparently minor or straightforward innovations should have such consequences. Innovations that change the way, in which the components of a product are linked together, while leaving the core design concepts (and thus the basic knowledge underlying the components) untouched, are defined as *architectural innovations* (Henderson & Clark, 1990). This is the kind of innovation that challenged Xerox with its traditional plain-paper copiers (competitors developed smaller copiers), and RCA with the portable transistor radio receiver (Sony used the concept to enter the USA market). It destroys the usefulness of a firm's architectural knowledge but preserves the usefulness of its knowledge about the product's components.

The distinction between the product as a whole – the system – and the product in its parts – the components – has a long history in the design literature. The distinction between the product as a system and the product as a set of components underscores the idea that successful product development requires two types of knowledge. First it requires component knowledge, or knowledge about each of the core design concepts, and the way in which they are implemented in a particular component. Second, it requires architectural knowledge, or knowledge about the ways in which the components are integrated and linked together into a coherent whole. The distinction between architectural and component knowledge, or between the components themselves and the links between them, is a source of insight into the ways in which innovations differ from each other.

10.2.3 Linking Innovation to Technology

The notion that there are different kinds of innovation, with different competitive effects, has been an important theme in the literature on technological innovation. The literature has characterised different kinds of innovations in terms of their impact on the established capabilities of the firm (see Figure 10.4, which covers a proposed classification for innovations along two dimensions). These dimensions resemble two concepts of Systems Theory: the distinction between structure (= architecture) and elements (= components). The horizontal dimension captures an innovation's impact on components, while the vertical captures its impact on the linkages between components. This framework therefore focuses mostly on the impact of an innovation on the usefulness of the existing architectural and component knowledge of the firm. Although these types of innovation have been recognised in literature, yet they have not been connected through a classification along the two proposed dimensions, structure and elements.

Framed this way, radical and incremental innovations are extreme points along both dimensions. Radical innovations establish a new dominant design and, hence, a new set of core design concepts embodied in components that are linked together in a new architecture. Incremental innovations refine and extend an established design. Improvement occurs in individual components, but the underlying core design concepts and the links between them remain the same.

Figure 10.4 shows two further particular types of innovation: those that change only the core design concepts of a technology and those that change only the relationships between them. The first is *modular innovation*, like the replacement of analogue with digital telephones. To the degree that one can simply replace an analogue dialling device with a digital one, means that it is an innovation that changes a core design concept without changing the product's architecture. The innovation, which has great influence, however, is the second type of innovation shown in the matrix: innovation that changes a product's architecture but leaves the components, and the core design concepts that they embody, unchanged. The essence of architectural innovation is the reconfiguration of an established system to link together existing components in a new way. This does not mean that the components themselves are untouched by architectural innovation. Architectural innovation is often triggered by a change in a component – perhaps size or another parameter of its design – that creates new interactions and new linkages with other components in the established product. The important

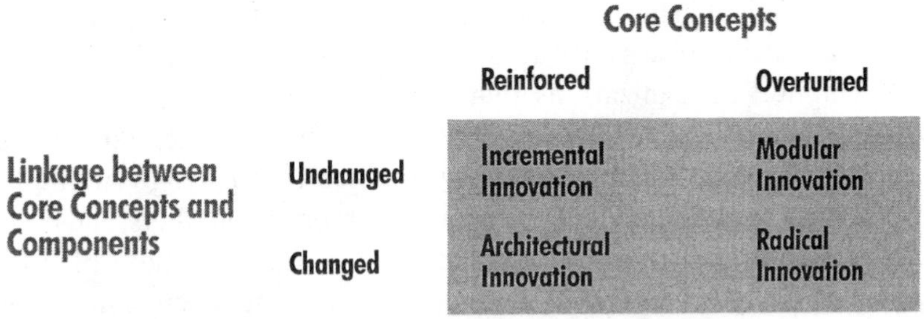

		Core Concepts	
		Reinforced	Overturned
Linkage between Core Concepts and Components	Unchanged	Incremental Innovation	Modular Innovation
	Changed	Architectural Innovation	Radical Innovation

Figure 10.4: Different concepts of innovation (Henderson & Clark, 1990). Two dimensions connect these concepts: linkage (or architecture) and core concepts. Each of these innovation concepts has a different impact on existing dominant designs.

point is that the core design concept behind each component – as well as the associated scientific and engineering knowledge – remains the same.

The distinctions in Figure 10.4 are important because they give us insight into why established firms often have a surprising degree of difficulty in adapting to architectural innovations. Incremental innovation tends to reinforce the competitive positions of established firms, since it builds on their core competencies or is competence enhancing. In the context of the framework developed here, it builds on the existing architectural and component knowledge of an organisation. In contrast, radical innovation creates unmistakable challenges for established firms, since it destroys the usefulness of both architectural and component knowledge.

Architectural innovation presents established firms with a more subtle challenge. Much of what the firm knows is useful and needs to be applied to the new product, but some of what it knows is not only not useful but may actually handicap the firm. Recognising what is useful and what is not and acquiring and applying new knowledge when necessary may be quite difficult for an established firm. This is mainly caused the way knowledge – particularly architectural knowledge – is organised and managed. An organisation's communication channels, both those that are implicit in its formal organisation, and those that are informal, are the interactions that are critical to effective design (Galbraith, 1973). They are the relationships around which the organisation builds architectural knowledge. An organisation's communication channels will come to stand for its architectural knowledge of the critical linkages between components. As a product evolves, information filters and communication channels develop and help engineers to work efficiently, but the evolution of the product also means that the engineers face recurring kinds of problems. The strategies the designers use, their channels for communications, and their information filters emerge in an organisation to help it cope with complexity. They are efficient precisely because they do not have to be actively created each time a need for them arises. The operation of channels, filters, and strategies may become implicit in the organisation. Since architectural knowledge is stable once a dominant design has been accepted, it can be encoded in these forms, and become implicit. Organisations that are actively engaged in incremental innovation, which occurs within the context of stable architectural knowledge, are likely to manage much of their architectural knowledge implicitly by embedding it in their communication channels, information filters, and problem-solving strategies. Component knowledge, in contrast, is more likely to be managed explicitly because it is a constant source of incremental innovation.

10.2.4 Processes of Innovation

The introduction of this section has already presented the outline of processes that yield innovations, from discovery to commercial production focusing on the value of the innovation itself. Which intermediate steps do exist in addition to the model of Herbig? Schippers (2003) has found 7 models to describe the innovation processes (they apply equally well to technology management):

- the innovation process according to Rothwell (1994), especially his third-generation model. The fourth and fifth generation models focus on aspects only;
- the breakthrough model (in 't Veld, 1998), as part of Systems Theory (Appendix B);
- the Innovation Arena (Janszen, 2000);
- the life-cycle model (ten Haaf et al., 2002);
- the interrelationships between major innovative activities (Burgelman & Sayles, 1986);
- the interactive innovation model (Kline & Rosenberg in van Gunsteren (1992));
- the innovation model (Tidd et al., 1997).

These models have been elaborated in Appendix F. All have similar stages, more detailed or more global, but differ in the detailed steps they recognise within product development and commercialisation of products. The scope of the research does not require a detailed comparison of these models for the innovation processes. The research aims at revealing which processes and structures fit adaptation; hence if necessary we should connect other concepts to such processes and structures. Innovation processes constitute such processes since innovations assist companies in adaptation.

The choice to continue within this research and refer to the breakthrough model, has roots in the characteristics of all the models of the innovation process, the scope of the model, and the presence of control processes; additionally, this research questions the validity of Systems Theory, and the use of the breakthrough model does not conflict with other processes. All these models recognise the importance of specific characteristics of innovation processes. First of all, the processes connect to determining strategy to innovation processes. Secondly, all seven innovation models end with the introduction of products (and the results of process improvements) to the market arena. Thirdly, the innovation processes in the models have a strong iterative character. Between the models, the exact stages differ, although the main steps have strong similarities. The exact link between the partial processes differs too but has no significant influence on the description of the innovation processes. The breakthrough model covers innovation processes, process innovation processes, and organisational improvement processes; this makes it more suitable than the others to serve as a background model for this particular research which covers a wide scope of adaptation processes. Additionally, it contains control processes, and the verification and evaluation of the primary process of breakthrough. Since, management wants to exert some kind of control over the development of a company; this link might assist in setting up more viable models for the processes and structures of companies for adaptation.

10.3 IMPLEMENTATION OF TECHNOLOGY AND INNOVATION

The implementation of technological advancements and innovations should increase the firms' competitiveness when organisations manage to create an adaptation that affects its fitness in relation to their environments. Such an improvement of fitness depends strongly on the relation between the visible traits, the phenotype, and the internal structure of the organisation, the genotype. In course of time, many have reported about the introduction of technologies and innovation, and most reported on the change management model needed to succeed in integrating the advancements in an organisation. Granstrand (1998) notes that management of a technology-based firm and of innovations requires quite different approaches to theory than classical economical theories. Chapter 13 deals with the matter of change management. This section will focus on the internal processes and structures that support adaptation of an organisation through technology and innovation.

Table 10.1 lists the authors that have conducted research in the domain of technology management and innovation (whom will be mentioned in this section and Section 10.4); only those authors have been listed who have performed quantitative analysis on a sample of companies or who carried out in-depth case studies. The table relates their findings to the reference model to assess the usability for the research questions. Furthermore, the table tells whether these researches support or refute the refined hypotheses.

10.3.1 Successful Implementation of Technologies

A study into the strategies of survival in fast-changing industries shows the importance of dominant design in adaptation and the need for a long term strategy (Christensen et al., 1998, p. 208, 219). Through an economic analysis of the industrial branch of disk-drives from 1975 to 1990, which has undergone tremendous figures of growth and change, they arrive at two conclusions. Firstly, the firms that incorporated key elements of the emerging product design had a twice higher probability of survival than those who did not. Ignoring the emerging design seems hardly a fruitful strategy whether a firm enters the market just before, during or after the establishment of dominant design. Secondly, a window of opportunity seemed to precede the era of the dominant design, in fact just prior to it. Companies entering well before that period face a higher failure rate[44]. Christensen et al. suggest that these companies developed capabilities for a broader architectural variety and low volume-per-model manufacturing in that competitive environment. These capabilities might not have equipped them very well for the competition that characterised the industry after the emergence of the dominant design. The only way out for early innovators is monitoring the convergence towards architectural standardisation. After the presence of a dominant design, attention should focus on component-level innovation. Additionally, Christensen et al. generate two findings. The first one being that elements of a dominant design that are salient to a company's survival are indeed architectural in nature. Henderson & Clark (1990) arrive at the very same conclusion. Their second insight tells that those firms whose entry strategies involved using proven component technologies, which facilitated the emergence of new markets, had significantly higher probabilities of survival than those firms that offer new component technologies for established markets.

A longitudinal study into the practice of innovation at fourteen companies drives Wagner & Kreuter (1999, pp. 69, 71-72) to conclude that successful innovation thrives on a number of factors determined by the organisation itself. They classified the fourteen companies into more innovative and less innovative companies based on market value parameter (based on stock value, even though one might doubt the value of this parameter). These companies were based in Germany, Japan, and the USA, and differentiated themselves from each other through a higher or lower score on the market value. In general, the findings suggest that innovative companies pay more attention to the softer factors, organisational culture, leadership, human resource management, and communication, in comparison to the hard factors, innovation strategy, organisational structure, and organisational processes. From the soft factors, the score on leadership hardly differs between the two groups of companies. Especially, the differences attributed to the importance of communication seem very strong, comprised of both formal and recessive communication, and internal and external communication structures. Japanese companies accredit communication and human resource management higher than the German and American companies. All these findings lead Wagner & Kreuter to the final statements that:

- innovation is strongly determined by the organisation's approach. Companies should focus on both hard factors and soft factors to create business prosperity through innovation;

---

44 *Please note the similarities between this approach and the model of growth from Baum & McGahan (2004), presented in Subsection 2.2.1.*

Table 10.1: Overview of findings of authors in the field of technology management and innovation related to the reference model. The last column of this table converts these findings to the refined hypotheses and indicates which of the hypotheses are supported and which ones opposed.

Author(s)	Study	Findings	Relation to Reference Model	Evidence for Refined Hypotheses
Christensen et al. (1998)	Hard disk-drive industry 1975-1990, based on data collection and interviews with key people in industry	Variables related to managerial choice rather than factors in the environment are the primary factors driving firm survival.	Confirmation that the generation of variation leads to selection by the environment and support for the capability of foresight.	
		Firms that incorporate key elements of an emerging dominant design had a probability survival twice of those that ignored the convergence.	Developmental pathways exist for innovation (minor innovations lead to major innovations). Mutations of innovations led by foresight.	Supports A.2: supports it, changes in competitiveness through 'dominant design.
		"Window of opportunity" just prior to the emergence of a dominant design during which entry was particularly advantageous.		Supports B.1.A: adaptive walks depends on presence of dominant design and window of opportunity.
		Firms whose entry involved using proven component technologies that facilitated the emergence of new market segments have significantly higher probabilities of survival than did firms that entered established market segments with new component technologies that offered better performance.	Dispersal (evolvability) more effective with proven component technology than local optimisation (sustained fitness) with new component technology. Given a dominant design, local optimisation only possible; dominant design equals Evolutionary Stable Strategy.	Opposes B.1.B: given structures hard to change. Supports B.2.B: entry based on proven component technology.
Wagner & Kreuter (1999)	5 German, 4 Japanese, 5 U.S. firms on innovation (based on questionnaires and stock-market value).	Successfull companies value organisational processes for innovation more than less successful companies.	Adaptive walks and developmental pathways depend on presence of processes for innovation.	
		Less successfull firms adhere more to innovation strategy, culture, Human Resource Management, and communication.		
Jenkins et al. (1997b)	5 case studies of product development.	Formal life-cycle management process necessary for reducing time-to-market.	The need for organisational processes stressed again.	
		Cross-functional approach to eliminate or reduce unnecessary iterations.		
Leonard-Barton (1988)	12 in-depth case studies of new technology (large corporations).	Clear strategy for business planning with technical and business strength for competitive advantage.	Adaptive walks should lead to increased fitness through the capability of foresight.	Supports B.1.A: increased fitness through developmental pathways based on capabilities.
		Implementation of new technologies is a dynamic process of mutual adaptation between the technology and its environment. Adaptation cycles necessary to manage the implementation of new technologies and align these to the strategy.	Refers to the concept of adaptive walks and developmental pathways (more in terms of regulatory genes). Can be applied to both sustained fitness and evolvability.	Support B.1.A: increased fitness through developmental pathways.

Source	Data / Method	Findings	Interpretation	Support
Tyre & Orlikowski (1993)	3 case studies of manufacturing and service organisations adapting new technology (U.S. and Europe). Comparative study with Japanese practices.	Ongoing adaptation is an important success factor for implementing and using new technologies. The more experience that users gain with a new technology, the more they rely on established routines and habits.	Points to managing both sustained fitness and evolvability. Also, it tells that ongoing adaptation (adaptive walks) is a continuous process.	Supports B.1.A: increased fitness through developmental pathways.
Brown & Eisenhardt (1997)	6 case studies in companies in highly dynamic markets.	Episodic cycles of change and stability might benefit the introduction of technologies more than on a gradual, continuous basis.	Although presented as discontinuous, adaptation is continuous and necessary. Alternatively, the authors suggest to alternate change and stability.	
		Time-paced change takes place at given intervals which gives management and work-force ample time to prepare for these changes.	Although presented as discontinuous, adaptation is continuous and necessary. Management should divide time between exploitation and preparing change; change is implemented during short intervals.	
King & Tucci (2002)	Disk-drive industry 1976-1995, based on data collection, news reports, interviews of industry executives and experts.	Experience in one market provides a competitive advantage in new market niches. Experience contributes to dispersal into other product-market combinations.	Dispersal relates to activities in other market-domains. Hence, dispersal connects to sustained fitness.	Supports B.2.B: success rate of dispersal increases with experience; need for more continuous dispersal.
Fleming & Sorenson (2001)	Analysis of U.S. patents granted in May/June 1990 (n=17,264), and underlying patents 1790-1989.	Technological evolution differs from evolution of biological systems. Technological evolution reaches beyond the simple search patterns (hill-climbing, random combination).	Points to the invalidity of recombination as pattern for adaptive walks in fitness landscapes. Indicates the need for adequate foresight.	Supports B.2.B: integration of technologies (component and architectural innovation) creates more opportunities.
		Modularity in the design of products benefits long-term development of products. Allows architectural innovation.		Supports B.2.B: modularity allows component and architectural innovation, which creates more opportunities.
Meyer & Utterback (1993)	Retrospective study of product families in disparate industries.	Product families based on product platforms constitute the competitive advantage.	Innovation concepts of Henderson & Clark determine developmental pathways.	Supports B.1.A weakly: product families set out paths for developmental pathways.
Boer & During (2001)	Comparison of three types of innovation. Product innovation in 30 SME's representing wide range Dutch industries.	Companies tend to concentrate on the development of the new product, and to neglect production and market-side. Insufficient communication within the organisation about innovation goals and progress.	The phenotypical effects of product development get too little attention but do drive product innovation.	Opposes B.1.A weakly: singular focus on product development rather than integrated approaches.
		Organisational adaptation required for the innovation process did receive insufficient attention.	Adaptive walks require developmental pathways that integrate components and changes in structures.	Supports B.1.A: product development requires integral approaches.
Grant et al. (1991)	3 Case studies in U.S. manufacturing. General analysis of industry.	Incremental approach to technology upgrading and organisational aspects more important than technology.	Adaptive walks through incremental increase of fitness. Integration more important than technologies.	Supports B.1.A: continuous incremental steps for increasing fitness.

- all three cultures attach higher values to soft factors than to hard factors. Especially, Japanese companies pay attention to communication;
- structural measures should be taken in companies to stimulate innovation, like project organisations, knowledge structures, and evaluation points. This should not lead to restrictive policies that slow down creativity;
- informal communication seems to be the stronghold of innovative companies, and internal policies should stimulate such.

Their study points to a total approach towards successful implementation of innovation and technology management. They hardly highlight that the most outstanding distinction between the more successful and less successful companies constitutes the attention for organisational processes for innovation (according to their own study). This confirms the necessity to look at processes and structures that support adaptation.

Jenkins et al. (1997b, pp. 388-392) looked at five case studies of product development and concluded that a formal life-cycle management process proves necessary (a) for reducing the time-to-market and (b) for learning from each new development project. They also point to the inevitability of a cross-functional approach to eliminate or reduce unnecessary iterations. Furthermore, companies should have a clear strategy for business planning and technology planning resulting in products that together with technical and business strength leverage the products a competitive advantage. Exploring portfolio management of R&D projects, Mikkola (2001, p. 426) proposes the R&D Project Portfolio Matrix to depict the competitive advantage and customer value of new and existing products. According to her, the well-known portfolio techniques, such as the Boston Consultancy Group Growth-share matrix, the McKinsey Matrix, Product Portfolio Matrix, have limited definitions of project success. She reflects her study on the competitive advantage of innovations in the batteries for electric vehicles and hybrid electric vehicles. Assessment and management of innovation requires an evaluation of competitive advantage and customer value (Mikkola, 2001, p. 424).

Leonard-Barton (1987, p. 18) proposes that managing the integration of new technologies in the organisation yields better results than when companies adhere to an original strategy and implementation plan. She even states that *implementation is innovation* (Leonard-Barton, p. 265). Based on empirical research and a model for adaptation by Berman (1980), she concludes that companies should allow adaptation cycles to actively link the actual implementation of technologies to the strategy. In the case of the introduction of an expert system at Digital, the success of the technology has depended on the interactive process to altering the technology to fit the organisation, and the simultaneously shaping of the user environment to exploit the full potential of the technology (Leonard-Barton, 1987, p. 7). Douthwaite et al. (2001) do also confirm the conclusion that the more complicated the technology, the more it requires interaction between the inventors, researchers, and the user environment. A simple top-down approach is not sufficient any more. This leads Leonard-Barton (1988) in a later paper to the proposition of small and large adaptation cycles to exist within the organisations. Misalignment between the strategy and objectives are viewed as normal, and the misalignment evoke an adaptation cycle where both the merits of the technology and the impact on the strategy are considered. The larger the adaptation cycle, the more factors it affects within companies. Each evaluation of performance of the technology leads to considering the adaptation at aggregation strata given the impact of the misalignment.

Tyre & Orlikowski (1993) expand these adaptation cycles and direct their research to further understanding of actively managing the technological improvements in companies. By comparing the practices at American and Japanese companies, they arrive at the insight that Japanese companies deploy a discontinuous process of change with conscious and careful timing of technological improvements. American companies continuously introduce improvements and have to manage operations and improvements at the same time; Japanese companies prepare and collect improvements which they introduce within a set (limited) time frame, and suggestions or necessities for improvements are always collected for the next window of opportunity. The adaptation cycles connect product innovation to manufacturing innovation on strategic, tactical, and operational level. Brown & Eisenhardt (1997) generate a similar concept for time-paced change based on empirical findings among six companies in highly dynamic markets. Time-paced change takes place at given intervals which gives management and work-force ample time to prepare for these changes. The cycle of freezing and unfreezing yields better operational results and clarity for communication, although it requires quick responses by the adaptation cycles (the last part of the statement is not addressed by Brown & Eisenhardt [1997] nor is it mentioned in Eisenhardt & Brown [1998]).

10.3.2 Achieving Architectural Innovation

The adaptation cycles connect to the architectural innovation at higher levels (strategic and sometimes tactical). Differences in the way in which architectural and component knowledge are managed within an experienced organisation give us insight into why established companies often find it difficult to achieve architectural innovation. These problems have two sources: the time lag needed to identify architectural innovation and the time needed to build the relevant knowledge.

Firstly, established organizations require significant time (and resources) to identify a particular innovation as architectural. This is partly due to the fact that architectural innovation can, often, initially be accommodated within old frameworks. Radical innovation is rather obvious – the need for new modes of learning and for new skills becomes apparent quickly. But the information filters and communication channels that embody old architectural knowledge may screen out information that a particular innovation might have an architectural opportunity. This effect is analogous to the tendency of individuals to continue to rely on beliefs about the world that a rational evaluation of new information should lead them to discard (Kahneman et al., 1982). Researchers have commented extensively on the ways in which organisations facing threats may continue to rely on their old frameworks – or in other terms on their old architectural knowledge – and hence misunderstand the nature of a threat. They shoehorn the bad news, or the unexpected new information, back into the patterns with which they are familiar (Dutton & Jackson, 1987).

Once an organisation has recognised the nature of an architectural innovation, it faces a second major source of problems: the need to build and to apply new architectural knowledge effectively. Simply recognising that a new technology is architectural in character does not give an established organisation the architectural knowledge that it needs. It must first switch to a new mode of learning, and then invest time and resources in learning about the new architecture. It is handicapped in its attempt to do this, both by the difficulty all organisations experience in switching from one mode of learning to another and by the fact that it must build new architectural knowledge in a context in which some of its old architectural knowledge may be irrelevant. An established organisation setting out to build new architectural knowledge must change its orientation from one of refinement within a stable architecture to one of active search for new solutions within a constantly changing context. Many organisations encounter difficulties in their attempts to make this type of transition. New entrants, with lesser commitments to older ways of learning about the environment and organising their knowledge, often find it easier to build the organisational flexibility for the transition than those that have to abandon old architectural knowledge and building new.

Once an organisation has succeeded in the re-orientation itself, the building of new architectural knowledge still consumes time and resources. This learning may be quite subtle and difficult. New entrants in the industry must build the architectural knowledge necessary to exploit an architectural innovation, but since they have no existing assets, they can optimise their organisation and information-processing structures to exploit the potential of a new design. Established firms are faced with an awkward problem. Because their architectural knowledge is embedded in channels, filters, and strategies, the discovery process and the process of creating new information (and rooting out the old) usually takes time. The organisation may be tempted to modify the channels, filters, and strategies that already exist rather than to incur the significant fixed cost and considerable organisational friction required to build new sets from scratch (Arrow, 1974). But it may be difficult to identify precisely which filters, channels, and problem-solving strategies need to be modified, and the attempt to build a new product with old organizational tools can create significant problems.

Architectural innovation may have very significant competitive implications. Established organisations may invest heavily in the new innovation, interpreting it as an incremental extension of the existing technology or underestimating its impact on their embedded architectural knowledge. But new entrants to the industry may exploit its potential much more effectively, since they are not handicapped by a legacy of embedded and partially irrelevant architectural knowledge.

10.4 ADAPTATION CAPABILITY OF TECHNOLOGY AND INNOVATION

The adaptation capability of an organisation depends on the way it treats these matters, technology and innovation should result in products and processes that suit the demands by the environment. The issues that the comparison of these fields with the reference model should yield an expansion of insight and opportunities for adaptation strategies by companies. Before doing so, the introduction of this section will briefly review the theories and practices so far.

The thoughts of Schumpeter triggered insight on innovation, and we know that technological advancement and innovation contribute to today's competitiveness of industrial companies. Achieving a continuous stream of innovations requires an active management of technology and innovation:

- the emergence of dominant designs landmarks the establishment of a technology or a group of technologies since an innovation might require more advances in technologies than one. Industrial companies should monitor their environment for trends towards dominant designs, and include key features for these in their own innovations. Once a dominant design has established itself, improvement has to focus on component level rather than overall designs until a new era of fermentation arrives;
- the occurrence of incremental and component innovation should be assessed at architectural integration and architectural innovation, does the integration of innovations at component level offer new opportunities? Radical innovations seem rare since each innovation seems to build on previous ones at incremental level or component level.

- for managing innovation, companies should pay attention to both hard and soft factors. Especially, communication within companies, formal and informal, contributes to a higher level of innovations. For the hard factors, the report has so far highlighted several approaches to modelling innovation processes; these seem all to consist of similar steps. All authors recognise the importance of the iterative process through feedback loops, and therefore the choice for either of these does not matter. The breakthrough model offers the unique feature of including the control of the innovation process.
- implementing technologies and managing innovations requires adaptation cycles within companies and interchanging periods of freezing and unfreezing.

10.4.1 Evolutionary Mechanisms for Technology and Innovation

The notion that the development of technology follows patterns of evolution got already long before attention from scholars. Already Gilfillan (1935, p. 275) noted that

> ... the nature of invention ...is an evolution, rather than a series of creations, and much resembles a biological process.

A similar insight led Schumpeter (1942, p. 82) to propose that the effects of innovations

> ... illustrate the same process of industrial mutation - if I may use that biological term - that incessantly revolutionizes the economic structure from within incessantly destroying the old, incessantly creating a new one.

More recently, Abernathy & Utterback (1978) argued that technologies follow a technological life-cycle - like living organisms, they are born, mature, obsolesce, and die. Additionally, Tushman & Anderson (1986) draw on palaeontology (Eldredge & Gould, 1972) by arguing that technology moves through punctuated equilibria by intervals of rapid change. Ruttan (1997) argues that sources of technical change find their base in theories of induced innovation, evolutionary theory, and path dependence when reviewing macroeconomic and microeconomic approaches. It makes him call for a more integrated approach towards theories of technological change. Hence, the search for adaptation has already its forebodes in past research into phenomena related to technology and biological evolutionary models.

When considering the development of technology from the perspective of evolutionary models, the question comes to mind what constitutes the generation of variants. In other words, what does constitute the "technological" genome, memes or replicators? Kauffman (1995, pp. 202-206) has clearly attempted to connect learning about technologies to his NK-model; these thoughts develop further in later work (Kauffman et al., 2000). Technologies themselves are taken as basic units for recombination for searching fitness landscapes. Mokyr (1990, pp. 352-354) states that technologies mostly require a number of microinventions before taking effect. Only few major technological advances revolutionised a whole technical mode in one bold stroke. By similar reasoning Fleming & Sorenson (2001) build on this notion by using fitness landscapes to analyse patents as an expression of searching for technologies. They conclude that technological evolution differs from biological evolution, mainly because social processes for inventors do not compare to recombinatory processes. This has mostly to do with the design and integration of components, and it might point to the concepts of architectural and component innovation of Henderson & Clark (1990). It seems that technology creation follows laws governed by (biological) evolutionary models, though the exact mechanism (recombination of memes, replicators or otherwise) remains unknown.

Building on the evolutionary mechanisms, Figure 10.5 connects the findings from this chapter to the model presented in Subsection 8.1.3; it mainly uses the results from Table 10.1. From the figure it becomes clear that the research considered within the scope of technology and innovation management reflects on parts of the evolutionary mechanism for organisations. In fact, all research together points to the importance of the evolutionary mechanism as missing link between all the individual studies. At the same time, it confirms the existence of evolution for technology and innovation linked to the development of organisations. The links between all individual studies gives the impression of the paramount importance of continuous adaptation through a focus on incremental innovation, which should end in an altered phenotype for selectional processes.

10.4.2 Phenotype and Genotype

The theories on technology management and innovation acknowledge the difference between the internal genotype and the external oriented phenotype, the competitiveness of industrial firms. The link between technology and innovation to the exact definition of a phenotype is weaker. The models of Adaptive Dynamics tell us that with each bifurcation, the dimensions of the state space increase, does this mean that each technology and innovation has a similar effect on the state space in which companies compete?

The proof from such effects as bifurcation arrives from the opposite side of reasoning. The ongoing specialisation of firms, an indication of the increase of state space dimensions, should create more dependencies on collaborations. Indeed, Jonash (1997) refers to the research report entitled *Leveraging Technology in the Global Company* published in 1993 when noting that most companies

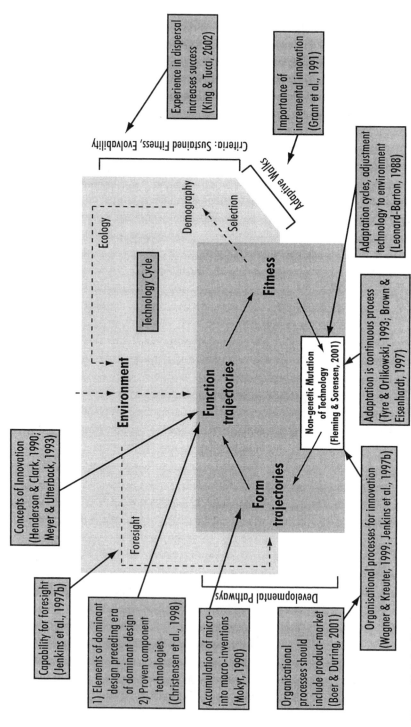

Figure 10.5: Studies into technology and innovation management related to the evolutionary mechanism for organisations. The individual studies have drawn conclusion mostly relating to the individual parts of the total evolutionary mechanisms.

believe that close to 50% or more of their technological competitiveness will be derived from external technology sourcing and partnering during the 1990's. He emphasises the need for connecting technology to the corporate strategy, and the need for integration of technology management in terms of collaboration with partners. The overall corporate strategy should address then the technology needs of corporations for the next 5-10 years, and define the technologies that the company will develop and husband internally and those it will satisfy through external collaborations. This drives companies not only to consider their own technological and innovative capability but also those of their partners, suppliers, and its networks.

Especially, pacing technologies qualify for external collaborations. Little (1981), Roussel et al. (1991), and Hamilton (1997) point out that the portfolio of technologies should meet business demands when presenting a classification of these:

- Base technologies, essential to business, but they do not lead to any identifiable competitive advantage. In fact, these base technologies have a wide availability through manufacturing equipment and suppliers.
- Key technologies, which provide an identifiable advantage over one or more competitors. They might link to the competencies of the firm, ensuring current competitive advantage.
- Pacing technologies, incipient technologies with the potential to become key technologies. These might have an impact on the short or medium term.
- Emerging technologies, technologies that may have competitive impact in the future. If the technological capability is strong, optimising the technological capability to reinforce the potential competitive advantage is called for.

According to Hamilton, firms expecting to build or sustain competitive advantage from technology should include pacing technologies in their technology portfolio. Therefore, the agenda of management should contain the selection of pacing technologies to contribute to the overall health of a company. Bessant (1997) stresses connecting technological capabilities to a strategic framework for the overall strategy.

For coping with unstable market conditions caused by innovation and increasing intensity and diversity of competition, Grant (1996) argues that industrial companies should base their (long-term) strategy on organisational capabilities rather than product-market strategies. Selecting product-market combinations becomes a tactical issue rather than a strategy, and requires a higher state of awareness of the organisation and high speed of adapting to the changed market conditions (Dekkers, 1996). Hence, the active management of technologies should cause the phenotype to change, through form and function trajectories, which in its turn will allow a company to adapt to the dynamics of the product-market combination it is operating in.

10.4.3 Adaptive Walks and Developmental Pathways

So far, it has been suggested that early entrants in a new market, with a broader variety in architecture of products and a low volume-per-model, hinder the capability to effectively deal with changes in that market and convergence towards a dominant design. King & Tucci (2002) also investigated the disk drive market like Christensen et al. (1998) did, and arrived at somewhat different conclusions. They show that experience in previous markets increased the probability that a firm would enter a new market, in fact this experience contributed for a large part in the success the firm would have in that new market.

Building on the same thoughts, Fleming & Sorenson (2001) link the NK-model from Kauffman to technology seen as a Complex Adaptive System. By investigating USA patents granted in the period May-June 1990, and tracing these back to earlier patents in the period 1790-1989, they found that the model of Kauffman holds true for technological inventions. The model predicts that the higher the degree of correlation in fitness landscapes, the more opportunities exist for inventors to find matches between components and technologies. Practically, this means that architectural innovation stands a greater chance when it requires the integration of diverse technologies although the niche of operation decreases; this statement finds its base in further specialisation on product-market combinations.

Meyer & Utterback (1993) describe how individual products are the offspring of product platforms over time. Product families and their successive platforms are themselves the applied result of a firm's underlying core capabilities. In well-managed firms, such core capabilities tend to be of much longer duration and broader scope than single product families or individual products. Companies should keep a long run focus in enhancing core capabilities which includes identifying what they are and how they are applied and synthesized in new products.

All these studies and their results point to path dependency of the evolution of organisations. The studies reflect mostly on mass or large series production, we might assume that findings hold sufficient validity for other types of industry. They build on previously gained experience and knowledge to acquire new technological skills to generate innovations and to enter new markets. The concepts linked to architectural innovation acts as pivots for initiating change or retaining the current dominant design.

The concept of architectural innovation elects as powerful mechanism for dispersal of companies into new markets. Through the assessment of innovations at their potential to turn into new concepts, companies might develop new markets (sometimes resulting in bifurcation), and create breakthroughs in existing product-market combinations. Whether experience hinders or strengthens such a development, remains an open question. Boer & During (2001, pp. 95-96, 99, 103) report on product innovation that the 30 companies they investigated tended to concentrate on the product development process, and neglected the production and, particularly, the market side of the new product. The main motive of these companies was the need to develop new products, often driven by the demands of just one customer, or the desire to penetrate new markets by developing new products or adapting existing products. Alignment of the constituent processes and stages therein was generally insufficient. Also, these companies did little to communicate the innovation goals to other than those involved in the innovation process. The organisational consequences for the innovation process to evolve got little attention, if even recognised. The authors trace the difficulties the companies experienced to overestimation of the relative advantage of the new product, the complexity of the innovation (it required more than just developing a product), and the compatibility between organisation and the new market. These phenomena occurred especially in companies that had to implement considerable adaptations to their organisations (new production processes, new distribution channels, entering a new market segment). They indicate that lack of experience with managing innovations might cause many of the observed problems.

10.4.4 Sustained Fitness

Research shows that the appropriate technology of a business depends critically on the circumstances of that business with regard to its strategic goals, its resources, the resource availability within its regional and national economy, and the characteristics of its product-market environment (Grant et al., 1991). This seems to follow the ideas of Porter on competitiveness (1980). According to Grant et al. (1991), the critical requirement for sustainable competitive advantage is that a company seeks for continuous optimisation. The research indicates that firms are likely to find the most attractive opportunities for improving performance in business systems and organisational aspects of technology (embedding technology in the organisation and its structure) rather than in the adoption of advanced capital equipment.

Especially, incremental improvements and incremental innovations represent the local search for optimisation, sustained fitness. In highly correlated landscapes of technology and markets, this process of optimisation, yields better results than evolvability. Yet, within the issues of the reference model, the search for evolutionary stability seems pointless. Even in the eras of a dominant design, continuous pressure on companies forces them to incremental innovation, small steps within a framework of the dominant design. This looks more like the principle of convergence stability wherein companies reach for a stable situation but did not arrive at it, yet. Product-market combinations might experience invasion by new entrants, although the research so far in this area has not exactly revealed the importance of gains in experience. Contradictory views hold on this matter. Under no circumstance, industry and industrial branches are at equilibrium, rather Red Queen dynamics[45] dominate industrial development.

Continuous monitoring (aided by foresight) will ensure timely reactions to shifts at both incremental innovation level and radical innovation level. The monitoring should look for pacing technologies that might become part of the dominant design, i.e. looking for acceptance by customers, and architectural solutions. Additionally, the technologies and innovations that offer higher mutation rates will eventually have higher changes for incorporation into the dominant design (Loch & Huberman, 1997), based on research into technology diffusion. This looks very much like the findings of Arthur (1989) on the dynamics of the technological lock-in, presented in Section 3.1. However, too early reactions and too early introduction of products might threaten industrial leadership or future competitive positions in the market.

10.4.5 Evolvability

Kauffman et al. (2000) explore the search possibilities of companies on technology landscapes. The core of their approach resides in the assumption that technological improvements mean higher efficiency when viewing a company's production plan. They find that early in the search for technological improvements, if the firm's initial position is poor or average, it is optimal to search far away on the technology landscape. As the firm succeeds in finding technological improvements, it is optimal to confine search to a local region of the technology landscape.

The invading potential of technology management resides in the concept of architectural innovation. When looking at the consequences of incremental changes and modular innovations that overturn core concepts, the opportunity arises to assess whether the innovations allow the emergence of new products and concepts. Companies might asses then whether these products and concepts allow for invading potential into existing markets and dispersal in new markets.

The dimorphism stability has hardly been addressed in management literature, although present in practice, e.g. spin-off on ventures. Splitting of lineages might occur when companies seek the opportunity to develop more specialised products for different market niches (specialisation) or when architectural innovation

---

[45] *For an explanation of the origin of Red Queen Dynamics, see the introduction to Part III.*

occurs. Iwai (2000) demonstrates that industry at best will reach a statistical equilibrium of technological disequilibria which maintains a relative dispersion of efficiency in a static balanced form. The analysis grounds in simple evolutionary models to describe the industry structure as a dynamic process moved by complex interactions among innovations, imitations, and investments of satisfying firms striving for growth and survival. Loch & Huberman (1997) have used a model for technology diffusion in which an old and a new technology are available, both of which improve their performance incrementally over time. Technology adaptors make repeated choices between the established and the new technology based on their perceived performance, which is subject to uncertainty. Both technologies exhibit positive externalities or performance benefits from others using the same technology. They find that the superior technology will not be broadly adopted by the population. Externalities cause two stable usage equilibria to exist, one with the old technology being the standard and the other with the new technology being the standard (the existence of two equilibria indicates a strong similarity to bifurcation processes). Punctuation in these equilibria determines the patterns of technology diffusion. The time for equilibrium punctuation depends on the rate of incremental improvement of both technologies, and on the system's resistance to switching between equilibria. If the new technology has a higher rate of incremental improvement, it is adopted faster and adoption precedes performance parity if the system's resistance to switching is low. Adoption of the new technology trails performance parity if the system's resistance to switching is high.

10.4.6 Self-Organisation

The concept of self-organisation as one of the key points in adapting to the environment has hardly been addressed by management literature on innovation and technology. The principle of dissipative structures indicates that during periods of turmoil an intense interaction with the environment takes place. The emphasis on user interaction makes one suspect that for technology management and innovation, communication with the user constitutes this key point.

When we review the meaning of self-organisation and dissipative structures, potentially these concepts should have a meaning for technology management and innovation. First of all, at industrial level, during periods of technological turmoil and ferment new profiles of industrial competition will appear; the most recognisable feature is the architectural innovation. It stems from intense interaction with the environment, companies offers a diversity of solutions to customers from which the dominant design emerges and at the end fixes in the population. Secondly, these periods of turmoil require intensive monitoring of the environment by individual companies. Thirdly, self-organisation and

Table 10.2: Theories and findings in the field of technology management and innovation. This table gives an overview of the main topics of this chapter classified according to the items of the reference model.

	Phenotype/Genotype	Adaptive Walks	Developmental pathways	Sustained Fitness	Evolvability	Self-organisation
Technology Product Innovation	How do technological advances and product innovation contribute to competitiveness?	Which paths do lead to increased fitness of an organisation? Does technological lock-in decrease or increase fitness? How does technology and product innovation link to foresight? How do periods of turmoil affect industrial companies? Does time-pacing offer a solution for dynamics environment?	Can one distinguish between major and minor inventions? Do minor inventions accumulate into major breakthroughs? Which inertia exist? Does technological lock-in set out developmental pathways? Do technology and innovation relate to core competencies?	How do technological advances contribute to sustained fitness? And product innovations? Should organisations specialise or generalise (depending on environment)?	How do technological advances contribute to evolvability? And product innovations? Do the pluralism and competition mean anything in this respect?	Which intense interactions enhance state transitions? Role of suppliers and customer base?
Technological discontinuities	Dominant design	Technology cycles: era of ferment, of dominant design, of variation, of incremental change. Higher probabilities for proven technologies for new markets.	Minor inventions building up to major inventions. Window of opportunity just before era of dominant design.	Incremental change.	Dominant design.	Emergence of dominant design.
Concepts of innovation	Architectural innovation. Radical innovation.		Core capabilities determine product platforms (product families).	Incremental innovation.	Radical innovation. Modular innovation. Architectural innovation.	
Organisational factors		Both soft factors (culture, leadership, human resource management, communication) and hard factors (strategy, structure, processes).	Informal communication.			
Integration of technologies	Optimised performance.	Experience with new technologies in new markets. Alignments within the company with other areas of business.	Adaptation cycles, discontinuous improvements. Organisational aspects of technology have large impact.			External technology sourcing and partnering.

dissipative structures appear also during the innovation processes, product development, and breakthrough processes when within cross-functional teams interactions occur; the necessary boundary condition would be undoubtedly that these teams interact with their environment before the design solution can be stabilised.

10.5 SUMMARY

No doubt that technology and innovation contribute to the competitiveness of a firm, and holds strong parallels to the evolutionary development of industrial organisations (see Table 10.2). The well-known model of the technology cycle resembles the ideas behind the theories of punctuated equilibrium. Eras of relative stability interchanged by eras of turmoil, resulting in a dominant design that dictates the further development of such an architectural concept. During the eras of ferment and selection of the dominant design, companies should monitor their environment to include the key components of that emerging dominant design. Incremental steps during the next stages take place at component level. The continuous monitoring of the environment should also link the innovations and product developments to achieving competitive advantage and customer value through adaptation cycles.

Internally, companies should pay attention to a number of factors to achieve successful technology management and innovation:

- companies should monitor the environment for the emergence of the dominant design during periods of variation and technological discontinuities. Monitoring should comprise the identification of components that will become part of that design and the accumulation of skills and knowledge to deal with such. Additionally, the monitoring should yield the opportunities for architectural innovation which might boost the growth of companies in new directions, applications or products;
- innovation depends on different types of innovations during different periods. Incremental innovation and modular innovation belong to periods after the appearance of a dominant design. Architectural innovation and radical innovation prelude a period of instability;
- innovation depends on both hard and soft factors. The paramount importance of communication, especially informal communication, contributes to increases competitiveness on long-term;
- learning from product development, the implementation issues of product life cycles, becomes necessary. Technology development and innovation processes constitute of iteration all through, and rely on adaptation cycles whereby at subsequent levels of aggregation reviews of chosen strategies

and pathways take place. Even when reaching the market place, this process of iteration resembles the processes connected to the learning organisation;
- innovation and technology management require integrated approaches, like cross-functional teams and integrated development. Cross-functional teams assist the organisations in improving the scope of the technology development and innovation. Integrated development indicates that organisations should not only focus on the technological solution but also at organisational impacts and impacts for the product-market combination: technologies should fit the organisation and vice versa;
- time-paced change offers opportunities for control of the introduction of innovation and technologies, according to one theory. Another theory states that during small windows of opportunity within an organisation, the introduction of changes becomes possible. Experience increases the capability of an organisation to deal with technological developments and innovations;
- innovation and technological advancements depend on the network of suppliers and partners.

All these factors constitute parts of the evolutionary mechanisms for organisations, pointing to both the incompleteness of theories and methods so far and the need for a more integral approach.

11 PROCESS INNOVATION AND BUSINESS PROCESS RE-ENGINEERING

The previous chapter has mainly dealt with innovation and technology seen as contributing factors to enter new markets, and the need for product innovations to sustain competitiveness. The contents of this chapter focus on the organisation of resources to increase competitiveness in more or less given markets. Some authors, like Boer & During (2001), distinguish between product innovation, process innovation and organisational innovation. Within the context of this report, process innovation, and organisational innovation are considered alike since this chapter also pays attention to Business Process Re-engineering. These approaches under the aggregate of process innovation and Business Process Re-engineering include the design methodology for organisations according to the Delft School Approach. Where the focus of technology and innovation as presented in the previous chapter directly affects the output of a company, this chapter deals with the deployment of resources and the belonging organisational models.

Since long, companies have always sought to improve business performance through optimisation of the organisational structure. These attempts have not always been successful, the painful upheavals in many companies during the recent years reflect the failure of companies, considered one-time industry leaders, to deal with industry change. In fact, practitioners have experienced the many ideas and concepts about optimisation brought forward by management scientists, some of them more successful than others. The large variety of research in this domain makes it impossible to cover all theory, and to do justice to each scientist who has generated a particular idea. Therefore, Section 11.1 will describe process innovation derived from the work of Wigman (2000). Especially, he has classified the several approaches to increasing the revenue of companies; during this study, we will restrict his research as much as possible to the findings on process innovation. To convert his line of thought to the current quest, the notion of resources deployment and utilisation replaces the concept of costs he adheres to. However, to maintain a holistic approach, this section will also partially draw on the concepts of technology and innovation from Chapter 10. Additionally, the first section pays also attention to Business Process Re-engineering, which got a lot of attention during the 1990's. Section 11.1 expands on the design methodology of the Delft School Approach. One of the starting points of the research was the doubts whether this methodology addresses sufficiently the challenges imposed by the dynamics of the environment. The implementation of process innovation and Business Process Re-engineering follows in Section

11.2. This section includes the assessment of six cases in which postgraduate students examined problems within industrial companies and proposed solutions after an extended analysis. The assessment has been performed during 2002, some years after the generation of the proposals and their possible implementation into the business practice. The evaluation of all these approaches by relating them to evolutionary biological models constitutes the contents of Section 11.3. This leads to preliminary conclusions on the adaptation processes by companies.

11.1 PROCESS INNOVATION FOR MEETING PERFORMANCE REQUIREMENTS

Changes in the contemporary market-environment have given rise to reconsider how a company remains competitive in the current environment. Hammer & Champy (1993) identified three forces responsible for the harsh competitive, contemporary market-environment:

- *The customer takes charge.* Since the early 1980's, the dominant force in the seller-customer relationship has shifted. Whereas in the past, the seller had the upper hand, now the customers do. Today a large number of customers tell what they want, when they want it, and how they want it. This trend caused a huge trunk of the mass market to break into pieces. Customers want to be treated individually, creating the need for individualised differentiated products (Hammer & Champy, 1993).
- *Competition intensifies.* In the past, the company that could get to market with an acceptable product or service at the best price would get a sale. Now not only does more competition exist, it is of many different kinds (Hammer & Champy, 1993; Hamel, 1998).
- *Change becomes constant.* As well as the customer and the competition have changed, so has the nature of change. It has become persistent and pervasive. Moreover, the pace of change has accelerated (Maira & Thomas, 1999; Hammer & Champy, 1993; van Someren, 1998; Hamel, 1998; Wagner & Kreuter, 1999; Quinn, 1999). Product life cycles have gone often from years to months; the time-to-market has been reduced in equal terms.

11.1.1 Competitiveness

Because of these changes and the difficulties companies experience in remaining competitive, competitiveness as a concept for business management needs further investigation. Competitiveness may be considered as the ability to continually create substantial margins in the difference between revenue and cost. All related issues of competitiveness are embedded in the three keywords: Continuity, Revenue, and Costs (Wigman, 2000). By adhering to the statement in the introduction of this chapter, we should replace *Costs* by *Utilisation of Resources*. To increase competitiveness, either the utilisation of resources will have to be improved, or revenue will have to increase, both fulfilling the boundary condition of resulting in a sustainable and continuous advantage. The keyword continuity will be used to evaluate initiatives of improved utilisation and increasing revenue.

Other definitions, such as the definition of the Dutch Ministry of Economic Affairs, include the same aspects. They describe competitiveness (for countries) as the ability to create wealth and jobs (Ministry of Economic Affairs, 1997). To increase competitiveness the same initiatives have to be undertaken, either improve the utilisation of resources or increase the revenue. Creation of wealth depends on the ability of companies and countries to create new products and services, which will increase the standard of living for everyone. Obviously, the creation of new products and services is achieved by the ability of companies to develop a substantial margin in the difference between revenue and utilisation, which will in turn free resources for the purpose of growth.

Another approach to competitiveness comes from The Economic Council of Canada (1998). They suggest that competitiveness can be broken down into three different components: efficiency, innovation, and adaptation. Firstly, efficiency is defined as the utilisation degree of resources (e.g. in 't Veld, 1998, p. 317). This can be deduced to the margin between utilisation and revenue: if the intended deployment of resources is less than the actual use of resources, the result will be a lowered margin in the difference between revenue and utilisation. Secondly, innovation involves the search for better products and better techniques to produce existing products (product and process innovation). Through improved or new products as well as through better techniques revenue may alter. Finally, adaptation is defined by the Council as "the speed of imitation of superior techniques", which means the implementation of process improvements developed in other countries, with the goal to enhance the ability to adopt and to adapt innovations from abroad. Therefore, it relates to the previously discussed innovation.

Summarising, competitiveness is the ability to create substantial margins in the difference between revenue and utilisation of resources. Based upon the definition stated in the previous section, to increase competitiveness simply induces either improving utilisation or increasing revenue. It is hardly that simple though. Everything is intertwined, so usually initiatives to improve utilisation of resources, i.e. offer products similar to those of competition at considerable lower price, will also yield an increase in revenue. Secondly, the constraint that the initiatives should result in a sustainable competitive advantage requires a more encompassing concept than just improve utilisation or launch a new product. Considering the oversimplified utilisation-revenue loop, see Figure 11.1, we will tackle this problem by starting to study the existing methodologies from one of the two starting points in the loop.

Figure 11.1: Revenue and utalisation loop. The figure shows the interlocking cycle of revenues and utilisation, which can not be disconnected. Restructuring aims mostly at improving utilisation; likewise Business Process Re-engineering and Vertical de-integration intend the same. Mergers and acquisitions primarily aspire to increase revenues.

11.1.2 Restructuring

When talking about restructuring, it equals *cutting assets and headcount*, state Hamel & Prahalad (1994). *The dramatic strategic and organizational changes that companies have undergone in order to adjust their strategies, structures, and management systems to the environment of competition, instability, and low rates of economic growth that have characterized most of the 1980's and 1990's*, says Grant (1995). Performance is usually measured by economic parameters to achieve higher rates of efficiency and productivity[46]. Managers know that raising net income proves likely to be a harder slog than cutting assets and headcount. Therefore, under intense pressure for a quick improvements, they tempt to reach for the lever that will bring the quickest, surest improvements - resulting in layoffs and reorganisations. Restructuring in this way seldom results in fundamental improvement in the business (Micklethwait & Wooldridge, 1996, p. 14). A study by Hamel & Prahalad (1994) of 16 large companies in the USA with at least three years of restructuring experience found that although restructuring usually did improve a firm's share price, the improvement was almost always temporary. The three years reviewed showed that the share prices of the companies surveyed were on average lagging even further behind index growth rates than they had when restructuring began. Although events as such at stock markets do not necessarily reflect the internal management of companies, these markets do react to the performance of companies in the long term. The findings of Hamel & Prahalad's study have been confirmed by Forte et al. (2000), Laitinen (2000), Ruef (1997), showing that organisations gained little from restructuring, and often reverted to old organisational structures. Therefore, these studies indicate that restructuring seems a poor strategy for evoking business growth and sustainability.

Grant (1995) states that the primary objective of restructuring is to increase profitability by improving margins through reducing costs (directly linked to

---

[46] *Productivity and efficiency follow the definitions by in 't Veld (1998, pp. 315-329). Efficiency is seen as an indicator of the real utilisation of resources, productivity as results vs. resources.*

the utilisation of resources). To do this, several restructuring activities have taken place:

- plant closures to improve capacity utilisation, and to eliminate obsolete technology;
- outsourcing of components and services wherever internal suppliers are less cost efficient than external suppliers;
- increasing managerial efficiency through *delayering* to reduce administrative overhead, and the application of rigorous financial targets and its control to provide incentives for aggressive cost reduction.

Is the achievement of restructuring incremental or continuous? Both Hamel & Prahalad (1994) and Grant (1995) agree that improved utilisation of resources rooting in restructuring efforts may no longer guarantee security and profitability in today's fast-changing market, but constitutes in almost all industries a prerequisite for success. Besides, restructuring, in the way Grant defined it, is built on very different aspects. It cannot be considered a systematic approach to lower cost, let alone that it will result in a continuous improvement. Restructuring only yield results when connected to a business strategy and business growth that meets criteria for evolution.

11.1.3 Mergers and Vertical De-integration

One of the ways to increase revenue is to gain a greater share in existing markets. Firstly, this section will deal with merger and acquisition, and secondly, with vertical integration as initiatives to increase revenue. The question rises if the increase in revenue may be considered as an ongoing and continuous improvement.

A natural result of any merger or acquisition is that the total balance of a company expands; the revenue has increased. The purpose of this increase is in general to cut overall cost as to create a higher profit margin. The most important reasons for mergers and acquisitions are:

- Economies of scale. Economies of scale exist, in short, *wherever proportionate increases in the amounts of inputs employed in a production process result in a more than proportionate increase in total output* (Grant, 1995). Economies of scale may be divided into three sub-aspects: technical input/output relationships, indivisibility, and specialisation. The first aspect relates to the fact that for some activities increases in output do not require proportionate increases in input. E.g. ordering large numbers of a component will decrease the price per unit; or the inventory does not necessarily need to be increased proportionate to the increase of sales and output. The second aspect relates to the fact that some resources are indivisible below a certain size. The last aspect means that larger volumes of output require the employment of more input, which permits increased specialisation of the tasks of individual inputs. This enables accelerated development of competencies.

- Economies of learning. The principal source of experience-based cost reduction is learning by employees, based either on the experience curve or because of refinement of organisational routines within a company.
- Capacity utilisation. At long term, firms can adjust the scale of their plants to vary output, at short and medium term, however, plant capacity is more or less fixed. Variation in demand causes variation in capacity need. This usually results in an increase of cost. Economies of scale originate from the possibility to balance capacity.

Mergers and acquisitions will increase revenue, no matter how. Nevertheless, the purpose of mergers and acquisitions is always to lower cost. Different reasons are found for achieving lower cost per unit. The cost of integrating two cultures, two systems, however, is not discussed in literature. It is often thought that these costs will be far less than the cost advantage that comes with mergers or acquisitions. Very often the integration of two cultures is far more difficult than considered, reducing cost advantages from the previously mentioned sources. Besides, this is also an incremental improvement. Thus, mergers and acquisitions are more of a catch-up initiative than a getting-to-the-front initiative.

Another initiative to increase competitiveness is vertical de-integration, or going back to one's core business. Vertical integration, the opposite of competency thinking, is defined as *the extension of a company's activities over the value chain, i.e. integration either forward into the sequential stages in the value chain or backward into the preceding stages or both ways* (Porter, 1985; Grant, 1995; Drucker, 1974). The usefulness of integration comes from the ability to lower transport and administration costs, to improve the interface between successive stages in the value chain, and to be more independent of suppliers in scarce times (Bikker et al., 1998). The drawback to integration is that it requires more organisational, coordination effort across stages, increasing overhead, and more importantly the risk that the focus on essential technological developments is lost, resulting in loss of competitive advantage. That the latter has become an issue, is suggested by the contemporary trend of outsourcing and competency thinking. Grant (1995) argues that vertical de-integration has become a powerful trend in most industrial sectors. Hamel & Prahalad (1994), Quinn (1999), and Hagel III & Singer (1999) all speak of the virtues of competency thinking. The key message is not cost but intellectual value, focusing on knowledge development of unique capabilities. Thinking in terms of competencies is no longer focused on wisely outsourcing supportive functions, but on outsourcing functions along the value chain as well (de Wit & Mol, 1999; Quinn, 1999; Hagel III & Singer, 1999).

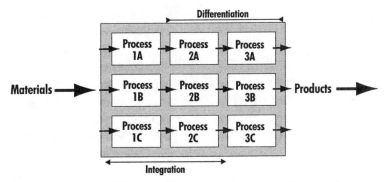

Figure 11.2: Integration and differentiation in the value chain. Outsourcing compares to differentiation and focuses companies on their competencies.

Baaij et al. (1999) and de Wit & Mol (1999) warn for blindly following the differentiation trend. Baaij et al. (1999) argue that since competencies are almost impossible to measure, and their flexibility is very limited, outsourcing of what might look like supporting functions should be a well-founded decision. De Wit & Mol (1999) distinct two different bases for outsourcing, transactional cost reduction, and long-term partnership. Transactional cost reduction refers to outsourcing on an incremental basis, whereas the latter one, obviously, refers to long-term relationships with the supplier. Besides the fact that there is no one best way to outsource, many of the companies they surveyed had no idea of the long-term implications and the risks of outsourcing.

Though many think that outsourcing and focusing on competencies is a permanent trend (Quinn, 1999; de Wit & Mol, 1999; Hagel III & Singer, 1999; Grant, 1995), some distinguish a cyclic pattern (de Wit & Mol, 1999; Grant, 1995). The cycle between going from vertical integration back to competencies, or differentiation (see Figure 11.2), however, is not likely to go around in an identical way. The new vertical integration is based on a close cooperation between partners, creating so-called strategic alliances or networks of partners (Maira & Thomas, 1999; de Wit & Mol, 1999; Hagel III & Singer, 1999).

When looking back at mergers and acquisitions, it is likely to see companies merge less based on vertical integration, and more by combining alike or supplementary competencies. Obviously, the focus on competencies is not directly aimed at increasing revenue, it aims at the development of unique competencies for achieving competitive advantage.

11.1.4 Product and Process Innovation

The efforts of process innovation look much like the ones for product innovation, as presented in Chapter 10, increasing competitiveness. Both aim at *the effort to*

Figure 11.3: Innovation tree, based on levels of aggregation. On the left-hand side the different levels and innovation that relates to these levels is displayed. On the right-hand side examples clarify these levels.

create purposeful, focused change in an enterprise's economic or social potential (Drucker, 1998), *renewal* (Wagner & Kreuter, 1999), *the creation of something new that replaces the old or integrates the old into the new* (van Someren, 1999). Clearly, innovation is about creating something new. What we have to ask ourselves though is the purpose of creating something new. Therefore, innovation is looked at in terms of levels of aggregation. This is a way to structure innovation through building a 'tree' that reflects the different levels of aggregation. The result is shown in Figure 11.3. Market innovation is to create completely new markets, such as the creation of a global system for telecommunication. Customer innovation or product-group innovation is closely related to product innovation. Both aim to create a new market space in existing markets, going beyond just adding new features to existing products. A good example is how Chrysler created a market for minivans in the 1980's. Though they did not create a transport market, they did create new market space. Through their product (concept) innovation of a minivan they were able to exploit a whole new range of customers. These innovation initiatives, however, are not aimed to lower cost, but to 'increase' (renew) revenue. Process innovation consists of two types: innovation based on technological improvements, and innovation based on structural improvements. The first one is about advancements in resources (e.g. new or more productive and effective machinery), whereas the latter refers to the way the resources are utilised (streamlining the processes).

Porter (1980) reports that the first type of process innovation will change the industry structure. It can make the process more or less capital intensive, increase or decrease economies of scale, change the proportion of fixed cost, increase or decrease vertical integration, affect the process of accumulating experience, and so on. These manufacturing innovations can come from outside the industry as well as from within, necessitating a broader view of technological change beyond industry boundaries. Therefore, to achieve durable competitive advantage, process innovation should be performed as a continuous in- and outward focused process. This can only be achieved through a culture that supports innovation (Markides, 1998).

The second option for process innovation, streamlining the processes, has found its way to the world of companies in the approach of Business Process Re-engineering (see next subsection), alignment approaches for change management (see Section 13.2), and other design and engineering methodologies, like the Delft School Approach (see Subsection 11.1.6). Both manufacturing innovation and structural innovation will strengthen a company's competitiveness by enhancing its performance. Manufacturing innovation can be seen as innovation at the levels of components, compare with Figure 10.4. Besides minor improvements to either the combination of components or the choice of components to build a process, it may occur that a new combination starts a chain of upward innovating possibilities: architectural innovation. Since products and processes relate to each other, a minor innovation may cause the emergence of a new opportunity, for example a new product. However, this new product may be itself the cause of a new product-group emerging. Architectural innovation causes a Domino effect, enabling the creation of new products, product-groups and even markets, at the level of products and processes. The theories of emergence and of catalyst systems (Cowan et al., 1994; Waldrop, 1993; Farrell, 1998) should be considered a support of the existence of architectural innovation. Hamel (1998), Baaij & van den Bosch (1999), and Maira & Thomas (1999) deal with strategy in relation to emergence, and exactly that approach could be used to better understand architectural innovation. This means that the same conclusions for strategy in relation to emergence and complexity theory also hold for architectural innovation.

Is the achievement of process and component innovation incremental or continuous? Technology cycles are characterised by different eras: periods of incremental change and periods of radical change. Considering the product life cycle (Henderson et al., 1998), we see that every product or service will eventually enter a saturation phase, with decreased markets and competitor shake-out (akin the model of Baum & McGahan [2004], Section 2.2.1). Therefore, periods of renewal and radical change are required to achieve sustainable competitiveness, in terms of products and performance of processes; in other words, both process and product innovation should be embedded as continuous processes in the organisation. This attitude is also a prerequisite for identifying architectural innovations.

11.1.5 (Business Process) Re-engineering

The movement of Business Process Re-engineering aims at reviewing and improving the utilisation of resources. *The fundamental rethinking and radical redesign of business processes to achieve dramatic improvements in critical contemporary measures of performance such as cost, quality, service, and speed* (Hammer & Champy, 1993, p. 32). Hammer & Champy debate that Re-engineering is the only way for companies to regain their competitiveness. Companies should no longer organise their work around the principles of Adam Smith, around which most companies are still organised, but around processes. Today fragmented organisations display appalling diseconomies of scale, quite the opposite of what Adam Smith envisioned. The diseconomies do not show up in direct labour but in overhead. With the changed environment companies are paying much more for the coordination efforts, e.g. management, of the organisation than for the real work – a recipe for trouble, say Hammer & Champy. Therefore, companies should reorganise their tasks around the business processes, instead of the other way around.

In their publication, Childe et al. (1994, p. 22) point out that the Business Process Re-engineering movement holds a different view than traditional improvement schemes. These existing approaches often fail to go beyond functional boundaries that exist in organisations structured along traditional lines. Business Process Re-engineering views the business process as a horizontal flow of activities while most organisations are formed into vertical functional groupings (they label them *functional silos*) (Kanter, 1983, pp. 28-31; Morgan, 1997, p. 28). The approach resides partially in the information systems departments, which did hold a cross-functional perspective since they provided services to various business areas within organisations. Additionally, the expected radical improvements did not occur which shifted the attention to the integration of information systems into business processes.

Childe et al. (1994, p. 23, 30, 32) connect the movement of Business Process Re-engineering to time-based competition, Lean Production and Kaizen. Each of these beholds certain aspects of Re-engineering and do focus on identifying and improving business processes. According to Childe et al., the benefits of adopting the approach of Business Process Re-engineering constitute of:

- the definition of business processes and their internal or external customers;
- the modelling and analysis of the processes that support these products and services;
- the highlighting of opportunities for both radical and incremental business improvements through the identification, and removal of waste and inefficiency;

- the implementation of improvements through a combination of IT and good working practices;
- the establishment of mechanisms to ensure continuous improvement of the redesigned processes.

Despite these differences, they conclude also that all the publications so far lack a clear methodology despite the interest by many.

The method of Re-engineering as originally proposed by Davenport (1993) fuses information technology and human resource management. The aim of Re-engineering directs itself to more radical, discrete innovations than the lower level and incremental steps of process improvement. The method consists out of five steps:

- identifying processes for innovation. This step is mainly driven by the search for the main processes, assessment of its strategic relevance, "health" and qualification of the quality and culture of each process. Davenport states *the fewer and broader the processes, the greater the possibility of process integration and the greater the problems of understanding, measuring, and changing the process.* He points to strategic-planning and systems-planning approaches for describing the processes. For selecting relevant processes, he proposes four criteria: (1) the process's centrality to the execution of the firm's business strategy, (2) process health driven by performance indicators and Pareto-like ratio, (3) process qualification by gauging the cultural and political climate of a targeted process, and (4) manageable project scope by focusing on a product line or geographic location;
- identifying change levers. After describing the difficult implementation of computers and its applications in business practices, Davenport states that *process improvement and innovation are the best hope for getting greater value out of our vast information technology expenditures.* Information technology should be seen as an enabler of processes rather than a means to help the implementation of a process, in other words the use of information technology has matured beyond the stage of simple automation of tasks. In addition, it has become clear that yields in productivity by deploying adequate information technology strongly relate to human resource innovations, like self-organising teams. The relation between processes and information, resident in performance monitoring, customisation, integration, etc. provides excellent opportunities for expanding the role of information technology in business practices. The direction of greater empowerment and participation in decision-making resulting in flatter organisational hierarchies or broader spans of control enables process innovations as well;
- developing process visions. The first step for developing a process vision targets at assessing the existing business strategy for process innovation.

Davenport stresses the importance of expanding a strategy beyond financial matters. This statement making clear that governing a company requires more than financial management, at that time pretty novel, has hardly found its way into management practice. The customer's perspective has an essential role in the development of the process vision as depicted in Figure 11.4;

- understanding existing processes by describing the current process flow, measurement of the process in terms of the new process objectives, assessment of the process in terms of the new process attributes, identifying problems with or shortcomings of the process, identification of short-term improvement in the process, and assessing the current information technology and organisation. Under the methods for business process improvements, Davenport lists: Activity-Based Costing, Process Value Analysis, Business

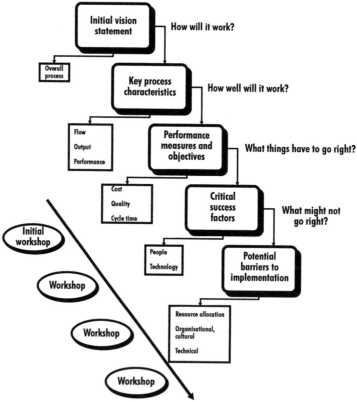

Figure 11.4: Visioning process for Re-engineering, according to Davenport (1993, p. 132). The process combines both analysis of the processes based on business criteria as well as creating support within the organisation. Especially, the workshops contribute to further understanding of the processes within the organisation when attention is paid to specificity of objectives and criteria.

Process Improvement (rooted in Total Quality Management), Information Engineering, and Business Process Innovation. The deployment of the methods has to fit the overall objectives of the innovation effort;

- designing and prototyping the new process. After brainstorming the design alternatives, stages follow that include (1) the assessment of feasibility, risk and benefit of design alternatives, and the selection of the preferred process design, (2) the prototyping of the new process design, (3) the development of a migration strategy, (4) the implementation of new organisational structures and systems.

The approach of Davenport combines indeed the process innovation itself and the change management process that comes along; organisational not technical barriers present the major challenges in process innovation efforts. The approach has an internal focus, it accounts for the identification of business criteria derived from customers' input, and the organisation reviews its internal handling.

Since its emergence, many have propagated the merits of Business Process Re-engineering and many have expressed doubts. Hammer & Champy (1993) estimate that only 30% of the efforts succeed; a study by Jarrar & Aspinwall (1999) shows that only 25% of Re-engineering cases reaches acceptable performance improvements. Sabherwal et al. (2001, p. 193, 195) point out that alignment between strategy and structure is hardly achieved and a redesign is often inhibited by cultural and structural inertia. Some, like Bryant & Chan (1998), attribute the low success rate to Business Process Re-engineering as a covert way for downsizing. Additionally, authors have already pinpointed that many different approaches exist which makes it difficult to define what exactly Business Process Re-engineering constitutes (Braganza & Myers, 1998; Choi & Chan, 1997, p. 40) and to define its methodology (Childe et al., 1994, p. 23, 32). The expected radical improvements do not occur, which shifts the attention to integration of information systems into business processes, a technological perspective. Most of all, many writers attribute the failure of Re-engineering efforts to leadership, culture, change management, etc. (e.g. Braganza & Myers, 1998; Choi & Chan, 1997, pp. 44-47; Drago & Geisler, 1997, pp. 298-300).

Smeds (2001, p. 2) calls for a capability of continuous process innovations (equalling the use of process innovations and Business Process Re-engineering). The competitive environment of enterprises leaves them with no possibility to rely on but process innovations, she adds. Her introduction to the special issue of the *International Journal of Technology Management* shows that parallels exist between product development and process innovations.

Is the achievement of Re-engineering incremental or continuous? Although Re-engineering as well as restructuring are prerequisites for survival, Hamel & Prahalad (1994), and Hamel (1998) point out that Business Process Re-engineering is more about catching up than getting to the front. Hammer & Champy (1993) report that sadly enough many companies that start Re-engineering do not succeed at achieving major performance improvements. Their estimate is that about 50 – 70% of the organisations that undertake the Re-engineering effort do not achieve the dramatic results they intended. Grant (1995) concludes that some of the most interesting and substantial sources of cost reduction have arisen from fundamental rethinking of the activities undertaken by the firm, and the ways in which it organises them. He does not report though, whether these activities ensure long-term advantage. Therefore, Re-engineering can help companies reduce cost, but not in such a way that it leads to a continuous, sustainable improvement; because if all companies have successfully re-engineered their processes, such spectacular results can not be achieved again by Re-engineering.

11.1.6 Design of Industrial Organisations (Delft School Approach)

That business processes offer an opportunity for process innovation has not only been recognised by Davenport (1993) and Hammer & Champy (1993). The shifting requirements as imposed on operations management call for the redesign of the organisational structure to meet market demands. However, translating these requirements directly into a hierarchy will not ensure the integration of processes across organisational units, and guarantee desirable performance. That the hierarchy does not meet as such the performance requirements, became already clear during case studies performed in the 1970's. The conclusion was drawn that organisational changes should affect working processes to be viable (Mervis & Berg, 1977).

Recently, some authors draw our attention to the importance of process mapping. Biazzo (2000, pp. 103-104, 111) classifies alternative approaches to business process analysis along two dimensions, strategy and focus. When the analysis looks at the behaviour of actors, the approach for a pragmatic construction is action analysis, and for a rational construction strategy coordination analysis. When the analysis concerns systems, the approach is either social grammar analysis (pragmatic) or process mapping (rational). Biazzo sees process mapping exclusively as a rational approach focused on systems, comprising of defining boundaries, inputs and outputs of processes, workflow, conducting interviews with those responsible for the various activities, studying available documentation, creating a model, and step-by-step revising this model for purposes of analysis. He stresses the importance of selection the proper approach, and remarks that practitioners pay insufficient attention for the social context of work. Bond (1999) reasons that business process modelling should precede the design of an information system, that way aligning the information system with the organisational requirements. Lee & Dale (1998, p. 215) indicate that Business Process Management intends to align the business processes with strategic objectives and customers' needs but requires a change in a company's emphasis from functional to process orientation. Preiss (1999, pp. 42-45) pays explicit attention to the role of process improvement in the context of extended enterprises by modelling. He concludes that sufficient tools are available for analysis. The statements of the authors underline the importance of business process modelling.

The implication of similar notions during the 1960's and 1970's required the development of a design approach for organisations through empirical studies and based on literature. The main features of the design methodology became the method for analysis and the organelle structure (in 't Veld, 1998). The organelle structure connects the strategy to the product flow (Dekkers, 2000). Thereto, a design methodology has been developed for revealing these relations and the practical implications (Bikker, 1993). During a number of case studies in the 1970's and 1980's, this methodology has been refined, and includes now the design of variants for the organelle structure with their own performance capabilities (in 't Veld, 1981; Bikker, 1993), ranging between the functional organisation and the product flow organisation. The application of the theory has lead to four design issues of an organisational structure: the primary process, the control processes, the organelle structure, and the hierarchy (see Appendix B).

11.2 IMPLEMENTATION OF PROCESS INNOVATION AND BUSINESS PROCESS RE-ENGINEERING

Process innovation, Business Process Re-engineering, and the Delft School Approach support reaching higher levels of competitiveness if the focus of these approaches shifts to:

- connecting the redesign of the business process to performance criteria dictated by product-market combinations;
- emphasising the redesign of the business processes rather than merely restructuring, mergers, etc. as long as the redesign meets business criteria;
- assessing the impact of redesign much like the principles of architectural innovation.

Both the Re-engineering method of Davenport and the methodology of the Delft School Approach encompass these notions (although more explicitly present in the second approach). Yet, the method of Davenport acknowledges the importance of change management.

Table 11.1 lists the authors that have conducted research in the domain of process innovation and Business Process Re-engineering (and whom will be mentioned in this section and Section 11.3); the table accounts only for those

Table 11.1: Overview of findings of authors in the field of process innovation and Business Process Re-engineering related to the reference model. The last column of this table converts these findings to the refined hypotheses and indicates which of the hypotheses are supported and which ones opposed. (CAD/CAM = Computer Aided Design/Computer Aided Manufacturing, FMS = Flexible Manufacturing System)

Author(s)	Study	Findings	Relation to Reference Model	Evidence for Refined Hypotheses
Boer & During (2001)	7 in-depth longitudinal case studies into process innovation.	Introduction of FMS's mostly considered as technical problem; manufacturing engineers and management dominated the process. Little involvement of other departments.	Necessity of integration points to developmental pathways to be followed.	
		Lack of organisational adjustments that needed to be made. Adjustments difficult to manage.	Resembles concepts of epigenetic and regulatory genes connected to developmental pathways.	Opposes A.2: organisational changes difficult to manage.
	2 in-depth case interview-based survey in a sample of 98 companies (TQM).	Sufficient attention to formal aspects (tasks, instructions, responsibilities, authority), less on culture and leadership. Internal diffusion largely neglected.		
McGahan & Silverman (2001)	Analysis of U.S. patent activity 1981-1994.	General level of patent activity is not lower in mature industries than in emerging industries. No evidence for shift from product to process innovation.	Equal attention for both product and process innovation indicates integrative character of process innovations.	
Beatty (1992)	Case studies of the implementation of CAD/CAM in 10 companies.	Implementation of these technologies requires a skilled champion of change management processes. Companies need a plan for integration. Cooperation necessary between departments.	Stressing the importance of the integrative character of process innovations.	
Jarrar & Aspinwall (1999)	Review of 79 cases of Business Process Re-engineering.	Only 25% of BPR aims at customer benefits. Successful organisations install Continuous Improvement after BPR. Results from BPR rather poor.	Adaptive walks undertaken by changes in phenotype necessity.	Supports B.2.B: BPR efforts have most chances when linked to external opportunities.
Leiponen (1997)	Comparative study between Finnish innovative and non-innovative firms.	Process innovation links to better economic performance. On the long run product innovation should too.	Process innovation linked to sustained fitness, and product innovation to evolvability.	Supports B.2.A: Process innovation contributes to firm's performance.
Romanelli & Tushman (1994)	Investigation of 25 microcomputer manufacturers.	Organisational transformations occur in short, discontinuous bursts.	Model of punctuated equilibrium for individual organisations.	Supports B.1.B: Punctuated equilibrium indicates the presence of long jumps.
Llora (2002)	About 2000 Spanish firms on productivity growth.	Process innovation has biggest influence on firm's productivity.	Process innovation linked to sustained fitness.	
Yung & Chan (2001)	Case of small manufactures (Hong Kong).	Business Process Re-engineering most effective when linked to external opportunities.	Adaptive walks undertaken by changes in phenotype necessity.	Supports B.2.B: BPR efforts have most chances when linked to external opportunities.

authors who have conducted quantitative analysis of samples of companies or who have performed in-depth case studies. The table relates the findings to the reference model to assess their usability for the research questions. Furthermore, the table tells whether these researches support or oppose the refined hypotheses.

During their study into organisation innovation (i.e. process innovation), Boer & During (2001, pp. 97-98, 100-101) remark that the implementation of Total Quality Management in companies fell short on duration and reaching intended benefits. The two in-depth cases and an interview-based survey in 98 companies showed that each of the companies paid very little attention to internal diffusion. The organisational adaptations focused sometimes more on tools and structures while neglecting culture and leadership. They conclude that most companies underestimated the complexity of Total Quality Management and did not achieve the potential results.

Many, such as Kerkhof (1993), have suggested that process innovation follows product innovation during a product life-cycle; during later stages of the life-cycle the importance of process improvement exceeds the efforts on product innovation. This stresses the importance of manufacturing technology as contributing factor to process innovation. Boutellier & Kiss (1996) underline the importance of manufacturing aspects when deploying the model introduced by Utterback (1994) when mentioning the three phases of dominant design: fluid phase, transition phase, rigid phase. During these phases the emphasis shifts from product design to process design. It is therefore important that companies consider the manufacturing aspects of product development during later stages of the product life-cycle equally as important as product innovation. An analysis of patent activity in the USA pharmaceutical industry shows no evidence that product innovation declines during the mature phase in favour of process innovation (McGahan & Silverman, 2001). The analysis shows that separate markets and industries have their own pace and kind of innovation, and industrial leaders do not keep their top position only by having intense innovation efforts directed at products only.

11.2.1 Six Cases Studies

To establish the effectiveness of the design methodology of the Delft School Approach, and of revealing its weak points and strongholds, six cases have been reviewed. These cases have been drawn from the reports of postgraduate dissertations at the Section Industrial Organisation and Management, Delft University of Technology. A postgraduate dissertation is the final project of a student, and the students have to demonstrate their ability to apply the methodologies taught during the undergraduate and graduate program. Those students that choose to specialise in Industrial Organisation and Management

Table 11.2: Description of the six case studies. The table compares mainly the contents of the studies and briefly the contents of the solution. Additionally, it shows for each case the implementation of the solution and whether the solution was modfied. Question marks indicate that no information was obtained on the topic.

Company	AgriCo	EngOf	ToolIt	PlasticCo	Blue Sky	Compult
Main business area	Agricultural equipment	Power technology and Process automation	Electric power tools (DIY)	Engineering Thermoplastics	Airline	Medical equipment, Test solutions, Software
Customer requirements	Seasonal sales, Price-oriented market, Fast delivery	Fixed-price contracts	Competitive quality/price	Delivery on order	Adherence to flight schedule	Customer demands, customer orientation
Bottle-neck	Stock levels of final products, reconfiguration of completed products	Increase of engineering hours despite investments in IT Tools	Disruption in production due to changes of products and processes	Logistics dispute handling due to change of delivery system	Disruptions during execution of flight schedule, maintaining efficiency	Internal focus on innovation, no assessment of customer demands
Problem statement of graduation thesis	Reduce stock levels	Evaluation of IT Tools	Processes for control of changes in production	Evaluate and design logistics dispute handling system	Minimise disruptions and reduce wrong interventions	Implement Customer Relations Management
Solution	Change of COEP Assembly in docks Production control	Generic method for evaluation of software tools Modifications of software	Change process management model	Control of dispute handling Organisational structure	Spare capacity Monitoring of relevant process parameters	CRM-model Introduction of team
Implementation of solution	No	No	Yes	Yes	?	?
Modifications			Minor (adjustments)	Minor (integration into software)	?	?
Current challenges		Reduce stock levels	Shift from projects to process management	Competitive industry	Efficiency	?

enter a training program to master the methodology as outlined in Appendix B. During a dissertation, a company assigns a real problem to postgraduate students, whom should solve it and propose feasible solutions. Typically, the assignment consists of two phases: the analysis of the current situation and the design of a solution; the total period of case study covers about nine months providing ample time to conduct interviews within the company, collect data, verify the solution, etc. Therefore, these six case studies represent in-depth studies of companies providing detailed information about the company and the specific problem at hand.

Each case has been reviewed about two years after the implementation. These cases represent almost a random draw from the available reports. Firstly, the first case has been selected by looking at a report, which was delivered to the examination board about one-and-half years before. This time-delay should be enough for a company to implement the proposal (some of them require investments) and gain experience; if necessary, companies will have made modifications to the solutions provided by the students. Secondly, the five adjacent reports of an older age have been taken chronologically from the files for review, no matter any characteristics, covering case studies ending within the same half a year. Going back in time much further would have created the danger of reviewing reports from which the solutions have been overtaken by recent developments, and newer solutions would have been implemented. Additionally, such a journey in time would make it extremely difficult to find people in companies to remember the studies, their history and their implementation. Therefore, these case are a limited and random sample from the studies performed but might provide us with sufficient insight to draw preliminary conclusions about the adaptation capability of industrial companies.

The characteristics of the six cases have been listed in Table 11.2. It shows that these cases cover a wide range of topics of industrial companies which will make it more difficult to draw conclusions on adaptation strategies. Before evaluating these cases against the reference model, a short description of each will follow to give an impression of the company, the need for the assignment of the graduation thesis, the solution, and its implementation.

The first company concerns a manufacturer of agricultural equipment that experiences problems with aligning stocks to seasonal demands and manufacturing setups (see Appendix H). At Agrico, the proposed solution has not been implemented due to political reasons; a new director did draw right away the conclusion that an ERP-implementation would solve all problems, later followed by a strong push for Just-in-Time. Ironically, the study had rejected these solutions based on their low effectiveness to resolving the problems of the company.

The second case concerns an engineering office for capital equipment, specialised in power technology and process automation (see Appendix I). The company faced with changes in its markets, started a cultural change program drive to meet the need for Lump Sum Turn Key projects. These projects rely on a much more integrated approach towards the execution of projects, and therefore needed more advanced IT tools to support these processes. In contrast to expectations, the number of hours was rising rather than decreasing. The IT tools were blamed for causing these increases but in fact, no evaluation was available to substantiate the inference. Therefore, the student has developed a generic model for the evaluation of IT tools. During the review two years later, the organisation had not yet adapted to the new required working methods, and the model had not been implemented. The organisation still faces an increase in hours while departments are still battling for control, and adhere to the old way of working.

ToolIt, a company supplying electric hand tools to mainly the consumer market, constitutes the third case (see Appendix J). The company experienced many difficulties during the introduction of new products in the production department and the implementation of process improvements. Because of the high mix flexibility and high innovation rate, this resulted in loss of efficiency; the company operates in a highly competitive market. The main problem areas, during new product introduction or process improvements, were found in the improvements that effected production equipment, the introduction of new equipment or modifications. The study developed a total process design for production changes, including control loops and quality control. To guide the practical implementation, documentation was provided as well as a system for registering and monitoring of changes. The objective of the proposed design was to reduce the disruptions in production to less than 50%. During the interview, it became clear that this goal had been reached, and that ToolIt had made only minor adjustments to the total solution to tailor it to its own needs.

The dispute handling system of PlastiCo has seen an increase in customer complaints about delivery, the fourth case (see Appendix K). An initial program aimed at improving internal quality did not yield customer benefits. In 1999, the company introduced deliver-to-order, which should result in short throughput times for distribution and in improved performance aligned with customer demands. Consequently, the number of disputes rose, and the question did emerge whether the dispute handling system was fit to handle disputes effectively. The outcomes of disputes were not transferred to business process improvements. A coordinating control was proposed as well as internal control loops for the departments involved in dispute handling. During the interview, the company pointed out that they had implemented the improved dispute handling system; only minor modifications were made to fit it to the existing software solutions.

Blue Sky constituted the fifth case as an airline with efficiency losses due to a tight flight schedule, sub-optimisation of resource usage leading sensitivity for disruptions (see Appendix L). The turnaround at airports suffered from disruptions due to delays in flight schedules and technical failures. The study proved the lack of spare capacity to be the cause for these frequent events. In addition, the performance indicators based on the balanced score card and the network performance monitor, did not provide adequate information for effective interventions. Hence, the solution contained a proposal for key performance indicators. Also, the study proposed Blue Sky to invest in spare capacity on the European destinations to reduce the chances of cascading and accumulating delays, and he proposed buffering for technical failures of planes during flight execution. No information could be gathered whether the airline had implemented these proposals.

The sixth and final case study was about CompuIt (see Appendix M). A move from the strong orientation on product divisions towards a customer orientation meant a change in the way the Customer Information Management Department handles its database with customer data. The study concerned the design and implementation of a Customer Relation Management System. The system comes along with different working methods and a stronger need for analysis of customer data. Especially, activating customers into active interaction with CompuIt might provide the organisation with valuable information about product needs, leads and initiation of product development. Segmentation of customers would assist in addressing effectively market opportunities. The review of the case demonstrates that change management needs more attention to improve leverage in the organisation. Additionally, the proposed working methods to improve customer loyalty will not guarantee success since it focuses on part of the customer base and the analysis of customer needs is one-sided.

11.2.2 Evaluation of Case Studies

These cases have been confronted with the hypotheses as formulated in the previous research; the results are found in Table 11.3 (the background for the validation of hypotheses is found in Appendix N). Each case has been reviewed on how an organisation wants to improve its competitive position by the assignment, and on the proposed solutions of the studies. The information has been profound and proven insightful when related to the redesign of business processes. The limited scope of the graduation theses entails that conclusions on the adaptations to the dynamics of the environment should be drawn with more care. The primary objective was to evaluate the adaptation process supported by the design methodology as practised at Delft University of Technology. The belief was that these redesigns should strongly contribute to the competitiveness of the industrial companies involved. The six case studies show partially that these graduation theses relate to issues of competitiveness, and at the same time, they demonstrate the limited scope of the methodology compared to necessary adaptation processes.

Table 11.3: Findings of each case. The table lists the evaluation of the case studies against the hypotheses. The details about the assessment against the features for the hypotheses are found in Appendix N.

Company	AgriCo	EngOf	Toollt	PlasticCo	Blue Sky	Compult
Main business area	Agricultural equipment	Power technology and Process automation	Electric power tools (DIY)	Engineering Thermoplastics	Airline	Medical equipment, Test solutions, Software
A.1 Mutations	Yes	Yes	Yes	Yes	No	Yes
A.2 State transition	No	No	No	No	No	No
B.1.A Adaptive Walks	No	No	No	Yes	No	Yes
B.1.B Long Jumps	No	No	No	No	No	No
B.2.A Sustained Fitness	Yes	Yes	Yes	Yes	Yes	Yes
B.2.B Evolvability	No	No	No	No	No	No
B.2.C Complexity Error Catastrophe	No	No	Yes	No	Yes	Yes

The first set of hypotheses tells about how companies interact with the environment to set out the path for increased fitness. All six companies have initiated process changes without any interaction with the environment, rather they did choose to improve their performance by internally inducing changes. These changes have not been implemented in all cases (two are known to have done so). The hypothesis about the transition state requires that in dynamic environments the exchange with the environment should increase. Certainly, EngOf elects for that cause but in fact did not even change its way of working while changing demands should have had a large impact. Resistance to change maintained a status quo rather than initiating a culture that puts the customers at their centre. Compult also tries to adapt to a changing environment, from product division orientation to customer orientation, but wants to keep the interaction under control. All together, the reviews of these hypotheses indicate the weak interaction between organisations and their environment even when acting in highly competitive markets.

The second set of hypotheses shows that none of the companies exerts long jumps (one-time interventions). Rather, they focus on increasing sustained fitness through incremental changes that limited effects for their phenotypes, in three cases that seems hardly to be the case; neither do the companies utilise the implementations for increasing fitness, or its assessment. Some of them aim to change and create a different orientation, like PlastiCo and Compult. The limited changes they implement root in incremental changes rather than the drastic changes they want to create. The efforts look a lot like those of Continuous Improvement but even then how will they sustain the competitive advantage. The three companies, Toolit, Blue Sky and Compult, which face a highly competitive market should revert to increasing fitness along competitive dimensions. They attempt to do so but neither seems to evaluate the effects on their performance.

From the review of the hypotheses a few conclusions can be drawn. When doing so, please remember that the sample of these cases is very limited in size. First, it seems that these companies' interaction with clients remains at distant levels, clients are seen as objects; clients are not seen as a potential source for innovation, except partially the case of Compult. The drive for the assignment in the case of Compult has the danger that the interaction is framed into self-cognition and therefore limited to the already existing beliefs of the organisation. Secondly, the methodology of the Delft School Approach directs partially it efforts to increasing competitiveness of firms. Most of the studies have an internal focus. They emerge from within the companies, and rely on the self-cognition of a firm in its environment. Not necessarily, this vision of customers is the same vision that the customers themselves have from the company. Finally, companies hardly have implemented mechanisms to deal successfully with the changing market, whether it concerns changing customer requirements or it addresses the competitive environment of the companies.

11.3 ADAPTATION CAPABILITY OF PROCESS INNOVATION AND BUSINESS PROCESS RE-ENGINEERING

The success rates of Business Process Re-engineering and the implementation of process innovation signify that the reference model based on biological evolutionary models seems to have little place in the mindset and approaches to adaptations by industrial companies; the companies adapt to changing environments by exerting one-time interventions even though the odds are against these. Yet, the evolutionary framework seems valid, and taken for true, it pinpoints that companies should more than ever include the developmental pathways into account when accounting for sustainable growth. The interaction with the environment, described by fitness models, game theories, and Adaptive Dynamics, should guide the way for organisational development. It requires efforts from academia to provide more realistic and valid models to support business development.

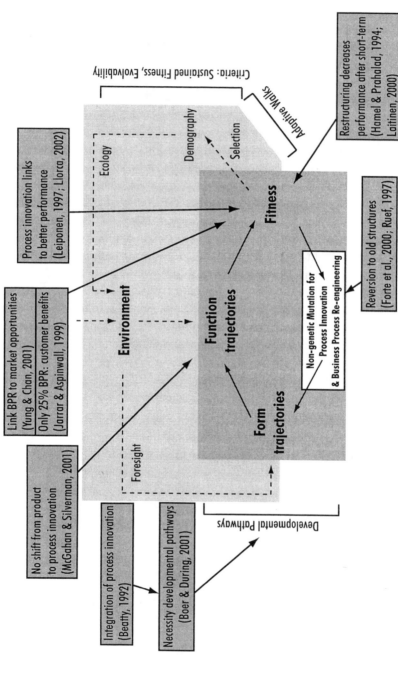

Figure 11.5: Studies into process innovation and Business Process Re-engineerins related to the evolutionary mechanism for organisations. The inidividual studies have drawn conclusions mostly relating to the individual parts of the total evolutionary mechanisms.

11.3.1 Evolutionary Mechanisms for Process Innovation and Business Process Re-engineering

The theories of process innovation and Business Process Re-engineering describe how organisations might evolve into fitter mutants by redesign of the business processes and organisational structures. The theories lack a clear base how these mutations fit into the concept of developmental pathways. Sometimes the theories refer to the combination with change management for the factual implementation in an organisation, e.g. Davenport (1993), a topic found in Section 13.2. From an evolutionary perspective, the approaches do hardly account for the development of the organisation into fitter successive mutants. In general, the theories derive organisational design and systems from business opportunities or criteria. The business requirements are translated into the design of the business process and the belonging organisational structures (i.e. form trajectories).

The assessment whether the evolutionary step of process innovation and Business Process Re-engineering acts as evolutionary trigger has not been established yet. Leiponen (1997) performed a comparative study between innovating firms and non-innovating firms in the Finnish manufacturing industry. By analysing profitability on the attributes of levels and fields of education, patents, process innovations, he arrives at the conclusion that product innovations as such do not appear to be associated with better economic performance, but process innovation does; we should note that on the long term, however, it seems reasonable that product innovation accounts for competitiveness of firms. The results of his research suggest that the complementaries between research competencies and general capabilities are more important for successful product innovation, whereas process innovation tends to rely on learning on the job, which is enhanced by a general skill level.

The mutations caused by process innovation and Business Process Re-engineering associate mostly with form trajectories as part of the evolutionary mechanisms (see Figure 11.5). Changes in the organisational structure and improvements of process execution come about through mutations based on the available resources. These range from the implementation of process technologies to changes in the control structure (IT applications), from regrouping of tasks into new organelles with a different hierarchy. Changes affect the organisational structures and intend to deliver a better performance; they do not directly result in function trajectories on which selection acts. Akin to macromutations, the interventions by process innovations and Business Process Re-engineering should include the epistatic interactions, avoiding partial solutions and aiming for integral solutions for organisations. The likelihood of succeeding becomes low since one might assume that companies operate in highly correlated fitness landscapes where long jumps display low effectiveness.

According to Drago & Geisler (1997, p. 297-300) four categories of problems constitute the many problems associated with implementing Business Process Re-engineering. Firstly, the lack of planning might cause problems associated with Business Process Re-engineering through (a) the reaction of management for the perceived need of discontinuous change, (b) the planning of the change process itself aligned with the overall direction of the organisation, (c) the adequate scope of the Re-engineering process, and (d) the lack of holistic view not accounting for effects on other organisational processes outside the scope of the changes. Secondly, there are problems associated with the implementation itself. These consist of a lack of commitment from top and middle managers, the lack of commitment of non-managers sometimes resulting in an actual increase of the costs of human resources, the poor development of effective process teams, and the ineffective decision-making during implementation (especially focusing on minor corrections or improvements and trade-offs for reaching the optimal solution). The latter problems looks very much like the necessity for adaptation cycles as proposed by Leonard-Barton (1988), and were discussed in the previous chapter. Thirdly, organisational weaknesses constitute a source for troublesome implementations, caused by companies close to a crisis mode, and the all-present entrenched hierarchy and rigid supporting processes. Finally, Business Process Re-engineering has some inherent weaknesses, like the link between the organisational structure and the redesign of processes. Note that the tradition of the Delft School Approach has overcome such by introducing the organelle structure. Strong interdependence between processes also inhibits an effective application of Re-engineering. Furthermore, Drago & Geisler (1997, p. 300, 302) state that the organisation theorists belief the perfect organisational structure does not exist, organising around processes emphasises specialisation within processes just as organising by function requires functional specialisation. Downsizing, coming along with a reduction in hierarchical levels, might also cause greater inconsistency in decisions made. Drago & Geisler conclude that despite these problems Business Process Re-engineering should not be discarded. Rather, continuous learning must occur to improve the success rate.

11.3.2 Phenotype and Genotype

Many of the Business Process Re-engineering efforts fail to deliver promised results; a study by Jarrar & Aspinwall (1999) shows that only 25% of Re-engineering efforts originate in increased customer demands or have customer benefits in sight. They come to this statement after reviewing 79 cases in Business Process Re-engineering that have been reported in published case studies. They classified the improvements or results in three categories: (a) radical, when in excess of 60% improvement over the old way of working, appeared in about

69% of the cases, (b) major, when between 30% and 60% improvement over the old way of working, happened in 28% of the cases, and (c) incremental, when less than 30% improvement over the old way of working, occurred in 2% of the reported cases. About 53% of the cases undertook Re-engineering to face the changes in the business world, such as increased competition, government legislation, IT implementations. The review of the cases considered the necessary success factors: the experiences in changing the culture and applying change management, the actual application of Re-engineering, the use of information technology in the change program, and the implementation and communication of the Re-engineering effort. The pitfalls and challenges indicate the importance of learning during the Re-engineering experience. Furthermore, the Re-engineering efforts need to pay attention to the human aspect of organisations; job contents are affected and resistance needs to be overcome. Even to the extent, that top-down approaches have proven their ineffectiveness in most cases. Keeping momentum of change provides another challenge, given that radical changes need preparation and lengthy implementations. The expectations about information technologies obstructed Re-engineering, mostly because of believing too much in technology, technology selection, and investments. Jarrar & Aspinwall conclude from their findings that:

- the primary use of Business Process Re-engineering was directly aimed at benefiting the organisation, assuming that customers and other stakeholders may also gain from improved performance results;
- a shared determination exists at all successful organisations not to stop after succeeding and *to go on to the next step*, mainly defined by Continuous Improvement. Vakola & Rezgui (2000, pp. 242, 248-249) also stress the importance of evaluation and ongoing process improvement as an important facet of Business Process Re-engineering methodologies;
- many of the cases reviewed were undertaken to achieve medium term cost and time savings rather than longer term strategic benefits. A greater focus on working and learning at the expense of a preoccupation with cost and time could increase the strategic impact of many Re-engineering applications. In general, human factors tended to be overlooked, and there needs to be a greater concentration of effort on improving employees' work environment and learning processes;
- no matter how good the organisation is, it pays to improve. The main theme for successful organisations will be a continuous stream of change;
- from the few experiences that were documented about organisations that failed Re-engineering, it appears that some of them pick up half an understanding and then install half of it. Additionally, some managers

approach Re-engineering as a quick-fix, which will not generate the expected results as well.

11.3.3 Adaptive Walks and Developmental Pathways

The main characteristics for adaptive walks are steps. These steps of process innovation and Business Process Re-engineering look more like long jumps than incremental steps, although some connect the theories directly to Continuous Improvement as a follow-up. For example, Kock & McQueen (1996, p. 19) do mention that business process redesign practitioners in general should pay more attention to information flow analysis and redesign (meaning: fitting the information technology adequately in the organisational structure).

Useem (1994, p. 57) strongly argues that organisational change should follow the pattern of architectural innovation. Changes in the organisation should lead to integration with other aspects to achieve effect at all. The integration should lead to strategic alignment, the deployment of resources to achieve company's objectives. Hence, it points to the need to connect initiatives of Business Process Re-engineering and process innovation to the company's objectives and strategy, and to ensure integration. The methodology of the Delft School Approach has reserved a central place for this notion. From the cases we do notice that to maintain this connection seems more difficult than thought before.

Beatty (1992) reports about the companies failing to implement advanced manufacturing technologies. At ten companies, representing a diversity of industries, she followed with her team the implementation of computer aided design and manufacturing systems (CAD/CAM). The results indicate three potholes. Firstly, the implementation of such technologies requires a skilled champion of the change management process coming along with the technological switch. Where the implementation failed, mostly an engineer was appointed champion rather than a senior (technical) manager. Secondly, the companies need a plan for integration since these technologies thrive on the premise that integration of separate functional databases becomes possible. Companies need to consider developing a strategy that addresses compatibility issues, both present and future, and they need to plan at a high enough level to overcome parochial orientation. To do so, they must either develop a degree of technological sophistication at the strategic level or obtain expert advice from inside or outside the organisation. Finally, the implementation of advanced technologies depends on the true cooperation of design and manufacturing. Teambuilding across the organisation increases the sustainability of advances made by the organisation, and requires adequate attention of management. In short, Beatty states that three rules stand out as the most necessary and powerful: develop an effective champion, plan for a high level of systems integration, and use integration techniques.

In addition, the research by Boer & During (2001, pp. 96-97, 100) on the implementation of the flexible manufacturing systems indicates the technical aspects of the innovation got most attention. They performed 7 in-depth longitudinal studies into the implementation of these manufacturing systems in the Netherlands, Belgium, UK During the implementation, the organisational prerequisites were largely neglected before the factual introduction. They state that the major reason may be found in the companies' lack of experience with this type of innovation and the consequences that this should have for the organisation and the management of the innovation process. In fact, the implementation was not merely the introduction of a new piece of equipment but required a techno-organisational innovation.

Romanelli & Tushman (1994) emphasise the validity of the models of the punctuated equilibrium. By examining 25 minicomputer manufacturers they find that organisational transformations occur in short, discontinuous bursts involving most or all key domains of organisational activity. They also found that small organisational changes do not accumulate to produce evolutionary transformations, strengthening the evidence for the punctuated equilibrium model. Major changes in environmental conditions resulting in declining performance increase the likelihood of fundamental, revolutionary transformation. The economical analysis shows the importance of the punctuated equilibrium, however, within the framework of the evolution of organisations, it does not account for the accumulation of changes that might result in revolutionary change. Hence, when finding revolutionary change, the attribution to earlier, small incremental steps remains unclear.

11.3.4 Sustained Fitness

Process innovation and Business Process Re-engineering seem to focus on optimising local fitness. The mutations do not result in different markets or different products. Rich & Mifflin (1994, p. 113) remark that Re-engineering is often cast in the guise of a primary strategy, becoming the focus rather than the means. In totally redesigning either individual or multiple business processes, Re-engineering aims at achieving relatively sudden and dramatic improvements, such as moving to world class, reducing costs by 40%, etc. Re-engineering can play a profound role in strategy, primarily by changing how a company competes. Nhira (2001) stresses the importance of the Re-engineering approach for the competitiveness of African industries. But its results will be unsatisfactorily in a company that does not determine (1) what primary strategic purpose Re-engineering fulfils, and (2) how it will impact the alignment of relationships and strategies. Llorca (2002) has investigated the economic relationship between process innovation, product innovation, and productivity growth for about 2000 firms in the Spanish manufacturing industry. He concludes that process innovation has the biggest influence on a firm's productivity. All these findings suggest that the role of process innovation and Business Process Re-engineering is restricted to increasing competitiveness; the impact on evolvability only comes around when initiatives in this area connect to value innovation.

Coulson-Thomas (1996, p. 20) also remarks that the findings in the project suggest that many organisations have a clear preference for incremental and evolutionary change, and that they may actually seek to avoid change that is perceived as radical or revolutionary. The organisations justified in incrementalism in various ways, including reference to a total quality management philosophy and references to the risks, uncertainties, and costs of large steps. As he states, an incremental approach can sometimes be rationalised in terms of being responsible and prudent. Promising developments were not progressed because of their likely impact on an existing market. One of the companies that decided against an innovation thought that it would have wiped out past investments in building up a capability that overnight could be rendered inappropriate. This points to resistance from within the organisation that prevents adaptation, being a matter of culture.

Most authors do directly link Business Process Re-engineering to Continuous Improvement; Section 12.3 will deal with this approach specifically. Nihra (2001, p. 12) mentions Continuous Improvement as the last phase of Business Process Re-engineering (Davenport, 1993). One of the reasons is that the approaches for process innovation might yield a initial, reasonable improvement in performance. The efforts for improvements become harder to attain when they operate near the local fitness peak, and less likely by long jumps.

11.3.5 Evolvability

The six case studies show that organisations tend to favour sustained fitness rather than evolvability. Even when it is clear that external shifts require a different response from an organisation, the internal momentum seems not to be reached to introduce new approaches for increasing fitness. Yung & Chan (2001) tell the story of a Hong Kong based small manufacturing enterprise. The company acted as an Original Equipment Manufacturer for foreign companies. During the years, accumulating in 1996, the company experienced a tremendous pressure to reduce costs. A first Business Process Re-engineering initiative failed to speed up and to smoothen the product development process. This was mainly caused by the individual influence of senior management, the centralisation of authority, and the functional specialisation within the organisation. At the same time, the

Table 11.4: Theories and findings in the fields of process innovation and Business Process Re-engineering related to the reference model.

	Phenotype/Genotype	Adaptive Walks	Developmental pathways	Sustained Fitness	Evolvability	Self-organisation
Process Innovation Business Process Re-engineering	How does Process Innovation contribute to the phenotype? How about Business Process Re-engineering?	Does the capability of foresight relate to Process Innovation and Business Process Re-engineering? Do these concepts improve fitness?	Does the implementation of Process Innovation and Business Process Re-engineering account for developmental pathways? Do they affect organisational routines? Do they consider core competencies?	Do Process Innovation and Business Process Re-engineering enhance sustained fitness? Do they link to generalisation or specialisation?	How does Process Innovation contribute to evolvability? And Business Process Re-engineering?	Which intense interactions enhance state transitions? Role of suppliers and customer base?
Delft School Approach	Does it differ from Business Process Re-engineering?	idem	idem	idem	idem	idem
Restructuring		Seldomly fundamental improvements.	Connected to other strategies to be effective.			
Mergers Vertical De-integration		Merger/acquisition: catch-up initiative.	Vertical de-integration (e.g. outsourcing).			
Process innovation	Strong influence on productivity (performance).	Technological improvements. Structural improvements.	More emphasis on process innovation near end of life-cycle. Model of punctuated equilibrium seems to hold. Team building across the organisation.		Organisational change should follow patterns of architectural innovation. Assessment of radical improvements necessary.	
Business Process Re-engineering	Too less focus on customer demands or benefits.	Modelling of business processes. Catching-up more than moving to the front.	Highlighting radical and incremental business improvements.	Continuous improvement. Too much emphasis on IT technology.	(Long jumps but ineffective).	
Delft School Approach	Connection through Sol-policy.		Integration with business strategy and in organisation intended. In practice, more on optimisation.	Mostly supporting sustained fitness.		

company tried to convert from an Original Equipment Manufacturer to an Original Design Manufacturer. Initially, this did not succeed. However, once an opportunity arose, and the earlier attempt of Business Process Re-engineering connected to this chance, a new head of the Engineering Department managed to get the process improvement implemented. This particular case study suggests that Business Process Re-engineering efforts prove most effective when they link to external opportunities, and that internally evoked changes are more difficult to implement.

Such lack of evolvability could be compensated by mechanisms that assess the opportunities arising from relevant mutations. Especially, the criteria for invading potential, dispersal, and bifurcation, get very little attention in the management literature on process innovation and Business Process Re-engineering. Hence, the stability conditions are not examined, and that will result in attempts for local optimisation. In an evolving environment, this creates the danger that fitness of the organisation's performance will decrease, creating the need for intervention by restructuring or Re-engineering. These jumps start to look more like the long jumps of Kauffman's model, with increased danger of not finding a local fitness peak. Even high mutation rates will not suffice for the search in the adaptive landscape (the occurrence of the complexity error catastrophe without a fitness peak).

11.3.6 Self-organisation

The approaches of process innovation and Business Process Re-engineering hardly pay attention to the concept of self-organisation. First, this is caused by the emphasis on developing a blueprint of an organisation. A blueprint does not necessarily evolve from the intense interaction between an organisation and its environment. It rather comes about through the organisation's perception of the outside world, cognition, and what it has learned from interactions with the environment (organisations as allopietic systems). The dissipative structures dictate that a lot of energy flows into the organisation causing a period of internal turmoil before reaching the (fragile) equilibrium of a new state, a concept hardly studied. Sabherwal (2001), with the doubts raised in Subsection 2.2.4, has investigated these phenomena, using the external oriented model of the punctuated equilibrium. At the moment, no proper leads exists that connects self-organisation to adaptation by process innovation and Business Process Re-engineering.

11.4 SUMMARY

No doubt, process innovation and Business Process Re-engineering assist companies to adapt to the environment (see Table 11.4). The results of such actions increase competitiveness but it hardly yields a competitive advantage to the companies. The integration of business improvements needs attention, not only one aspect should be addressed, the other affected factors or aspects should be accounted for. The methodology for the Delft School Approach does so, however, in practice the scope of the assignments seems limited to partial problems within a company and therefore has less effects than possible. In addition, the evaluation of the implementation of generated proposals shows similar results. When not implemented, companies still struggle with the same problems as the reason for the assignments. In fact, the companies seem not to get a grip on changing customer demands.

The evolutionary pathways of process innovation and Business Process Re-engineering have got little attention, in theory and practice. All findings in management literature point to managing change and cultural transformation (see Section 13.3), assuming that change is enforced top-down, with or without participation of other levels in the organisation. Viewed from the reference model for evolutionary adaptation, the following notions are made:

- The developmental pathways of process innovation and Business Process Re-engineering seem to be based on long jumps with risks of misfits (literature consistently reports a failure rate in the magnitude of 70%). If not, the efforts concentrate on sustained fitness with its limited reach and ignoring evolvability.
- The accumulation of changes and subsequently creating momentum for toppling, the principle of regulatory genes similar to the innovation modes of architectural and modular innovation, has been hardly addressed in literature and managerial practice. The learning during implementation, i.e. adaptation cycles, has not been adequately noticed in management literature.
- The extensive interaction with the environment to create dissipative structures has not been elaborated in literature and managerial practice.

The evolutionary scope of approaches for process innovation and Business Process Re-engineering seems limited to increasing the sustained fitness. Connecting the theories of process innovation and Business Process Re-engineering to evolutionary impact might yield more valuable theories than currently available. The efforts taken into this direction require that companies integrate their redesign very well into the organisational structure, covering a wide range of aspects. Process innovation comes along together with managing change in an organisation. Furthermore, it is often mentioned that Business Process Re-engineering is followed by Continuous Improvement.

12 LEARNING ORGANISATION AND KNOWLEDGE MANAGEMENT

The adaptation of industrial organisations to the dynamics of the environment happens also through cognition and learning. This notion has received considerable attention since the publication of the work of Argyris & Schön (1978). The most famous scholar advocating the concept of the Learning Organisation has become Senge (1992). This notion of the Learning Organisation coincides with looking at organisations like an biological system. Especially, viewing an organisation like an allopietic system (Section 8.1.2) means the acknowledgement of self-cognition, self-reflection, and self-consciousness: all elements necessary for effective learning.

Learning results in expansion of skills and knowledge of the resources available to an organisation. Hence, it expands the capabilities of an organisation to deal with the dynamics of the environment. The concept of the Learning Organisation much written about over the last decade, dates back to early work in the 1920's and 1930's on learning organisms and learning systems, according to Coulson-Thomas (1996, p. 16). In a variety of scientific fields a relatively rich body of literature exists, following the investigations of such pioneers as von Bertalanffy (1956) in biology, Boulding (1956) in economics, and Parsons & Shils (1962) in sociology. Consideration of how organisations use external inputs and feedback loops to learn, and adapt to a changing environment has lead to a distinct approach in many disciplines. Recent years have seen a rise in publications about the concepts of the Learning Organisation.

This chapter deals with the concepts that got a lot of attention during the past decades. Section 12.1 describes the concepts of the Learning Organisation. Following the ideas laid down by de Geus (1999, p. 111) about learning, in turn inspired by the works of Maturana & Varela (1980), Senge et al. (1998) have expanded these theories and gained recognition about the importance of the continuous process of gathering understanding about the interaction between organisation and environment. Shortly afterwards, the movement of Knowledge Management came to rise, topic of Section 12.2. Knowledge Management has a more internal focus than the Learning Organisation, and emphasises the interaction between actors in gathering new skills and knowledge. Recently, management literature has seen a increasing number of publications addressing Continuous Improvement. The approach of Continuous Improvement links to the concept of incremental innovation, and has been mentioned as the final phase of Business Process Re-engineering (Section 11.3.4); sometimes authors do view Continuous Improvement as part of organisational learning (Terziovski & Sohal,

2000, p. 539). Section 12.3 explores these publications briefly, and expands the existing approaches to the adaptation of organisations to the dynamics of the environment. Sections 12.4 and 12.5 conclude this chapter by reviewing the implementation of these concepts in practice, and by assessing their value for adaptation.

12.1 LEARNING ORGANISATION

The concept of learning has already found its way into business practices for a long while. For example, the learning curve as applied in the aerospace industry focuses on the improvement of working methods (Teplitz, 1991; Wright, 1936). The application of this concept requires the systemic follow-up of the production process, the implementation of process improvements, and the monitoring of progress; additionally, it puts conditions to operational management, like the minimisation of disruptions.

Argyris & Schön (1978) expand the existing concepts of learning at that time by looking at different levels. Senge (1992, p. 142) defines learning as the ability to produce the results we truly want in life; therefore it expands beyond the absorption of information to a lifelong, generative learning. Swieringa & Wierdsma (1990, pp. 21-22) emphasise the relationship between learning and action. A learning process aims at creating more effective behaviour, and they state the learning only occurs when the behaviour has truly changed. Learning also indicates the possibility to gather knowledge that might not directly result in new behaviour but to the expansion of the behaviour potential: the sustainable arsenal of behaviour embodied in knowledge, understanding, and skills. Such a definition is found in Fiol & Lyles (1985, p. 811). This concept requires the interrelationships between actions in the past and future actions.

12.1.1 Learning Processes

Human learning follows a defined pattern, according to Senge et al. (1998, p. 60), the wheel of learning as they call it (Figure 12.1). They state that their primary source of the learning cycle constitutes of the work of Kolb (1984). Kolb synthesised and expanded upon theoretical work by American educational philosopher John Dewey, organisation psychology pioneer Kurt Lewin, and learning philosopher Jean Piaget. Additionally, Senge et al. (1998, p. 60) refer to the Shewhart cycle (Plan-Do-Study-Act cycle) as base for the theory. Each step of the learning cycle demands deliberate attention before people can move on to the next: Reflecting, Connecting, Deciding, and Doing. During the stage of reflection, an individual becomes observer of its own thinking and acting. Senge et al. (1998, p. 60) remark that many organisational cultures influence people to skip this stage, partly because of assumptions about the way people spend their time. One looks for links between potential actions and other patterns of behaviour in the system surrounding them. New forms of ideas and possibilities might appear. While deciding, people settle on a method for action, including the consideration of alternatives. Kim (1990, p. 5) uses the same model as Senge et al. but calls it the Plan-Do-Check-Act cycle. The learning cycle indicates that learning takes place continuously, and each phase should follow from the previous and connect to the next one.

Huber (1991) identifies four constructs linked to organisational learning that he labels knowledge acquisition, information distribution, information interpretation, and organisational memory. Implicit in this formulation is that learning progresses through a series of stages. Huber does not connect this framework to organisational action, since to him it alters the range of potential behaviour. Nevin et al. (1995, p. 74) follow this framework but transform it into three stages: knowledge acquisition (the development or creation of skills, insight, and relationships), knowledge sharing (the dissemination of what has been learned), and knowledge utilisation (the integration of learning so it is broadly available and can be generalised to new situations). They state that most studies up until that time have been concerned with the acquisition of knowledge, and to a lesser extent with the sharing and dissemination of the acquired knowledge. Huber (1991) refers to the assimilation and utilisation process as organisational memory.

Within literature, there is a strong recognition of different levels of learning. Some authors recognise two levels, others three, but without doubt the most known and used one stems from Argyris & Schön (1978, pp. 18, 22, 26-27).

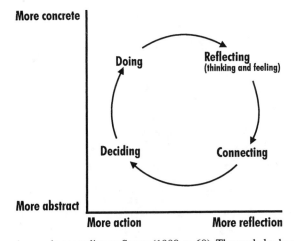

Figure 12.1: Learning cycle according to Senge (1998, p. 60). The cycle looks much like the Plan-Do-Study-Act cycle. People learn in cyclical fashion, passing between action and reflection, between activity and repose.

Single-oop learning aims mostly at correcting mistakes and failures directly. It does not exceed the current architecture of products and processes, and does not entail the complete reconfiguration of a concept. Double-loop learning reviews current solutions within an existing architecture and the why's and how's. By reflective learning or deutero learning it becomes possible to search for integration of innovation, Subsection 10.2.2 called that architectural innovation, and adapt new models for governing business, including shifting performance requirements (denoted by breakthrough, see introduction to Chapter 10). Even the learning process is at stake, and it might result in innovation of learning strategies or the development of new strategies. Moldaschl (1998, p. 18) mentions that feedback constitutes the key to institutional learning (Figure 12.2). Fiol & Lyles (1985, p. 807) distinguish two levels of learning: lower-level learning and higher-level learning. This distinction between lower-level learning and higher-level learning strongly resembles the difference between single-loop learning and double-loop learning by Argyris & Schön. The same applies to the definition of levels by Kim (1990, p. 2): operational and conceptual learning. Bomers (1990, p. 23) and Senge (1992, p. 14) talk in this matter about learning aiming at improvement and learning aimed at renewal. Bomers emphasises that learning aimed at renewal has a stronger external focus. Changes in the environment force companies to adapt their strategy or learning aimed at renewal. Ghemawat & Costa (1993, p. 59) denote two aspects of learning: static and dynamic efficiency. Putting it all together for the purpose of this study, three levels of learning can be distinguished: single-loop learning, double-loop learning, and deutero learning; at each level the learning cycle applies (Swieringa & Wierdsma, 1990, p. 47).

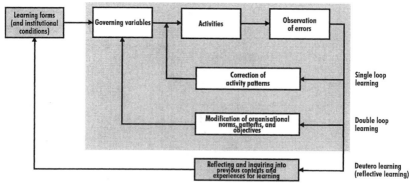

Figure 12.2: Learning cycles from Argyris & Schön (adapted from Moldaschl, 1998, p. 18). The first cycle, single-loop learning, directly corrects deviations of actions, mostly by compensating. Double-loop learning has a more preventive character, attempting to resolve the recurrence of aberrations. Deutero-learning directs itself to finding new pathways, including those for learning.

12.1.2 Organisational Learning

Carneiro (2000, p. 93) states that organisational learning should be viewed as one of the most important responsibilities of top management. In fact, organisations may use the individuals' learning activities, and learn through them to create an organisational learning system, which provides the possibility of enhancing the capacity to generate new offering proposals (Coopey, 1995; Sinkula, 1994; Senge, 1990). Some authors consider that organisational learning includes the ability to increase the understanding level from experience through analysis of problems, experimentation with solutions, and evaluation of results (e.g. McGill & Slocum, 1994; McGill et al., 1992). Vigil & Sarper (1994, p. 189) state that organisational learning concerns the improvement of integral group activities, so that a company learns and improves the making of products. Individual learning restricts itself to specific tasks. Several authors indicate the importance of individual learning for organisations, an organisation learns through individuals; however, organisational learning is not simply the combination of individual learning cycles (Fiol & Lyles, 1985, p. 804; Swieringa & Wierdsma, 1990, p. 37; Warnecke, 1993, p. 21).

In addition to individual learning, Senge et al. (1998, pp. 61-63) distinguish team learning (Figure 12.3). Each phase of the learning cycle has an equivalent for teams: public reflection, shared meaning, joint planning, and coordinated action. According to them, the activities and points of attention do not differ for both individual learning and team learning. By deploying teams, the learning capability increases by collective discussions and dialogues in which members

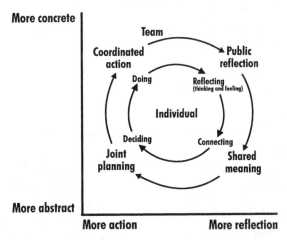

Figure 12.3: Team learning wheel, according to Senge (1992, p. 61). Each point on the learning wheel has a team equivalent; the reflection stage is public because it takes place within the domain of the total organisation.

might exert specific roles for specific phases. The purposeful use of dialogue and discussion serve as a base for learning within a team (Senge, 1992, p. 237).

Kim (1993) connects individual learning to organisational learning by using the concept of mental models. He builds on the concepts of operational (single-loop) learning and conceptual (double-loop) learning to differentiate between the learning modes of individuals and the organisation. The individual learning cycle looks like the one in Figure 12.1, but Kim denotes the stages: Observe (concrete experience), Assess (reflect on observations), Design (form abstract concepts), and Implement (test concepts). The distinction in these stages connects better to organisational learning, according to him. Individual learning results in the possession of individual mental models (frameworks and routines) that guide the individual in its behaviour as a response to environmental stimuli. The level of complexity increases tremendously when we go from a single individual to a

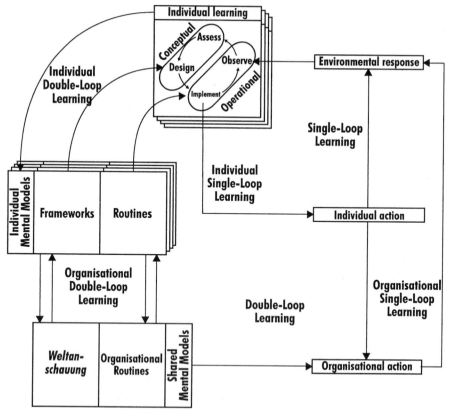

Figure 12.5: Organisational learning (Kim, 1993, p. 44). Transfer of learning takes place through the exchange of indvidual and shared models. Organisational learning is dependent on individuals improving their mental models; making those models explicit is crucial to developing new shared models.

large collection of diverse individuals, and models for such should cope with this complexity. Hence, Kim proposes an alternative model for organisational learning than existent in literature so far, see Figure 12.4. Essential to organisational learning is sharing of mental models that are embedded in individual frameworks and routines, which will result in a shared vision of the world, *Weltanschauung*, and organisational routines, operating procedures.

12.1.3 Concept of the Learning Organisation

Simsek (1993, p. 81) sees a difference between organisational learning and the Learning Organisation. An organisation learns when individuals, teams or groups within an organisation learn. Only when an organisation incorporates the learning of people and groups into a conscious, systematic and fundamental strategy, we can talk about a Learning Organisation. Mills & Friesen (1992, p. 146) use a similar description but add that other goals exist also within the reach of a strategy, the Learning Organisation does not suffice to warrant the continuity of a firm. In addition, Swieringa & Wierdsma (1990, p. 77) state that learning is not sufficient but that organisations should learn to learn.

The core of the learning organisation work is based upon five learning disciplines, lifelong programs of study and practice according to Senge et al. (1998, pp. 6-7):

- personal mastery. This discipline of learning expands our personal capacity to create the results we most desire, and creates an organisational environment, which encourages all its members to develop themselves towards the goals and purposes they choose;
- mental models. This concerns the reflection, continuous clarification, and improvement of our internal pictures of the world and the observations how they shape our actions and decisions;
- shared vision. By building a sense of commitment in a group, by developing shared images of the future, we seek to create, and the principles and guiding practices by which we hope to get there;
- team learning. The transformation of conversational and collective thinking skills, so that groups of people can reliably develop intelligence and ability greater than the sum of individual members' talents;
- systems thinking. This final discipline is a way of thinking about and a language for describing and understanding the forces and interrelationships that shape the behaviour of systems. It helps us to see how to change systems more effectively and to act more in tune with the larger processes of the natural and economic world.

Garvin (1993, p. 81) describes the Learning Organisation not by characteristics, he mentions five skills of such an organisation: the systematic solving of problems, the experimenting with new methods, the learning from the past and own experiences, the learning from experience and experiments of others, and the transfer of knowledge throughout the organisation in a fast and efficient way. Additionally, the roadmap to a Learning Organisation is determined by (Fiol & Lyles, 1985, p. 805):

- the strategy, the choice between alternative ways and resources to achieve a set goal. Senge (1992), Swieringa & Wierdsma (1990, p. 79), and Drucker (1990, p. 267) point to the importance of a strategic mission;
- the organisational structure;
- the culture. The culture of an organisation consists of the shared vision, the ideas and the standards that influence the development of behaviour and the knowledge of an organisation. Changes and the drive to learn often affect the necessity of a learning culture (Fiol & Lyles, 1985, p. 804). Bomers (1990, p. 25) recognises the importance of a learning culture in which norms and standards prevail the positively influence learning. Management has an important task by installing a learning culture (Morgan, 1990, p. 87).

The creation of the strategy, the structure, and the culture will never finish. A start will be made and each of the three components requires updating to the circumstances.

Nevis et al. (1995) have studied four companies, Motorola, MIC, EDF, Fiat, looking for less-defined, more subtle embodiment rather the linear approaches to learning in organisations. They found four core themes that constitute the model of the Learning Organisation. The first core theme states that all organisations are learning systems. All companies have formal and informal processes and structures for the acquisition, sharing, and utilisation of knowledge and skills. Members of those organisations that Nevis et al. studied communicated broadly and assimilated values, norms, procedures, and outcome data, starting with early socialisation and continuing though group communications, both formal and informal. Secondly, learning conforms to culture. The nature of learning and the way in which it occurs are determined by the organisation's culture or subcultures. For example, the learning in a entrepreneurial culture relies more on informal, individual approaches while a group culture hinders the learning across groups. Thirdly, the style varies between learning systems. There are a variety of ways in which organisations create and maximise their learning. Basic assumptions about the culture lead to learning values and investments that produce a different learning style from a culture with another pattern of values and investments. Nevis et al. relate these variations to a series of learning orientations: knowledge source (internal or external), product-process focus, documentation mode (personal vs. public), dissemination mode (formal vs. informal), learning focus (incremental vs. transformational), value-chain focus (design vs. deliver), and skill development focus (individual vs. group). The fourth theme covers the generic processes to facilitate learning. They identify ten factors that induced or facilitated learning: scanning imperative, performance gap, concern for measurement, experimental mind-set, climate of openness, continuous education, operational variety, multiple advocates, involved leadership, and systems perspective.

The model that results from this research is depicted in Figure 12.5 (Nevis et al., pp. 76-77, 82). They conclude that two general directions exist for enhancing learning in an organisational unit. One way is to embrace the existing style, and improve its effectiveness. This approach builds on the notion that full acceptance of what has been accomplished is validating and energizing for those involved. The second direction is to change learning orientations, which has a more profound effect on the organisation, even viewed as an attack on the organisation's culture.

The creation of a systematic Learning Organisation seems to assist companies in adapting to the market. However, key point in the setup is the combination of individual learning and organisational learning, a point that has not yet been leading up to strong concepts for management. Following the thought of Nevis et al., all organisations are learning systems but how?

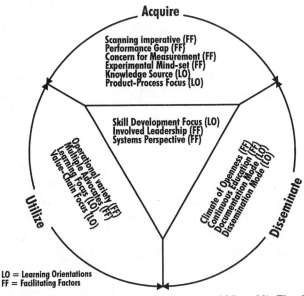

Figure 12.5: Organisational learning system (Nevis et al., 1995, p. 82). The three main process within a learning organisation have attributes from learning orientations and facilitating factors.

12.2   Knowledge Management

Knowledge Management builds on the change of the learning directions. In that perspective, Swan et al. (1999) write that from the 1990's onwards the emphasis on innovation has been seen to replace efficiency and quality as the main source of competitive advantage for firms. Note that this statement of Swan et al. should be rewritten to fit the contemporary situation for most firms: innovation, quality, and efficiency contribute to the competitiveness of organisations. According to Zack (1999), management is increasingly aware that knowledge resources are essential to innovation, and to the development of their organisations. After all, every strategic position within the market is linked to some set of intellectual resources and capabilities. Carneiro (2000) states that the strategic choices for innovation that a company makes have a profound influence on the required knowledge. However, with few exceptions, most firms have difficulties in developing a viable strategic knowledge system. There are manifold reasons for this but certainly a major one is the omnibus nature of knowledge. Knowledge flows within the organisation in a continuous but unsystematic manner, probably because of the amount and characteristics of the required knowledge resources vary by level of management activity. Furthermore, Knowledge Management efforts tend to focus on knowledge exploitation rather than knowledge exploration, and on technical rather than organisational issues (Zack, 1999).

12.2.1 Types of Knowledge

Literature on Knowledge Management extensively describes the concept of data and knowledge. Often the distinction between data, information, and knowledge is made (Boersma & Stegwee, 1996; Preiss, 1999; Skyrme, 1997; Carneiro, 2000, p. 89), although each author on this topic might deploy different terminology and definitions. Many authors do see data as pure values of parameters while they connect knowledge to the capability for change, particularly the relationship between the organisation and its environment.

It makes more sense that data become information when connected to a model; the model represents a structure for capturing data as values for relevant parameters and relating these parameters to each other. According to Preiss (1999, p. 37), data are qualitative or quantitative descriptions of a physical or abstract entity. Therefore, data exist of two elements: the name of the attribute referred to and the value of that attribute. Data becomes information when it serves a meaningful purpose in a certain setting (Bierly III et al., 2000, p. 599; Boersma & Stegwee, 1996). Preiss (1999, p. 37) mentions that information constitutes a collection of facts together with relationships between them, which contributes to or enables the performance of a certain task. Especially, the denotation of relationships points to the existence of a model to define the relationships between data and attributes.

Knowledge, in its turn, should exceed simple facts and figures. In fact, knowledge consists of (Ploegmakers, 2000, p. 6):

- facts, information, and skills acquired by a person through experience or education: the theoretical or practical understanding of a subject;
- awareness or familiarity gained by experience of a fact or situation.

Knowledge retains itself to the scope of different models, which individuals and organisations possess to solve particular problems. We can speak about wisdom when the knowledge exceeds the purposeful application, and when a person becomes capable to select models that fit problems including the understanding the limitations of these for any problem at hand (e.g. Bierly III et al., 2000, p. 599-602). Data and information are carriers of knowledge, and in that way essential to organisations (Boersma & Stegwee, 1996). If data is arranged in meaningful patterns (Davis & Botkin, 1994), and in its turn these patterns are conceptualised with norms, cognitive frameworks, contact, and culture, its becomes knowledge (Rowley, 2000). Blumentrit & Johnston (1999) mention that knowledge needs other tools to be managed than information.

The potential capability embedded in knowledge should yield appropriate actions by receiving , interpreting, and evaluating information (Boersma & Stegwee, 1996). Skills as mentioned before might indicate the ability to execute an action successfully within the scope of a given model. Preiss (1999, p. 37) tells that knowledge is a collection of data and of rules and relationships that enable one to create new data or new rules from a given collection of knowledge. Then knowledge resembles the upgrading of models and adoption of models, leading to new data, new interpretations, new actions in different circumstances, shortly the behaviour of an entity. Examination of literature on learning and knowledge development tells that learning aims at creating adapted behaviour either through increasing skills (repeating behaviour with a higher accuracy) or through adapting new behaviour. Following the reasoning, new behaviour assumes the implementation of new models in the structure of processes and organisations, and it will allow an entity to connect to changing circumstances.

12.2.2 Knowledge Exploration and Exploitation

Carneiro (2002, p. 89) states that the firms' search for information can be viewed as part of a process, through which an organisation adapts to its external environment in order to survive and to become more competitive. Later on, he formulates that a company can decide its competitive advantage as a function of the capability to generate radical change in its processes and technologies, and of the flexibility to adapt its resources to the strategic formulation (Carneiro,

2000, p. 91). This view takes Knowledge Management as an explicit part of the strategic processes. Knowledge represents the gathering of data and interpretations of the external world and the linkage to internal innovation initiatives to increase competitiveness (e.g. Sprenger, 1995; Zack, 1999).

The link between innovation and knowledge becomes visible in the distinction between exploration and exploitation (Swan et al., 1999; Zack, 1999). When a company operates in an environment that is changing, the organisation has to explore new knowledge to keep pace with the industry's innovation. The organisation has to absorb (external) or generate (internal) the required knowledge. The organisation has to exploit acquired knowledge within the industry to turn it into a tangible, profitable product or service. Exploration and exploitation exist simultaneously in an organisation. Exploration provides the knowledge capital to explore new markets and to stay viable on longer term. Exploitation of the acquired knowledge ultimately provides the resources to fuel the successive rounds of exploration (Zack, 1999).

Exploration and exploitation typically occur in different parts of an organisation because they consist of different efforts, and deal with different criteria and constraints. They are separated both organisationally as well as culturally (Schein, 1996). The question arises what efforts do both processes, exploration and exploitation, consist of and how do they link to innovative processes within an organisation. Thereto, Ploegmakers (2000, pp. 22-32) has connected these processes to the breakthrough model (Subsection 10.2.4 has pointed out the breakthrough model as most adequate model to describe renewal). To connect the processes of knowledge, he has also linked strategic, tactical, and operational management to the breakthrough model as shown in Figure 12.6. Exploration matches the focus at the strategic level: the discovery of new and innovative practices and means to fulfil the environmental needs (i.e. raising efficacy), and the extension of the company's capabilities. Exploration corresponds with the operational focus to gain profit out of (new) resources and to reach higher levels of efficiency.

Further examination of the process of exploration teaches us that two primary sources of knowledge might be distinguished. The first one, internal knowledge, is knowledge generated within a firm that tends to be unique, specific, and tacit. It is difficult to imitate and has great potential to deliver competitive advantage. The second one, external knowledge, is absorbed from the environment. This type of knowledge is generally costly to obtain, and widely available for competitors, making it hard to obtain competitive advantage out of it (Zack, 1999). Mostly, an organisation uses both sources to explore new knowledge. Part of the knowledge is generated, part of it is copied from competitors and general resources, leading Ploegmakers (2000, p. 24) to conclude that the

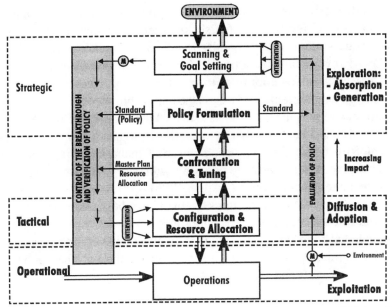

Figure 12.6: Knowledge Management and levels of control (Ploegmakers, 2000, p. 27). Each level has distinct operandus modi for managing knowledge and control.

distinction is hard to make. For instance, Bhatt (2000) uses the term adoption for both the absorption of external knowledge from the environment and the generation of knowledge by adapting existing knowledge. Bhatt (2000, p. 17) also distinguishes four different kinds of generation and absorption in the development cycle, from which two address the knowledge development at an individual level, namely:

- knowledge creation (pure generation). It concerns the ability to generate novel, useful ideas and solutions. Knowledge creation is not a systematic process that can be planned and controlled but rather continually evolves;
- knowledge adoption consisting of (a) imitation of competitor's knowledge (pure absorption), (b) replication of one's experience during another project or situation and translating it into new knowledge (both absorption and generation), and (c) substitution of products and processes by ones with similar functionality (both absorption and generation).

At the organisational level Bhatt (2000, pp. 17-18, 20) distinguishes two more phases since organisational knowledge is not equated with individual knowledge in the firm:

- knowledge distribution. Knowledge needs to be distributed and shared throughout the organisation before it can be exploited at the organisational level. How organisations are structured can have a direct bearing on knowledge distribution;

- knowledge review and revision. One of the important tasks for management becomes to review and replenish knowledge clusters of a distributed knowledge system in the organisation. These knowledge clusters can be reviewed, revised, and reconfigured. The review and revision of knowledge clusters matters for coping with environmental stimuli, solve current organisational problems, and assess the applicability and risk of knowledge in current circumstances. This phase in the knowledge development cycle is of special concern to firms that are operating in highly dynamic technological and globally competitive environments. Self-managed teams in a firm and collaborative arrangements provide firms with many opportunities to manage knowledge review processes (Inkpen, 1996).

The processes and belonging findings of Bhatt have been summarised in Table 12.1. As indicated, a company needs both sources, generation and absorption, to combine external knowledge with unique internal knowledge into new and unique insight. These might provide competitive advantage through the innovation of new or better products and services.

12.2.3 Diffusion and Adoption

The ultimate objective of knowledge exploration, diffusion, and adoption, is to innovate and to turn knowledge into a competitive advantage. To do so, an organisation has to exploit the newly acquired knowledge within its existing value adding process. Exploitation is concerned with the incorporation of

Table 12.1: Strategies for the knowledge development phases (Bhatt, 2000, p. 24). Each of the four stages has specific characteristics for the absorption of external knowledge and the generation of internal knowledge at the level of organisations.

Strategic actions	Knowledge creation	Knowledge adoption	Knowledge distribution	Knowledge review and revision
Plans	Experimentation	Standardisation	Diffusion	Refinements
Control mechanism	Consistency	Reusability	Information access and retrieval	Thoroughness
Measurement goals	Early checks to eliminate inconsistencies	Early checks to find the relevance of knowledge	Flexible format in information/knowledge representation	Checks to refine knowledge
Issues	Freedom to experiment	Knowledge storage	Infrastructure connectivity	Training and expertise
Prime objectives	Innovation	Interpret past in terms of current realities	Assessing changing knowledge requirements and relevance	Collaboration and peer supports

knowledge into the fabric of the operational process, and into its products and services. The balancing of both efforts, exploration and exploitation, relies heavily on knowledge diffusion and adoption.

However, one has to connect the two basic processes. Ploegmakers (2000, p. 25) proposes the tactical level of control to play a crucial role in this process of interchange between diffusion and adoption. The tactical level concerns the development and assignment of knowledge resources. Its objective is to make the strategic desired knowledge available at the operational level and to decide where, how and when to assign it. It follows that the main criteria of the processes at the tactical level are that the new resources and developments consist of availability and adoptability to increase productivity.

The efforts of diffusion focus on making new knowledge available throughout the company. Knowledge needs to be distributed and shared throughout the organisation, before it can be exploited at the operational level (Nonaka & Takeuchi, 1995). In reality, distribution and sharing is not an easy task. The natural tendency is to hoard our knowledge and look suspiciously upon that of others (Davenport, 1997). The motivation of people and a proper infrastructure to share knowledge is crucial for the process of diffusion. At this point, the distinction between information and knowledge might be recalled. Sharing data and information is relatively easy, compared to the diffusion of knowledge. However, the availability of data and information does not necessarily alter the organisation's competitiveness, the interpretation of information and acting on it might.

Adoption efforts are directed at incorporating new knowledge into the fabric of the organisational process. When the new knowledge is diffused, it has to be integrated into existing resources to make it applicable at the operational level. Figure 12.6 illustrates the position of the four Knowledge Management efforts (exploration, exploitation, diffusion, adoption) within the breakthrough model.

12.2.4 Conversion Processes of Knowledge

With diffusion and adoption being the central activities of Knowledge Management, linking exploration to exploitation, two types of knowledge can be distinguished, tacit and explicit. Bhatt (2000, p. 17) traces the distinction between explicit knowledge and tacit knowledge back to Polanyi (1967). Tacit knowledge is knowledge that is not visible but that influences employees's decisions and efforts. It is formed by a company's culture, personal experience, and skills. It is deeply rooted in action and in an individual's commitment to a specific context, tacit knowledge is deeply rooted in individual work routines (Bhatt, 2000, p. 17). It has an important cognitive dimension: subjective insight, intuition, and know-how fall into this category of knowledge (Nonaka, 1991).

Explicit knowledge is the knowledge that is tangible, visible, and exchangeable. Contrary to tacit knowledge, explicit knowledge is formal and systematic (Nonaka, 1991). It might be expressed in words and numbers, and can be easily communicated and shared in the form of hard data, scientific formulae, codified procedures or universal principles (Nonaka & Takeuchi, 1995). The definition of explicit knowledge shows the close relation to data and information. Most authors follow the distinction introduced by Nonaka, like Preiss (1999, pp. 37-38).

The distinction between tacit and explicit knowledge suggests four basic patterns for creating and converting knowledge (Nonaka, 1991; Nonaka & Takeuchi, 1995):

- tacit to tacit (socialisation). During this process individuals acquire knowledge directly from others. Only direct conversation, observation, imitation, and practice support this kind of knowledge sharing. This socialisation-process is time-consuming but especially important for operational processes. Besides, it is very difficult to monitor and verify the progress of the socialisation process;
- tacit to explicit (externalisation). This is the articulation of knowledge into tangible form through dialogue. This form of knowledge sharing allows tacit knowledge to be shared with others in the organisation. The knowledge gathered in the head of an individual takes the shape of metaphors, analogies, concepts, and models. It extends the company's knowledge by innovative new approaches based on tacit knowledge developed over the years. This articulation process is essential for the diffusion of knowledge;
- explicit to explicit (combination). This is the combination of discrete pieces of explicit knowledge into a new whole. The knowledge is different in the sense that it synthesises information from many different sources. Nonaka & Konno (1998) distinguish three processes within the process of combination: capturing and integrating new explicit knowledge, disseminating explicit knowledge, and editing it to fit for use. The absorption of external knowledge and the generation of internal knowledge start with this type of knowledge sharing;
- explicit to tacit (internalisation). This type of knowledge creation occurs when employees internalise explicit knowledge, and they use it to broaden, extend, and reframe their own tacit knowledge (this should happen when reality does not fit any the implicit contemporary models people are holding). This process is crucial for the adoption of knowledge. An example is learning by doing where individuals internalise knowledge from documents into their own body of experience (Skyrme, 1997).

During the stages of the breakthrough process, the emphasis shifts between these various types of knowledge conversion (see Figure 12.7):

- externalisation (tacit to explicit) and internalisation (explicit to tacit) are typical types of conversion during diffusion and adoption of knowledge throughout the company. Diffusion demands that tacit knowledge at a certain level of control (strategic, tactical or operational) is made explicit to distribute it efficiently. Once distributed, it has to become tacit again to use the specific knowledge in a specific context. For this adoption of knowledge, internalisation is the most important form of conversion;
- socialisation might be the most efficient way to share tacit knowledge. However, a lot of constraints should be met to share tacit knowledge directly. Firstly, socialisation is time-consuming, and secondly, it requires people to be at the same place. As it is concerned with the transfer of skills by observation, imitation, and practice, socialisation is typical for operational efforts;
- the combination of knowledge is used at the strategic level to combine technologies and explicit knowledge of the environment with internal knowledge. Combination is used at the operational level to exchange data and tangible information.

A point of continuous discussion within the field of Knowledge Management is how to measure the efficacy of the efforts made. These difficulties of evaluation

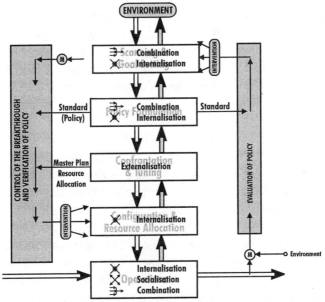

Figure 12.7: Conversion processes and their relation to the breakthrough model. Each stage of the breakthrough process has its own typical knowledge conversion processes.

and verification partially arise because the different efforts cannot be measured with the same standards. On the subject of performance measurement, Armistead (1999) distinguishes the creation, transfer, and embedment of knowledge. In the context of organisational efficacy, the knowledge creation process should be purposeful, i.e. with a client for the outputs. Verification and evaluation of the success of knowledge creation need to include the assessment of: fitness for use, innovative potential, reliability of knowledge, and completeness. Verifying the success of knowledge transfer process includes review of the acceptance of new knowledge. Furthermore, it should consider the aspects of accessibility, availability, and the cost of the transfer process. More importantly, verifying knowledge transfer means verifying the motivation of employees to adopt new knowledge. The only way to do this is by taking interviews, conducting surveys, etc. The knowledge embedding process is concerned with organisational efficiency through the incorporation of knowledge into organisational processes and into products and services. Metrics of the process should be concerned with individual learning and organisational learning as well as with knowledge productivity and the evidence of best practice.

12.2.5 Dynamic Capability of Knowledge

The question arises whether Knowledge Management contributes to the dynamic capability of firms. If so, how? Bogman (2000, p. 1) refers to the concept of dynamic capabilities as presented by Volberda (1998, pp. 108-111), who strongly focuses on the role of management. The dynamic capabilities encompass: dynamic competition, broad knowledge-base/variety of managerial expertise, absorptive capacity, managerial experimentation, broad managerial mindsets, development time, and higher level learning. Volberda uses the concept of dynamic flexibility to solve the problem of being flexible and remaining stable enough to exploit the necessary changes in the company to fit the environment. Bogman (2000, pp. 4, 15-17) connects the basic process of the dynamic capability to the breakthrough model by distinguishing four basic processes: reading the environment, interpreting the findings, designing and redesigning, implementing the redesign and its decisions. Dynamic capabilities distinguish themselves from specialised routines that merely replicate previously performed tasks (Grant, 1996; Teece et al., 1997; Volberda, 1998, p. 109).

Expanding on the dynamic capability as indicated by Volberda, the broad and deep knowledge base is necessary to solve complex problems (Volberda, 1998). In analogy to Systems Theory, the broad and deep knowledge base constitutes the buffer that contains the tacit and explicit knowledge. The high absorptive capacity consists of the ability to absorb new knowledge, and filter this knowledge by review and evaluation to company's norms to usable knowledge in the future (Cohen & Levinthal, 1990). The absorptive capacity enables companies to quickly point out new knowledge from various sources including those outside the company (Cohen & Levinthal, 1990, pp. 148-149; Volberda, 1998). This process is based on active and broad scanning for new knowledge. Dynamic capabilities cannot be developed quickly (Teece et al., 1997). They must be built by skill acquisition and learning (Volberda, 1998). Grant (1996) points out that the dynamic capabilities can only be developed by integrating a broad base of knowledge. This process of higher learning integrates a broad base of knowledge and of selected knowledge provided by the absorptive process into surplus knowledge for the knowledge base, comparable with the knowledge spiral mentioned by Nonaka & Takeuchi (1995).

Morgan (1997) discusses a form of control necessary for knowledge handling and information handling in the Learning Organisation. He points out that control of knowledge and information has an emergent quality, and cannot be pre-designed or imposed. Both Morgan (1997) and Volberda (1998) agree that handling knowledge demands dynamic control. Morgan introduces the gatekeeper that opens and closes the channels of communication, and while doing that filters and summarises. The gatekeeper reacts every time in a different manner depending on new insight, beliefs, and mindsets.

The Learning Organisation and the dynamic capability have some similarities (Bogman, 2000, p. 21). The five processes of Garvin (Subsection 12.1.3) show that the dynamic capability is partly a tool for the Learning Organisation. If implemented, the dynamic capability reflects the last three processes: learning from own experience and past history, learning from the experiences and best practices from others, transferring knowledge quickly and efficiently through the organisation. The dynamic capability represents a tool that enables a company to adjust quickly to changes in the environment. Some adjustments to the Learning Organisation are necessary to include the whole process of the dynamic capability. Thereto, the knowledge development cycle (according to Bhatt, 2000; see Subsection 12.2.2) links to the model of the dynamic capability (see Figure 12.7), especially, the verification and the evaluation processes.

12.3 CONTINUOUS IMPROVEMENT

Continuous efforts on adapting are also found in the Continuous Improvement movement that relies mostly on the concepts of the Deming Cycle (or Shewhart cycle) and the Kaizen concept. Imai (1986, p. 3) defines the essence of Kaizen as ongoing improvement involving everyone, including both managers and workers. The resistance to change has been overcome by addressing the critical issues (Imai, 1986, p. 217):

• constant effort to improve industrial relations;

- emphasis on training and education of employees;
- developing informal leaders among the workers;
- formation of small-group activities such as Quality Circles and improvement teams;
- support and recognition for workers' Kaizen efforts (process-oriented thinking);
- efforts for making the workplace a situation where employees can pursue goals;
- bringing social life into the workplace as much as practical;
- training supervisors so that they can communicate better with workers, and that they can create a more positive involvement with workers.

Bessant et al. (2001, p. 68) state that high involvement in incremental innovation is not new (they view Continuous Improvement as incremental innovation). It is based on the premise that all human beings are capable of creative problem-solving. Many historical examples exist of encouraging participation in innovative activities; for example, Denny's shipyard in Dumbarton in the 19th century and the *hundred-headed* brain at NCR at the turn of the previous century. The more recent discussion has been strongly influenced by experience in Japan on Kaizen or Continuous Improvement. Although strongly associated with the quality movement of the 1980's, Continuous Improvement as concept has roots in many other fields, including socio-technical systems design (see also Stoker & Verweij, 2003), the human relations movement, and more recently, Lean Production.

Delbridge & Barton (2002, p. 682) mention that recently research has begun to focus on the organisational matters behind the Kaizen headlines. The current topics focus on how Japanese firms manage innovation, the evolution of systems, and the adoption of continuous improvement practices; and case studies on the implementation in Western companies should support the research. Especially, matters like the behavioural models receive attention, like Bessant et al. (2001). Delbridge & Barton (2002, p. 689) suggest that managers in the companies they investigated in the UK and the USA seek involvement of shop-floor operators in both problem solving and Continuous Improvement activities. These managers also incorporate the skills and expertise of technical specialists in some form of cross-functional grouping. The initial findings point as well to interorganisational interaction, particularly in the areas of product development, quality management, and cost reduction. They conclude that the first-tier auto component manufacturers have taken greater strides in developing internal organisational processes and practices than they have in establishing innovative and collaborative networks.

In the 1990's, Continuous Improvement emerged as one of the key issues of not only quality management but also organisational design. It offers the possibility of flexible adaptation to changing requirements at the operative level of organisations, and simultaneously, a vehicle for meaningful employee participation (Lillrank et al., 2001, p. 42). The design of Continuous Improvement varies mostly depending on the process characteristics and design. In this view, highly standardised tasks call for incremental innovation based on teams, like Quality Circles, and explicit (financial) reward systems (Lillrank et al., 2001, pp. 50-53). Custom-engineering companies with their different product and process characteristics should focus on target-oriented teams and individual performance evaluation.

12.4 IMPLEMENTATION OF LEARNING ORGANISATION AND KNOWLEDGE MANAGEMENT

Table 12.2 lists the authors that have conducted research in the domain of the Learning Organisation, Knowledge Management, and Continuous Improvement (and whom will be mentioned in this section and Section 12.5); the table accounts only for those authors who have conducted quantitative analysis of samples of companies or who have performed in-depth case studies. The table relates the findings to the reference model to assess their usability for the research questions. Furthermore, the table tells whether these researches support or oppose the refined hypotheses.

A case study by Leonard-Barton (1992) shows the application of the Learning Organisation at Chaparral, the tenth largest steel producer in the USA that time but undoubtedly the most productive one by far. At the core of her review are the knowledge assets of a firm: integration of external knowledge, integration of internal knowledge, independent problem solving, and continuous innovation and experimentation. The case description tells how the learning system and the involvement of all employees at all levels contribute to the firm's innovation potential. Although factories are traditionally not seen as environments for learning, this case demonstrates otherwise. The most important characteristic of such organisations is that they are totally integrated systems. They are difficult to imitate because every employee, from CEO to line operator, is technically capable and interested in learning. Moreover, the whole organisation is designed around the creation and control of knowledge. The four subsystems described above are not only internally linked but also tremendously dependent on each other. Continuous education depends upon the careful selection of willing learners. Continuous learning depends upon the sense of ownership derived from the incentive system, upon the pride of accomplishment derived from special educational systems, upon values embedded in policies and managerial practices as well as upon specific technical skills. Paradoxically, the system's interdependence is also a potential weakness. A learning laboratory may have trouble recreating itself. According to Leonard-Barton, experts suggest that three critical elements are required for altering current practices: (a) dissatisfaction

Table 12.2: Findings in the field of the Learning Organisation, Knowledge Management, and Continuous Improvement related to the reference model. The last column of this table converts these findings to the refined hypotheses and indicates which hypotheses are supported.

Author(s)	Study	Findings	Relation to Reference Model	Evidence for Refined Hypotheses
Leonard-Barton (1992)	In-depth case study of Chaparral.	Learning part of the total company's system and all employees involved (or learning system should be integrated).	Cognition is the basis for evolutionary development at higher levels of Boulding. Need for integrative approaches towards processes and structures of companies.	
Winfield & Kerrin (1994)	Case study of Toyota Motor Manufacturing UK Ltd. and its effects on the suppliers in the region.	Role model of Toyota for learning. Other suppliers focus on aspects only of total approach. Inter-firm connectivity and inter-firm learning an integral part of Japanese manufacturing techniques.	The fuzzy boundaries of companies allow mutual interaction towards optimisation.	Supports A.2 weakly: Interaction points to fuzzy boundaries and collaboration pays off.
Murray & Donegan (2003)	Investigation of large (26) and small (15) contractors in New South Wales construction industry.	Organisational learning appears to be useful when combined with competency development.	Adaptive walks of allopietic systems should focus on development of capabilities which will increase fitness.	Supports B.1.A: adaptive walks increase fitness.
		Learning at all levels not present in large firms. Management and learning competencies absent in small firms, but technical and operational competencies present.	Small companies and large companies do differ, different focuses of competencies development.	
Bessant et al. (2001)	Case studies of 103 organisations on the implementation of Continuous Improvement.	Competence building in Continuous Improvement is a continuous process. At the higher levels it connects to strategic goals of companies.	Continuous Improvement is search for sustained fitness and evolvability. Both searches are integrated at higher levels of experience.	Supports B.2.A: Continuous Improvement is an adaptive walk leading to increased fitness searching for a local peak.
		Continuous Improvement does extent beyond operational routines, e.g. innovation.	Search for evolvability moves at level of innovation, driven by the search for sustained fitness.	Supports B.2.B weakly: Continuous Improvement might lead to evolvability, aligning it with strategic intents (= capability for foresight).
Gertsen (2001)	Survey of 87 manufacturing units in Denmark.	Larger companies are more likely to have Continuous Improvement.	Differences might exist between larger and smaller companies.	
		Manufacturers of modularised products tend to have more experience with Continuous Improvement than manufacturers of standardised products.	(Macro)mutations possible in output, depending on configuration of products; related to concepts of innovation which indicates developmental pathways.	Supports B.1.A weakly: increased fitness possible through accumulation of changes. Supports B.2.B weakly: accumulation of innovations leads to possibilities for survival.
Terziovski & Sohal (2000)	Survey into Continuous Improvement practices in Australian manufacturing industry (n=385)	Implementation of Continuous Improvement has a positive correlation with performance. The approach seems mostly restricted to parts of their operations, e.g. manufacturing.	Search for sustained fitness increases performance of companies.	

with the status quo, (b) a clear model of what the changed organisation will look like, and (c) a process for reaching that model, that vision of the future. The precise process for implementing these principles will differ markedly from company to company. It is possible to interrupt a factory's current systems by introducing new equipment, new learning skills and activities, new knowledge creating management systems or new values. If a learning capability is to be developed, the whole system must be addressed.

Winfield & Kerrin (1994) show the importance of imitation of practice by studying the effects of the settlement of the Toyota-plant in the UK on the environment of suppliers. They looked at how the companies supplying took advantage of the Toyota Production System when it started up production. Their initial thought was that if learning occurred at organisational level, the suppliers should take the advantage of the contacts with Toyota to learn and implement best practices in their own organisation. Indeed, the initial survey indicated that many suppliers started to assimilate parts of the Toyota Production System. Whereas the general practice of companies in the UK was only to do cherry-picking, and therefore not reach the full effects of the approaches.

The study by Murray & Donegan (2003) suggests that a firm's competitive advantage can be increased as a result of competencies that are established from a learning culture. The purpose of the study was to explore the links between organisational competencies and learning cultures. According to the authors, much has been written about the principles of organisational learning but no attention has been given to link it to the internal techniques or procedures. Such principles seem more valuable when superior organisational competencies are linked to a learning culture, when the improvement of behavioural routines can be traced to the existence of superior learning. In addition to revealing this relationship, they have found that differences exist between larger and smaller construction companies (they conducted a survey in the Australian construction industry among 41 contractors). While large firms display differences in learning across most competency groups, where some levels (e.g. simple, structure and efficiency-driven learning in technical competencies) will be more dominant, small firms are less disparate, meaning there is similar learning evidence across levels in a broad competency group. Current learning in the industry however appears to be impoverished to the extent that individuals and groups lack the complexity and diversity to interpret complex environments (both internal and external); old learning cultures dominate the learning agendas.

Skyrme & Amidon (1997) present a study into the creation of the Knowledge-based Business. The study covers theoretical backgrounds of Knowledge Management and case studies, giving an overview mostly aimed at managers. They claim that the implementation of Knowledge Management might yield a wide range of opportunities and benefits, such as developing a deeper understanding of and anticipating customer needs, improving efficiency, and being more adept to innovation. The research of Skyrme & Amidon found that the state-of-practice at that time was focused on two main areas: the sharing of existing knowledge throughout an organisation and the creation of new knowledge. Many knowledge agendas start with the first, which is seen as easier to tackle, but often quite quickly realise that the second strand is likely to be the most valuable to the organisation in the long-term. The state-of-practice is at that early stage of evolution very much an art form. The development of theory lags behind mainly due to highly philosophical content of writings, which management has difficulties to get grasp with. They point to the theoretical constructs of Nonaka & Takeuchi (1995) on the knowledge-creating spiral and the tacit-explicit conversion process. Based on the difference between leaders and laggards in the implementation of Knowledge Management, Skyrme & Amidon (1997, p. 33) identify seven key factors:

- a strong link to a business imperative. Knowledge programs and processes are visibly supporting business objectives. There is a vital understanding of what knowledge is vital to the organisation's future prosperity;
- a compelling vision and architecture. Generally, some framework is provided as the hook around which to build a common language and momentum for change. It may also define key domains of knowledge and core knowledge value-enhancing processes;
- a knowledge leadership. This is usually a knowledge champion with support from top management. But knowledge leadership qualities are also developed in individuals throughout the organisation;
- a knowledge creating and sharing culture. One that empowers individuals, supports informal networking and encourages knowledge sharing across the organisation and geographic boundaries;
- continuous learning. Learning takes place at all levels. Individuals are encouraged to ask questions, to challenge, and to learn. The organisation learns from its successes and mistakes. Learning is shared;
- a well-developed technology infrastructure that supports collaboration of knowledge workers. As well as explicit knowledge databases, its supports computer conferences and structured conversations. It must be accessible and easy to use;
- systematic organisational knowledge processes for identifying, capturing, and diffusing important knowledge in a structured way. Sources of knowledge must be identifiable and accessible, whether in databases or human brains.

Although the Learning Organisation and Knowledge Management aim at achieving guidance for adaptation, the implications of the theory seem difficult to capture and hard to transfer to managerial reality.

12.5   ADAPTATION CAPABILITY OF THE LEARNING ORGANISATION, KNOWLEDGE MANAGEMENT, AND CONTINUOUS IMPROVEMENT

Nevertheless, these concepts should be connected to ongoing initiatives for business improvement. Coulson-Thomas (1996, p. 20) reports on the possible outcomes or implications of Business Process Re-engineering (see Subsection 11.3.3). It appears that an incremental approach can sometimes be rationalised in terms of being responsible and prudent. In reality, while most of the organisations observed either employed, or has access to, people with competence to undertake process improvement exercises, they usually lacked the skills required to undertake Re-engineering of the radical change variety. Some evidence suggests that, as with learning, organisations do not pursue innovation at all costs. In fact, in most of the cases observed radical change was avoided rather than actively sought. Other interviews suggested that top management has a tendency not to think through the likely consequences of innovations involving corporate structure, or the adoption of a different model of organisation, for their own roles.

12.5.1 Evolutionary Mechanisms for the Learning Organisation and Knowledge Management

The principles of the Learning Organisation, Knowledge Management, and Continuous Improvement direct themselves at incremental change of the organisation and its output (products). Especially, the concepts of the Learning Organisation are directed at creating new behaviour and output towards the environment. Since organisations possess characteristics of allopietic systems, self-cognition, self-reflection, and self-consciousness make learning from actions towards the environment possible; the observation of the effects of its own behaviour allows an organisation to adapt actions to achieve (preset) outcomes. None of the three discussed theories tells in more detail how to accomplish objectives.

Besides, all three approaches have a strong focus on the internal mechanisms for achieving a better fit with the environment. The processes of learning, managing knowledge, and incremental improvements get a lot of attention in the found literature. The movement of Continuous Improvement stresses mostly the external focus. Some authors within Knowledge Management highlight the importance of acquiring external knowledge to expand the capabilities of the firm. The intangible nature of some knowledge makes it difficult to imitate by others. How exactly to connect the generation of knowledge and the learning processes to the evolutionary mechanisms at this stage remains unresolved; no mechanism as such becomes apparent. Yet, all three theories describe the processes necessary for the generation of variation. That indicates that the reach of the

272

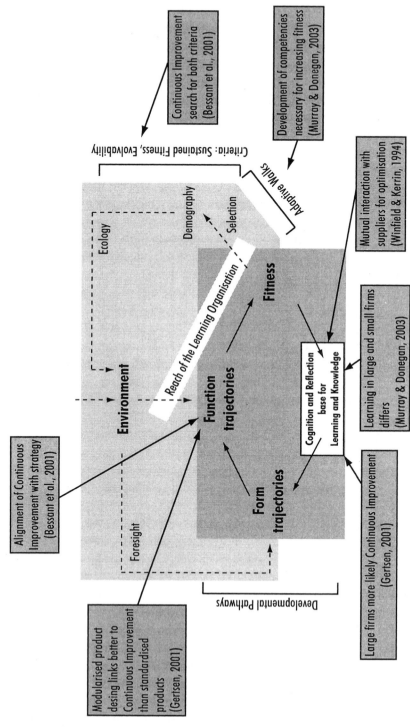

Figure 12.8: Studies into the Learning Organisation, Knowledge Management, and Continuous Improvement related to the evolutionary mechanism for organisations. The individual studies have drawn conclusions relating to the individual parts of the total evolutionary mechanisms. Most notably, the generation of variation is part of the allopietic properties of organisational systems; no direct link exists to recombination.

three approaches is mostly directed at form and function trajectories (Figure 12.8), and less at the external expression of mutations by the organisation.

12.5.2 Phenotype and Genotype

The efforts from the Learning Organisation, Knowledge Management, and Continuous Improvement focus mostly on internal processes to improve competitiveness and achieve higher levels of innovativeness. The concept of a genotype seems absent, although the skills and capabilities present in the organisation form the base for learning and adapting. The connection to the environment is mostly weak in most cases, although some of the authors use external criteria for analysis. To achieve change, most of the approaches require extensive review of internal processes. Once these redesigns align with the purpose of the Learning Organisation and Knowledge Management, the companies might profit from continuous efforts to adapt to the environment. Therewith the three approaches do not distinguish concepts that look like the concepts of phenotype and genotype in evolutionary mechanisms.

In some of the models, the exploration of the environment gets explicit attention. The environment is seen as a resource for advancing the company and in this sense collaboration is sought with suppliers, customers, knowledge centres, etc. The mutual shaping of the environment through the actions of a company gets less attention. Within the scope of the models for evolutionary development of organisations, both issues should be addressed, gathering information and knowledge and interacting with the environment.

12.5.3 Adaptive Walks and Developmental Pathways

The interaction with the environment sets out path for the evolutionary development of organisations. Bessant et al. (2001) have studied and viewed Continuous Improvement as a set of skills and routines that organisations need to develop. Based on Action Research, they arrive at different levels of Continuous Improvement:

1. No Continuous Improvement activity. The dominant mode of problem-solving within a company is by specialists which means there is no continuous impact.
2. Trying out the ideas. Continuous Improvement has only minimal and local effects. Within the company, there is improvement in morale and motivation. Continuous Improvement happens as a result of learning curve effects associated with a particular product or process - and then fades out again. Or it results from a short-term input - a training intervention, for example -, and leads to a small impact around those immediately concerned with it. These effects are often short-lived and very localised. Problem-solving happens at

random and there are no formal efforts or structure. Occasional bursts of improvement occur punctuated by inactivity and non-participation.

3. Structured and systematic Continuous Improvement. There is measurable Continuous Improvement activity - e.g. number of participants, ideas produced. The measurable performance effects are confined to projects with little or no bottom line impact. The organisation makes formal attempts to create and sustain Continuous Improvement by use of a formal problem-solving process. There is use of participation and training in basic tools. A structured idea management system exists together with a recognition system. Often Continuous Improvement is a parallel system to operations, which can extend to cross-functional work but on an ad hoc basis.

4. Strategic Continuous Improvement. Policy deployment links local and project level activity to broader goals. Monitoring and measurement drives improvement on these issues, which can be measured in terms of impact on bottom line - for example, cost reductions, quality improvements, time savings, etc. Further extension of the practice of Continuous Improvement happens by formal deployment of strategic goals, and the monitoring and measurement of improvement effects against these goals.

5. Autonomous innovation. Improvement yields strategic benefits, including those from discontinuous, major innovations as well as incremental problem solving. There is a further expansion of practice plus responsibility for mechanisms, timing, etc. devolved to problem-solving unit. High levels of experimentation exist.

6. Learning Organisation. Strategic innovation arises with its ability to deploy the competence base to achieving a competitive advantage. Continuous Improvement has become the dominant way of life. There is automatic capture and sharing of learning. Everyone is actively involved in innovation processes, consisting of incremental and radical innovation.

A survey of 87 business units in Denmark's industry by Gertsen (2001, pp. 317-318) confirms these results. Experience makes a difference to the level of implementation of Continuous Improvement, in fact larger companies tend to have more likely an implementation of Continuous Improvement. Another finding of this study is that manufacturers of modular products tend to have more experience with this approach than manufacturers of standardised products. In contrast, manufacturers with unique products tend to have the least experience. The more the experience, the more the integration of Continuous Improvement in regular work patterns, the higher the degree of decentralisation, and the higher the degree of diffusion and participation. Also as shown by Bessant et al., the more experience, the more it connects to achieving strategic business objectives.

12.5.4 Sustained Fitness

The evolution of companies through incremental improvements resembles the criterion of sustained fitness. A study by Terziovski & Sohal (2000) into the relationship between a company's performance and the implementation of Continuous Improvement demonstrates that this approach has a positive correlation to a firm's prosperity. Based on the response of 385 firms with each more than a $10 million sales turnover, they conclude that organisational performance linked to the length of time Continuous Improvement had been implemented and to the extent of its implementation. The implementation of the approach seemed mostly restricted to part of their operations, i.e. manufacturing and production. A vast majority of companies had adopted the approach.

Do the theories of the Learning Organisation, Knowledge Management, and Continuous Improvement address the criterion of sustained fitness? One of the subcriteria of sustained fitness concerns the evolutionary stability. The theories in this chapter presume that the organisation has to upgrade itself continuously to remain competitive whether that involves different types of learning or Knowledge Management processes. Hence, the organisation on the move, evolving itself, adapts to the environment, and has not yet reached an evolutionary stable point. Even reaching convergence stability seems hardly addressed by the implications of these theories. However, the danger exists that an organisation views it own development process from the point of view of convergence stability, each step becoming harder to reach to local fitness peak, and does not consider the further evolvability.

12.5.5 Evolvability

The evolution of organisations should result in evolvability. Emblemsvåg & Bras (2000, p. 646) remark that change is inevitable, and that organisations that try to resist it will fail. They compare this process with those of organisms: Continuous Improvement through incremental changes is not sufficient on the long-term, innovation is needed as well. The explicit criteria of evolvability, dispersal, invading potential and bifurcation, get no attention in literature revolving around the concepts of the Learning Organisation, Knowledge Management, and Continuous Improvement.

It is more or less assumed that learning and gathering of knowledge will automatically result in evolvability. The reference model shows that this is not necessarily the case, especially, the subcriteria of evolvability have not been addressed effectively in management science, both in theory and practice (most publications describe IT applications for Knowledge Management). This contrasts the amount of literature in technology management, innovation, process innovation, Business Process Re-engineering where a vast amount of literature

Table 12.3: Theories and findings in the field of Learning Organisation, Knowledge Management, and Continuous Improvement related to the reference model. This table aims at generating a summary of the main topics.

	Phenotype/Genotype	Adaptive Walks	Developmental pathways	Sustained Fitness	Evolvability	Self-organisation
Learning Organisation Knowledge Management Continuous Improvement	How do these concepts relate to the phenotype? Do they focus on genotypes or phenotypes?	Do these concepts relate to adaptive walks to increase fitness? How do they link to the capability of foresight? Relation to time-pacing?	Do these concepts relate to core competencies? And to organisational routines?	Do these concepts increase sustained fitness? Do they link to generalisation and specialisation?	How do these concepts contribute to evolvability?	Which intense interactions enhance state transitions? Role of suppliers and customer base?
Learning Organisation		Learning process generates more effective behaviour. External orientation of learning.	Feedback on actions. Organisational learning vs. individual learning. Organisations prefer incremental and evolutionary change. Need for assessing impact of improvements: innovations, organisational structure.	Single-loop learning. Double-loop learning.	(Double-loop learning). Deutero-learning.	
Knowledge Management	Knowledge connects to innovation: exploitation and exploration.	Knowledge Management as part of the strategic processes. Knowledge conversion processes. Anticipating customer needs.	Both internal knowledge (creation) and external knowledge (imitation, replication, substitution). Knowledge diffusion and adoption. Being more adept to innovation.	Improving efficiency.	(Dynamic capability).	
Continuous Improvement		Linking Continuous Improvement to strategic objectives. Longer implementation, more benefits in performance.	Team-based approach. Modular product design enhances Continuous Improvement.	Focus on incremental innovation. Measurable performance.		Team-based approach.

is available on both theory and all kind of practical aspects. May be, the academic world is still digesting these theories and assessing them on usability. Within the scope of the research at hand, the theories of the Learning Organisation and Knowledge Management present some manifestations for the adaptation of processes and structures. The models of these approaches need further upgrading before they connect to evolvability on business level. The newly presented models for the knowledge conversion processes might demonstrate a possible link to dispersal and invading potential.

12.5.6 Self-organisation

Additionally, self-organisation has been hardly addressed during the research on the Learning Organisation, Knowledge Management, and Continuous Improvement. Especially, the opportunities for employee participation should enable active involvement of all employees in a company during the adaptation. In addition, intense communication with the environment should create dissipative structures that move to new states. Rather, within the discussed theories the environment is seen as an object of study.

12.6 SUMMARY

The concepts of the Learning Organisation, Knowledge Management, and Continuous Improvement aim at establishing a continuous process of adjustments in know-why and know-how. The accumulation of knowledge should result in improved ways to deal with the environment (see Table 12.3). Additionally, the organisations should be able to deal with the changes taking place in the environment. The theories address in this matter the need for evolutionary change by companies and their capability to adapt.

However, they do not do so explicitly. Reviewing all the theories using the reference model for organisations, the findings emerge that although the concepts address internal matters of adaptation, possibly pointing to necessary processes and structures, they have not been linked to the external needs for adaptation. Within the presented theories, the following conclusion may be drawn:

- all three categories of theories attempt to improve and to increase the capabilities of an organisation. These improvements are not always linked to the phenotype of the organisation making it difficult to understand how these theories result in increased competitiveness of organisations;
- the theories of the Learning Organisation, Knowledge Management, and Continuous Improvement describe internal processes of organisations and how these link to actions of individuals, teams, groups, and organisations. These processes have not yet been linked to regular processes and structures

within organisations. The only attempt that classifies for this link is Volberda's dynamic capability;

- the learning processes and knowledge management processes can be connected to the breakthrough model. This chapter has presented a new model based on this relationship, the model for conversion processes. Yet, the mapping has not resulted in addressing the total issue of adaptation; missing links to the Framework for Dynamic Adaptation call for further development of the theories in a comprehensive theory;
- the theories of the Learning Organisation and Knowledge Management have not yet elevated from the conceptual theories to profound practical implications.

The insight of the Learning Organisation, Knowledge Management, and Continuous Improvement should be combined with the earlier findings of technology management, innovation management, and process innovation to result in a more comprehensive approach.

13 Preluding the Dynamic Adaptation

The dynamic capability for adaptation, not adaptation as an one-time intervention but as a continuous process, has been stressed as one of the prominent challenges for management in dynamic environments. The research has sought to find those theories that sustain the evolutionary development of organisations meeting the particular phenomena of dynamic environments. At this moment, it becomes possible to look at the indications and evidence presented in all the management theories and research found in literature to support or contradict these refined hypotheses (Section 13.1). Yet, the belonging questions mentioned in Chapter 8 have been addressed partially during the preceding three chapters. Section 8.2 has formulated refined hypotheses used for reviewing the theories and the six case studies in Section 11.2. Section 13.2 will summarise the findings of the review of theories from management science and the case studies; and it will briefly indicate which questions still need answers. This summary will reveal in how far the findings from other theories in management science effectively deal with the effects of changes in the environment.

Additionally, authors did refer regularly to the necessity of change management and the impact of culture during the previous chapters; the research has not addressed these matters so far. No matter the profound approaches to technology management, innovation, process innovation, Business Process Re-engineering, the Learning Organisation, Knowledge Management, Continuous Improvement, all did touch on the matters of change management and culture. In any circumstance, the review of the management theories point to that a technocratic view on organisations does not hold. The approach of change management aims also at creating a new organisational structure within a company, that way concerning itself with processes and organisational design. Ultimately, the final goal looks much like achieving process innovation, like Berger (1994, p. 5) states: *it is clear that any company that wants to succeed in the 1990's and beyond must have a systematic and well-oiled change management process in place.* Change management differs mostly in its approach to reach the goal, namely through the emphasis on and inclusion of changing the attitude and behaviour of employees. Section 13.3 will pay attention to change management. Section 13.4 will shortly expand on the matter of culture; the text is mostly based on the work of Dronrijp (2000).

To conclude this part of the research, Section 13.5 will discuss the outlines of a framework for the adaptation strategies, processes, and structures for companies to react to the dynamics of the environment. During the previous three chapters, specific topics of management literature have been discussed on their merits for adaptation by industrial companies. The main themes resulting from this search are listed and linked so that the outline of a Framework for Dynamic Adaptation gets shape.

13.1 Collected Evidence for the Adaptation Strategies (and Refined Hypotheses)

This chapter will start with looking at the hypotheses presented in Section 8.2. Each of these hypotheses represents an adaptation strategy, which an organisation could follow to react or anticipate on the dynamics of the environment. Evidence pro or contra these hypotheses has been found during the literature reviewed:

- the evolutionary models for business growth in Chapter 3 and their review in Section 8.3;
- the management of technology and innovation in Chapter 10;
- the approaches of process innovation and Business Process Re-engineering in Chapter 11;
- the theories about the Learning Organisation, Knowledge Management, and Continuous Improvement in Chapter 12.

None of these surveys in the previous chapters might be complete due to the vast amount of literature present in each of these fields; the research has attempted to collect most relevant outcomes of these during the past decades. The overall indications seem to point to a much more appropriate, gradual approach than most of the management scientists propagate. Before drawing these conclusions, this section will elaborate on the findings of the four main topics mentioned in the list. Note that findings relevant to the research questions have been accounted for, concepts and theories that have little grounding have been omitted. Additionally, the findings related to the hypotheses have found their way in the overview in Table 13.1.

13.1.1 Evolutionary Models for Business Growth

With respect to processes and structures, the social-economical perspective has brought forward the notion that microinventions prelude macroinventions. After the introduction of a macroinvention, further optimisation occurs through successive microinventions. Such a thought fits the concepts of developmental pathways and adaptive walks, increasing fitness occurs through microinventions and accelerates around the appearance of macroinventions.

Within organisational ecology, a number of studies have found that age and size matter for the probability of survival. Additional findings in this type of research indicate that turbulent environments will favour generalists (dispersal into new habitats) while their success might attract specialist entrants for short periods. One might conclude that age and size most likely connect to becoming generalists, however, this has not been confirmed yet in studies on this matter. Research into population dynamics has indicated that new entrants might stand a chance when their technologies dissolve existing frameworks or competencies (note the parallel with the concepts of innovation presented in Subsection 10.2.3). At the same time, technological lock-in hinders competition between technologies. Generalists in the development of a product-market combination tend to increase in scope and size. Therefore, these generalists tend to focus mostly on their competencies, maintaining their homeostatic view on the development of their organisations.

The life-cycle of organisations has indicated that phases of stability exist interchanged by periods of internal turmoil. The periods of turmoil are explicitly present in the Growth Model of Greiner, although not expanded on. The prerequisite for the state transition based on the principles of self-organisation has not been addressed adequately by literature. The concepts of the developmental pathways stress the presence of organisational routines based on knowledge, the concept of Nelson & Winter (1982), and time-pacing (Brown & Eisenhardt, 1997). Yet, these concepts that link to adaptive walks do tell little about how companies should or might evolve. Regularly, literature stresses the importance of the punctuated equilibrium model for organisational and technological change; these observations are mostly based on retrospective views and do hardly account for predictive modelling. We might conclude that the search and development for processes and structures to support the development of industrial organisations stretches beyond existing, generic concepts.

13.1.2 Technology Management and Innovation

The findings in the domain of technology management and innovation point to more smooth transitions than assumed so far. Although the popular model of the punctuated equilibrium dominates the research in this area, all models and theories depend on the continuous evolution of technological progress. To assist this more continuous approach, internal adaptation cycles have been proposed by Leonard-Barton (1987, 1988), and additionally, the concepts of innovation support these thoughts of processes within organisations.

Evidence has been compiled that outsourcing and collaboration will contribute to companies' competitiveness. To achieve so, companies should link technology to their strategy and establish collaborations to enhance the total capabilities. Especially, the identification and development of pacing technologies will contribute to increasing the overall fitness of an industrial company. The theoretical study of Kauffman et al. (2001) indicates that companies might exert long jumps in the technological landscape for finding new optima. It tells also that combining technologies might prove a successful strategy for finding new

Table 13.1: Compilation of findings, classified to the hypotheses. The table lists findings found in literature about the application of theories in practice as discussed in Chapter 3, 8, 10-12; for completion, specific references have been denoted. Theoretical concepts have been mostly eliminated. A * indicates findings and conclusions drawn in this research.

Hypothesis	Refined hypothesis	Management literature		Cases Delft School Approach	
		Confirmed	Falsified	Confirmed	Refuted
A Homeostasis The principle of boundary control based on homeostasis limits the evolution of organisations in response to the dynamics of the environment.	**A.1 Mutations** The organisation maintains its homeostasis through the introduction of small changes to its phenotype, outer traits, to adapt to the dynamics of the environment.	Reversion to old organisational structures after restructuring.* Importance of incremental innovation.*	Incremental innovation moves mostly at operational level.*	5	1
	A.2 State Transition In dynamic environments, organisations should increase their exchange with the environment and create a dissipative structure through which new behaviour and structures arise.	Growth Model of Greiner recognises periods of transition. Collaboration with suppliers and partners.* Emergence of dominant design during periods of turmoil.	No evidence of dissipative structures.*		6
B Continuity Adaptation to the environment constitutes of continuous processes within the organisation rather than one-time interventions	**B.1.A Adaptive walks** An organisation undertakes continuous adaptive walks to increase its fitness in the landscape it operates thereby taking the characteristics of the landscape into account. These adaptive walks follow developmental pathways by which the fitness increases.	Micro-inventions accumulate into macro-inventions (Mokyr, 1990); micro-inventions contribute to further optimisation after a macro-invention. Age and size increase the probability of survival. Organisational routines and time-pacing. Adaptation cycles (Leonard-Barton, 1987, 1988; Tyre & Orlikowski, 1993). More experience with continuous improvement the more it connects to business strategies (Bessant et al., 2001).	Singular focus on product development rather than integrated approaches (Boer & During, 2001). Exploration and Exploitation as separate issues (Volberda, 1998); partially theoretical.*	3	3
	B.1.B Long jumps An organisation exerts one-time interventions taking into account the Hamming distance, they exceed the differences necessary for reaching a nearby adaptive peak in the landscape.	Evidence for punctuated equilibrium (e.g. Romanelli & Tushman, 1994); note the parallel with evolutionary biology.* Initial position of firm poor or average on technology landscape, long jumps prove more beneficial (Kauffman et al., 2000); theoretical study.*	Strongholds of Dutch economy (Golden Age-20th century) have hardly changed.* Business Process Re-engineering efforts partially succeed (25-30%).		6

B.2A Sustained fitness The organisation maintains its homeostasis through the introduction of small changes to its phenotype, outer traits, to find a local optimum. Through gradual steps, it becomes gradually harder to reach the local fitness peak.	Technological lock-in (Arthur, 1989). Process innovation contributes to firm's performance; should exist besides product innovation. Continuous Improvement leads to increase of company's performance (e.g. Terziovski & Sohal, 2000).	Considerable adaptations prove difficult to manage (Boer & During, 2001). Restructuring seldomly results in viable improvements.*	6 6
B.2B Evolvability A company moves into new adaptive zones either by deploying and appropriate strategy, dispersal and invading, or by bifurcation.	Analyser-strategy of Miles & Snow (1978) finds support in case studies. Prospector strategy has found less support. Specialist entrants in existing markets (Freeman & Hannan); more chances when dissolving or replacing existing technologies. Architectural innovation (Henderson & Clark, 1990). Entry strategies based on proven component technologies (Christensen et al., 1998). Integration of technologies (component and architectural innovation) creates more opportunities (Fleming & Sorenson, 2001). Collaborations on technological base will contribute to increasing fitness; identification of pacing technologies necessary*. Dispersal into product-markets increased by previous experience (King & Tucci, 2002); need for more continuous dispersal. Business Process Re-engineering efforts most chances when linked to external opportunities.*	Sometimes the Defender and Reactor strategy of Miles & Snow prevails. Turbulent environments favour generalists (Freeman & Hannan). Technological lock-in might restrict development of new markets.	
B.2C Complexity Error Catastrophe An increasing number of competitors, mutations, diversity in the product-market combination(s) force a company to reposition itself by choosing either to increase sustained fitness or to search for a nearby local fitness peak.	Generalists vs. specialised entrants (Freeman & Hannan). Opportunities for combination of technologies on landscapes (Kauffman et al., 2000).		3 3

optima. It points again to the need for collaboration combined with technology management as source for technological competitiveness.

Firms become more successful by entering markets based on proven component technologies, a possibility to meet the criterion of evolvability. The combination of technologies opens more opportunities in highly correlated landscapes, following Kauffman's thoughts. Experience in entering previous markets eases the entrance of new markets, underlining the necessity for dispersal. This should result in managing specialisation, the focus on specific product-market combinations while increasing the scope of the firm (size increases the chances of survival, and through focusing companies might tend to become specialists).

In general, product development gets much attention in management literature, in comparison to the manufacturing domain and the market side. Managing innovations should account for all areas of business management. At the same time, it seems that considerable adaptations to the organisation will prove difficult to manage for industrial companies. Henceforth, companies should follow integrative approaches, and introduce changes that are more gradual.

13.1.3 Process Innovation and Business Process Re-engineering

The efforts of process innovation and Business Process Re-engineering direct themselves mostly to radical changes in the structure of the company. Business Process Re-engineering has known little success. It also happens quite often that organisations revert to old organisational structures after restructuring. Despite these alarming signals, advancement of industrial companies depends on both the need for product innovation and process innovation. The success of organisational improvements relies on integration of both product innovation and process innovation into organisational structures, this includes technological improvements of processes.

The six case studies of the Delft School Approach confirm that sustained fitness rather than evolvability acts as driver for improvement of business processes. Companies might find the best opportunities for process innovation, when they link these to external opportunities; this way the improvements of the execution of processes will meet the criterion of evolvability. Although the companies studied introduced relatively small changes, these do not lead to increased fitness according to the principles of adaptive walks. This traces back to whether organisational changes will benefit the companies. The Delft School Approach might yield slightly better results than the approaches of Business Process Re-engineering (we should not that the number of case studies in this research has been limited).

13.1.4 Learning Organisation and Knowledge Management

Linked to the concepts of the Learning Organisation and Knowledge Management, exploration and exploitation are seen as separate issues mostly, e.g. by Volberda (1998, 2000). This appears as a theoretical thought, in practice companies seek to fulfill both criteria, sustained fitness and evolvability, to adapt to the environment. The concept of adaptive walks dictates that mutational steps should yield benefits for both criteria.

Within the domain of the Learning Organisation and Knowledge Management, the importance of incremental innovation emerges; though it moves mostly at operational levels and sometimes at tactical levels. Leonard-Barton (1992) shows the importance of integration at all levels of the organisation by discussing the Learning Factory. For incremental changes, the learning culture becomes important, and is closely related to Knowledge Management and Continuous Improvement. Several studies point to the more experience companies gain, the more the incremental changes connect to business strategies. Hence, incremental innovations and Continuous Improvement only succeed when it leads to connections to the business strategy, irrespective of experience.

Some authors note that radical change is sometimes purposely avoided. The ambiguity for not taking a step might reside in the mentality as they suggest or alternatively managers might have doubts about the effectiveness of radical change. The research so far has generated little proof for the need and the conditions to exert one-time interventions.

13.1.5 Validity of Main Hypotheses

This brings the study to the original two hypotheses as launched in Chapter 4. So far, the evidence has been collected to support or contradict the refined hypotheses. Will the main hypotheses hold in view of all the indications and findings?

The first hypothesis directs itself at the maintenance of homeostasis, and the specific role of the organisational boundaries. Yes, it seems that introducing small mutations seems beneficial, that way exerting control at the boundary of the organisation. The intense exchange with the environments does hardly occur. The question arises whether this comes about because of the traditional view on an organisation as a closed entity, and therefore that managers and management scientists do not recognise the possibilities of such intense interaction. Research also suggests that the interaction with the environment might contribute to a firm's competitiveness, e.g. through the collaboration with suppliers and partners. Further research into this phenomenon of state transition through intense interaction with the environment might yield better insight. At the moment, this gives the impression of an under-researched area. The homeostatic model of organisations holds, most likely due to inadequate theories for state transitions.

The evidence for the second hypothesis looks supportive; at large, the results for the refined hypotheses support mostly the main hypothesis. Long jumps sort little effect while their call on the resources of the organisation might even cause setbacks for companies. The difficult concept of the complexity error catastrophe sometimes occurs and sometimes not; a more specific study might yield specific findings on this topic. The adaptive walks that should yield a higher fitness do not always occur; some of these should be traced back to managerial decision-making, an issue left out from this study. Throughout the entire study, the relevance of continuous change and adaptation resonates.

13.2 ELABORATION OF THE REFERENCE MODEL

For studying all this phenomena, the research has yielded a reference model for the continuous adaptation of organisations to the dynamics of the environment during Part I (Subsection 8.1.3). The continuity as Red Queen dynamics occur because of the mutations by industrial companies on the dimensions of allopietic systems whereby the research should account for two major differences between organisms and organisations, the openness of the boundary and the capability for foresight. Chapter 5 did outline that organisms have a structurally closed boundary and organisations might shift their boundaries. The second difference is the capability for foresight, not equalled in the evolutionary models for organisms. Both differences still allow the application of the reference model to the selected theories of management science and the case studies.

The reference model connects to three major fields in management science: (1) technology management and innovation, (2) process innovation, (3) Learning Organisation and Knowledge Management. A wide variety of theories and research has been reviewed on their connections to the reference model and their merits for adaptation during Part II.

13.2.1 Yield of Management Science

The investigation into the theories and practice of technology management and innovation generated a model for assessment of diverse innovation initiatives. The concepts cover: incremental innovation, radical innovation, modular innovation and architectural innovation. During innovation processes, and even after the establishment of innovations, companies should assess whether accumulated insight might affect current product configurations, and whether radical innovations appear. These assessments will lead to setting standards for convergence stability in existing product market combinations or possibilities for entering new markets (or dispersal in existing markets not yet explored by the company). Furthermore, industrial companies need to monitor the environment during transitions from one dominant design to the next; the monitoring is aimed at revealing which elements will become part of the dominant design. Technologies and innovations that have relatively quick reaction times for tuning to the demand of the market should be preferred over those will take longer to improve (e.g. investments in highly capitalised assets do not have this type of flexibility, in general).

Process innovation and Business Process Re-engineering render limited possibilities for evolvability. Rather these approaches increase the competitiveness of firms without necessarily expanding its base. If companies succeed in connecting the methods to generate added value and to formulating a product-market strategy then the chances that the implementation will be successful increase. During case studies it appears that in practice companies limit themselves to the tools and methods, thereby neglecting principles of change management, cultural change, and leadership. Additionally, Continuous Improvement is seen as the final phase of Business Process Re-engineering making it necessary that companies extend their efforts beyond an one-time intervention. Furthermore, it appears necessary to deploy the concept of adaptation cycles. The adaptation cycles, also found in the study into technology management and innovation, demand flexibility from an organisation to adjust procedures, structures, strategy, etc. during the implementation of business improvements. Throughout the learning stages of implementation, results show the true potential of the changes, which will deviate from initially set goals and objectives. Hence, the need arises to continuously adapt to ongoing implementation of process innovations and Business Process Re-engineering.

The modes of the Learning Organisation and Knowledge Management aim at adapting organisations to the changes in the environment. Both have a strong internal orientation like in autopoietic and allopietic systems. Characteristic for these approaches is the different levels of information processing and feedback systems. The learning processes should connect to the adaptation processes for firms; Knowledge Management models yield more insight into these processes since they move at the organisational level rather than the individual or team level. Especially, the models reflecting the knowledge efforts and knowledge conversion have been connected to dynamic adaptation. The models have been expanded to address the dynamic adaptation by organisations and have resulted in models incorporating knowledge conversion processes.

The review of six cases led to further insight about adaptations by industrial companies in practice. Although most of these companies were confronted by shifting environments, they concentrated mainly on local optimisation. This optimisation results from the changes taking place. Yet, the improvements did not lead to consideration of further evolution of the internal structures to meet future demands, resulting in increased changes for one-time interventions (long jumps). When companies operate in highly correlated landscapes, these long jumps will have hardly effects.

13.2.2 Remaining Issues

Looking back at the findings so far, the theories reviewed in Chapter 10-12, especially the concepts of the Learning Organisation, Knowledge Management, and Continuous Improvement link weakly to the phenotype. Although intended to connect the organisation to the outer world, most of these approaches rely on internal processes and structures, reinforcing the characteristics of organisations as allopietic systems. The only clear relationship to the phenotype exists in the systems approach of the Learning Organisation (Senge et al., 1998, pp. 87-190); this has nothing to do with the original systems theories but with its focus on mapping and causal diagrams. Within the fields of process innovation, Business Process Re-engineering, and the Delft School Approach not a clear relationship exists between those efforts and the phenotype. For Business Process Re-engineering the customer demands serve as a base for redesign of the organisation and the Delft School Approach deploys an examination of the *Soll*-policy for such. It appears though that technology management and innovation directly contribute to the phenotype of organisations.

The capability for foresight hardly appears in any of the theories. This capability constitutes a huge difference between organisms and organisations. Although monitoring the environment assists companies in adapting, particularly during the era of ferment for the appearance of a dominant design, it differs from the capability for foresight. This issue should become an essential keystone for the dynamic adaptation by connecting the internal efforts to the developments of the environment.

In terms of evolutionary development, the issues that deserve more attention within management science are evolvability and self-organisation. The danger lures that industrial companies focus on sustained fitness, hardly paying attention to evolvability. On the long run, the criterion of evolvability determines the roadmap for industries, and therefore that of individual companies, by finding adaptive zones. No doubt technology management and innovation connect to these adaptive zones, yet, better methods should become available to support companies on issues of evolvability. The characteristics of the concepts of innovation (incremental innovation, radical innovation, modular innovation, and architectural innovation) fit to these thoughts, most likely, by extending them to the overall breakthrough, process innovation, and integration themes. Evolvability operates at the edge of chaos where the principle of self-organisation applies.

Although it seems that self-organisation plays a critical role in the evolution of companies, the implications have not been detailed. Attempts, like Zuijderhoudt et al. (2002), show the complications that it brings along to transfer the thoughts to managerial practice. The dissipative structures require an intense interaction with the environment, something we find indications about in management science. In particular, the cooperation with suppliers or partners elects for such interaction, thereby not excluding the interaction with customers. Hence, the dynamic adaptation relies on both the connected issues of evolvability and self-organisation for which management science has not reached the stage of predictive modelling.

The only topics that have not yet been addressed in the research are change management and culture, though they are mentioned as part of the findings in the previous chapters. Wagner & Kreuter (1999, pp. 71-72) underline the importance of culture and leadership for the practice of innovation. The concept of architectural innovation is embedded in the organisational and communication structures of the organisation (see Subsection 10.3.2), and requires change management when introducing a new architecture. Boer & During (2001, pp. 97-99) remark that organisational consequences of innovation get little attention, and organisational adaptations fall short on culture (and leadership). Beatty (1992) mentions change management as cornerstone for the implementation of computer aided design and manufacturing systems. The methods of Business Process Re-engineering include approaches to change management, in practice they fail to recognise these issues, according to Drago & Geisler (1997). The domain of the Learning Organisation, Knowledge Management, and Continuous Improvement regularly refers to creating a supportive culture. Will these two concepts, change management and culture, overcome the difficulties for adaptation by companies?

13.3 ADAPTATION AND CHANGE MANAGEMENT

Change management becomes a necessity during one-time interventions, which do often have a top-down approach as mentioned in Section 1.2. Berger (1994, p. 7) defines successful change as the continuous process of aligning an organisation with its marketplace, and doing it more responsively and effectively than competitors. In this view, alignment constitutes the continuous synchronisation of four key management levers: strategy, operations, culture, and reward. Within the model he proposes, two basic concepts dominate: the strategic alignment and the process of change itself. The assessment of strategic alignment follows the approach by Porter (1980) with its business classification of Grow, Earn and Harvest. For the change process itself, Berger (1994, pp. 18-20) presents the Change Plan:

- Formal communication of the new alignment blueprint to all stakeholders in ways appropriate to each group.
- Symbolic change in the organisation to signify the enhancement or change in a business classification and the basis for the resulting alignment model. These changes could involve replacement of key executives and change of the organisational structure.
- Introduction of a new performance management system (the main change driver) focusing on goals, measures, and rewards necessary for the realignment of the organisation to its market situation. Berger advises to use cascading goals, measurements, and rewards to drive the company objectives to the lowest levels of the organisation while creating training programs to introduce new skills and competencies. These include the initiation of technology, process and facilities restructuring, and team development.
- Creation of a vision group (a multifunctional, multilevel unit) made up of change agents and change managers around key customers, competitive or internal alignment issues. These people will take scanned information, and drive it through the organisation in the form of proposed action plans. This process must incorporate the capability to discuss the "indiscussable". Change agents and managers should have sponsorship from top management.
- Gaining control of the gatekeepers (recruitment, promotion, and termination processes) and immediately link them to the requirements of the alignment blueprint. A correct culture mix should be developed to meet business requirements. This step includes a mandatory job movement program encompassing all jobs, through promotions, job rotation, and skills enhancement. Such a planned movement will embed the change process into the infrastructure.
- Training of people in self-discipline and the process of managing change. People must see the benefit of the change or they will resist it. Commitment without compliance will not lead to real change.
- Ensuring the correct distribution of change agents, change managers, facilitators, buffers, and resistors for the business classification. This will ensure that the change will be introduced and managed in an orderly way.
- Establishment and promotion of a core set of business ethics (change stabilisers). This code must survive any change in alignment.
- Continuous communication of the status of the company's market and internal alignment in an open and constructive way.
- Codification of the trigger scanning process to continually assess opportunities and threats to the customer base, competitive position, and internal alignment. The empowerment of the scanners and ensuring that the board is part of the scanning process. There must be continual assessment of

the market and internal alignment as well as assessment of readiness to change.

• Experimentation with change. Some changes will be linear, other geometric, others quantum, and still others will be metamorphoses.

Beer (1994) argues that the top-down changes have little effect in contemporary working environments (note the Anglo-Saxon view on the prominent role of leaders), since the attitude of employees have changed towards leadership. Most change programs do not work because they belief that changes in attitude lead to changes in individual behaviour, and these changes in individual behaviour, repeated by many people, will result in organisational change (Beer et al., 1990, p. 159). Rather the process of change requires involvement at all levels of a corporation whereby top management monitors progress but does not push the change program, which guarantees more chances for strategic alignment. The writing of Beer (1994) sometimes suggests that involvement moves at the level of middle management, business unit managers, etc. rather than at the shop-floor level. Useem (1994, p. 53) mentions that distinction between success and failure in organisational change was task alignment. This entailed a sharpening of employee understanding of company objectives, a focusing of company resources around these objectives, and a tightening of organisational support, such as linking performance appraisal and compensations more explicitly to the objectives. Beer et al. (1990, p. 166) conclude that companies need a particular mind-set for managing change: one that emphasises process over specific content, recognises organization change as a unit-by-unit learning process rather than a series of programs, and acknowledges the pay-offs that result from persistence over a long period of time as opposed to quick fixes (such a mind-set is difficult to maintain in an environment that presses for short-term earnings).

Schein (1993) discusses the concept of learning for the support of change as a prerequisite to survival. He distinguishes eight steps for creating the organisational learning process. It starts with that leaders must learn something new so they can teach learning to others. The next step is the creation of a Change Management Group (also called Steering Committee), again with the same purpose that they learn something new, and then help the rest of the organisation. The Steering Committee must go through its own learning process. During the fourth step the Steering Committee must design the organisational learning process which will lead to the creation of task forces. Consecutively, the task forces must learn how to learn. The sixth step covers that task forces must create specific change programs for the specific areas they are assigned to. Throughout the process, the Steering Committee must maintain communication. Finally, the Steering Committee must develop mechanisms for continuous learning. All the same, the process that Schein proposes still has a strong leader focus, the leader of the company endows his vision on the organisation. He proposes a traditional change management program. Also, Davenport (1993, pp. 171-197) connects Change Management to Business Process Re-engineering. Change management is seen again as a top-down driven approach.

A case study by Nelson (2003) shows that organisational change constitutes rather a dynamic process than a static model, moving from the status quo to a new, desired configuration to better match the environment. Analysis of this case at PowerCo in Australia reveals a number of issues related to changes aimed at achieving a more commercial, profit-oriented focus. Nelson visualises it as dynamic rather than static, having a temporal setting, which has multiple causes acting as loops rather than simple lines. The demands of maintaining momentum, controlling variables, and adjusting strategies as the process of change progresses and the context changes, were key aspects that contributed to frustration and disfunctional consequences. The need to monitor progress, and act on feedback information so that strategies can be altered accordingly should be a normal part of introducing change (note the parallel to adaptation cycles). This enables change to be understood as a discontinuous phenomenon having the benefits, without the limitations of rational contingency models.

Johnston et al. (2001) have studied the often-mentioned reward systems in relation to Continuous Improvement and step-wise change. They have looked at Continuous Improvement as requiring employee involvement for target setting and reward systems focusing on non-financial rewards. They assumed that step-wise change leads to top management autonomously setting targets and a focus on financial rewards. The analysis of the responses did not reveal a major contrast between the two approaches: targets are set based on past performance and internal benchmarks, they were mainly imposed by management and financial rewards dominated. Johnston et al. conclude that managers adopting radical change strategies should not set targets based on past performance, which makes it difficult to achieve the desired revolutionary step-change in performance, but should explore external benchmarks. Secondly, the differences between Continuous Improvement and radical change are small, although they require totally different handling by management. Hence, the continuum of adaptation, ranging between continuous and radical change, marks the difference between internal and external benchmarks and comes along with a variety of management approaches to drive change.

Looking at this brief review of change management, it looks like the Business Process Re-engineering efforts, only directed at affecting the changes in the organisation. Mostly driven top-down, it hardly seems to meet the challenges of adaptation; does cultural change do?

13.4 ADAPTATION AND CULTURE

The intensity and rapidity of change in the external environment oblige a company to change continuously in order to increase its performances. However, without a fundamental shift in the organisational culture, there is little hope of enduring improvement in organisational performance; as noted in Section 1.1 cultural change is difficult to implement. As history shows, many efforts, like Total Quality Management, Business Process Re-engineering, and downsizing, failed to improve organisational performance because of the fact that the fundamental culture, i.e. the core values, remained the same. Furthermore, we need to know in which direction cultural change is needed and how cultural change can be achieved.

The organisational culture has a significant influence on the organisational performance. This is mainly because corporate culture serves as a sense-making and control mechanism that guides and shapes the attitudes and behaviour of employees. Because corporate culture is narrowly interwoven with many other organisational aspects, the corporate culture exerts a lot of influence on the functioning of an organisation. Organisational change, therefore, is most likely to succeed if the corporate culture is supportive and well-matched to these changing aspects of an organisation.

To stay competitive, an organisation has to match its performance with the criteria of success, which follow from the external environment. In other words, the internal environment has to be aligned with the external environment. Because the corporate culture has a significant contribution to the organisational performance by its influence on the internal environment by means of the ability, the motivation, and even the choice of resources, the corporate culture also has to be matched to the criteria of success that result from the external environment.

Because the organisational environment is ever-changing, and determines the criteria whether or not organisational performance will be successful, only cultures that will help organisations to anticipate on and to adapt to an environmental change might be associated with excellent performance over time. However, adapting the corporate culture to every single change in the external environment is also very inefficient, if not rendered quite impossible. One has to consider the corporate capabilities, including the organisational culture, which are hard to change. Therefore, one needs to find an equilibrium between optimising the corporate strategy on the basis of current organisational capabilities or fully optimising the corporate strategy to the external environment by adapting these capabilities.

Because changing corporate culture will require a lot of time, i.e. in order of years, one should distinguish a short- and a long-term strategy. This means that on the short-term one cannot fully optimise a company's strategy, but organisations should match the strategy with current capabilities. On the long-term however, it is possible to change these capabilities in order to avoid strategic drift and to optimise the organisation's strategy. Where exactly a line can be drawn between short-term and long-term strategy depends on the costs in terms of management attention and investment.

Difficult however, is to predict whereto an organisation should change. In order to be adaptive, an organisation should predict the future criteria of success several years in advance. Although many criteria are of importance in determining the characteristics of organisational culture, it is possible to provide a framework of preferable characteristics of future corporate cultures. Because almost all companies tend to grow through a predictable pattern of organisational changes, in which every period is characterised by some dominant management problem that must be solved before growth can continue (i.e. the implication of the life-cycle model of Greiner, see Section 3.3).

The management problems of the several phases of growth can be reduced to two dimensions that are representative: flexibility versus stability and internal versus external oriented. Together these two dimensions form four clusters of criteria, each representing a distinct set of cultural values and behaviour. These clusters of cultural values and behaviour, adhocracy, clan, hierarchy, and market,

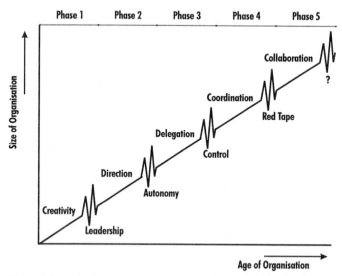

Figure13.1: Cultural Growth Model (Dronrijp, 2000). Based on the life-cycle model of Greiner, types of cultures have assigned to phases of growth. The adhocracy culture points to flexibility, specialisation, and dynamics. In the next phase, the clan culture dominates, characterised by teamwork and employee development. Formalisation and structure determine the hierarchy culture. The market culture is oriented towards the external environment instead of the internal issues of the other cultures.

precisely match the phases of growth. Resulting in the Cultural Growth Model (see Figure 13.1), organisations should successively go through adhocracy-, clan-, hierarchy-, market-, and again adhocracy-oriented culture types.

However, it should not be forgotten that many other criteria ask for numerous other cultural characteristics that have to be taken into account. Therefore, the Cultural Growth Model should not be considered as a panacea, but as a useful framework in which individual cases should be considered on their unique characteristics.

There are two parts to cultural change: auditing the culture to determine what needs to be changed, and developing and implementing culture change strategies. Although every case should be considered on its unique features and merits, it is possible to indicate some general guidelines that have to be observed in order to have a successful cultural change. These guidelines are combined to the following eight principles of cultural change:

1. Unsettle. Make conscious that current ways of business have to be broken through. Show external and internal threats to establish a sense of urgency.
2. Unite. Create a critical mass of people with enough power at all levels to lead the change.
3. Visualise. Provide a clear message with regard to the strategic values and activities of an organisation.
4. Communicate. Use every vehicle to get the message out: big or small meetings, memos, company newsletters, formal and informal interactions.
5. Construct. Change conflicting processes and structures. Since culture is embedded in structures and processes, changing them can change the culture.
6. Succeed. Gain success with relation to the pursued culture as soon as possible.
7. Reinvigorate. Concentrate on reestablishing and reinvigorating the personnel's self-confidence. Take care of having the right people on the right job.
8. Confirm. Promptly and positively confirm all behaviour that is in line with the preferred culture. Also alter rewarding, promotion and succession to reflect the new vision.

These principles of cultural change are active on a broad range of organisational aspects. Therefore, it seems that cultural change programs are most likely to succeed if all principles of cultural change are part of a cultural change strategy. Focusing on corporate cultures alone, and trying to shape them will not change an organizational culture. A true change of corporate culture asks for organisational changes throughout the organisation, by which the change will slowly seep to the unconscious of the organisation.

According to Morgan (1997, pp. 146-150) the organisation as a metaphor of culture has four major strengths. Firstly, it directs attention to the symbolic significance of almost every aspect of organisational life. Furthermore, it shows how an organisation ultimately rests in shared meaning, hence in the actions and interpretive schemes that create and recreate their meaning. Additionally, the metaphor encourages to recognise that the relations between an organisation and its environment are also socially constructed. Finally, the cultural metaphor helps to understand organisational change and that this implies always cultural change. The disadvantages, according to Morgan (1997, pp. 150-152), are that it might evolve into ideological manipulation and control as an essential managerial strategy, and that there is more culture than meets the eye, partially because of the reduction of culture to a phenomenon with clearly defined attributes.

Again, like change management, based on this brief review, it seems that models of cultural change hardly address the needs for adaptation, certainly they do not lead to processes and structures for adaptation.

13.5 OUTLINE OF FRAMEWORK FOR DYNAMIC ADAPTATION

The need arises to create an integrated framework based on the pro's and con's of the theories evaluated so far, the results of the evaluation of six case studies, and the reference model for adaptation. Similarly, Ruttan (1997) advocates also integration of models for technical change rooting in three economic models[47]: induced innovation, evolutionary theory, and path dependence. These concepts have also been found in the theories of evolutionary biology, and some of the theories in the fields of management science presented in this research. The lead to construct a framework of adaptation is found in the differences and similarities between organisms and organisations.

One of the two major differences between organisations and organisms resides in the capability of foresight. Recombination and random mutation thrive evolution of biological species, especially recombination has great potential as Kauffman points out. However, organisations have the capability of foresight, and therefore should be able to create organisational mutations that might yield benefits during selection. So far, the theories about technology management, innovation, Business Process Re-engineering, the Learning Organisation, Knowledge Management, and Continuous Improvement have linked their efforts to strategy but weakly converted these links into practical approaches. Therefore, one of the parts of the framework is the development of an adequate model for foresight.

The second difference between organisations and organisms we do find in the open boundaries of an organisation. Although organisations are structurally closed (a derivative from the theories of autopoiesis), they have the possibility

---

[47] *Rather than economic models we should denote these as evolutionary models.*

to shift boundaries. This results in the notion that companies can mutate themselves by shifting boundaries (e.g. outsourcing, specialisation, mergers, acquisitions, etc.). At the same time, the interaction with the environment shows the principles of homeostatic behaviour, creating boundary control and maintaining a boundary to the environment. The concept of state transition has been contradicted during the review of the hypotheses, yet, it might also result from a lack of adequate theories. The interaction with the environment should be managed, the exact mechanisms are not yet established. Additionally, the system boundaries of an organisation introduce the concept of self-cognition, and therewith the need for learning processes to be present in organisations.

The similarities between organisations and organisms tend to conclude that organisations do follow similar evolutionary pathways as biological entities. They both mutate step-wise, and will have to follow certain paths during their development to maintain or to increase fitness levels. Accumulation might lead to effects for toppling of regulatory genes (found in theories of technology management, innovation, process innovation, Learning Organisation, Knowledge Management). Criteria for development reside in the criteria of sustained fitness and evolvability. The notion of sustained fitness gets substantial attention in the review of the theories and approaches of management science, evolvability less. Adaptation is therefore a dynamic process for both organisations and organisms where organisations have the advantage of shaping their future.

Some of the previous perspectives of management approaches did yield additional insight to those arriving from the theories of evolutionary biology to lay the foundations for the Framework for Dynamic Adaptation. First of all, the assessment of the concepts of innovation, particularly architectural innovations (impact of innovations), constitutes one of the foundations for effective adaptation. Secondly, the need for learning processes should reflect on both the internal processes for developmental pathways and the effect of environmental changes. Thirdly, the framework should include the Knowledge Management processes and their relation to dynamic adaptation. Fourthly, resulting from the case studies the need emerges to exceed the emphasis on sustained fitness, i.e. local optimisation, especially concerning the impact on strategic levels. From the evolutionary biological models, it has become clear that both sustained fitness and evolvability drive evolution. Finally, the fields of technology management, innovation management, and Knowledge Management point to the importance of partnerships, the influence of external relationships with suppliers, etc. to enhance the capabilities of individual firms.

During a market transition, turmoil caused by technological advances and innovation, it becomes of paramount importance to monitor the environment for the emergence of features of the dominant design. Maybe, this applies to process innovations and organisation innovations, too, then monitoring is not only applicable to technology and innovation but any major breakthrough might elect for monitoring. Such monitoring might facilitate principles of self-organisation if the boundary of the organisation is seen as fuzzy (focusing on the intense interaction with suppliers and customers). The theory of state transition does not equal the theory of the punctuated equilibrium, the evidence to support this has been retrospective. In analogy to evolutionary biology, the punctuated equilibrium theory looks at fast-evolving mutations with greater impact than the regular mutations, e.g. the selection of dominant designs. Although the model of the punctuated equilibrium has advanced research in biology, current findings have integrated it into theories of macromutations, developmental pathways, adaptive walks, etc.; this is not the case for management science. Monitoring the environment in conjunction with diffusion processes in the organisation becomes an essential capability for adaptation.

Looking back at the exploration of the variety of theories in this report, all of them contribute pieces of the puzzle for the adaptation processes and structures. Technology management and innovation management yielded more focus on the impact of innovations and the belonging assessment model. Furthermore, active monitoring of the environment during periods of turmoil contributes to adapting. The experiences with process innovation and Business Process Re-engineering point to integrative approaches; the tuning of the organisation, the adjustments made should all fit in the total strategy, the organisational processes, and the organisational structure. If not, companies concentrate on sustained fitness while the fulfilment of the criterion of evolvability ensures long-term health; hence, the focus on sustained fitness endangers the adaptation on the long run. The concepts of the Learning Organisation and Knowledge Management point to the internal learning processes necessary for the dynamic adaptation by firms.

PART III: FRAMEWORK FOR DYNAMIC ADAPTATION

"Now! Now!" cried the Queen. "Faster! Faster!" And they went so fast that at last they seemed to skim through the air, hardly touching the ground with their feet, suddenly, just as Alice was getting quite exhausted, they stopped, and she found herself sitting on the ground, breathless and giddy. The Queen propped her up against a tree, and said kindly, "You may rest a little now."

Alice looked round her in great surprise. "Why, I do believe we've been under this tree the whole time! Everything's just as it was!"

"Of course it is," said the Queen. "What would you have it?"

"Well, in our country," said Alice, still panting a little, "you'd generally get to somewhere else - if you ran very fast for a long time, as we've been doing."

"A slow sort of country!" said the Queen. "Now, here, you see, it takes all the running you can do to keep in the same place. If you want to go somewhere else, you must run at least twice as fast as that!"

(Lewis Caroll. Through the looking glass. 1946, pp. 178-179).

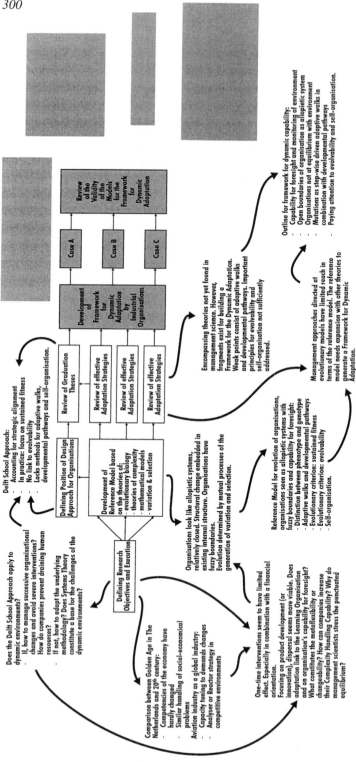

Figure III.1: Overview of the research, completed with the findings from Part II. Contemporary management theories address insufficiently and incompletely the mechanisms of adaptation, and it requires the development of a Framework for Dynamic Adaptation in Part III. The Delft School Approach needs modification and expansion to fit the requirements of adaptation. Adapting to the environment is a more difficult and slower process than anticipated in management science.

Avoiding the Red Queen dynamics or coping with it, becomes the ultimate challenge for industrial companies; avoiding seems hardly realistic. The static strategies do not work any more (Volberda, 2000, pp. 27-28), but what to do? According to Volberda, his palate of different organisation types (Network Corporation, Dual Corporation, Oscilating Corporation, and Balanced Corporation) offers managers choice. For example, the Balanced Corporation might shift its emphasis to exploitation or exploration following internal forces in such a company. Likewise, the reference model indicates that successive mutations as such follow the selectional forces, incorporating both sustained fitness and evolvability. Yet, the models of Volberda and the other approaches presented in Chapter 3 only address partially the challenges posed by dynamics of the environment.

So far, the quest into the adaptation by industrial organisations to the dynamics of the environment has yielded insight into evolutionary development of organisations and mechanisms that support this development. The insight of evolutionary biology shows the power of generating diversity followed by selectional processes, and they indicate more detailed schemes how entities evolve. This insight came together in a reference model that also accounts for the differences between organisations and organisms. The six case studies show that most likely managerial practice, esp. in the case of Re-engineering efforts, focuses on local optimisation rather than evolvability. The review of management theories has contributed to connecting this reference model to technology management, innovation management, Business Process Re-engineering, Learning Organisation, Knowledge Management, and Continuous Improvement.

The next step in the research would be to weld the models together in an encompassing framework. Although the approaches do come from different backgrounds, they share common grounds, which should allow the models to be integrated in approaches for the Framework for Dynamic Adaptation. This seems to be the case for the innovation modes, the adaptation cycles for technology, the levels of learning, and the levels in Knowledge Management. In addition, the importance for interaction with the environment, especially the relationships with suppliers more than customers, is such a common feature. In other ways, the theories behold complementary views, and give ground to additional modes for adaptation. The extensive monitoring of the environment during periods of technological turmoil, the need for integration found in technology management, innovation management, process innovation, the interaction processes of learning and Knowledge Management, all represent those complementary thoughts and approaches. Some of the topics within the evolutionary models need more attention like the capability of foresight and the possibility of shifting boundaries. Finally, this framework should be prepared for the application in industrial companies.

The review of cases has been very limited, and conclusions drawn have therefore limited value; nevertheless, the outcomes of the six case studies and the review of the management literature give rise to the notion that change in companies happens more gradually than thought (see Chapter 13). To ensure validity, the case studies should be expanded in number, and they should cover a diversity of topics, since this study limited the case studies to Re-engineering. Studies of this type will require many resources since this field of evolutionary development of organisations is broad, both in knowledge and in reach. Then, research might also yield more refined approaches to the evolutionary development of organisations since this study represents a first step.

During all the research into these areas of management science, little information has been found on approaches to foresight and the fuzziness of boundaries of firms. Yet, these two characteristics account for the complexity of the eight' level of Boulding and should get attention during the compilation of the Framework for Dynamic Adaptation by organisations.

Chapter 14 will expand on these models to find processes and structures that support adaptation by industrial companies. This part of the development of the research will concentrate on managing breakthrough, learning and knowledge, strategy formulation, and collaboration. The models describe the basic processes and structures within industrial organisations to adapt to the dynamics of the environment.

These models serve as a base for expanding the models of Strategic Capacity Management in Chapter 15. Already some models have been developed for Strategic Capacity Management during earlier research, yet these have not been completed. Some of the interaction models will directly result from the Framework for Dynamic Adaptation.

Chapter 16 describes three cases to which the models of the Framework for Dynamic Adaptation and Strategic Capacity Management have been applied. Three cases seem a limited base to draw definite conclusion on the validity of the models, and to expand the models for application in industry; the rather extensive studies have prevented a more-in-depth exploration of practices following the Framework for Dynamic Adaptation.

14 DEVELOPMENT OF FRAMEWORK FOR DYNAMIC ADAPTATION

The effects of the dynamics of the environment, the external changes, link to the concept of the Complexity Handling Capability, the ability of a company to cope with changes occurring in its environment, and affecting organisational performance. Boswijk (1992), when introducing this concept, stresses that complexity is imposed on organisations, which differs from the internal complexity that finds its creation in the processes and structures of organisations. Reducing and managing (internally) complexity within organisation aims mostly at structuring the organisation, and implementing organisational changes, like Child et al. (1991) propose. No matter how companies build on existing capabilities, present in available resources and current structures, choices for coping with the external changes remain limited. At the end, companies will have to adapt to the external changes taking place through increasing the Complexity Handling Capability[48], which means building on existing capabilities for new situations or incorporating new knowledge for creating new capabilities (Boswijk, 1992, p. 100). Essential is the handling of the complexity of issues pouring into the organisation from the environment (Wiendahl & Scholtissek, 1994). Stimulated by information technology and telematics, these interactions take place in a different way than before but also more chaotic and less visible. The boundary of the organisational system dissolves, and companies experience the involvement of the customer within the boundary control of processes. The closeness to the customer will prevent sudden changes and developments, which might eventually lead to drastic measurements later on.

Dehaëne (1997) notes that the complexity imposed on organisations prevents us from recognising, understanding, and foreseeing these developments. Time presents the only possibility for coping with complexity. In course of time, organisations will find ways to understand external changes, and transform these into actions for coping (see also Grant [1996]). After a while, when these actions become more and more successful, the Complexity Handling Capability has reached the stage of capability, which might turn into a competency. The situation being out of balance has acted as driver for adaptation on the boundary of the organisation as an allopietic system.

---

[48] *The concept of the Complexity Handling Capability has strong similarities to the concept of Law of Requisite Variety (Beer, 1972, p. 54). This cybernetic principle limits the reach of internal complexity reduction and states that internal variety should reflect the variety imposed by the environment.*

This chapter expands on the concepts from the first two parts of this research that support the capability of organisations to deal with its environment. Section 14.1 will focus on the similar concepts within technology management, innovation, Learning Organisation, Knowledge Management to arrive at the first models of the Framework for Dynamic Adaptation: the Innovation Impact Point Model and the Model for the Dynamic Adaptation Capability of organisations. The combination of the breakthrough model with the knowledge conversion processes and the implication for the Model for the Dynamic Adaptation Capability will be discussed in Section 14.2. The true distinctions between organisations and organisms, the capability for foresight and the shifting boundaries, are the topics of Sections 14.3 and 14.4. Section 14.3 will propose leads how companies might deal with strategy and foresight in the dynamically changing environment. Section 14.4 will introduce a model for collaboration, which finds its origins in the literature survey by van der Meiracker (2001).

14.1 INNOVATION IMPACT POINT

The findings from Part II point to the importance of a range of similar concepts within innovation, technology management, the Learning Organisation, and Knowledge Management. From innovation and technology management the main types of innovation arrive, see Figure 10.4. The distinction between single-loop learning, double-loop learning, and deutero learning consists the core of the theories for the Learning Organisation (see Figure 12.2). From Knowledge Management the distinction between data, information, knowledge (and wisdom) arrives. What commonality do these concepts have? When establishing this relationship, how do these concepts link to the breakthrough model that we have taken as overall concept for describing innovation and renewal in general?

14.1.1 Impact of Advancements

Looking at the different types of innovation, it becomes clear that the assessment of the impact of innovations determines the impact on adaptation. Incremental and modular innovation move at the level of sustained fitness, while architectural innovation and radical innovation determine the evolvability. For the sake of reasoning, we denote the architecture as a model of linkage between components whether that architecture covers products, processes, organisational structures or any combination of these. Then only innovations classified as architectural or radical by nature will overturn the existing model of linkage, and introduce new product platforms. From social-economic history, it is known that these architectural and radical innovations emerge as a result from earlier "microinventions". This reasoning resembles the ideas of regulatory genes having control of a number of other genes, and once an accumulation occurs, a macromutation becomes possible. Hence, the critical decision point is the overturning of the dominating model preceded by the accumulation of minor changes.

The concepts of the Learning Organisation distinguish between single-loop learning, double-loop learning, and deutero learning. Single-loop learning occurs within a given framework, and aims mostly at reinforcing the status quo (it has many characteristics of the feedback, part of the boundary control within the steady-state model of Systems Theory). Double-loop learning tries to improve the existing situation through a systematic learning cycle that should lead to an improved concept, e.g. modular or architectural innovation; either within the existing concept a lasting solution will resolve problems encountered or a new concept should overcome contemporary barriers. Replace the concept of a concept by architecture, and a similar reasoning appears as with the innovation types. The innovation types have a more refined classification of impacts of innovations in comparison to the learning types.

But what do deutero-learning and reflective learning constitute? Might they resemble radical innovations or do they indicate other mechanisms of learning? Some authors point to the core of deutero-learning as learning about learning (Jacobs, 2001), see Figure 14.1. Reflective learning might also point to the shifting of criteria and the assessment of what types of improvement are necessary. In that case, i.e. reflective learning, it would supersede the assessment of the types

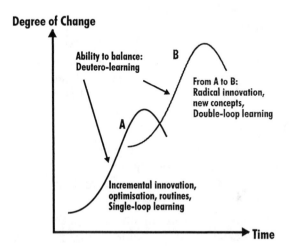

Figure 14.1: Different types of learning, according to Jacobs (2001). Simge-loop learning aims at correcting deviations leading to optimisation while double-loop learning aims at implementing improved or new concepts. Deutero-learning constitutes the capability to reflect on learning itself.

of innovation, and it will provide the framework for assessment of the impact of innovations.

Knowledge Management distinguishes between data, information, knowledge, and wisdom. Data turn into information when placed within a model, without meaning data have no relevance. Knowledge means then upgrading models to make them more effective (incremental or modular innovation) or simply introducing a new model (architectural or radical innovation). We can follow a line of thought that compares to the one about the learning cycles. Then, wisdom has a strong link to reflective learning. Additionally, the model of Bogman (2000, p. 18), which itself is based on the breakthrough model from Systems Theory, the knowledge base, and absorptive capacity derived from Volberda (1998),) offers a possibility to connect learning to the concepts of Knowledge Management.

All together, even though the definitions of the concepts differ in great extent, they all share the same intent, the assessment of the impact of improvements. Better, they intent to seek actively for improvements, and to understand how improvements have an impact on the behaviour of people, the skills, the capabilities, and the organisational system. The adaptation cycles as proposed by Leonard-Barton (1988) aim at the same cycle, the assessment of impacts, and the evoking of decision-making related to the impact or scope of changes.

14.1.2 Breakthrough Model

Combining the learning processes with the breakthrough model shows the impact of improvements into the strategic renewal processes. The breakthrough model arrives from Systems Theory, and is depicted in Figure 14.2. It shows the iterative processes from scanning the environment to the operational control at the lowest level of the model. The deployment of the breakthrough model aligns with the necessity to have organisational processes in place, as found in Subsections 10.3.1. and 10.4.3 based on the findings of Boer & During (2001), Jenkins et al. (1997b), and Wagner & Kreuter (1999). The learning processes distinguish three types of learning. Single-loop learning aims mostly at correcting mistakes, aberrations, failures directly. It does not exceed the current architecture of organisations, products, and processes. Double-loop learning reviews current solutions and possibilities to improve within an existing architecture (for any type of breakthrough). By reflective learning, it becomes possible to search for integration of innovation, the so-called architectural innovations, and to adapt new models for governing business, including the anticipation of shifting performance requirements. The further the learning and the adaptation penetrates into the breakthrough model, the more the impact on the strategic decision processes,

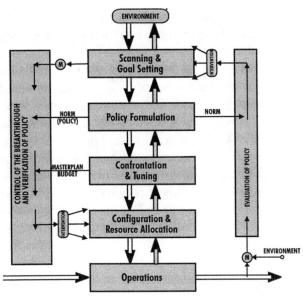

Figure 14.2: The breakthrough model (in 't Veld, 1998, p. 332) indicates the overall processes
necessary for implementing changes into the structure of operations. By scanning
the environment new or adapted goals are set and the derived policy acts as a
reference for the review of tactical and operational decisions. The process of
confrontation and tuning takes the possibilities into account leading to specific
decisions on the utilisation of resources and structures for operations. Through the
development and construction process the actual implementation of the structural
changes in operations takes place. The evaluation of strategies might create new
input for the breakthrough processes. The verification enables companies to follow
the progress of the breakthrough processes.

and the more the need for reflection to get the maximum out of innovation and
learning processes.

The different types of learning move on different levels of the breakthrough
model. Single-loop learning restricts itself to the processes of Operations and
Development & Construction. Learning takes place without questioning the
dominating model seen as a whole. Double-loop learning aims at changing the
model: architectural or radical innovation. It overturns concepts as they exist.
Deutero learning is found at the levels of goal setting, policy formulation, by
deriving goals and criteria from the environmental setting, and by using internal
wisdom (or knowledge) to set priorities. Each of the types of learning hooks to a
different level of the breakthrough model, and they indicate quite different modes
of learning.

Therefore, the impact of learning from the evaluation of experience might
have different impacts on and different entries to the processes of the breakthrough

model. The so-called Innovation Impact Point thereto serves as an indicator for management to evaluate the ongoing innovation processes, and evokes the involvement of the managerial levels with the consequences for business processes (see Figure 14.3). At the lowest level, the Innovation Impact Point 1 tells that changes only address standards and optimisation within a given configuration, while total architecture and components remain intact. Innovation Impact Point 2 indicates redesign of components, i.e. incremental innovation and modular innovation. At Innovation Impact Point 3 an organisation has to reconsider its architecture either by radical innovation or architectural innovation or accumulation of incremental innovation resulting in a breakthrough. Such decisions require fine-tuning of business requirements with the possibilities of innovation, e.g. dispersal. These decisions might affect either the policy (Innovation Impact Point 4) or even its objectives (Innovation Impact Point 5).

14.1.3 Dynamic Adaptation Capability

The distinction of the Innovation Impact Points shows us the importance of managing innovations, and the central role of *Confrontation and Tuning*. This should lead to the timely recognition of ongoing developments as drivers for business renewal. The central role of *Confrontation and Tuning* points to the capability of adapting to the dynamically changing environment. Fed by bottom-

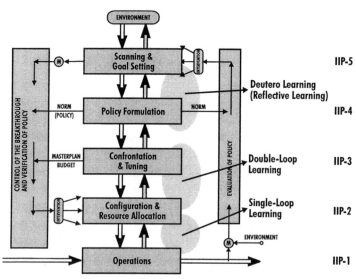

Figure 14.3: Model for the Innovation Impact Point. The breakthrough model shows the learning modes and the identified Innovation Impact Points (IIP). The higher the Impact Point, the more changes and innovations from lower levels affect organisational decision-making. Architectural, and often radical, changes and innovations might come about through accumulation of minor changes and minor innovations.

up innovations through the learning cycles and the technological improvements, improvements through collaboration and outsourcing, and driven by the dynamics of the market itself, continuous reflection on possibilities and opportunities leads to a continuous stream of innovations to the market. Both product and process innovations match than with the changing customer demands. Through the stage-wise decision-making process the innovations will connect better to the actual market developments. The ability to maintain a scope of strategies with related innovations creates the opportunity for anticipation (Paré, 2001). Thus, companies avoid the static view of strategy which might result in missing opportunities and not recognising the value and impact of innovations (Section 14.3 will expand on this matter).

Thereto I do propose a new Model for the Dynamic Adaptation Capability as depicted in Figure 14.4. This model has two components: the Dynamic Capability and the Internal Innovation Capability. Both these capabilities determine the Dynamic Adaptation Capability. The Dynamic Capability has strong similarities to the concept as introduced by Teece et al. (1997, p. 515): (a) the ability to renew competencies so as to achieve congruence with the changing business environment, and (b) the adaptation, the integration and reconfiguration of internal and external skills, resources and functional competencies to match the requirements of a changing environment. Both capabilities might be considered as major components of the Complexity Handling Capability as

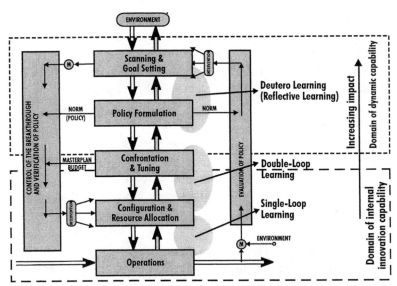

Figure 14.4: Model for the Dynamic Adaptation Capability. Expanding on the model of the Innovation Impact Points, this particular model distinguishes the Internal Innovation Capability and the Dynamic Capability with its external orientation.

defined by Boswijk (1992). We find the separation between these capabilities at one of the defined Innovation Impact Points, at the level of *Confrontation and Tuning*. Above and inclusive this level the strategic adaptation takes place while at lower levels in the breakthrough model and learning cycles a continuous flow of innovations is generated.

However, when the Innovation Impact Point of the streams of innovations mainly moves at lower levels in this model, the innovations will not be assessed on its potential value for customers thus not leading to timely adaptations to the market. These adaptations might be necessary to guarantee a competitive position within the market. It indicates also in these cases that initiatives and product development might be obliterated by managerial levels; these innovations have to find their own course without management paying attention to the integration in the organisation and considering the value for (prospective) customers.

During 2000, Daimler-Chrysler faced decision-making in this respect when they reviewed their policy on product development driven by cost reductions (announced publicly). Management officials announced that they wanted to maintain the continuous stream of new products in order to ensure a competitive position within the market. Within the Model for the Dynamic Adaptation Capability this last effort aligns with the characteristics of dynamic capability, although we have little information if stage-wise decision-making takes place during the *Confrontation and Tuning* process for this particular case.

14.2 ADAPTIVE LEARNING AND KNOWLEDGE MANAGEMENT

Cognition and learning constitute major differences between technical systems and forms of life; therefore, it appears that cybernetic approaches like Systems Theory do not appraise the nature of humans (seventh level of Boulding) and organisations (eight' level of Boulding). Hence, adaptation differs from the cybernetic approach underpinning the methodology of the Delft School Approach. The research has shown that the concepts of the learning organisation have to be incorporated into models for adaptation. Knowledge Management has gone a step further than the concepts of the Learning Organisation. After connecting the learning processes to the breakthrough model in the previous section, the need arises to explore the concepts of Knowledge Management, and incorporate these into the processes and structures necessary for adaptation.

14.2.1 Processes and Knowledge Conversion

Before discussing the model about conversion processes that links the approaches of knowledge distribution and knowledge conversion, it is necessary to depict the learning processes; to do so, we should look at a generic approach to processes. Assume that a process requires an input, material or information, to convert it

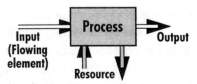

Figure 14.5: Process according to Applied Systems Theory. The depiction shows the interaction between the flowing elements and the resources. Each process as an interaction leads to changes of states of both flowing elements and resources. Note that two systems exist, one comprising the flowing elements and one the resources.

into output, then resources are needed to execute the process; this line of thought follows the basic idea of a process expressed in Applied Systems Theory (Dekkers, 2002) and Soft Systems Methodology (Checkland, 1981, p. 164), see Figure 14.5, which emphasises the interaction with resources. It deviates from the process as defined by in 't Veld (1998, p. 34), and accounts for the interaction between diverse resources in its generic representation. As the resource to conduct a process can be a human or a group of humans, the possibility emerges to connect this construct to learning and knowledge conversion processes.

The evaluations, learning is about reflection on performance, express the learning that takes place, and also the influence on knowledge (see Figure 14.7). Two processes exist, one that links the evaluation to control and to intervention at an organisational level, and one that increases the knowledge of individuals or groups (smaller subsets than those of the organisation). This reflects the thoughts of Kim (1993, p.44) who states that organisational learning directly

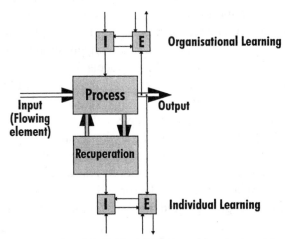

Figure 14.7: Organisational and Individual Learning. Organisational learning leads to new operational routines; individual learning adapts the behaviour of a resource. The diagram shows that tuning between organisational and individual learning prevents divergence between the organisation and its members (individuals or groups).

intervenes into operational routines (Subsection 12.1.2). Following the roots of Systems Theory, single-loop learning occurs mainly within the steady-state model of the operations, the evaluation process within the boundary control. Double-loop learning follows the pathways of the breakthrough model leading to adjustments in concepts. This type of learning questions the current model and searches for improvement independent of their nature according to the classification of the types of innovation.

The contribution of resources to process execution is also embodied in the knowledge base of the resources. The theories of Nonaka (1994) about the knowledge spiral distinguish between levels of individuals to levels of organisations indicating that knowledge primarily resides in individuals and groups of these. Hence, it represents a grouping closely related to the hierarchy of organisations. Therefore, the processes of Knowledge Management seem strongly connected to the chain of command in an organisation. Next, tacit knowledge is per definition embodied in individuals, hence learning at an individual level extends itself to tacit and explicit knowledge. The bigger the group, the more the need arises to manage the organisational knowledge processes, focusing more and more on organisational learning which seems more explicit than tacit.

The learning of individuals (and small groups) leads to recursive behaviour from agents in organisational processes. Stacey (1996, pp. 168-169) elucidates on this matter when discussing recessive schemes and shadow systems within Complex Adaptive Systems. Within an organisation recessive schemes and shadow systems exist in conjunction with the formal systems embedded in organisational routines and the organisational structure. Formal behaviour of agents is linked to the organisational procedures, hence organisational learning occurs at least at the level of groups within the organisation or the organisation as a whole. Recessive schemes, e.g. those models for modes of operation that have not been formalised in organisations, seem linked to tacit knowledge, the knowledge residing in individual agents not embraced and embedded by the organisation. The dynamics that Stacey shows is that these recursive behaviours play an important role in the adaptation of organisations to the dynamics of the environment, especially at the edge of chaos. However, these dynamics carry the danger of disintegration of the organisation. This appears particularly when organisational learning and individual learning diverge. Here lies an important task of management to give ground for both organisational and individual learning.

This leads to a more differentiated view on the knowledge conversion processes connected to the breakthrough model. Tacit knowledge at an operational level can be learned and taught through imitation, i.e. externalisation. The operational level gives less space for combining knowledge unless the organisational structure comprises a mix of skills in the organelle structure. More specialised forms of resources, as present in the functional structure, will enhance the particular skills and tacit knowledge giving less space for combination and more for socialisation. An individual person will have the chance of internalisation, the learning dynamics do quite differ for groups and individuals. The transfer of the breakthrough model to the operational processes strongly depends on externalisation. Combination and internalisation are the driving forces during development of new systems for operations. The intertwining of alternate combination, externalisation, internalisation, and socialisation drives the knowledge processes of the breakthrough model (Figure 14.8).

14.2.2 Enhancing the Model for the Dynamic Adaptation Capability

The earlier proposed Model for the Dynamic Adaptation Capability builds on the knowledge conversion processes, and links it to learning and a knowledge base. As already demonstrated in the previous subsection, the processes have

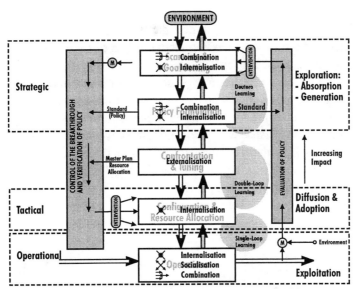

Figure 14.8:   Model for the Dynamic Adaptation Capability and knowledge conversion processes. The model combines the levels of decision-making (Ploegmakers, 2000, p. 31) and the outline of the Model for the Dynamic Adaptation Capability. The internal innovation capability consists of diffusion and adoption, and exploitation. The dynamic capability comprises of exploration, i.e. absorption and generation. At the different levels of the breakthrough model the dominant knowledge conversion processes have been mentioned. The dynamic control as proposed by Bogman (2000, p. 47) is translated into the Innovation Impact Points, the verification process, and the evaluation processes.

been integrated in the new model. With a slight modification we can enhance our understanding of knowledge conversion processes, in particular knowledge distribution has received little attention. Thereto, the interaction between groups horizontally and vertically beholds the possibility for knowledge distribution.

The horizontal and vertical interaction does have quite different implications for managing learning and knowledge. Horizontal interaction mostly aims at establishing skills and knowledge for performing tasks. Both tacit and explicit knowledge play an important role in establishing operational routines that ensure execution of processes and tasks within the scope of business requirements. Vertical interaction needs twice a process of externalisation with its scope of breakthrough, innovation and renewal, once when breakthroughs are enforced top-down, and the other time when bottom-up innovations require reconsidering the strategy. Externalisation requires the transfer of tacit knowledge in explicit knowledge, a process that might be both times questioned. The underlying process of the breakthrough already depends on iterations and feedback. The externalisation loads these transformations for making clear why matters should be as they are. These two interactions, horizontal and vertical, link to the Innovation Impact Points at all levels.

Within the Model for the Dynamic Adaptation Capability, the verification process embodies the state of the knowledge gathered by the organisation for the adaptation processes. Is it possible to derive from the characteristics of the verification the state of adaptation processes? Most likely, the options can be found in the resource allocation, and its link to the choices the subsequent phases have to make. The continuous need for iteration indicates the lack of effective knowledge embedment in the verification process. However, the call on adaptation cycles, iterations will be there as an organisation goes through a learning process.

Do the processes of the adaptation capability give leeway for iterations? Set-based Concurrent Engineering provides such a possibility (Ward et al., 1995). By not fixing on one single solution but by successively limiting the range of

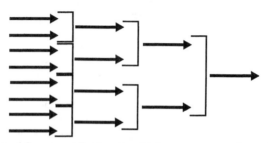

Figure 14.9: Set-based Concurrent Engineering. Options are generated or active during the first phases of decision-making. At the end of each stage, decision-making leads to elimination of alternatives; the remaining alternatives are elaborated during the next stage. Every round of decision-making leads to more precise criteria.

solutions as knowledge progresses and the target comes closer. Also, the criteria for decision-making become more defined. This way, a successive staging of decisions, narrowing down options, expanding criteria, allows an organisation to react more refined to changes in the environment, and improves the reaction time (see Figure 14.9).

14.3 MODELS FOR FORESIGHT

Hence, the strategic process should provide a more flexible approach for finding optimal solutions, therefore this section will explore the themes of strategy and foresight in connection to the adaptation processes. Additionally, the *Confrontation & Tuning* in the breakthrough model depends on externalisation as a process. To what extent does a more flexible approach to strategy and foresight at the programming at this level coincide with externalisation? Thereto, we should explore the meaning of strategy and foresight within the context of adaptation.

14.3.1 Strategy

In 't Veld (1998) describes strategy as the choice between alternative ways and resources to achieve a set of goals, Burgelman et al. (1995) divides strategy into resource–based strategy and product-market strategy. Porter (1996) defines the essence of strategy as choosing a unique and valuable position rooted in systems of activities. Quinn (1980) says: *a strategy is the pattern of plans that integrates an organisation's major goals, policies and actions sequences into a cohesive whole*. A well–formulated strategy helps to marshal and allocate an organisation's resources into a unique and viable posture based on its relative internal competencies and shortcomings, anticipated changes in the environment, and contingent moves by opponents.

In the early days of strategic management, Ansoff (1965) proposed a matrix of four strategies, which became quite well known – market penetration, product development, market development, and diversification. But this was hardly comprehensive. Fifteen years later, Porter (1980) introduced what became the best-known list of *generic strategies*: cost leadership, differentiation and focus. But the Porter list was also incomplete: while Ansoff focused on *extensions* of business strategy, Porter focused on *identifying* business strategy in the first place. Ten major schools now characterize the strategy literature, says Mintzberg (1999), see Appendix O. All the different schools of strategy were developed in a time of relative environmental calmness. Because of this calmness, there is a general lack of dynamics in most of these strategies. Most of the existing strategy schools are based on the assumption of competition in a stable and static environment, but technological advances and global changes have created a more dynamic, complex climate. Technology has lowered the market's entry boundary, and geographical barriers are decreasing. Porter (1980) has developed a model of forces affecting industry competition, subsequently threat of entry, powerful suppliers and buyers, substitute products, jockey for position. Rivalry among existing competitors takes the familiar form of jockeying for position - using tactics like price competition, product introduction, and advertising. The forces described by Porter still exist, but they have changed in magnitude. We may conclude that the threat of entrants has increased and that at the same time buyers are able to get better through combining their forces. However, suppliers have lost some of their bargaining power, amongst others through the globalisation of the market. What we see is an increased rivalry among existing firms and new entrants, with an increased pace of change.

14.3.2 Dynamic Strategies

These changes are forcing industries to react quickly to changes anywhere on the world market, in other words strategies need to be dynamic. In this context, there are two general interpretations for the dynamic strategy: constantly changing over time, or multiple strategies. Markides (1999) finds that:

> Designing a successful strategy is a never-ending, dynamic process of identifying and colonising a distinctive strategic position. Excelling in this position while concurrently searching for, finding, and cultivating another viable strategic position. Simultaneously managing both positions, slowly making a transition to the new position as the old one matures and declines and starting the cycle again.

This phrase can be split into two parts; in the first part we find the assumption that strategy is a given position, which should be taken in by a company. The second part is more concerned with the problems of competing today while preparing for tomorrow. The key here is that strategy is a never-ending, dynamic process. This is a big difference from conventional conceptions of strategy. In the early days it was common that a strategy could be seen as a long-term process; meaning that once formulated strategies would serve the company for many years. As we find ourselves in an ever faster changing environment, we see that dynamics are becoming an essential part of strategy. The more uncertain the future we have to deal with, the more sense it makes to create multiple scenarios, different strategies.

Beinhocker (1999) recommends cultivating and managing populations of multiple strategies that evolve over time, because the forces of evolution acting on a population of strategies makes them more robust and adaptive. Note the similarity to evolution in populations where several alleles are present at the same time ensuring adaptation to changing environments. In high-velocity, intensely competitive markets, traditional approaches to strategy give way to *competing on the edge* creating a flow of temporary, shifting competitive advantages and strategies. Eisenhardt (1999), in her research on entrepreneurial and diversified businesses, demonstrates that successful firms in these markets have fast, and high-quality, strategic decision-making processes. This is also what Williamson (1999) concludes: the success rate of strategies can be greatly enhanced when they are not too specific. A company must keep tactical opportunism within the bounds of its overall strategy, ruling out options that might cause it to deviate from its long-term strategies.

A dynamic strategy consists of multiple strategies; these strategies should grow within the preset bandwidth. Only in this way can we be more secure of the long-term success of companies in a fast changing and global surrounding. This is visualised in Figure 14.10, in which one sees a current position from which multiple strategies are pursued. These strategies are not strictly formulated, they have some variance in the set bandwidth. When an organisation finds that one of the possible strategies is not viable that strategy is terminated, as shown. The pursuit of the remaining strategies could be done by implementing the variety of strategies in its overall business process or create separate business units.

Many of the organisation's problems are rooted more in past decisions than in present events or they come about no matter the market dynamics (Greiner, 1998). He states that outside forces may less determine the future of an

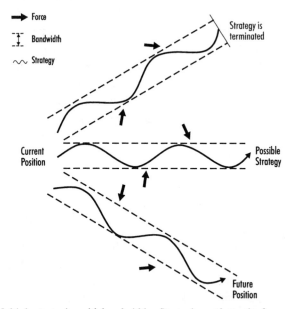

Figure 14.10: Multiple strategies with bandwidths. Strategies undergo the forces of the environment and companies will have to adapt these during time.

organisation, and that it depends more on the organisation's history. Companies fail to see that many clues to their future success lie within their own organisation, and their evolving states of development. Moreover, the inability of management to understand its organisational development problems can result in a company becoming "frozen" in its present stage of evolution or, ultimately, in failure, regardless of market opportunities.

Burgelman (1999) agrees that in successful organisations there is a tendency for inertia, because of given success, and with that for the focus on the successful strategy. In relative stable surroundings, the inertia of an organisation can be successful; there is a possibility that the efficiency and the efficacy of the organisation will increase. As a result, the flexibility and innovative potential may reduce and, if an organisation is operating in a fast changing environment, this inertia can create serious problems. Besides deducting strategy direction from organisational growth phases, inertia can also be conquered through the active search for new opportunities. In other words, a company has to innovate.

Kim & Mauborgne (1999a, 1999b) have studied companies of sustained high growth and profits. All pursue a strategy, value innovation, which renders competition irrelevant by offering new and superior buyer value in existing markets or by enabling the creation of new markets. Value innovation places equal emphasis on value and innovation, since innovation without value can be too strategic or wild, too technology-driven or futuristic. Hence, value innovation is not the same as value creation. Although value creation on an incremental scale creates some value, it is not sufficient for high performance. To innovate by considering value creation, managers must ask two questions: *Is the firm offering customers radically superior value?* and *Is the firm's price level accessible to the mass of buyers in the target market?* A consequence of market insight gained from creative strategic thinking, value innovation focuses on redefining problems to shift the performance criteria that matter to customers.

The reshaping of the industrial landscape seems to be hardly addressed by the traditional strategy schools, giving us reason to explore other possibilities to define the changing landscape in which companies operate.

14.3.3 Forecasting

As one of the possibilities for defining the position of a company, forecasting dates back to the 1930's, according to de Geus (1999, p. 41). The main objective of forecasting was to deal systematically with the future; in the centuries before, forecasting existed but was not yet incorporated into a process. A series of tools became available under the generic name of planning, and managers used these tools during decision-making. Mostly, forecasting took place in separate back-rooms, planning departments, and resided within the financial departments. This seemed logical because of the availability of figures, the data collection, and their objectives, resulting in balance sheets, profit-and-loss-accounts, budgets, etc. The planners handed the management within the organisation their reports supposing they would execute the plan. Essential to these planning processes, called forecasting, was the emphasis on the development of a plan based on historical figures, and only one route to achieve certain objectives.

This top-down approach continued until the early 1960's. After that more and more companies started with bottom-up planning. When asked for a forecast by management, the planners went firstly to e.g. the district managers for predictions on sales figures for next year, two years or even five years. When all the data were collected, the planners added up the figures according to their own thoughts, and generated budgets and forecasts. The predictions became part of the Management by Objectives movement, led by the well-known management guru Drucker (1978, pp. 100-113). At the end of the 1960's, forecasts became an internal contract, based on little external information, and derived from the same introvert process. It created also a culture of handing down safe figures so that performance of individual managers could be ensured.

The forecasting process turned from a simple one-minute job for line management into a complex and time-consuming process, not only for the planning department but for the whole company. Every choice has to be double-checked and agreed upon. In times of prosperity, this poses no problem to companies but in times of crises and turbulence, the process takes long and leads to totally wrong predictions also caused by the elapsed time. For example, that was the case during the oil-crisis in the 1970's (van der Heijden, 1996; de Geus, 1999).

Millet & Honton (1991) state that predicting the future by trend analysis is still the most popular technique for technology forecasting. The different techniques have all some common assumptions and features, namely:
- the future is a continuation of the recent past, and can be expressed quantitatively, as human behaviour follows natural laws as in physics and chemistry;
- there is one future, and it is predictable if you understand the underlying laws as shown in the trend data.

This does not represent a realistic view of the world. Most environments of companies are so complex that it will be impossible to understand all underlying laws, and, even so, all these laws governing human behaviour are so complex that there are too many exceptions to the rule. Forecasting will only work in a perfect world.

14.3.4 Scenario Planning

Hence, scenarios might offer a way out of the complexity of factors acting on organisations, and at the same time increase the capability of an organisation to deal with the effects of these factors. Scenarios can be traced back to the Oracle of Delphi and Nostradamus. The first modern scenario developer was Kahn (Kahn & Wiener, 1967). Working for the US Air Force, Kahn developed scenarios to imagine what the opponents might do, and to prepare alternative strategies to react to the opponent. Brouwer (2002, p. 9) states that this is one of the reasons that scenarios and strategies are regarded as the same thing, which is not the case. During the 1960's, Kahn refined his scenario development tools to fit business prognostications. The scenarios of Kahn are developed in three steps (Kahn & Wiener, 1967, pp. 5-10):

- First, the Basic, Long Term Multifold Trends are described. These trends come from historical data, and do not change over the period that the scenario covers. They provide the basic structure on which the scenarios are built. Examples of these trends are birth rates, consumption of consumer goods, etc.

- After that, the Surprise Free Projections and the Standard World are described. These projections are based on basic trends at the time of the development of the scenario. Experts assess these trends, and draw plausible conclusions from them (for example, high and low trend developments of birth rates under different circumstances). These projections are intended to be used as basic vehicles for further discussion, explanation of underlying assumptions, and systematic consideration of major alternatives.

- The last step in developing the different scenarios is the introduction of the Canonical Variations. These are designed to raise certain issues. The introduction of these issues leads to scenarios that are out of the expected Surprise Free Projections. In these Canonical Variations issues, such as a sudden rise on costs of energy or crude oil due to a war, can be introduced.

In his book, Kahn uses 13 basic trends and 8 Canonical Variations. Most of the time, these variations affect two or more basic trends. This way, 9 different scenarios are developed. Kahn's methods were widely used until the 1970's when the work of Wack came to rise.

Wack worked for the Royal Dutch/Shell in a newly formed department, called Group Planning (de Geus, 1999, pp. 58-60). This group successfully predicted the oil crisis in 1973. After working in the Planning Department for several years, Wack came to the conclusion that the key point of scenario planning was not a clear picture of the future but what he describes as the *gentle art of perceiving*. He changed his efforts to liberating people's insight so that they can perceive different pictures of the future, and act on changing circumstances.

After Wack left Royal Dutch/Shell, Schwarts and de Geus continued his work there, building scenarios, training management, production personnel to understand the mental models, and learning how to work with these. They combined organisational learning, systems thinking, and scenario development.

Brouwer (2002, p. 10) describes scenarios as a hypothetical sequence of events with causal processes based on shared mental models. The sequence of events might help to generate a step-by-step description of multiple possible futures of the external world. The description arrives from exploring the definitions given by Kahn & Wiener (1967), Jantsch (1967), and van der Heijden (1996). Appendix P lists different types of scenarios, covering many aspects. Different scenarios might take place in the transactional and contextual environment as depicted in Figure 14.11. Accounting for the time span, forecasting is used for the near future, and scenarios for the future further away; in the far future, even scenarios become not useful. According to van der Heijden (1996), scenarios are useful to create structure in events and patterns in the environment, to identify irreducable uncertainty, to confront different views with each other through dialectic conversation, to reveal individual knowledge of members of an organisation, to introduce external perspectives, and to translate the above in a suitable form for corporate strategic conversation.

Ringland (1997) identifies three types of methods in scenario development (Table 14.1 gives an overview of the methods and their steps):
- Trend-impact analysis (used by Futures Group). Trend-impact analysis is concerned with the effects of trends, for instance in markets or populations. The work done to isolate the important trends may well be similar to that used in what is more generally called scenario planning; however, the basic

Figure 14.11: Different environments of an organisation. The transactional environment consists of players (e.g. customers) and competitors. The transactional environment is influenced by driving forces from the contextual environment.

Table 14.1: Steps of the three scenario development methods. More or less the same steps are present in each of the methods.

Scenario writing (Global Business Network)	Cross-Impact Scenario Analysis (Battelle)	Intuitive Scenarios (Shell traditionally)
Identify focal issue or decision	Define and structure the topic question	Analyse strategic concerns and decision needs
Identify key forces in the corporate environment	Identify most important issues in response to topic questions	Identify key decisions factors
List driving forces of the macro-environment	Select descriptors from most important issues	Identify key environmental forces
Rank driving forces by a) Importance b) Uncertainty	Prepare descriptor white papers with projected alternative outcomes and a priori probabilities	Analyse the key environmental forces
Select scenario logics structured by 2 axes and 4 quadrants	PC-base cross-impact analysis	Define scenario logics (typically 2 critical issues)
Flash out at least 4 scenarios and product narratives	PC-based scenarios generated from cross-impact matrix (sorting out of descriptor outcomes into alternative scenarios)	Elaborate on two detailed descriptive scenarios
Draw implications and conclusions	Draw business-related implications from 5 scenarios and derive robust strategies	Draw implications for scenarios for strategic concerns and decision needs
Select leading indicators/sign posts for continued monitoring	PC-based strategy simulations and scenario sensitivity analysis, including disruptive events	Make conclusions and recommendations
	Briefing, discussions, and implications focus groups	
	Monitoring, updates and revisions	

assumption within scenario planning is that we are looking for the unexpected, in other words what will upset the trends. Nevertheless, the trend-impact analysis can provide multiple pictures of the future. This method closely resembles the method developed by Kahn. Most of the time, the scenarios look alike and cover a high, a medium, and a low trend of a certain event. The risk exists that a company will always choose the medium prediction just to be on the safe side (Ringland, 1997, p. 47, 92). Such a deployment of predictions within scenario development looks more like forecasting;

- Cross-impact analysis (used by Battelle). Cross-impact is a technology for the analysis of complex systems. It concentrates on the ways in which forces on an organisation, external or internal, may interact to produce effects bigger than the sum of the parts, or to magnify the effect of one force because of feedback loops. It has been used successfully where the dominant forces can be identified, and the modelling mechanism can be used to increase management's understanding of the relative importance of various factors. Interactive Future Simulations is a futuring method created by Battelle to generate alternate scenarios for long-term business environments. It is used to orient strategic thinking about new products, technologies, and marketing towards most likely future market conditions, including the net effects of various customers, regulatory, competitive, economic, and technological trends. Futuring anticipates long-term (beyond three years) customer behaviour when customers themselves cannot articulate their own future behaviour. It also serves as a computer-based tool to simulate *what-if* questions to see how actions and events may change the baseline (most likely) scenarios. Simulations test potential business investments and strategies. Most likely scenarios are compared with most desirable scenarios to identify critical success factors.

An Interactive Future Simulations project starts with the formulation of an explicit topic question relevant to the strategic objectives (see Figure 14.12). The topic question provides focus for the project, and assures that the results are responsive to business decision-making requirements. Having established a topic question, the next challenge is to identify the most important trends, issues and factors to be included in the scenarios, the so-called specification of the model. Expert judgment is used to provide this input, most often in the form of one to five expert focus groups. Each expert focus group generates a list of 35-50 ideas, and votes on those considered being most important. These expert lists provide inputs to the project team, which distils the inputs

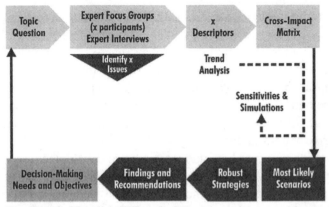

Figure 4.12:   Flow chart of Batelle's IFS method. A topic question provides the focus for the cycle of scenario planning. After going through the stages of the method, decision-makers will arrive at a picture of the future and will draw inferences from it.

into descriptors for the cross-impact analysis. Descriptors might include Strategic Positioning, Demand Growth, Point of Sale, Customer Satisfaction, and Margins.

Each descriptor is researched, and documented in a 1-3 page paper. The research paper includes an in-depth definition of the descriptor, describes its importance, status, historical trends, and alternative outcomes to the target year. With the descriptor paper, the author and project team also complete a cross-impact guide describing how the outcome of each descriptor state affects each of the other descriptors. This procedure explicitly interrelates all the descriptors to one another. The cross-impact guide asks whether one descriptor has any direct impact on each of the other descriptors, whether the impact is positive (making it more likely to occur) or negative (making it less likely to occur), and whether the impact is strong (3), moderate (2), or weak (1). The descriptors, alternative outcomes, probabilities and cross-impact information are then input into the IFS software. The software adjusts all a priori probabilities up and down to 1.0 (occurs) or 0 (does not occur), and organises all occurring descriptor states into scenario groups. The larger the grouping of same scenarios, the more likely that type of scenario is to occur;

- Intuitive Logistics (used by Royal Dutch/Shell and Global Business Network). The essence of this method is to find ways of changing mindsets so that managers can anticipate futures, and prepare for them. The emphasis is on creating a coherent and credible set of stories of the future as a *wind tunnel* for testing business plans or projects prompting public debate or increasing coherence. The term wind tunnel is used because intuitive scenarios can be seen as wind tunnels in which strategy models can be tested under different circumstances.

  Key factor in Intuitive Logistics is the recognition of events and how these events form causal relationships under different circumstances. This can be visualised by systems thinking in the way Senge (1992) explains, with cause and effect diagrams. Another way uses hexagons that can, connected together like a jigsaw puzzle, explain underlying trends, patterns, and structures.

The three methods support scenario development but not all do address multiple strategies. Each of them is a way of arriving at a scenario, only the latter method does not arrive at a vision for one state.

The question becomes how do these scenario development methods relate to the evolutionary development of organisations? Brouwer (2002, pp. 43-47) has reviewed these scenario methods with game theories, and arrives at the conclusion that the methods hardly account for the principles of game theories, especially those focusing on Evolutionary Stable Strategies. Although he sees the game theory is impractical for scenario planning, and while many data are needed to evaluate strategies, these approaches explain better the evolution of organisations and industrial branches. The theories of Adaptive Dynamics might even lead to better predictions for scenario planning.

14.4 INTERORGANISATIONAL COLLABORATION

Scenarios might also be developed for collaboration, the study has highlighted that collaborations in any kind solidify the base for adaptation, they shift the boundaries of organisations; the research has already outlined that key-point as one of the major differences between organisms and organisations. Many biologists now believe that the whole ecosystem evolves, and that the process of evolution can really be understood only at the highest aggregation level: total ecology; this seems very much like the point of view found in organisational ecology. This suggests that evolution is always evolution of a pattern of relations embracing organisms and their environments. As Boulding once has put it, evolution involves the "survival of the fitting", not just the survival of the fittest. When we attempt to understand the ecology of organisations with this perspective in mind, it becomes necessary to understand that organisations and their environments are engaged in a pattern of "co-creation". Once we recognise this, it becomes clear that, in principle, organisations are able to influence the nature of their environment (Morgan, 1997). With the environment becoming more complex and turbulent, an organisation alone is experiencing a decrease in possibilities to influence the environment. Close collaboration with suppliers on technology, innovation, indicative learning, and knowledge absorption might enhance the competitiveness of organisations.

14.4.1 Cooperation between Organisations

The ecological perspective emphasises the importance of cooperation between organisations, which gives them the possibility of playing an active role in shaping their future. From the ecology metaphor the importance of cooperation for influencing an organisation's future followed. Until recently though, cooperation has been regarded as something that might have benefits. For example, Contractor & Lorange (1988) identified seven more or less overlapping objectives that cooperative arrangements can achieve: (1) risk reduction, (2) economies of scale and/or rationalisation, (3) technology exchanges, (4) co-opting or blocking competition, (5) overcoming government-mandated trade or investment barriers, (6) facilitating initial international expansion of inexperienced firms, and (7) vertical quasi-integration advantages of linking the complementary contributions of the partners in a value chain. In the broadest sense, they argue like Porter

(1980), the combined efforts of all partners must add up to a value chain that can produce a more competitive result.

Beforehand, competition was primarily resource-based, i.e. based on factors like economies of scale and scope, market position, and financial power, which can all be related to the seven objectives for cooperation from Contractor & Lorange. Now, competition is increasingly knowledge-based, as firms strive to learn and to develop capabilities faster than their rivals. In knowledge-based competition external acquisition of technology is an even more important success factor than in traditional situations (van Aken & Weggeman, 2000), because technological developments are becoming more complex, thereby creating the need for more specific skills and knowledge than most organisations can develop alone with proper speed (Glas, 1996; Sen & Egelhoff, 2000). This is also due to the demands and constraints from the market, which increase the imposed complexity on the organisation (Dekkers, 2000).

This turns the picture full scale. If organisations fail to innovate continuously, they will lose their competitiveness. Because successful product and process innovation asks for more resources and capabilities than most organisations can develop and maintain in-house, cooperation becomes a prerequisite for success (Botter, 1994; Glas, 1996; Rycroft & Kash, 1999; Sen & Egelhoff, 2000). Recent research, plus over 50 worldwide interviews with CEO's and CTO's confirm that most companies now believe that close to 50% or more of their technological competitiveness will be derived from external technology sourcing and partnering (Jonash, 1996). It is even observed from the ecology metaphor that interorganisational relations emerge as a natural response to complexity and turbulence in the environment (Morgan, 1997). The question is now which cooperative arrangements are available.

14.4.2 Types of Cooperative Arrangements

Cooperation can take place in four directions; Reve (1990) described these directions (a similar view is found in ten Haaf et al. [2002, p. 478-485]). The strategic core consists of the assets of high specificality that are governed within the boundaries of the firm. He states that with no strategic core, there is no economic rationale for the existence of the firm. Having defined and delimited the strategic core, the next step in strategic analysis is to analyse which directions can be followed from the strategic core basis. Reve identifies four directions, each representing a strategic expansion path. Reve (1990) stresses that these expansions not only can take place in the form of mergers, but also in the form of strategic alliances. The first one, upstream vertical integration, means cooperating with suppliers, while downstream vertical integration means cooperating with customers. Thirdly, horizontal integration, or parallelisation

(Botter et al., 1994), usually takes place through mergers and acquisitions, in order to obtain scale advantages, but it can also be obtained by joint ventures. A creative use of horizontal strategic alliances is to form such alliances in order to obtain advantages in vertical relations; retailers form voluntary chains to be able to obtain better terms of trade with their suppliers, and industrial vendors form joint venture companies to obtain large contracts with demanding customers. The fourth path of strategic expansion is by exploiting economies of scope through related diversification. Related, because economies of scope arise when common skills are shared or utilised jointly. Such skills are found within the strategic core of the firm. Economies of scope give a more precise meaning to the broader notion of synergy (Reve, 1990).

In fact, diversification as used by Reve (1990), is also a form of horizontal integration. The distinction between diversification and horizontal integration can be made using the concepts: related supplementary and related complementary (Sen & Egelhoff, 2000). The horizontal integration, like Reve uses it, is related supplementary, or in other words: more of the same. Horizontal integration in the sense of diversification is related complementary. The same distinction can be applied to vertical integration, but then in a broader sense: a company that outsources assets at different stages of the value chain is related complementary. This makes a 'remote' type of supplementary relation possible if the company involves more players at the same stages in the value chain. This distinction makes sense, because these different (for example) suppliers do not have to be integrated horizontally in any way.

14.4.3 Vertical and Horizontal Integration

The advantages of vertical integration are the ability to lower transport and administration cost, to improve the interface between successive stages in the value chain, and to be more independent of suppliers in scarce times. The drawback to vertical integration is the organisational efforts it requires across stages, it increases overhead costs, and more importantly, it sets the risk that the focus on essential technological development is lost, resulting in loss of competitive advantage. That the latter has become an issue is suggested by the contemporary trend of outsourcing and competencies (Hamel & Prahalad, 1994; Glas, 1996; Wigman, 2000). In other words, companies are differentiating instead of integrating.

There are two rationales for horizontal cooperation that have to be considered, though. The first is technology development by two or more companies (e.g. Philips and Sony) in situations where the individual companies do not possess the financial means, the required skills, and the knowledge to develop products themselves (Glas, 1996). Of course they have to see the profits for this cooperation. This kind of cooperation is usually temporarily, while it is formed to exploit specific, fast changing opportunities. When the goal driving the cooperation is achieved, the cooperation will, by prearrangement, dissolve (Rycroft & Kash, 1999). The second rationale is based on cooperation with complementors to enlarge the market for yourself and your complementors. A company can have a competitor that is at the same time its complementor. This is the case when this competitor produces services or products that influence the value of the services or products of the company. This means that companies that compete with each other are dependent from each other at the same time, so it could be interesting to cooperate. This is called co-opetition (de Bruijn & ten Heuvelhof, 1999).

Many companies are both competitors and complementors with respect to their suppliers. This was already identified in Subsection 14.4.2, where it was mentioned that horizontal relationships could be used to obtain advantages in vertical relations. Brandenburger & Nalebuff (1996) add that as we continue with moving into the information economy, supply side complementaries will become increasingly the norm. There is a big up-front investment in learning to make something, and then variable costs are relatively modest. So the more people that want a knowledge-based product, the easier it is to provide. For vertical relations, where the outsourcing company can picture itself as supplier in the value net, this view supports the formation of networks of suppliers.

It should be emphasised that supplier relations are just as important as customer relations. And the fact that companies can be both complementors and competitors explains what the advantage of horizontal cooperation can be: as complementors companies can create and enlarge markets, because together they offer more value. Of course, as competitors they will have to divide it up (Brandenburger & Nalebuff, 1996).

14.4.4 Virtual Vertical Integration

Since vertical integration means operating in a network of organisations, we will have a closer look at virtual organisations. First called quasi-vertical integration or vertical quasi integration (Grant, 1991; Contractor & Lorange, 1988), this vertical integration is generally referred to as virtual vertical integration or just virtual integration (Margretta, 1998; Mrakas & Kelly, 1998). This gives reason to assume a resemblance with the concept of virtual organisations. Indeed, Bultje & van Wijk (1998) suggest that a virtual organisation *is primarily characterised as being a network of independent, geographically dispersed organisations with a partial mission overlap.* Within the network, all partners provide their own core competencies and the cooperation is based on semi-stable relations. The products and services provided by a virtual organisation are dependent on innovation and are strongly customer based. So in situations where vertical cooperation takes place in a virtual integrated way, the emerging network can be called a virtual organisation.

The underlying concept of virtual integration is that the resources are not integrated. The integration moves up to the level of knowledge and skills. Analogous to the shift of competition from resource-based to knowledge-based, the vertical cooperation shifts from resource-based to knowledge-based. Cooperation then is aimed at transferring and integrating skills and knowledge, instead of integrating resources. These skills and knowledge cannot be represented only through an organisation's files, which record its actions, decisions, regulations, and policies or in the maps, formal and informal, through which organisations make themselves understandable to themselves and others. The knowledge and skills are also held in the minds of individual members of the organisation, and in the physical objects that members use as references and guideposts. And they are embedded in routines and practices which may be inspected and decoded even when the individuals who carry them out are unable to put them into words (Argyris & Schön, 1996).

Therefore it is important to explicitly consider the members of the organisation, when dealing with knowledge-based cooperation. Johanson & Mattsson (1992) have suggested a network model. It views networks as sets of connected relationships between actors, which stand for members of the organisation. Further, a distinction is made between two levels in the industrial system: the network of exchange relationships between industrial actors and the production system, where resources are employed and developed in production. The network of exchange relationships is viewed as a structure governing the production system. This network should support the transfer and integration of skills and knowledge in order to make continuous innovation possible. This thought yields the Collaboration Model in Figure 14.13. Assets are a part of the resources of a company. It follows that core capabilities and assets are closely interconnected: complementary assets are necessary to get a product in the market. Rycroft & Kash (1999) state that complementary assets can be either generic or specialised. Generic assets are those that do not need to be tailored for a particular innovation process, whereas specialised assets must fit with and be integrated into the overall design of the particular innovation. Specialised complementary assets are generally knowledge intensive assets, which have a high degree of interdependence with the core capabilities.

In handling these two types of complementary assets, the same distinction should be made as Stuart & McCutcheon (2000) apply: shaping the relation on the basis of cooperative tension or strategic alliance. Generic assets are then commonly accessed by arm's length contracting, in which the organisation

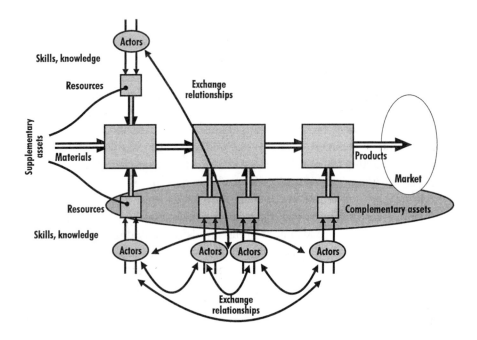

Figure 14.13: Collaboration Model. Exchange relationships occur through vertical and horizontal integration.

holding core capabilities uses detailed product or process specifications and suppliers are chosen based on price; the interaction is relatively predictable.

A different pattern emerges where the holders of core capabilities require highly specialised assets. Then the holders of core capabilities often perform the role of strategic coordinators, rather than trying to control specific transactions (Rycroft & Kash, 1999). Holders of core capabilities can have specialised assets inside their organisation, but they could also be found in other organisations, e.g. universities. This possibility is pictured in the Collaboration Model (Figure 14.13) by letting two resources participate in the middle value chain position. While specialised complementary assets are found within the different organisations in the virtual integrated network, the strategic coordination should be based on close cooperation.

To make full use of the innovative potential in specialised complementary assets more companies with comparable core capabilities should be linked to the virtual integration network of exchange relationships. This way the network is provided with supplementary assets. Although they are competitors for their part of the value chain, in the perspective of the entire value chain they could both be interested in providing the virtual integration network with innovative potential. This might lead to profitable product-market combinations for which they could be the supplier of certain components, especially when they are the first to offer the needed components. Sometimes it might even be interesting for companies with comparable core capabilities and supplementary assets to cooperate directly with each other. This horizontal cooperation comes down to technology development or co-opetition.

The customers, or users, should not be forgotten as possible complementary assets. Not only may the use of an innovation by experienced buyers generate new information about user requirements, it may suggest routes to product improvement. For example, many software developers are technologically oriented, and know little about customer applications of their product. Customers can contribute greatly to the software company's fortunes by reporting new applications, bugs, flaws in menu construction, and links to other software packages. The complementary assets embodied in lead user's (the first to employ a new technology) experience, much of it tacit, can be invaluable, especially when user-producer linkages facilitate constant and rapid processes of self-organisation.

14.5 CONCLUSIONS

This chapter has elaborated on the models of the previous parts and converted these into models to describe adaptation processes for industrial organisations (see Table 14.2 for the relationship between these models and the reference model). The first model, Model for the Dynamic Adaptation Capability, connects learning processes and assessment of innovations, regardless of their nature (product, process, organisational structure) to the processes of the breakthrough model. Following this model, one can distinguish between the Dynamic Capability and the Internal Innovation Capability. The Internal Innovation Capability tells how much companies improve their sustained fitness, based on given concepts like the dominant design (architecture and core concepts of product, process and organisation). Cumulation within the Internal Innovation Capability might lead to architectural innovation. Then it denotes the Dynamic Capability, which focuses more on the evolvability of the organisation, addressing issues like the search for new equilibria, dispersal, bifurcation, etc. External changes in the environment might also induce internal changes. However, these issues should reside in capabilities present within the organisation so that the organisation can reach new states through successive mutations.

The strategic process should also allow a wider scope of strategies to be active. Current strategy schools assume relative stable situations to describe strategy formulation and enactment. Uncertainty about development calls for strategies based on scenario planning that allow multiple futures to be present.

Table 14.2: Models from the Framework for Dynamic Adaptation in relation to the reference model. For each new model the link has been made to the components of the reference model.

	Phenotype/Genotype	Adaptive Walks	Developmental pathways	Sustained Fitness	Evolvability	Self-organisation
Innovation Impact Point Model	Higher impact points affect phenotype.	Increasing fitness possible through consideration of impact innovations. Integrative consideration of impacts.	Choices for concepts of innovation: incremental, component, architectural, radical. Adaptation cycles continually active.	Innovation Impact Points at lower levels. Mostly incremental innovation, sometimes component innovation.	Innovation Impact Points at higher levels. Mostly radical and architectural innovation, sometimes component innovation.	
Model for Dynamic Adaptation Capability	Distinction between phenotypical and genotypical change.		Accumulation of impacts on lower levels might lead to change at the level of the business.	Internal Innovation Capability.	Dynamic Capability: industry level and business orientation.	
Process Model			Interaction between processes and resources.			
Scenario Planning				Traditional strategy focus and forecasting enhance local optimisation.	Scenario Planning prepares companies for uncertainties in the environment. Connects also to more dynamic environments.	
Collaboration Model		Increasing fitness by horizontal and vertical collaboration.	Resource interaction in combination with managing processes.			Interaction with suppliers might create dissipative structures.

Under driving forces of the environment, such scenario planning methods should not direct the company to a preset future, creating the trap of a combination of forecasting and backcasting. The application of game theories, especially Adaptive Dynamics, might yield new theory in this domain.

Successful adaptation requires the application of interaction and process models. Learning processes and Knowledge Management rely on interaction models between entities, groups, organisation, and environment. An enunciation or a modification, according to others, of the basic model of Systems Theory helps to describe both the processes and interaction models. Hence, the learning processes and Knowledge Management can be connected to the breakthrough model. The same extension of the model for processes allows expanding on the interaction between organisations and their suppliers for horizontal and vertical integration. The model for collaboration in the value chain shows the relations between both types of integration, and the need for active management by organisations. This fits entirely into the picture that through active collaboration companies will adapt more effectively to changes in the environment.

15 APPLICATION TO STRATEGIC CAPACITY MANAGEMENT

After the development of the components of the Framework for Dynamic Adaptation in the previous chapter, the study will transfer the concepts to the domain of Strategic Capacity Management. In Chapter 4, Strategic Capacity Management has been selected as an application domain for the research into adaptation. Strategic Capacity Management came about by requests of industrial companies to support strategic decision-making for the manufacturing domain; the question arises how the concepts of the framework might complete the models of Strategic Capacity Management. The cases that Chapter 16 will present have a strong relationship with the concepts of Strategic Capacity Management. When industrial requests for case studies addressed Strategic Capacity Management (e.g. Spoelstra, 1998) no satisfactory methodologies existed at that point in time; current literature has very few references on capacity management from a strategic or tactical point of view. Neither did the application of the Delft School Approach, including the steady-state model and the breakthrough model, suffice.

Research that relates to Strategic Capacity Management focuses mostly on the design of the organisational structures. Most companies have maintained efficiency as the main objective of their production departments, as Avella (1999) remarks. Since Skinner's publication in 1969, many more authors have recognised that manufacturing can be a fundamental cornerstone for achieving a competitive advantage. Although manufacturing contributes for a large part to the current performance of companies, few companies deal systematically with issues related to Strategic Capacity Management.

The market and competition drives industrial companies to improve continuously the way they run their overall operations. This concerns the total primary process of these companies, innovation, and product development as well as the manufacturing operation. For the manufacturing operation it involves issues as:
- The development of manufacturing processes and technology.
- The initiation of process innovation to meet performance requirements.
- The utilisation and acquisition of resources, qualitative and quantitative.
- Management and organisation of the company's resources and the value chain.

For example, when companies fail to initiate timely development of new processes, the non-availability of these processes might result in poorer products, higher overall cost and increased lead-times. The research into Strategic Capacity Management has mostly concentrated on developing an approach to models for decision-making on outsourcing, for continuous process innovation, and for management of manufacturing technology. During case studies, fragments of these methods have been implemented in several industrial companies, particularly the management of outsourcing and the design of organisational structures (as reported in Dekkers [2003]).

This chapter will address the overall concept that has been developed for Strategic Capacity Management, and its elements. Furthermore, this chapter links Strategic Capacity Management to the Framework for Dynamic Adaptation. Section 15.1 starts with describing the components of Strategic Capacity Management. The general model points also to additional models to describe the interaction between the components of the approach. Section 15.2 explores the three components of the general model, in particular strategy, technology, and organisation. Section 15.3 expands on the four interaction models. These four interaction models partially reside in the Framework for Dynamic Adaptation (Chapter 14). Additionally, Section 15.3 reviews the position of the framework in relation to Strategic Capacity Management.

15.1   OVERALL APPROACH TO STRATEGIC CAPACITY MANAGEMENT

Assuming that manufacturing directly contributes to competitive advantage, how should we optimise the total manufacturing processes? Most literature describes the balancing of organisations with the environment taking into account the strongholds of companies in relation to their evolution (following the thoughts about competencies of Prahalad & Hamel [1990], Section 3.4). Others do stress aspects of capacity management, like Wüpping (1998b) when underlining the advantages of manufacturing cells. However, to address the contemporary issues for manufacturing, industrial companies need an integral approach to bridge strategy and operations.

To arrive at a coherent approach we have to revert to the core of manufacturing and operations. It concerns the transformation from materials into products as a primary process. To succeed, resources are needed; this line of thought follows the definition of a process in Applied Systems Theory (Subsection 14.2.1). Additionally, the structuring of resources implies the organisation of manufacturing. The primary process is also driven by the development of process technology to sustain competitiveness. Overall, the transformation process and its organisation structure should follow the requirements as set by the environment, consisting of primarily the organisational entity it is part of, and the customer base or markets in which it operates. Hereto, Sun & Ove Riis (1994) have generated a model that connects strategy through management with technology and organisation. Since, Strategic Capacity Management aims at managing resource utilisation, etc., management as concept is oblivious, and more emphasis should be given to the underlying models that govern effective management in this field (see Figure 15.1). The model of Sun & Ove Riis relies on the following governing principles:

- organisation, technology, and strategy are strongly linked to each other;
- organisation and technology should support the strategy;
- management is required to implement changes;
- organisational and technological changes should be implemented synchronously.

The model of Figure 15.1 shows that four models are needed to describe the interaction between technology, organisation, and strategy:

- a strategic method for assessing manufacturing technologies;
- an adaptation model for strategy following the scan of technologies;
- an integration model for organisation and technology;
- a change model that interacts between the components: organisation and strategy.

15.2   COMPONENTS OF STRATEGIC CAPACITY MANAGEMENT

Manufacturing management faces the challenges, mentioned in the introduction of this chapter, when defining the strategy, with only a few methods available to manage capacity at a strategic level, and for the initiation of process innovation (manufacturing technologies and improvements). Manufacturing is part of the total primary process of companies as depicted in Figure 15.2. Manufacturing provides the market place with products by being a subsystem on its own as well as that it connects the processes of product development and engineering to the market. Therefore, whenever talking about manufacturing and determining strategies, we should address the link with product development and engineering, and the link with the market demands.

Figure 15.1: Framework for Strategic Capacity Management. The original model of Sun and Ove Riis (1994) showed also management as a component. This has been replaced by models to govern actions.

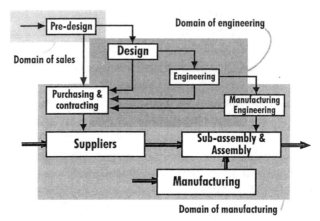

Figure 15.2: Total primary proces. The domain of manufacturing connects to the sales and engineering domains. Product development and engineering connects to manufacturing through manufacturing engineering.

Especially, the relationship between manufacturing and product development needs elaboration through adequate research. Conducting a study into sequential and simultaneous approaches to engineering, Riedel & Pawar (1998) highlight that the concepts of design and manufacturing are not connected in literature and that the interaction between product design and manufacturing strategy is under-researched. Spring & Dalrymple (2000) came to the same conclusion when examining two cases of product customisation, manufacturing issues got little attention during design and engineering.

15.2.1 Manufacturing Strategy

Since manufacturing is part of the total process, the strategy is too. Figure 15.3 represents this thought, showing the breakdown of the overall strategy in its components: marketing strategy, product development strategy, and manufacturing strategy. Although each component of the strategy will generate more details, these substrategies should have a strong common link. Particularly, the execution of these strategies might diverge during implementation, thus reducing the total efficacy from strategy formulation and implementation.

Manufacturing management is confronted with increasing pressure on improving overall performance and reducing costs. The issues for management relate to the setup of the primary process and control, leading to increased competitiveness in today's global market. Key issues for capacity management in industrial companies focus on:

- Which activities should a company focus on and allocate its resources to?

- How to maintain competitive leads through outsourcing and using partnerships? In which aspect(s) of business does a company excel and which ones does it want to enhance?
- How to reduce cost-prices and still meet customer needs in terms of variety and quality of products and performance?
- How does an industrial company match capacity with forecasts and product development?

Pfeifer et al. (1994) refer to this matter when mentioning: *In view of the variety and complexity of changing boundary conditions, the question presents itself as to what methods can be best employed to sustain the competitiveness of a company.* An extensive study by Corbett & Claridge (2002) of the Manufacturing Future Surveys 1996 excavates that manufacturing capabilities should link to the individual business strategy, and that contingencies might strongly determine each firm's capability to retain its competitiveness. Schroeder et al. (2002) argue that managing resources and creating competitive advantage by meeting performance requirements does not suffice, since creating unique proprietary processes and assets contributes strongly to profitability and long-term competitiveness. In effect, their notion links to research undertaken into the adaptation of organisations to the dynamic changes of the environment. This points to major issues within the manufacturing strategy: capabilities relate to outsourcing and process innovation, and capabilities relate to strategic and tactical resource management.

Hence, strategy articulates the ways in which the opportunities that result from the capabilities will be exploited (see Subsection 14.3.1). Thereto we should connect the manufacturing area to the overall primary process, improve the overall performance of resources, and structure the utilisation of resources. Explicit decision-making on outsourcing, whether it concerns suppliers, alliances or partnerships, provides an opportunity to enhance the capabilities (Heck, 2000) and adapt more flexible to the changing market demands imposed on industrial firms.

Figure 15.3: Components of strategy. The three domains of strategy, market, product development, and manufacturing should be derived from the overall strategy.

15.2.2 Decision-making on Outsourcing

As an important aspect of Strategic Capacity Management, outsourcing provides the opportunity for acquiring manufacturing technologies to expand capabilities and to level capacity over a horizon of two years or more. At the same time, it enhances the focus on the firm's own capabilities to achieve levering of the performance of its manufacturing system (Friedrich, 2000). Thus, outsourcing evolves from both technological demands and performance requirements. The recognition of competencies creates insight in the load on the available resources and the remaining capacity of resources is available for optimising the performance of manufacturing through in- and outsourcing.

Decision-making on outsourcing takes place at strategic, tactical, and operational levels within a company. Distinguishing these three levels will help assigning specific frameworks and requirements for each of these three processes. Burt (1989) stresses also the two procurement functions: (a) support during engineering and (b) management of the value chain as part of the current manufacturing process.

Industrial companies do not always manage the outsourcing in an effective and efficient way. This reflects on strategic decision-making as well as on operations management. Regularly, decisions with regard to outsourcing come about during the phase of production planning when suppliers only fulfil a buffer function with regard to overflow in capacity. It is a common practice that during the early stages of product development, neither practical availability of suppliers and alliances is taken into account nor any other standard than strictly technical and commercial aspects. Therefore, Manufacturing Departments cannot manage

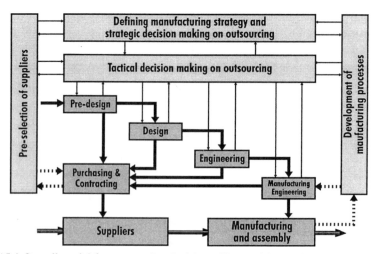

Figure 15.4: Overall model for outsourcing decisions. The models consists of strategic, tactical and operational decision-making.

the total manufacturing process at a strategic and tactical level while in most companies operational management of outsourcing concentrates on fire-fighting.

Through the Action Research at a Food Equipment Manufacturer (Vorstermans, 1997) and some literature surveys (e.g. van der Velde, 1999) a new model for the processes and the decision-making on outsourcing has been developed (Dekkers, 2000b). This model includes decision-making on outsourcing during the first stages of product development. Decisions differ in each stage of product development; during pre-design, it concerns mostly subsystems of equipment, and during later stages it turns to detailed production planning. It requires close cooperation between engineering and manufacturing, including procurement, to implement this model either through simultaneous engineering or through blackbox-engineering[49] (Köppel, 2000).

The model (see Figure 15.4) depicts a model for early supplier involvement during the design and engineering phases to operational decisions during manufacturing. As a side effect of such decision-making, the company at the end of a value chain will concentrate on its own competencies as well as the capabilities of the suppliers to the company. Hence, there will be a strong need to identify but also to maintain these competencies. All companies, investigated during the development of the concepts of Strategic Capacity Management, applied the principle of Engineering-to-Order with lead-times in excess of one year; this makes it difficult to determine which improvements do contribute to overall performance. However, the companies involved reported that staff on outsourcing did not increase although the number of outsourced orders rose to levels of 150% or more of the original volume. Furthermore, outsourcing was not viewed any more as a bottleneck for logistic management.

15.2.3 Manufacturing Technology

Another source for process development is the technological development as such. By analysing the current performance against objectives set by the manufacturing strategy, management sets goals for further improvements by applying appropriate manufacturing technologies. This will enable a company to review potential benefits of manufacturing technologies.

Research shows that the appropriate manufacturing technology of a business depends critically on the circumstances of that business with regard to its strategic goals, its resources, the resource availability within its regional and national economy, and the characteristics of its product-market environment (Grant, 1991). The critical requirement for sustainable competitive advantage is that

---

[49] *Blackbox-engineering refers to that the specification considers the component to be developed as a blackbox. The connections to the total systems are defined and the internal solution irrelevant to the total product under development.*

manufacturing seeks for continuous optimisation. Firms are likely to find the most attractive opportunities for improving manufacturing performance in business systems, and organisational aspects of manufacturing technology rather than in the adoption of advanced capital equipment, indicating the need for effective resource management.

Jonash (1997) refers to the research report entitled *Leveraging Technology in the Global Company* published in 1993 when noting that most companies believe that close to 50% or more of their technological competitiveness will be derived from external technology sourcing and collaboration during the 1990's. He emphasis the need for connecting technology to the corporate strategy and stresses the collaborations with partners. Likewise, Lei (1997) indicates the importance of technology fusion by blending older, current, and emerging technologies to create higher-order products and competencies. The overall corporate strategy should address then the technology needs of a corporation for the next 5-10 years; it should also define the technologies that the company will develop and husband internally, and those it will satisfy through external collaborations or partnerships that require commitment and attention by management (Heck, 2000). Again, this points to the importance of collaboration in the value chain as discussed in Subsection 14.4.4.

15.2.4 Manufacturing Organisation

Aside from resource acquisition, resource management also invokes the structuring process among resources to create and to manufacture products meeting business demands. Industrial companies achieve so by managing the total value chain, and by creating proper organisational structures.

Organisational structures within a company should meet the challenges of managing the value chain, and they should align the internal structure with business demands. Through developing proper structures, companies might reduce costs with 10% or more (Wüpping, 1998). Although structuring a company as such does not contribute to sustained competitiveness on the long-term, it is necessary to create a continuous flow of resources. Wigman (2000) claims that product innovation strategies do serve as base for creating continuous growth. Additionally, structuring creates short-term competitive advantages, necessary for creating space for future growth (especially through the increase of the Return-On-Assets). Restructuring meeting benchmarks on yesterday's performance constitute a fragile base for (business) growth (Friedrich & Hinterhuber, 1998). Companies tend to seek improvement within their existing system without questioning the system as such, a prerequisite for implementing business change. Thereto, interventions in the organisational structure do not retain unless they connect to the (future) product-market strategy.

Bessant (1997) demonstrates this notion when introducing three cases of organisational redesign by evolving manufacturing capability, through stage-wise change. Linking utilisation of resources to external opportunities and shifting demands is necessary for creating overall value. The integration between technology and the organisation, including appropriate information structures, is a keystone for developing strategic health.

15.3 INTERACTION MODELS FOR STRATEGIC CAPACITY MANAGEMENT

The four interaction models have already been partially elaborated in earlier publications on Strategic Capacity Management (e.g. Dekkers, 1999, 2003). They link the three components from the framework for Strategic Capacity Management (in Figure 15.1) to each other and describe the interactions that will take place. First, this section will elaborate on the method for assessment of technologies.

15.3.1 Strategic Framework for Assessment of Technologies

This emphasises the need for developing a method and tools for a manufacturing technology scan and implementation. The continual requests from industries strengthen the need for developing this method and related tools. An important feature of the method will be the indication of possible increases in performance.

In his publication on strategic technology scanning, van Wyk (1997, p. 23) advances four relevant propositions, mostly related to materials and product technology (van Wyk focuses on the strategy for product development):

1. Accepted procedures for strategic technology scanning are hard to find.
2. The necessary theoretical basis for scanning can be found in strategy technology analysis.
3. Scanning procedures, based on strategic technology analysis, are being developed for practical use.
4. Better scanning leads to improved strategic focus.

In addition to the literature used for the propositions and this scan, Chiesa et al. (1996, p. 111) mention as references for the formulation of a manufacturing strategy: Hill (1993), Hayes & Wheelwright (1984). The implementation of new processes is dealt with by Voss (1992), Leonard-Barton (1988), Tyre (1991), Drazin & Kazanjian (1986) but not to the extent that either of them presents a complete method. This created the need for searching a method for scanning manufacturing technologies; such a scan differs from ones for materials and product because manufacturing operates within boundaries set by product development.

Firstly, the method should formulate a manufacturing strategy or should review the existing strategy. Doing so, it will set the product requirements by the market, and it will identify the needed competencies for the related manufacturing processes. The strategy should meet the performance requirements as well, i.e. cost-price, flexibility, quality, delivery. By analysing the current performance, the tool sets goals for further improvement by applying appropriate manufacturing technologies. This will enable to review potential benefits of selected manufacturing technologies.

The next step would be the analysis of the available technologies to meet the suggested improvements. This matches the strategic technology analysis. According to van Wyk (1997, p. 27), tools of strategic technology analysis consist of six frameworks:

- a format for describing the essential features of a given technology;
- a system for classification of technologies;
- a model for tracking technological trends;
- a matrix for reviewing technological interactions;
- a chart of potential technological breakthrough zones;
- a profile of social preferences with respect to technology.

The latest framework does not directly comply with the goals of a tool for scanning and assessing manufacturing technology; for manufacturing, such a profile might direct itself to the social-economical consequences of the implementation at the shop-floor and its environment.

The scan itself should consist out of a number of steps. The four-step scanning process as suggested by van Wyk (1997, p. 28) does not directly apply to the scan for manufacturing technology. The scanning process relates more to the explorative search for products and materials technology rather than manufacturing technology. The four steps of van Wyk are:

- preparation: defining the landscape that has to be scanned and setting up an agenda;
- observation: exploring the technological frontier;
- interpretation: identifying landmark technologies that serve as indicators of the main thrust of technological advance;
- evaluation: using the list of landmark technologies to identify technological potential and re-examining the company's own technological base.

The design of a new method for technology scanning and implementation for the domain of manufacturing is depicted in Figure 15.5 (Dekkers, 1997, 2001); the proposed concept finds its roots in the approach by van Wyk but has been converted for the specific requirements of manufacturing. Especially, this conversion is found in the step of characterisation of product (families), manufacturing, and in the definition of performance indicators. As the figure shows, the selection of appropriate technologies takes place after assessing the current performance, and the identification of the competencies. The evaluation of selected technologies consists of determining the consequences of the

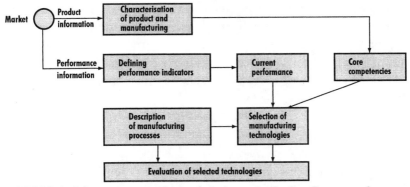

Figure 15.5: Method for assessment of manufacturing technologies. Current performance and competencies drive the selection of manufacturing technologies.

technology for the layout of the processes, the changes in the performance of the manufacturing operation, and the impact on the organisation. Furthermore, this evaluation should reveal constraints for the application of the choices. This step will mean an integration of methods and tools, already present in today's literature on this subject.

15.3.2 Adaptation Model for Technology

During the publications so far (Dekkers, 1999, 2003), the assessment of technology on its consequences for strategy has been poorly dealt with. Technology affects the capabilities of an organisation for deploying skills and knowledge in the manufacturing domain. The question arises whether the yield of the Framework for Dynamic Adaptation might offer an opportunity to complete the models of Strategic Capacity Management.

When referring to capabilities we note the strong parallel with the utilisation and creation of knowledge, as Mohanty & Deshmukh (1998) do. Knowledge Management refers directly to anticipate on the changing demands and requirements pouring in from the environment. This notion implies Knowledge Management aims at refining the present models and creating new models. The Model for the Dynamic Adaptation Capability, as introduced in Subsection 14.1.3 , has two components: the Dynamic Capability and the Internal Innovation Capability.

In analogy to Knowledge Management, technology management should aim at two different processes for a continuous flow of process innovations:
- Integrating new skills and resources into the existing infrastructure of resources with their specific knowledge and skills (the capability to introduce new models and adapt existing models).

- Cultivating existing skills and knowledge to improve contemporary competitiveness (the capability to learn from current practices and optimise within the business model).

These processes represent the dynamic adaptation by organisations for managing their base of manufacturing technology, and they determine the effectiveness of Strategic Capacity Management.

15.3.3 Integration Model for Organisation and Technology

For the integration between organisation and technology, a company should rely on the adaptation cycles, as present in the Innovation Impact Point Model. Through learning modes and subsequent adaptation of goals and objectives, changes in the organisation and technology reflect on the direction an organisation is taking. Introducing manufacturing technologies is partially a process of experimentation. Outcomes are not always predictable, and therefore organisations need to follow up on the introduction of the technology through continuous evaluation, the reflection by assessing the impact of the development, and the implementation of the technology; equally well organisations should consider the changes in the organisation.

It has been mentioned that collaboration with suppliers and technology providers has a paramount importance for companies to adapt to the dynamics of the environment (see Section 14.4); therefore, the models of Strategic Capacity Management might be expanded with the developed Collaboration Model. As manufacturing technologies represent capabilities to perform processes, vertical integration makes less sense. Rather through ongoing specialisation and differentiation, companies will revert to competencies and outsourcing technologies. This creates the possibility for collaboration on technologies with suppliers, hence it requires the mutual sharing of knowledge and Knowledge Management. An industrial organisation should possess sufficient key technologies to differentiate from competitors. To remain competitive an organisation should collaborate or develop technologies (pacing or emerging technologies). Base technologies, which do not create competitive advantage, should be elected for outsourcing. These outsourcing activities require vertical integration along the value chain. Collaboration with suppliers should be directed mostly at technologies that might turn into essential technologies to increase competitiveness.

It seems logical now that the decision-making on outsourcing as presented in Subsection 15.2.2 should also account for the possibilities to advance in technology on the long run. The decision-making on outsourcing as presented earlier concentrates on resources utilisation. The model on collaboration generates additional criteria to complement decision-making.

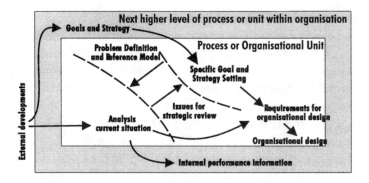

Figure 15.6: Framework for analysis and design of organisations. Although similar to the model of Bikker (1993) it has added the embedding of the processes and organisational units in the total organisation.

15.3.4 Change Model for Strategy and Organisation

The new view on the redesign of organisations as an element of industrial networks required the development of a new approach through empirical studies and based on literature. Thereto, a decision model has been developed for revealing these relations, and the practical implication. The approach is rooted in the methodology the Section Production Technology and Organisation has practised for many years. Yet, it required an adaptation to distinguish clearly between external and internal criteria.

This framework for analysing organisational problems that affect the business process, and the structure of the organisation, is based on Thompson (1991) and notes by Bikker (1993). Essentially, this framework derives the requirements for the structure and processes of organisations to meet the desired performance. Once the requirements have been set, the analysis of the current situation within an organisation takes place, indicating where and how to improve the organisation. The next step consists of developing alternative solutions, and choosing between them. Finally, management will set structural changes in motion. This kind of approach applies either when the environment changes or when the organisation wishes to improve its own performance.

Figure 15.6 marks the core of the framework consisting of the evaluation of the set strategy against external developments and internal performance information. This will result in deviations that make up the elements to define the problem. Such a definition compromises mostly main criteria and the problem domain for investigation and analysis. Even though that the main external criteria might be efficacy, productivity, lead-times, and flexibility, the specific set of criteria should match the contingencies of the situation[50]. Besides the internal organisation should meet performance criteria set by the strategy. The design of an organisation should be based on integration of aspects (Gold, 1991). The selection of an organisational structure should not merely depend on one single point of view but should match as well with the integrative aspects of the strategy. This points to including the bottlenecks and performance requirements into the selection of the organisational structure.

Once the performance requirements are known, the design of a proper organisational structure, incorporating the opportunities provided by product and process characteristics should be carried out. The hierarchy does not necessarily reflect business processes and therefore does not directly create the alternatives for strategic choices (see Appendix B). For connecting strategy to choices, we should combine activities within the manufacturing system from a strategic point of view. Such combinations are called the organelle structures. Strategic choices relate the organelle structure to external performance criteria dictated by product/market-combinations and internal performance criteria.

To implement the changes, the change model for strategy and organisation should be complemented with a change management approach. From the evolutionary approaches, it would be logical to define steps related to sustained fitness and evolvability. These steps or mutations should lead to increased fitness on a fitness landscape. None such approach does yet exist, an approach based on these principles should guide organisations to assess their current situation and move towards more viable competitive positions. Additionally, the scope of strategies should be wide enough for these step-wise mutations might take a long term, let us say more than 2-5 years; during such a period in more dynamic markets, the environment has been reshaped. No method has been developed yet to assist such changes in combination with a scope of strategies.

15.3.5 Dynamic Adaptation and Strategic Capacity Management

The development of the models for Strategic Capacity Management originates in requests by industrial companies to assist in strategic decision-making. Traditionally, such decision-making leads to interventions, most likely one-time interventions. Although some continuity has been present in the models, like in the model for outsourcing, this issue has not been sufficiently addressed. Following the thoughts of the earlier Chapters 13 and 14, a more continuous approach becomes necessary for industrial companies to enhance competitiveness.

Some of the models of the Framework for Dynamic Adaptation by industrial organisations have been used to complete the earlier developed models of Strategic

---

[50] *Bikker (1993) strongly recommends to set criteria on the extent of control efforts, the control competencies and the organisational learning capabilities (as expressed in the evaluation loops of the steady-state model and the breakthrough model) into the new design of the organisational structure..*

Capacity Management. These models are the Innovation Impact Point Model, the Model for the Dynamic Adaptation Capability, the knowledge management processes, the Collaboration Model. Additionally, the thoughts about step-wise mutations and adaptive walks have been used to describe the evaluation of technological and organisational improvements as well as pathways for industrial organisations to develop. The evolutionary approach serves as a useful base for expanding Strategic Capacity Management.

At the same time, the further development of Strategic Capacity Management depends on the conversion of evolutionary biological models to the domain of organisations. Currently, the research into adaptation did expand the models, and did contribute to understanding evolutionary development but a more definite description of evolutionary models for industrial organisations might create the possibility for quantification.

15.4 CONCLUSIONS

Strategic Capacity Management thrives on the integration of technology and organisation to meet business demands. The realisation of the strategy depends of the appropriate manufacturing technology along with creating competencies as a base for managing the value chain, implementation of an effective outsourcing policy, and organisational structuring. The integration should result in transparent decisions on capacity bottlenecks and process development, mainly appropriate manufacturing technology, and the integration should define suitable business organisational structures for adapting to shifting market demands.

The methods as described provide both management and engineers during development the opportunity for reviewing manufacturing aspects: manufacturing strategy, meeting technological as well as performance requirements, core competencies, and outsourcing. This leads to the inclusion of manufacturing strategy in decision-making during the stages of product development. A continuous evaluation of technological developments against performance requirements and product-market developments serves as source for adaptation. Through a well-defined process of strategy development and implementation, manufacturing might anticipate better on market developments and product development. That enables manufacturing to create sufficient utilisation of its own resources as well as to initiate process development. A prerequisite is a strong link to the product development strategy and the market development strategy.

The evolutionary models have expanded the range of models in Strategic Capacity Management by adding the Innovation Impact Point Model, the Model for the Dynamic Adaptation Capability, and the Collaboration Model. Yet, these models have not been tested at their validity for adaptation. A smoother approach to implementing effective changes resides in the developmental pathways and adaptive walks of the evolutionary models.

16 CASE STUDIES

The comprehensive models have not yet allowed conducting many case studies fully based on the theory. The development of new theory has absorbed a lot of lead-time, leaving little time in the current study to revert to extensive case studies. Secondly, the execution of case studies requires the development of an integral, specific research method, involving many disciplines and access to a lot of data and people within companies. The current technological and social-economic settings involving the capabilities of management of many companies have led to further restrictions on information and sources within companies limiting the outcomes of such studies.

Within the scope of the search for a Framework for Dynamic Adaptation, three case studies have been conducted. These case studies have been spread over the duration of the study and did investigate mechanisms, processes, and structures of adaptation within industrial companies. All these case studies represent an investigation in which a postgraduate student solves a problem within an industrial company. All three specific case studies have been performed under close supervision linking the progress of the students to the actual research and guarding useful outcomes for the problems companies are experiencing. From each case study, the contribution to the research will be mentioned. It should be remarked that these case studies are not directed at the testing of earlier hypotheses, rather they are concerned with the application of the models developed so far.

The first of the three case studies took place during 1998 at a company developing and manufacturing vision systems. The case served as a base for both the development of concepts for Strategic Capacity Management and the research into adaptation by industrial companies (Section 16.1). The second case study concerned a developer and manufacturer of communication sets (Section 16.2). The case builds on the early models and expands the models to integral problems. The third case study was about a company executing infrastructure projects (Section 16.3), which lost its market leadership preceding the case study in 2000-2001. All three cases will be evaluated against the developments made at the time of the study and the Framework for Dynamic Adaptation.

16.1 CASE A - VISION SYSTEMS

Before expanding on the problem definition, a short description of the company follows. Vision Systems produces dedicated vision systems and control systems for professional applications for a wide variety of customers having their own specific requirements. The total lead-time for specific orders (product development and manufacturing) amounts to five years, the planned lead-time is exceeded by 50% or more. Manufacturing costs account for 65-70% of the sales per order, lot-sizes for orders vary between a few systems to sometimes 30 pieces of identical equipment. The years before 1998 have seen a shift from customers having sizeable budgets for specific products and projects to customers faced with major cut-downs in budgets. The market, consisting of suppliers like Vision Systems, has to react by offering a different scope of products more directed at becoming Original Equipment Manufacturers, thus offering more commonality at lower price levels.

16.1.1 Problem Statement

The clients have not only adjusted their budgets, they impose more stringent criteria to the costs of orders, and they require timely delivery. The old style of working embedded in project management practices does not suffice any more, causing more and more deviations from internal targets for budgets and delivery. The project-oriented views give little space for developing long-term production plans and schedules. Additionally, the Manufacturing Department encounters problems to produce within budget and schedule for specific orders. The investigation aims at developing a methodology for Strategic Capacity Management for the manufacturing domain to address the dynamically changing environment.

16.1.2 Analysis

During the first half of the 1990's, a reorganisation leads to a considerable reduction of the work force (41%), partially achieved by outsourcing components and production technology. Especially, the core activities do focus on strategic interests of the company. Even in current times, the order processing is characterised by design-to-order and make-to-order. Therefore, each order requires the execution of the complete cycle from development to manufacturing. Sales have focused mostly on wheeling clients in since these clients have yearly budgets for expenditures and next years these budgets might vaporise. During the sales process, the Sales Department does not completely account for the available capacity as well as the technological feasibility of clients' specifications. Originally, the market is characterised as a seller's market based on calculations afterwards and space for profit margins. Because of external market developments, Vision Systems has entered a market that consists of smaller systems with a higher degree of standardisation. Additionally, the contracts contain more and more penalties for late delivery and other breaches, because of the increased buying power of the clients. The deadlines and cost targets are not linked to the long-term production plan and schedule, hence it becomes more and more difficult for the Manufacturing Department to deliver in-time.

Still, the management of internal processes relies on project management, based on a matrix structure. The focus of project management is on fast delivery within set budgets for each program separately. Such a management structure holds for large and complex products and small orders sizes with low commonality. The Manufacturing Department has to consider the production of units per period and has a different view. The long-term planning is based on the units per period, no matter for which program they are. The strong project orientation allows limited planning and scheduling on long-term. The current performance of the company indicates that the structure based on project management inhibits sustained competitiveness in a market that undergoes major changes.

Looking at the setting of business objectives, the strategy process encompasses the compilation of four plans for the Strategic Business Unit Vision Systems (see Figure 16.1):

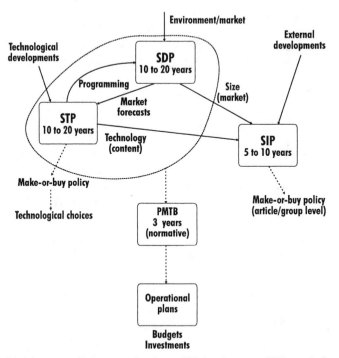

Figure 16.1: Link between all the strategic plans of Vision Systems. SDP stands for the Strategic Domain Plan, PMTB for Plan for Medium-Term Budgetting, STP for Strategic Technology Plan, and SIP for Strategic Industrial Plan.

- Strategic Domain Plan. This plan describes the mission, the corporate policy, the market developments, the competitive situation, the operational and functional requirements for systems and products. It highlights the recommended strategic alliances and collaborations. It should also describe effects of strategic scenarios on results of the business unit. It contains business definitions, competitive positions, strategic collaborations, SWOT-analysis, capital expenditures, objectives, and action plans;
- Plan for Medium-Term Budgeting. The Strategic Domain Plan is transferred into budgets for the three years to come.
- Strategic Technology Plan. This document describes the current situation in fifteen disciplines, ranging from information technology to mechanical systems. In each of these fields, the technological developments are described. Decisions are made about the internal development of technologies or purchasing these technologies; collaboration with third parties is possible. The document lists actions and a plot of technologies compared with intended programs.
- Strategic Industrial Plan. This plan contains strategic highlights for the Manufacturing Department. Furthermore, it describes, the internal requirements for the make-or-buy policy, the policy and agreements for international cooperation, co-production, and specific outsourcing agreements. The second section contains capacity requirements for the departments within the Manufacturing Department (the reliability of these plans is low). The third section of the plan transfers the capacity requirements to production technologies and their development.

The study into Strategic Capacity Management reflects on the Strategic Industrial Plan. Investigations showed that both the Strategic Technology Plan and the Strategic Industrial Plan are developed separately bottom-up, yielding a low correlation between them. The departments of Vision Systems view mostly the consequences for the Manufacturing Department as a side-effect of their own plans, even the development of a Strategic Industrial Plan is considered obsolete.

Further investigation reveals that most problems are caused by not considering manufacturing aspects during product development. Typically, an old design concept includes one main sensor per system for receiving signals, a new concept introduces a hundredfold of smaller sensors. The consequences for manufacturing are not considered. This results in a relatively high cost price and above all manufacturing lead-times increase by 300%.

In addition, the Manufacturing Department does not succeed in following a strategy. Firstly, because of the unpredictable lead-times of product development they cannot set out an adequate strategy. During product development, the Engineering Department determines mostly manufacturing aspects without considering the consequences, as shown above. Secondly, the Manufacturing

Department does not translate objectives into programs for improvement and does not anticipate changes for the business. This is mainly due to having insight only at a total level of load on capacity, which does not trigger decisions on capacity investments, process technology improvement, and structures to meet performance requirements.

16.1.3 Solution

The solution of a redesign of the strategic processes has been based on the breakthrough model. Requirement for the development of the strategic process is to act as a continuous process yielding discrete plans. Main themes are the integration of the different plans into a whole, the evaluation of the performance to allow adjustments during the periods of a plan, and to generate valid plans during future strategic processes. The implementation of the strategic decision process for the manufacturing domain takes also into account: outsourcing, and organisational structures for manufacturing. Furthermore, a link has to be established between product development and manufacturing, especially for outsourcing. The generic strategic process has been depicted in Figure 16.2.

Two years later, the decision-making on outsourcing during product development has taken full effect. During private interviews, middle and senior

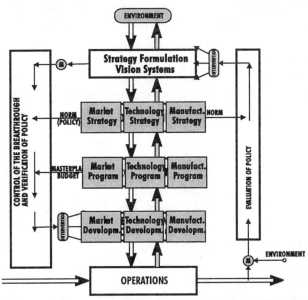

Figure 16.2: Industrial strategy model for Vision Systems. The three fields of strategy have been linked at the different levels of the breakthough model. The Plan for Medium-Term Budgeting serves as driver for the verification process and an evaluation process has been added which was not present before.

managers have accounted for the differences in strategic decision-making process. Yet, it appears that the operational management of outsourcing requires more attention as a consequence of the ongoing call for flexibility and capital expenditures.

16.1.4 Framework for Dynamic Adaptation

Looking back at this case study, it seems plausible that the company strived for increasing sustained fitness rather than issues of evolvability. At the time, the Innovation Impact Point Model was not available; though it was recognised that the developments at different levels of the breakthrough model should lead to consideration by management. Later on this thought connected to the concepts of innovation and the Innovation Impact Points to ensure both sustained fitness and evolvability. The perception was also that the company should undertake small steps to improvement in the manufacturing area rather than trying big leaps forward.

During this case study, the first outlines appeared for the Framework for Dynamic Adaptation. Firstly, the breakthrough model served as a base for designing the strategic process; no adequate model was available (being generic, covering all aspects, process oriented). A short study revealed that no other strategic process could cope with the requirement of continuity. Eventually, the outcomes of the study led to the literature survey by Paré (2001) which confirmed these findings (see Subsection 14.3.2). Also during these study, it became clear that the need arose to assess internal and external developments, both market and technological, on their merits for the organisation. No clear methodology was available for such. This case study evoked the literature surveys by Meijs (1999) and Wigman (2000) into innovation management to find mechanisms, evaluation criteria, and processes of innovations.

16.2   Case B - Communication Sets

The company in this case study develops, manufactures, and markets a wide range of personal communications products. The main manufacturing site employs about 2800 people and it produces about 6 million products, its market share well beyond other competitors. The company has suffered heavy losses during the years preceding the case study.

16.2.1 Problem Statement

Management assumes that the major cause for these losses should be found in the delays of the introduction of new products. For two years, the company has not introduced any new product concepts that has resulted in loss of market share as well. Through improvements in the management structure, the management wants to regain competitiveness. Thereto, they have introduced the *Supply, Demand, and Support* model (see Figure 16.3) which should address the problem, according to them. The supply group (including manufacturing, research and development) designs products and sells them at a transfer price to the demand group. The supply group will be measured on its delivery of competitive products in terms of quality, price, and delivery-as-scheduled. The demand group sells those products that it acquires from the supply group to customers. The demand group is measured on order generation, revenue, profit, and cash.

To increase its profitability, the control of the New Product Introduction process should meet the performance requirements. Currently, this process does not meet targets: the time-to-market exceeds deadlines, the quality level is poor, and the costs are higher than scheduled. The assignment focuses on proposing an effective organisation capable of controlling the New Product Introduction process, mostly focused on the supply group.

16.2.2 Analysis

The fast technological evolution in the market and the continuous stream of new communication sets introduced by competitors has created a situation in which the customer's value perception of a specific product deteriorates rapidly; retail prices drop about 30% annually. Consequently, the economic life-cycle is limited to about 12 to 24 months. The delays of introduction of about two years have resulted in the launch of obsolete sets from the market perspective. The disconnection in the management structure between the supply group and the demand group weakens the focus of new product development on perceived market value of new products. Hence, an effective management structure should

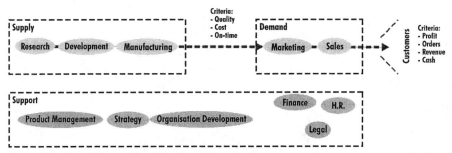

Figure 16.3: Supply, Demand, and Support Model for the company Communication Sets. It shows that the company tries to separate operations from sales thereby introducing accountability. Especially, the supply group did not meet its objectives.

account for the throughput of the product development process and customer focus during the development process.

Furthermore, the pressure on market introduction has resulted in the release of products that do not meet quality standards yet. The dilemma the company faces is that later introduction of products will make developments obsolete or reduce possible market reach or direct introduction will result in quality problems to be absorbed by the organisation. The latter decision has resulted in that about 30% of sold products is sent back due to quality problems. This indicates that the product development process should also account for release of products that are more effective by increasing the internal quality of new products.

Until recently, the organisation is based on a matrix structure of purely functional departments, like Development, Purchasing, Logistics, Production, and project teams per product. Within the current situation, the functional department manager has much more power than the project manager does; the functional groups are dispersed into geographical locations on the site hampering communication. The interests between projects managers and functional departments clash at the expense of the lead-time of the project. Recently, the management has added focus groups for realising a part of the product by using the necessary skills from the functional departments. A Product Architecture and Integration Team has the responsibility for realising the total product. The total effectiveness of the matrix structure remains low and a slight performance improvement might be expected.

A further investigation into the development process reveals that the number of so-called prototype production runs was higher than anticipated and that delays in planned prototype production runs occurred. The excess of prototype production runs is occurring due to incomplete data of previous runs and quality problems. Every time such a run is prepared, it has to fit into a manufacturing slot, to use the equipment of the Manufacturing Department. That means that the availability of all materials, support, and equipment should be tuned to this slot. In practice, it appears that materials and tools are not available on time. During production runs, many problems appear that need to be addressed after the prototype production run. Some of the problems are due to the quality of delivered products, some of them due to integration problems, some of them due to lack of coordination within the time limits of the previous troubleshooting periods. The company does not succeed in fully resolving these problems to prevent recurrence.

The product development process shows very little control of coordination between the different fields of expertise while a high degree of collaboration is needed. The integral management of the product development process does focus on local optimisation of functional departments, skill groups or focus groups.

Hence, many delays occur because of coordination during product development and insufficient absorption of quality problems.

16.2.3 Solution

The proposed solution finds its origin in models of Strategic Capacity Management, especially the Model for the Dynamic Adaptation Capability. The first partial solution is to create small product teams with core specialists addressing the need of that particular product. These small product teams are linked to the Marketing Department by programs, consisting of a few products, to ensure customer focus during ongoing development and incorporate customer requirements as much as possible. This partial solution comes about from a predecessor of the Innovation Impact Point Model and is supported by team composition to indicate the impacts of problems and solutions more quickly. The second partial solution addresses the application of adaptation cycles and quick responses to problem-solving. Again, problems are assessed on their impact on the specific product development and the total development process of related products. Information about encountered problems are issued to related products so that they can benefit from the experience of other groups. Thirdly, the support in terms of manufacturing, logistics, quality control is also linked to these small product groups. Additionally to this partial solution, one production line is converted for experimental use by product development, but operated by manufacturing personnel (which improves the knowledge transfer between product development and manufacturing).

Initially, these improvements moved many product development projects near completion. At the moment, these products were reaching the market introduction, the conglomerate of which this company was part of, enforced a reorganisation during the second half of 1999, cutting down the number of jobs by more than 30%. The management was changed and a new product market strategy was developed with severe consequences for the organisation.

16.2.4 Framework for Dynamic Adaptation

The principles of adaptation and the Innovation Impact Point Model served as a major drive for the acceleration of the product development process, for both increasing sustained fitness and evolvability. To create a more continuous stream of innovations, the management of projects should address the impact on the organisation. Hence, the concepts for the solution did account for concepts of innovation and integrative thoughts across product innovation and process innovation. Within the business planning, the purposeful application of mutations leading to both sustained fitness and evolvability emerged. Slowly, the style of managing product development and manufacturing turned around until the announcement of the cutdown in jobs.

Additionally, the focus on the market proved an important aspect for ensuring innovations and product development directed at true market needs rather than showing that project would meet aims set by the organisation. The separation between functional entities did not meet the requirement of adaptation to fast-changing market needs. This indicated the importance of an overall link from the organisation to the market as part of adaptation processes.

16.3   CASE C - INFRASTRUCTURE COMPANY

This case study concerns a company that executes major projects in infrastructure. To do so, the company deploys equipment, many smaller pieces of equipment, and few bigger pieces of equipment. The market is characterised by its capital intensity and competitiveness. The Infrastructure Company employs 2200 people and generates about € 330 million in sales. The projects, this company executes, require the selection and deployment of proper equipment to match the soil conditions, the terrain, the environmental constraints, and a delivery within schedule and budgets (equipment costs amount to 65-75% of the budgets of projects). The deployment of equipment entails also the modification of equipment and the construction of new pieces of equipment.

The organisation is characterised by specialists working in functional departments with a strongly technical orientation. The orders are executed by assigning people from these departments to projects, which might have a duration up to 4 years. The organisation has an innovative orientation and if necessary, it brings people together from different fields to solve problems. The need to react to changes in demand (large projects with relatively short lead-times for quotations) forces the long-term vision to the background. Information transfer and decision-making take place informally and few formal procedures do exist. The hierarchy is flat and allows a swift response to the environment.

16.3.1   Problem Statement

The Infrastructure Company has lost its market leadership in the years before and wants to regain its competitiveness. The competitiveness will be reached if the composition of the base of equipment matches to the requirement the markets pose on the execution of projects. The past years have proven that (a) modifications take longer than scheduled and do not deliver the expected results, (b) equipment that has been build, proves not to be competitive because of design choices, and (c) the process of construction of equipment and modifying equipment lacks transparency which causes that the tuning to the market requirements absorbs too much time. The company is the only one that did not invest in the so-called super class of equipment while the other companies consistently have invested in this segment (the development and construction of such equipment takes 2-3 years). The assignment focuses on increasing the efficacy of the process for construction and modification of equipment, and the development of a framework to increase productivity.

16.3.2 Analysis

The market demands that companies offer infrastructure projects on the base of costs (competition is fierce) and quality (environmental requirements are at stake). According to Volberda (1998), these market demands are translated into efficiency, quality, and organisational flexibility. In the case of this company, one should also add: product flexibility. The execution of projects depends on the project organisation, outside the scope of the assignment, and the deployment of the equipment. Equipment determines in great extent the quality of the projects and the efficiency. Hence, the system logistics have a strong impact on the profitability of projects and the future capabilities to accept projects.

The most recent acquired equipment has a efficiency rate of more than 100% while the efficiency of older equipment moves at levels of 70%[51]. Extension of the lifetime of equipment relies on the modifications and upgrades in between periods of deployment. The timely development of new equipment is essential to remain competitive. Especially, as noted, the company has been reluctant to invest in the so-called super class (pieces of equipment with a relative high capacity). The company is not prepared to submit any information about the strategic decision-making process although it seems that they not meet any of the requirements for strategic planning and scenario planning. Additionally, it does not become clear how the allocation of equipment relates to the execution of projects, making it impossible to evaluate the actual performance. Hence, the attention of the investigation shifts to the process for modifications and upgrades of equipment.

Because of the separation between project evaluation and equipment performance evaluation, mainly aiming at efficiency rather than productivity, the management of equipment focuses mostly on budget spending. Through examples, it becomes clear that this particular decision-making process is not meeting business demands. Equipment is used successfully during the first years of exploitation and becomes quickly obsolete through absence of regular upgrades and modifications. A closer examination of the development process shows that (a) decision processes to start a project takes a long time, (b) not all people are

---

[51] *Efficiency rates within this company are defined by the actual utilisation degree against the budgetted utilisation. An efficiency rate of 100% means then more hours deployed that foreseen (financially).*

involved at the right times during the development process, (c) not all knowledge is incorporated in decisions at strategic, tactical and operational level of the development process, (d) unstructured commissioning of the equipment takes place.

16.3.3 Solution

The solution comprises of (1) a link between project evaluation and equipment performance evaluation, and (2) a process for processing and distributing knowledge. The first part of the solution will allow the company to assess the deployment of equipment and its performance to introduce both operational improvement sand modifications of equipment. During these evaluations, the productivity of the equipment is reviewed and possible areas for improvement are identified. The items might cover the specification, the effectiveness of improvements, operational procedures, etc. Such an evaluation should be staged according to the knowledge conversion processes. The second part of the solution thrived on the application of Knowledge Management and its models gathered during the research into adaptation, especially the models for knowledge conversion and distribution.

Although, the solution met all demands and criteria, it was never implemented. Just before implementation, the company was taken over by a competitor and lost its independence in decision-making. However, the company assessed the methodology as useful and started the implementation before the effects of the takeover were known to integrate it into their procedures.

16.3.4 Framework for Dynamic Adaptation

More than the models for Strategic Capacity Management, the solutions for this assignment relied on the Framework for Dynamic Adaptation. Most elements were present in the solution. However, the modifications to the strategic processes were never at stake since the directors refused to elaborate on these matters.

The company had not sufficiently anticipated on the developments in the market. Its core business relied in previous times on innovative approaches to projects, which were of smaller size at that time. The flexible deployment of equipment helped the company to maintain leadership in its markets. The change in the market became apparent when major projects were announced on which competitors were able to react faster by providing equipment with much higher capacity. The company did not join the mainstream of companies active in the infrastructure market and lost consequently its market position.

16.4 Review of the Framework for Dynamic Adaptation

All three cases have used the models of the Framework for Dynamic Adaptation for increasing the reach of the offered solutions. Without the insight about adaptation processes, some features would be impossible to develop. Yet, there is a longer way to go since all three cases were conducted during the execution of the study and during the ongoing development of models. In Table 16.1 the case studies have been projected against the reference model; this table also indicates which of the models have been used to solve the problems of the companies. The choice for the reference model rather than the Framework for Dynamic Adaptation follows from the need to assess its validity.

Looking at the validity of the framework, the three cases struggled with connecting their organisation, the processes and structures, to market demands. The first two cases struggled more with matching the internal processes to meet market demands while the case of the Infrastructure Company experienced more troubles with matching equipment to (sometimes unknown) projects and that way affecting decision-making. In the first and third case the capabilities and capacities of "manufacturing" comprised the topics of the studies, the second one the internal processes and structures. Increasing fitness in a market domain becomes not only a matter of strategy, as some of the schools in Appendix M tell, but also a matter of resource management and internal processes and structures. Hence, the phenotype of organisations depends on its internal structure and processes, an assumption taken at the beginning of this study.

Secondly, organisational changes seem more viable when market opportunities arise. All three companies wanted to capture market opportunities and to adapt to the changing market conditions; not all three could do so without changing their internal structures. Yet, the very idea that adaptations, preferably continuously, by those companies gave leeway to enter market opportunities acted as driving force to base the organisational structure on principles of continuous change. Before the case studies, behavioural actions, on the management level or the company as total, should have established the necessary changes; they did not. The negative images of one-time interventions (resistance to change, doubts about effectiveness) were avoided. The follow-up on two of the case studies has been weak because of organisational changes, even out of managerial control. We might conclude that market opportunities enhance adaptation when they fit to organisational changes and create better opportunities for organisations to adapt in a more continuous way.

Thirdly, the principle and the consequences of self-organisation have found little support again. The dissipative structures do not exist or they present a new challenge for companies. The interaction with partners and suppliers comes closest

Table 16.1: Case studies and the reference model. The table lists also the models used for solving the problems of the companies.

	Phenotype/Genotype	Adaptive Walks	Developmental pathways	Sustained Fitness	Evolvability	Self-organisation
Vision Systems	Internal focus on technology has to change to customer-orientation. Additionally, the company should become OEM.	Customer orientation beholds developing own product range rather than project orientation of unique solutions. Company offers attractive range of products, yet, does not succeed in reducing lead-time, costs and reliability. *Model: Pre-model for Innovation Impact Point*	Both product development and manufacturing should get attention. Especially, since recurrence becomes more dominant in products. Systematic sourcing decisions become necessary to develop the manufacturing capability. *Model: Pre-model for Innovation Impact Point*	Focus of manufacturing on optimisation.	Component innovation and architectural innovation open the pathway for dispersal. Connecting product development to manufacturing. *Model: Pre-model for Innovation Impact Point*	Sourcing decisions allow interaction with suppliers
Communication Sets	Focus on use of components rather than on customer demands. Rapid decline of customers' value perception.	Increased pressure on product development for launching new products. Products launched lag behind and have a poor quality image. Separated responsibilities and lack of co-ordination. *Model: Pre-model for Innovation Impact Point*	Co-operation necessary between all disciplines. Adaptation cycles absent and needed for managing business processes. *Models: Pre-model for Innovation Impact Point; Adaptation cycles (precedessor dynamic capability)*	More focus on sustained fitness to manage quality problems. Impact on organisation of product development to be highlighted. *Models: Pre-model for Innovation Impact Point; Adaptation cycles (precedessor dynamic capability)*	Products should connect to the market demands and market strategy. Continuous assessment of development of products necessary. *Models: Pre-model for Innovation Impact Point; Adaptation cycles (precedessor dynamic capability)*	
Infrastructure Company	Capital intensity.	Innovative orientation. Long-term vision lacks due to environmental changes.	Development of equipment needs to connect to market demands and strategy. *Model: Dynamic Adaptation Capability*	Modifications should find their way to all equipment and projects. *Model: Dynamic Adaptation Capability*	Development and modification of equipment should connect to opportunities. *Model: Dynamic Adaptation Capability*	

to this concept, nevertheless the intense exchange with the environment has not yet its place in management science.

Fourthly, the models of the Framework for Dynamic Adaptation assisted in solving the strategic issues of the companies. Both the Innovation Impact Point Model and the Model for the Dynamic Adaptation Capability served as cornerstone for the solutions in the three cases. Although these models were not totally available, especially during the first two cases, their underlying mechanisms generated guidelines for implementing more effective solutions than without the knowledge about adaptation.

Fifthly, the dynamic adaptation assumes a more gradual change than one-time interventions with their negative effects. All three cases stress that both main hypotheses are true. Organisations maintain homeostatic boundary control and continuous change prevails in effectiveness. Adaptation to the environment besides being a necessity and consists of more continuous processes than mostly thought about.

Finally, two out three cases experienced tremendous changes caused by the conglomerate they are part of. Even to the extent that they could not implement changes they wanted to. When talking about the adaptation industrial organisations have been approached as single unit serving a product-market combination. Dispersal meant exploring different but related markets. Conglomerates consist out of many business units, sometimes directed at total different product-market combinations which might have weak relationships. Such conglomerates exert governance on business units based on (financial) performance criteria, which might differ from the criteria needed for the evolution of companies.

The evolutionary approach to industrial companies seems to behold promises. The development of these models requires much more attention to convert them to practical approaches for companies. The current models are the first outcome of evolutionary approaches to companies at the level of the organisation and the models did not find their match in any other methodology. Change management and cultural change realise a more gradual transformation of the organisation, but they often come along with one-time interventions. With the effectiveness of these interventions being limited, the big chance that organisations revert to their old structure and ways of working, one-time interventions open little possibility that they will work out. To prove that evolutionary models and approaches yield definite results, more research should generate additional insight and studies should focus on longer periods.

16.5   CONCLUSIONS

The three case studies were conducted at moments that strategic choices were the focal points of management. Although different in nature, each of the cases concerned the production processes (and departments). In two cases external developments did not allow the proposed solutions to take full effects; however, all cases let the study use the developed models to support analysis and implementation of solutions.

In course of time, the models of the Framework for Dynamic Adaptation were developed and introduced in these cases along with the models of Strategic Capacity Management. The three cases showed that the implementation of dynamic adaptation enhances current industrial models. In each of these cases the implementation showed improvements although the actual changes were influenced by decision-making outside the scope of management of the business units. Only through long case studies such phenomena can be studied and linked to the developed models for the Framework for Dynamic Adaptation and Strategic Capacity Management.

The Innovation Impact Point Model and the Model for the Dynamic Adaptation Capability capture both the sustained fitness and evolvability. The concepts of adaptive walks and developmental pathways need further attention.

EPILOGUE

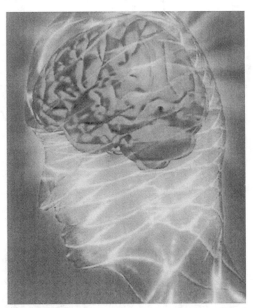

The dynamic adaptation by organisations comprises the capabilities of self-cognition of individuals, the self-conscience (or Persona of de Geus), and the capability of foresight. Despite these differences, the development of organisations seems to have many characteristics of the evolution of organisms.

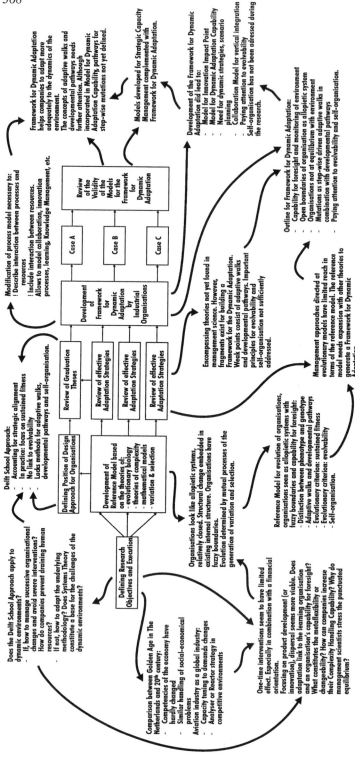

Figure 17.1: Overview of the research. The prologue has raised questions to the development of companies based on two studies, one of the Netherlands and one of the aviation industry. Current management approaches did not suffice to explain the phenomenon of adaptation. The research has explored evolutionary biological models during Part I, resulting in a reference model for the development of organisations. The research used the reference model to review existing management approaches in Part II. Additionally, the methodology of the Delft School Approach has been looked at as well, leading to conclude that it focuses on sustained fitness and that it lacks methods for adaptive walks and developmental pathways. During Part III of the research a Framework for Dynamic Adaptation has been developed.

17 CONCLUSIONS

Returning to the original quest for this research, this chapter draws conclusions based on the earlier findings of this study (see Figure 17.1, opposite page). For it is the purpose of this particular study to investigate whether processes and structures exist for adaptation avoiding the exertion of severe interventions (main proposition in Section 4.1). After the search for models of adaptation in Part I and Part II, the Framework for Dynamic Adaptation has outlined thoughts and models in Part III. These models mean a shift from static approaches to capturing the dynamics of external change into the dynamic capability and the internal-oriented adaptation capability.

Section 17.1 will shortly review the models for adaptation and reflect on the move from static to dynamic thinking, necessary to sustain adaptation. The underlying thoughts about evolutionary models constitute Section 17.2. So far, most authors in management literature have emphasised the punctuated equilibrium as main evolutionary model to describe the dynamics organisations experience. The models of fitness landscapes, game theories, and Adaptive Dynamics have enhanced the interaction between entities and their environment with mathematical models. Finally, Section 17.3 will review the validity of the Delft School Approach. Additionally, it will elaborate on modifications of this methodology to match with the requirements for adaptation.

17.1 ADAPTATION OF INDUSTRIAL ORGANISATIONS TO THE DYNAMICS OF THE ENVIRONMENT

Answering the question: *Do processes and structures exist that support adaptation?*, this research has shown that industrial organisations might deploy mechanisms to do so. These mechanisms range from internal mechanisms to actively seeking the interaction with the environment. The study has already noted the proposition of Boulding (1956, p. 201) that processes of growth differ from processes of steady-state.

17.1.1 Static versus Dynamic Thinking
The principle of homeostasis, present in most theories and therewith implicitly describing a steady-state, views the environment as certain. Even theories that aim at creating change often take the state of the environment as given and hardly take the interaction between organisations and the environment into account. From such a snapshot of the environment, organisations can derive demands and requirements they should meet for continuity. Yet, the driving

principles of evolution have shown that continuous interaction between the generation of mutations and the selection process in the environment enables the development of organisations. Especially, the mathematical models demonstrate this interaction to the extent that organisms (and therefore also organisations) might influence their environment as a continuous process.

Hardly, any equilibrium exists. Even when we observe or experience such a state, relatively speaking, dynamic movements are happening. Through successive minor modifications, potential major shifts are being prepared, creating a latent lake of potential opportunities for sustained fitness, seen as optimisation within the current product-market combination, and evolvability, comprising of bifurcation and dispersal. The changes take place because of the continuous interaction between the generation of variation and the selectional processes (van den Bergh, 2003, p. 3).

17.1.2 Review of Original Hypotheses

The research did address a wide scope of models from evolutionary biology, focusing on speciation and landscape fitness, and management science, all centring to generate answers to the two following hypotheses, launched in Section 4.1:

> **Hypothesis A**
> *The principle of boundary control based on homeostasis limits the evolution of organisations in response to the dynamics of the environment.*
> **Hypothesis B**
> *Adaptation to the environment constitutes of continuous processes within the organisations rather than one-time interventions.*

The review of these hypotheses is found in Section 13.1, a brief outline will be presented now.

The testing of the first hypothesis did indicate that we have to revise the main principle that seems to dominate management science. Indeed, it has been shown that homeostasis does not fit as model for change when talking about dynamically changing environments, rather both the environment and organisations are on the move. The maintaining of homeostasis leads organisations to behave as allopietic systems, structurally closed and change embedded in their internal structure. Unlike allopoietic systems, organisations have the possibility to adapt their boundaries and deploy intense interaction for creating change. The so-called dissipative structures have found little support in this study; it remains unclear whether a lack of theory causes such or that this phenomenon hardly applies to organisations.

The testing of the second hypotheses has been found in the generation of variation, mutational steps, that constantly leads selection by the environment to find viable mutations that fix. Internal processes drive the variation, accumulation leads possibly to macromutations. Possible explanations of periods of turmoil find their origin in retrospective views on phenomena ruling out the more complex interactions of mechanisms to create that turmoil. For sure, one-time interventions do have limited effects, even sometimes negative effects as noted in the literature of management science.

17.1.3 Synthesis of Reference Model and Framework for Dynamic Adaptation

The reference model has served as basis for exploring existing management approaches and the six case studies. According to the reference model, organisations develop as allopietic systems with fuzzy boundaries and the capability for foresight, taking into account five issues:

- the distinction between genotype and phenotype. This points to the fact that internal changes will only lead to adaptation if they result in changes in the visible traits;
- the undertaking of adaptive walks. An adaptive walk in the fitness landscape should increase the fit between the organisation and its environment;
- the existence of developmental pathways. Path dependence exists in many ways, controlled by the equivalent of regulatory genes and epigenetic structures present in organisations;
- the criteria sustained fitness and evolvability. These two criteria specify that organisations should look for both local fitness peaks and global fitness peaks. Evolvability is driven by invading potential, the capability to penetrate new or other product-market combinations, and bifurcation, the capability to split companies (specialisation) or have a different focus for each product-market combination;
- the principle of self-organisation. This principle appears from theories on complex systems but has hardly been operationalised in management science. Weak evidence exists that the intense interaction with suppliers yields evolutionary results.

The reference model has been based on biological models for evolution; so far, the findings in management science have not really contradicted the validity of the reference model. Derived from the comparison of organisations and organisms, the reference model points to the gradual changes taking place that might have more effects than one-time interventions. Alike the macromutations in evolutionary biology (networks of developmental genes, heterochrony, heterotopy, epigenetics), one-time interventions appear to be deleterious, indeed, sometimes organisations are worse off. Some evidence exists that in course of time organisations revert to old structures after such interventions; also the relative low success rate of process innovations and Business Process Re-engineering efforts support this view. Hence, it seems reasonable to assume that transformations take place more gradually than expected; does a Darwinistic view on organisations hold?

The input of the review did lead to the creation of models within the Framework for Dynamic Adaptation. These models differs from the reference model in that extent that they focus more on the internal processes and structures of industrial companies (except the Collaboration Model, which focuses on the interaction with suppliers). The output of the models of the framework should meet the requirements of the issues of the reference model. The distinction between phenotype and genotype is found in the Innovation Impact Point Model (and the Model for the Dynamic Adaptation Capability). The assessment of innovations at the levels of breakthrough model constitutes the adaptive walks, supported by the capability for foresight through a new method for scenario planning. Integration of all aspects should be ensured by the Model for the Dynamic Adaptation Capability; the integrative aspect was stressed by several management studies and it can be encountered with the assessment of concepts of innovation at all levels for products, processes and organisational structures. A more flexible approach should reside in strategy approaches, this research propagates the use of dynamic strategies and scenario planning to address this matter. We might conclude that the models from the Framework for Dynamic Adaptation support the evolutionary development of organisations.

17.1.4 Dynamic Adaptation by Organisations

Moving away from the static approaches, the dynamics between the organisation and environment require an active role of the organisation. The dynamic capability of organisations depends on the ability of organisations to explore, to interpret the environment, and to actively generate variation.

The exploration of the environment consists of monitoring and scenario planning (a shift from views about strategy as relatively static to anticipation and consideration of alternatives). During periods of technological ferment, it becomes important for organisations to scan the environment for the emergence of features of dominant designs. The active reading of the environment will result in the more timely recognition of these features and their impact on the organisation (e.g. the development of internal capabilities or the search for horizontal collaboration). Such development might take place on (relatively) short term. A long-term approach based on scenario planning assists companies preparing for the future, not focused on one possible outcome but an array of alternative routes for different futures. Game theories provide a theoretical base for such analysis; however, they should not be used to predict one possible future, consisting of a mix from different strategies. Hence, the exploration of the environment exceeds the application of System Dynamics[52] for learning, promoted by Senge (1992).

Especially, the connection with suppliers (and other partners), aiming at horizontal and vertical integration, expands the possibilities to adapt to the dynamics of the environment. Interacting with suppliers enables companies to extend their base of capabilities and through organisational learning broaden the base of knowledge and skills. The active interaction between suppliers and organisation means (a) managing the business processes, the steady-state as supply chain and the breakthrough as business development as well as (b) managing the exchange relationships and interaction between resources. These two strands require different approaches although they meet each other in the actual capability of an organisation to adapt to the environment (Dekkers et al., 2004, pp. 67-68).

The active generation of variation, comprising all three types of breakthrough: product, process, and organisation innovation, serves as the base for companies to adapt. Without variation no evolutionary processes take place. The management of variation becomes possible through managing the Innovation Impact Point, an extension of the breakthrough model.

17.2 EVOLUTIONARY MODELS

The research into adaptation explored evolutionary models and did draw an analogy with the domain of organisations. This has resulted in a reference model for assessing the evolutionary development of organisations. This research was merely a start to explore the analogy between organisations and organisms. During the exploration, the importance of the punctuated equilibrium became clear. Additionally, the theories of the fitness landscapes and game theories yielded insight into the interaction between (genetic) variation and selectional processes.

17.2.1 Punctuated Equilibrium

The interest into the mechanisms of the punctuated equilibrium by many management scientists roots in its inherent inference for explaining alternate periods of turmoil and stasis. Within the field of biology, the emergence of this theory triggered new insight. Yet, after the turmoil this theory caused its merits for understanding evolutionary change move at the level of species and genera while still not yet make clear the factual mechanisms of mutations. This seems very well the case for management science, too. Elucidating sudden movements

---

[52] *System Dynamics aims at investigating the mechanisms of the environment, e.g. by looking at the dynamics of the beer supply chain (Senge et al., 1998, pp. 87-190).*

at industrial level, it leaves the question unanswered what and how to change. The work of Brown & Eisenhardt (1997) is a typical representation of this type of research.

The punctuated equilibrium has been brought forward to explain revolutionary changes, like Romanelli & Tushman (1994) do. These explanations rely on retrospection by which the changes are assessed and reviewed. Following the path of evolutionary biological models and the example of macro- and microinventions by Mokyr, these changes had their preludes. Most of the studies have not yet tried to look for the accumulation of changes and regulatory *genes* that govern the paths at which periods of turmoil occur.

Yet, individual companies have a large role in the visible changes at industrial level which follows the patterns of the punctuated equilibrium. Not only through active monitoring of emerging features of dominant designs but also by the generation of variation in all its aspects leading to changes in the phenotypes as perceived by the market. In evolutionary processes, both phenotypical changes and selection rule, therefore mutations do not always guarantee success, for companies too.

Putting it all together, especially the one-time interventions seen as representation of the punctuated equilibrium have very limited evolutionary effects for the development of industrial organisations. Successive changes, minor, cumulative or major, will lead to adaptation if accounted for the selectional process by the environment. The changes reside in the capability of organisations themselves to adapt by generating the mutations. Such a capability resides strongly in the skills and knowledge of the individuals in the organisations. Hence, adapting an organisation to the dynamics of the environment requires the participation of all within and related to the company.

17.2.2 Game Theories

A new stream of evolutionary models resides in the application of game theories to the domain of evolutionary biology. Originating from economic game theories, these theories describe speciation and related phenomena. Similar phenomena appear at the level of organisations and game theories seem to behold promises to explain these.

The game theories describe the interaction between entities, groups, and species in reactions between them and as response to the environment. Initially, these game theories limited themselves to detecting Evolutionary Stable Strategies and convergence stability in evolutionary biology based on the premise of static pay-offs. The route with Adaptive Dynamics creates the understanding of the more complex interactive behaviour between organisms and environments. These evolutionary models might have applications in the domain of organisations.

Within the context of this research, new routes for scenario planning methods might open based on the application of game theories. The danger arises that these methods will resemble again forecasts, predicting one possible future. Certainly, for evaluating proposals and explaining dynamics of change, scenario planning will be enhanced by using game theories.

17.2.3 Fitness Landscapes and Adaptive Dynamics

The application of game theories in evolutionary biology has paved the way for understanding the interaction between organism and environment. Similarly, we might think about organisations like organisms and then the game theories should have applications in the domain of organisations. Essential to understanding the interaction is the fitness landscape. These landscapes describe the fitness of organisations and they might vary from highly correlated to uncorrelated, from rugged to relatively flat. The concept of adaptive walks describes how organisations might improve their fitness by looking for local fitness peaks or global fitness peaks. The findings in biological research show that long jumps, equal to severe one-time interventions, aiming at finding global fitness peaks yields poor results. Multi-step mutations reaching for local fitness peaks creates more chances for finding optimal mutations. Game theories make us understand the mutual influence between organism and environment, between organisation and environment.

Adaptive Dynamics open the possibility for taking it all one step further. Speciation comes along with increased dimensions of the state space in which organisations operate. The ever-increasing specialisation in our industrial society enlarges the number of state space dimensions. On the fitness landscapes as defined by Kauffman, the correlation increases following the thoughts about the NK-model therewith decreasing the effectiveness of long jumps. Adaptive walks by step-wise mutations determine the future fitness of companies.

17.3 APPLIED SYSTEMS THEORY

The implications of adaptive walks should be integrated in the methodology of the Delft School Approach. The Delft School Approach has as main characteristics (see Appendix B):

- the interaction between goals, policy, and organisational structures;
- the mapping of processes (transformations), functions, and systems (transformations and control);
- the analysis and the design of process structures, organelle structures, and hierarchy at each stratum of the organisation;
- the modelling of these structures for the approach of analysis and design;

- the integral assessment of the policy and the organisational structure on main criteria.

As the methodology beholds a more static view on organisations the limitations for continuous change and adaptation emerging the study. The contemporary dynamic environments, the evaluation of existing approaches, and the creation of a Framework for Dynamic Adaptation with its models have shown the limits of the Systems Theory. A number of modifications are necessary; a further development based on the findings in this study has been labelled Applied Systems Theory (Dekkers, 2002). The modifications concern in particular the model for processes and the breakthrough model. Additionally, the principle of homeostasis has been questioned.

17.3.1 Equifinality and Homeostasis

Typically for engineering approaches, the principle of equifinality has found its way into the methodology. The research has shown that a dynamic approach calls for a more open view on boundaries and restrictions for possible solutions. Only designing organisations does not suffice, the design has to account for adaptive walks and developmental pathways, even though not fully developed yet. Equifinality, applicable at the third and fourth level of the systems hierarchy of Boulding, hardly holds for the complexity and evolution of organisations.

As part of the methodology, the main models within the Delft School Approach, the steady-state model, the breakthrough model, the design approach have embedded the principle of homeostasis. Organisational change is introduced periodically rather than continuously. The boundaries of the main process, i.e. the transformation process, are enclosed in processes aiming at maintaining homeostasis. Additionally, the initiating processes and evaluation processes contribute by setting feasible standards for the processes in the boundary of the steady-state model. The breakthrough model assumes implicitly that an organisation operates in relative isolation from the environment. The principles seem directly connected to the thoughts about autopoiesis and allopietic systems.

Homeostasis hardly guides the development and evolution of organisations. Through the open boundary that can be shifted by the organisation itself, through the interaction that drives internal variation and external evolution, the artificial boundary of an organisation is created by the entities constituting the organisation. The purposeful creation and maintenance of a boundary might even limit the long-term development of an organisation, as proven in Section 13.1. This phenomenon has created the need for models that describe interaction between entities.

17.3.2 Processes

To allow the description of interaction, the original generic model for processes as developed by in 't Veld (1998, pp. 32-35) does not suffice; Subsection 14.2.1 proposes a modification that shows that a process expresses the interaction between a flowing system and a residing system, a resource. This model opens up the possibility for modelling interactions.

Additionally, interaction takes place between resources participating in conducting a process. The process generates the outcomes by the transformation that occurs enacting on the flowing element, often resulting in the true output of the organisation (towards the environment). Resources provide the necessary means for the transformation, exploration, and their behaviour determines the performance of the company. Thus, improvements occur either by the changing allocation of resources to the process flow, the thought behind process innovation and Business Process Re-engineering, or through the changed behaviour of the resources themselves. Interaction, such as collaboration and learning, influence the behaviour of resources and might alter the output and the performance.

Additionally, this modified model might help to understand the relation between systems of organisations and cultures. Cultural change aims at changing the individual behaviour of agents (resources) as part of an organisation and therewith tries to influence outcomes of the process. Organisation seen as systems design leads to structural changes in processes, their interrelations to each other and to departmental structures of companies. Traditionally seen as two opposing models for an organisation, the metaphor of organisations as organisms, in his view meaning mostly systems theories (Morgan, 1997, pp. 33-71) and the metaphor of organisations as cultures (Morgan, 1997, pp. 199-152), these theories meet each other in the adapted model for processes. In management literature, these concepts hardly meet and when they do, like in Davenport (1993), they are treated separately. The connected processes of evaluation and learning enable organisations to advance in both the organisational systems and the cultural aspects. The new model for processes serves as a starting point for understanding this particular relationship.

17.3.3 Breakthrough Model

The modification for evaluation is also found in the breakthrough model. Both the learning processes and the adapted process model describe the structures needed to support continuous adaptation in combination with the Innovation Impact Point. The principle of the Innovation Impact Point means that improvements might affect any of the levels of the breakthrough model. This model shows that the impact only takes place at the highest level, the evaluation process (Innovation Impact Point 5). Therefore, the model has to be modified on this particular issue.

The second issue for modification concerns the strongly related setting of objectives and policy making, two parts of the breakthrough model. In 't Veld explicitly presents these processes as iterative, the determination of the objectives of a company followed by the setting of a policy while iterations lead to refinement; the allocation of resources, part of the policy, should follow the objectives. May be true as an inference, the evolutionary models shows a strong intertwining between these constructs and suggest to pronounce the intertwining. The resources at the disposition of an organisation (organisations have the freedom to choose their resources) determine the pathways of development, organisations as allopietic systems, and therewith the future of an organisation. In fact, this means a return to the original model of Malotaux (Malotaux & in 't Veld, 1969), not making this distinction present in the breakthrough model (see Figure 17.2).

17.3.4 Emergence of Organisations

Following the thoughts of this research, organisational processes and structures emerge rather than they are designed. McMaster (1996, p. 9) was right after all: *Companies emerge rather than being designed*. First, pathways determine the development of the organisation, the step-wise mutation that yields improvements and advantages in the selectional processes by the environment. During these step-wise mutations, the directional selection by the environment indicates the improvement of fitness. These step-wise mutations give the organisation space

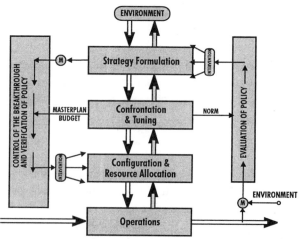

Figure 17.2: Adapted Breakthrough Model. The original breakthrough model has been changed to fit with the insight about adaptation by organisations. The processes of Goal Setting and Policy Formulation have been integrated in Strategy Formulation following the thoughts of evolutionary models.

to adapt to the changes rather performing a long jump that might not yield fitness advantages. Secondly, improvements are accumulated during step-wise mutations. Internal variation and accumulation of these will lead to mutations in the phenotype of an organisation, the mutation is not created but accumulated. The organisation should monitor the Internal Innovation Capability to assess the effect of variation, changes, and improvements. The organisation emerges through the developmental pathways and active monitoring, the Internal Innovation Capability.

The only case for intended organisational design appears when environmental changes call for a response. The organisation translate the changes in a possible

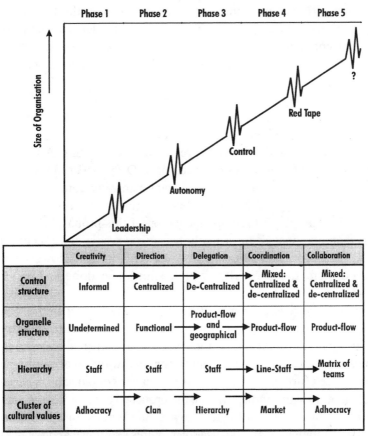

	Creativity	Direction	Delegation	Coordination	Collaboration
Control structure	Informal	Centralized	De-Centralized	Mixed: Centralized & de-centralized	Mixed: Centralized & de-centralized
Organelle structure	Undetermined	Functional	Product-flow and geographical	Product-flow	Product-flow
Hierarchy	Staff	Staff	Staff	Line-Staff	Matrix of teams
Cluster of cultural values	Adhocracy	Clan	Hierarchy	Market	Adhocracy

Figure 17.3: Proposal for developmental pathways connected to the Delft School Approach. Each phase has its own characteristic choices for the control, organelle and hierarchical structure connected to the life-cycle model if Greiner. Additionally, the findings about the cultural values have been added to the model. This proposal has not been tested and does not account for issues of the reference model, e.g. fuzzy boundaries, evolvability.

blueprint for the organisation, it might concern the products, processes or the organisational structure. Such an approach carries the danger of predicting one possible future, which will be impossible to reach. Alternatively, through scenario planning, several pathways might appear as possible routes, though management has to decide in time, the dimension time will tell which one will be the ultimate answer to challenges the organisation faces. Again, both ways do call on the organisation again to develop step-by-step to such a future rather than implementing a radical change in one time.

The theories known as the Delft School Approach, including Systems Theory, should be expanded with theories of developmental pathways. As part of such a pathway, the research proposes in Section 3.3 a life-cycle model based on the life-cycle model of Greiner; this can be expanded with the Cultural Change Model as presented in Section 13.4. The integrated model is depicted in Figure 17.3. The current models of this research should be seen as a first attempt in this direction but do certainly not behold a complete approach to the challenges of change.

A first case study showed already positive indications for the life-cycle approach. In this case, the organisational structure for the emergency services required renewal, the objectives for performance were not fully met while expectations were mounting due to increased public spending. After analysis, a blueprint was made for the new organisational design; that design was reviewed using the life-cycle model and developmental pathways from Figure 17.3. The outcome of the review pointed to a different structure in between the old situation and the original proposal; the implementation of this proposal caused far less problems than anticipated, most likely because it was a more natural path to follow than the more radical approach from the redesign. However, it is too early to confirm these results, which should be done 1-2 years after implementation.

The current models comprise of the Innovation Impact Point Model, the Model for the Dynamic Adaptation Capability, the scenario planning, the Collaboration Model; additionally, the research has launched a modified model for processes. The concepts of developmental pathways, evolvability and self-organisation need further expansion to the domain of organisations. The careful examination of the environment within the proposed approach provides already the possibility for a snapshot to increase sustained fitness on the short run; the long-term development of an organisation requires additional approaches to fully assess evolvability.

18   RECOMMENDATIONS

What should change? Section 18.1 will discuss the implementation of the generated concepts in industry. It will deal with which mechanisms industrial organisations might deploy to ensure continuous change and briefly indicate the changing role of management. Although having clear implications for industry, the research needs to continue to result in viable models for companies. Clearly, this strand of research needs the interaction between a range of related scientific domains to yield progress. Also, much more empirical research is needed to sustain the models and thoughts. Section 18.2 will expand on this matter.

18.1   IMPLEMENTATION IN INDUSTRIAL COMPANIES

Industrial thinking should convert from the ideas and behaviour based on the effectiveness of one-time interventions to managing continuous change (Chanaron [1990, p. 532] proposes a similar notion for technological genesis). So far, one-time interventions have dominated management science and practice based on the classical view on leadership as invested power. The research has shown that changes takes place at all levels within the organisation and the environment. Hence, static thinking has only its place in relatively calm environments, which we perceive as existing less and less. The dynamics of the environment call on different ways of managing industrial organisations, according to this particular research directed to continuous change happening in and around the organisation.

Active monitoring of the environment becomes an essential ingredient. This means not only looking for the emergence of dominant designs, possibilities for architectural innovation, but also more dynamic approaches to strategy, like scenario planning. The scanning for dominant designs and architectural innovations links directly to technological developments causing phenomena like the punctuated equilibrium. Active monitoring assists companies in timely recognition of trends. Scenario planning looks across the border of the trends manifesting itself, into the far future where uncertainties rule but not so that it makes it totally unpredictable. The anticipation on multiple futures resulting from scenario planning helps companies to be prepared when the future shapes up definitely.

Companies seen as allopietic systems with fuzzy boundaries (How would we call such systems?) seek active cooperation with suppliers and interaction with the environment. Through active cooperation new opportunities will emerge on which companies might act. Intense interaction supports dissipative structures in which new internal structures arise that suit the conditions of the environment.

Operating at the edge of chaos, yet ... Awareness by management that such enfolds without having a full grip seems most challenging, especially in environments that call on managers to achieve performance.

The deployment of the models of this research should assist managers in envisioning the development within the organisation and the trends of the interaction with the environment. These models, the Innovation Impact Point Model, the Model for the Dynamic Adaptation Capability, the Collaboration Model, and the proposed scenario planning, stand for tools for managing the changes occurring at the different levels in the organisation. Small nucleus groups in the organisation seem a possibility to manage the organisation, although not thoroughly investigated. However, management should avoid of getting trapped by interfering with the ongoing developments caused by innovations. Rather they should create awareness and cohesion. When organisations have nucleus groups, with their own expertise and innovation processes, and processes for breakthrough, the attention of management will shift to:

- determining which competencies are needed to achieve business goals for product-market combinations. These competencies might be assigned to units within the organisation in-house or might get shape through alliances with other firms. The strategy to follow depends on the overall strategy of the company, either following the path of specialisation in product market combinations or differentiation within the total supply chain; the differentation in the supply chain calls for adequate approaches to collaboration as expressed by the Collaboration Model;
- assuring and strengthening the bond between employees and the company as well as the relationships with partners and suppliers. In the case of innovations employees will participate in various projects and alliances. These contemporary collaborations and alliances cross each other at the same units at the same time. Therefore it might reinforce the feeling of belonging to certain projects and alliances rather than the own company. For people to be part of a team, they need to feel the backup of the mother company. Management should provide this security while at the same time the future holds uncertainties how the organisation will continue;
- increasing alertness and responsiveness on all levels and within each unit following developments in global markets, technology, etc. This alertness directs itself to as well solving quality problems, meeting changing clients' demands, developing new products, and maintaining its own expertise. For achieving goals in innovation not directed at incremental steps but on the long term, management needs to have visions extending over the horizon of lead-time of research and development. This will support creating the necessary stability for sustained growth.

Maintaining business growth through innovation strongly relies on the effective adaptation to changing market conditions and the incorporation of inventions, technologies, and internal innovations. To achieve so, the learning organisation proves of value as model for allowing knowledge development as driving force for architectural innovation, internally and by collaborations. The Innovation Impact Point indicates the need to adapt strategies to these innovations and create new business models together with adjusted performance requirements. Effective management of the cultural changes will finalise the transformation from one-time interventions to dynamic adaptation.

18.2 FURTHER RESEARCH

Although this study has generated some model to deal with continuous change and adaptation, the research into adaptation has just begun. Viewing the study as an initial analysis, the cooperation between fields of sciences might result in further expansion of the reference model; the focus of the current research has been on the interaction between environment and entity. The study has not looked at knowledge and skills as base for analogies with recombination, one of the powerful drivers of organisms for adaptation. Furthermore, this study did not cover all the relevant literature on evolutionary biological models, like models of co-evolution and altruism. Even though it reflects the state-of-the-art, it became impossible to review all relevant literature in biology due to its enormous extent, biologists are indeed productive. What can be learned is that advances in biology come about through active cooperation between disciplines, something unequalled in management science.

One of the further studies might focus on empirical studies of companies based on the knowledge of this research, combining different fields of management science, history, economy, evolutionary biology, etc. The analysis of the aviation industry might serve as an example. Section 2.2 used the available models of Miles & Snow and Farjoun to analyse this industry. The research has added additional insight to these models, to the already existing literature on organisational forms[53] and organisational ecology, justifying a more detailed analysis of this industrial branch. Possibly, such an investigation might direct itself to other industrial branches. Much might be gained from predictive modelling in this respect; most of the studies in this field have a retrospective character, emphasising explanations that are descriptive, such as the punctuated

---

[53] *The concept of organisational form has not sublimated in a new description. Even though it has the characteristics of the phenotype in biology, it is advised to the academics of management science to operationalise this notion by using the biological understanding of phenotype to enhance it and transform it in a more practical way.*

equilibrium. The individual life-cycle of companies defined by mutational steps should find its way into these investigations. The phenomena of adaptive walks and developmental pathways have received too little attention so far from a heuristic point of view. These investigations might profit from quantitative modelling like in Adaptive Dynamics, even though these models have a theoretical base with quite practical implications.

The particular research of this research had to restrict itself to the review of six case studies from the Delft School Approach. An expansion of the survey base from six to 20-30 cases, if possible more, will yield more reliable findings to determine the applicability of this approach and its relation to the adaptation by industrial companies. In itself successful, the number of implemented solutions from the approach is relatively high by indication, the question remains how effectively industrial problem solving at postgraduate level contributes to the adaptation processes by companies. A further extension of the Delft School Approach by complementing and modifying with some of the models found here will enhance the methodology. In any case, the concepts of adaptive walks and developmental pathways have potential to assist in implementation and increase utilisation of the underlying methodology.

To arrive at models for adaptation, the research reviewing the existing management literature has yielded models that did not exist before:

- the concepts of innovation in relation to decision-making (Subsection 10.2.3);
- the implications of architectural innovation (Subsections10.2.2, 10.3.2);
- the modelling of the Learning Organisation (Sections 14.1.2, 14.2.1);
- the modelling of Knowledge Management (Subsections 12.2.2, 12.2.4).

These models and proposals need reviewing on their merits to these fields of management science. The breakthrough model has served as background for modelling the Learning Organisation and Knowledge Management, though it seems incomplete in some ways to deal with issues in these fields, e.g. dynamic control and absorptive capacity. Within the scope of this research, these models paved the way for Framework for Dynamic Adaptation.

Within the proposed framework, the models for industrial application, i.e. the Innovation Impact Point Model, the Model for the Dynamic Adaptation Capability, the scenario planning based on game theories, the Collaboration Model, need further development. During the application in the field of Strategic Capacity Management, these models served as background for analysing and solving challenges for adaptation. These models have not reached the stage of totally practical tools and methods, a prerequisite for companies to implement these in practice; for example, decision-making on the concepts of innovation linked to the Innovation Impact Points requires more attention. The impact from static to dynamic thinking requires attention since most practitioners presume that the power of one-time interventions is unequalled. Meanwhile, practitioners experience problems with continuing static views: the reality of inertia present in the organisation and its structure forces them to take a different look at the challenges they face.

The concept of self-organisation has hardly been addressed by the models developed so far. Nevertheless, this seems of utmost importance to the development of organisations, what does self-organisation constitute, and how might we create dissipative structures? It is suggested that semi-autonomous groups provide excellent opportunities for self-organisation. Management science has paid little attention to this matter, it should be integrated with other views like happened in evolutionary biology. In any case, evolutionary biology acted as a breeding ground for a more profound look at daily reality in ecological systems, may be evolutionary management science will provoke the same for industrial systems.

REFERENCES

Abell D.F. Defining the Business. Englewood Cliffs: Prentice-Hall, 1980.

Abernathy, W., Utterback, J. Patterns of industrial innovation. *Technology Review*, 80(7), 1978: 40-47.

Abernathy, W., Clark, K. Innovation: Mapping the Winds of Creative Destruction. *Research Policy*, 14(1), 1998: 51-61.

Achilladelis, B., Antonakis, N. The dynamics of technological innovation: the case of the pharmaceutical industry. *Research Policy*, 30(4), 2001: 535-588.

Adler, P.S., Cole, R.E. Designed for Learning: A Tale of Two Auto Plants. *Sloan Management Review*, 34(3), 1993: 85-94.

Aken, J.E. van, Weggeman, P. Managing learning in informal innovation networks: overcoming the Daphne –dilemma. *R&D Management*, 30(2), 2000: 139-149.

Ansoff, I. Corporate Strategy. New York: McGraw-Hill, 1965.

Argyris, C., Schön, D.A. Organizational learning: a theory of action perspective. Reading: Addison-Wesley, 1978.

Armistead, C. Knowledge Management and process performance. *Journal of Knowledge Management*, 3(2), 1999: 143-154.

Arrow, K. The limits of organization. New York: Norton, 1974.

Arshad, A. Evolution and the Qur'an. [online] The Talks.Origin Archive, 24 November 1996 [cited 27 January 2003]. Available from Internet: <http:/www.talkorigins.org/origins/postmonth/nov96.html>.

Arthur, W.B. Competing Technologies, Increasing Returns, and Lock-in by historical Events. *The Economic Journal*, 99(394), 1989: 116-131.

Avella, L. Focal points in manufacturing strategic planning in Spain. *International Journal of Operations and Production Management*, 19(12), 1999: 1291-1317.

Baaij, M.G., Lekkerkerk, P., Weerdt, N. van der. Kerncompetentiesbenadering Prahalad en Hamel slechts beperkt uitvoerbaar. *Holland Management Review*, 16(67), 1999: 24-29.

Baker, F. Introduction: Organizations as Open Systems. *In:* Baker, F. Organizational Systems, General Systems Approaches to Complex Organizations. Homewood: Richard D. Irwin, 1973: 1-25.

Barnett, W.P. The organizational ecology of a technical system. *Administrative Science Quarterly*, 35(1), 1990: 31-60.

Barnett, W.P. The Dynamics of Competitive Intensity. *Administrative Science Quarterly*, 42(1), 1997: 128-160.

Baum, J.A.C. Organisational ecology. *In:* Clegg, S.R., Hardy, C., Nord, W.R. Handbook of Organisation Studies. London: Sage, 1996: 77-114.

Baum, J.A.C., McGahan, A.M. Business Strategy over the Industry Lifecycle. [online] [cited 18 June 2003]. Available from Internet: <http:/www.rotman.utoronto.ca/~buam/v21_toc.html>.

Baum, J.A.C., Oliver, C. Institutional embedddedness and the dynamics of organizational populations. *American Sociological Review*, 57(4), 1992: 540-559.

Beatty, C.A. Implementing Advanced Manufacturing Technologies: Rules of the Road. *Sloan Management Review*, 33(4), 1992: 49-59.

Beer, M. Managing Strategic Alignment. *In:* Berger, L.A., Sikora, M.J. The Change Management Handbook. Chicago: Richard D. Irwin, 1994: 33-48.

Beer, M., Eisenstat, R.A., Spector, B. Why Change Programs Don't Produce Change. *Harvard Business Review,* 68(6), 1990: 158-166.

Beer, S. Cybernetics and Management. New York: John Wiley, 1959.

Beer, S. Brain of the Firm, The managerial cybernetics of organization. London: Allen Lane The Penguin Press, 1972.

Beer, S. Diagnosing the system for organizations. Chichester: John Wiley, 1985.

Beinhocker, E.D. Robust Adaptive strategies. *Sloan Management Review,* 40(3), 1999: 95-106.

Bell, Michael A. Bridging the gap between population biology and paleobiology. *Evolution,* 54(4), 2000: 1457-1461.

Berger, L.A. Change Management. *In:* Berger, L.A., Sikora, M.J. The Change Management Handbook. Chicago: Richard D. Irwin, 1994: 1-23.

Berggren, C. Point/Counterpoint: NUMMI vs. Uddevalla. *Sloan Management Review,* 35(2), 1993: 37-50.

Bergh, J.C.J.M. van den. Firm Behaviour and Organisation from an Evolutionary Perspective. *In:* Groot, H.L.F. de, Nijkamp, P. Entrepreneurship in the Modern Space-Economy: Evolutionary and Policy Perspectives. Cheltenham: Edward Elgar Publishing, 2003.

Bergh, J.C.J.M. van den, Dekkers, R. Beyond Simplified Economic Darwinism: Advanced Evolutionary Concepts in Economics and Management Science. *Journal of Evolutionary Economics* (forthcoming)

Bergh, J.C.J.M. van den, Gowdy, J.M. The microfoundations of macroeconomics: an evolutionary perspective. *Cambridge Journal of Economics,* 27(1), 2003: 65-84.

Bergh, J.C.J.M. van den, Stagl, S. Coevolution of Economic Behaviour and Institutions: Towards a Theory of Institutional Change. *Journal of Evolutionary Economics,* 13(3), 2003: 289-317.

Berman, P. Thinking about Programmed and Adaptive Implementation: Matching Strategies to Situations. *In:* Ingram, H., Mann, D. Why Policies Succeed or Fail. Beverly Hills, Sage: 1980: 205-227.

Bertalanffy, L. von. General System Theory. New York: Braziller, 1973.

Bessant, J. Developing technological capability through manufacturing strategy. *International Journal of Technology Management,* 14(2/3/4), 1997: 177-195.

Bessant, J., Caffyn, S., Gallagher, M. An evolutionary model of continuous improvement behaviour. *Technovation,* 21(2), 2001: 67-77.

Bhatt, G.D. Organizing knowledge in the knowledge development cycle. *Journal of Knowledge Management,* 4(1), 2000: 15-26.

Biazzo, S. Approaches to business process analysis: a review. *Business Process Management Journal,* 6(2), 2000: 99-112.

Bierly III, P.E., Kessler, E.H., Christensen, E.W. Organizational learning, knowledge and wisdom. *Journal of Organizational Change,* 13(6), 2000: 595-618.

Biggiero, L. Are Firms Autopoietic Systems. *In:* Geyer, F., Zouwen, J. van der. Sociocybernetics: complexity, autopoiesis and observation of social systems. Greenwood: Westpoort, 2001.

Bikker, H. Lecture notes wb5413. Delft: Delft University of Technology, 1993.

Bikker, H., Dekkers, R. The Order Entry Matrix: Keystone for Productivity of Design and Manufacturing. *In:* Proceedings of the 2nd International Conference Product Development Management on New Approaches to Development and Engineering, Göteborg, 1994: 44-58.

Blumentritt, R., Johnston, R. Towards a Strategy for Knowledge Management. *Technology Analysis & Strategic Management*, 11(3), 1999: 287-300.

Boeing. News Releases. [online] Boeing Company, 1997-2003. Available from Internet: <http://www.boeing.com/news/releases/>.

Boer, H., During, W.E. Innovation, what innovation? A comparison between product, process and organization innovation. *International Journal of Technology Management*, 22(1/2/3), 2001: 83-107.

Boersma, J.S.K.Th, Stegwee, R.A. Exploring the issues in Knowledge Management. [online] Groningen: University of Groningen, 1996 [cited 29 September 2000]. Available from Internet: <http://www.docserver.ub.rug.nl/eldoc/som/96A09>.

Bogman, N.J. Creating a Dynamic Capability based on Knowledge. Delft: Delft University of Technology/Section Production Technology and Organisation, 2000.

Bomer, G.B.J. De Lerende Organisatie. *Harvard Holland Review*, (22), 1990: 21-31.

Bond, T.C. Systems analysis and business process mapping: a symbiosis. *Business Process Management Journal*, 5(2), 1999: 164-177.

Boswijk, H.K. Complexiteit in evolutionair en organisatorisch perspectief; het zoeken naar balans tussen vermogens en uitdagingen. Rotterdam: Erasmus Universiteits Drukkerij, 1992.

Botter, C.H., Boer, H., Fisscher, O.A.M. Industrie en organisatie. Den Haag: Kluwer Bedrijfswetenschappen, 1994.

Boulding, K.E. General Systems Theory. The skeleton of science. *Management Science*, (2), 1956: 197-208.

Boulding, K.E. Ecodynamics: a new theory of social evolution. London: Sage, 1981.

Boutellier, R., Kiss, E. Wie Industrie-design und Innovation neue Märkte schaffen. *io Management Zeitschrift*, 65(4), 1996: 24-28.

Bowen, H.K., Clark, K.B., Holloway, C.A., Wheelwright, S.C. Development Projects: The Engine of Renewal. *Harvard Business Review*, 72(5), 1994: 108-120.

Boyer, K.K., Pagell, M. Measurement issues in empirical research: improving measures of operations strategy and advanced manufacturing technology. *Journal of Operations Management*, 18(3), 2000: 361-374.

Braganza, A., Myers, A. Issues and Dilemmas Facing Organizations in the effective Implementation of BPR. *Business Change and Re-engineering*, 3(2), 1998: 38-51.

Brams, S.J. Biblical Games, Game Theory and the Hebrew Bible. Cambridge: MIT Press, 2003.

Brandenburger, A.M., Nalebuff, B.J. Co-opetition. New York: Currency Doubleday, 1996.

Brandligt, S.M. Management bij stagnatie. Delft: Delft University of Technology/Section Industrial Organisation and Management, 1992.

Brouwer, A. Trend Watching through Scenario Planning. Delft: Delft University of Technology/Section Production Technology and Organisation, 2002.

Brown, J.S., Vincent, T.L. A Theory for the Evolutionary Game. *Theoretical Population Biology*, 31, 1987: 140-166.

Brown, S.L., Eisenhardt, K.M. The art of Continuous Change: Linking Complexity Theory and Time-Paced Evolution in Relentlessly Changing Organizations. *Administrative Science Quarterly*, 42(1), 1997: 1-34.

Brown, W.B. Systems, Boundaries, and Information Flow. *In:* Baker, F. Organizational Systems, General Systems Approaches to Complex Organizations. Homewood: Richard D. Irwin, 1973: 236-246.

Bruggeman, J.P. Formalizing Organizational Ecology. Amsterdam: ILLC Publications, 1996.

Bruijn, J.A. de, Heuvelhof, E.F. ten. Management in netwerken. Utrecht: Lemma, 1999.

Bryant, T., Chan, D. BPR – to Redesign or not to Redesign. *Business Change and Re-engineering*, 3(2), 1998: 52-61.

Buckler, B. A learning process model to achieve continuous improvement and innovation. *The Learning Organization*, 3(3), 1996: 31-39.

Bultje, R., Wijk, J. van. Taxonomy of virtual organizations, based on definitions, characteristics and typology. *VoNet: The Newsletter*, 2, 1998: 7-21.

Burgelman, R.A., Maidique, M.A., Wheelwright, S.C. Strategic Management of Technology and Innovation. Chicago: Irwin, 1996.

Burgelman, R.A., Sayles, L. Inside corporate innovation, Strategy, Structure, and Managerial Skills. New York: Free Press, 1986.

Burt, D.N. Managing Product Quality through Strategic Purchasing. *Sloan Management Review*, 31(3), 1989: 39-48.

Bush, G.L. (1998). The conceptual radicalization of an evolutionary biologist. *In:* Howard, D., Berlocher, S. Endless Forms: Species and Speciation. Oxford: Oxford University Press, 1998: 425-438.

Campbell, D.T. Variation, selection and retention in sociological evolution. *General Systems*, 14, 1969: 69-85.

Cánez, L.E., Platts, K., Probert, D.R. Developing a framework for make-or-buy decisions. *International Journal of Operations & Production Management*, 20(11), 2000: 1313-1330.

Carillo, M.R., Zazzaro, A. The Enigma of Medieval Craft Guilds: A Model of Social Inertia and Technological Change. *In:* Salvadori, N. Old and New Growth Theories. Cheltenham: Edward Elgar, 2001.

Carneiro, A. How does knowledge management influence innovation and competitiveness? *Journal of Knowledge Management*, 4(2), 2000: 87-98.

Casagrandi, R., Gatto, M. Habitat Destruction, Environmental Catastrophes, and Metapopulation Extinction. *Theoretical Population Biology,* 61(2), 2002: 127-140.

CBS. Vijfennegentig jaar statistiek in tijdreeksen (1899-1994). Den Haag: SDU, 1994.

CBS. Standaard Bedrijfsindeling (SBI) 1993. [online] Voorburg: CBS, 2003 [cited 23 February 2003]. Available from Internet: <http://www.cbs.nl/nl/standaarden/classificaties/sbi>.

CBS. De Nederlandse economie in 2000. Voorburg: CBS, 2001.

Chanaron, J.J. Towards and Ecogenetics of Technological Change: an Essay. *In:* Khalil, T., Bayraktar, B. Proceedings of the 2nd Internation Conference on Management of Technology. Miami: University of Miami, 1990: 525-534.

Chanaron, J.-J., Dekkers, R. Technology Leadership in the 21st Century: Global Challenge for East and West. *e-Journal of the International Forum on Technology Management*, 1, 2004: 1-7.

Checkland, P. Systems Thinking, Systems Practice. Chichester: John Wiley, 1981.

Checkland, P., Scholes, J. Soft Systems Methodology in Action. Chichester: John Wiley, 1993.

Child, P., Diederichs, R., Sanders, F.-H., Wisniowiski, S. SMR Forum: The Management of Complexity. *Sloan Management Review*, 33(1), 1991: 73-80.

Childe, S.J., Maull, R.S., Bennett, J. Frameworks for Understanding Business Process Re-engineering. *International Journal of Operations & Production Management,* 14(12), 1994: 22-34.

Choi, C.F., Chan. S.L. Business process re-engineering: evocation, elucidation and exploration. *Business Process Management,* 3(1), 1997: 39-63.

Christensen, C.M., Suárez, F.F., Utterback, J.M. Strategies for Survival in Fast-Changing Industries. *Management Science,* 44(12), 1998: 207-220.

Cohen, W.M., Levinthal, D.A. Absorptive Capacity: A New Perspective on Learning and Innovation. *Administrative Science Quarterly,* 35(1), 1990: 128-152.

Colby, C. Introduction to Evolutionary Biology. [online] The Talks.Origin Archive, 7 January 1996 [cited 31 May 2002]. Available from Internet: <http://www.talkorigins.org/faqs/faq-intro-to-biology.html>.

Cole, K.C. The universe and the teacup. New York: Harcourt Brace, 1998.

Contractor, F.J., Lorange, P. Why should firms cooperate? *In:* F.J. Contractor, Lorange, P. Cooperative Strategies in International Business. Lexington Books, 1988.

Cooper, R., DeJong, D.V., Forsythe, R., Ross, T. Forward Induction in the Battle-of-the-Sexes. *American Economic Review,* 83(5), 1993: 1303-1316.

Corbett, L.M., Claridge, G.S. Key manufacturing capability elements and business performance. *International Journal of Production Research,* 40(1), 2002: 109-131.

Coulson-Thomas, C.J. BPR and the learning organization. *The Learning Organization,* 3(1), 1996: 16-21.

Cowan, G.E., Pines, D., Meltzer, D. Complexity; metaphors, models and reality. Reading: Addison-Wesley, 1994.

Darwin, C.R. On the Origin of Species by Means of Natural Selection. 1859.

Davenport, T.H. Process Innovation, Reengineering Work through Information Technology. Boston: Harvard Business School Press, 1993.

Davenport, T.H. Ten Principles of Knowledge Management and Four Case Studies. *Knowledge and Process Management,* 4(3), 1997: 187-208.

Davis, S., Botkin, J. The Company of Knowledge-Based Business. *Harvard Business Review,* 72(5), 1994: 165-170.

Dawkins, R. The Selfish Gene. Oxford: Oxford University Press, 1989.

Dehaëne, P. La Défi de la Complexité. [online] [cited 13 August, 1997]. Available from Internet: <http://edfgdf.fr/im/html/fr/bib/bic17/13.htm>.

Dekkers, R. Trends for Management and Organisation of Innovation. *In:* Proceedings of the 6th International Forum on Technology Management. Amsterdam, 1996: 415-430.

Dekkers, R. Concurrent Engineering and Project management as Tools for Product Development. *In:* Proceedings of the 4th International Product Development Conference. Stockholm, 1997a: 241-250.

Dekkers, R. Global Manufacturing: Technology Assessment and Outsourcing. *In:* Proceedings of the 7th International Forum on Technology Management. Kyoto, 1997b: 288-295.

Dekkers, R. Integrated Product Development: Manufacturing Aspects in Product Development. *In:* Proceedings of the 6th International Product Development Management Conference. Cambridge (U.K.), 1999: 21-334.

Dekkers, R. Strategic Capacity Management. *In:* Proceedings of the 15th International Conference on Production Research. Limerick, 1999: 213-216

Dekkers, R. Models for Decision-Making on Outsourcing. *International Journal of Production Research*, 38(17), 2000a: 4085 – 4096.

Dekkers, R. Organelle Structures: Strategic Choice of Performance Management of Manufacturing. *In:* Proceedings of the First World Conference on Production and Operations Management. [CD-ROM] Sevilla, 2000b.

Dekkers, R., 2001, Strategic Framework and Adaptation Model for Technology Assessment. *In:* Proceedings of the 10th International Conference on Management of Technology. [CD-ROM] Lausanne, 2001.

Dekkers, R. Strategic Capacity Management: Balancing Technological Demands and Performance Criteria. *Journal of Materials and Processing Technology*, 139(1-3), 2003: 385-393.

Dekkers, R. Lecture Notes wb5428 Applied Systems Theory. Delft: Delft University of Technology/ Section Production Technology and Organisation, 2002.

Dekkers, R. Contemporary Approaches for Adaptation Strategies - Review and Evaluation, 3rd interim report. Delft: Delft University of Technology/Section Production Technology and Organisation, 2003.

Dekkers, R., Sauer, A., Schönung, M., Schuh, G. Collaborations as Complex Systems. *In:* Gregory, M., Shi, Y. (eds.) Designing and Operating Global Manufacturing & Supply Networks, Proceedings of the 9th Annual Cambridge International Manufacturing Symposium. Cambridge: IMNet/CIM, 2004: 60-77.

Dekkers, R., Sopers, F.P.M. Production Control and the Order Entry Point. *In:* Proceedings of the 16th International Conference on Production Research. [CD-ROM] Prague, 2001.

Delbridge, R., Barton, H. Organizing for continuous improvement, Structures and roles in automotive plants. *International Journal of Operations & Production Management*, 22(6), 2002: 680-692.

Deschamps. J., Nayak, P.R. Product Juggernauts: how companies can mobilize to generate a stream of market winners. Boston: Harvard Business School Press, 1995.

Dienel, H., Lyth, P. Flying the flag. Chippenham: Antony Row, 1998.

Dorak, M.T. Introduction to Evolutionary Biology. [online] 2 May 2002 [cited 3 June 2002]. Available from Internet: <http://www.dorkamt.tripod.com/evolution/intro.html>.

Douthwaite, B., Keatinge, J.D.H., Park, J.R. Why promising technologies fail: the neglected role of user innovation during adoption. *Research Policy*, 30(5), 2001: 819-836.

Drago, W., Geisler, E. Business process re-engineering: lessons from the past. *Industrial Management & Data Systems*, 97(8), 1997: 297-303.

Dronrijp, D.J. Shaping the corporate culture to enhance organizational performance. Delft: Delft University of Technology/Section Production Technology and Organisation, 2000.

Drucker, P.F. Management in de Praktijk. Amsterdam: J.H. de Bussy, 1978.

Drucker, P.F. Met het oog op de toekomst. Schiedam: Scriptum Management, 1993.

Drucker, P.F. The Discipline of Innovation. *Harvard Business Review*, 76(6), 1998: 149-157.

Dutton, J.E., Jackson, S.E. Categorizing Strategic Issues: Links to Organizational Action. *Academy of Management Review*, (12), 1987: 76-90.

Eisenhardt, K.M. Strategy as Strategic Decision Making. *Sloan Management Review*, 40(3), 1999: 65-72.

Eisenhardt, K.M., Brown, S.L. Time Pacing: Competing in Markets that won't stand still. *Harvard Business Review,* 76(2), 1998: 59-68.

Eldredge, N., Gould, S.J. Punctuated Equilibrium: an alternative to phyletic gradualism. *In:* Schopf, T.J.M. Models in Paleobiology. San Fransisco: Cooper & Co., 1972: 82-115.

Elsberry, W. Punctuated Equilibria. [online] The Talks.Origin Archive, 4 February 1996 [cited 31 May 2002]. Available from Internet: <http://www.talkorigins.org/faqs/punc-eq.html>.

Emblemsvåg, J., Bras, B. Process thinking - a new paradigm for science and engineering. *Futures*, 32(7), 2000: 635-654.

Emery, F.E. Systems Thinking. Middlesex: Penguin, 1972.

Emery, F.E., Trist, E.L. Socio-technical systems. *In:* Emery, F.E. Systems Thinking. Middlesex: Penguin, 1972: 281-296.

Encyclopaedia Brittannica. The Theory of Evolution. *In:* Encyclopaedia Brittannica, Vol. 18. Chicago: Encyclopaedia Brittanica, 1986: 981-1011.

Faber, M., Proops, J.L.R. Evolution, Time, Production and the Environment. Heidelberg: Springer, 1990.

Farjoun, M. Towards an organic perspective on strategy. *Strategic Management Journal*, 23(7), 2002: 561-594.

Fiol, C.M., Lyles, M.A. Organizational learning. *Academy of Management Review*, 10(4), 1985: 803-813.

Fischer, D., Hafen, U. Immer wieder die gleichen Fehler; Weshalb Reengineering-projekte in KMU so oft scheitern. *io Management*, 66(6), 1997: 38-45.

Fleming, L., Sorenson, O. Technology as a complex adaptive system. *Research Policy*, 30(7), 2001: 1019-1039.

Fokkema, J.T. Twee culturen. *de Ingenieur,* 115(9), 2003: 54-57.

Forte, M., Hoffman, J.J., Lamont, B.T., Brockmann, E.N. Organizational Form and Environment: An Analysis of Between-Form and Within-Form Responses to Environmental Change. *Strategic Management Journal*, 21(7), 2000: 753-773.

Fowler, S.W., King, A.W., Marsh, S.J., Victor, B. Beyond products: new strategic imperatives for developing competencies in dynamic environments. *Journal of Engineering and Technology Management*, 17(3-4), 2000: 357-377.

Freeman, J., Hannan, M.T. Niche width and the dynamics of organizational populations. *American Journal of Sociology*, 88, 1983: 116-145.

Friar, J., Horwitch, M. The Emergence of Technology Strategy: A new Dimension of Strategic Management. *Technology in Society*, 7(2-3), 1985:143 – 178.

Friedrich, S.A. Was ist "Core" und was ist "Non-Core"? *io Management*, 69(4), 2000: 18-23.

Friedrich S.A., Hinterhuber, H.H. Restrukturierung auf dem Prüfstand: Streben wir nach einer "falschen" Wettbewerbsfähigkeit? *io Management*, 67(1/2), 1998: 16-21.

Galbraith, J., Designing complex Organizations. Reading: Addison-Wesley, 1973.

Garvin, D.A. Building a learning organization. *Harvard Business Review*, 71(4), 1993: 78-91.

Geritz, Stefan, A.H. and Metz, J.A.J., Kisdi, Éva, Meszéna, Géza. Dynamics of Adaptation and Evolutionary Branching. *Physical Review Letters,* 78(10), 1997: 2024-2027.

Geroski, P.A., Mazzucato, M. Modelling the dynamics of industry populations. *International Journal of Industrial Organization,* 19(7), 2001: 1003-1022.

Gertsen, F. How continuous improvement evolves as companies gain experience. *International Journal of Technology Management*, 22(4), 2001: 303-326.

Geus, A. de. The Living Company. London: Nicholas Brealy Publishing, 1999.

Ghemawat, P., Costa, J.E. The organizational tension between static and dynamic efficiency. *Strategic Management Journal*, 14, 1993: 59-73.

Gilfillan, S. Inventing the Ship. Chicago: Ship. Follett Publishing: 1935.

Glas, G.F. Industriële Netwerken. Groningen: Rijksuniversiteit Groningen, 1996.

Glaser, B.J., Strauss, A.L. The Discovery of Grounded Theory. Chicago: Aldine, 1967.

Gleick, J. Chaos, Making of a New Science. New York: Penguin, 1988.

Goethe, J.W. von. Faust. München: Wilhelm Goldman Verlag, 1832.

Gold, B. Towards the increasing integration of management functions: needs and illustrative advances. *International Journal of Technology Management*, Special Publication on the Role of Technology in Corporate Policy, 1991: 10-20.

Goldstone, J.A. Efflorescenes and Economic Growth in World History. *Journal of World History*, 13(2), 2002: 323-389.

Gomory, R.E., Schmitt, R.W. Science and Product. *Science*, (240), May 1998: 1131-1204.

Goold, M., Campbell, A. Desperately Seeking Synergy. *Harvard Business Review*, 76(3), 1998: 130-143.

Gordon, S.S., Stewart, W.H., Sweo, R., Luker, W.A. Convergence Versus Strategic Reorientation: The Antecedents of Fast-paced Organizational Change. *Journal of Management*, 26(5), 2000: 911-945.

Gould, S.J., Eldredge, N. Punctuated equilibria: the tempo and mode of evolution reconsidered. *Paleobiology*, 3, 1977: 115-151.

Gould, S.J. Is a new and general theory of evolution emerging? *Paleobiology,* 6 (1), 1980: 119-130.

Granstrand, O. Towards a theory of the technology-based firm. *Research Policy*, 27(5), 1998: 465-489.

Grant, R.M. Prospering in Dynamic Competitive Environments: Organizational Capability as Knowledge Integration. *Organization Science,* 7(4), 1996: 375-387.

Grant, R.M., Krishnan, R., Shani, A.B., Baer, R. Appropriate Manufacturing Technology: A Strategic Approach. *Sloan Management Review*, 33(1), 1991: 43-54.

Gray, M.W. The evolutionary origins of organelles. *Trends in Genetics,* 5(9), 1989: 294-299.

Griffiths, R.T. Industrial retardation in the Netherlands, 1830-1850. The Hague: Martinus-Nijhoff, 1979.

Griffiths, R.T. Achterlijk, achter of anders? Aspecten van de economische ontwikkeling van Nederland in de 19ᵉ eeuw. Amsterdam: Vrije Universiteit, 1981.

Greiner, L.E. Revolutions as Organisations Grow. *Harvard Business Review,* 76(3), 1998: 55-67.

Gromko, M.H. What is frequency dependent selection? *Evolution,* 31, 1976: 438-442.

Gunsteren, L.A. van. Management of industrial R&D, a viewpoint from practice. Delft: Eburon, 1992.

Haaf, W. ten, Bikker, H., Adriaanse, D.J. Fundamentals of business engineering and management. Delft: Delft University Press, 2002.

Hagel III, J., Singer, M. Ontbundeling van de onderneming: welk proces is uw core-business? *PEM*, 15(3), 1999: 3-15.

Hagen. E.E. Analytical Models in the Study of Social Systems. *In:* Baker, F. Organizational Systems, General Systems Approaches to Complex Organizations. Homewood: Richard D. Irwin, 1973: 73-84.

Hamel, G., Prahalad, C.K. Competing for the future. Boston: Harvard Business School Press, 1994.

Hamel, G. Opinion: Strategy Innovation and the Quest for Value. *Sloan Management Review*, 39(2), 1998: 7-14.

Hamilton, W.F. Managing technology as a strategic asset. *International Journal of Technology Management*, 14(2/3/4), 1997: 163-176.

Hammer, M., Champy, J. Reengineering the corporation. New York: Harper Collins, 1993.

Hanes, J. What is Darwinism? [online] The Talk.Origins Archive [cited 14 February 2003]. Available from Internet: <http://www.talkorigins.org/faqs/darwinism.html>.

Hannan, M.T., Freeman, J. The Population Ecology of Organizations. *American Journal of Sociology*, 83(4), 1977: 929-984.

Hannan, M.T., Freeman, J. Organizational ecology. Cambridge: Harvard University Press, 1989.

Heck, A. Strategische Partnerschaften zum operativen Erfolg führen. *io Management*, 69(4), 2000: 24-31.

Heijden, K. van der. Scenarios, the art of strategic conversation. Chicester: Wiley, 1996.

Henderson, R., Clark, K. Architectural Innovation: The Reconfiguration of Existing Product Technologies and the Failure of Established Firms. *Administrative Science Quarterly*, 35(1), 1990: 9-30.

Herbig, P.A., The innovation matrix: culture and structure prerequisites to innovation. Westport: Quorum Books, 1994.

Heylighen, F. Fitness Landscapes. [on-line] Principia Cybernetica Web, 22 July 1999 [cited: 20 February 2005]. Available from Internet: <http://pespmc1.vub.ac.be/FITLANDS.html>.

Hines, W.G. Strategy stability in complex populations. *Journal of Applied Probability*, 17, 1980: 600-610.

Hjalager, A-M. Organisational ecology in the Danish restaurant sector. *Tourism Management*, 21(3), 2000: 271-280.

Hoffmann, A.R., Hercus, M.J. Evironmental Stress as an Evolutionary Force. *BioScience*, 50(3), 2000: 217-226.

Hofstede, G. Cultures and Organizations, Intercultural Cooperation and its Importance for Survival. London: Harper Collins Business, 1994.

Huber, G. Organizational Learning: The Contributing Processes and Literature. *Organization Science*, 2(1), 1991: 88-115.

Iansiti, M., Clark, K. Integration and dynamic capability. *Industrial and Corporation Change*, 4(3), 1994: 557-605.

Imai, M. Kaizen: The Key to Japan's Competitive Success. New York: McGraw-Hill, 1986.

Ingram, P., Baum, J.A.C. Chain affiliation and the failure of Manhattan hotels, 1980-1989. *Administrative Science Quarterly*, 42(1), 1997: 68-102.

Inkpen, A.C. Creating knowledge through collaboration. *California Management Review*, 39(1), 1996: 123-140.

Iwai, K. A contribution to the evolutionary theory of innovation, imitation and growth. *Journal of Economic Behaviour & Organization*, 43(2), 2000: 167-198.

Jablonski, D. Micro- and macroevolution: scale and hierarchy in evolutionary and biology. *Paleobiology*, 26(4), 2000: 15-52.

Jacobs, D., Waalkens, J. Innovatie, vernieuwingen in de innovatiefunctie van ondernemingen. Deventer: Kluwer, 2001.

396

Jägers, H.P.M. et al. Characteristics of Virtual Organizations. [online] Available from Internet: <http://www.Virtual-Organization.net>, 1997.

Jansma, K., Schroor, M., Abma, G. Onze vaderlandse geschiedenis. Lisse: Rebo Productions, 1991.

Janszen, F. The Age of Innovation, kaming business creativity a competence, not a coincidence. London: Pearson Education, 2000.

Jarrar, Y.F., Aspinwall, E.M. Business process re-eingineering: Learning from organizational experience. *Total Quality Management*, 10(2), 1999: 173-186.

Jenkins, S., Forbes, S., Durrani, T.S., Banerjee, S.K. Managing the product development process - (Part I: an assessment). *International Journal of Technology Management*, 13(4), 1997a: 359-378.

Jenkins, S., Forbes, S., Durrani, T.S., Banerjee, S.K. Managing the product development process - (Part II: case studies). *International Journal of Technology Management*, 13(4), 1997b: 379-394.

Johanson, J., Mattsson, L.G. Network positions and strategic action. *In:* Axelsson, B., Easton, G. Industrial Networks: A New View of Reality. London: Routledge, 1992.

Johnson, P.E. What is Darwinism? *In:* Baumann, M. Man and Creation: Perspectives on Science and Theology. Hillsdale: Hillsdale College Press, 1993.

Johnston, R., Fitzgerald, L., Markou, E., Brignall, S. Target setting for evolutionary and revolutionary process change. *International Journal of Operations & Production Management*, 21(11), 2001: 1387-1403.

Jonash, R.S. Strategic Technology Leveraging: Making Outsourcing Work for You. *IEEE Engineering Management Review*, 25(2), 1997: 90-95.

Kahn, H., Wiener, A.J. The year 2000: a framework for speculation on the next thirty-three years. New York: McMillan, 1967.

Kahneman, D., Slovic, P., Tversky, A. Judgment under Uncertainty: Heuristics and Biases. Cambridge: Cambridge University Press, 1982.

Kanter, R.M. The Change Masters. New York: Simon & Schuster, 1983.

Kast, F.E., Rosenzweig, J.E. Organization and Management, a Systems Approach. Tokyo: McGraw-Hill Kogakusha, 1974.

Katz, D., Georgopoulos, B.S. Organizations in a Changing World. *In:* Baker, F. Organizational Systems, General Systems Approaches to Complex Organizations. Homewood: Richard D. Irwin, 1973: 120-140.

Kauffman, S.A. The Origins of Order. New York: Oxford University Press, 1993.

Kauffman, S. At Home in the Universe. New York: Oxford University Press, 1995.

Kauffman, S., Lobo, J., Macready, W.G. Optimal search on a technology landscape. *Journal of Economic Behaviour & Organization*, 43(2), 2000: 141-166.

Kerkhof, M. Innovation in Service Organisations. *In:* Proceedings of the 4th International Production Management Conference, Management and New Production Systems, 1993: 325-337.

Keys, L.K. Management and organizational challenges to technology (paradigm) S-curve change management. *International Journal of Technology Management*, 14(2/3/4), 1997: 265-276.

Kim, D.H. Toward learning organizations: integrating total quality control and systems thinking. Cambridge: Pegasus Communications, 1990.

Kim, D.H. The Link between Individual and Organizational Learning. *Sloan Management Review*, 35(1), 1993: 37-50.

Kim, W.C., Mauborgne, R. Strategy, Value Innovation and the Knowledge Economy. *Sloan Management Review*, 40(3), 1999a: 41-53.

Kim, W.C., Mauborgne, R. Creating New Market Space. *Harvard Business Review,* 77(1), 1999b: 83-93.

King, A.A., Tucci, C.L. Incumbent Entry into New Market Niches: The Role of Experience and Managerial Choice in the Creation of Dynamic Capabilities. *Management Science*, 48(2), 2002: 171-186.

Knudsen, T. Economic selection theory. *Journal of Evolutionary Economics*, 12, 2002: 443-470.

Kock Jr., N.R., McQueen, R.J. Product flow, breadth and complexity of business processes, an empirical study of 15 business processes in three organizations. *Business Process Re-engineering & Management Journal*, 2(2), 1996: 8-22.

Kolb, D. Experiental learning: Experience as the Source of Learning and Development. Englewood Cliffs: Prentice-Hall, 1984.

Köppel, R. Strategische Lieferanten verändern den Innovationsprozess. *io Management*, 69(5), 2000: 63-67.

Kramer, N.J.T.A., Smit, J. de. Systeemdenken. Leiden: Stenfert Kroese, 1974.

Krebs, J.R., Davies, N.B. Behavioural Ecology: An Evolutionary Approach. Oxford: Blackwell, 1984.

Kuhn, T. *Die Struktur wissenschaftlicher Revolutionen.* Frankfurt am Main: Suhrkamp, 1998.

Laitinen. E.K. Long-term Success of Adaptation Strategies: Evidence from Finnish Companies. *Long Range Planning,* 33(6), 2000: 805-830.

Landes, D.S. The Unbound Prometheus. Technological change and industrial development in Western Europe from 1750 to present. Cambridge: Cambridge University Press: 2003.

Landström, B. Het Schip. Hoofddorp: Septuaginta, 1972.

Leavitt, F. Evaluating Scientific Research. Upper Saddle River: Prentice-Hall, 2001.

Lee, R.G., Dale, B.G. Business process management: a review and evaluation. *Business Process Management Journal*, 4(3), 1998: 214-225.

Lei, D.T. Competence-building, technology fusion and competitive advantage: the key roles of organizational learning and strategic alliances. *International Journal of Technology Management*, 14(2/3/4), 1997: 208-237.

Leiponen, A. Dynamic Competences and Firm Performance. Laxenburg: International Institute for Applied Systems Analysis, 1997.

Lemmon, Alan R. Phyletic Gradualism vs. Punctuated Equilibrium. [online] [cited 14 May 2002]. Available at Internet: <http://ucsu.colorado.edu/~lemmon/Research/Paper-EG4-Gradualism.htm>.

Leonard-Barton, D. The Case for Integrative Innovation: An Expert System at Digital. *Sloan Management Review*, 31(1), 1987: 7-19.

Leonard-Barton, D. Implementation as mutual adaptation of technology and organization. *Research Policy*, 17(5), 1988: 251-267.

Leonard-Barton, D. The Factory as a Learning Laboratory. *Sloan Management Review*, 36(1), 1992: 23-38.

Lewin, A.Y., Volberda, H.W. Prolegomena on Coevolution: A Framework for Research on Strategy and New Organizational Forms. *Organization Science,* 10(5), 1999: 519-534.

Lewin, A.Y., Long, C.P., Carroll, T.N. The Coevolution of New Organizational Forms. *Organization Science,* 10(5), 1999: 535-550.

Lievegoed, B.C.J. Organisaties in Ontwikkeling. Rotterdam: Lemniscaat, 1972.

Lillrank, P., Shani, A.B., Lindberg, P. Continuous improvement: Exploring alternative organizational designs. *Total Quality Management*, 12(1), 2001: 41-55.

Little, A.D. The Strategic Management of Technology. Cambridge: 1981.

Llorca, R. The impact of process innovations on firm's productivity growth: the case of Spain. *Applied Economics*, 34(8), 2002: 1007-1016.

Loch, C.H., Huberman, B.A. A Punctuated Equilibrium Model of Technology Diffusion. Fontainebleau: INSEAD, 1997.

Lönnig, W-E. Johann Gregor Mendell: Warum seine Entdeckungen 35 (72) Jahre ignoriert wurden. [online] 2001 [cited 3 June, 2002]. Available at Internet: <http://www.mpiz-koeln.mpg.de/~loenning/mendel/mendel.htm>.

Luhmann, N. The Autopoiesis of Social Systems. *In:* Geyer, F., Zouwen, J. van der. Sociocybernetic paradoxes: Observation, Control and Evolution of Self-Steering Systems. London: Sage Publications, 1986.

Maira, A.M., Thomas, R.J. Vier principes om innovatie en efficiëntie te combineren. *Holland/ Belgium Management Review*, 63, 1999: 44-51.

Malotaux, P.Ch.A., Veld, J. in 't. Industriële Organisatie A. Delft: Delft University of Technology, 1969.

Margretta, J. The Power of Virtual Integration: An Interview with Dell Computer's Michael Dell. *Harvard Business Review*, 76(2), 1998.

Markides, C. Strategic Innovation in Established Companies. *Sloan Management Review*, 93(3), 1998: 31-42.

Markides, C. A Dynamic View of strategy. *Sloan Management Review*, 40(3), 1999a: 55-63.

Markides, C. In Search of Strategy. *Sloan Management Review*, 40(3), 1999b: 6.

Maturana, H.R. Autopoiesis. *In:* Zeleny, M. A Theory of Living Organization. New York: North Holland, 1981.

Maturana, H.R., Varela, F.J. Autopoiesis and Cognition: The Realization of the Living. London: Reidl, 1980.

Max, E.E. The Evolution of Improved Fitness, By Random Mutation Plus Selection. [online] The Talks.Origin Archive, 1 September 2001 [cited 27 May 2002]. Available from Internet: <http://www.talkorigins.org/faqs/faq-intro-to-biology.html>.

Maynard Smith, J., Price G.R. The Logic of Animal Conflict. *Nature*. 246(2), 1973: 15-18.

Maynard Smith, J. Evolution and the Theory of Games. Cambridge: Cambridge University Press, 1982.

Maynard Smith, J. The causes of extinction. *Philisophical Transaction of the Royal Society of London*, 325, 1989: 241-252.

Maynard Smith, J., Burian, R., Kauffman, S., Alberch, P., Campbell, J., Goodwin, B., Lande, R., Raup, D., Wolpert, L. Developmental constraints and evolution. *The Quarterly Review of Biology*, 60(3), 1985: 265-287.

Mayr, E. Systematics and the Origin of Species. New York: Columbia University Press, 1942.

Mayr, E. Diversity and the Origin of Life. Cambridge, MA: Belknap Press, 1976.

McCarthy, I.P. Toward a Phylogenetic Reconstruction of Organizational Life. *Journal of Bioeconomics*, 2005 (forthcoming).

McGahan, A.M., Silverman, B.S. How does innovative activity change as industries mature? *International Journal of Industrial Organization*, 19(7), 2001: 1141-1160.

McKendrick, D.G., Carroll, G.R. On the Genesis of Organizational Forms: Evidence from the Market for Disk Arrays. *Organization Science,* 12(6), 2001: 661-682.

McMaster, M.D. The Intelligence Advantage, Organizing for Complexity. Boston: Butterworth-Heinemann, 1996.

Mervis, B.N., Berg, D.N. Failures in Organization Development and Change. New York: Wiley, 1977.

Meszéna, G., Kisdi, É., Dieckmann, U., Geritz, S.A.H., Metz, J.A.J. Evolutionary Optimisation Models and Matrix Games in the Unified Perspective of Adaptive Dynamics. *Selection,* 2, 2001: 193-210.

Meyer, M.H., Utterback, J.M. The Product Family and the Dynamics of Core Capability. *Sloan Management Review,* 34(3), 1993: 29-47.

Meyerson, J.M. Enterprise systems integration. Baco Raton: CRC Press, 2002.

Micklethwait, J., Wooldridge, A. *The witch doctors.* London: Heinemann, 1996.

Mikkola, J.H. Portfolio management of R&D projects: implications for innovation management. *Technovation,* 21(7), 2001: 423-435.

Mikulecky, D.C. Life, Complexity and the Edge of Chaos: Cognitive Aspects of Communication between Cells and other Components of Living Systems. [online] 27 November 1995 [cited 23 February 1998]. Available from Internet: <http://views.vcu.edu/~mikulecky/rev/htm>.

Milberg, J., Dürrschmidt, S. Planning Methodology for Changeable Logistic Systems. *Production Research,* 9(1), 2002: 63-68.

Miles, R., Snow, C. Organizational Strategy, Structure, and Process. New York: McGraw-Hill, 1978.

Miller, D., Chen, M.-J. Sources and consequences of competitive inertia: A study of the U.S. airline industry. *Administrative Science Quarterly,* 39(1), 1994: 1-23.

Miller, E.J., Rice, A.K. Systems of Organization, the Control of Task and Sentient Boundaries. London: Tavistock Publications, 1970.

Millett, S.M., Honton, E.J. A managers guide to technology forecasting and strategy analysis methods. Columbus: Battelle Press, 1991.

Mills, D.Q., Friesen, B. The learning organization. *European Management Journal,* 10(2), 1992: 145-156.

Miner, A.S., Amburgey, T.L., Stearn, T.M. Interorganizational linkages and population dynamics: Buffering and transformational shields. *Administrative Science Quarterly,* 35(4), 1990: 689-713.

Mingers, J. Self-Producing Systems: Implications and Applications of Autopoiesis. New York: Plenum Press, 1995.

Mintzberg, H., The structuring of Organizations: a synthesis of the research. Englewood Cliffs: Prentice-Hall, 1979.

Mintzberg, H., Lampel, J. Reflecting on the Strategy Process. *Sloan Management Review,* 40(3), 1999: 21-30.

Mintzberg, H. Managers not MBAs: A Hard Look at the Soft Practice of Managing and Management Development. San Francisco: Berrett-Koehler, 2004.

Mokyr, J. Punctuated Equilibria and Technological Progress. *American Economic Review,* 80(2), 1990: 350-354.

Mokyr, J. Technological Inertia in Economic History. *The Journal of Economic History,* 52(2), 1992: 325-338.

Mokyr, J. Cardwell's Law and the political economy of technological progress. *Research Policy,* 23(5), 1994: 561-574.

Moldaschl, M. Kultur-Engineering und Kooperative Netzwerke. *io Management,* 67(6), 1998: 16-22.

Moran, L. The Modern Synthesis of Genetics and Evolution. [online] The Talks.Origin Archive, 22 January 1993 [cited 31 May 2002]. Available from Internet: <http://www.talkorigins.org/faqs/modern-synthesis.html>.

Morgan, G. De Nieuwe Manager. Schiedam: Scriptum Management, 1990.

Morgan, G. Images of Organization. Thousand Oaks: Sage, 1997.

Morone, J. Winning in high tech markets; the role of general management; how Motorola, Corning, and General Electric have built global leadership through technology. Boston: Harvard Business School Press, 1993.

Morrison, S.A. The evolution of the airline industry. Washington, D.C.: The Brookings Institution, 1995.

Mrakas, C., Kelly, W. Building the Perfect Corporation: From Vertical Integration to Virtual Integration. Axio Executive Whitepaper Series, 1998.

Murray, P., Donegan, K. Empirical linkages between firm competencies and organisational learning. *The Learning Organization,* 10(1), 2003: 51-62.

Nakane, J. Manufacturing Futures Survey in Japan: A Comparative Survey 1983-1986. Tokyo: Waseda University, 1986.

Nash, J. Non-Cooperative Games. *Annals of Mathematics,* 54(2), 1951: 286-295.

Nedin, C. Archaeopteryx: Answering the Challenge of the Fossil Record. [online] The Talks.Origin Archive, 17 June 2002 [cited 27 January 2003]. Available from Internet: <http://www.talkorigins.org/faqs/archaeopteryx/challenge.html>.

Nelson, L. A case study in organisational change: implications for theory. *The Learning Organization,* 10(1), 2003: 18-30.

Nelson, R.R., Winter, S.G. An Evolutionary Theory of Economic Change. Cambridge: Belknap Press, 1982.

Neumann, J. von, Morgenstern, O. Theory of Games and Econmic Behaviour. Princeton: Princeton University Press, 1944.

Nevis, E.C., DiBella, A.J., Gould, J.M. Understanding Organizations as Learning Systems. *Sloan Management Review,* 36(2), 1995: 73-85.

Nhira, N. Business Process Re-engineering. *Management Services,* November 2001: 8-13.

Nicolis, G., Prigogine, I. Self-organisation in Nonequilibrium Systems. New York: Wiley Interscience, 1977.

Nieuwstad, J.P.M. De organisatie als complex adaptief systeem. Delft: Delft University of Technology/Section Industrial Organisation and Management, 1997.

Nola, R., Sankey, H. A Selective Survey of Theories of Scientific Method. *In:* Nola, R., Sankey, H. After Popper, Kuhn and Feyerabend, Recent Issues in Theories of Scientific Method. Dordrecht: Kluwer, 2000: 1-65.

Nonaka, I. The Knowledge-Creating Company. *Harvard Business Review,* 69(6), 1991: 96-104.

Nonaka, I. A Dynamic Theory of Organizational Knowledge Creation. *Organization Science,* 5(1), 1994: 14-37.

Nonaka, I, Konno, N. The concept of "Ba": Building a foundation for knowledge creation. *California Management Review,* 40(3), 1998: 37-51.

Nonaka, I., Takeuchi, H. The Knowledge-Creating Company. New York: Oxford University Press, 1995.

Olson, M. The logic of collective action, public goods and the theory of groups. Cambridge: Cambridge University Press, 1965.

Olson, M. The rise and decline of nations, economic growth, stagflation and social rigidities. New Haven: Yale University Press, 1981.

Olson, R. Answering Dr. Edward Max Challenge to Dr. Duane Gish. [online] TCCSA [cited 27 January 2003]. Available from Internet: <http://tccsa.freeservers.com/articles/answering_max.html>

Paré, A.G.M. Strategies in the New Economy. Delft: Delft University of Technology/Section Production Technology and Organisation, 2000.

Parsons, T., Shils, E.A. Towards a General Theory of Action. New York: Harper & Row/Torchbooks, 1962.

Pfeifer, T., Eversheim, W., König, W., Weck, W.M. Manufacturing Excellence, The competitive edge. London: Chapman & Hall, 1994.

Ploegmakers, J.H.P. Strategic, Tactical and Operational Knowledge Management. Delft: Delft University of Technology/Section Production Technology and Organisation, 2000.

Polanyi, M. The Tacit Dimension. New York: Doubleday, 1967.

Popper, K.R. Logik der Forschung. Tübingen: J.C.B. Mohr, 1966.

Popper, K. All Life is Problem Solving. London: Routledge, 1999.

Porter, M.E. Competitive Strategy: Techniques for Analyzing Industries and Competitors. New York: The Free Press, 1980.

Porter, M.E. The technological dimensions of competitive strategy. *Research on Technological Innovation, Management, and Policy*, (1), 1983:1-33.

Porter, M.E. The Competitive Advantage of Nations. *In:* Michael E. Porter on Competition and Strategy. Boston: Harvard Business School, 1991.

Porter, M.E. What Is strategy? *Harvard Business Review*, 74(6), 1996: 61-78.

Prahalad, C.K., Hamel, G. The Core Competence of the Corporation. *Harvard Business Review*, 168(3), 1990: 79-91.

Preiss, K. Modelling of knowledge flows and their impact. *Journal of Knowledge Management*, 3(1), 1999: 36-46.

Price, I, Evans, L. Punctuated equilibrium: an organic model for the learning organisation. [online] [cited 3 July 2001]. Available from Internet: <http://member.aol.com/ifprice/peqforum.html>.

Prigogine, I. From Being to Becoming. San Francisco: Freeman, 1980.

Prothero, D.R. Punctuated Equilibrium at Twenty: a Paleontological Perspective. *Skeptic*, 1(3), 1992: 38-47.

Quinn, J.B. Strategic outsourcing: Leveraging knowledge Capabilities. *Sloan Management Review*, 40(4), 1999: 9-21.

Rance, H. f25 Phyletic Gradualism. [online] [cited 27 May 2002]. Available from Internet: <http://geowords.com/histbooknetscape/f25.htm>.

Rich, A.C, Mifflin, K.E. Game Plan for the Next Dynamic. *In:* Berger, L.A., Sikora, M.J. The Change Management Handbook. Chicago: Richard D. Irwin, 1994: 105-121.

Riechert, Susan. E., Hammerstein, Peter. Game Theory in the Ecological Context. *Annual Review of Ecological Systems*, 14, 1983: 377-409.

Riedel, J.C.K.H., Pawar, K.S. The strategic choice of simultaneous versus sequential engineering for the introduction of new products. *International Journal of Technology Management*, 6(3/4), 1998: 321-334.

Riedl, R. A systems-analytical approach to macro-evolutionary phenomena. *The Quarterly Review of Biology*, 52(4), 1977: 351-370.

Ringland, G. Scenario planning; managing for the future. Chicester: Wiley, 1997.

Romanelli, E., Tushman, M.L. Organization Transformation as a Punctuated Equilibrium: An Empirical Test. *Academy of Management Journal*, 37(5), 1994: 1141-1166.

Romme, A.G.L., Witteloostuijn, A. van. Autopoiesis, Chaos en Zelforganisatie in de Bedrijfskunde. *Bedrijfskunde*, 69(2), 1997: 63-71.

Rossem, M. van. Het poldermodel en het buitenland. *Amsterdamse Boekengids*, 18, 1999: 5-14.

Rothwell, R. Towards the Fifth-generation Innovation Process. *International Marketing Review*, 11(1), 1994: 7-31.

Roussel, P.A., Saad, K.A., Erickson, T.J. *Third Generation R&D*. Boston: Harvard Business School, 1991.

Rowley, J. From learning organisation to knowledge entrepreneur. *Journal of Knowledge Management*, 4(1), 2000: 7-15.

Ruef, M. Assessing Organizational Fitness on a Dynamic Landscape: an Empirical Test of the Relative Inertia Thesis. *Strategic Management Journal*, 18(11), 1997: 837-853.

Ruttan, V.W. Induced innovation, evolutionary theory and path dependence: sources of technical change. *The Economic Journal*, 107(444), 1997: 1520-1529.

Rycroft, R.W., Kash, D.E. The complexity challenge: technological innovation for the 21st century. London: Pinter, 1999.

Sabherwal, R., Hirscheim, R., Goles, T. The Dynamics of Alignment: Insights from a Punctuated Equilibrium Model. *Organization Science*, 12(2), 2001: 179-197.

Samuelson, L. Evolutionary games and equilibrium selection. Cambridge: MIT Press, 1997.

Sanderson, S., Uzumeri, V. Managing Product Families. *Research Policy*, 24(5), 1995: 761-782.

Saris, B.G. The tarot cards for the future opened? Delft: Delft University of Technology/Section Production Technology and Organisation, 2003.

Savage, J.M. Evolution. New York: Holt, Rinehart and Winston, 1969.

Schein, E.H. How Can Organizations Learn Faster? The Challenge of Entering the Green Room. *Sloan Management Review*, 34(2), 1993: 85-92.

Schippers, M. Controlling the innovation process. Delft: Delft University of Technology/Section Production Technology and Organisation, 2003.

Schroeder, R.G., Bates, K.A., Juntilla, M.A. A resource-based view of manufacturing strategy and the relationship to manufacturing performance. *Strategic Management Journal*, 23(2), 2002: 105-117.

Schumpeter, J.A. The Theory of Economic Development. Cambridge: Harvard University Press, 1934.

Schumpeter, J. Business Cycles. New York, McGraw-Hill: 1939.

Scott, W.G. Organization Theory: An Overview and an Appraisal. *In:* Baker, F. Organizational Systems, General Systems Approaches to Complex Organizations. Homewood: Richard D. Irwin, 1973: 99-119.

Seaborg, David M. Evolutionary Feedback: a New Mechanism for Stasis and Punctuated Evolutionary Change Based on the Integration of the Organism. *Journal of Theoretical Biology,* 198 (1), 1999: 1-26.

Selz, O. Über die Gesetze des geordneten Denkverlaufs, erster Teil. Stuttgart: Spemann, 1913.

Sen, F.K., Egelhoff, W.G. Innovative Capabilities of a Firm and the Use of Technical Alliances. *IEEE Transactions on Engineering Management,* 47(2), 2000: 174-183.

Senge, P.M. The fifth discipline: the art & practice of The Learning Organization. Kent: Century Business, 1990.

Senge, P.M., Kleiner, A., Roberts, C., Ross, R.B., Smith, B.J. The Fifth Discipline Fieldbook, Strategies and Tools for Building a Learning Organization. London: Nicholas Brealey, 1998.

Sepers, H.J.M. De implementatie van nieuwe procestechnologiën. Delft: Delft University of Technology/Section Industrial Organisation and Management, 1998.

Simon, H.A. The architecture of complex systems. *Proceedings of the American Philosophical Society,* 106, 1962: 467-482. *Reprinted in:* Simonn, H.A. The Sciences of the Artificial. Cambridge: MIT, 1981: 192-199.

Simsek, S.G. De Lerende Organisatie: definitie, modellering en kenmerken. *Personeelsbeleid,* 29(5), 1993: 81-85.

Singh, J.V., Lumsden, C. Theory and research in organisational ecology. *Annual Review of Sociology,* 16, 1990: 161-195.

Sitter, L.U. de, Naber, J.L.G., Verschuur, F.O. Synergetisch Produceren. Assen: van Gorcum, 1994.

Skyrme, D.J. From Information to Knowledge Management: Are You Prepared? [online] December 1997 [cited 16 February 2002]. Available from Internet: <http://www.skyrme.com/pubs/on97full.htm>.

Skyrme, D., Amidon, D. The Knowledge Agenda. *The Journal of Knowledge Management,* 1(1), 1997: 27-37.

Smeds, R. Implementation of business process innovations: an agenda for research and action. *International Journal of Technology Management,* 22(1/2/3), 2001: 1-11.

Smeets, G.H.M. A study of the evolution of the aviation industry to find dynamic interaction models of organizations with their environment. Delft: Delft University of Technology/Section Production Technology and Organisation, 2003.

Smith, A. The Wealth of Nations. London: Stratton & Cadell, 1776.

Someren, T.C.R. van. Factor tijd is cruciaal voor groei. *Holland Management Review,* 66, 1999: 64-71.

Sorenson, O. Letting the Market Work for You: an Evolutionary Perspective on Product Strategy. *Strategic Management Journal,* 21(5), 2000: 577-592.

Southgate, C., Negus, M.R. Self-Organisation and the Development of Complexity. [online] [cited 3 July 2002]. Available from Internet: <http://www.counterbalance.net/ghc-evo/selfo-body.html>.

Spoelstra, H.L. Strategic Capacity Management. Delft: Delft University of Technology/Section Industrial Organisation and Management, 1998.

Sprenger, C.C. Vier competenties van de lerende organisatie. Den Haag: Delwel Uitgeverij, 1995.

Spring, M., Dalrymple, J.F. Product customisation and manufacturing strategy. *International Journal of Operations & Production Management,* 20(4), 2000: 441-467.

Stacey, R.D. Strategic Management and Organisational Dynamics. London: Pitman, 1993.

Stacey, R.D. Complexity and Creativity in Organizations. San Fransisco: Berrett-Koehler, 1996.

Stoker, J., Verweij, M. Participatie na de Sitter en in 't Veld, de Sociotechniek als oerstructuur. *Bedrijfskunde*, 75(1), 2003: 76-84.

Stuart, F.I., McCutcheon, D.M. The manager's guide to supply chain management. *Business Horizons*, 43(2), 2000: 35-44.

Sun, H, Ove Riis, J. Organizational, Technical, Strategic, and Managerial Issues along the Implementation Process of Advanced Manufacturing Technology - A General Framework of Implementation Guide. *International Journal of Human Factors in Manufacturing*, 4, 1994: 23-36.

Swan, J., Newell, S., Scarbrough, H., Hislop, D. Knowledge Management and Innovation: networks and networking. *Journal of Knowledge Management*, 3(4), 1999: 262-275.

Swieringa, J., Wierdsma, A.F.M. Op weg naar een Lerende Organisatie: over het leren en opleiden van organisaties. Groningen: Wolters-Noordhoff, 1990.

Tabrazi, B.N., Eisenhardt, K. Accelerating adaptive processes: product innovation in the global computer industry. *Administrative Science Quarterly*, 40(1), 1995: 84-110.

Tashakkori, A., Teddlie, C. Mixed Methodology, Combining Qualitative and Quantitative Approaches. Thousand Oaks: Sage, 1998.

Teece, D.J., Pisano, G., Shuen, A. Dynamic Capabilities and Strategic Management. *Strategic Management Journal,* 18(7), 1997: 509-533.

Teed. The Phyletic Gradualism - Punctuated Equilibrium Debate. [online] [cited 3 July 2001]. Available from Internet: <http://lrc.geo.umn.edu/people/teed/papers/macroev.html>.

Teplitz, C.J. The learning curve deskbook: a reference guide to theory, calculations and applications. Westport: Quorum Books, 1991.

Terryberry, S. The Evolution of Organizational Environments. *In:* Baker, F. Organizational Systems, General Systems Approaches to Complex Organizations. Homewood: Richard D. Irwin, 1973: 178-195.

Terzioviski, M., Sohal, A.S. The adoption of continuous improvement and innovation strategies in Australian manufacturing firms. *Technovation*, 20(10), 2000: 539-550.

Theobald, D. All you need to know about Punctuated Equilibrium (almost). [online] 13 March 2002 [cited 27 May 2002]. Available from Internet: <http://ucsu.colorado.eud/~theobal/PE.html>.

Thompson, J.L. Strategic Management: Awareness and Change. London: Chapmann & Hall, 1991.

Tidd, J., Bessant, Pavitt. Managing Innovation, integrating technological, market and organizatinal change. London: Wiley, 1997.

Tushman, M., Anderson, P. Technological discontinuities and organizational environments. *Administrative Science Quarterly*, 31(3), 1986: 439-465.

Tushman, M.L., Anderson, P. Managing strategic innovation and change. Oxford: Oxford University Press, 1997.

Tushman, M.L., Newman, W.H., Romanelli, E. Convergence and Upheaval: Managing the Unsteady Pace of Organizational Evolution. *California Management Review,* 29(1), 1986: 29-44.

Tyre, M.J., Orlikowski, W.J. Exploiting Opportunities for Technological Improvement. *Sloan Management Review*, 35(1), 1993: 13-26.

University of California Museum of Paleontology. Trends in Evolution. [online] University of California Museum of Paleontology, 2004 [cited 7 Febr. 2004]. Available from Internet: <http://evolution.berkely.edu/evosite/evo101/VIIDTrends.shtml>.

Useem, M. Driving Systemic Change. *In:* Berger, L.A., Sikora, M.J. The Change Management Handbook. Chicago: Richard D. Irwin, 1994: 49-59.

Utterback, J.M. Mastering the Dynamics of Innovation. Boston, 1994.

Vaart, R. van der. Autopoiesis! Zin of Onzin voor organisaties? Delft: Delft University of Technology/Section Production Technology and Organisation, 2002.

Vakola, M., Rezgui, Y. Critique of existing business process re-engineering methodologies: the development and implementation of a new methodology. *Business Process Management Journal*, 6(3), 2000: 238-250.

Varela, F.J. Describing the Logic of the Living. *In:* Zeleny, M. A Theory of Living Organization. New York: North Holland, 1981.

Veld, J. in 't. Organisatiestructuur en Arbeidsplaats. Amsterdam: Elsevier, 1981

Veld, J. in 't. Analyse van Organisatieproblemen. Houten: EPN, 1998.

Velde, J.P. van der. Models for Decision-Making for Outsourcing. Delft: Delft University of Technology/Section Industrial Organisation and Management, 1999.

Vigil, D.P., Sarper, H. Estimating the effects of parameter variability on learning curve model predictions. *International Journal of Production Economics*, 34(2), 1994: 187-200.

Vits, J., Gelders, L. Performance improvement theory. *International Journal of Production Economics*, 77(3), 2002: 258-298.

Volberda, H.W. Building the Flexible Firm, How to Remain Competitive. New York: Oxford University Press, 1998.

Volberda, H.W. Blijven Strategisch Vernieuwen, het Herschikken van de Multi-Unit Onderneming. *Bedrijfskunde,* 72(2), 2000: 20-29.

Vorstermans, P. Uitbesteding. Delft: Delft University of Technology/Section Industrial Organisation and Management, 1997.

Vries, Joh. de, Woude, A. van der. Nederland 1500-1815, de eerste ronde van moderne economische groei. Amsterdam: Balans, 1995.

Wagner, M., Kreuter, A. Succesfactoren in innovatieve bedrijven. *PEM*, 15(1), 1999: 65-72.

Walker, P. A Chronology of Game Theory. [online]. May 2001 [cited 21 October 2003]. Available from Internet: <http://www.econ.canterbury.ac.nz/hist.htm>.

Wallace, Bruce. Hard and soft selection revisited. *Evolution,* 29, 1975: 465-473.

Walsh, S.T., Linton, J.D. The Competence Pyramid: A Framework for Indentifying and Analyzing Firm and Industry Competence. *Technology Analysis & Strategic Management,* 13(2), 2001: 165-177.

Ward, A., Liker, J.K., Cristiano, J.J, Sobek II, D.K. The Second Toyota Paradox: How Delaying Decisions Can Make Cars Faster. *Sloan Management Review*, 36(3), 1995: 43-61.

Warnecke, H.-J. The fractal company: a revolution in corporate culture. Berlin: Springer Verlag, 1993.

Wennekes, W. De aartsvaders, grondleggers van het Nederlandse bedrijfsleven. Amsterdam: Atlas, 1993.

Wezel, F.C., Lomi, A. The Organizational Advantage of Nations: An Ecological Perspective on the Evolution of the Motorcycle Industry in Belgium, Italy and Japan, 1894-1993. *In:* Baum J.A.C., Sorenson, O. *Geography and Strategy.* Greenwich CT: Jai, 2003.

Whetten, D.A., Organizational Decline: A Neglected Topic In Organizational Science. *Academy of Management Review,* 5(4), 1980: 577-588.

Wiendahl, H.-P., Lutz, S. Production in Networks. *Annals of the CIRP,* 51(2), 2002: 573-586.

Wiendahl, H.-P., Scholtissek, P. Management and Control of Complexity in Manufacturing. *Annals of the CIRP,* 43(2), 1994.

Wigman, J. How to stay competitive? Shaping the Corporate Strategy to Allow Business Growth. Delft: Delft University of Technology/Section Production Technology and Organisation, 2000.

Wilkins, J. So You Want to be an Anti-Darwinian. [online] The Talk.Origins Archive, 21 December 1998 [cited 27 January 2003]. Available from Internet: <http://www.talkorigins.org/faqs/anti-darwin.html>.

Williamson P.J. Strategy as Options on the Future. *Sloan Management Review,* 40(3), 1999: 117-126.

Winfield, I.J., Kerrin, M. Catalyst for Organizational Learning, The Case of Toyota Manufacturing UK Ltd. *The Learning Organization,* 1(3), 1994: 4-9.

Wit, B. de, Mol, M. Uitbesteden, topprioriteit en valkuil. *Holland Management Review,* (66), 1999: 47-57.

Wobben, J.J. Complexiteitstheorie in de bedrijfskunde, een managementconcept in ontwikkeling. Groningen: Rijksuniversiteit Groningen, 2001.

Wollin, A. Punctuated Equilibrium: Reconciling Theory of Revolutionary and Incremental Change. *Systems Research and Behavioural Science,* 16, 1999: 359-367.

Womack, J.P., Jones, D.T., Roos, D. The Machine that Changed the World. New York: Harper, 1990.

Wood, M. Legacy, a Search for the Origins of Civilization. London: Network Books, 1992.

Worden, R.P. A Speed Limit for Evolution. *Journal of Theoretical Biology,* 176, 1995: 137-152.

Wright, S. The shifting balance theory and macroevolution. *Annual Review of Genetics,* 16, 1982: 1-19.

Wright, T.P. Factors affecting the cost of airplanes. *Journal of Aeronautical Sciences,* 3, 1936: 122-128.

Wüpping, J. Logistikgerechte Produktstrukturen bei marktorientierter Variantenvielfalt. *io Management,* 67(1/2), 1998a: 76-81.

Wüpping, J. Zeitnahe Prozessorganisation durch produktorientierte Fertigungsinseln. *io Management,* 67(7/8), 1998b: 36-41.

Yung, K.L., Chan, W.Q. The adoption of business process reengineering in SMEs: a diffusion of innovation approach. *Journal of Manufacturing Technology Management,* 3(4/5), 2001: 361-374.

Zack, M.H. Developing a knowledge strategy. *California Management Review,* 41(3), 1999: 125-145.

Zajac, J.Z., Kraatz, M.S., Bresser, R.K.F. Modelling the dynamics of strategic fit: a normative approach to strategic change. *Strategic Management Journal,* 20(3), 2001: 257-265.

Zanden, J.L. van. Een klein land in de 20ᵉ eeuw, economische geschiedenis van Nederland 1914-1995. Utrecht: het Spectrum, 1997.

Zeeman, E.C. Population dynamics from game theory. *In:* Nitecki, Z., Robinson, C. Global Theory of Dynamical Systems. New York: Springer, 1980: 471-497.

Zuijderhoudt, R., Wobben, J.J., Have, S. ten, Busato, V. De logica van chaos in veranderingsprocessen. *Holland Management Review,* (82), 2002: 59-67.

Glossary

Adaptation	Adaptation is the (biological) process by which advantage is conferred on those organisms that have structures and functions enabling them to cope successfully with the conditions of the environment.
Adaptive Dynamics	Mathematical framework for dealing with evolutionary processes in dynamic fitness landscapes, conceived as an extension of polymorphic game theory to more complex ecologies and longer time scales.
Adaptive radiation	Adaptive radiation describes the rapid speciation of a single or a few species to fill many ecological niches. This is an evolutionary process driven by mutation and natural selection.
Allopatric speciation	Splitting of a species into two related species occurring in separate non-exchanging areas. The genetic difference may arise by chance, or as a side effect of local adaptation, and is followed by a decrease of the reproductive success on hybridisation, caused by the difference in genetic arrangements.
Allopietic systems	Systems that have three main characteristics of autopoiesis: structurally closed, autonomy, and self-reference. These systems do not possess the property of self-production, typical for autopoietic systems.
(Applied) Systems Theory	Theory for describing business processes and control processes, for the purpose of analysis and design. Systems Theory refers to the original theory written down by in 't Veld; Applied Systems Theory is a further development of this theory including the modifications necessary to describe continuous change.
Autopoietic systems	Autonomous systems that self-reproduce and are therefore structurally closed. These characteristics separate living entities from cybernetic systems.
Bifurcation	Splitting of lineages into separate branches as a biological evolutionary process which results in allopatric speciation or sympatric speciation. For organisations, it might mean the shift or the specialisation by companies on product-market combinations.
Breakthrough	Redefining the position, the activities and the policy of a company. The renewal is called breakthrough to distinguish it from innovation directed at product market combinations. Innovation might be part of the total breakthrough for a company.
Complex Adaptive System	This system consists of a number of components, or agents, that interact with each other according to sets of rules that require them to examine and respond to each other's behaviour in order to improve their behaviour and thus the behaviour of the system they comprise.

Complexity	Perception of not being able to explain phenomena or behaviour by liniear relations between cause and effect.
Complexity error catastrophe	The phenomenon where due to a size increase in the hereditary code the overall mutation rate starts to exceed the stabilising selection keeping a population on its adaptive peak. In particular there is little chance of reaching a different adaptive peak, as the system is in too much a disarray, or too incoherent, to move in any particular fashion; mutations dominate over direction imparted by selection.
Complexity Handling Capability	Ability of a company to cope with changes occurring in its environment and affecting organisational performance.
Developmental homeostasis	The result of the genetic assimilation of stabilising selection forces occurring at evolutionary equilibrium, resulting in a developmental system that is well buffered against both environmental and mutational impacts, and therefore shows little phenotypic variation.
Dimorphism	Occurence of two distinct forms. A process in evolutionary biology that results in speciation, splitting of lineages.
Dynamic capability	Capability for organisations to respond to changes in the environment.
Epigenetics	Development involving gradual diversification and differentiation of an initially undifferentiated entity.
Equifinality	Achieving a set objective through a dynamic balance during changing circumstances.
Evolutionary Stable Strategy	A strategy or a coalition of strategies that can persist together indefinitely and are resistant to invasion by rare mutant strategies.
Evolvability	Capacity to search a reasonable fraction of the space in which species operate to find new local fitness peaks.
Genetic drift	Change in the gene pool of a small population that takes place strictly by chance. Genetic drift can result in genetic traits being lost from a population or becoming widespread in a population without respect to the survival or reproductive value of the alleles involved.
Genome	The genome of an organism is the whole hereditary information of an organism that is encoded in the DNA (or, for some viruses, RNA).
Genotype	Genetic constitution of an individual organism.
Gradualism	The idea that the change in and development of diversity in life forms proceeds in small steps only, which are difficult to detect, and would initially appear to have little significance for natural selection.
Hamming distance	Number of positions on which two lists of N components differ.
Heterochrony	Deviation from the typical embryological sequence of formation of organs and parts as a factor in evolution.
Heterostasis	Maintainance of a relatively stable equilibrium between an entity and its environment through the changes in one or more parameters.

Heterotopy	Displacement in or difference of position of an organ from the normal position.
Homeostasis	Maintainance of a relatively stable equilibrium between an entity and its environment. Homeostasis assumes processes in the boundary to uphold this equilibrium.
Innovation	The conversion from inventions and technologies into products and services. This includes developing new products or the application of existing products in new markets.
Linkage disequilibrium	Assocation between alleles at different loci, sometimes sustaining variants despite their individual appearance. Interrelated traits might favour individual traits that would be deleterious.
Knowledge	Knowledge encompasses the conscious deployment of models. Data and information are related to a specific model. Data has no meaning without a framework (model) that turns it into information.
Macroevolution	Evolutionary change involving relatively large and complex steps such as transformation of one species to another and bifurcation, especially over long periods of time.
Macromutations	Complex mutations involving concurrent alteration of numerous characteristics of species. Might give rise to new species or subspecies if adaptive to the environment.
Memes	Memes are self-propagating units of cultural evolution having some resemblance to genes. The difference lies in the replicative potential and minimally required resources to replicate. Memes can represent parts of ideas, languages, elemental particles, tunes, designs, skills, moral and aesthetic values, and anything else that is commonly learned and passed on to others as a unit.
Microevolution	Evolutionary change resulting from selective accumulation of minute variations, ending in evolutionary differentiation. Micro-evolution takes place at the level of individual species, especially over shorter periods of time.
Natural selection	Natural process whereby organisms better adapted to their environment tend to survive and produce more offspring. Resulting from the interaction of the organism in its entirety with all the factors of the environmental complex although any one factor may appear to be decisive for survival or extinction.
NK-model	Model that describes fitness landscapes to explain the search for phenotypic variation to find local or global fitness peaks. N denotes the number of genes and K the connection between the genes.
Organelle structures	The specialisation of groups on activities, based on either tasks or products, within a total process or organisation.
Phenotype	Observable characteristics of an organism from the interaction of the genotype with its environment. Phenotypes might consist of many thousands of traits.

Point mutations	Point mutations are a type of mutations that cause the replacement of a single base pair with another pair. Point mutations are usually caused by chemicals, malfunction of DNA replication, and exchange a single nucleotide, an organic molecule, for another.
Punctuated equilibrium	Change occurs through periods of turmoil, eventually, caused by changes in the environment, during which there will be a burst of new species creation. Initially, the separation of new species as offspring of a dominant variant might attribute to their chances of survival before being exposed to the competitive environment in which the original variant is present.
Red Queen dynamics	Biological phenomenon in which all species keep changing and changing their phenotypes indefinitely in a never-ending race merely to sustain their fitness level.
Self-organisation	Phenomena in a Complex Adaptive System appearing at the edge of chaos. Behaviour and structure constantly change at a far-from-equilibrium state, between the stable equilibrium and chaotic behaviour.
Self-reference	Principle of autopoiesis stating that initiation of changes resides in the internal structure of a system.
Speciation	Formation of biological species or the process leading to this end whether constituting gradual divergence from related groups or occuring abruptly.
Sustained fitness	Incremental adaptation for optimisation, the search for increased fitness in the direct neighbourhood of local fitness peaks.
Systems Theory	See Applied Systems Theory.

INDEX

Appendix A: Boeing - Press Releases

This appendix gives an overview of press releases by Boeing (1997-beginning 2005), concerning public announcements of interventions to adapt its business of jetliners (Commercial Airplane Group) to the changes Boeing experiences. This interpretation of the press releases is not meant to be complete but serve as an illustration of how companies deal with changes.

Aug. 4, 1997   First day of single company after merger of Boeing with McDonnell-Douglas.

Aug. 27, 1997   Increasing numbers of airplane orders lead to measurements. Shift of some employees from the 767 production line to work on the 747 lines. Considering options for additional resources, implementing new manufacturing and business processes, providing additional training, adjusting internal work schedules to streamline production, eliminate waste, and cut costs.

Sept. 15, 1997 Announcement of Plan to deal with delayed deliveries. Challenges are: parts shortages, stretched supplier base, influx of new employees. The plan includes: working closely with suppliers to obtain needed parts, shifting personnel among production lines, working overtime, talking with the unions, exploring delivery-schedule changes. Boeing still expects to deliver 340-350 aeroplanes this year.

Oct. 3, 1997   Announcement of Production Recovery Plan. Boeing experiences problems raising the output from 18 planes per month to 40 planes per month. Part shortages are the biggest cause for delays, especially for the 747-program and 737-production. The 747 production line will be stopped for 20 days. Expected delivery of the new 737-700 delayed because of design change for horizontal stabiliser. Expected delivery of aeroplanes in 1997: 335.

Oct. 6, 1997   Expected output 1997: 375-385 aircraft.

Oct. 24, 1997   Third quarter earnings reduced by $1,6 billion (pre-tax) due to unplanned and abnormal production inefficiencies, and late-delivery costs associated with the accelerated production increases on the 7-series commercial aircraft programs. Earnings will continue to be negatively impacted by these production inefficiencies in 1998, which is the expected production recovery period. The problems Boeing experiences: raw material shortages, internal and supplier parts shortages, and productivity inefficiencies with adding thousands of new employees. Both the 747 and 737 production lines are halted for approximately one month. Announcement of assessment of commercial aircraft programs of the Douglas Products Division.

Nov. 3, 1997   Strategy for Douglas Product Division. Continuation of MD-11 (especially freighters), ending of production of MD-80 and MD-90 by mid 1999, first production lot of 50 MD-95's will be produced, future MD-95 dependant on reduction of production costs.

Dec. 16, 1997   Overtime announced during Christmas holidays to meet production schedules. Employment will reduce by 12.000 people during second half of 1998 (the Boeing Commercial Airplane Group employees 118.000 people). Production 1997 will vary between 375-385 aircraft.

Oct. 22, 1998   Phase-out of MD-11. Production rates of 747 will be reduced from five to three and a half, and of the 777 from seven to five.

Dec. 1, 1998   Boeing announces reducing production rates for some of its commercial airplane programs by the end of 1999. Lower rate of growth in passengers will affect orders for aeroplanes. Deliveries estimated at 1998: 550, 1999: 620, 2000: 490 aircraft.

Dec. 30, 1998   550 Aeroplanes delivered and in accordance with production target. The expected production in 1999 will be about 620 jetliners. Higher number of people worked during holiday time to meet customer demands (13% instead of 3%).

Jan. 26, 1999   Total of 559 aircraft delivered during 1998. Delivery of aircraft in 1999: 480 (expected).

March 29, 1999 The company has taken a further step to reduce internal costs, and to increase efficiency by implementing simpler ways of configuring and producing commercial aeroplanes.

April 15, 1999 Production rate of 737 to 24 per month. Further improvement of the learning-curve of 737 and 777. Announcement of pricing pressures and price-escalation trends.

July 7, 1999   Planning for 1999: 620 aeroplanes.

Sept. 20, 1999 50% of production costs come from suppliers. Partnerships with suppliers and aiming for cost reduction. Shift to delivering assemblies rather than parts.

Jan. 19, 2000   Delivery of 620 aeroplanes during 1999. Reduction of work force from 118.000 to 93.000.

April 19, 2000   Strike decreased the deliveries in the first quarter from 125 to 75 jets. Recovery to original plan for 490 jets expected.

June 29, 2000   Increase of production rate of 737 from 24 to 28 per month per third quarter.

Aug. 18, 2000   Announcement of relocation of jobs in- and outside the company for manufacturing and assembly for three factories.

Jan. 2, 2001   Total delivery 2000: 489 jets.

July 5, 2001   Target for deliveries in 2001: 530 aircraft.

July 18, 2001   Delivery in 2001: 530 (from 530) and in 2002: 510-520 aeroplanes.

Sept. 18, 2001   Possible reduction of employment by 20.000 to 30.000 people by the end of 2002. Expected delivery of 533 aircraft could be as low as 500. 2002 deliveries estimated at low 400's, compared to the 510-520 forecast. The downward trend might continue.

Nov. 28, 2001   Boeing signs agreement with Aerosud (South Africa) to manufacture parts for use across a range of models. Operations to start April 2002. Boeing supplies specialised capital equipment, tooling, and transfer of necessary production technology.

Dec. 13, 2001   Production of 717-program will continue at a lower production rate and revised delivery projections. Expected deliveries of 522 aeroplanes in 2001, 350-400 deliveries in 2002 and continued downward trend for 2003.

Jan. 3, 2002   Deliveries in 2001: 527 aeroplanes.

March 20, 2002 767-program deploys moving line principle with related changes from the automotive lean manufacturing methods in Japan. The moving line moves at a steady pace, allowing employees to gauge status at a glance and reduce the amount of work-in-progress.

April 17, 2002   Moving line production of the high-volume 737-program. Outlook for deliveries in 2002: 380 aeroplanes.

Aug. 15, 2002   Assembly of 757-program on moving line.

Sept. 3, 2002   On Demand Manufacturing for selective laser sintering technology in venture.

Oct. 16, 2002   Outlook for 2003: 275-285 aeroplanes.

Jan. 6, 2003   Delivery in 2002: 381 aeroplanes.

Jan. 30, 2003   Employement reduced by approx. 30.000 people since

September 2001. Airplane production rates at half. Recovery of market expected beginning of 2005.

April 23, 2003	Lower planned deliveries of airplanes.
June 16, 2003	Forecast for total market during next 20 years released (market growth: 18.400, replacement: 5.900, currently flying: 9.700).
July 17, 2003	Announcement for reducing number of employees by 4.000-5.000 (targeted workforce year-end 2003: 55.000-56.000).
July 29, 2003	Expected increase of freighter airplane fleet by twofold during the next two years.
Oct. 16, 2003	Boeing has decided to complete the production of the 757-program late 2004.
Oct., 29, 2003	Lower planned deliveries for 2003.
Jan. 6, 2004	Delivery in 2003: 281 airplanes.
Jan., 29, 2004	Recovery of market expected beginning 2006.
April 28, 2004	Expected delivery in 2004: approx. 285 airplanes. Slight raise of demand expected in 2005.
July 28, 2004	Delivery forecast for 2005 changed from approx. 300 to 315-320 airplanes. Increased demand for 737-program.
Nov. 12, 2004	Focus of airplane design and production to twin-aisle, long-haul airplanes for direct routes.
Jan. 5, 2005	Delivery in 2004: 284 airplanes.
Jan. 6, 2005	Net orders increased, planned production 2005: 320 airplanes.
Jan. 14, 2005	Announcement to end production of the 717-program.
Jan. 27, 2005	Reduction of lead-time final assembly 737 by 50% to 11 days (in comparison to 1999). Reduction of work-in-progress inventory by 55%. Due to implementation of lean manufacturing techniques.
Feb. 2, 2005	Company experiences increasing demand, esp. 737's and 777's. Delivery forecast 2006: 375-385 airplanes.

During the period 1997-2005, the company has announced regularly upgrades of existing planes (longer range, etc.) and the development of a few new airplanes, like the 787 (first known as the 7E7 Dreamliner).

APPENDIX B: DELFT SCHOOL APPROACH

This appendix summarises the main elements of the Delft School Approach: the Systems Theory, the differentiation of the organelle structure, and the design principles present in it. The approach roots in the developments at the Delft University of Technology. In 1968, two chairs were defined: Business Engineering and Management (prof.ir. P.Ch.A. Malotaux) and Industrial Organisation[54] (prof.ir. J. in 't Veld), at two different faculties. The collaboration resulted in the methodology that has been named *Delft School Approach*. The methodology, as it is today, profited from the cooperation and elaboration by others working for the two chairs. The book written by Adriaanse, Bikker and ten Haaf reflects the cooperation between these two groups (ten Haaf et al., 2002).

The topics of Section B.1, i.e. the main concepts of the Systems Theory, systems, subsystems, aspect systems, steady-state model, breakthrough model, are derived from the seventh edition of the book: *Analyse van Organisatieproblemen* (in 't Veld, 1998). The theory originates in thoughts about systems as did emerge at the end of the 1960's and the beginning of the 1970's (for example: Baker, 1973). The organelle structure relates to the process modelling of Systems Theory, and connects the design of these structures to performance requirements (Section B.2, based on the lecture notes of Bikker, 1993); originally the base for these concepts are found in in 't Veld (1998, 1981). The design of the organelle structure can be traced back to the thoughts of Emery & Trist (1972, p. 293) on differentiation and grouping into units, departments. Section B.3 touches on the design and engineering aspects of the Delft School Approach (Bikker, 1993, no. 183).

B.1 SYSTEMS THEORY

Central to Systems Theory is the concept of a system, in which the internal elements do have mutual relationships between each other and with elements in the environment of a system. The quality system of a company might exist out of quality procedures, policies, guidelines, and at the same time, it will link to the environment through relationships with stakeholders, customers, and suppliers. Through a structure, we describe the relationships elements do have within the system as well as with elements outside the system. For example, a manufacturing

---

[54] *Industrial Organisation has more the meaning of Industrial Engineering, Operations Management than the contemporary meaning of the external relationships of an organisation which emerged during the 1980's and the 1990's.*

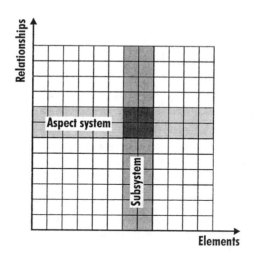

Figure B.1: Subsystems and aspect systems, according to in 't Veld (1998, p. 31). Subsystems are a partial set of the elements of the system and an aspect system a partial set of relationships.

system might consist of pieces of equipment performing processes (the resources), and it connects to the environment by the materials and parts supplied to it, and through the final products it delivers (the primary process). Although we attempt to isolate a system from its environment for the sake of a study, it maintains its relationships with its environment, the external structure, defining its purpose within the whole or universe.

When our search and analysis takes us further into the structure of a system, we have two options for exploring a system. Look at the financial system of a company, being the categorisation of mutations and the overview of the current financial position. Either we concentrate on certain elements of the system (subsystem) or we focus on certain types of relationships within the system (aspect), see Figure B.1. The overviews in the financial administration related to deliveries by suppliers represent a subsystem while the cash flow is an aspect system. The progress and results of the analysis and search determines which options to choose for further refinement and investigation: a subsystem or an aspect system.

According to Systems Theory when implementing a control strategy, differences exist between directing and controlling. Both however assume some principles for exerting control on a system:
- there should be a target state for the system;
- the system should be capable of reaching this target state;
- there should be ways for influencing the outcome and behaviour of the system.
Practically this means that the system should react predictably to a signal to achieve a certain outcome or state. To determine the signal and related actions

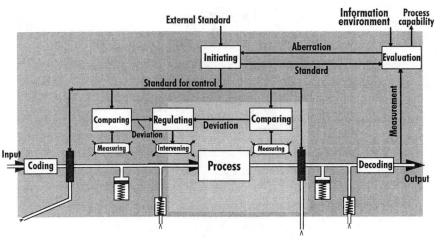

Figure B.2: Steady-state model for one aspect (in 't Veld, 1998, p. 238), simplified version. Horizontally we do find the primary process flow. The flowing elements are coded, checked, and buffered before the actual transformation. After the transformation, flowing elements are checked, buffered, decoded before crossing the boundary zone into the environment. Control processes, consisting of feedforward and feedback, maintain standards set by the initiating control process. Additionally, evaluation takes place to ensure attainable standards.

or interventions one should deploy a model of intervention. In the case of directing, the control restricts itself to giving a one-time signal, presupposing that the system will react and achieve this outcome. This also tells that the control does not verify whether the state has been achieved. It presumes an ideal situation in which no disturbances will occur after setting the original process. Practically, this never takes place even when it concerns a repeating process. Thereto, feedback measures the (value of the) output. The corrective actions aim to get the next output to the preset objectives (standard). This allows reactions to unknown and immeasurable disturbances. In the case of feedforward the control corrects the input of the system to achieve the desired output. Feedforward measures the disturbance in the input of a system, and compensates. The comparing process checks the measurements to a standard, and when finding a deviation an intervention happens.

The steady-state model (Figure B.2) adds the control for the system boundary in addition to these two control processes. For tuning the system control to the environment, the steady-state model deploys the initiating process and the evaluation process. Through the initiation process the standard, as imposed by the environment, transforms into standards suitable for use by the internal control processes. By evaluating the actual performance and information from the

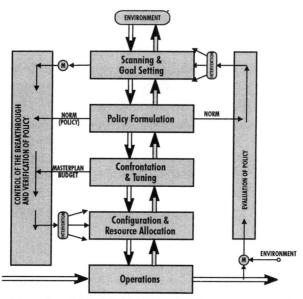

Figure B.3: Breakthrough model (in 't Veld, 1998). The primary process consists of transforming environmental input, changes into primary process for operations (e.g. the steady-state model). Note the two control processes at the left and right of this transformation. The policy evaluation aims at comparing the output of the system with goals set, such might lead to changes in goals and policy. The policy verification finds its base in a master plan for reaching organisational objectives by stating intermediate steps and milestones (these do not guarantee the outcomes).

environment, the initiating process issues new standards, and relays the capability of remaining within its own standards to the environment.

The breakthrough model (Figure B.3) describes indicates the overall processes necessary for implementing changes into the structure of operations. By scanning the environment, new or adapted goals are set, and the derived policy acts as a reference for the review of tactical and operational decisions. The process of confrontation and tuning considers the possibilities for specific decisions on the utilisation of resources and structures for operations. Through the development and construction process, the actual implementation of the structural changes in operations takes place. The evaluation of strategies might create new input for the breakthrough processes. The verification enables companies to follow the progress of the breakthrough processes.

B.2 ORGANELLE STRUCTURE AND HIERARCHY

The design of the organisation should combine activities within the manufacturing system from a strategic point of view (i.e. the re-design of an organisation might cause a breakthrough); that means grouping the tasks and activities into an

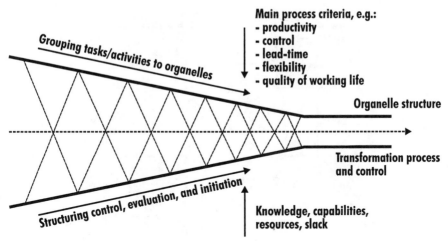

Figure B.4: Design process for the organelle structure (Bikker, 1993, pp. 183-188). The organelle structure affects both the grouping of tasks in the primary process as well as the control processes. By subsequent integration and iteration, the design of the organelle structure meets performance requirements.

organelle structure according to criteria (see Figure B.4). The design of organelle structures depends strongly on the imposed performance criteria. Strategic choices relate the organelle structure to external performance criteria dictated by product-market combinations and internal performance criteria. Bikker (1993, no. 182) gives an overview of organelle structures, ranging from the functional structure (job-shop) to the product flow organisation with their impact on design requirements for organisational structures. Factually, the organelle structure represents the trade-off between the requirements for control and the utilisation of resources.

The hierarchy represents the management of the resources. Thereto, leadership issues, span of control, and communication structures play an paramount role in the choice for the most adequate structure. However, the choices for this structure might undergo the forces of politics.

The design of an adequate organisational structure should incorporate the opportunities provided by product and process characteristics as well as it should meet all performance requirements. It should be noted that the management of resources incorporates both the primary process and control processes. Each of these processes deploys resources, with specific skills and knowledge, to achieve outcomes whether it concerns the manufacturing of products or the transformation from signals into interventions (the domain of control processes). Optimisation by management, the hierarchy, concentrates on all available resources for the primary process and control processes to reach organisational objectives.

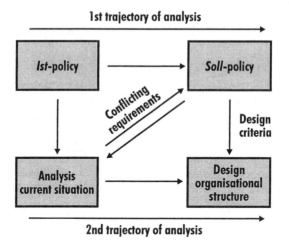

Figure B.5: Methodology to (re-)design organisations (Bikker, 1993, pp. 181-187), simplified version. The first trajectory aims at investigating prevailing policies for the *Ist*- and *Soll*-situation. The second trajectory analysis the current organisational structure (primary process, control process, organelle structure, hierarchy) and arrives at a redesign of the total organisational structure. The two trajectories are interlaced through the criteria, for analysis and redesign.

B.3 DESIGN AND ENGINEERING OF ORGANISATIONS

The design methodology follows two principles. Firstly, an organisation is analysed, and after the analysis of bottlenecks, the design follows the requirements of the strategy from the company (see Figure B.5). Changes in the general strategy, external developments, internal performance information or any combination of these factors set new requirements for an organisation. External developments might concern market investigations, technological changes or other information from the outside that influence the business processes. According to some authors and management sources, the development of a successful business strategy depends on the gathering of information about external developments. The internal information refers to the data about the performance, the structure, and the working methods of the organisational unit. The changes in general policy, external developments, and internal information should lead to either a radical or an incremental upgrade of the organisation. Secondly, the performance requirements reflect on the different design issues. So far, the design approach has relied on the step-wise approach: first, the setup of the primary process, then the design of the control processes, followed in iterations by consecutively the organelle structure and the hierarchy. During each stage, potential performance of possible solutions is compared with design requirements.

Appendix C: Case Welding Job-shop

The production manager of a welding shop did ask the general manager for an assistant to his position. The company, employing 35 people, concentrated on a variety of specialised welding techniques performed for a base of clients, which had expanded during the past years. The shop-floor, including the production manager and a production administrator, consisted of 28 people. The production manager had regularly filled 14 hrs./day during the past months partially due to an increase in orders.

An analysis revealed that the delivery time had become the most important performance requirement for clients; many clients accepted the higher level of cost since they contacted the company for outsourcing, mostly for reasons of capacity, or they needed the technological capability of the welding job-shop. About 50% of the orders exceeded the agreed delivery time. Waiting time and shortages of materials caused 75% of all late deliveries mainly due to a lack of overview by the production manager, and due to the issue of all specific production orders by himself (see Figure C.1). All orders were split into instruction sets, varying from a few minutes to some hours. The amount of workload on the production manager was attributed to a lack of overview, and the continuous stream of issuing instruction sets for each production employee, resulting in late deliveries that caused intense communication with clients.

The characteristics of the flow or orders allowed a division into three sub-streams: orders for welded sub-assemblies, orders for sheets, and orders for a

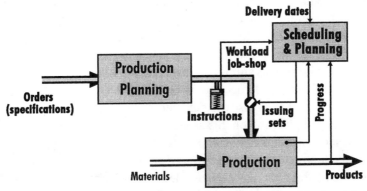

Figure C.1: Process model of the Job-shop Welding, for the logistic control. In the original situation, the production manager issued each set of instruction personally to workers. This centralised way of scheduling and issuing prevented a flexible control for reacting to changing circumstances.

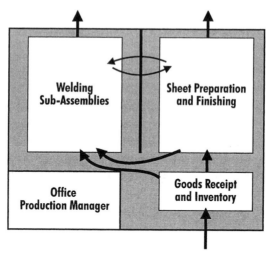

Figure C.2: The new general lay-out for the Job-Shop Welding. The changes in the way of working and the organisational structure implied a change in lay-out that was more in accordance to the requirement imposed on the company. The lay-out was derived from the organelle structure and the hierarchical structure.

specific welding process (this concerned only two persons); this division might reduce workload by introducing manufacturing cells with semi-autonomous groups. Validation of this proposal yielded a match with only 11% of the orders requesting a close interaction between the two main groups on sharing resources; the group would *Welded Sub-Assemblies* consist of 15 people, and the group *Sheet Preparation and Finishing* of 9 people. Finally, the graduate student prepared a detailed proposal for the layout of the two groups (see Figure C.2), equipment, and made a proposal for the allocation of personnel.

The implementation came along with moving equipment and assisting the semi-autonomous groups with the planning process. An evaluation revealed that the late deliveries decreased to less than 5% while maintaining organisational performance, and that no assistant to the production manager was needed. The hierarchy for operations was simplified using the semi-autonomous groups.

Half a year after the implementation, the company reported an adjustment in planning concerning the crossover between the two groups; the production manager centralised planning on this aspect.

The case showed that the control processes had to be adapted in connection with the organelle structure. Although treated briefly here, the analysis consumed a lot of time and effort to connect the problem to bottlenecks (it was not clear at all how work orders were issued), and the identification of solution strategies. To make the organelle structure fully work out, a change in the hierarchy proved necessary: the introduction of semi-autonomous groups.

Appendix D: Analysis Aviation Industry

This appendix describes the analysis of data of the aviation industry by Smeets (2003), as a part of this research. This investigation will examine airlines; they comprise the heart of the aviation industry, and they embody the reaction to changes in the environment. The purpose of the study is to indicate how an industry anticipates on environmental changes. Although there will be changes affecting the relationships between the airlines, airplane builders, airports, and suppliers of the industry, the focus will be on the airlines; an extensive study will require the cooperation of many disciplines to reveal all factors contributing to the dynamics in an industry. Such a study is beyond the scope of the research that only focuses on preliminary conclusions on adaptation.

The empirical analysis uses the dynamic model displayed in Figure D.1. This model arrives from the model of Farjoun introduced in Subsection 2.2.2; all four factors are going to be evaluated, the model has been expanded using the design approach of Bikker (see Section B.3). The appendix starts with an explanation of the used data: the environment, the organisational structure, the strategy, and the performance will be assessed. The appendix finishes with an analysis of the available data using two methods of investigation.

D.1 Data Acquisition

The data about airlines between 1970 and 1990 are found in six sources. The Air Transport Association (2003) and the Bureau of Transportation Statistics (2003) have both data available on the Internet. Furthermore, the International Air

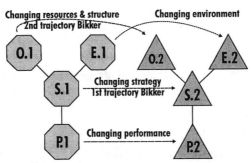

Figure D.1: Dynamic model as proposed by Smeets (2003, p 19). The four factors, Organisation (O), Environment (E), Strategy (S), Performance (P), influence each other mutually. The change in strategy looks like the 1st trajectory from Bikker as presented in Section B.3. The organisation consists of the resources and the structure (2nd trajectory of Bikker).

Totals of air transport for all large certificated air carriers

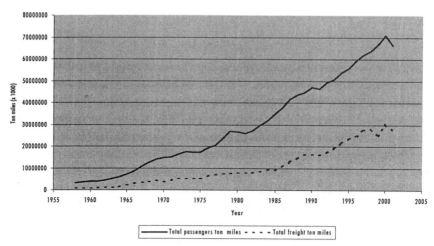

Figure D.2: Progress of air transport 1958-2001. The aviation industry has experienced a gradual rise of demand until 2001; at the end of that year unexpected events caused a downwards reaction.

Transport Association (1970-1990) publishes every year the *World Air Transport Statistics*. These figures were completed with the Annual Reports available at the Erasmus University Rotterdam at the Faculty of Economical Sciences, the data from Dienel & Lyth (1998), and the data from Morrison (1995). The currencies were all translated with historical exchange rates data (2003) to the historical dollar rate.

The airlines examined during the analysis are all major airlines in the USA and Europe. The data about these major airlines are more available than information about smaller airlines, and it makes a comparison possible between similar companies. Seven airlines based in the USA were examined; three of them stopped operating during the period, and all of them were seen as trunk carriers (Air Transport Association, 2003). In Europe, four airlines were investigated: the three largest airlines and KLM (which merged with Air France during 2004). An overview of airlines and major events is listed in Table D.1.

D.2 GLOBAL ANALYSIS

The analysis starts with a global overview of the total airline industry. Figure D.2 shows the transported passengers ton-miles and freight ton-miles of the total airline industry between 1958 and 2001. These data are extracted from the Bureau of Transportation Statistics (2003). A *passenger ton-mile* represents one ton-mile per passenger that is carried by the industry. This graph indicates a few points that mark the development of the aviation industry. From 1965 on a growth in air travel is seen, and this growth can be attributed to the boom of the first jet decade. In 1971, the impact of the recession on the industry becomes visible. During the next few years, the oil crisis and the recession slow down the further development of air transport. From 1975 on, the numbers of passengers and the freight start to rise again until 1979 when the second oil crisis appears. This crisis is followed by a strike of the air traffic controllers in the USA, which has a big influence on the passenger flows. In 1978, the Deregulation Act is introduced in the USA, by which all routes have free access for competitors. The influence of this regulatory change is discussed later on. In 1989, another economic crisis hits the market, and during the first Gulf Crisis in 1991 a dip can be noticed. The last decrease of passengers can be observed in 2001, which is caused by the terrorist attack on the World Trade Centre in New York, and the global SARS crisis.

Based on the general development of the aviation industry, a period is chosen to limit the extent of the research. Because 1978 marks an important change in the aviation history, i.e. the introduction of the Deregulation Act, statistics are gathered around this date. A choice is made for data between 1970 and 1990. By using these figures, a good impression can be created about the influence of the Deregulation Act, which should affect competitive pressures.

D.3   FACTORS FROM THE DYNAMIC MODEL

This section evaluates the environment, the organisational structure, the strategy, and the performance of the period between 1970 and 1990, based on the modified model from Farjoun. The investigation starts with the analysis of the environment by using the dynamic model from Figure D.1.

D.3.1   Environment

The environmental changes are market changes and technology changes (Dekkers, 2000a, pp. 7-9). During this period, market changes occur mostly through incidents causing variations in passengers demand. Other changes like *change of sort* or *change of routes* become not visible by analysing the available data. The change of sort encompasses the changes in service, price or quality demand, and the change of routes covers the changing demand per route or upcoming new routes. Because the actual strategy and the change of routes and of sort are closely linked together, these variations will appear in the strategy. A deployed strategy sometimes might even lead to variation of demand on a certain route (e.g. low fare routes to insignificant destinations). Furthermore, governmental influence is exerted in 1978 by the introduction of the Deregulation Act, which does affect the changes of sort and of routes but will not become visible in the available data. New aviation technologies do not influence the market by dominant designs during this period. In the beginning of the 1970's, Boeing

Table D.1: Timeline of airlines investigated during this research (Smeets, 2003, p. 47-48). Major events have been listed during the time span of 1970-1991.

Historical events	American Airlines Inc.	United Airlines Inc.	Delta Air Lines Inc.	Trans World Airlines Inc.	Eastern Airlines	Braniff International	Pan American World Airways	British Airways	Lufthansa	Air France	Royal Dutch Airlines
Code	AA	UA	DL	TW	EA	BN	PN	BA	LU	AF	KL
1970	Massive loss			First 747 service							
1971											
1972			Merger Northeast Airlines							Large management reorganisation	
1973 Oil crisis								Merger of BOAC and BEA			
1974 Recession											
1975											
1976											
1977 Oil shortage; UK/USA agreements						Concorde service Europe				Government funding	
1978 Deregulation Act; Bilateral Air Transport Agreement KLM/USA			Transatlantic service			32 new routes					Open Skies Treaty USA
1979						transpacific, Asia scale back services Europe					
1980 Attack on Iran from Iraq											
1981 Strike of the air traffic controllers in USA			FFP					High loss			

441

Historical events	American Airlines Inc.	United Airlines Inc.	Delta Air Lines Inc.	Trans World Airlines Inc.	Eastern Airlines	Braniff International	Pan American World Airways	British Airways	Lufthansa	Air France	Royal Dutch Airlines
Code	AA	UA	DL	TW	EA	BN	PN	BA	LU	AF	KL
1982					Hired routes from Braniff	Bankruptcy					
1983		First transpacific routes									
1984 Bilateral Anlgo-Dutch Treaty								Largest airline in pax miles			
1985					flights to UK and South America						
1986 Package of deregulating measures for Europe		Purchase PN Pacific Division		Purchase Ozark Airlines							
1987 Single European Act	Purchase Aircal routes		Merger Western Airlines								
1988			Operations in Asia					London Stock Exchange	Joint venture Air France		14,9% in Air UK
1989 Gulf Crisis Economic crisis					Bankruptcy						
1990											Investment in Northwest
1991							Bankruptcy				
1992 Full scope of EC liberalisation											

starts to sell its 747, and Airbus joins this market with its A-300 a few years later. However, it should be mentioned that a good hub and spoke system appears to be an advantage to feed all routes after 1978. This can be seen as a dominant design but is not included in this research.

The used variables for the changes in the demand for passengers travel are the *Revenue Seats Kilometre* (RSK) and the *Revenue Ton Kilometre* (RTK); the RTK indicates the total tons an airline has transported each one kilometre. These data will be used in the further research. Additionally, an overview of the most important events is found in Table D.1.

D.3.2   Organisation

The changes in the organisational structure reflect mostly on the resources of the companies. Through acquisitions of airplanes and allocation of personnel, an airline is capable of changing its organisation. Unfortunately, changes in the composition of the organelle structures of airlines are not measurable with a global investigation, and a more specific examination would be necessary for such an assessment. This research only investigates the changes in resources. Hereto, it uses the *Available Seats Kilometre* (ASK), the *Available Ton Kilometre* (ATK), and the total number of employees; the ASK indicates the total available seats per kilometre per year, and the ATK the available flight capacity.

D.3.3   Strategy

The strategy of the airlines defines the market position, which the company wants to be in. Gudmundsson (1998a) differentiates the strategic options in three aspects: (1) operating strategies, (2) marketing strategies, and (3) financial strategies. The first category deals, for example, with the routing, equipment or feeding possibilities. This connects to the environmental changes in demand and changes of routes. The second includes the pricing strategy, the service, the offered quality, and the promotion, and is linked to the environmental changes in sort and changing organisational form. The third category contains the cost structure, and it is an indication for the organisational form.

Taking into account the available data, this research applies the following variables, which are linked to the organizational types from Miles & Snow (1978) in Subsection 2.2.2:

- The *total employees per RPK* (Revenue per Passenger Kilometre) are an indication of the offered service, and the investment in the clients of the airline. This could lead to a higher quality offering to its passengers. A relatively high figure points to the Prospector type.

- The *total operating expenses per ATK* gives an idea of the financial strategy used by the airline, a relatively low figure indicates a Defender type.
- The *total operating revenues per RTK* shows the pricing strategy of the organisation. A high figure implies again the Prospector type. The Analyser type has a high service level but lower than that of the Prospector, and the other factors are close to the mean. The Reactor is totally allocated to the grand mean.

These indicators are shown in Table D.2. As can be noticed, the operating strategy has not been covered. This has two reasons: moving into other routes is hard to capture in a generic model, and the implication on the performance is hard to detect. It could be portrayed by the initiation of new agreements for routes with other airlines, partially captured in Table D.1. These data will be used as a sidetrack of this analysis.

D.3.4 Performance

The last factor from the dynamic model is the performance. The process of changing the strategy and the organisational structure determines the dynamic fit with the environment, which should ultimately lead to a better performance. A strong correlation between the ASK and the RSK or between the ATK and the RTK implies that the airline did adapt to the changes in the environment. A growing load factor denotes a better fit. By staying on the same routes and using constantly the same strategy, a company adapts to the changing demand in the market, which is visible in the correlation factor mentioned above. By moving into other routes or adopting other strategies, companies can move to better performance. For companies it is important to understand which changes will lead to a higher fit and to an improved performance. This will eventually lead to profit, and it will secure the survival of the company. Therefore, the variables for performance in this research will be the *weight load factor* and the *operating*

Table D.2: Strategic forms of Miles & Snow for the airline industry. The theoretical dimensions of these forms have been parametrised into three theoretical dimensions of the aviation industry: service, cost, price.

Strategic Form	Theoretical dimensions		
	Service	Cost	Price
Prospector	Highest	Highest	Highest
Defender	Lowest	Lowest	Lowest
Analyser	Mean	High	Mean
Reactor	Mean	Mean	Mean

margin. The first is the RTK as factor of the ATK, in fact how much revenues cover the available capacity of an airline, and the latter the total operating profit as factor of the total operating revenue.

D.3.5 Interrelationships between Factors

The proposed variables in the last four subsections are visualised in Figure D.3. This diagram shows all investigation possibilities in the range of the Organisation-Environment-Strategy-Performance model given the available data. The paths of the investigation are highlighted in the diagram though more paths might be possible.

D.4 ANALYSIS OF DATA

This section proposes two methods for the analysis to examine the dynamic model with the available data. The first method investigates the total market. The second method investigates the airlines from the database separately. Both analyses use the paths from Figure D.3.

D.4.1 Investigation of Total Market

Figures D.4-D.10 display the interaction between the proposed variables. From Figure D.4 we can derive that the ASK follows more or less the RSK, indicating that the organisational structure follows the changes in the environment (i.e. the capacity follows demand). Also the changes in the total employees become obvious. After 1978 a decrease and after 1985, a clear increase of these variables happens due to the changed environment (the Deregulation Act respectively the deregulation measures in Europe). The differences in the RSK and RTK might

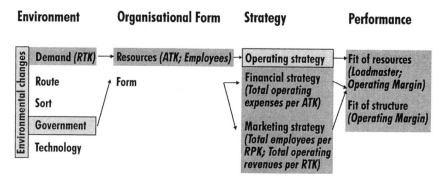

Figure D.3: Possibilities for investigation within the range of the Organisation-Environment-Strategy-Performance model. In this figure the dark shaded areas represent the analysis extracted directly from the statistical data. The lightly shaded areas indicate the investigations used from observed events not present directly in the data. The white areas have not been examined in the analysis.

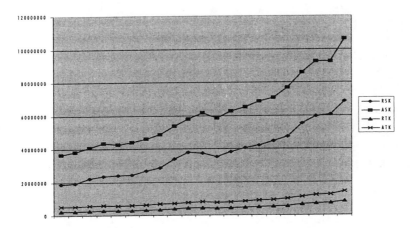

Figure D.4: Totals for the variables RSK, ASK, RTK, ATK for all examined airlines.

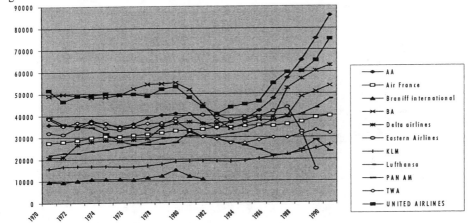

Figure D.5: Totals of the employees per airline.

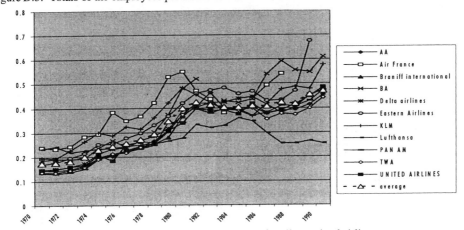

Figure D.6: Expenses per ATK (Available Ton Kilometre) for all examined airlines.

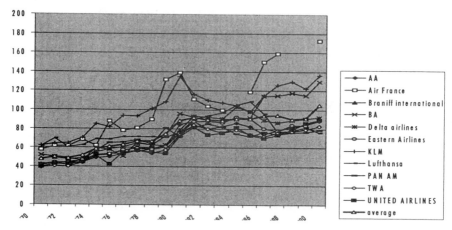

Figure D.7: Revenue per RTK (Revenue Ton Kilometre) for all examined airlines.

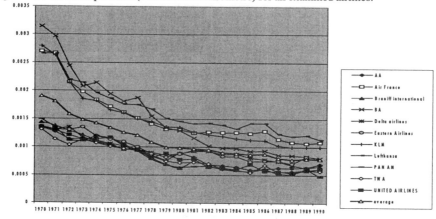

Figure D.8: Employees per passengers kilometer for all examined airlines.

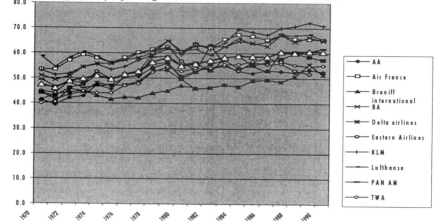

Figure D.9: Weight loadfactor for all examined airlines.

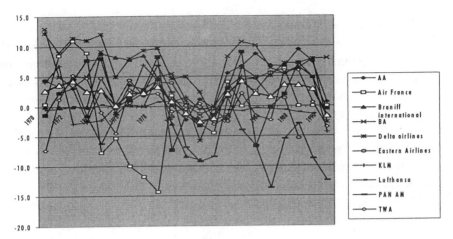

Figure D.10:   Operating margins for all examined airlines.

be explained with the historical events in the aviation industry from Table D.1. More interesting is the strategic variable of the employees per RSK; the total of the employees increases (Figure D.5), and the number of employees per PAX km decreases (Figure D.8). The variables decrease over the whole period but not all on the same level, the European airlines remain clearly a fraction above the American ones. A general higher cost level or a chosen strategy could cause this phenomenon. In Figure D.6, the operating expenses per ATK, and in Figure D.7, the operating revenue per RTK, the effect of the historical events can again be noted. After the Deregulation Act in 1978, the variable increases at a higher level, this points to the influence of increased levels of competition: airlines have to pay more effort to gain customers. From 1981, the variable decreases, probably as a reaction to the economic crisis. The European airlines move again at the higher ranges of the graph. Furthermore, the weight load factor increases over the entire period. This means that the airlines are better capable to adjust there ASK with the actual RSK, only in the year 1980 to 1982 a slow decrease can be seen for the American airlines. The operating margins show a general decrease between 1979 and 1983 and in 1990, caused by the two economic crises. At the beginning of the 1980's, the airlines decrease their capacity.

The general overview of the events in the period discussed here is not sufficient for a complete impression. The next subsection will look at the individual airlines in more detail (second method of analysis).

D.4.2   Investigation of Airlines

The investigation will continue with looking at the correlation between the ASK and RSK in conjunction with the ATK and RTK of all individual airlines, see Figures D.11a-k for these variables. These figures show again that the available tons or seats follow the passengers' numbers. However, there are differences between the airlines:

- After the Deregulation Act, Braniff International shows a strong growth in ATK. This is accompanied by an increase in load factors but also by a high increase in expenses per ATK. The revenue per RTK follows not until 1980. This leads to a decreasing operating margin from 1978 on.

- British Airways had a decrease of RTK from 1980. The expenses per ATK had risen from 1978 till 1981 on a high pace. However, the number of employees dropped from 1979 to 1983. The load factor went down by 5 percent from 1979 to 1980. The year 1981 was a record loss for the British Airways. It could be concluded that the strategy of increasing the expenses per ATK and of decreasing the number of employees was not successful.

- Delta Air Lines displays a clear increase of ATK in 1987. This can be connected to the merger with Western Airlines. From 1987 on, the expenses per ATK and the revenue per RTK are rising. The load factor and operating margin follow this trend. In general, the expansion of the network was a logical step for all airlines according to the rise of ATK and the number of employees. For Delta Air Lines, the merger seemed to be profitable. The higher price was compensated by the expansion of the network.

- KLM and Lufthansa show a more or less steady growth in ATK and RTK. After 1980, Lufthansa has lower financial indicators. KLM stays in the higher region and has a decreasing figure between 1980 and 1984. KLM seems to be more sensitive to the international fluctuation, for example, due to the *Open Skies Treaty* it has with the USA.

- Air France is affected more by the oil crisis in 1973 than at the end of the 1980's as seen in the operating margin. In 1973, it was less capable of adjusting its prices due to institutional restrictions.

- Pan Am peaks with the ATK in 1980. However, it has relatively stable financial indicators. The losses are major between 1980 and 1982 and stayed negative until the end of the company in 1991. The expansion of the ATK did not seem to be a good strategy at that particular time.

These cases show the fluctuation in performance by all airlines. However, it could be more interesting to show the differences between all airlines. This could reveal the changes in strategy, as proposed in Subsection D.2.3, of the organisational types from Miles & Snow (1978), between the airlines. Hereto, *the averages* and *the standard deviations* of the airlines are being calculated. With these data, the deviation from the average is calculated by presuming the standard deviation at 1. This method makes it possible to put the variables in one picture and to focus on the differences of the airlines with the grand mean. In this manner, the changes in time are filtered from the data.

Only the American airlines are going to be investigated during the next step of the analysis. As shown in the previous subsection, the European airlines had a quite different performance than those from the USA. Most likely because of the more intense competition (also before 1978), the performance indicators were closer together in the USA. Using the European airlines in the analysis would pollute the data. Figure D.12 shows the result of this examination.

In general, as found in the last section the load factors decrease and the expenses per ATK increases after the Deregulation Act in the USA. This implies a change to Analysers of all airlines (see Table D.2). A few characteristics can be distinguished:

- Eastern Airlines scores much higher than the other airlines, especially in the expenses per ATK. Therefore, also the figures without Eastern Airlines are shown in Figure D.13. Eastern Airlines and Delta Air Lines can be seen as the Prospectors of the population of airlines (see Figure D.14). With their financial structure and service in the higher region of the graphs, they perform particularly well before 1980. During the second phase of the period with the introduction of the Deregulation Act, they perform significantly worse.
- Pan Am and TWA are most of the time Defenders. In a short period after 1978, however, they turn into Analysers. This change is even visible in comparison with the other airlines. For TWA the operating margins increase from 1979. The Defender structure seems to be better than the Prospector structure for TWA after 1978.
- United Air Lines, with its high expenses per ATK, is an Analyser. Only in the period 1978 to 1973 it changed to a Reactor status. This leads surprisingly to a higher operating margin in this period. During the other periods, the airline performs moderately.
- Braniff International and American Airlines move during the whole period more or less near the averages of the graphs. This points to a Reactor structure. For American Airlines this leads to a higher performance after 1979. Braniff, however, did not survive the turmoil period after 1978. In this period, the ATK decreases clearly for American Airlines and for TWA. For Braniff, the rapid growth did finally lead to the bankruptcy in 1982.

These observations show that before the Deregulation Act the Performer structure worked out well. After the Deregulation Act, the Analyser structure performed better, and the best structure to be in just after 1978 was the Reactor status. In this turmoil, it can be seen that all airlines tend to move towards a more fitting structure.

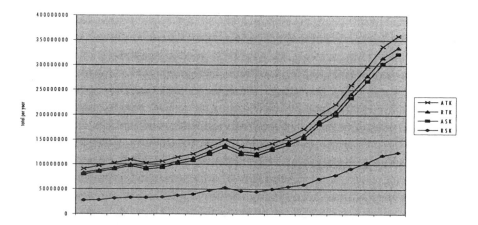

Figure D11a: Relationship between ATK, RTK, ASK, RSK for American Airlines.

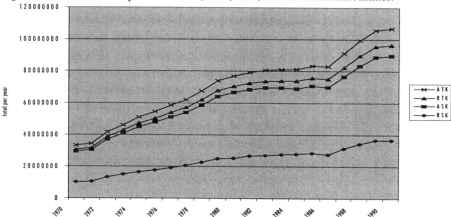

Figure D11b: Relationship between ATK, RTK, ASK, RSK for Air France.

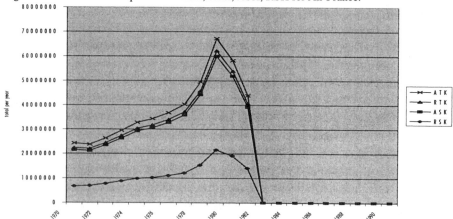

Figure D11c: Relationship between ATK, RTK, ASK, RSK for Braniff International.

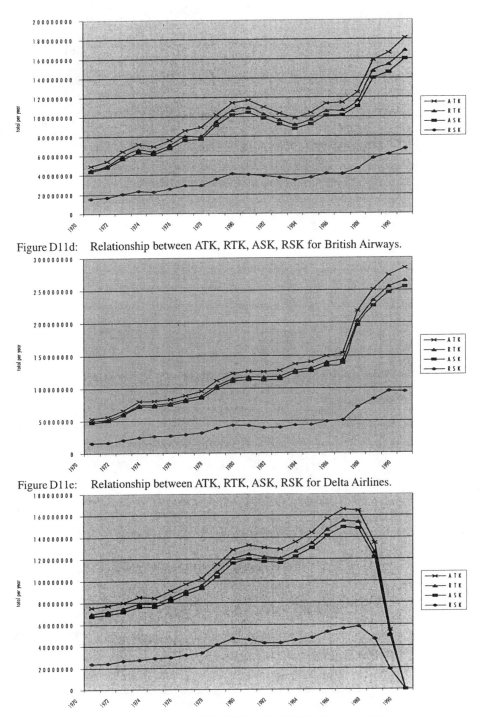

Figure D11d: Relationship between ATK, RTK, ASK, RSK for British Airways.

Figure D11e: Relationship between ATK, RTK, ASK, RSK for Delta Airlines.

Figure D11f: Relationship between ATK, RTK, ASK, RSK for Eastern Airlines.

452

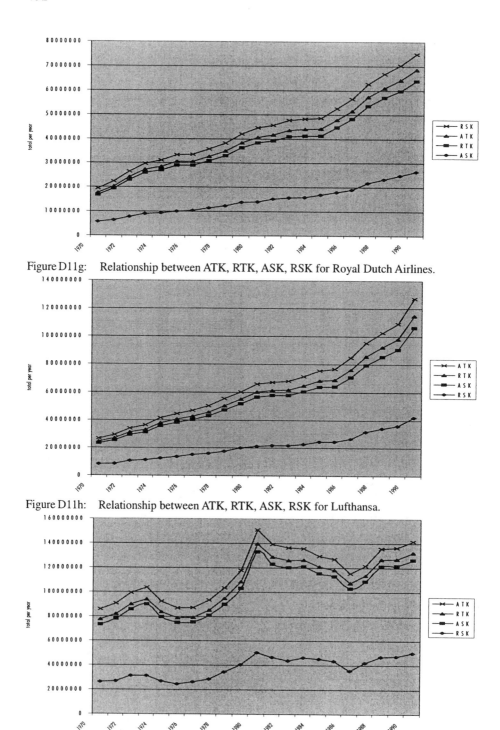

Figure D11g: Relationship between ATK, RTK, ASK, RSK for Royal Dutch Airlines.

Figure D11h: Relationship between ATK, RTK, ASK, RSK for Lufthansa.

Figure D11i: Relationship between ATK, RTK, ASK, RSK for PanAm.

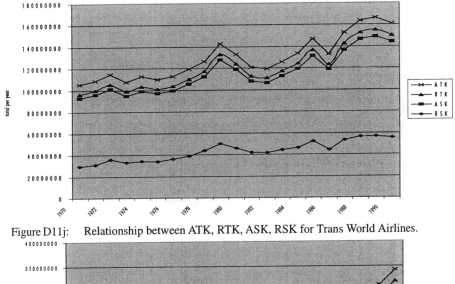

Figure D11j: Relationship between ATK, RTK, ASK, RSK for Trans World Airlines.

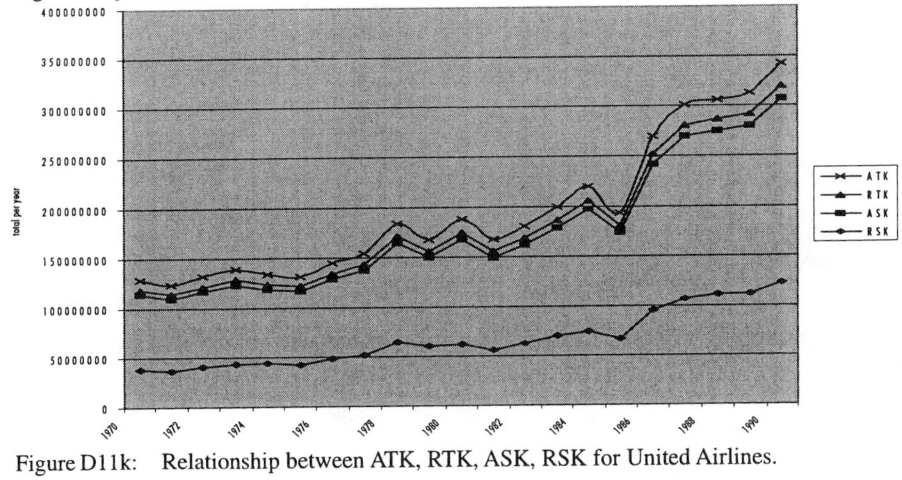

Figure D11k: Relationship between ATK, RTK, ASK, RSK for United Airlines.

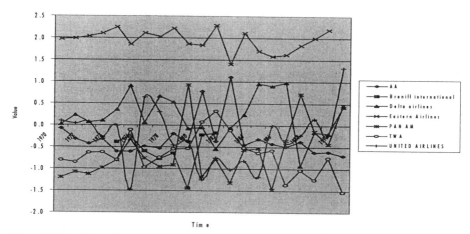

Figure D.12a: Operating expenses per ATK for American airlines (including Eastern Airlines).

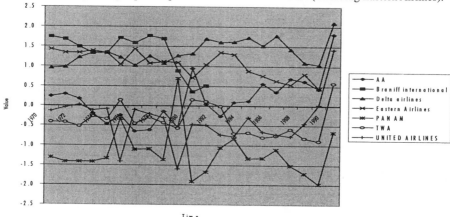

Figure D.12b: Operating revenue per RTK for American airlines (including Eastern Airlines).

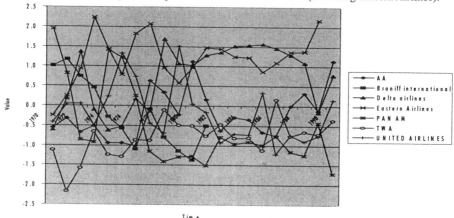

Figure D.12c: Employees per passenger kilometre for American airlines (including Eastern Airlines).

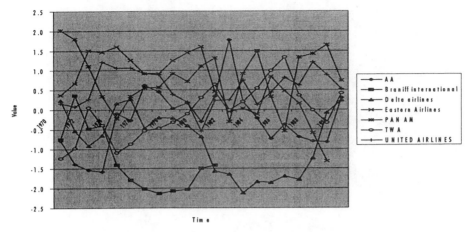

Figure D.12d: Weight Loadfactor for American airlines (including Eastern Airlines).

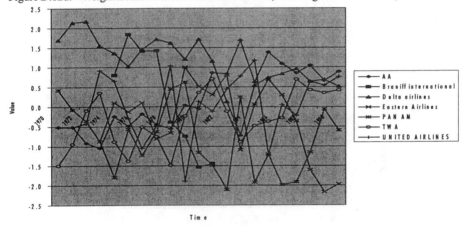

Figure D.12e: Operating margin for American airlines (including Eastern Airlines).

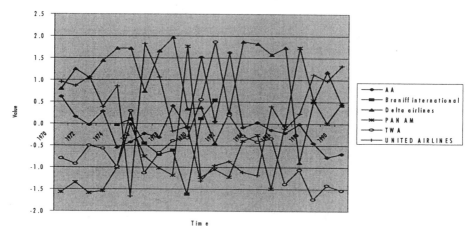

Figure D.13a: Operating expenses per ATK for American airlines (excluding Eastern Airlines).

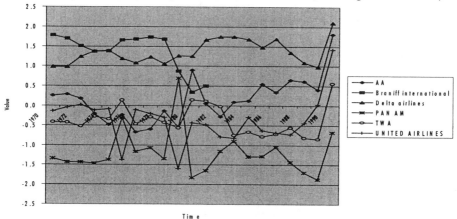

Figure D.13b: Operating revenue per RTK for American airlines (excluding Eastern Airlines).

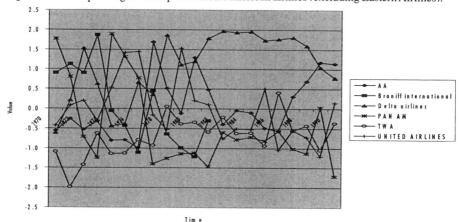

Figure D.13c: Employees per passenger kilometre for American airlines (excluding Eastern Airlines).

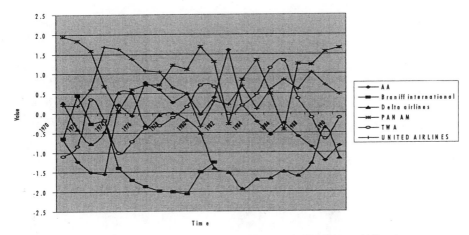

Figure D.13d: Weight Loadfactor for American airlines (excluding Eastern Airlines).

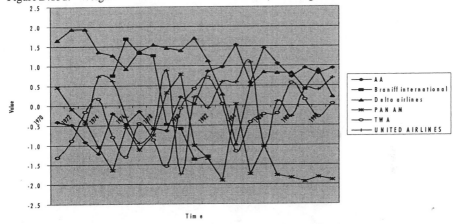

Figure D.13e: Operating margin for American airlines (excluding Eastern Airlines).

458

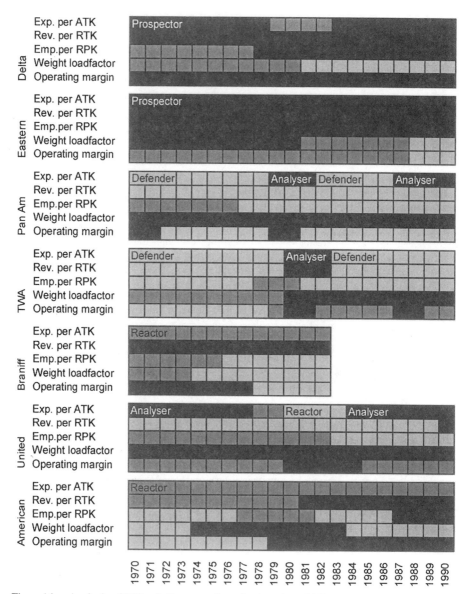

Figure 14: Analysis of Miles & Snow typology for American Airlines during the period 1970-1990.

APPENDIX E: INTRODUCTION TO GAME THEORIES

Game Theory has always been part of human existence. Brams (2003) traces it back to the implications of game theory to the Hebrew Bible, and he gives numerous examples of behaviour of individuals guided by moral principles. Walker (2001) gives an overview of the application of game theories dating back to the Babylonian Talmud; especially, the marriage contract problem has posed challenges to scholars to understand it, in 1985 it turned out to be an example of cooperative games. In this respect, Riechert & Hammerstein (1983, p. 378) propose the following definition of game theory:

> Game Theory is the study of conflict of interests in which the value of a particular set of actions undertaken by a "decision maker" depends not only on his own but also on others.

When we look at how individuals make choices, Classical Game Theory describes such (Section E.1). When looking at choices of larger groups, we will have to turn to Evolutionary Game Theory (Section E.2) and Evolutionary Stable Strategies (Section E.3). This leads to the recognition of levels in game theory (Section E.4) and the belonging models (Section E.5). Section E.6 expands on Adaptive Dynamics, a version of evolutionary game theory, to describe biological evolutionary processes of speciation.

E.1   CLASSICAL GAME THEORY

The most famous example of Game Theory is the *Prisoners Dilemma*, because it contains most of the basic elements of game theory (e.g. the Nash-equilibrium, common knowledge, and trust). In the Prisoners Dilemma, two criminals are arrested for a minor crime (Riechert & Hammerstein, 1983, p. 379). This crime is generally punished with a one-year sentence. However, they are also suspected of being guilty of another major crime for which they will be imprisoned for an additional 9 years. While there is a firm evidence of the first charge, the evidence of the second is insubstantial and a confession is essential to the prosecutor's case. A deal is offered to the criminals by the District Attorney. If one of the criminals confesses that both have committed the major crime, he will be freed immediately, whereas his partner will get a ten-year prison term. However, when both confess they will be forgiven the minor crime but not the major crime. When both deny everything, they will be sentenced for the minor crime. Both suspects are interrogated simultaneously and in separate rooms, which makes this a non-cooperative game. With this deal, the District Attorney has placed the criminals in a situation where they have a conflict of interest. The situation is

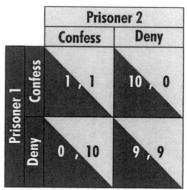

Figure E.1: Pay-off matrix for the Prisoner's Dilemma. The best options for both players is to confess, the so-called Nash-equilibrium, being the optimal strategy.

shown in the pay-off matrix in Figure E.1. Each would be best off if he confessed and the other did not.

To analyse the game, it is useful to think in terms of best-reply strategies. How should Prisoner 1 act in order to maximise his pay-off? When Prisoner 2 chooses to deny, it is clear that Prisoner 1 should confess since 10 years saved is more than 9 years saved. So confessing would be the best-reply strategy in case of Prisoner 2 denying. When Prisoner 2 chooses to confess, Prisoner 1's best reply would be still to confess (1 year saved against 0). Therefore, the only obvious conclusion for both prisoners would be to confess, putting them in their third-best situation, which is the Nash-equilibrium of this game. The Nash-equilibrium is a collection of strategies, one for each player, that are mutual best replies in the sense that each player's strategy is optimal given the strategy of other players (Nash, 1951, p. 287).

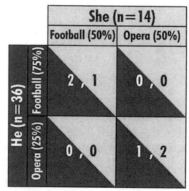

Figure E.2: Pay-off matrix for the Battle of the Sexes. If both go to their favourite event, they will not enjoy it (pay-off 0). They will both enjoy the favourite event of the other less (pay-off 1) than their own favourite (pay-off 2).

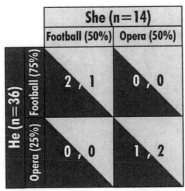

Figure E.3: Results of the Battle of Sexes when players choose according to their own gender.

Driving forces in a game include also time and power, as demonstrated by the *economic* game called the *Battle of the Sexes*. Imagine a couple that has different plans for the evening, he wants to go to a football match, and she wants to go to the opera (see Figure E.2). Cooper et al. (1993) have done extensive research on this game, and the different strategies to be played. Their results were published in 1993, the outcomes show that there is more to game theory than just pay-offs. In an experiment in 1999, students were asked to play the Battle of the Sexes where the row player was called *He* and the column player was called *She*. Students were asked to play the game in the role of the player that fitted their gender: 68% of the students did choose their own preferred action. In comparison, about 63% of the subjects in any of the two roles did choose their preferred action. Since the students were asked to play the game in the role that fitted their gender, we can compare the choice of the students according to their gender. 75% of the males choose their preferred action whereas the females were equally divided between the two actions (Figure E.3). The experiment was repeated several times with different circumstances (see Figure E.4). In the first case, Player 1 can make an announcement about the choices but does not do so, silence is seen as a sign of weakness. This reflects in the higher percentage of Player 2 choosing the favourite option, the opera. The choices of the players are influenced by the assumptions of the students of whom the most powerful player in the game is. In the next case, Player 1 clearly states that he will choose his favourite, the football match, seen as a sign of strength or determination. The very high percentage (94%) of Player 2 choosing the second best option illustrates this. The same pay-offs can result in different choices with different people playing the game and different circumstances (with or without announcements).

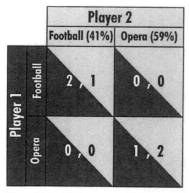 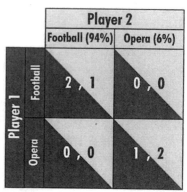

Figure E.4: Two scenarios for the Battle of the Sexes. On the left hand, it shows the results when Player 1 can make an announcement but does not. On the right hand, the results are shown when Player 1 announces to go to the football match.

E.2 EVOLUTIONARY GAME THEORY

When we look at evolution, we also find traces of game theory. One of them is the equal division of men and women. Darwin argued that natural selection would act to equalise the sex ratio (Walker, 2001). If, for example, births of females are less common than males, then a newborn female will have better mating prospects than a newborn male, and therefore can expect to have more offspring. Parents genetically disposed to produce females tend to have more than the average number of grandchildren, and that way the genes for female-producing tendencies spread, and female births become more common. As the ratio 1:1 is approached, the advantage associated with producing females dies away. The same reasoning holds if males are substituted for females throughout. 1:1 is the equilibrium ratio.

The evolution of species is not determined by rational choices but only by competitive advantages. It is simply the result of a strategy that is followed by chance, initiated by mutations. When this different strategy leads to a higher pay-off, i.e. to a competitive advantage of it's own species enemies, the chances of this so-called mutation to survive grow. Depending on how fast the mutation population can grow the mutant takes over the whole population or dies out. Riechert & Hammerstein (1983) address this by stating:

> the evolutionary application of this construct (game theory) focuses on decisions "made by" the process of natural selection - individual plants and animals are merely the performers of an inherent program.

E.3 EVOLUTIONARY STABLE STRATEGIES

Samuelson (1997, p. 38), Meszéna et al. (2000), Geritz et al. (1997), and many others have written about the phenomenon Evolutionary Stable Strategies (ESS).

Evolutionary strategies provide insight into phenomena like bifurcation and range from simple games to more complex games.

The most common setting is to discuss this evolutionary stability in a two-player symmetric game, both players have equal options and information, but the theories themselves also discuss asymmetric games, in which players have different options and information. This legitimate because the effect of a different strategy is always measured against:

- another player from the same set (following the old strategy) or
- another player from another set (assumed to follow the same strategy he normally does).

In both cases different strategies and pay-offs are evaluated against each other. An example of the first case, a player from the same set, are plants competing for the same water source where the different strategies might be different root systems (Riechert & Hammerstein, 1983, pp. 387-395). The second case is explained by the *Battle of the Sexes* where in the first game males and females battled against each other, although the differences between the players are not very large. More distinct asymmetric games are those of buyers-sellers, firm-union, etc. As long as the conditions are stable, symmetric as well as asymmetric games can be used in the ESS-theory.

Now the question arises: When is a strategy an ESS? Consider two players in a game with a set of different strategies $S=\{s_1, ..., s_n\}$. When one player plays strategy s_i and the other plays strategy s_j then $P(s_i, s_j)$ is the pay-off of both players playing s_i given that the other player chooses s_j. When the players choose mixed strategies (multiple strategies for the same number of games), we define the pay-off as $P(m, m')$ with m and m' as part of S (a combination of one or more different strategies of S).

Now strategy m^* is an ESS if

$$P(m^*, m^*) > P(m, m^*) \text{ and} \qquad (Eq.\ E.1)$$
$$P(m^*, m^*) = P(m, m^*) \Rightarrow P(m^*, m) > P(m,m) \qquad (Eq.\ E.2)$$

in words:

(1) Given that the opponent plays strategy m^*, there is no strategy with a higher pay-off than strategy m^* (for Player 1).

(2) If the pay-off is equal, the opponent might play another strategy m. Given that the opponent plays any strategy m, there is no strategy with a higher pay-off than strategy m^* (for Player 1).

Therefore the strategy m^* is the best response to any other strategy and called the Evolutionary Stable Strategy. This ESS condition is a combination of a Nash-equilibrium (Eq. E.1) and a stability requirement (Eq. E.2) (Samuelson, 1997, p. 40). When these two conditions do not hold, it is possible for a mutant playing strategy m to invade the population playing strategy m^*.

This proof holds for symmetric games and asymmetric games. When looking at reality, symmetric games are seldomly played. Most of the time because players come from different sets but also because perceptions of the outside world are subject to the mental models (Senge, 1990) of the players. In this case, the players are symmetric, but the pay-offs are not.

Instead of one equilibrium, there can also be more equilibria. When this happens, we speak about Neutrally Stable Strategies (NNS). In this case, a mutation can invade a population but it can not take over the whole population. The mathematical form can be found in Equation E.3 and E.4:

$$P(m^*, m^*) \geq P(m, m^*) \tag{Eq. E.3}$$
$$P(m^*, m^*) = P(m, m^*) \Rightarrow P(m^*, m) \geq P(m, m) \tag{Eq. E.4}$$

Again, the first formula points to a Nash-equilibrium, the second formula in this case ensures that the mutant cannot earn a higher pay-off. In this case, a mutant can coexist with the normal population playing the normal Neutrally Stable Strategy. The problem is (according to Samuelson, 1997, p. 53 and others) that a neutrally stable game might not be stable enough. Especially when the Nash-equilibrium is just on the brink of being a Nash-equilibrium.

E.4 LEVELS IN GAME THEORY

When reading about different types of game theory, it becomes clear that there are different levels in game theory that can interact with each other. A simple example by McEwan (1997) might provide a good example of these different levels. The story starts at a picnic at a hot-air balloon festival where suddenly a balloon becomes adrift. In the balloon basket is a terrified 10-year old boy. A number of men hold on to the ropes of the balloon, stopping it from climbing any higher. The situation suddenly changes, the wind gets hold of the balloon and the men are pulled from the ground. They are in a terrible dilemma. When they hold on they might save the boy, but they might also fall to the ground when the balloon keeps gaining altitude and they cannot hold on any longer. In that case, they will fall to their death. But every man that saves himself by letting loose puts the other men in more danger, letting the balloon climb faster and faster. In the story all but one man let loose. Resulting in the death of the man trying to save the boy. In this example, it becomes clear that pay-offs for individuals can be totally different for groups of individuals, even when a group of individuals with a common goal is put in the same situation.

Olson (1965, p. 2) states in his research about this subject: *unless the number of individuals is quite small, or unless there is coercion or some other special device to make individuals act in their common interest, rational, self interested individuals will not act to achieve their common or group interests.* This investigation of Olson questions the fact that logic of groups can be explained by game theory and that game theory about individuals (Classical Game Theory) can be connected to the game theory of groups. Cole (1998) arrives at the same conclusion. In an investigation by the University of California, people were observed when they had to choose between relative risks (for example, acid gasses) and possible profits (e.g. more jobs). The research showed that individuals change when someone becomes part of a group. Although an individual can consider a deal to be fair, a group consisting of the same individuals can object to the deal because it conflicts with the group's interest. Although the basic process of game theory is the same on all levels (individual, groups, and may be even larger groups at higher evolutionary levels), the outcomes are different.

E.5   MODELS FOR EVOLUTIONARY LEVELS

On the highest level of aggregation, the input is *different players,* which can be any amount of players above two. They enter the game theory process, in this process the players are matched with each other and they can win or loose a game or, in case of symmetrical games, break even. The pay-offs and strategies determine the winners and losers of the game, as displayed in a pay-off matrix.

According to the findings in the previous section, choices of people in groups are influenced by the voice of the group. The process of choosing on this level still stays the same, but now a player also has to take the pay-offs of the group into account. Brouwer (2001) shows has this might be put into a pay-off matrix, see Figure E.5. Another method might be to make all possible combinations between Player 1, Player 2, Group 1, and Group 2 and play all games simultaneous. But to evaluate the choices made, every player has to look at four matrices, his strategy against the other player, his own group, the other group

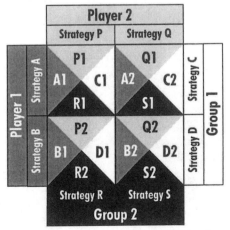

Figure E.5: Pay-off matrix for group level. Pay-offs of individual actions relate to group decisions.

and finally, between the two groups. The overall picture gets lost considering all these options.

Although the group level is more complicated than the individual level, the group level can still be understood. But what if the groups have to play a game against other groups? The matrix shown in Figure E.5 will be even larger or there will be so many different matrices that have to be compared to each other that nobody can remember all different pay-offs exactly, thus resulting in an educated guess instead of a rational and objective choice. Still there has to be a connection between the individual and the evolutionary level as in both levels the strategies are measured against each other.

Following the process of game theory, the distribution of the strategies in the population will shift to all X or all Y, see Figure E.6. The figure shows the Nash Equilibria, XX and YY, where XX is a pay-off dominant equilibrium, and YY a risk-dominant equilibrium. Since both points are end state equilibria, a never-ending tournament between players only with strategy X and Y will result in a situation with all players adopting strategy X or all players strategy Y.

But how do we know what the end result will be? This depends on a number of factors, e.g. the composition of the group and the mutation rate allowed by the model. First of all, a number of players with random distribution between strategy X and Y are put together. Then the players are randomly put together two-by-two, so $N/2$ games are played. The results of the game are remembered by the players and they learn from the outcomes; so when they loose they adopt the strategy of the opponent (learning can also be seen as dying of the individual who loses the game, and replacing this individual by a new one with the winning strategy). The outcomes of the original games are win, loose and break-even, but after the learning phase only the winning breaking-even strategies survive. Next, all players are subject to mutation, in which a number of players will switch between strategy X and Y. After, the mutation players are matched to each other

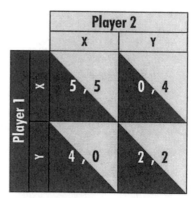

Figure E.6: Pay-off matrix with multiple equilibria. It shows two Nash equilibria: XX and YY.

and the total process is repeated. Looking at the different combinations of strategies in this game, we see that

- *XX* results in break-even and no learning, these players stay with *X;*
- *YY* results in break-even and no learning, these players stay with *Y;*
- *XY* (or *YX*) results in a loss for X, so these players switch to Y.

The division is 1:2 so that the critical mass for all *X* and all *Y* lies on *2/3*. This means that to reach a state where the whole population plays *X*, at least *2/3* of the population has to be *X*. Only *1/3* of the population has to play *Y*, to reach the equilibrium of *YY*. Depending on how large the mutations are and how fast they die out, one of these equilibria can be abandoned for the other.

The examples given do not address directly the domain of evolutionary biology Nevertheless, from these models one can conclude that on the evolutionary level:

- the basic game theory process is the same as on the individual level;
- the real difference between evolutionary and individual levels is that individuals can learn new strategies;
- the players can always be successful by copying a successful strategy, though the advantages decrease over time.

E.6   ADAPTIVE DYNAMICS

The models of the Evolutionary Stable Strategies have evolved to models that do not take fitness as a constant but as a variable. The application of these so-called Adaptive Dynamics yields additional insight into the evolution and co-evolution of species and populations (Geritz et al., 1997, Meszéna et al., 2001). This section will firstly describe *Pairwise Invasibility Plots*, then move on the stability requirements for assessing Evolutionary Stable Strategies, and finally pay attention to the impact of these models on evolution of species.

Geritz et al. (1997, p. 2025) claim that a Pairwise Invasibility Plot allows convenient display of how mutants spread in a given population. It indicates the effect of a mutant with strategy y in an equilibrium population with x strategists (see Figure E.7). Note the parallels with the work of Kauffman about fitness landscapes, which in this case is more explicitly present, though the focus of Kaufmann is on fitness landscapes themselves. Adaptive Dynamics directs itself at the evolution of a population. Figure E.7 shows the intersection of the diagonal with another curve on which $s_x(y)=0$ which corresponds to a singular strategy. Eight possible generic local configurations of the PIP exist, as depicted in Figure E.8. Each of these configurations represents a different evolutionary scenario that can be interpreted in terms of four properties of stability:

a) Evolutionary stability. A singular strategy is evolutionary stable if no initially rare mutant can invade, in other words, of $s_{x*}(y)<0$ for all $y \neq x^*$. This concerns all the diagrams in which the vertical line through x^* finds itself

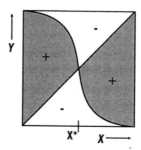

Figure E.7: Example of Pairwise Invasibility Plot showing fitness gradients. On the main diagonal $s_x(y)$ is always zero. A "+" just above the diagonal and a "-" just below inidicate a positive fitness gradient ($s_x(y)>0$), i.e. moving in the direction of the positive fitness gradient proves beneficial for the population because of increased fitness: the mutant will spread. The opposite indicates a negative fitness gradient, meaning a loss of fitness ($s_x(y)<0$).

entirely within regions marked with "-". (Meszéna et al., 2001, p. 202; Geritz et al., 1997, p. 2025).

b) Convergence stability. A singular strategy is convergence stable if a population of nearby phenotypes can be invaded by mutants that are even closer to x^*; that means $s_x(y)>0$ for $x<y<x^*$ and $x^*<y<x$. A convergence stable singular strategy is an evolutionary attractor in the sense that a monomorphic population will remain in its neighbourhood. A singular strategy that is not convergence stable is a repeller from which populations tend to evolve away (Geritz, 1997 et al., p. 2025). The singular strategy moves towards an asymptotically stable fixed point of the canonical adaptive dynamics: a sequence of small steps that constitute a stochastic evolutionary path (Meszéna et al., 2001, pp. 201-202).

c) Invading potential. A singular strategy can spread in other populations when itself is initially rare if $s_y(x^*)>0$ for all $x \neq x^*$, in other words if in the PIP the horizontal line through x^* on the y-axis lies entirely in a region marked "+". A singular strategy that is evolutionary stable and convergence stable may nevertheless be incapable of invading other populations if initially rare itself (Geritz, 1997, p. 2025). Meszéna et al. (2001, p. 202) remark that this requirement differs from convergence stability. Such a singular strategy can be reached only asymptotically through a series of ever-decreasing evolutionary steps.

d) Dimorphism stability (Geritz, 1997, pp. 2025-2026). Two strategies x and y can mutually invade and give rise to a dimorphic population, if $s_x(y)>0$ and $s_y(x)>0$. The set of pairs of mutually invasible strategies near x^* is given by the overlapping parts of the "+" region. The evolutionary significance of mutual invasibility depends on the combination with the other properties of the singular strategy. If x^* is convergence stable and ESS, the mutually invasible strategies are necessarily on the opposite sides of x^*. A mutant strategy with strategy y can invade a population with x_1 and x_2 (with $x_1 < x_2$) only if $x_1 < y < x_2$. The mutant may replace both x_1 and x_2, or only the one that is not on the same side of x^* but further away. In the long run dimorphism effectively disappears as the populations gradually evolves towards x^* through a series of monomorphic and (converging) dimorphic population states. However, if x^* is convergence stable but not ESS, then a strategy y can invade only if $y < x_1$ or $y > x_2$. Since always the middle strategy is ousted, the two remaining strategies become progressively more distinct with each successive invasion. This process of divergence of strategies is evolutionary

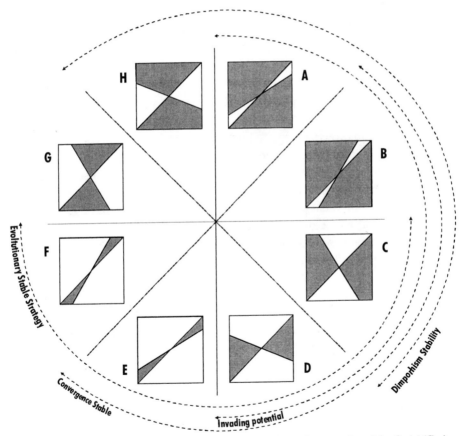

Figure E.8: Classification of the singular strategies according to the second partials of $s_x(y)$ (Geritz, 1997, p. 2025). Each pairwise invasibility plot represents a different evolutionary scenario which can be interpreted in the four properties of the singular strategy: evolutionary stability, convergence stability, invading potential and dimorphism stability.

branching, and the singular strategy in the PIP is a branching point. The dimensionality of the environment sets an upper limit to the number of different types that can coexist, and hence to the maximum diversity that can be reached by branching of the evolutionary tree. The picture of evolution that arises is that of a random walk in a state space of a dimension given by the number of the different strategies present. The direction of the steps is given by the local fitness gradient. At each branching event, the dimension of the state space increases.

These four different kinds of stability indicate different kinds of modes for a singular strategy. To determine the position of a singular strategy and to evaluate the evolutionary potential, assessment of all these four different kinds of stability should take place. Please note that in Figure E.8 one situation reflects a position of total instability. None of the four different types of stability apply for that situation. Evolutionary change occurs when the requirement of evolutionary stability is not met.

The application of these models exceeds the thoughts of the NK-models as proposed by Kauffman (1993, pp. 41-43). In the NK-model, the type with the highest fitness peak will in the long-run out-compete all others since the separate fitness peaks possess unequal heights (Geritz et al., 1997, p. 2027). Although Kauffman explains coexistence and branching, he deploys additional qualitative descriptions to arrive at conclusions towards the diversity of life. During the discussion of the adaptive walks two main criteria appeared: sustained fitness and evolvability. The first two stability requirements, evolutionary stability and convergence stability, have strong parallels with sustained fitness. Evolvability resembles invading potential and dimorphical stability. The models of Adaptive Dynamics effectively explain the underlying mechanisms of selection but hardly connect explicitly to the genotype as is the case with the NK-model of Kauffman.

Appendix F: Features for Hypotheses Testing

This appendix describes the qualitative parameters that have been used to test the refined hypotheses. To use quantitative measures, longitudinal data should be available of the companies; for the moment being, the link between processes and structures and data is considered weak. Therefore, this assessment has reverted to the evaluation of qualitative parameters, which make it also possible to compare the six different cases.

Critical features have been defined to review the cases, see Table F.1. Each of these features arrives from the evolutionary theories and their meaning for the domain of organisations. Since this study focuses mainly on industrial organisations, the features direct themselves to those directly linked to the primary process of companies. For example, the output of the companies links it to the customers in specific product-market combinations. According to organisational ecology, other factors should be also taken into account, like institutionalisation; these have been omitted because of the scope of the study and the information present in the reports about the graduation theses.

Table F.1: Features for hypotheses to assess the research in management science and the case studies of the Delft School Approach.

Refined hypothesis	Features
A.1 Mutations The organisation maintains its homeostasis through the introduction of small changes to its phenotype, outer traits, to adapt to the dynamics of the environment.	Visible traits should change: - product - market - performance
A.2 State Transition In dynamic environments, organisations should increase their exchange with the environment and create a dissipative structure through which new behaviour and structures arise.	Dynamics of the environment: - changes in competitiveness or industry Dissipative structure: - intense interaction with customers, suppliers
B.1.A Adaptive walks An organisation undertakes continuous adaptive walks to increase its fitness in the landscape it operates thereby taking the characteristics of the landscape into account. These adaptive walks follow developmental pathways by which the fitness increases.	Adaptive walks result in increased fitness: - fitness of solutions in comparison to current situation - landscape characteristics (rugged, smooth) Developmental pathways: - accumulation of internal changes - combining these internal changes into major changes
B.1.B Long jumps An organisation exerts one-time interventions taking into account the Hamming distance, they exceed the differences necessary for reaching a nearby adaptive peak in the landscape.	One-time interventions: - severe organisational changes of processes, structures, etc. Hamming distance: - new structure deviates much from current operations
B.2.A Sustained fitness The organisation maintains its homeostasis through the introduction of small changes to its phenotype, outer traits, to find a local optimum. Through gradual steps, it becomes gradually harder to reach the local fitness peak.	Small changes of phenotype: - product - market - performance Reaching local fitness peak: - effect of changes - stability (at local fitness peak) or convergence (approaching)
B.2.B Evolvability A company moves into new adaptive zones either by deploying and appropriate strategy, dispersal and invading, or by bifurcation.	Dispersal and invading: - new products - new markets Bifurcation: - internal specialisation
B.2.C Complexity Error Catastrophe An increasing number of competitors, mutations, diversity in the product-market combination(s) force a company to reposition itself by choosing either to increase sustained fitness or to search for a nearby local fitness peak.	Market: - increasing number of competitors - increasing number of new products Repositioning: - Strategy

APPENDIX G: PROCESSES OF INNOVATION

Subsection 10.2.1 has already presented the outline of processes that yield innovations, from discovery to commercial production focusing on the value of the innovation itself. Which intermediate steps do exist in addition to the model of Herbig (1994)? Schippers (2003) has found 7 models to describe the innovation processes (they apply equally well to technology management):

- innovation process according to Rothwell (1994);
- breakthrough model (in 't Veld, 1998);
- Innovation Arena (Janszen, 2000);
- life-cycle model (ten Haaf et al., 2002);
- interrelationships between major innovative activities (Burgelman & Sayles, 1986);
- interactive innovation model from Kline & Rosenberg (Jacobs, 2001);
- innovation model (Tidd et al., 1997).

G.1 ROTHWELL'S COUPLING MODEL

Rothwell (1994) distinguishes five generations of innovation models when looking at the history of innovation over the past decades. The final fifth generation model does approach innovation not merely as an aspect of organisation, but rather as an multi-factor process which requires high levels of integration within an industrial company and its network. The fourth and fifth generation models hold perspectives on cooperation and collaboration more the organisational processes; therefore, the next paragraph will discuss the preceding model.

Figure G.1 presents Rothwell's own coupling model of innovation, which is a third generation model. Within the model, he distinguishes five main processes: idea generation, development, prototype production, manufacturing, marketing & sales, each of them linked to each other with feedback loops. Also, Jenkins et

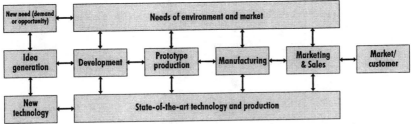

Figure G.1: Rothwell's coupling model of innovation (third generation). Innovation processes are driven by market demans (technology pull) and technological developments (technology push).

al. (1997a, pp. 371-377) arrive at the conclusion that an integrative approach succeeds more likely than just a stage-wise approach, which appear to serve more as a management tool. They recognise also the need for iteration and feedback loops within the product development process. Additionally, they advocate the deployment of cross-functional teams supported by senior management and allowing the team to exert control over the project. Thirdly, they stress the simultaneous development of the product itself and the manufacturing system. Similarly, conducting a study into sequential and simultaneous approaches to engineering Riedel & Pawar (1998) highlight that the concepts of design and manufacturing are not linked in literature, and that the interaction between product design and manufacturing strategy is under-researched. Spring & Dalrymple (2000) come to the same conclusion when examining two cases of product customisation, manufacturing issues got little attention during design and engineering.

G.2 BREAKTHROUGH MODEL

The breakthrough model (in 't Veld, 1998) indicates the overall processes necessary for implementing changes into the structure of operations (see Figure G.2). By scanning the environment, new or adapted goals are set and the derived policy acts as a reference for the review of tactical and operational decisions.

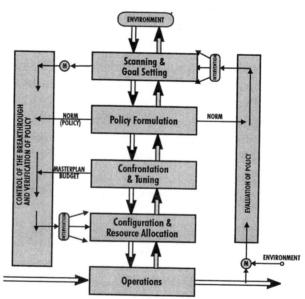

Figure G.2: Breakthrough model (in 't Veld, 1998). The model shows the processes of scanning the environment, the implemtation of changes, operations, and control of the breakthrough process itself.

The process of confrontation and tuning takes the possibilities into account leading to specific decisions on the utilisation of resources and structures for operations. Through the development and construction process the actual implementation of the structural changes in operations takes place. The evaluation of strategies might create new input for the breakthrough processes. The verification enables companies to follow the progress of the breakthrough processes. This model might apply to product development, process development, changes in organisational structures, etc., having a wide scope for any breakthrough.

G.3 INNOVATION ARENA

The Innovation Arena characterises the innovation process as a process that moves from chaos to orderly producing in time. Therefore, an organisation has to move from conducting non-linear processes at the start on an innovation to linear processes during manufacturing and sales. An innovation process has four main aspects with which it can be described: technology, application, market segment/customer groups, organisation. Figure G.3 depicts how these four aspects do relate, they are not independent from each other. Within this arena, the position of an organisation denotes the state of the innovation process, each change of position stands for an innovation. After the determination of its position in the Innovation Arena, an organisation can conduct the Dynamic Business Model. The five steps consists of: the determination of the position of the organisation (Innovation Arena), the allocation of resources (people and means), the determination of processes (internal and external), the application of mechanisms (non-linear), and the modification of behaviour (market and organisation). The Dynamic Business Model recognises also three stages:

- first stage. In this stage, an analysis is made of existing business systems, encompassing three steps, (a) boundary setting, determination of present and future position of the organisation and goal setting, (b) analysis of the

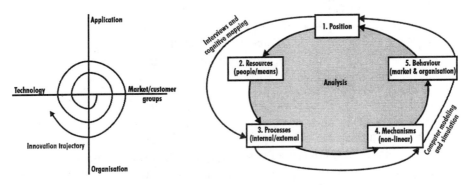

Figure G.3: Innovation Arena (on the left) and the Dynamic Business Model (on the right).

important players for the organisation (for development of new products and markets), (c) analysis of all processes (internal and external) that are part of the innovation process;

- second stage. This stage consists of analysing the non-linear mechanisms that affect the potential dynamics of the new product or business development process as well as the behaviour of the innovation process;
- third stage. This stage consists of building Dynamic Business Models that create a Learning Organisation.

Non-linear mechanisms are at the heart of this approach since these constitute the reality of the innovation process; in contrast, management wants to control processes within firms from a linear mechanism (causal relation known on beforehand). An early conversion from the non-linear mechanism to linear control facilitates understanding of management of the issues at hand (private conversation with F. Janszen). The non-linear mechanisms can be divided in (Janszen, 2000, p. 132):

- reinforcing loops. These consist of virtuous loops (new products lead to new markets, because that market did not exits before), and vicious loops (e.g. new product has bugs, service-engineers send to field work, reduced capacity to develop new version for product, hence competitors have greater chance to introduce a better product);
- limiting loops. These comprise of control mechanisms (the control of the innovation process itself), capacity and performance limits (every market gets satiated), and constraints (customer requirements, environment, technology);
- lock-in mechanisms. Switching costs are a key constraint of the organisation, its customers and its competitors;
- time delays, described by negative feedback loops (like in cybernetic control, maintaining homeostasis), and large time variation of processes (puts a demand on the organisational flexibility);
- selection mechanisms: market, intra-organisation, and governmental (technology push or pull, opportunities);
- variation and creation mechanisms. These include the possible sources of innovation (science, suppliers, and competitors) and the options an organisation has for decision-making.

G.4 LIFE-CYCLE MODEL

The life-cycle model of ten Haaf et al. (2002, pp. 166-312) has seven phases as depicted in Figure G.4, covering the scanning of market needs and demands to the disposal or renovation of products. The innovation process within this life-cycle concept consists of the phases A-E. The organisation has several drivers

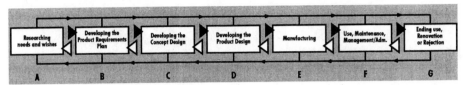

Figure G.4: Life-cycle model of ten Haaf et al. (2002).

to perform research and a scan of the environment to find out what the market needs, now and in the future. Input can come from stakeholders (customers, producers and suppliers, governments), organisational processes, and characteristics from the system. During the next phase these market needs and requirements are translated into functional requirements for the system to be developed. The functional criteria result in the generation of alternative system concepts followed by an evaluation of the best system concept. Up until this phase the phases of A-C are not a linear process but iterative. During the final phase of development, the construction of the product takes place during phase D. The subsequent phases F-G provide information about design requirements with respect to usage, maintenance, and disposal.

G.5   Interrelationships between Major Innovative Activities

Burgelman & Sayles (1986) developed a model depicting the interrelationships between the major innovative activities of innovation processes (see Figure G.5). Similarly to the other models, it describes how to transform an idea or a market need to an actual product or production process that creates that particular product. From the corporate knowledge domain an initiation for a research program starts, sometimes resulting from an environmental scan. The exploratory research starts with defining envelopes, which set the boundaries and parameters (divergent thinking) after which narrowing down takes place (convergent thinking); the exploratory research ends by defining objectives and programs. After exploratory research (in which knowledge of the past can be used), several alternative opportunities arise. A trade-off decision leads to the further detailing

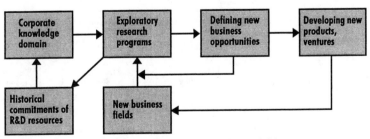

Figure G.5: The interrelation between the major innovative activities.

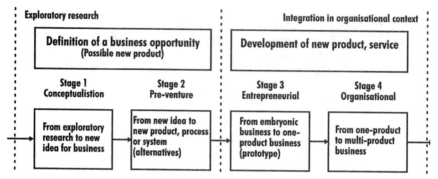

Figure G.6: Stages in product development. The model is an expansion of activitiy of "Developing new products, ventures" in the model of the interrelation between major innovative activities, as presented in Figure G.5.

of the chosen opportunity into new ventures of products or processes. As a result of a new product, new markets or business fields might originate in which new innovations might fit. The newly acquired knowledge is put into the database of the historical commitments of the R&D resources. Additionally, Burgelman & Sayles describe the transformation from the definition phase to the development phase in more detail (see Figure G.6).

G.6 INTERACTIVE INNOVATION MODEL

Kline & Rosenberg (Jacobs, 2001) developed the interactive innovation model. Typically, for this model is the inclusion of feedback loops while traditional models depict linear transformations from research to the development of a new product (see Figure G.7). Firstly, within the new model an environmental scan is performed after which potential products and product concepts are created. If knowledge is needed for the innovation process, which does not yet exist in the organisation, additional research is done. During every stage of the process, feedback locks in

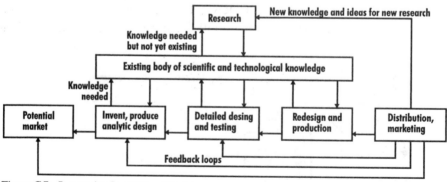

Figure G.7: Interactive Innovation Model.

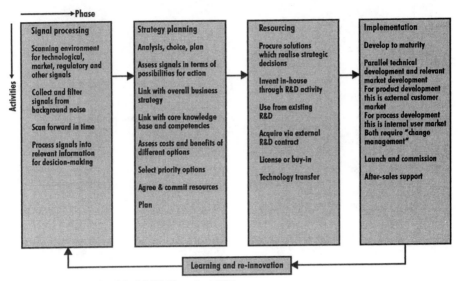

Figure G.8: Innovation Model (Tidd et al., 1997).

the previous stages and the existing body of knowledge to evaluate the designs for functionality. The model emphasises the knowledge flows and interactions between different functions in the firm (departments, etc.), according to Leiponen (1997, p. 7).

G.7 Innovation Model

The innovation model from Tidd et al. (1997) recognises four phases during the product and process innovation trajectory (see Figure G.8). These phases are also known as the routines underlying the process of management. The phases of this model compare to those of military experience (Tidd et al., 1997; Janszen, 2000): (1) describe understand and analyse the environment, (2) determine a course of action in line with the analysis, and (3) carry out the decided course of action.

APPENDIX H: CASE AGRICO

Since 1998, AgriCo belongs to a concern, one of the largest specialised producers and distributors of agricultural and viticultural implements in the world. AgriCo produces various agricultural machines in three types: spreaders, sprayers, and mowers. The production figures for 1998 were: 8.398 spreaders, 4.762 mowers and 452 sprayers. The investigation by the postgraduate student, during 1999 and 2000, has been narrowed down to the production process of two mowers: one that is pulled by a tractor (KM), and one that is mounted on the tractor (FM); each of them delivered in varying sizes and with different options. The seasonal demand had forced AgriCo to deploy a strategy of keeping products at stock for fast delivery to clients. Fast delivery and competitive pricing are the most essential ingredients for sales in the agricultural market, a truly competitive environment with relatively low margins.

H.1 CONTENTS OF GRADUATION THESIS

The investigation initially started with the request to investigate options for reviewing the make-to-stock strategy and to reduce stock levels of products. The student undertook an analysis of the production process, its control processes, and the relation between forecasts, production scheduling, and actual production. The analysis also contained a detailed review of the forecasts produced by strategic processes, the marketing data generated by the sales offices, and the actual production figures during a number of years.

Problem Analysis
At the highest level of aggregation, the production processes for the two types of mowers have equal transformation steps; at a more detailed level differences do exist, however these do not have any impact on the findings for the overall control of the production process. Various conclusions can be drawn:
- Seasonal influence. The output rate of the production process fluctuates throughout the year. The production of the FM and KM mowers is highly affected by seasonal demand. The assembly of the mowers starts at the end of October and finishes at the end of June. The production peak is slightly ahead of the sales' peak of the mowers.
- Influence on stock. Because of the seasonal influence on production, AgriCo produces FM and KM machines at stock. They estimate that the cost of stock constitutes about 15% of the cost price, with 190 mowers per month at

stock, the costs of stock are about € 260.000,- a year; the KM type causes most of the stock cost.

Bottlenecks in the Production Processes

The student arrived at the following findings for the order processing:

- The sales predictions are not very accurate. However, it is not feasible to expect accurate predictions so that the stock will be reduced to minimum levels. Hence, the production system should absorb the uncertainties surrounding sales predictions and meet as much as possible the actual demand.
- Once an order has been accepted, the customers want a quick delivery of the product. The logistics and production system should allow fast processing of orders reducing the current delivery time.
- This means that the company should deliver all the products out of stock within the current situation. Because the orders are not always compliant with the stock, sometimes the delivery times are very long or costly (make-to-order or conversion from stock) or the product will not be made at all.
- Due to the seasonal influence there is an alternating over- or undercapacity present in the factory.

The analysis of the supply of raw materials, parts, and components revealed as problems:

- Some materials and some parts have a long lead-time.
- Some parts are delivered beyond the scheduled dates.

For the delivery of finished products and the stock replenishment, he concluded:

- The stock levels exceed the required minimum levels at large due to the inaccurate sales predictions.
- The machines get more and more complex, making them even more expensive to keep at stock. This indicates the need to develop a control and production system that reduces stock to acceptable levels.
- The wrong machines are kept at stock during the sales season resulting in conversion of already finished mowers into types requested by clients.
- The capacity of the manufacturing process is not large enough to cover the seasonal peak, making production to stock inevitable.

Another conclusion from the analysis is that the assembly department has limited workspace, which means that the storage area for the parts is very limited. In the existing assembly line, every day production management and workers struggle to free the necessary workspace for parts and assembly activities.

Criteria

The criteria that the solutions will have to meet are:

- A short delivery time of end products to the customers.

- The mower production process should be able to operate as both assembly-to-order and assembly-to-stock. The seasonal sales do not allow solely assembly-to-order because of the difference between off-season sales level and the sales peaks.
- A reduction of costs mainly through reduction of inventory. Current costs include the costs of inventory, the conversion costs, and the costs of operational logistics at the shopfloor.

H.2 Proposed Solution

The redesign of the assembly process consists of the following adjustments:
- Assembly of the machines in a dock structure.
- Changing the Customer Order Entry Point (for an explanation of this issue, see: Dekkers & Sopers, 2001).
- Modification of the organisation and the control of the production process.

By producing in a dock, the mix-flexibility of the process increases. The proposed structure (one module dock, one T-dock, one R-dock, one kart-dock, and one final assembly dock) has a nominal capacity of one hundred mowers a month. Because of the seasonal influence, a stock level of 115 mowers is required, just before the peak of the sales season. The number of orders remain constant throughout the year which has the following advantages:
- Less docks are required and a larger part of the assembly is done by AgriCo's own personnel rather than involving large numbers of temps.
- The assembly of series of specific types is still possible.
- The stock levels can be regulated much more easily.
- The process can be adjusted quickly when the reliability of the sales prognoses increases.

Changing the Customer Order Entry Point means changing AgriCo from a make-to-stock company to an assembly-to-order company. The Customer Order Entry Point is placed before the final assembly. As a consequence, during the season it will be possible to produce a subassembly and all the required parts for final assembly for an order in just one day. Off-season, it will be possible within two or three days.

The production process before the Customer Order Entry Point will be initiated by the forecasts, the process after the Customer Order Entry Point will operate on orders. The main control principles in the entire process are: adjusting the intake of orders, giving orders priority and steering of capacity.

When this proposal is implemented, the final stock will decrease with at least 50%, while the stock in between sub- and final assembly will only increase with 12%. The process will be easier to control and AgriCo's own staff can do a

larger part of the assembly. This implies a reduction of costs with at least €
136.000,-.

Since the lay-out and space occupation presented also two major concerns
of production management, the student has evaluated the alternatives for
production on these aspects. The necessary space for production is at least 1600
m². The optimal space requires 2300 m². Two alternatives have been studied:
Alternative 1, the redesign of the existing assembly facility (1600 m²), and
Alternative 2, the construction of a new facility (2300 m²). The cost of investment
of the Alternatives 1 and 2 are respectively € 90.000,- and € 900.000,-, with a
pay back time of one respectively five years. Alternative 1 seems more attractive
now, but on the long-term Alternative 2 is the better option. In the case of
Alternative 2, due the extra space that would become available a more effective
production process will be possible, not only in the assembly line, but throughout
the whole facility of AgriCo.

H.3   INTERVIEW

Date: March 2002
Interviewee: Manager Production and Logistics AgriCo

Situation after 3 years

At the start of the interview, it became clear that there had been some
miscommunication. The Manager Production and Logistics was not aware of
the fact that there had been a student who had been writing a report about his
department until the report was finished (the former Manager Logistics had
never communicated about the study to other departments). Nevertheless, the
manager had studied the contents of the report.

He pointed out that there has been an upper management change at AgriCO,
with consequences for the corporate strategy. At the time of the report, the
management wanted KANBAN, now it wants JIT, and a stock reduction of
50% (note: these issues have been evaluated by the student and found infeasible).
Due to the change of strategy, the proposed solution has not been implemented.

However, seasonal influences remain, still demanding a decrease in stock
and a flexible production. The recommended dock structure is now available for
the KM machines, subassemblies are made, and more attention is paid to the
workspace and the stock.

The management holds on to a JIT approach, although the staff is not
convinced that it presents the right strategy, since they do not see clear benefits
for quality or lead-time. The stock has to be reduced with such an amount that
flexible production almost becomes impossible. In three years, it is already reduced

by a quarter, while the target is a reduction by half. This year's stock has increased slightly due to a take-over of a product from another company within the concern; some problems occurred while starting up with manufacturing and an increase of stock was necessary.

The mowers are partially built by estimated sales figures, and every month there is a meeting about the stock and sales predictions. Some critical components remain to have a delivery time larger than three or four months; while in-house production of parts may yield some flexibility, the suppliers of this facility are quite harder to manage but more cost-effective. Yet, AgriCo manages to have a reliability of delivery of about 75%. Sometimes the delivery dates are set too short, even for delivery directly out of stock.

The communication between the various AgriCo departments could be improved. Within the Production Department, it is all right, but the Purchasing Department might warn in advance if parts will not arrive on time and the Sales Department could check with production if the delivery time that has been set is correct.

The main problem for AgriCo is that the headquarters have centralised their organisation. Since AgriCo makes various product market combinations, and is the only one within the entire group with this position, the staff at headquarters does not always understand the different requirements for AgriCo, causing extra difficulties.

APPENDIX I: CASE ENGOF NETH

The EngOf Group is a conglomerate of companies in power and automation technologies that enables utility and industry customers to improve performance. The EngOf Group of companies operates in more than 100 countries and employs around 150.000 people. In recent years however, EngOf has shifted its focus from large-scale solutions to alternative energy sources, and to the advanced products and technologies in power and automation that constitute its Industrial IT offering.

I.1   Contents of Study

EngOf Neth is part of the EngOf Group. It provides project services that include Engineering, Procurement, and Construction of large-scale equipment. EngOf defines these projects as the integrated activity of several different functional disciplines that interrelate over time to produce a comprehensive production process. The primary process of EngOf Neth is to provide certain process techniques. EngOf offers its clients a service that contains technical knowledge and project management. The scope of this service is up to the customer's needs. EngOf Neth also conducts feasibility studies and other types of studies for its customers.

Market Changes
Due to mainly two developments, the market changed from primarily reimbursable projects (also called cost plus contracts) to primarily major Lump Sum Turn Key (LSTK) projects (fixed price contracts):
- In the past the client was involved during all phases of the contract. Because experienced clients went through processes of cost saving, they only wanted to focus on their core business and did not want to be involved in all phases of the contract any more.
- Less experienced clients need project funding. Funding by banks require lump sum commitments to have a constant clear view on the costs, this requires Lump Sum Turn Key contracts.

Faced with a changing market, EngOf Neth had to adapt its way of working. To keep up with, or better stay ahead of, its competitors, and to anticipate on the changing market and low market conjunctures EngOf started a change of culture. This culture change had been introduced with a program named "Driving into the future" and approximately would take five years to implement. This program was started to gain perspective, to develop management skills, and to start a fire prevention program, instead of fighting fires during project execution. It concerns changes and investments in the aspects Structure, Processes, People, and Tools. New company goals will have impact on all aspects of the company, therefore an integral solution concerning all elements of the organisation is very important.

Problem Analysis

Due to a changing market the demand for LSTK projects is increasing. This resulted in a change of culture at EngOf as said above. To maintain a good overview of the major projects, the management and control of these and to anticipate on low conjunctures, EngOf invested in modern IT-tools.

In this case, Information Technology (IT) can be defined as all the resources used for automated data processing. Many disciplines in EngOf's organisation will be influenced by IT applications for different reasons. For instance, within the primary processes they substitute human actions by automated actions to reduce man-hours or to improve quality. Within the controlling and supporting processes, they provide decision-makers with valuable information to rationalise their decision processes. Each tool should fulfil a certain function with its own goals and support the primary process to increase productivity.

Bottlenecks in the Control Process

In contrast to the expectations and in spite of the investments in IT-tools, the overruns of engineering-hours spent on projects was increasing instead of decreasing. Management could not say if implementing IT-tools resulted in a efficiency improvement. Together with the conclusion from the analysis, made during the first phase of the research, it could be stated that simply evaluating IT tools only on efficiency was not correct. The gap in the IST situation, where there is a shortage of information about the added value of IT tools, that creates the need for a method to evaluate the performance of IT-tools, the SOLL situation.

I.2   PROPOSED SOLUTION

The designed model represents a system to manage the IT tool's performance. The model shows the life-cycle of a tool as a process with the control structures to determine, and to regulate the performance. The following aspects are integrated into this model:

- The functional aims of EngOf Neth.
- The different levels in the organisation and its goals.
- The functions a tool fulfils in the primary processes.
- The different types of costs and results.

functional departments still prevails, driven by the resistance at upper and middle management levels. The proper implementation of IT tools requires the proper interaction between the personnel involved of different departments. The IT tools will shift power from functional departments and project management to integrated process-oriented approaches, which barely happens at the moment.

Appendix J: Case ToolIt

ToolIt is a worldwide operating producer of electrical power tools. It is mainly focused on the Do-It-Yourself market. From 1996 on, another conglomerate of companies owns the company. ToolIt has 400 employees of which 300 are related to the production process. It has a turnover of € 90.000.000. The following departments are found in the Dutch site:
- The European Headquarters (Management, Finance and Marketing).
- The Benelux Sales Office.
- The production of parts and assembly of tools.
- The European Warehouse.
- The Product Development Department.

The goals are to develop, produce, sell, and service portable power tools of high quality for the 'Do-It-Yourself' market in Europe. It operates in the market segment where low prices are very important. Because ToolIt is a part of a conglomerate with companies that operate in the same market, it should not compete with other brands, which cover the high end of the market. ToolIt wants to be flexible in the product range they produce as well as in the volume of products to be produced; this is called the mix flexibility and the innovation flexibility. To reach high levels of flexibility in both areas, the performance of both the development of products and the production process should excel. The policy of the company focuses on reducing the overhead costs, the purchasing costs, and the costs of inventory (e.g. through Just-In-Time). ToolIt's organisation is informal, flexible with fast communication in order to anticipate on changes and disruptions.

Every product consists of a few parts and a motor. The parts are partially produced in-house and partially purchased. The motor consists of purchased and produced components. The produced parts, the purchased parts, and the motor are assembled for each specific product.

J.1 Contents of Assignment

The emphasis on a high level of mix flexibility and innovation flexibility implies the importance of the development process and its structure, in particular the change-over to new products and the introduction of specific production processes. The lead-time of changes should be as short as possible, their costs should be minimised and the quality of the processes maximised. When changes are implemented in the production process, all kind of tuning problems arise. Disruptions can occur in newly designed, tuned, and maladjusted machines. Because of disruptions in the production process, the quality level of the products can not be reached within the given time frame. When the quality of the change-overs is not well controlled, the lead-time may become too long, the costs may increase, and the quality of the total change process may decrease. Herewith, the mix- and innovation flexibility can be endangered. At the end, this will prohibit ToolIt from reaching its strategic objectives.

Problem Analysis

The changes in the production process can be divided into changes in the production equipment and of the assembly line. Changes in production equipment are related to improvements of the production process and to corrections caused by disruptions. These changes concern all machines and all tools in the production process. The changes in the assembly line are caused by product changes, these changes concern the material flow and the standards for quality checks.

Changes in the assembly line cause small disruptions of the production process. They have a direct influence on the supply of parts and on the quality of the used parts during production. The costs related to this are relatively the smallest of the three groups of disturbances. This is why changes in production equipment are seen as the main group that causes disturbances.

The assignment covered the development of a controlled design process for the changes in production equipment. Important requirements for the production process should result from the process development. Therefore, the design of a new production process before production release should be improved. The assignment covered also the possibility for monitoring and documenting changes to enhance insights in execution and control.

J.2   PROPOSED SOLUTION

The design of the SOLL situation concerns the quality control of the production planning. In this case, the production planning can be seen as the design of the production process within the total development of a product. The (re)design consists of:

- Adding feedback loops, evaluation, and initiating processes for the control of the change process. This is done for the design processes, the production processes, the implementation processes, and the test processes.
- Implementing control loops within the departments by defining the organelle structure (see Delft School Approach, Appendix B).
- Subdividing the changes in three categories in such a way that not every change is treated the same way. These three categories are:
  1. Changes that result in a change in production (production method), e.g. automation of a production step. This covers also improvements of the production layout.

2. Changes where only a part of production equipment has to be designed. The production method remains the same, only the current production equipment has to be adjusted or improved.
3. Changes where existing parts are produced and the overhaul of production equipment is done.

In the newly designed quality control system, the most important control loops are implemented:

- Documentation of the change process so that the employees can work with this new method. Documentation consists of the documentation of the specific activities, the checklists for the process functions and the listing of the most important results (deliverables) during the change process.
- Starting up of project teams for the second group of changes mentioned above. To monitor the teams' progress a steering committee is started up.
- Using a change document for recording all relevant data concerning an change and the observed problems.
- Introducing a plan to control the changes in drawings, mainly done by marking unedited drawings.
- Making people conscious of the activities in the control loops via quality activities.

The model for the change process was extended with extra control loops for product development for which it can also be used. Also, the standards for the production release were reviewed.

J.3 REVIEW OF ANALYSIS AND SOLUTION

The redesign will establish an improved control of the changes and subsequently the (total) disturbances of the production process caused by changes will decrease with more or less 50%. Because the development, the structure, and the change of the processes are controlled better, the monitoring of the mix and innovation flexibility will improve; the upgraded change process should result in:

- that the production equipment will cause less disruptions during production;
- that the requirements and specifications of the product parts are linked better to the tuned processes;
- that because of the change document and the registration of the process, the implemented changes will be known better to everyone;
- that as a result of the project teams everyone's responsibility and competence will become clearer;
- that by defining standards, the moment of the production release during the product development can be clearly pinpointed.

J.4   INTERVIEW

Date: May 2002
Interviewee: Technical Manager ToolIt

Situation after 3 years

ToolIt has implemented the proposed change processes and only modified slightly to make it work. The goals have been achieved although the effect on market performance has been minor.

Appendix K: Case PlastiCo

PlastiCo is a division of PlastiHolding. In the Netherlands, the close proximity of the Technical Centre and the major manufacturing facility provides exceptionally fast response for capturing market opportunities in adapting PlastiCo's engineering plastics to specific customer requirements. The company produces engineering thermoplastics, such as resin, silicones, special chemicals, and structured products. This project focuses on the resin business. The resin products are stored in the warehouse before they are transported to the customers. Defects may occur as a result of handling and transportation. PlastiCo operates a logistic dispute handling system in order to settle the disputes about defects. Based upon customer's demands the following facets are important to this logistic dispute handling system:

1. The system's throughput time.
2. The recurrence of disputes.
3. The system's fairness.

K.1 Contents of Assignment

In 1996, PlastiCo started a project to increase the added value for customers by improving internal quality, resulting in major cost reductions. However, the customers enjoyed little of these rewards. This resulted in a change of course in 1999. Instead of working at internally defined projects for products, the customer's requirements became the point of departure, which created a strong focus on integral order-processing. The main objective for the Distribution Department became the reduction of throughput times. Performance measurements were no longer based on *agreed delivery time* but on *required delivery time*. The logistic dispute handling system was part of the Distribution Department. The objectives of the Distribution Department were not formally translated into objectives for the logistic handling system. Despite lack of formal objectives, the logistic dispute handling system was influenced by this renewed customer focus. It was felt that the service provided by the logistic dispute handling system was dropping below acceptable levels. Furthermore, the number of disputes did increase, and, in addition, the amount of money paid for compensation almost doubled in 1999.

Problem Statement
The assignment of this investigation is to return the service level to the previous levels by answering these questions:

1. How to reduce the throughput time and the recurrence of disputes in a sustainable way?

2. How to control the throughput time and the recurrence of disputes?

Problem Analysis

During this project a process model has been proposed, stating two main processes for a dispute handling system. The first process is the Settle Dispute and the second process is the Improve Business, which executes improvements to reduce the overall number of disputes, based upon aggregated information from the Settle Dispute process. The processes of the Settle Dispute cause no major problems. The focus of this project will therefore be on the design of the Improve Business processes.

Criteria

Formal aims for both processes of the logistic dispute handling system are determined:

1. Settle Logistic Disputes, which are issued by the customer, in a controlled way that is fair, within a reasonable throughput time and against acceptable costs.
2. Improve the Business processes in a controlled way in order to reduce the overall number of disputes to a reasonable level against acceptable costs.

Process criteria are derived based upon these aims, including effectiveness, efficiency, and control.

K.2   PROPOSED SOLUTION

The structures of the Improve Business process are designed. The same organisational units that cause the disputes should execute these processes: the forwarders, the plants, and the warehouse. Analysis of groups of disputes should lead to changes in processes and procedures in order to eliminate defects.

Control loops for the recurrence of disputes are designed, including both internal control loops and boundary control loops (part of the steady-state model, see Appendix B). The internal control loops control the Improve Business functions' processes. Each organisational unit that executes these processes performs its own internal control loop. A higher-level control loop by the logistic dispute-handling organisation ensures their coordination.

Also control loops for the throughput time are designed. They include both internal control loops, controlling the throughput time of the Settle dispute function, and boundary control loops. Each sub-process of the Settle Dispute function performs its own internal control loop. A higher level internal control loop by the logistic dispute organisation ensures the coordination between the sub-processes.

Preliminary Conclusions for the Developed Method
- Objectives are derived for PlastiCo's logistic dispute handling system. They focus on helping customers fast and fair, at the same time they should reduce the number of disputes.
- Following the new aims, process criteria are derived. They state the system's efficiency in settling disputes and its effectiveness per facet. In addition, they state criteria for control.
- An Improve Business function is designed. Its processes, input and output criteria, and relations with other processes are defined. The Improve Business function should realise a considerable reduction of the number of recurring disputes by executing improvement projects.
- Control loops are designed for the facet recurrence of disputes. These include both boundary control loops and internal control loops.
- Control loops for the facet throughput time are designed. These include both boundary control loops and internal control loops.
- Implementation: In order to reduce the number of recurring disputes and to reduce the settle dispute's throughput time, the Improve Business function and the control loops should be implemented at the plants, the forwarders, and the warehouse as soon as possible. Priority should be given to the plants and the forwarders, given the number of disputes they cause.

Recommendations
1. This project was performed for one location specifically. This project's best practices should be implemented as soon as possible by the other five logistic dispute handling systems. Emphasis should be placed on the implementation of the Improve Business function at all European plants.
2. As a consequence, the above-mentioned implemented measurements are European wide performed. This means that the above-mentioned recurrence measurements are not only performed for the three finishing plants at that location, but for all finishing plants of the European resin business. In addition, throughput time measurements are performed for all European Analyse Dispute and Compensate Customer processes.
3. PlastiCo should strive to eliminate the detour flow. Its existence is mainly the result of a deficit in capacity for the Analyse Dispute process and caused an increase of credited disputes by 10%. As long as the detour flow operates, it is recommended that random checks on the validity of the detour disputes are performed. A reduction of accepted and credited disputes could compensate for the extra resources necessary to keep up to the throughput time standard.

4. A system should be set up that handles 'internal disputes'. Their number is unknown, but a considerable amount is expected. In addition, they should be categorised and handled by the Improve Business function to prevent them from recurring.

5. The information transfer between the input border area and the Analyse Dispute process should be improved. A standard checklist could be used at the Customer Assistance Department. This checklist ensures that all necessary information is available in the Analyse Dispute process. This improves the quality of the root cause analysis and reduces the requests for additional customer information.

6. The categorising of disputes should be simplified. The current categorisation raises many questions. It is doubtful whether all European logistic dispute handlers accept and categorise disputes the same way. A one-on-one relation between root cause's originator and the liable department should be created.

The following actions were already taken:

- The measurements for the control loops of the facet recurrence of disputes are implemented for the plants.

- The measurements for the control loops of the throughput time are implemented at the logistic dispute handling organisation and the Customer Assistance Department. All Customers Assistance Teams received a refreshing course on (logistic) dispute handling. The enforced standard and the correct way of entering data in the dispute management system were communicated.

- The response time for the plants and the main forwarders to deliver information to the Analyse Dispute process is reduced. In addition, the standard for the forwarder to return PoD ('proof of delivery') within four days is formalised. This standard was added as a service level when PlastiCo's entered into a new contract with its main forwarder.

K.3 INTERVIEW

Date: May 2002
Interviewee: Dispute Handling Manager

During a telephone conversation, the manager indicated that the complete proposal has been implemented and the objectives have been reached. Only some minor modifications have been made to the proposal due to the integration into software solutions.

Appendix L: Case Blue Sky

Blue Sky is a worldwide operating airline. In a strong alliance with one partner and in cooperation with other European and international network partners, Blue Sky offers more than 160.000 connections worldwide, covering over 500 cities, in 90 countries, and on six continents. During 1999, Blue Sky transported 15 million passengers and 578,000 tons of cargo and airmail. The average age of the 117 aircraft is 8 years, making the fleet one of the youngest in the world. The company employs about 28000 people and had a turnover of about 6 billion Euro in 1999. The main corporate objectives are:
- Offering a high quality product at a competitive price.
- Strengthening market presence, partially through alliances.
- Achieving internationally competitive costs, on a sound financial base.
  The external objectives can be summarised as:
- Transport of passengers through the air.
- Offering air cargo services: transport, distribution and information.
- Maintenance of the aircraft, its engines and various components.

High quality, productivity, and growth constitute the main criteria for managing the airline. According to Blue Sky, quality means offering many destinations with a high punctuality, having a good customer service, operating under high safety levels, and reducing environmental damage as much as possible.

L.1 Contents of Assignment

The primary objective of Blue Sky is the transport of cargo and passengers, which constitutes more than 90% of the turnover. The primary process centres around two parts for realising the transport process:
- Preparing the flight schedule.
- Executing the flight schedule.

The schedule is made four times a year and is the result of tuning the available resources and the demand for air transport. The various Blue Sky services such as Capacity and Service Provider, Flight Service, Cabin Crew Services, Technical Services, and Ground Services provide information on their capacity for that period as well. With the result of this process the actual flight, meaning the transport of passengers and cargo, takes place. During turnarounds, passengers and cargo are shipped off and a fresh load of passengers and cargo is shipped in at every airport. Following this, the actual flight takes place, in which the crew flies to the destinations as given in the flight plan. This flight plan must be approved before every flight. Landing and departure slots are appointed using these flight plans.

Problem Analysis

To execute the flight schedule, eight distinct resources are necessary: fleet, maintenance capacity, ground handling capacity, cabin crew, cockpit crew, airport capacity, air space capacity, and fuel. Some of these resources can be planned and buffered, such as crew and fleet, others like air space capacity (slots plus flight plan) cannot. The limited reserve capacity (fleet and crew are very expensive) or, sometimes, non-existing spare capacity makes the entire system very inflexible and makes it hard to recover from disruptions.

Bottlenecks for Scheduling

The scheduling method for flights centres around the efficient deployment of the available aircraft. The airline executes more flights in a sequence. This means that when an airplane gets delayed in its first flight of the day, due to whatever problem, it becomes almost impossible to catch up with the flight schedule. Consequently, this delay affects other flights by that plane and the scheduling of resources, which calls for intense control and communication. The two major causes of disturbances are: the disturbances during a turnaround and the disturbances of flights. Also, the flight schedule is made in such a way that it is not completely executable without disruptions.

L.2 PROPOSED SOLUTION

Enlarging the possibilities to intervene might increase productivity. This can be achieved by installing more spare capacity at the main airport, so that more disturbances can be met. The presence of spare capacity (fleet, cockpit crew, and cabin crew) will reduce the disturbances caused by technical failures and late arrival of incoming flights. As a result, altering the fleet planning can be used to solve late arrivals.

An initial estimation brought about a possible productivity increase of about 10 to 40 million Euro on an annual base through the availability of 5-6 extra airplanes, only for the execution of European flights. The optimal amount and the optimal airplane type have to be determined by statistical methods. The execution of intercontinental flights and the placement of spare capacity on airports other than the main airport should also be examined.

The current performance measurement systems do not deliver much useful information. Monitoring the right performance indicators could supply the Air Traffic Management department with adequate information for improving the effectiveness of the process. The low effectiveness is currently accountable for a large amount of the primary process' non-punctuality.

L.3   REVIEW OF ANALYSIS AND SOLUTION

Although the solution seems feasible, it means also a departure from a strategy strongly directed at efficiency. No information could be obtained to what extent Blue Sky has implemented this solution. Indirectly, information shows that Blue Sky has not yet implemented this solution.

Appendix M: Case CompuIt

During 1999, CompuIt had about 80.000 employees worldwide. CompuIt focuses on the product lines of medical electronic equipment, test and measurement systems, computerised test systems, systems for chemical analysis, networks and systems management software. The Customer Information Management Department is responsible for the maintenance of the customer profile, the handling of responses, telemarketing, and database analysis. The goal of the CIM Department is to increase the productivity of Sales, Marketing, and Service & Support. Currently it is a data-processing department, which offers technical solutions like lead management, campaign management, funnel management, and contact management.

M.1   Contents of Graduation Thesis

CompuIt has always been a product-oriented company and structured in such a way that the product divisions control the marketing and sales departments. The products always sold well, so seldomly there was a large gap between what the market asked for and what the company pushed to the market. As a result, the divisions are powerful within the company. By founding other divisions with different product groups, the structure did not really change, resulting in lack of communication between different product divisions and departments. The customers in the end-user market start to experience the effects of the communication. Because information is difficult to find or unavailable at times, it takes a lot of time to prepare a customer visit and to respond to customers' requests.

Problem Statement

CompuIt's goal is to improve the individual customer profitability while establishing growth of market share, without losing the original goals of the company. To make this possible, CompuIt has to become a customer-oriented organisation. The company has recognised it has to build relations with its customers, to learn their needs, and to be able to serve the end-user with a solution, not a product only. The company wants to implement a Customer Relationship Management system, which will make customer information widely available throughout the company. Implementing the CRM could lead to new ways of dealing with customers, enabling CompuIt to retain its customers and improve margins.

Problem Analysis

The study focused on the possibilities of using the information that the CRM tool might contain, what the effect will be, and how the customer data should be handled and interpreted; especially managing the relation with the customer, defining how the customer base can best be segmented, defining how the business processes Sales, Marketing, and Service should communicate with these different customer segments. A customer relation model was designed combining all active interactions, which enables to manage the relationships between Compult and its customers.

The task of CRM is to combine, to compare, and to present the available information about the customers and solutions in such a way that a clear insight is obtained about the status of the customer and the customer base, therewith creating market possibilities. The relationship with the customer can be measured by measuring the results of interactions with the customer.

According to CRM theory, the provider should react on created needs from customers in a more structured manner: the provider changes them into orders for a solution and then should try to keep these customers. If the provider does not succeed in this, the customer will leave the active communication system of the provider and the provider has to revert to passive, mostly unidirectional communication. This should be prevented for the most interesting and lucrative customers. The system border makes the difference in the type of interaction: active or passive interaction. Within the system border, the interactions between the provider and the customer are bidirectional, that is to say an active relationship. Outside the system border, the relationship is passive, restricted to telemarketing and requalification to acquire and update information and marketing actions to create new external needs.

The relationships inside the border are more effective in creating new business because there is much more interaction and information than outside the system. If CRM is implemented successfully, customers will not leave the system of the provider and you might call the customer loyal to the provider. Inputs are new needs and if the system works correctly the output, lost active customer relationships, is minimised. Therefore, the system of the provider should expand in four areas:

- New needs can be found inside and outside the system border from existing customers and from potential customers. Converting potential customers into customers makes the customer base grow. Fulfilling new needs from existing customers is the beginning of up-selling and cross-selling.
- Creating orders out of generated leads is essential for staying in business. In this phase, it is already possible to look for cross-sell opportunities.

- Implementing the solution and operational service of the solution in the customer's productive environment is probably the longest phase. This phase will end as soon as the customer decides to stop using the solution.
- The termination of the solution is the last opportunity to offer a new solution while having an active relationship with the customer. If the provider is not able to get a follow-up lead and it has not succeeded in getting another lead before, the customer will leave the system.

By exploiting the active relationship with the customer, the company can sell more to the same customer while at the same time expanding the total customer base by acquiring new customers too. To implement CRM successfully, these four different processes are very important to control:

- The creation of leads out of external needs.
- The creation of orders out of leads.
- The implementation and the operational service of the solution.
- The creation of leads out of internally generated demands.

M.2 PROPOSED SOLUTION

To find out at which moment in the interaction with the customer measurements should be taken and to what purpose, a customer relation model is designed. The CRM process model connects five defined processes as follows:

- The needs entering the providers' environment are transformed into leads. The needs the provider cannot transform leave the system again as unmatched needs.
- The interesting leads are transformed into orders. If the transformation was not successful, the leads leave the system as missed orders. During the process of designing a solution, the provider tries to generate new leads to better fulfil the need of the possible customer. These leads are immediately included in the order proposal.
- The solution is implemented and used in the environment of the customer. During this period, the provider is actively looking for and creating new needs. If the solution of the provider is not suited for its job any more, the customer will stop using the solution.
- This means the termination of the operational service time of the solution. The provider is able to get a follow-up need, or the customer does not want to give this follow-up need to the provider. If the provider did not get a different internally created need before, the active customer relationship between the customer and the provider is lost.
- The provider will try to transform internally created needs into new leads.

If all the results of the interactions are consequently recorded in the database during these five processes, the provider is able to analyse the relationship it has with its individual customers.

Customer Segmentation.

Segmentation is necessary because no single company with a large customer base can implement 1:1 personal relationships in a cost-efficient way. Segmenting the customer into different groups of importance makes cost efficient differentiation in allocation of resources possible. Three major factors define the importance of a customer to the provider:
- Customer profitability.
- Size of the customer.
- Strategic value of the customer.

The customers are divided into four groups, each group requiring a different strategic response from the company. In the future all orders will be entered in the new CRM tool, which means it is easy to find about a specific customer. The third criterion is reflected by giving the customer a virtual higher profitability or size, raising the importance of the customer. This thinking leads to the definition of a profitability index, a customer size index, and a strategic value index. Together these indices can define one index: the customer priority index. Therefore, the customer segment classification should be a dynamic process. The evaluating function should control the norm of the classification; this means the definition of the customer segment and the transfer of customers from and to the segments.

Implementation

The requirements, to make the customer information analysis contribute successfully to managing the relationship with the customer, are:
- Quick analysis and reaction times.
- Dedicated job function to make sure the analysis is done.
- Direct report line to customer account management.
- Direct link to R&D to pass on analysed feedback about offered solutions.

The necessary condition to perform the analysis is that relevant data are entered in the database.

To guarantee that these requirements are met, a new team completely dedicated to Customer Information Analysis (CIA) is proposed. The CIA organisation should report to the account manager and take part in his team, but not be absorbed in his team completely as it would make segmentation of the customer accounts more difficult. The CIA organisation is responsible for all customers. To be able to closely follow overall company strategies and to guarantee the customer importance to the company, the CIA organisation should connect to top management. This results in a much higher level of customer orientation inside the Compult and separates the interests of the sales results from the customer relationship. The CIA organisation will be focused on analysing the information and gathering missing information to understand the status of the customer to advice Sales, Marketing, and Service & Support.

Data Management

Building a relationship with a customer implies collecting a lot of data. The new CRM tool will increase considerably the availability of data. It will be possible to enter, to update and to search data from all over the organisation anywhere in the world. Two problems are likely to arise while using the database:

- Handling the growing data volume, there is a restriction on the amount of information that can be kept.
- Handling the data quality, related to the ageing of the information.

M.3   REVIEW OF SOLUTION

The handling of information, although supported by computer tools, seems complex. Additionally, it appears that focusing on targeted customers might result in narrowing the customer base; especially, the combination with the shift from a product-oriented company to a customer-oriented company seems a long way. Inside information revealed that this shift is hardly taking place.

Appendix N: Case Studies Delft School Approach and Hypotheses

This appendix describes the conversion from the contents of the case studies, presented in Appendices H-M, to the testing of the refined hypotheses presented in Section 8.2. The hypotheses have been tested by using qualitative parameters. To use quantitative measures, longitudinal data should be available of the companies; for the moment being, the link between processes, structures, and data is considered weak. Therefore, this assessment has reverted to the evaluation of qualitative parameters, which makes it also possible to compare the six different cases.

N.1 Review of Cases

The features of Table F.1 have been described briefly in Table N.1 for each of the six case studies. The information has been obtained from the reports of the case studies and the conducted interviews; in the case of Blue Sky Airlines it has been complemented with public announcements about the strategy and the course of action. The analysis of the Delft School Approach includes the assessment of strategies and their relevance to investigation during a graduation thesis; the findings of these assessments have been used to determine the performance of the companies on the features. Subsequently the outcomes of Table N.1 have been linked to the hypotheses, see Table N.2. Sometimes the remarks have been changed into concise statements not distorting the information of the original ones.

N.2 Findings of the Review

The second set of hypotheses shows that none of the companies exerts long jumps (one-time interventions). Rather, they focus on increasing sustained fitness through incremental changes that have limited effects for their phenotypes, in three cases that seems hardly to be the case; neither do the companies utilise the implementations for increasing fitness or assessment to that matter. Some of them aim to change and create a different orientation, like PlastiCo and CompuIt. The limited changes they implement root in incremental changes rather than the drastic changes they want to create. The efforts look like Continuous Improvement but even then how will it sustain the competitive advantage? The three companies: ToolIt, Blue Sky, and CompuIt that face a highly competitive market should revert to increasing fitness along competitive dimensions. They attempt to do so but neither seems to evaluate the effects on their performance.

Table N.1: Review of the cases against the features of the hypotheses. The row with the grey colour indicates the solution proposed during the case study. Below that row the solution implemented by the management of the company is listed.

Feature	AgriCo	EngOf	ToolIt	PlastiCo	Blue Sky	Compult
Environmental changes						
Changes in competitors or industry	Not really, ongoing fierce competition, seasonally bound.	-	Competition to retail outlets.	-	Increased competition.	Fierce competition.
Increasing number of competitors	-	-	-	-	Yes, niche; No, mergers.	-
Increasing number of new products	Company produces regularly new products.	-	Regularly new products, variants are introduced.	Clients request new product tailored to specifications.	-	Streams of new products.
Landscape characteristics	Rugged due to agricultural culture. Slowly changing.	Changing and correlated.	Rugged.	Smooth.	Rugged and correlated.	?
Gradual change of customers base	Customers buy according to price and delivery; fierce competition.	Customers shift from reimbursable project to lump sum turnkey projects.	Product range expands more than customer base.	Customer-orientation becomes more important.	Customer-orientation becomes more important.	?
Strategy and Performance						
New products, new markets	-	Shift in projects.	Introduction of stream of products.	Clients' requests.	-	Introduction of products.
Strategy of repositioning	-	No, but address market needs.	-	No, but address market needs.	-	-
Changes in product, market, performance	Continuous pressure on pricing and shorter delivery times	Managing of deadline and integral performance of product.	Product flexibility.	Quality performance. Reliability of delivery.	Better performance expected at lower prices.	Coherent approach necessary towards clients.

Intense interaction with customers, suppliers	-	Reduced on customer side.	-	-	-	Defining needs of clients.
Stability or convergence	Convergence towards optimal sales performance.	Convergence towards project performance.	Stability.	Convergence towards optimal points.	Convergence.	Convergence.
Internal changes						
Accumulation of internal changes	Complexity of products increases over time.	Graduation thesis part of internal changes.	-	Delivery became bottle-neck after quality drive.	Gradual changes were not effective.	Graduation thesis should contribute.
Combining changes in major change	No	Intended but not realised.	-	-	-	-
Severe organisational change of processes, structures, etc.	Local optimisation of part of manufacturing	Intended integration of management, tools, processes, people.	-	-	-	-
New structures deviate much from current operations	Calls for more control of capacity.	Focus on processes more than projects.	Fits into the current organisational routines.	Fits into the current organisational routines.	Orientation on flights more than resources.	Availability of information.
Internal specialisation	-	-	-	-	-	-
Effects of change	Lower stock levels. Shorter delivery time; will increase flexibility	Evaluation of tools resulting in more adequate tools.	Increase in productivity of change-overs for products.	Decrease of disputes. Increase reliability delivery.	Increase of reliability of flight schedule.	Increase of effectiveness towards customers.
Fitness of proposed solution (graduation thesis) in comparison to current situation	Shorter delivery time; better financial performance expected.		Better productivity.	Better performance.	Better performance.	Increased sales performance.
Fitness of solution (by management) implemented to current situation	Managerial proposal (JIT, etc.) might decrease fitness.	Focus remains on projects. No changes in working methods.	Solution implemented.	Solution implemented.	Financial orientation.	?

Table N.2: Outcomes of features rearranged for hypotheses. The validation of hypotheses has followed the implementations by management. Doubtful outcomes have been seen as negative.

Hypothesis	AgriCo	EngOf	Toollt	PlastiCo	Blue Sky	Compult
A.1 Mutations	No new products, markets. Performance improvement in price and delivery; will increase competitiveness. (Yes)	Shift in requests for projects by customers (lump sum turn key); more competitiveness. (Yes)	Continuous introduction of new products (variants). Increased product flexibility. (Yes)	Quality performance. Reliability of performance. Customer orientation becomes more important. (Yes)	Better performance expected at lower prices. Customer orientation becomes more important. Not implemented. (No)	Coherent approach necessary towards clients. (Yes)
A.2 State Transition	Ongoing competition, continuous pressure on price and delivery time. (No)	Reduced interaction on customer side. (No)	Competition to retail outlets. (No)	- (No)	Increased competition. (No)	Fierce competition. Defining needs of clients necessary. (No)
B.1.A Adaptive walks	Complexity of products increases over time. Proposal graduation theses will increase fitness. Management policy will not. Rugged landscape due to agricultural culture. Slowly changing. (No)	Proposal graduation thesis supports required working methods. Actually, no changes happen in working methods. Changing and uncorrelated landscape. (No)	Proposal increases productivity. Rugged landscape. Proposal does not increase fitness as such and does not fit into a larger plan. (No)	Better performance (quality and delivery). Smooth landscape. Delivery became bottleneck after quality drive. (Yes)	Better performance needed. Financial orientation prohibits improvement. Rugged and correlated landscape. Gradual changes were not effective. (No)	Increased sales performance. Graduation thesis should contribute. (Yes)
B.1.B Long jumps	No severe intervention; more control of capacity allocation needed. Management proposal has more profound but limited effects. (No)	Intended integration of management, processes, tools, people. Factually, no change taking place. (No)	Fits into current organisational routines. (No)	Fits into current organisational routines. (No)	Orientation more on flights rather than resource utilisation. (No)	Availability of information. (No)

B.2.A Sustained fitness	Performance will improve: reliability of delivery and higher flexibility. Convergence. (Yes)	Managing of deadline and integral performance of product. Proposal should contribute to increased performance, affects only partial processes. Convergence. (Yes)	Product flexibility increases. Increased productivity for creating product flexibility. Stability. (Yes)	Quality of performance. Reliability of delivery. Decrease of disputes. Convergence towards optimal points. (Yes)	Better performance for lower prices expected. Increase of reliability of flight schedule. Convergence. (Yes)
B.2.B Evolvability	Customers buy according to price and delivery; fierce competition. (No)	Address different market needs, but no different product-market combination as such. (No)	Easing the existing stream of products; does not create new markets or products as such. (No)	- (No)	- (No)
B.2.C Complexity Error Catastrophe	Companies launch regularly new products. (No)	To address market needs. (No)	Regular introduction of new products. Increases becomes possible. (Yes)	Clients request new products tailored to specifications. (No)	Niche market operators appear; fierce competition on price and routing. Mergers happen also. (Yes)

Coherent approach necessary towards clients. Increase of effectiveness towards customers. (Yes)
Introduction of products. Defining needs of clients. Does not yield directly new products. (No)
Streams of new products. (Yes)

Appendix O: Schools of Strategy

Ten major schools characterise the strategy literature, says Mintzberg (1999). This summary of the ten schools of strategic management (including their origins) can be divided into two groups, three prescriptive (or "ought") and seven descriptive (or "is"):

1) *Design School: A Process of Conception.* The design school sees strategy formation as achieving the essential fit between internal strengths and weaknesses, and external threats and opportunities. Senior management formulates clear, simple, and unique strategies in a deliberate process of conscious thought – which is neither formally analytical nor informally intuitive – so that everyone can implement the strategies.

2) *Planning School: A Formal Process.* With the planning school precise intentions are formulated and articulated by a central leadership, and backed up by formal controls to ensure their surprise-free implementation in an environment that is being controllable or predictable (to ensure no distortion of intentions); these strategies are therefore highly deliberate. The process is not just cerebral (like the design school) but formal, decomposable into distinct steps, delineated by checklists, and supported by techniques. This means that staff planners replaced senior managers, de facto, as the key players in the process.

3) *Positioning School: An Analytical Process.* The third of the prescriptive schools is labelled positioning. With formalised analyses of industry situations, the organisation is placed in a so-called environment. By doing so, the organisational structure becomes the match between organisation and environment, between the internal and external context. This position can be pre-selected through a plan and/or can be reached, or even found, through a pattern of behaviour. Strategy as positioning has been preceded by a long literature on military strategy dating back to Sun Tzu in 400 BC. The formalised analysis of industry proved especially lucrative to consultants and academics, who could sink their teeth into hard data and promote their "scientific truths" to journals and companies. This literature grew in all directions to include strategic groups, value chains, game theories, and other ideas – but always with this analytical bent.

4) *Entrepreneurial School: A Visionary Process.* The entrepreneurial school has a different approach to strategy (descriptive). Like the design school, the process is focused around one person. But unlike the design school and opposite to the planning school, it roots that process in the mysteries of intuition.

Intentions exist as the personal, unarticulated vision of a single leader, and so are adaptable to new opportunities; the organisation is under the personal control of the leader and located in a protected niche in its environment; these strategies are relatively deliberate but can emerge too. That shifts strategy making from precise designs, plans, or positions to vague *vision* sense, often through metaphor. This focuses the process on particular contexts – start-up, niche, or private ownership, as well as "turnaround" by a forceful leader – although the case was certainly put forth that every organisation needs the vision of a creative leader. In this view, however, the leader maintains such close control over *implementing* his or her formulated vision that the distinction central to the three prescriptive schools begins to break down.

5) *Cognitive School: A Mental Process.* The cognitive school sees a clear limit to the information handling capacity of the strategy maker. The principle of intended rationality implies that any approach to implementing strategy must confront two problems. First, the limited rationality of strategy makers requires that large strategic problems be factored into more local and manageable proportions to reduce the complexity of implementation activities. Second, long-term strategic objectives must be factored into short-term operating objectives, and control mechanisms must be established to ensure consistency of individual and organisational rationality in pursuing these objectives. On the academic front, the origin of strategies generated considerable interest. If strategies developed in people's minds as frames, models, maps, concepts, or schemes, what could be understood about those mental processes? Research has grown steadily on cognitive biases in strategy making and on cognition as information processing, knowledge structure mapping, and concept attainment, important for strategy formation, yet the progress has been minimal. Another, new branch of this school adopted a more subjective *interpretative* or *constructive* view: that cognition is used to construct strategies as creative interpretations, rather than simply to map reality in some more or less objective way, however distorted.

6) *Learning School: An Emergent Process.* People are born with intrinsic motivation, self-esteem, dignity, and curiosity to learn. If an organisation could have the same adaptation this would be increasingly interesting in a dynamic, interdependent and unpredictable world. But adaptation is only the first stage in moving towards learning organisations. The impulse to learn in children goes much deeper than desires to respond and adapt more effectively to environmental change. The impulse to learn, at its heart, is an impulse to be generative, to expand our capability. Generative learning is about creating, as well as adaptive learning, which is about coping. In the learning organisation

strategies are emergent, strategists can be found throughout the organisation, and so-called formulation and implementation intertwine, in so doing the learning school cuts across all the prescriptive schools, and challenges them.

7) *Power School: A Process of Negotiation.* A small part of strategy making focuses on strategy rooted in power. Here we can find two different approaches. One is *Micro* power and attains the development of strategies *within* the organisation as essentially political. Through mutual adjustment, various members converge on patterns that pervade the organisation in the absence of central or common intentions, and confrontation among actors who divide the power. This is mostly a rather emergent process. The second is *Macro* power; the organisation uses its power over others and among its partners in alliances, joint ventures, and other network relationships to negotiate "collective" strategies in its interest.

8) *Cultural School: A Social Process.* Hold power up to a mirror and its reverse image is culture. Whereas the former focuses on self-interest and fragmentation, the latter focuses on common interest and integration – strategy formation as a social process rooted in culture. Again, there is only a thin stream of literature, focused particularly on the influence of culture in discouraging significant strategic change.

9) *Environmental School: A Reactive Process.* Environment refers to various characteristics of the organisation's outside context: markets, political climate, economic conditions, and so on. Perhaps not strictly strategic management, if one defines the term as being concerned with how organisations use degrees of freedom to manoeuvre through their environments, the environmental school nevertheless deserves some attention for illuminating the demands of environment. In this category, we include so-called "contingency theory" that considers which responses are expected of organisations facing particular environmental conditions and "population ecology" writings that claim severe limits to strategic choice. "Institutional theory," which is concerned with the institutional pressures faced by organisations, is perhaps a hybrid of the power and cognitive schools.

10) *Configuration School: A Process of Transformation.* A configuration is seen as a coherent cluster of characteristics, structures and behaviours. There are seven common configurations, entrepreneurial, machine, professional, diversified, adhocracy, ideological, and political. There are however few circumstances where these configurations constitute effective organisations. More often, the conflicting demands placed on the organisation require managers to build their own unique solutions instead of slotting themselves into one of the seven configurations. The contingency approach tells to adapt the strategy process and content to the organisational context.

Hence, the organisation matters - strategy may influence the organisational forces and forms, but the opposite is also the case. Structure follows strategy as the left foot follows the right. Finally, we come to a more extensive and integrative literature and practice. As an organisation is placed in one of these configurations, it could also be placed in another one by *changing* the organisation and thus creating a different organisation. And so, a literature and practice of transformation – more prescriptive and practitioner oriented (and consultant promoted) – developed. These two different literatures and practices nevertheless complement one another and so belong to the same school.

These descriptions have just served as background for assessing the *static* views of many of these schools. None of these strategy schools fits the dynamic thinking.

Appendix P: Types of Scenarios

This appendix lists the different types of scenarios and their application in the planning processes:

Environmental scenarios   Scenarios on how the environment of an organisation could develop in the future. These scenarios help people understand the driving forces outside the organisation.

Strategic scenarios
1. Scenarios that describe possible events in the near future. These scenarios are more dedicated to action and strategic choices that have to be made. Most of the time a Business as Usual (BuA) scenario is developed. Along with a BuA scenario two or three other scenarios are developed, one of them a worst-case scenario.
2. Scenarios that describe possible strategies, which are then judged by their consequences. In this case strategic scenarios fit in environmental scenarios and are a logical step after the development of environmental scenarios.

Means allocating scenarios   These scenarios go one step further than strategic scenarios. Here we try to decide which means suit best for the chosen strategic scenario. Most of the time, this reaches beyond the meaning of scenario development towards an operational level.

Projective scenarios   Scenarios developed by extrapolation of trends. They are projections of the here and now towards the future, based on continuity. Comparable with the Basic, Long Term Multifold Trends of Kahn.

Prospective scenarios   Scenarios developed by backcasting. They set a desired future (state) and then develop a way to reach this future. Another method working with backcasting is the Delphi method.

There are many types of prospective scenarios; they are listed below:

Normative scenarios   Consists of targets that are thought of as feasible and desirable. The case for internal scenarios of van der Heijden.

Table P.1: List of scenario types and their application in scenario methods.

Scenario types	Trend-impact analysis	Intuitive Logistics	Cross-Impact Analysis	Back-casting from DFS
Environmental		x		
Strategic	x		x	
Means-allocating	-	-	-	-
Internal		x		x
External		x		
Projective	x			
Prospective				x
- normative				x
- contrast		x		x
- descriptive				x
- exploratory		x		x
- anticipatory				x

Contrastive scenarios	Consists of targets that are on the limits of what is thought to be possible.
Descriptive scenarios	Same as normative, scenarios are not judged on desirability. This way it is easier to develop different scenarios that are equally possible to happen. Van der Heijden describes this as an external scenario.
Exploratory scenarios	Exploratory scenarios are developed to generate insight in possible effects of environmental developments on the users organisation, market or field of investigation. The users have reasonable knowledge about these developments.
Anticipatory scenarios	Anticipatory scenarios are the opposite of exploratory scenarios. The user knows about the effects that happen on certain moments but does not know what causes these effects. Scenarios are developed to help the user to explain the phenomena. These scenarios are retrospective.

Table P.1 links the different types of scenarios to the scenario methods.